ALPHABETICAL QUICK REFERENCE TO BIRD GROUPS

Accipiters	90	Falcons	110	Nightjars	246	Shearwaters	2(
Akalats	444	Finches	652	Nigritas	686	Sheathbills	15(
Albatrosses	16	Finfoots	138	Noddies	196	Shelducks	6(
Alethes	442	Firefinches	692	Olivebacks	686	Shrikes	574
Antpeckers	688	Fiscals	576	Orioles	382	Siskins	718
Apalises	512	Flamingos	54	Ospreys	74	Skimmers	188
Avocets	172	Flufftails	134	Ostriches	286	Skuas	182
Babblers	400	Flycatchers	546	Owls	236	Snake-eagles	80
Barbets	298	Francolins	120	Oxpeckers	612	Snipes	170
Batises	564	Frigatebirds	40	Oystercatchers	152	Social-weavers	656
Bee-eaters	280	Gallinules	142	Palm-thrushes	454	Sparrowhawks	90
Bishops	680	Gannets	42	Paradise-flycatchers	558	Sparrowlarks	348
Bitterns	52	Geese	64	Parisomas	494	Sparrows	646
Bluebills	696	Go-away-birds	224	Parrots	212	Sparrow-weavers	656
Boobies	42	Godwits	172	Peacock	118	Speirops	644
Boubous	584	Goshawks	90	Pelicans	58	Spinetails	260
Bristle-bills	428	Grebes	36	Penduline-tits	390	Spoonbills	54
Broadbills	326	Greenbuls	412	Penguins	36	Spurfowl	124
Buffalo-weavers	654	Grosbeaks	730	Petrels	20	Starlings	598
Bulbuls	410	Ground-hornbills	286	Petronias	652	Stilts	172
Buntings	726	Guineafowl	118	Phalaropes	180	Stints	178
Bush-shrikes	584	Gulls	184	Picathartes	106	Storks	58
Bustards	146	Hamerkop	46	Piculets	316	Storm-petrels	32
Buttonquails	132	Harriers	84	Pigeons	202	Sugarbirds	614
Buzzards	96	Helmet-shrikes	596	Pipits	368	Sunbirds	614
Camaropteras	536	Herons	46	Pittas	326	Swallows	356
Canaries	714	Hobbies	114	Plantain-eaters	224	Swifts	258
Chanting goshawks	88	Honeybirds	314	Plovers	160	Tchagras	582
Chats	460	Honeyguides	310	Pratincoles	156	Terns	190
Cisticolas	496	Hoopoes	266	Prinias	520	Thick-knees	154
Citrils	720	Hornbills	288	Prions	24	Thrushes	436
Cliff-chats	472	Hyliotas	544	Puffbacks	580	Tinkerbirds	300
Coots	142	Ibises	54	Pytilias	688	Tit-babblers	494
Cormorants	44	Illadopsis	406	Quailfinches	698	Tits	392
Coucals	232	Indigobirds	708	Quail Plover	134	Trogons	266
Coursers	158	Jacanas	152	Quails	132	Tropicbirds	38
Crab Plover	152	Kestrels	108	Queleas	678	Turacos	218
Crakes	140	Kingfishers	270	Rails	136	Twinspots	690
Cranes	144	Kites	72	Ravens	388	Vultures	76
Creepers	396	Korhaans	148	Redstarts	460	Wagtails	364
Crimsonwings	692	Lapwings	164	Robin-chats	448	Warblers	474
Crombecs	532	Larks	328	Rock-jumpers	398	Wattle-eyes	570
Crows	386	Linnets	730	Rock-thrushes	432	Waxbills	700
Cuckoos	226	Longbills	542	Rollers	276	Weavers	658
Cuckooshrikes	376	Longclaws	366	Ruff	174	Wheatears	466
Curlews	172	Lovebirds	216	Rufous thrushes	432	Whimbrels	172
Darters	44	Malimbes	674	Sandgrouse	198	White-eyes	640
Doves	206	Mannikins	698	Sandpipers	174	Whydahs	710
Drongos	380	Martins	350	Saw-wings	354	Widowbirds	682
Ducks	62	Moorhens	142	Scimitarbills	270	Wood-hoopoes	268
Eagles	100	Mousebirds	264	Scrub-robins	456	Woodpeckers	316
Egrets	48	Nicators	430	Secretarybird	286	Wren-warblers	538
Eremomelas	528	Nightingales	454	Seedcrackers	696	Wrynecks	314

COLOUR-CODED QUICK REFERENCE TO BIRD GROUPS

16-17: Albatrosses, petrels, prions, shearwaters, storm-petrels, grebes, penguins, tropicbirds, frigatebirds, gannets, boobies, cormorants, darters, Hamerkop, herons, egrets, bitterns, flamingos, spoonbills, ibises, pelicans, storks, ducks, geese

72-117: Diurnal raptors: kites, Osprey, fish-eagles, vultures, snake-eagles, harriers, hawks, accipiters, buzzards, eagles, falcons, kestrels, hobbies

118-151: Peacocks, guineafowl, francolins, spurfowl, quails, buttonquails, Quail Plover, flufftails, rails, crakes, coots, moorhens, gallinules, finfoot, cranes, bustards, korhaans

152-197: Charadriiforms: jacanas, oystercatchers, Crab Plover, thick-knees, sheathbills, pratincoles, coursers, plovers, lapwings, painted snipes, snipes, waders, avocets, stilts, sandpipers, stints, skuas, gulls, skimmers, terns, noddies

198-235: Sandgrouse, pigeons, doves, parrots, lovebirds, turacos, go-away-birds, plantain-eaters, cuckoos, malkohas, coucals

236-285: Owls, nightjars, swifts, spinetails, mousebirds, trogons, hoopoes, wood-hoopoes, scimitarbills, kingfishers, rollers, bee-eaters

286-325: Ostriches, Secretarybird, ground-hornbills, hornbills, barbets, tinkerbirds, honeyguides, honeybirds, wrynecks, piculets, woodpeckers

326-375: Pittas, broadbills, larks, sparrowlarks, martins, saw-wings, swallows, wagtails, longclaws, pipits

376-431: Cuckooshrikes, drongos, orioles, crows, ravens, penduline-tits, tits, creepers, rock-jumpers, picathartes, babblers, illadopsises, modulatrixes, bulbuls, greenbuls, bristle-bills, nicators

432-473: Rufous-thrushes, rock-thrushes, thrushes, akalats, ground-robins, robin-chats, nightingales, scrub-robins, redstarts, stonechats, chats, wheatears, cliff-chats

474-545: Warblers: reed warblers, woodland warblers, parisomas, tit-babblers, cisticolas, apalises, prinias, eremomelas, crombecs, camaropteras, wren-warblers, longbills, hyliotas

546-613: Flycatchers, paradise-flycatchers, crested flycatchers, batises, wattle-eyes, shrikes, puffbacks, tchagras, boubous, gonoleks, bush-shrikes, helmet-shrikes, starlings, oxpeckers

614-685: Sugarbirds, sunbirds, white-eyes, speirops, sparrows, petronias, finches, buffalo-weavers, sparrow-weavers, social-weavers, weavers, malimbes, queleas, bishops, widowbirds

686-731: Olivebacks, nigritas, antpeckers, twinspots, crimsonwings, firefinches, seedcrackers, bluebills, quailfinches, mannikins, silverbills, grenadiers, waxbills, indigobirds, whydahs, canaries, seed-eaters, siskins, citrils, buntings, grosbeaks

A comprehensive
illustrated field guide

Birds

of Africa
south of the Sahara

Ian Sinclair • Peter Ryan

assisted by Patrice Christy and Phil Hockey

Illustrated by Norman Arlott, Peter Hayman & Alan Harris

For Jackie in millions and Daryn & Kiera. Ian Sinclair
For Coleen and Molly – may your patience persist. Peter Ryan

Struik Publishers
(a division of New Holland Publishing (South Africa) (Pty) Ltd)
Cornelis Struik House
80 McKenzie Street
Cape Town 8001

New Holland Publishing is a member of the Johnnic Publishing Group.
Visit us at **www.struik.co.za**
Log on to our photographic website
www.imagesofafrica.co.za for an African experience.

First published in 2003
1 3 5 7 9 10 8 6 4 2
Copyright © text: Ian Sinclair, Peter Ryan 2003
Copyright © maps: Ian Sinclair, Peter Ryan 2003
Copyright © published edition: Struik Publishers 2003
Copyright © illustrations: Norman Arlott 2003, David Chamberlain 2003, Struik Publishers 2003

Publishing manager: Pippa Parker
Managing editor: Helen de Villiers
Editors: Tracey Hawthorne, Piera Abbott, Katharina von Gerhardt
Proofreader: Tessa Kennedy
Design director: Janice Evans
Designer: Robin Cox
Typesetter: Heston Michaels
Cover design: Robin Cox
Cartography: Robin Cox, Heston Michaels

Reproduction by Hirt and Carter Cape (Pty) Ltd
Printed and bound by Times Offset (M) Sdn Bhd, Malaysia

ISBN 1 86872 857 9 (Standard edition)
ISBN 1 86872 876 5 (Sponsors' edition)
ISBN 1 86872 875 7 (Collectors' edition)

CONTENTS

FOREWORD

When I was a lot younger than I am now, I was thrilled to have met James Chapin shortly before he died in 1964. He had been one of my boyhood heroes, when I had gone through a phase of learning all that I could about Africa's explorer-naturalists. It was Chapin who, in an extraordinary piece of detective work and more than some dogged perseverance, 'discovered' the Congo Peacock in 1936. The species was responsible for having caused something of a sensation in the ornithological world of the time. Peacocks, you see, were not supposed to have occurred in Africa.

In any event, you need to persevere and you need to be a bit of a detective, together with some other sometimes 'abnormal' attributes, if you want to join the ranks of the world's top-class bird-watchers. These people are passionate about tracking down rare birds, and they will endure any amount of privation to gain sightings of their quarry. Sinclair and Ryan are very much in this bracket, but they also derive satisfaction from observing the everyday activities of easy-to-see common species. And, there are many more of these than there are rarities in Africa; the majority, indeed, being easily viewed and identified from the comfort of your camp chair or stationary motor vehicle. This book will help you to do just that, almost anywhere in sub-Saharan Africa. All watchers of African birds should be grateful to Sinclair and Ryan for making their avian-related activities a little easier.

The authors thank me for having encouraged them. Frankly, however, I cannot recall ever having said anything to them about producing a comprehensive field guide to the birds of Africa. Had they asked me about the book when it was still a twinkle in their eyes, I probably would have responded by playing the role of a doubting Thomas. They have proven my cautionary thinking wrong, and I am delighted. They can be proud of their book.

The book will help to bring pleasure to many people, for sure. But, it will do more than just that. It will assist in the further expansion of nature-based tourism and, hence, the economic development of Africa. Albeit in a relatively small way. Moreover, because of its virtual continental scope, it constitutes an expression of the importance of the notion of connectivity in the conservation of the avian resource. A cursory perusal of the book's geographical distribution maps exemplifies that not only nomads and migrants but most birds are no respecters of national boundaries or those of parks and reserves. In short, the fact of the matter is that plants and animals (and birds are animals, too) are dispersed according to a system of areas of sources and sinks. The future welfare of Africa's rich avian diversity, indeed its whole biodiversity, depends on how effectively such areas are protected and linked by corridors of connectivity.

Finally, I have to say again, mainly for those people who tend to take this sort of thing for granted, that the production of a field guide to the birds of Africa was no easy task. It has come together because of the talents and efforts of special people, synthesized in some measure by serendipity. To all concerned, illustrators, consultants and authors, congratulations on a job well done. Your book is bound to take a place among the classic publications of its kind. I feel confident in saying that James Chapin would have concurred.

Roy Siegfried

SPONSOR'S FOREWORD

It is a great privilege and pleasure to have been part of this milestone in ornithological history – the publication of *Birds of Africa south of the Sahara*. As an African company, we are proud to have sponsored this attractive, accessible and authoritative field guide to Afro-tropical birds. Detailing some 2 100 birds, it covers more species than any other bird field guide in the world.

The idea for the project was first conceived on a sultry African night in a remote village pub after an exciting day's birding. The conversation turned, as it often did, to an abiding problem: the absence of a competent field guide covering birds of the region – in fact, the absence of field guides to much of Africa's bird life. Clearly, such a significant gap in world bird literature would require the talents, experience and efforts of some truly intrepid author. Among the company was Ian Sinclair, renowned African birder, author and adventurer. Perhaps emboldened by the cold beer, Sinclair took up the challenge. The project was on course – and was to take more than five years to complete.

Africa holds undiscovered treasures of nature, pristine backdrops, and the certain thrill of adventure. Our cover bird, Prince Ruspoli's Turaco, for instance, is found only in juniper forests deep in the untamed south of Ethiopia. This stunning bird has eluded many an avid birder, but the chance of a sighting will continue to draw parties to the region.

The Turaco, the wild places and the wildlife of Africa are the elements of ecotourism, an emerging industry that offers local people the promise of a better life. And publications like this one are essential to such an industry – both to support ecotourism ventures by luring nature-lovers to the continent, and to document Africa's rich wildlife heritage.

Our Company has in the past sponsored a field guide, *Birds of the Indian Ocean Islands*, a second edition of which will soon be published. Now in 2003, Chamberlain's centenary year, we offer to conservation, to birds and birders, this important field guide, *Birds of Africa south of the Sahara*.

Philip and David Chamberlain

CHAMBERLAIN

1903 - 2003

ACKNOWLEDGEMENTS

AUTHORS' ACKNOWLEDGMENTS

Firstly, the team at Struik have been so patient and helpful on this long project and to them all: Pippa Parker, Helen de Villiers, Robin Cox, Heston Michaels, Tracey Hawthorne, Pierra Abbot, Katharina von Gerhardt, Emily Bowles and Tessa Kennedy, many, many thanks.

Norman Arlott has gone well beyond all our demands and requests to provide us with the finest set of images of African birds ever done … thanks. Peter Hayman and Alan Harris are also thanked for their fine artwork.

To the countless birders in the field who over the years have encouraged and helped us on this project go our appreciation, admiration and thanks. Those we wish to mention and thank personally are Niel and Liz Baker, James and Tanya Brown, Rod & Tamar Cassidy, David and Margot Chamberlain, Bill Clarke, Callan Cohen, Alvin Cope, Matthieu Le Corre, Harry Dilley, Gerold Dobler (Swarovski), Tony and Maureen Dixon, Dick Forsman, John Graham, Trevor Hardaker, Hans Jornvall, Rob Leslie, Alan Kemp, Olivier Langrand, Pete Leonard, Lyn Mair, David Moyer, Mel Ogola, Robert Payne (waxbills, whydahs and indigobirds), Richard Porter (Socotra endemics), Claire Spottiswoode, Isley Rasmussen, Barrie Rose, Albert Wannenmacher (Swarovski), Barry Watkins, and Giles and Barbara Webb. Thanks also to Roy Siegfried for his inspiration and encouragement over many years and for his foreword.

Thanks to Robert Prys-Jones at the Bird Room of the British Museum for access to research material.

Finally, to our long-suffering wives and children go our thanks, not only for enduring our too many absences in the field but also for their understanding of our passion in the pursuit of birds.

Ian Sinclair & Peter Ryan

ARTIST'S ACKNOWLEDGEMENTS

My thanks go to the following for their help in supplying answers to queries that cropped up during the preparation of my artwork: Roger Mitchell of Papyrus Tours UK, Dr John Fanshawe, Dr Richard Liversidge, and the staff of the British Museum at Tring – especially Peter Colston, Michael Walters and Dr Robert Prys-Jones for allowing access to their skin collection. I also owe a great debt to John G Williams, who inspired my fanatic interest in Africa and its birds, and an unpayable debt to my wife, Marie, for managing a home and family while I spent days and weeks researching in museum and field.

Norman Arlott

PUBLISHER'S ACKNOWLEDGEMENTS

The Publisher acknowledges with gratitude the generous sponsorship towards this publication by FH Chamberlain Trading; and extend their appreciation to Sasol Limited for permission to reproduce the artwork appearing in *Sasol Birds of Southern Africa* (3rd edition, 2002) alongside the new artwork in this publication.

INTRODUCTION

Africa is one of the best places to go birding. The continent is second only to South America in terms of numbers of bird species, and arguably offers more rewarding birding than other tropical regions – thanks to the large number of conspicuous species associated with savanna and woodland habitats. Africa is home to two endemic bird orders, 10 endemic families (with two more only reaching Madagascar or Arabia), and of the more than 2 100 species in sub-Saharan Africa, almost 1 400 are restricted to the region.

This book is a concise identification guide to the birds of sub-Saharan Africa. Preparing it has been a daunting task, given the very large number of species, but we believe it is useful to bring all the region's birds together in one volume. We hope that it will encourage greater interest in Africa's birds, and promote birding throughout the region. Historically, birding attention has been divided into three general areas: west Africa, east Africa and southern Africa. This balkanisation of birding activity was exacerbated by political differences and resulted in some unfortunate consequences. At a prosaic level, it led to regional differences in common names. More significantly, it greatly decreased our knowledge of areas outside the classic boundaries of areas of interest. For example, we know much more about the birds of southern than northern Mozambique simply because the southern part of the country lies south of the Zambezi River, and thus falls within the rather arbitrary limits of southern Africa. Similarly, east African birders have tended to stop their activities at the DRC border, in part because the DRC fell outside 'their' area. The aim of this book is to promote a more holistic view to birding throughout the continent, and to highlight species that fall outside the three regions covered in traditional field guides.

Scope of the book

The book covers all species that regularly occur in the Afrotropics (excluding south-west Arabia), one of the world's major faunistic zones. The boundary between the Afrotropics and western Palearctic runs through the centre of the Sahara Desert. Rather than following arbitrary political boundaries, we have taken the boundary to be 20°N. This excludes north Africa, which forms part of the Palearctic and is well covered in field guides for the western Palearctic. Coverage includes southern Mauritania and most of Mali, Niger, Chad and Sudan. However, some extremely marginal species that just enter the north of these countries are only mentioned as 'similar species'. These species, as well as vagrants recorded fewer than 10 times in the region, are not illustrated but are described briefly at the end of accounts for related species (*see below*).

The book includes seabirds regularly occurring within 200 nautical miles of the continent, as well as the birds endemic to the inshore islands off Africa: Bioko, São Tomé, Prìncipé and Annobon in the Gulf of Guinea, Pemba and Zanzibar off Tanzania, and Socotra off Somalia. It does not cover Madagascar and the Indian Ocean islands with affinities to Madagascar (Comoros, Seychelles and the Mascarenes); the birds of these islands are well covered by Sinclair and Langrand's *Birds of the Indian Ocean Islands* (Struik, 1998). It also excludes oceanic islands in the Atlantic such as the Cape Verdes (typically treated as part of the Palearctic), Ascension, St Helena and Tristan da Cunha.

Given the large number of species covered and the desire to give them adequate coverage within a package that remains a manageable size in the field, we have kept the introductory section brief.

Group introductions

The vast majority of the book is devoted to the species accounts, but we have included brief introductions to the main groups of birds. These may be useful for birders from outside Africa to give some idea of the general type of bird in each group. They are also used to save repetition in individual species accounts. For example, we use them to highlight potential confusion with other broad groups of birds, to identify common behavioural traits or to report the existence of short-lived juvenile plumages that are generally similar across the group.

11

VEGETATION MAP OF AFRICA

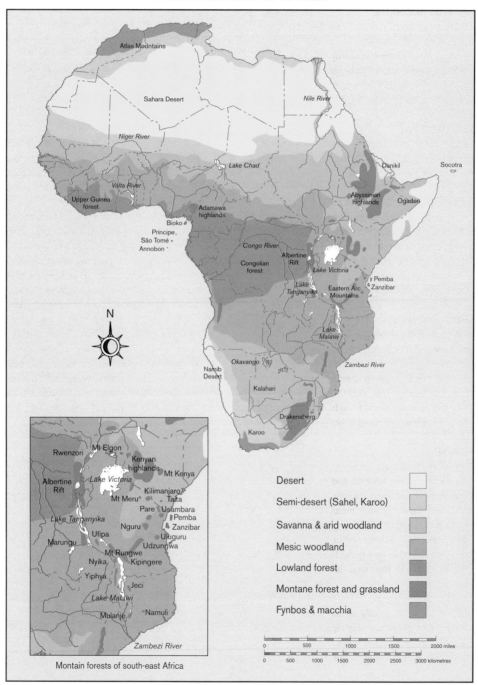

Desert

Semi-desert (Sahel, Karoo)

Savanna & arid woodland

Mesic woodland

Lowland forest

Montane forest and grassland

Fynbos & macchia

Montain forests of south-east Africa

12

Species accounts

The large scope of the book necessitates rather brief texts. Much of the information is conveyed through illustrations and range maps. However, we have attempted to convey as much germane information in the texts as possible, saving space by using abbreviated sentence structures. Each species account has four main sections: identification, habitat, status and voice. The header for each account gives the standard common name, with widely used alternative names given in parentheses, the scientific name, and the approximate size (length from bill tip to tail tip) in centimetres (cm).

Identification

The accounts focus primarily on identification. Where a species has a restricted range, this is highlighted first. We use N, S, E, W and C Africa for north, southern, east, west and central Africa, respectively. The text summarises the key identification features of each species in a comparative sense, rather than providing a detailed description of each bird (which is presented more succinctly in the illustrations). We highlight the diagnostic features that separate a particular bird from species with which it could be confused.

It is not always possible to illustrate all plumages in a field guide of this scope. Significant differences as a function of age and/or sex are reported in the text, although where similar juvenile plumages are common to entire groups of birds (e.g. the short-lived juvenile plumages of robins, chats, flycatchers, larks, etc.), they are merely mentioned in the group introductions. For brevity, juvenile (juv.) is used loosely to include pre-adult plumages, unless a separate description is given for immatures (imm.), in which case juvenile is the first post-fledging plumage, and immature means all subsequent plumages until adult plumage is attained. Unless otherwise specified, statements such as 'Female duller' are in relation to the male, and 'Juv. more streaked below' is relative to adult plumage (or female plumage if the adults are sexually dimorphic). It also isn't possible to illustrate all geographic variants, but the main racial differences are described briefly in the text. For most species, the accounts should be sufficient to identify most individuals, but for some species space constraints prevented as complete a treatment as we would have liked. For other species, the identification criteria for certain ages and sexes are not known adequately, and for still other species, definitive field characters are lacking. This adds to the challenge and enjoyment of birding in Africa, and offers the opportunity to birders to make novel contributions to our understanding of field identification characters. However, the reader should be prepared to accept that not all individuals in some groups can be identified reliably.

Habitat

This section briefly summarises the main habitats in which birds are found. The major terrestrial habitats are forest (divided into lowland and montane, gallery forest, and secondary growth or farm bush), woodland (broad-leafed, including miombo *Brachystegia,* and acacia woodland), savanna (grassland with scattered trees), grassland (treeless areas, typically at higher elevations), semi-desert (including Karoo, Sahel, etc.), desert and mountains (including heathland, mountain fynbos and alpine habitats). The gross distribution of these habitats is summarised in the map opposite, and repeated at the back of the book. Many montane forest species have very restricted ranges, especially in E Africa; the inset map opposite shows the location of most of these mountain ranges. Aquatic habitats include rivers, other inland wetlands (lakes, dams, marshes and various temporary wetlands including vleis and dambos), estuaries, the coastline and marine habitats. Seabirds are loosely ascribed to either coastal (inshore, usually over the continental shelf) or oceanic (offshore, usually off the shelf) waters. Where species occupy specific niches within these broad habitat types, these are also reported. Forest habitats are broadly divided into three vertical zones: understorey (forest floor up to about 3 m from the ground), canopy (the upper parts of the forest, typically with dense foliage) and the more open mid-strata in between.

Status

This section reports the relative abundance of each species. Status categories are, in decreasing order: abundant, common, fairly common, uncommon, scarce, rare and vagrant. These categories are subjective and related to the size and type of bird. Thus a 'common' raptor may be less numerous within an area than an 'uncommon' bulbul. Clearly the status applies only to the range of the bird, and should be interpreted in conjunction with the range maps. Most species vary in abundance within their mapped range, but we have acknowledged this only where there is a consistent geographic pattern in abundance (e.g. common in S, scarce in NE). The qualifier 'locally' (e.g. locally common) is used for species that are patchily distributed within the mapped range. For species listed as threatened by BirdLife International's (2000) *Threatened Birds of the World*, threat category is reported first: Critical, Endangered or Vulnerable.

The status section also reports on the seasonality and movements of each species. The default assumption is that species are resident unless otherwise stated. Migrant species are typically either intra-African migrants (which have both breeding and non-breeding areas within the continent) or Palearctic migrants, which breed to the north of the region and winter in Africa. The seasonality of occurrence of migrants (e.g. Oct-Apr) are broad generalisations, encompassing the main arrival and departure dates across the continent; they are unlikely to apply throughout. They also fail to consider birds which remain on the non-breeding grounds throughout the year (mostly immatures), which are regular in at least some migrant species.

Voice

This section attempts to describe the major songs and calls, which we acknowledge is highly subjective. Sonograms are more useful for people used to interpreting them, but space limitations precluded their inclusion in this book. Clearly the best way to convey bird calls is to listen to recordings. We thus annotate those species that are available on the two major commercial compilations for Africa: Claude Chappuis' (2001) *African Bird Sounds* (15 CDs covering some 1460 species) and Guy Gibbon's (1995) *Southern African Bird Sounds* (6 CDs of some 900 species). Numbering systems differ between these CDs. Chappuis has up to 99 tracks on each CD, occasionally resorting to two species per track (labelled a and b). Gibbons has 15 tracks per CD, each with usually 10 species per track. Thus C14.3a refers to the first part of track 3 on Chappuis' CD14, and G4.12.2 is the second cut on track 12 of Gibbon's CD4.

Similar species

Because of the vast scope of this field guide, we have not illustrated all vagrants to the region. Our cut-off was to leave out species that had been recorded fewer than 10 times, but we also omitted a few species that occur only in the extreme north of the area; these species are well treated in western Palearctic guides. Both the vagrants and marginal species are listed as 'similar species' at the end of the account of the species deemed to be most similar to them. The very brief accounts for these species are by no means definitive; they are merely intended to alert birders to the possible occurrence of these species in the region.

Illustrations

The book combines illustrations from Sinclair, Hockey & Tarboton's *Birds of Southern Africa* (Struik, 2002) and Kemp & Kemp's *Birds of Prey of Africa* (Struik, 1998) with new artwork commissioned specially for this project. Most of the new artwork was done by Norman Arlott, with additional plates by Peter Hayman and Alan Harris. Images were combined electronically, and although we attempted not to mix illustrations by different artists on the same plate, this was not always possible. Typically, single birds are not labelled; unless otherwise indicated, all birds depicted are adult males. Other plumages are labelled: juvenile (juv.), immature (imm.), sub-adult (sub-ad.), non-breeding (non-br.), breeding (br.), male (♂), and female (♀). Birds labelled as breeding or non-breeding are all adults. Single images are only labelled if there are sex or racial differences that are not illustrated.

Range maps

The distributions of all species are plotted on one of seven basic range maps. The small scale of these maps (especially the map of the entire region) necessitates some generalisations, especially for species with patchy distributions (e.g. species confined to mountain forests are often shown with much larger and less fragmented ranges than is actually the case). Small, isolated populations are highlighted with lines on the maps. The mapped ranges should be taken only as general guidelines of each species' range.

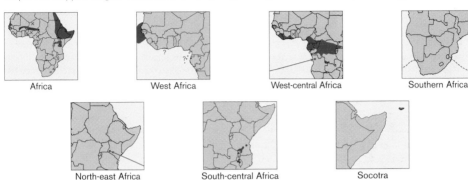

Africa	West Africa	West-central Africa	Southern Africa

North-east Africa	South-central Africa	Socotra

Ranges are mapped in red. There is no attempt to map breeding and non-breeding ranges of migratory species. Dashed lines are used to denote the extreme limits of mobile species such as seabirds. Crosses (x) indicate extra-limital records or vagrants. The ranges of many species are poorly known, and in some instances question marks (?) are used to show areas where species may occur, but there are too few data.

Species order, taxonomy and common names

In general, we have ordered plates according to the traditional taxonomic sequence. Although this is not representative of the evolutionary relationships among birds, there is considerable resistance among birders to a change from this sequence. We further justify our choice by noting that we have deviated from a strict evolutionary sequence to group species that look similar, or to balance the number of species on each plate.

The question of common names is perhaps more contentious. Each region of Africa has its own set of names, with the greatest differences between southern Africa and the rest of the continent. Southern Africa has the larger number of birders, whereas the rest of Africa covers a greater area. Southern Africa also has fewer birds, resulting in some inappropriate parochialisms such as Wattle-eyed Flycatcher and Puff-backed Shrike, akin to 'the' Swallow and Kingfisher in Britain. The decision on a single set of common names was taken out of our hands to some extent by the International Ornithological Committee, which set up a working committee under Frank Gill to come up with a single set of common names for all the world's birds. Stuart Keith chaired the African sub-committee, which after much heated debate came up with the list we use here. We do not personally like all the choices made, but in the interests of attaining a unified list we have adopted them. However, we retain major synonyms in parentheses.

Finally, bird systematics is in a state of flux, with molecular evidence and a switch to a more phylogenetic species concept combining to result in the splitting of many taxa – very often re-splitting species that were lumped in the mid-20th century. We have been liberal in adopting these splits, especially where our field experience suggests that they are well founded. We have broadly followed the recent literature, but also use unpublished data to raise well-marked subspecies to species status. Although not all these decisions may stand the test of further investigation, we believe that most will, and that by including them here we will encourage birders to be more critical in their observations and ultimately to contribute to the ongoing taxonomic debate.

GREAT ALBATROSSES

Huge pelagic seabirds, with pink bills and mostly white underwings at all ages. Plumage variation considerable; combination of upperwing and tail pattern important for identification. Adults have diagnostic white backs, but beware gannets (p. 42) and occasional Shy Albatrosses with white backs. Sexes alike.

1 WANDERING ALBATROSS *Diomedea exulans* 107-130 cm

A huge, hump-backed albatross with a pink bill. At all ages, has white underwing with narrow black trailing edge, tip and leading edge to carpal joint. Juv. is dark chocolate-brown, with white face and underwings. As birds age, they become progressively whiter: body becomes mottled ('leopard' stage); then all-white, with fine vermiculations concentrated on back and breast, forming shadow breast band; then upperwing starts to whiten, initially from centre of wing over elbow (not from leading edge, as in Southern Royal Albatross). Throughout these stages, birds have black tail tip (mostly white in Royal Albatross). Males whiten faster than females, and eventually, after 20-25 years, become all-white, apart from black flight feathers. These very old males differ from old Southern Royal Albatross by their pinker bill with no dark cutting edge. Feathering doesn't extend far onto lower mandible (as is case in royal albatrosses), giving a steeper-looking forehead. **Habitat:** Open ocean, breeding at sub-Antarctic islands; occasionally visits trawlers, but seldom joins feeding mêlée. **Status:** Vulnerable. Rare inshore, but more common beyond continental shelf. **Voice:** Harsh, nasal 'waaaak', seldom heard at sea. [G1.1.10] **Similar species: Tristan Albatross** *D. dabbenena* is slightly smaller, and breeds in darker, more juvenile plumage, but probably not separable at sea; abundance in African waters unknown.

2 NORTHERN ROYAL ALBATROSS *Diomedea sanfordi* 107-122 cm

Same size and shape as Wandering Albatross. Crisp black upperwing contrasting with white body and tail is diagnostic. Underwing is like Wandering Albatross's, but has broader black carpal patch. Bill is slightly yellower than Wandering Albatross's; black cutting edge is visible at close range. Juv. has some black in outer-tail and slight scalloping on back, but lacks brown body of juv. Wandering Albatross; has much less black in tail than Wandering Albatrosses with dark upperwings; black carpal patch is narrower than adult's. **Habitat:** Open ocean, mostly at shelf break. **Status:** Endangered. Rare visitor to South Africa. **Voice:** Silent at sea. **Similar species: Southern Royal Albatross** *D. epomophora* has upperwing whitening with age from leading edge; white tail separates it from Wandering Albatrosses, except for very old birds; juv. is similar to juv. Northern Royal Albatross; vagrant to South Africa.

SMALL ALBATROSSES (MOLLYMAWKS)

Large pelagic seabirds. Smaller and generally more common than great albatrosses, with dark backs. Species have diagnostic bill and underwing patterns, although bill colour changes with age; underwing becomes paler in some species. Sexes alike.

3 SHY ALBATROSS *Thalassarche cauta* 92-100 cm

Largest of the 'dark-backed' albatrosses. Upperwing and mantle are paler than those of other mollymawks; very rarely has white back. At all ages, underwing pattern is diagnostic (except for Salvin's and Chatham albatrosses): mostly white, with narrow black border and diagnostic black 'thumb-print' on leading edge near body. Adult has pale grey cheeks and white crown; bill is pale olive-grey with yellow tip. Juv. and imm. have grey-washed head, often with incomplete grey breast band; bill is grey with black tip. **Habitat:** Open ocean, mostly over continental shelf; large numbers scavenge at trawlers; generally occurs closer to land than other albatrosses. **Status:** Common year round; adults most abundant May-Aug. **Voice:** Loud, raucous 'waak' when squabbling over food. [G1.2.1] **Similar species: Salvin's Albatross** *T. salvini* adult has grey-sided bill with paler, yellowish band along upper and lower mandible, and dark spot on lower mandible tip; head and neck are washed grey, with paler crown; imm. is virtually identical to Shy Albatross, but black primary tips are slightly more extensive and head greyer; status poorly known, with only a few records from South Africa. **Chatham Albatross** *T. eremita* is even rarer; adult has yellow bill with dark tip to lower mandible, and dark, uniform grey head; imm. similar to imm. Salvin's Albatross; vagrant to South Africa.

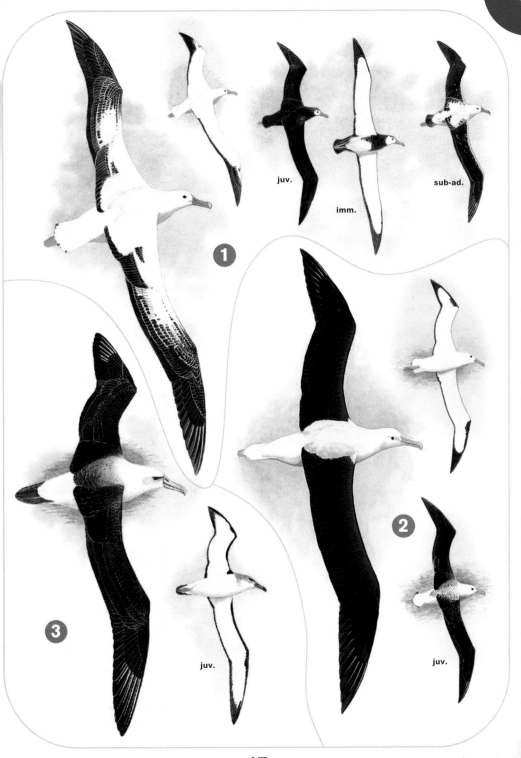

juv.

imm.

sub-ad.

juv.

juv.

1 BLACK-BROWED ALBATROSS *Thalassarche melanophris*   84-92 cm

Adult has a diagnostic orange bill with a reddish tip, and a small black eyebrow. Underwing has broad black leading edge and narrower trailing edge. Juv's underwing is all-dark, lightening with age. Juv. has dark horn-grey bill with black tip. Amount of grey on head and neck is variable, usually forming incomplete collar; lacks smooth grey mantle of juv. Grey-headed Albatross. Sub-adult's bill is dull yellow with black tip. **Habitat:** Open ocean, breeding at sub-Antarctic islands; scavenges at trawlers. **Status:** Common year round, but adults mostly Apr-Sep. **Voice:** Grunts and squawks when squabbling over food. [G1.2.2] **Similar species: Laysan Albatross** *Phoebastria immutabilis* resembles sub-adult Black-browed Albatross but has dark-washed cheek, brown lower back and black streaks on underwing coverts; feet project beyond tail tip in flight; vagrant from N Pacific to South Africa.

2 GREY-HEADED ALBATROSS *Thalassarche chrysostoma*   80-88 cm

Similar to Black-browed Albatross, but adult has uniform pale grey head and black bill with yellow stripe along upper and lower mandibles. Juv. has darker grey head; cheeks may become almost white but always has darker, more uniform grey crown and neck, merging smoothly into mantle, than juv. Black-browed Albatross. Juv's bill appears all-dark (not black-tipped), and soon develops yellow tinge to tip of upper mandible. **Habitat:** Open ocean, breeding at sub-Antarctic islands; joins other albatrosses feeding at trawlers. **Status:** Vulnerable. Rare, mostly juv. birds, Jun-Sep. **Voice:** Grunts and squawks when squabbling over food. [G1.2.3] **Similar species: Buller's Albatross** *T. bulleri* has neatly demarcated underwing like yellow-nosed albatrosses at all ages, and grey-washed head and neck with pale forecrown; adult's bill has broad yellow stripe along upper mandible and narrow stripe on lower mandible; juv. has dark horn bill with black tip; vagrant to South Africa.

3 ATLANTIC YELLOW-NOSED ALBATROSS
Thalassarche chlororhynchos   72-80 cm

A small, slender albatross with a relatively long bill. Underwing has crisp black margin, with leading edge roughly twice as broad as trailing edge at all ages. Adult has black bill with yellow stripe along upper mandible, becoming reddish towards tip. Differs from Indian Yellow-nosed Albatross by having grey wash on head and nape (slightly paler on forecrown); at close range, base of yellow stripe on upper mandible is broad and rounded (not pointed). Juv's bill is all-black and head is white; indistinguishable from juv. Indian Yellow-nosed Albatross. **Habitat:** Open ocean, breeding at Tristan and Gough islands. **Status:** Fairly common year-round in small numbers. **Voice:** Generally silent at sea; throaty 'waah' and 'weeeeh' notes when squabbling over food. [G1.2.4]

4 INDIAN YELLOW-NOSED ALBATROSS *Thalassarche carteri*   72-80 cm

Adult differs from Atlantic Yellow-nosed Albatross by having a mostly white head, with only a faint grey wash on the cheek; at close range, yellow bill stripe on upper mandible ends in a narrow point (not rounded). Juv's bill is all-black and head is white; indistinguishable from juv. Atlantic Yellow-nosed Albatross. **Habitat:** Open ocean, breeding at islands in Indian Ocean. **Status:** Vulnerable. Fairly common year-round, mostly May-Sep further N. **Voice:** Similar to Atlantic Yellow-nosed Albatross's.

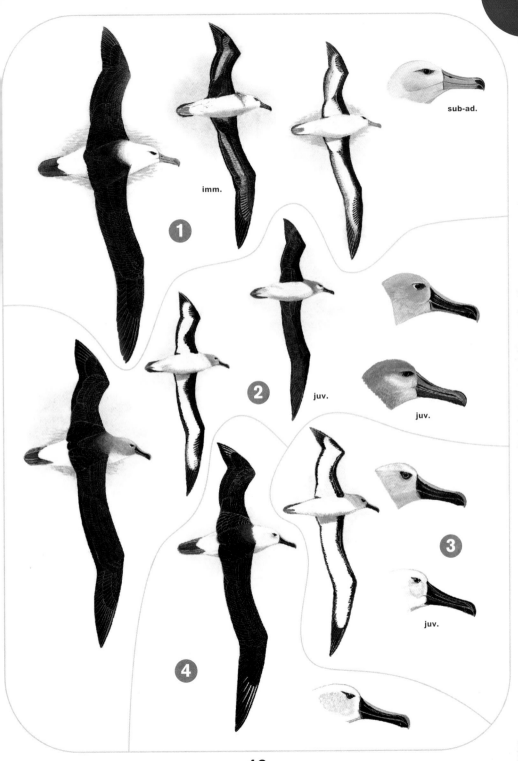

imm.

sub-ad.

1

2

juv.

juv.

3

juv.

4

1 SOOTY ALBATROSS *Phoebetria fusca* 84-89 cm

A dark brown, slender albatross with long, narrow wings and a long, wedge-shaped tail that usually appears pointed. Adult is all-dark, with pale shafts to primary and tail feathers. At close range, yellow stripe is visible on lower mandible. Juv. and imm. have conspicuous buff collar and mottling on back, but this does not extend to rump as in Light-mantled Sooty Albatross. **Habitat:** Open ocean; breeds at sub-Antarctic islands. **Status:** Vulnerable. Rare in oceanic waters; vagrant over continental shelf. **Voice:** Silent at sea. [G1.2.5] **Similar species: Light-mantled Sooty Albatross** *P. palpebrata* has pale mantle extending to rump; adult has lilac stripe on bill; vagrant to South Africa.

GIANT-PETRELS

Huge, lumbering petrels with humped backs like great albatrosses and massive, pale bills. At a distance could be confused with sooty albatrosses or juv. gannets (p. 42). Flight action is less graceful than that of albatrosses and, unlike albatrosses, they moult their primaries sequentially, often resulting in large gaps in the primaries. Often occur close to shore, especially near seal colonies, but rarely come ashore in Africa. Sexes alike.

2 SOUTHERN GIANT-PETREL *Macronectes giganteus* 86-99 cm

Adult has paler head and breast than Northern Giant-Petrel, but definitive identification requires seeing greenish bill tip. Juv. is dark brown, becoming lighter with age; greenish bill tip of juv. is not well defined. Rare white morph is white with few black spots. **Habitat:** Open ocean; breeds at sub-Antarctic islands. Scavenges at trawlers and around seal colonies. **Status:** Vulnerable. Fairly common in coastal waters, but decreasing in numbers. **Voice:** Harsh grunts and wheezes when squabbling over food. [G1.2.7]

3 NORTHERN GIANT-PETREL *Macronectes halli* 81-94 cm

Very similar to Southern Giant-Petrel, but has a reddish tip to the bill, which appears dark-tipped at a distance. Adult has pale face and foreneck, but seldom attains full pale head of adult Southern Giant-Petrel. No white morph. Juv. is dark brown, becoming lighter with age; reddish bill tip is less well defined than adult's. **Habitat:** Open ocean; breeds at sub-Antarctic islands. Scavenges at trawlers and visits seal colonies more frequently than Southern Giant-Petrel. **Status:** Fairly common in coastal waters. **Voice:** Grunts and wheezes, slightly higher pitched than Southern Giant-Petrel's. [G1.2.8]

FULMARINE PETRELS

Medium-sized, distinctively plumaged petrels. Keen ship followers, but seldom come very close to shore. Sexes alike.

4 PINTADO PETREL *Daption capense* 38-40 cm

A small, black-and-white petrel with chequering on the back and upperwing. Head is black; tail white, with black tip. Underparts are white; underwing is narrowly bordered black. **Habitat:** Open ocean; breeds on sub-Antarctic and Antarctic islands. Habitually follows trawlers. **Status:** Common visitor to coastal waters, mostly May-Nov. **Voice:** High-pitched 'cheecheecheechee' when feeding. [G1.3.1] **Similar species: Antarctic Petrel** *Thalassoica antarctica* is larger, brown above lacking chequering, with white subterminal band across wings and tail; Antarctic vagrant to South Africa.

5 ANTARCTIC FULMAR *Fulmarus glacialoides* 45-51 cm

A pale grey petrel with white underparts and white panels in the primaries. At close range, dark-tipped, pink bill with blue nostrils is diagnostic. Flight is light and buoyant. **Habitat:** Open ocean; breeds in Antarctica. Scavenges at trawlers, often among Pintado Petrels. **Status:** Rare visitor, mostly Jun-Oct. **Voice:** High-pitched cackle when squabbling over food. [G1.2.9]

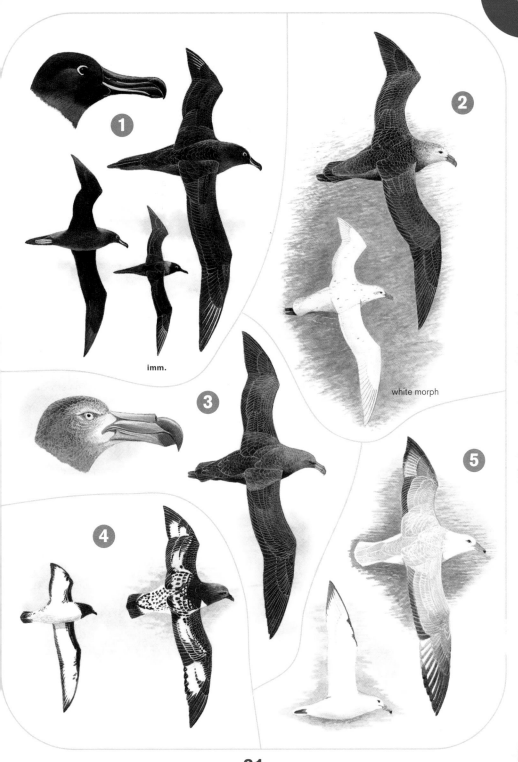

imm.

white morph

Medium-sized petrels characterised by erratic, towering and very rapid flight. Bills dark; shorter and deeper than shearwaters (p. 26). All-dark species could be confused with smaller Bulwer's and Jouanin's petrels (p. 32). Wings usually held more angled than shearwaters and other petrels. Birds of open ocean; seldom occur close to shore unless there are strong onshore winds. Sexes alike.

1 GREAT-WINGED PETREL *Pterodroma macroptera*   40-42 cm
A dark brown petrel with a short, stubby, black bill and relatively large head. Wings are long and slender, held angled at wrist. Wing and bill shape, dark (not silvery) underwing and short neck differentiate it from Sooty Shearwater (p. 26). Smaller than White-chinned Petrel (p. 26), with black (not white) bill and gadfly jizz. Soars high above water in typical gadfly action, but flight action tends to be more relaxed than other gadfly petrels'. **Habitat:** Open ocean; winter breeder on sub-Antarctic islands. **Status:** Common visitor, mainly Oct-Apr. **Voice:** Silent at sea. [G1.3.3]

2 KERGUELEN PETREL *Aphodroma brevirostris*   34-36 cm
A small, compact petrel. Shape resembles that of gadfly petrels, but has characteristic 'bull-neck' and large head with large, dark eyes; often appears hooded. Smaller and greyer than Great-winged Petrel, with silvery highlights, especially on leading edge of forewing. Often towers up to 50 m above sea, hanging motionless or even hovering kestrel-like with rapid, shallow wing beats. Flight is very rapid and erratic. **Habitat:** Open ocean; breeds on sub-Antarctic islands. **Status:** Vagrant, mostly Jun-Sep. Irrupts in fairly large numbers in some years. **Voice:** Silent at sea. [G1.3.6]

3 SOFT-PLUMAGED PETREL *Pterodroma mollis*   32-37 cm
A small gadfly petrel with a variable dark breast band and a white throat. White underparts contrast with dark underwings. Upperparts are grey, with faint, darker 'M' across upper wings. Rare dark morph lacks silvery highlights of Kerguelen Petrel, has more slender neck, and is often mottled on belly. Flight is rapid and erratic. **Habitat:** Open ocean; breeds on sub-Antarctic islands. **Status:** Uncommon in shelf waters, mostly Apr-Sep; common offshore year round. Status in N Atlantic uncertain (*see* Fea's Petrel). **Voice:** Silent at sea. [G1.3.4] **Similar species: White-headed Petrel** *P. lessonii* is larger, with a white head and tail; sub-Antarctic vagrant to S Africa; **Barau's Petrel** *P. baraui* has white underwing and breast; unconfirmed sight records from the SE coast.

4 FEA'S PETREL (GON-GON) *Pterodroma feae*   32-33 cm
Endemic to N Atlantic. Very similar to Soft-plumaged Petrel, which may also reach these waters. Has longer, more pointed wings and paler tail that contrasts with dark rump. Breast band is incomplete (usually complete in Soft-plumaged Petrel), and underwing is darker. **Habitat:** Open ocean. **Status:** Rare and little known in W African waters. **Voice:** Silent at sea. [C1.1a] **Similar species: Zino's (Madeira) Petrel** *P. madeira* is slightly smaller, with thinner bill, smaller head and relatively shorter, more rounded wings; flanks are slightly mottled. Status in African waters unknown: Critically Endangered; population fewer than 100 birds.

5 ATLANTIC PETREL *Pterodroma incerta*   44 cm
A large, brown gadfly petrel with a conspicuous white lower breast and belly; most likely to be confused with jaegers (p.182). Much larger than Soft-plumaged Petrel, with chocolate-brown (not grey) plumage and no dark 'M' on upperwing. In worn plumage, neck and mantle can appear mottled brown. **Habitat:** Open ocean; winter breeder at Tristan and Gough islands. **Status:** Vulnerable. Vagrant, mostly May-Sep. **Voice:** Silent at sea.

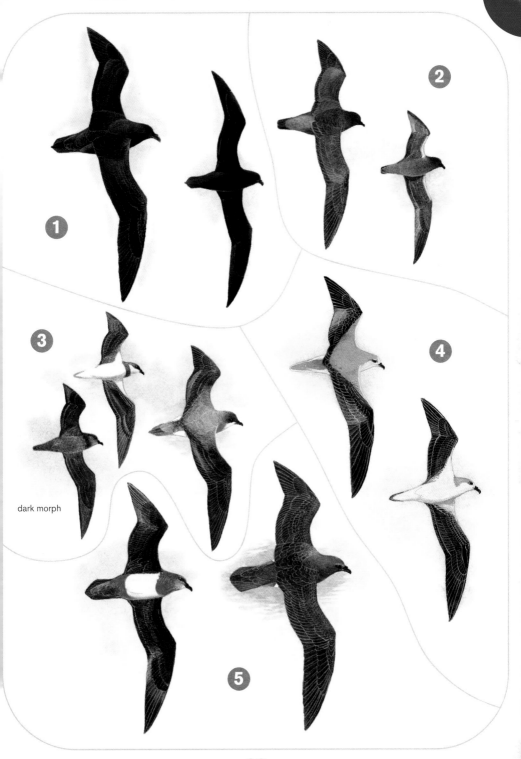

dark morph

1 BLUE PETREL *Halobaena caerulea* 28-30 cm

A small, blue-grey petrel with white underparts and underwings. Superficially similar to prions, but is larger, with diagnostic white-tipped tail; also has white frons, black crown and nape, and less well-defined, dark 'M' on upperwing. At a distance, has much darker partial neck collar, and body is more elongate, tapering from shoulders to relatively long tail. Flight action is more petrel-like than that of prions: faster and more direct, rising higher above water. **Habitat:** Open ocean; breeds at sub-Antarctic islands. Seldom strays N of 40°S. **Status:** Rare visitor, mostly Jun-Sep. Irrupts in fairly large numbers in some years. **Voice:** Silent at sea.

PRIONS

Small, blue-grey petrels with well-defined, dark 'M' marks across the upperwing and white underparts and underwings. Flight is fluttery and erratic. Easily separated from other petrels, but species identification is very tricky; depends on subtle differences in head and tail patterns. Most individuals not separable at sea. Sexes alike.

2 ANTARCTIC PRION *Pachyptila desolata* 25-28 cm

By far the most abundant species in African waters. Among broad-billed species, black tail tip is relatively narrow, with dark central stripe on undertail ('T'-bar). Bill is relatively narrow and bluish. Tends to have smaller breast smudges and cleaner face than larger Salvin's and Broad-billed prions, with relatively broad white supercilium, broadest behind the eye. **Habitat:** Open ocean; breeds at sub-Antarctic islands and Antarctica. **Status:** Common visitor, mostly late May-Aug, occurring in large flocks. Subject to 'wrecks' when large numbers of dead and dying birds come ashore. **Voice:** Silent at sea.

3 SALVIN'S PRION *Pachyptila salvini* 26-29 cm

Intermediate in size and coloration between Broad-billed and Antarctic prions. distinctly larger and darker than Antarctic Prion, with smaller, less distinct white supercilium and typically larger, darker breast patches. Very similar to Broad-billed Prion, although bill perhaps bluer at close range. In the hand, measurements overlap with Broad-billed and Antarctic prions. Most likely to occur in SE. **Habitat:** Open ocean; breeds at sub-Antarctic islands in Indian Ocean. **Status:** Uncertain; apparently rare visitor, mostly May-Sep. **Voice:** Silent at sea. [G1.3.8]

4 BROAD-BILLED PRION *Pachyptila vittata* 27-30 cm

The largest prion, identifiable at sea only if seen at very close range, when the broad, flattened, blackish (not blue as smaller prions) bill can be seen. However, bill size overlaps narrowly with that of Salvin's Prion, making positive identification in the field almost impossible. More likely to occur in SW. Head appears rather large, and grey smudges on sides of breast are well developed. **Habitat:** Open ocean; breeds at S temperate islands (Gough and Tristan). **Status:** Uncertain; apparently rare visitor, mostly May-Sep. **Voice:** Silent at sea.

5 SLENDER-BILLED PRION *Pachyptila belcheri* 25-27 cm

Similar to Antarctic Prion, but is slightly paler, especially on the head. At very close range, thin bill is diagnostic. Tends to have longer white eye-stripe than other prions. Grey breast smudges are usually reduced. Best feature is tail pattern: black tip is reduced, with outer 2-3 tail feathers white (only outer-tail feather is white in Antarctic Prion). Flight is rather more shearwater-like than that of other prions: wings are stiffer, with rapid bursts of flapping. **Habitat:** Open ocean; breeds at sub-Antarctic islands. **Status:** Poorly known; apparently rare in shelf waters, but large numbers irrupt in some years. **Voice:** Silent at sea. [G1.3.10]

6 FAIRY PRION *Pachyptila turtur* 24-26 cm

The smallest prion. Given a good view, this species is relatively easy to identify by broad black tip to tail and lack of dark central stripe on undertail. It appears paler than other prions, with pale, unmarked head and short bill. **Habitat:** Open ocean; breeds at sub-Antarctic islands. **Status:** Vagrant May-Sep; most records of beached birds. **Voice:** Silent at sea. [G1.4.1]

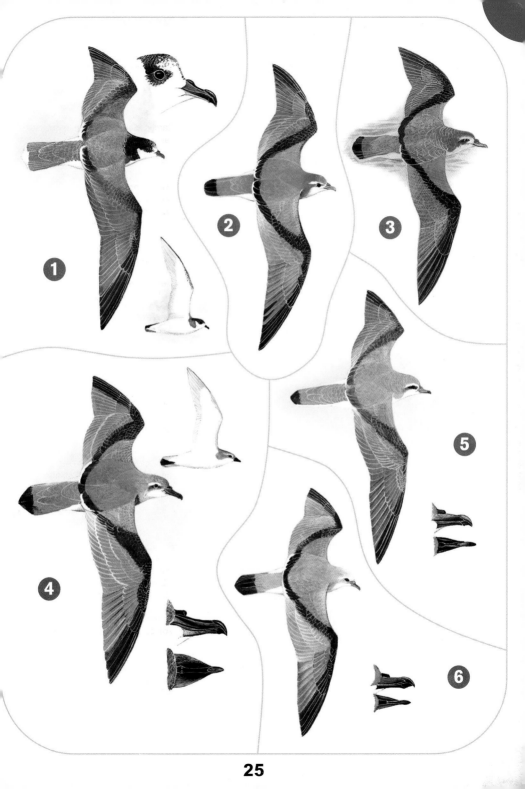

Large petrels and shearwaters with mostly dark brown or brown-and-white plumage. Flight is languid, with slightly angled wings in larger species, or more rapid, with stiff wings among smaller shearwaters. Some species occur in large flocks, and often occur fairly close to land. Sexes alike.

1 WHITE-CHINNED PETREL *Procellaria aequinoctialis* 51-58 cm
A large, all-dark-brown petrel (appears black in some light), with an obvious pale, whitish bill. At close range, black 'saddle' to bill is visible. White throat is variable in extent: conspicuous in some individuals, but greatly reduced or absent in others. Flight action is intermediate between gadfly petrels and shearwaters; wings are held slightly bent at wrist. **Habitat:** Open ocean; breeds at sub-Antarctic islands. Most abundant in shelf waters, where it scavenges at trawlers. **Status:** Vulnerable. Common year round, but probably decreasing due to longline fishing. **Voice:** High-pitched 'titititititi' when squabbling over food. [G1.4.2]

2 SPECTACLED PETREL *Procellaria conspicillata* 50-56 cm
Very similar to White-chinned Petrel, but has diagnostic white spectacle. Size of spectacle varies; incomplete in some birds, but when spectacle is narrow, it is not connected to white throat. Pale bill has slightly darker tip than White-chinned Petrel's. Some White-chinned Petrels have large white throat, and aberrant birds may have white head markings, often on nape. **Habitat:** Open ocean; attends trawlers. **Status:** Critically endangered. Rare visitor from Inaccessible Island, Tristan da Cunha, mostly Oct-Apr, but some records year round. **Voice:** Deeper than White-chinned Petrel's; seldom heard at sea.

3 SOOTY SHEARWATER *Puffinus griseus* 40-46 cm
A brown shearwater, differing from all other dark shearwaters by the silvery lining to the underwing (always visible, but varies with light conditions). Bill is long, slender and dark. Narrow wings are held straight, with little bend at wrist. Flight intersperses rapid bursts of flapping with short glides, but becomes petrel-like in high winds. **Habitat:** Open ocean, especially in coastal waters; breeds at sub-Antarctic islands. **Status:** Common., occurs throughout year in S, but most abundant May-Sep; in N Atlantic, mostly Jul-Oct. **Voice:** Silent at sea. [C1.6a, G1.4.7]

4 FLESH-FOOTED SHEARWATER *Puffinus carneipes* 45-50 cm
A dark brown shearwater with a dark-tipped, flesh-coloured bill and flesh-coloured legs and feet. Larger than Sooty Shearwater, lacking silvery underwing, but has pale primary bases; flight is more petrel-like, with wings more bent at wrist. Smaller than White-chinned Petrel, and pale bill is much more slender. Rounded tail and pale bill and feet distinguish it from Wedge-tailed Shearwater. **Habitat:** Open ocean; breeds at S temperate islands. **Status:** Uncommon to locally common visitor, mostly Jun-Aug in NE; small numbers present year round in S. **Voice:** Silent at sea. [G1.4.6]

5 WEDGE-TAILED SHEARWATER *Puffinus pacificus* 40-45 cm
A slender shearwater with a long, graduated tail that appears pointed in flight. Mostly dark-morph birds recorded from African waters: dark brown all over, with dark bill (but lacks bright fleshy feet of Flesh-footed Shearwater). Pale morph is brown above and white below, with clear-cut cap. Superficially resembles Great Shearwater (p. 28), but lacks pale rump and nape, and white underwing is mottled brown (not uniform white). Flight action is distinctive: light and buoyant on broad wings, held bowed forward and down. **Habitat:** Open oceans; breeds at tropical and subtropical islands. **Status:** Uncommon. **Voice:** Silent at sea. [G1.5.1]

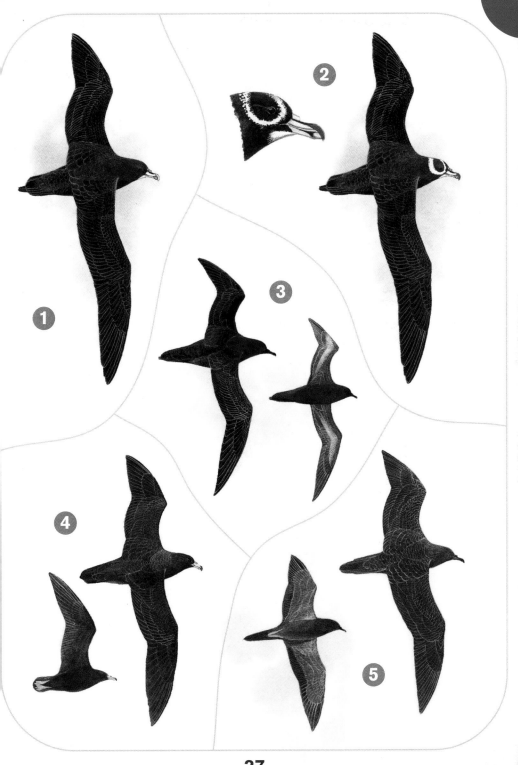

1 CORY'S SHEARWATER *Calonectris diomedea* 46 cm

An ash-brown shearwater with a yellow bill. Upperparts are rather uniform; paler than Great Shearwater's, but often shows pale crescent at base of tail. Flight is slow and languid on broad wings; stays close to water, not banking and shearing as much as other shearwaters. Atlantic race *borealis* has more robust bill and fully dark primaries on underwing (but this is tricky to see and dependent on light conditions). **Habitat:** Open ocean; breeds at islands in N Atlantic (*borealis*) and Mediterranean ('Scopoli's Shearwater' *diomedea*). Often forages in association with dolphins and tuna. **Status:** Common Palearctic migrant, mostly Oct-May. **Voice:** Silent at sea. [C1.2b,3a, G1.4.4] **Similar species: Streaked Shearwater** *C. leucomelas* has white face and streaked crown, nape and cheeks; vagrant to E coast.

2 CAPE VERDE SHEARWATER *Calonectris edwardsii* 42-44 cm

Slightly smaller and darker above than Cory's Shearwater, with a dark, more slender bill that looks relatively long. In flight, appears more slender, with narrower wings. Slightly darker crown gives capped appearance, but always lacks white nape and dark belly of Great Shearwater. Flight action is similar to that of Cory's Shearwater. **Habitat:** Open ocean; breeds at Cape Verde Islands. **Status:** Fairly common off W Africa; uncommon in Gulf of Guinea. **Voice:** Silent at sea. [C1.3b]

3 GREY PETREL *Procellaria cinerea* 48-50 cm

A pale, silvery-grey petrel with white underparts and a yellowish bill. Told from all pale-bellied shearwaters by grey (not white) underwing. Flight shape resembles White-chinned Petrel's (p. 26), but wing beats are curiously stiff and shallow. Grey-brown of head extends far down cheeks, with only narrow, white throat. **Habitat:** Open ocean, seldom straying N of 40°S; breeds at sub-Antarctic islands. **Status:** Rare visitor, mostly May-Oct. **Voice:** Silent at sea. [G1.4.3]

4 GREAT SHEARWATER *Puffinus gravis* 46-51 cm

A dark-capped shearwater with a diagnostic dark belly patch. Shows clear pale nuchal collar and broad white rump. Darker above than Cory's Shearwater, with dark bill. Underwing is mostly white, with indistinct lines across coverts. Flight action is more dynamic than Cory's and Cape Verde shearwaters', with more rapid wing beats and straighter wings. **Habitat:** Open ocean; breeds at Tristan and Gough islands. **Status:** In SW common Aug-Oct and Apr-May, fairly common Nov-Mar, scarce Jun-Jul; in NW fairly common Aug-Oct. **Voice:** Silent at sea. [C1.4a, G1.4.5]

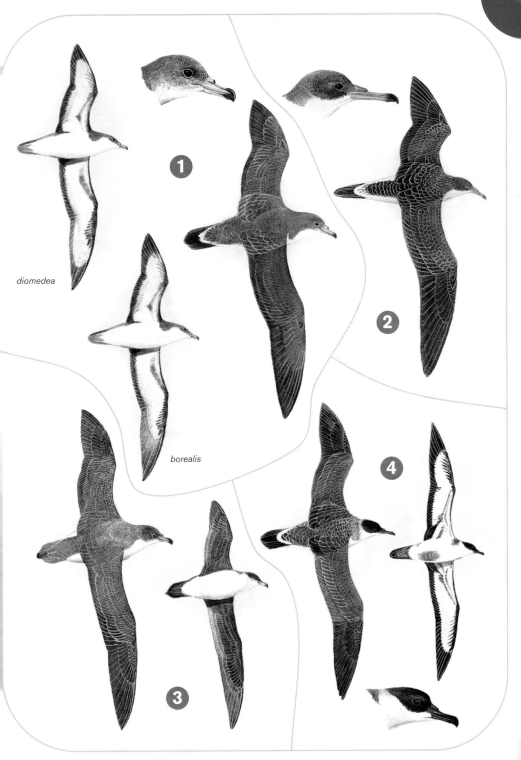

diomedea

1

2

borealis

4

3

1 MANX SHEARWATER *Puffinus puffinus*   30-36 cm
The largest black-and-white shearwater, with a relatively long, slender bill. Black (not brownish) upperparts contrast sharply with white underparts, unlike Balearic Shearwater's; often has white bands extending up onto sides of rump. Undertail coverts are white (not black or mostly black, as in Audubon's Shearwater). Black cap extends below eye, and underwing has broader black trailing edge than Little Shearwater's. Flight action is similar to Sooty Shearwater's (p. 26): long glides interspersed with rapid beats of stiff, straight wings (not rapid, fluttery flight of Little Shearwater). **Habitat:** Open ocean, over continental shelf, often with Sooty Shearwaters. **Status:** Uncommon Palearctic migrant, mostly Oct-Apr. **Voice:** Silent at sea. [C1.4b, G1.4.8]

2 BALEARIC SHEARWATER *Puffinus mauretanicus*   32-38 cm
Formerly considered a race of Manx Shearwater; slightly larger, with brown (not black) upperparts, and lacking sharp contrast on face. Typically has dark axillaries and dusky underparts and underwings, although this is variable. Some individuals are almost all dark, and could be confused with larger Sooty Shearwater (p. 26). **Habitat:** Open ocean, mostly in coastal waters; breeds at islands in W Mediterranean. **Status:** Uncertain; apparently rare Palearctic migrant Oct-Mar, with several records from South Africa. **Voice:** Silent at sea. [C1.5a]

3 AUDUBON'S SHEARWATER *Puffinus lherminieri*   30 cm
A small shearwater; intermediate in size between Little and Manx shearwaters. Bill is longer than Little Shearwater's, shorter than Manx Shearwater's. Dark brown above, appearing black in certain light. Has diagnostic dark (not white, as in Manx and Little shearwaters) undertail coverts (but Little Shearwater *boydi* from Cape Verdes has dark undertail). **Habitat:** Open ocean; breeds at Indian Ocean islands. **Status:** Uncommon in tropical and subtropical waters off E coast. **Voice:** Silent at sea. [C1.5b, G1.4.10]

4 LITTLE SHEARWATER *Puffinus assimilis*   25-30 cm
A tiny, black-and-white shearwater. Appreciably smaller than Manx Shearwater, with short, rounded wings and narrow black trailing edge to underwing (similar in width to leading edge, not twice as wide, as in Manx Shearwater). Flight action is distinctive: very rapid wing beats punctuated by short glides. N Atlantic has white-faced *baroli* (Canaries and Azores) and dark-faced *boydi* (Cape Verdes), which is browner above, with dark vent and flight feathers, and may be closer to Audubon's Shearwater. S Africa has both white-faced *tunneyi* (Indian Ocean and Australia) and dark-faced, silvery-grey *elegans* (sub-Antarctic islands). **Habitat:** Open ocean; in coastal waters. Often joins flocks of Sooty Shearwaters (p. 26). **Status:** Uncommon in NW; rare visitor in S, mostly May-Sep. **Voice:** Silent at sea. [C1.5b, G1.4.9]

white-faced races

BULWERIA PETRELS

Small, all-dark petrels with long, wedge-shaped tails. Could be confused with Matsudaira's Storm-Petrel (p. 34), or much larger Great-winged Petrel (p. 22). Sexes alike.

1 BULWER'S PETREL *Bulweria bulwerii* 26-28 cm

A small, dark brown petrel with a diagnostic long, wedge-shaped tail that is usually held closed and appears pointed. Superficially like a large *Oceanodroma* storm-petrel (p. 34), with deeper, stubby bill and paler grey-brown bar across upperwing coverts. Flight is buoyant and graceful. **Habitat:** Open ocean, seldom close to shore; breeds at N Atlantic islands. **Status:** Fairly common in NW; vagrant to SW. **Voice:** Silent at sea. [C1.2a, G1.3.2]

2 JOUANIN'S PETREL *Bulweria fallax* 30-32 cm

Similar to Bulwer's Petrel, but is larger, with a different flight action. Usually seen in calm, tropical oceans, where it flies low over the water with long glides interspersed with shallow, rapid flicks of the wings. In windy conditions, arcs and wheels high over the waves with dynamic, gadfly-like flight. Long, pointed tail could cause confusion with noddies (p. 196), but lacks pale crown, and bill is short and stubby. **Habitat:** Tropical Indian Ocean; breeding area unknown, presumed off Arabia. **Status:** Uncommon off E coast; possibly into Red Sea. **Voice:** Silent at sea.

STORM-PETRELS

Small pelagic seabirds often with white rumps. All-dark species could be confused with Bulwer's and Jouanin's petrels, but have forked (not wedge-shaped) tails. Flight rather erratic and fluttering in most species. Sexes alike.

3 WHITE-FACED STORM-PETREL *Pelagodroma marina* 19-21 cm

A very pale, long-legged storm-petrel with diagnostic white underparts and a prominent white eye-stripe. Upperwing coverts are pale brown; rump is pale grey. Direct flight is erratic, with jerky wing beats; long toes extend beyond tail tip. Feeding flight is buoyant, with legs swinging from side to side as it bounds over the water. **Habitat:** Open ocean, rarely inshore; breeds at Cape Verde, Tristan and Gough islands and Australasia; widespread in tropical and temperate waters. **Status:** Uncommon off NW Africa; vagrant to South Africa Apr-May and off E coast. **Voice:** Silent at sea. [C1.7a]

4 BLACK-BELLIED STORM-PETREL *Fregetta tropica* 19-21 cm

A fairly large, bulky storm-petrel with a broad white rump, black vent, white underwings and a white belly with a broad black line down the centre (unless the bird rocks right over, black belly line can be tricky to see in the field). Back and upperwing coverts are brown-tinged and darker than those of White-bellied Storm-Petrel. Flight action is characteristic: glides over the waves, seldom flapping. When feeding, appears to hit waves with its breast, almost stopping, then kicking forward with short-toed, triangular feet. **Habitat:** Open ocean, breeding at sub-Antarctic islands; often follows ships and attends trawlers. **Status:** Fairly common passage migrant off South Africa Sep-Oct and Apr-May; rare elsewhere. **Voice:** Silent at sea. [G1.5.6]

5 WHITE-BELLIED STORM-PETREL *Fregetta grallaria* 19-21 cm

Similar to Black-bellied Storm-Petrel, but belly is all-white, extending onto vent. Has paler, greyer back and upperwing coverts than Black-bellied Storm-Petrel due to grey-edged feathers. **Habitat:** Open ocean, breeding at south temperate islands; seldom follows ships. **Status:** Poorly known; rare over continental shelf; uncommon further offshore. **Voice:** Silent at sea. [G1.5.5]

1 WILSON'S STORM-PETREL *Oceanites oceanicus*   15-19 cm
A very small, dark petrel with a large, square, white rump. Long legs project beyond tail in flight and are obvious, dangling below bird when feeding, but can be retracted into belly plumage. Yellow webbing on feet is hard to see. Slightly larger than European Storm-Petrel, with square (not rounded) tail and broader, more rounded and flattened wings. Can show paler bar on underwing, but this is never white (unlike obvious white underwing stripe of European Storm-Petrel). Flight is swallow-like and direct, with frequent glides, but varies with wind strength. **Habitat:** Open ocean, breeding at sub-Antarctic islands and Antarctica; may occur at high densities, but seldom flocks; often follows ships. **Status:** Common year round in S; more abundant Apr-Sep; uncommon elsewhere. **Voice:** Silent at sea. [C1.6b, G1.5.4]

2 EUROPEAN STORM-PETREL *Hydrobates pelagicus*   14-17 cm
Slightly smaller and darker than Wilson's Storm-Petrel, with a short, rounded tail and diagnostic white bar on the underwing. Legs are short; feet never project beyond tail tip in flight. Flight action is typically more rapid and fluttery than that of Wilson's Storm-Petrel, with pale bar across upperwing coverts less pronounced. Often occurs in large flocks, pattering over water when feeding. **Habitat:** Open ocean, mostly over continental shelf; attends trawlers; breeds in NE Atlantic. **Status:** Common Palearctic migrant, mostly Oct-May. **Voice:** Silent in region. [C1.7b, G1.5.2]

3 LEACH'S STORM-PETREL *Oceanodroma leucorhoa*   19-22 cm
Larger than Wilson's and European storm-petrels, with a long, forked tail and narrow, 'V'-shaped white rump. Best identified by its long wings and languid flight action: glides low over waves, with wings held forward and bent at wrist, flapping infrequently, the deep wing beats causing erratic changes in direction. White rump is usually divided by dusky central line, and is rarely reduced or absent (unlike Swinhoe's Storm-Petrel). **Habitat:** Open ocean, breeding in N Atlantic and in small numbers at islands off South Africa; most occur, singly or in small groups, in oceanic waters beyond continental shelf; seldom follows ships. **Status:** Fairly common, mostly Oct-Apr. **Voice:** Silent at sea; musical chattering and trilling at night at breeding islands. [C1.8b, G1.5.3] **Similar species: Swinhoe's Storm-Petrel** *O. monorhis* is slightly smaller, with dark rump, paler forehead and more prominent pale panel on upperwing coverts; vagrant to NE coast (Feb-Aug). **Matsudaira's Storm-Petrel** *O. matsudairae* is larger, with long, broad wings, brown rump, very prominent panel across upperwing coverts and white shafts to primary bases; vagrant to E coast.

4 BAND-RUMPED (MADEIRAN) STORM-PETREL *Oceanodroma castro* 19-21 cm
Intermediate between Leach's and Wilson's storm-petrels, with a broad white rump and rather long tail with a shallow fork. Pale upperwing bar is not as pronounced as that of Leach's or Wilson's storm-petrels. Wing shape and flight action recall Leach's Storm-Petrel, but wing beats are generally shallower and progress less erratic. **Habitat:** Open ocean, mostly in tropical and subtropical waters; breeds at islands in central Atlantic; is usually solitary at sea and seldom follows ships. **Status:** Poorly known: fairly common off W Africa; migrant to Gulf of Guinea Feb-July. **Voice:** Silent at sea. [C1.8a]

GREBES
Distinctive, short-tailed diving birds mostly on fresh water. Seldom fly. Sexes alike, but plumage varies seasonally.

1 LITTLE GREBE (DABCHICK) *Tachybaptus ruficollis* 23-29 cm
A small, compact grebe with a pale, fleshy gape flange. Bill is short and relatively deep; head is rounded. In breeding plumage, has rich chestnut sides to neck; non-breeders are duller. Juv. has black-and-white striped cheeks. On water, sits with rump higher than back. **Habitat:** Lakes, dams and other freshwater bodies; rarely in estuaries and sheltered bays. **Status:** Common resident. **Voice:** Noisy; distinctive whinnying trill. [C1.10a, G1.1.8]

2 BLACK-NECKED GREBE *Podiceps nigricollis* 28-33 cm
Larger than Little Grebe, with longer, more slender neck. Bill is longer, with upturned tip; head is more angular. Eye is bright red. In breeding plumage has black head and throat, conspicuous golden ear tufts and chestnut flanks. Non-breeders and imms have white cheeks, throat and flanks. On water, sits with back higher than or level with rump. Preening birds often roll over, flashing white belly. **Habitat:** Lakes, pans and occasionally sheltered bays. **Status:** Fairly common but localised resident and nomad. **Voice:** Mellow trill during display. [C1.11, G1.1.7]

3 GREAT CRESTED GREBE *Podiceps cristatus* 45-56 cm
A large, long-necked grebe. Adult is unmistakable, with dark double crest and rufous-edged ruff ringing sides of head. Ruff of non-breeders is smaller and paler. Juv. has black-and-white striped head. Rarely seen in flight, when it has conspicuous white secondaries and lesser coverts. Wings are long and thin; flies with neck extended and legs trailing. **Habitat:** Large lakes and pans; rarely in estuaries and sheltered bays. **Status:** Locally common. **Voice:** Barking 'rah-rah-rah'; various growls and snarls. [C1.10b, G1.1.6] **Similar species: Red-throated Loon** *Gavia stellata* is larger, with shorter, thicker neck; lacks head ruff; Palearctic vagrant to NW coast.

PENGUINS
Flightless seabirds; only one species breeds in Africa. Sexes alike.

4 AFRICAN PENGUIN *Spheniscus demersus* 60-70 cm
Breeding endemic to S Africa. Adult has diagnostic black-and-white face and breast pattern. Some birds have double breast band, like vagrant Magellanic Penguin, but upper band is narrower; also lacks pink line at base of bill. Juv. lacks bold patterning, varying from greyish-blue to brown above; some partially moult heads to adult plumage. **Habitat:** Coastal; rare beyond 50 km from shore; breeds mostly on offshore islands. **Status:** Vulnerable. Common, but decreasing in numbers. **Voice:** Loud, donkey-like braying, especially at night. [G1.1.3] **Similar species: Magellanic Penguin** *S. magellanicus* is rare vagrant from South America: one South African record, probably ship-assisted.

5 ROCKHOPPER PENGUIN *Eudyptes chrysocome* 55-61 cm
Has a short, stubby, red bill and a yellow crest that starts just in front of eye (does not meet on forehead, as in Macaroni Penguin). Juv. is browner above, has dull red bill and lacks yellow crest, but has 'crest' of raised brown head feathers. Most records are of northern *moseleyi*, which has longer crest and more extensive dark tips to underflipper. **Habitat:** Pelagic S of 30°S; breeds at Tristan, Gough and sub-Antarctic islands. **Status:** Vulnerable. Rare visitor to S, mostly Nov-Mar; most records are moulting juveniles. [G1.1.4] **Voice:** Silent in Africa. **Similar species: Macaroni Penguin** *E. chrysolophus* is larger, with massive bill, pink gape and yellow crests meeting on forehead; sub-Antarctic vagrant to S Africa; **Gentoo Penguin** *Pygoscelis papua* and **King Penguin** *Aptenodytes patagonicus* are also very rare sub-Antarctic vagrants.

1

non-br.

br.

non-br.

2

non-br.

non-br.

br.

3

non-br.

br.

juv.

4

partial head-moult

juv.

5

imm.

Stiff-winged, tropical seabirds that typically fly high over the sea. Could potentially be confused with large terns (p. 190). Sexes alike. Adults readily identified by colour of bill, tail streamers and upperwing. Juvs more similar and require careful scrutiny.

1 RED-TAILED TROPICBIRD *Phaethon rubricauda*   45 cm (45 cm tail)
The palest tropicbird. Adult is mostly white (tinged pink when breeding), with red bill and red tail streamers. Compared to other adult tropicbirds, has thin (not broad) black primary tips on outer primaries and small black tips on scapulars. Juv. is more finely barred above than White-tailed Tropicbird, with less black in outer primaries; bill is blackish; lacks nuchal collar of juv. Red-billed Tropicbird. **Habitat:** Open ocean; occasionally visits coast, sometimes remaining at cliff sites for days or weeks. **Status:** Uncommon visitor to E coast, vagrant to SW coast; breeds at Indian Ocean islands. **Voice:** Deep 'kraak', similar to Caspian Tern's. [G1.5.7]

2 WHITE-TAILED TROPICBIRD *Phaethon lepturus*   40 cm (40 cm tail)
The smallest tropicbird. Adult has orange-yellow bill, extremely long, whispy, white central tail feathers (shafts are black), and neat black face mask. In flight, has two black patches on each wing (outer primaries and median coverts). Juv. is smaller than other juv. tropicbirds, with barred upperparts and black wing tips; bill is yellow, with dark tip. Barring is sparser than juv. Red-tailed Tropicbird's, and black eye patch does not form nuchal collar as in juv. Red-billed Tropicbird. **Habitat:** Open ocean and islands. **Status:** Fairly common; breeds at Gulf of Guinea islands and oceanic islands off E coast, dispersing widely through tropical oceans. **Voice:** Silent at sea. [C1.13, G1.5.8]

3 RED-BILLED TROPICBIRD *Phaethon aethereus*   50 cm (50 cm tail)
The largest tropicbird. Adult has large red bill and white tail streamers. Differs from Red-tailed Tropicbird by its finely barred back, which appears grey at a distance, and by its long, white (not red) tail streamers. Juv. is heavily barred above, with black eye patch extending to nape to form nuchal collar. Bill is yellow, with dark tip. **Habitat:** Oceanic islands and open ocean. **Status:** Uncommon. Breeds at islands off Senegal and in the Red Sea, dispersing through tropical oceans. **Voice:** Largely silent at sea. [C1.12]

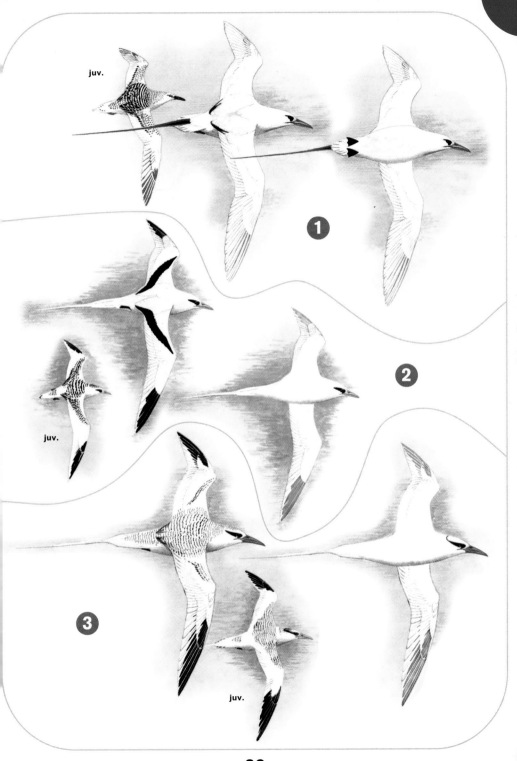

juv.

1

juv.

2

3

juv.

Distinctive large, black tropical seabirds with long, slender wings and deeply forked tails. Identification is complicated by a complex series of age- and sex-related plumage differences.

1 MAGNIFICENT FRIGATEBIRD *Fregata magnificens* 95-110 cm

The largest frigatebird, most likely to be seen off NW Africa. Might overlap with Ascension Frigatebird, although vagrant Greater and Lesser frigatebirds cannot be excluded from these waters. Adult male is all black (no paler upperwing bar, as in female and imm. frigatebirds), with blackish feet and red throat pouch; probably inseparable in the field from male Ascension Frigatebird. Adult female has pale breast with black chin and throat, blue eye-ring and red feet; differs from Ascension Frigatebird by having 3-4 wavy white bars on 'armpits' (visible only at close range). Juv. and imm. have pale feet and more extensive white on head and underparts than adult female, but generally less than same-aged Ascension Frigatebirds. Diagnostic wavy lines on armpits are present in all but the youngest birds, which never show white patches in underwing coverts as in Ascension Frigatebird. **Habitat:** Tropical oceans. **Status:** Rare in NW African waters; a few pairs breed at Cape Verde Islands. **Voice:** Silent at sea. [C1.20]

2 ASCENSION FRIGATEBIRD *Fregata aquila* 87-92 cm

Usually encountered in Gulf of Guinea, but might overlap with Magnificent and other vagrant frigatebirds. Bare-part coloration is same as Magnificent Frigatebird's; dark-morph adult males probably inseparable in the field. Pale-morph male has white lower breast and belly, with short spurs extending onto underwing. Female has broad brownish breast band; belly is black or white (as in males). Juv. has white head and underparts, with white blotches on underwing coverts. Imm. gradually develops dark breast band, then dark head and throat; unlike Magnificent Frigatebird it always lacks white wavy bars on armpits. **Habitat:** Tropical oceans. **Status:** Vulnerable; breeds only at Ascension Island. **Voice:** Silent at sea.

3 GREATER FRIGATEBIRD *Fregata minor* 86-100 cm

The common frigatebird off the E coast. Underwing is wholly dark, lacking white 'armpits' of Lesser Frigatebird. Male is black, with paler brown bar across upperwing coverts, reddish feet and red throat pouch. Female has white breast and throat, grey chin and red eye-ring and feet. Juv. has whitish or tawny head and throat, dark breast band and white lower breast and forebelly. Imm. is white from chin to belly, but gradually darkens. **Habitat:** Tropical oceans; occasionally roosts ashore in trees. **Status:** Fairly common at sea in tropical waters off E coast; vagrants reach South Africa, often after cyclones. **Voice:** Silent at sea. [G1.7.1]

4 LESSER FRIGATEBIRD *Fregata ariel* 71-81cm

Smaller and more angular than Greater Frigatebird, but this is only useful in direct comparison. Male is black, with diagnostic white 'armpits' extending from axillaries to sides of breast; lacks pale upperwing bars. Feet are dull red-black. Female has white breast extending as collar onto neck, red feet and red or blue eye-ring; differs from female Greater Frigatebird by black throat and white breast extending to armpits. Juv. has brownish head and mottled white breast. Imm. is variable, but typically has dark (brownish or black) throat, more extensive black on belly, and white breast extending to armpits. **Habitat:** Tropical oceans. **Status:** Rare off E coast; seen mostly after summer cyclones. **Voice:** Silent at sea.

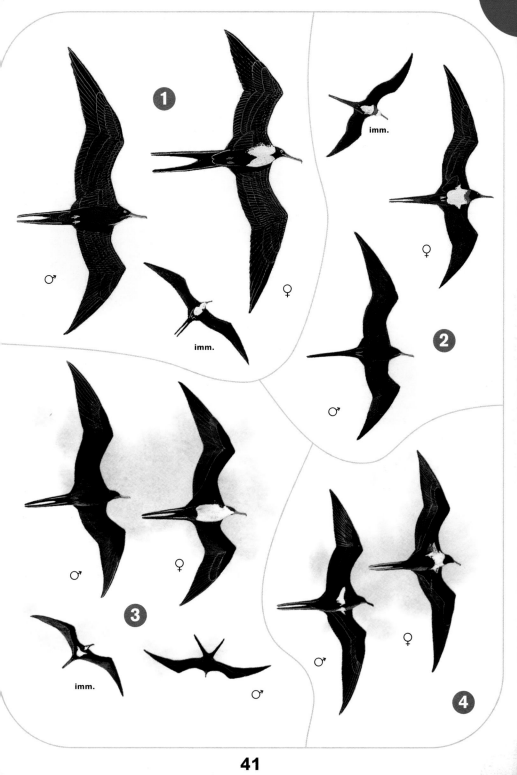

Large, plunge-diving seabirds with long, pointed wings and dagger-like bills. Breed colonially, but disperse widely at sea. Sexes alike; juvs distinctive.

1 NORTHERN GANNET *Morus bassanus* 90-100 cm

Adult is mostly white, with yellow wash to head and dagger-like bill. Differs from other gannets and Masked Booby by white (not black) secondaries and white tail (central tail feathers are occasionally dusky). Juv. is brown, with white spots; differs from Cape Gannet by short gular stripe. Imm. gradually acquires white adult plumage, going through various mottled phases; some white secondaries appear by third year. Juvs outnumber adults in W African waters. **Habitat:** Coastal waters, often attending fishing vessels. Roosts at sea. **Status:** Uncommon Palearctic migrant, mostly Oct-March. **Voice:** Raucous 'harrah', usually when foraging in groups. [C1.14]

2 CAPE GANNET *Morus capensis* 85-95 cm

Adult is similar to Northern Gannet, but has all-black (not white) secondaries and tail, and much longer gular stripe (seldom visible at sea). Juv. is brown with white spots, whitening gradually, typically starting with head. Juv. could be confused with Brown Booby, but is larger and lacks clear-cut brown bib and white belly. Juv. and imm. differ from other gannets by long gular stripe (seldom reliably identifiable at sea). **Habitat:** Coastal waters; often feeds at trawlers. **Status:** Vulnerable. Breeds at six islands off Cape and Namibia, dispersing N and E; range off W Africa poorly known due to confusion with Northern Gannet. **Voice:** Noisy 'warrra-warrra-warrra' at colonies and when feeding at sea. [G1.6.3]

3 AUSTRALIAN GANNET *Morus serrator* 83-92 cm

Very similar to Cape Gannet, but has a darker, greyish eye, more golden wash to head and much shorter gular stripe (but none of these features is useful for identification at sea). All confirmed records are of birds at Cape Gannet colonies, where they are best located by their higher-pitched call. Adult has white outer-tail feathers, but some Cape Gannets also show white outer-tail. Juv. differs from juv. Cape Gannet only by its short gular stripe. **Habitat:** Coastal waters and offshore islands. **Status:** Vagrant, but some birds return regularly to Cape Gannet breeding islands, and has bred with Cape Gannet. **Voice:** Higher pitched than Cape Gannet's. [G1.6.4]

4 MASKED BOOBY *Sula dactylatra* 80-90 cm

A large white booby. Lacks yellow head of adult gannets and has small black facial mask and broader black secondaries. Black (not white) tail and dark (not red) legs separate it from smaller, white-phase Red-footed Booby. Juv. resembles Brown Booby, but has narrow white collar around hindneck, less extensive brown on breast, and scruffy underwing with more extensive white coloration and dark central bar (clearly defined, smaller white area in Brown Booby; juv. Red-footed Booby has all-dark underwings). Usually solitary. **Habitat:** Tropical oceans and islands. **Status:** Fairly common along E coast, vagrant to W coast; breeds at islands from Red Sea to Tanzania. **Voice:** High double honk; generally silent at sea. [G1.6.1]

5 BROWN BOOBY *Sula leucogaster* 64-74 cm

Adult is dark brown, with a white lower breast and belly, and a broad white underwing patch. Bill and legs are yellowish. Uniform upperparts and crisply defined white underparts distinguish it from juv. gannets. Juv. is duller brown above; has brown flecks on white belly, but lacks white speckling of larger juv. gannets. Differs chiefly from vaguely similar juv. Masked Booby by solid and uniform upperparts and well-demarcated (not fuzzy) underpart pattern. **Habitat:** Tropical oceans and islands. **Status:** Common breeder at islands in Gulf of Guinea, Red Sea and Gulf of Aden; disperses through tropical waters, rarely reaching South Africa. **Voice:** Silent at sea. [C5.2b, G1.6.2]

6 RED-FOOTED BOOBY *Sula sula* 66-77 cm

A small, slender booby with a long, pointed tail and a pink-blue bill. Adult has bright red legs. Brown morph is plain brown; is much smaller than juv. gannets, and lacks pale-speckled plumage. White morph has yellow wash on head, but white (not black, as in adult Cape Gannet) tail, and in flight, has black carpal patch on underwing. Juv. is brown-streaked, with brownish bill and greyish-yellow feet. **Habitat:** Tropical oceans. **Status:** Uncommon in tropical waters along E coast; rare off W coast. **Voice:** Silent at sea.

imm.

sub-ad.

juv.

juv.

juv.

brown morph

Foot-propelled pursuit divers; often perch with extended wings. Cormorants have hook-tipped bills for grasping prey; darters spear prey with dagger-like bills. Sexes alike; juvs differ.

1 WHITE-BREASTED CORMORANT *Phalacrocorax lucidus* 80-100 cm
Largest African cormorant. Adult has white throat and breast (washed pink in marine populations), yellow skin at base of bill; eye turquoise. Breeding adult has white flank patches. Juv. has white underparts. Race *marocannus*, intermediate between White-breasted Cormorant and Great Cormorant *P. carbo*, with less extensive white breast, may occur in Mauritania. **Habitat:** Coastal and fresh waters. **Status:** Locally common. **Voice:** Grunts and squeals at colonies; otherwise silent. [G1.6.5]

2 BANK CORMORANT *Phalacrocorax neglectus* 76 cm
Endemic to Benguela upwelling region. A large, matt-black cormorant. More robust than Cape Cormorant, with thicker, woolly neck, heavier bill and diagnostic head shape: small crest on forecrown results in steep forehead and flat crown. Pre-breeding birds have white flecks on head and diagnostic white rump. Adult eye is unique: red above, turquoise below. Juv. has turquoise eye. **Habitat:** Rocky shores, islands and stacks; seldom moves more than 10 km from breeding islands. **Status:** Vulnerable. Locally common, but decreasing in numbers. **Voice:** Wheezy 'wheeee' at nest; otherwise silent. [G1.6.7]

3 CAPE CORMORANT *Phalacrocorax capensis* 61-65 cm
Breeding endemic to S Africa. A medium-sized cormorant with a short tail and long, slender neck. Adult has glossy blue-black plumage, yellow-orange throat patch, turquoise eye. Breeding birds have blue-spotted eye-ring and bright orange-yellow throat. Juv. is dark brown, with paler underparts and drab brownish-yellow throat. Imm. in worn plumage can be very pale brown. **Habitat:** Coastal waters, estuaries and lagoons. Often feeds and roosts in huge flocks. **Status:** Abundant, but numbers decreasing. **Voice:** 'Gaaaa' and 'geeee' noises at nest; otherwise silent. [G1.6.6]

4 AFRICAN DARTER *Anhinga rufa* 80 cm
Differs from cormorants by its long, slender neck and head and long, pointed bill. Adult has elongate, white-striped scapulars and wing coverts. Breeding male has rufous foreneck, with white stripe down neck. Female and non-breeding male have pale brown throat. Juv. has buffy neck; lacks streaking on back. When swimming, often only long neck and head visible. Often glides in flight, with broad wings, and long, broad tail. **Habitat:** Lakes, dams and slow-moving rivers; rarely coastal lagoons and estuaries. **Status:** Common. **Voice:** Croaks when breeding; otherwise silent. [C5.4a, G1.6.10]

5 REED (LONG-TAILED) CORMORANT *Phalacrocorax africanus* 50-55 cm
A small, short-billed, long-tailed cormorant. Adult has yellow-orange face, red eye, and small crest on forehead (pronounced when breeding). Back is scaled, with black-edged silver feathers. Juv. is dark brown above and white (not dark, as in Crowned Cormorant) below; may show darker breast; throat is pale. **Habitat:** Lakes, dams and rivers; also sheltered coastal waters outside S Africa. **Status:** Common. **Voice:** Cackles and hisses at colonies; otherwise silent. [C5.3b, G1.6.8]

6 CROWNED CORMORANT *Phalacrocorax coronatus* 50-55 cm
Endemic to Benguela upwelling region. Marine counterpart of Reed Cormorant, with slightly shorter tail. Adult has orange-red face, longer forehead crest (in breeding plumage) and less contrasting back scaling. Juv. has brown-washed (not white, as in Reed Cormorant) underparts, especially on throat and breast. **Habitat:** Offshore islands, coast, estuaries and lagoons. **Status:** Locally common. **Voice:** Cackles and hisses at colonies; otherwise silent. [G1.6.9]

7 SOCOTRA CORMORANT *Phalacrocorax nigrogularis* 80 cm
An all-dark marine cormorant. Smaller than White-breasted Cormorant, with shorter tail and dark grey (not black) bill, black (not orange or yellow) throat skin and dark green (not turquoise) eye. Juv. dark brown above, paler below. Differs from Cape Cormorant by narrow white margins to back feathers, creating distinctive, arrow-marked effect; ranges not known to overlap. **Habitat:** Coastal waters, roosting ashore; may breed occasionally at Socotra. **Status:** Vulnerable. Uncommon and sporadic. **Voice:** Silent in Africa.

imm.

1

br.

2

br.

juv.

3

4

juv.

juv.

♂

imm.

5

juv.

6

juv.

7

br.

1 HAMERKOP *Scopus umbretta*   48-56 cm
Endemic to Africa and Madagascar; monotypic family. A dark brown, heron-like bird with a heavy crest and a flattened, boat-shaped, black bill. Has rather long, black legs and shortish neck. Hammer-shaped head profile is diagnostic, but often rests with neck retracted, and crest lies along back. Flight is buoyant, showing finely barred tail at close range. **Habitat:** Lakes, dams and rivers. Nest is huge, domed structure of sticks, with small side entrance, usually in sturdy tree or on cliff ledge. **Status:** Common. **Voice:** Sharp 'kiep' in flight; jumbled mixture of querulous squawks and frog-like croaks during courtship. [C5.9b, G1.9.1]

HERONS
A diverse group of long-legged wading birds with dagger-like bills. Sexes alike, but plumage varies with age and seasons in some species. Polymorphic egrets pose greatest identification challenge.

2 GOLIATH HERON *Ardea goliath*   135-150 cm
The largest heron, with a massive bill. Rich chestnut head, neck and underparts recall much smaller Purple Heron, but has an unstriped head and dark (not yellow) legs and bill. In flight, the huge, broad wings beat slowly and deeply. Juv. is less rufous than adult, with foreneck, chest, belly and underwing coverts white, streaked with black. **Habitat:** Lakes, dams, large rivers and estuaries, usually where there are extensive reeds or papyrus. **Status:** Locally common. **Voice:** Loud, low-pitched 'kwaaark'. [C5.9a, G1.7.4]

3 PURPLE HERON *Ardea purpurea*   78-86 cm
The black-striped rufous head and neck and dark grey wings are distinctive. Much smaller than Goliath Heron, with yellow (not dark) bill and legs. Juv. is duller, with less well-marked head stripes and browner back. Flight more buoyant than large herons, with long legs and toes extending well beyond tail tip. **Habitat:** Wetlands, typically among sedges and reeds; seldom forages in the open. **Status:** Common. **Voice:** Hoarse 'kraaark'. [C1.29, G1.7.5]

4 GREY HERON *Ardea cinerea*   90-100 cm
A large, greyish heron told in flight from Black-headed Heron by its uniform grey (not contrasting dark and pale) underwing. Adult has mostly white head and neck, with black eye-stripe ending in wispy plume; bill and legs are yellowish. Juv. differs from juv. Black-headed Heron by underwing pattern, pale flanks, yellow (not dark) upper legs and white (not black) ear coverts. **Habitat:** Pans, dams, slow-flowing rivers, lagoons and estuaries. **Status:** Common. **Voice:** Harsh 'kraaunk' in flight. [C1.30/31, G1.7.2]

5 BLACK-HEADED HERON *Ardea melanocephala*   85-92 cm
Slightly smaller than Grey Heron, with contrasting dark flight feathers and pale underwing coverts in flight (not uniform grey underwing). Black-topped head and hindneck contrast with white throat. Bill and legs are black. Juv. has grey (not black) on head and neck; differs from juv. Grey Heron by dark legs and flanks, dark (not white) ear coverts and underwing pattern. **Habitat:** Grassland, fields and scrubland; also marsh fringes, but seldom forages in water. **Status:** Common. **Voice:** Loud 'aaaaark'; various hoarse cackles and bill clapping at nest. [C5.8b, G1.7.3]

1

2

juv.

3

juv.

4

juv.

5

juv.

1 YELLOW-BILLED (INTERMEDIATE) EGRET *Egretta intermedia*   65-72 cm

A medium-sized white egret with a yellow bill and dark legs and toes, with paler tibia. Smaller than Great White Egret with a shorter bill and neck, which is not held in such a pronounced 'S' shape; gape ends just below eye (behind eye in Great White Egret). Larger than Cattle Egret with a longer bill and more slender appearance. In breeding plumage, has long plumes on back and chest, red bill and upper legs, and lime-green lores. **Habitat:** Marshes and flooded grassland; rarely at estuaries. **Status:** Common resident and nomad. **Voice:** Typical, heron-like 'waaaark'. [C5.8a, G1.7.9]

2 GREAT WHITE EGRET *Egretta alba*   85-92 cm

A large white egret with a large, heavy bill; gape extends behind the eye. Larger and heavier-billed than Yellow-billed Egret. Lacks yellow toes of much smaller Little Egret. Structure recalls larger *Ardea* heron (p. 46). Legs and feet are black at all times. In breeding plumage, has elaborate plumes, black bill and lime-green lores. Non-breeding birds have yellow bill. **Habitat:** Lakes, dams, estuaries and lagoons. **Status:** Common. **Voice:** Low, heron-like 'waaaark'. [C1.28, G1.7.8]

3 LITTLE EGRET *Egretta garzetta*   55-65 cm

A smallish, white egret with black legs and contrasting yellow toes. Straight, black bill is more slender and slightly shorter than that of Western Reef Heron. Very similar to Dimorphic Egret but assumed to be absent from open coast in E Africa. Rare dark morph varies from grey to black; usually has white throat. Non-breeding birds have grey lores (usually yellow in Dimorphic Egret); breeding birds have mauve (not pink) lores and black (not pale yellow) eyes. Juv. lacks head plumes and aigrettes; toes are duller yellow. Often feeds by actively pursuing fish in shallow water. **Habitat:** Wetlands, coastal pools, mangroves and estuaries. **Status:** Common. **Voice:** Harsh 'waaark'. [C1.27, G1.7.8] **Similar species: Snowy Egret** *E. thula* is slightly smaller with shorter bill and more extensive yellow lores; Nearctic vagrant.

4 CATTLE EGRET *Bubulcus ibis*   48-54 cm

A small, compact egret with much shorter bill, neck and legs than Yellow-billed Egret. Legs are olive-yellow; bill is yellow. Adult has buff plumes on crown, mantle and breast, forming a shaggy bib; buff areas increase in breeding season, but are never as extensive as Squacco Heron's (p. 50). Pre-breeding birds have reddish bill and legs. Juv. has black legs immediately after leaving nest, but these soon pale. **Habitat:** Mostly in grasslands, often in association with cattle or game; roosts in large trees or reedbeds. **Status:** Common; highly gregarious. **Voice:** Heron-like 'aaaark' or 'pok-pok'. [C1.25, G1.8.1]

5 WESTERN REEF HERON *Egretta gularis*   56-66 cm

A coastal egret which differs from Little and Dimorphic egrets by having a very long, heavy, yellow-brown (not dark) bill and olive-yellow legs (not black with yellow feet). Occurs in dark and white morphs. Dark morph is dark grey, with white throat and variable white patch on primary coverts, visible in flight. Imm. is greyish-brown or white, diversely mottled with grey or grey-brown. **Habitat:** Coastal rocky beaches and mangroves. **Status:** Locally common. **Voice:** Harsh 'gaaar'. [C1.50] **Similar species: Little Blue Heron** *E. caerulea* has yellowish-green legs and pale grey bill with dark tip; adult is slate-grey, juv. is white, imm. is mottled; Nearctic vagrant.

6 DIMORPHIC (MASCARENE) EGRET *Egretta dimorpha*   55-65 cm

Occurs in dark and white morphs. White morph is very similar to Little Egret, but appears more slender, with longer-looking neck and bill; yellow of toes extends up front of tarsus. Compared to Western Reef Heron, legs are black (not olive-yellow) and bill is shorter and black (not brownish-horn). Some intermediate birds are mottled grey and white. In breeding plumage, feet and face are bright pink. Dark-grey morph has white throat and wing spot (not all dark grey as in Black Egret). Juv. is typically grey to blue-grey, with white throat and some brown feathering on wings and neck. **Habitat:** Apparently exclusively coastal, foraging in pools on exposed coral beds; breeds in colonies on coral islets. **Status:** Locally common. **Voice:** Very similar to Little Egret's.

non-br.

non-br.

br.

1

br.

3

non-br.

non-br.

br.

2

juv.

non-br.

4

non-br.

non-br.

br.

imm.

5

dark morph

white morph

dark morph

6

1 BLACK HERON (EGRET) *Egretta ardesiaca*   46-52 cm
A small, slate-black egret, with black legs and orange-yellow toes. Blacker than Slaty Egret, with dark (not dull yellow) legs. Shorter necked and lacks white or rufous throat and white wing patches of other dark egrets (p. 48). Often uses its wings to form an 'umbrella' over head, shading water. Adult has nape, back and breast plumes, which are pronounced in breeding season. Juv. slightly paler, lacking plumes. **Habitat:** Lakes and marshes; occasionally estuaries. **Status:** Locally common resident and nomad. **Voice:** Seldom calls; deep 'kraak'. [C5.7b, G1.7.10]

2 SLATY EGRET *Egretta vinaceigula*   48-58 cm
Endemic to S Africa. A dark grey egret with diagnostic rufous throat. Differs from Black Heron by greenish-yellow (not black) legs and feet; does not use its wings to shade water when feeding. Eye is yellow (black in pre-breeding birds). Juv. lacks head and breast plumes. **Habitat:** Marshes and vegetated lake shores. **Status:** Vulnerable. Uncommon; local nomad. **Voice:** Unknown.

3 SQUACCO HERON *Ardeola ralloides*   42-46 cm
A small, buff-and-white heron, with a heavy, greenish-yellow bill with a dark tip. Breeding adult has blue base to bill. At rest, appears mostly buff and brown, with white underparts, but in flight has prominent white wings and tail. Wings are broad and rounded. Juv. and non-breeding birds are less boldly streaked and blotched dark brown than Madagascar Pond Heron. **Habitat:** Vegetated margins of lakes, pans and slow-moving rivers; skulks in long grass, sitting motionless for long periods. **Status:** Common. **Voice:** Low-pitched 'kruuk'; rattling 'kek-kek-kek'. [C1.24, G1.8.2]

4 MADAGASCAR POND HERON *Ardeola idae*   45-48 cm
Slightly larger than Squacco Heron, with a heavier bill. Non-breeding bird is dark brown (not buffy) above, with much broader and darker streaking on throat and breast; tends to show a sharper contrast between streaked breast and white belly. Breeding plumage, seldom seen in Africa, is completely white. **Habitat:** Vegetated lake shores; often in more open areas than Squacco Heron. **Status:** Vulnerable. Uncommon visitor from Madagascar, mostly May-Oct. **Voice:** Louder 'kruuk' than Squacco Heron's. [C5.6b, G1.8.3]

5 RUFOUS-BELLIED HERON *Ardeola rufiventris*   38-40 cm
A small, dark heron with a sooty head and breast, and rufous belly, wings and tail. In flight, bright yellow legs and feet contrast strongly with dark underparts. Pre-breeding birds have red lores and legs. Juv. has rufous on forewing only and is dull brown (not blackish), becoming darker with age. Skulking; normally seen only when put to flight. **Habitat:** Dense marshes and flooded grassland. **Status:** Uncommon resident and local migrant. **Voice:** Typically heron-like 'waaaaak'.

6 GREEN-BACKED HERON *Butorides striata*   40-44 cm
A small, dark heron with an erectile black crown, dark grey-green back and paler grey underparts. Stands motionless in characteristic hunched posture. Legs are yellow (orange in pre-breeding birds). From behind, back is greener and more scaled than Dwarf Bittern's (p. 52). Black, wispy nape plume is not usually seen except when bird alights. Juv. is streaked brown and buff; fledgling has pink-orange legs. **Habitat:** Sluggish rivers overhung with trees, lake shores (often in rocky areas), mangroves and coral reefs at low tide. **Status:** Fairly common. **Voice:** Sharp 'baaek' when flushed. [C5.7a, G1.8.4]

umbrella
feeding

1

2

non-br.

br.

br.

imm.

3

imm.

imm.

4

non-br.

imm.

5

juv.

juv.

6

imm.

juv.

1 WHITE-BACKED NIGHT-HERON *Gorsachius leuconotus* 50-56 cm

A medium-sized heron with a large, dark head and conspicuous pale eye-ring. Dark back and wings with contrasting small white back are obvious in flight and during display; much darker than Black-crowned Night-Heron. Neck is rufous, with white throat. Juv. has streaked neck and is paler brown above, spotted white on wing coverts. Has black (not yellow) bill and larger cap than juv. Black-crowned Night-Heron, with plain mantle; white back develops with age. Roosts during day in dense cover; more nocturnal than Black-crowned Night-Heron. **Habitat:** Slow-moving rivers overhung with dense vegetation. **Status:** Uncommon; easily overlooked. **Voice:** Sharp 'kaaark' when disturbed. [C5.6a, G1.8.6]

2 BLACK-CROWNED NIGHT-HERON *Nycticorax nycticorax* 58-64 cm

Black crown, nape and back contrast with grey wings and tail, and white underparts. Juv. is grey-brown, with white spotting above; smaller than Eurasian Bittern, but is grey-brown (not tawny), and lacks black crown and moustachial stripes. Yellow (not dark) bill, spotted (not streaked) back, small cap and pale (not dark) eye distinguish it from juv. White-backed Night-Heron. Roosts communally in reeds and trees during the day, flying out at dusk to feed. **Habitat:** Lakes, rivers and rocky shores. **Status:** Common resident and Palearctic migrant. **Voice:** Harsh 'kwok' in flight. [C1.23, G1.8.5]

3 WHITE-CRESTED TIGER HERON *Tigriornis leucolopha* 66-80 cm

Smaller and more slender than Eurasian Bittern. Black, erectile cap is bisected by long white crest, but this is rarely seen unless bird is agitated. Lacks black moustache and foreneck stripes of Eurasian Bittern; back is barred (Eurasian Bittern has chevrons on back). Female is darker than male. Mostly active at night. **Habitat:** Reedbeds edging forest rivers, thick vegetation overhanging water and mangroves. **Status:** Uncommon; easily overlooked. **Voice:** Low, resonant booming, often repeated at dusk and at night. [C5.5b]

4 EURASIAN BITTERN *Botaurus stellaris* 70-80 cm

A large bittern, more often heard than seen. Tawny, heavily streaked plumage, with a black crown and broad, conspicuous moustachial stripes prevent confusion with other species. Larger and more heavily built than White-crested Tiger Heron; back has chevrons (not bars). Juv. is less heavily marked above, with reduced dark cap. Typically remains in dense cover. Flight is owl-like, with bowed, rounded wings. **Habitat:** Extensive reedbeds, sedges and flooded grassland. **Status:** Rare; resident and local migrant in S, Palearctic migrant in N. **Voice:** Deep, resonant, 3-5-note booming, similar to grunting of a distant lion. [C1.21, G1.8.9]

5 LITTLE BITTERN *Ixobrychus minutus* 27-36 cm

A tiny, rather pale heron. Pale upperwing coverts contrast with dark flight feathers in flight (lacks uniform dark upperwing of smaller Dwarf Bittern). Male has greenish-black back and crown; female is browner above, with striped foreneck. Palearctic *minutus* is slightly larger and paler than resident *payesii*, which has more rufous face and neck. Juv. is more heavily streaked below; smaller and more buffy than Green-backed Heron (p. 50), with greenish (not orange-yellow) legs. **Habitat:** Thick reedbeds. **Status:** Uncommon; *payesii* is resident with local movements; *minutus* is Palearctic migrant, mostly Oct-May. **Voice:** Short bark, 'rao', every few seconds when displaying during breeding season. [C1.22, G1.8.7]

6 DWARF BITTERN *Ixobrychus sturmii* 26-30 cm

A tiny, dark-backed heron. Adult is dark slaty-blue above and buff below, with broad, dark stripes running down throat onto breast and belly. Neck is rather broad. Can appear rail-like in flight. Juv. has upperparts scalloped with buff, and breast is more rufous. **Habitat:** Lakes and ponds surrounded by grass and trees; also mangroves. **Status:** Uncommon intra-African migrant, following seasonal rains. **Voice:** Barking 'ra-ra-ra-ra-ra...' in display, otherwise silent. [C5.5a, G1.8.8]

1

2

juv.

juv.

3

juv.

juv.

4

minutus

payesii

♂
minutus

payesii

5

♂

♀

juv.

6

53

FLAMINGOS
Distinctive, gregarious waterbirds. Easily identified given adequate views. Sexes alike.

1 GREATER FLAMINGO *Phoenicopterus ruber* 125-145 cm
The larger of the African flamingos, with very long legs and neck. Appears mostly white at rest (Lesser Flamingo appears pink); in flight, salmon-pink wing coverts contrast with white body. Bill is pink (not dark red), with black tip. Juv. is grey-brown, becoming paler with age, and has grey, black-tipped bill. **Habitat:** Shallow lakes, salt pans, lagoons and sandy beaches; feeds on large prey filtered from bottom sediments. **Status:** Common resident, intra-African migrant and nomad. **Voice:** Noisy, gooselike honking. [C1.37, G1.10.6]

2 LESSER FLAMINGO *Phoenicopterus minor* 80-100 cm
Smaller than Greater Flamingo, with a dark red (not pink) bill and face. Bill appears uniformly dark from a distance. Intensity of pink body colour varies, but is usually much brighter than Greater Flamingo's. At a distance, flocks appear pink (Greater Flamingos appear white). In flight, median coverts are crimson, but appear less contrasting than those of Greater Flamingo. Juv. is brown, becoming paler with age; best told from Greater Flamingo by all-dark bill. **Habitat:** Lakes, salt pans and estuaries; filters blue-green algae from water, often swimming in deep water. **Status:** Common resident, intra-African migrant and nomad. **Voice:** More muted honking than Greater Flamingo's. [C5.1.6a, G1.10.7]

SPOONBILLS
Large waterbirds with distinctive long, flattened, spoon-shaped bills. Fly with neck outstretched (unlike herons and egrets). Feed by sweeping bill from side to side. Sexes alike.

3 AFRICAN SPOONBILL *Platalea alba* 86-92 cm
Adult told from Eurasian Spoonbill by its grey (not black) bill with a red border and base; has bare red face and red (not black) legs. Juv. has shorter yellow-horn (not black or pinkish-grey) bill, dark legs and dark-tipped flight feathers. **Habitat:** Lakes, flood plains and estuaries. **Status:** Common resident and local migrant. **Voice:** Low 'kaark'; at breeding colonies emits various grunts and claps bill. [C5.15b, G1.10.5]

4 EURASIAN SPOONBILL *Platalea leucorodia* 80-92 cm
Adult differs from African Spoonbill by having black (not red) legs and a black (not grey and red) bill with a yellow tip. Face is feathered (not bare), and some have yellowish patch at base of neck. Juv's bill is pinkish grey (not yellow-horn, as in juv. African Spoonbill). **Habitat:** Wetlands, including estuaries. **Status:** Uncommon migrant, mostly Oct-Mar. **Call.** Silent in Africa. [C1.36]

IBISES
Large, long-legged birds with decurved bills. Sexes alike.

5 AFRICAN SACRED IBIS *Threskiornis aethiopicus* 66-84 cm
A large, white ibis with a heavy, decurved, black bill. Adult's head and neck are naked, wrinkled and black. Scapular feathers are black, making bird appear black-tailed at rest. Flight feathers are tipped black, giving narrow black edge to wing. Breeding adults have scarlet naked skin on underwing and yellow flank feathers. Juv. has white-feathered neck and slightly greyish cast to white plumage. Often flies in 'V' formation. **Habitat:** Open habitats, from offshore islands, wetlands and fields to grassland. **Status:** Common. **Voice:** Loud croaking at breeding colonies. [C5.15a, G1.10.1]

6 SOUTHERN BALD IBIS *Geronticus calvus* 75-80 cm
Endemic to Africa. A dark, glossy ibis. Adult is easily identified by its bald head with smooth, red crown. Legs are rather short; legs and bill are red. Juv. is duller, lacking coppery shoulder patch; head is covered in short, light brown feathers, and bill is red only at base; legs are brown. **Habitat:** Short grassland, often in burned areas; breeds colonially on cliffs. **Status:** Vulnerable. Locally common resident. Occurs in flocks. **Voice:** High-pitched, wheezing call. [G1.10.2] **Similar species: Northern Bald Ibis** *G. eremita* formerly wintered in NE Africa, but this population is extinct.

juv.

1

br.

2

juv.

juv.

3

4

juv.

5

br.

juv.

6

juv.

1 GLOSSY IBIS *Plegadis falcinellus*   55-65 cm
A rather small, slender ibis with long legs. Appears black from a distance. Breeding adult's head, neck and body are dark chestnut; wings, back and tail are dark, glossy green with bronze and purple highlights. There is a narrow white line around base of bill. Non-breeders have pale-flecked head and neck. Juv. resembles non-breeding adult, but body is dull, sooty brown. **Habitat:** Lakes, dams, pans, estuaries and flooded grassland. **Status:** Locally common. **Voice:** Normally silent; low, guttural 'kok-kok-kok' when breeding. [C1.34, G1.10.3]

2 HADEDA IBIS *Bostrychia hagedash*   76-89 cm
A large, stout, grey-brown ibis with glossy-bronze wing coverts. Lacks shaggy crest of other forest ibises. Grey face has white stripe running from bill to below and behind eye. Bill is dark grey, with red ridge on upper mandible. Juv. lacks red on bill and bronze wing patch. **Habitat:** Forest clearings, woodland, savanna, grassland, farmland and lawns. Usually in small parties; roosts in trees. **Status:** Common. **Voice:** Noisy on flights to and from roosts: loud 'ha-da' or 'ha-ha-da-da'. [C5.13b, G1.10.4]

3 WATTLED IBIS *Bostrychia carunculata*   80 cm
Endemic to Abyssinian highlands. A large, dark ibis with diagnostic white shoulder patches. Bill has broad base and rather slender tip. Thin wattles, white eye and wispy crest are visible at close range. **Habitat:** Grassland, fields and heathland from 1 500 m to 4 100 m, often near water; roosts and breeds on cliffs. **Status:** Common. **Voice:** Loud, far-carrying 'waaah waah' honking.

4 OLIVE IBIS *Bostrychia olivacea*   74 cm
A dark, crested ibis, very difficult to observe when it feeds on the forest floor, easier to see at dusk and dawn when flying to or from its roost. When flushed from the ground, is silent and perches on nearby branch. If seen well, shaggy crest, black face, and red bill and legs distinguish it from Hadeda Ibis. Larger than Spot-breasted Ibis, with plain (not spotted) breast and pale brown head contrasting with black face. Juv. is duller, with shorter crest. **Habitat:** Forest undergrowth, in moist areas; also mangroves. **Status:** Uncommon. **Voice:** Loud 'han-ha', often repeated, given in flight. [C5.14a]

5 DWARF OLIVE (SÃO TOMÉ) IBIS *Bostrychia bocagei*   62 cm
Endemic to São Tomé; the only ibis on the island. Smaller than Olive Ibis, with slightly darker head and smaller crest. Generally silent at dawn and dusk (unlike noisy Olive Ibis), and feeds on forest floor often far from water. **Habitat:** Primary forest in SW São Tomé, where it occurs in pairs or family groups in closed-canopy forest undergrowth, feeding on ground. When disturbed, flies to perch on larger limbs in mid-canopy. **Status:** Critically threatened. Local and very rare. **Voice:** Usually silent; various honking 'kah gah' nasal notes when going to roost.

6 SPOT-BREASTED IBIS *Bostrychia rara*   55 cm
A small, dark ibis with a diagnostic buff-spotted neck and breast. Smaller and more slender than Olive Ibis. Head is uniformly dark, with patches of bare blue skin around eyes (smaller in females). In flight, has broad wings and short tail; bill is rather short. Juv. is duller, with shorter crest. Best located at dawn and dusk by birds calling in flight; silent and furtive when feeding on ground. **Habitat:** Moist areas in lowland and riverine forest, often in wetter areas than Olive Ibis. **Status:** Uncommon to locally common. **Voice:** Loud, raucous 'ha-han' in flight. [C5.14b]

juv.

imm.

1

2

3

4

5

6

PELICANS

Huge waterbirds with long bills and elastic gular pouches used to catch fish. Strong fliers, often soaring in thermals. Sexes alike. Enigmatic Shoebill usually placed in its own family, but genetic evidence places it close to the pelicans.

1 GREAT WHITE PELICAN *Pelecanus onocrotalus*　　140-178 cm

A very large, white pelican with black flight feathers contrasting with white coverts in flight. Bill pouch is yellow, with more of a sag in middle than Pink-backed Pelican's. Breeding adult has pink-tinged underparts, bare pink-orange face, short crest, yellow breast patch and red nail at tip of bill. Non-breeders have yellow face. Juv. is brown, whitening with age. **Habitat:** Typically fishes in groups on open water (lakes, estuaries and sheltered bays); nests colonially on ground. **Status:** Locally common. **Voice:** Usually silent; deep 'mooo' given at breeding colonies. [C1.18, G1.59]

2 PINK-BACKED PELICAN *Pelecanus rufescens*　　135-152 cm

Smaller and greyer than Great White Pelican, with a pink back and a pinkish-yellow bill. Flight feathers are darker grey, but do not contrast strongly with coverts in flight. Breeding birds have grey crest. Juv. is dark brown, becoming greyer with age. Best distinguished from Great White Pelican by size. **Habitat:** Lakes and estuaries; typically fishes alone; nests colonially in trees. **Status:** Locally common. **Voice:** Usually silent; guttural calls at breeding colonies. [C5.4b, G1.5.10]

3 SHOEBILL *Balaeniceps rex*　　120 cm

Endemic to Africa, where it is one of the most sought-after species. An enormous blue-grey bird with a massive, mottled, yellow-grey bill and a small, erect crest. Flight surprisingly buoyant on massive wings. Possibly related to pelicans, but usually placed in a monotypic family. **Habitat:** Swamps, usually papyrus, but also reeds and sedges. **Status:** Uncommon to rare; pairs have large territories (5 km^2), but groups gather at prime feeding areas. **Voice:** Claps its bill, making loud, hollow 'dok'. [C5.13a, G1.9.2]

STORKS

Large, long-legged birds of wetlands or open habitats. Most species fly with necks extended (unlike herons); soar well, often using thermals. Sexes alike in most species.

4 MARABOU STORK *Leptoptilos crumeniferus*　　120-150 cm

A huge stork, with a grey, blade-like bill, a naked head and a pendulous throat pouch. In flight, head is tucked into shoulders, and dark grey wings contrast with white body. Juv's head and neck are covered with sparse, woolly down. **Habitat:** Savanna, grassland and wetlands; often around towns. Scavenges with vultures at game kills; also at refuse dumps and abattoirs. Breeds colonially in trees. **Status:** Fairly common resident or local migrant. **Voice:** Low, hoarse croak when alarmed; claps bill when displaying. [C5.12b, G1.9.9]

5 SADDLE-BILLED STORK *Ephippiorhynchus senegalensis*　　145 cm

A very tall, black-and-white stork with a diagnostic red-and-black banded bill with a yellow 'saddle' at the base. In flight, wings are striking black and white. Male has brown eyes (female's yellow), a small, yellow wattle (absent in female) and more black on wing in flight. Juv. is grey, and neck and head are brown; lacks yellow 'saddle' on bill; flight feathers are greyish, and leading edge of wing is dark. **Habitat:** Freshwater dams, lakes and rivers. **Status:** Uncommon; usually solitary or in pairs. Undertakes seasonal movements in some areas. **Voice:** Normally silent except for bill-clapping during display. [C5.12a, G1.9.8]

1

br.

juv.

imm.

non-br.

2

br.

non-br.

juv.

juv.

3

4

5

♂

♀

juv.

1 AFRICAN OPENBILL *Anastomus lamelligerus* 81-94 cm
A rather small, all-dark stork with an ivory-horn bill which has a diagnostic wide, nutcracker-like gap between the mandibles. Adult has glossy sheen to plumage. Juv. is duller and browner, with pale feather tips; fledges without noticeable bill gap, but this soon develops. **Habitat:** Freshwater lakes and dams, where it feeds mostly on snails and mussels. **Status:** Locally common intra-African migrant; breeds mostly S of equator. **Voice:** Seldom heard; croaking 'honk'. [C5.10b, G1.9.7]

2 WOOLLY-NECKED STORK *Ciconia episcopus* 85 cm
A glossy black stork with a diagnostic woolly white neck, white belly and white undertail coverts (which extend to tip of black tail, appearing all white from below). In flight, has white rump and lower back. Juv. is dull brown; black forehead extends further back on crown. **Habitat:** Wetlands, often along rivers and streams; also mangroves, coastal mudflats and reefs. **Status:** Uncommon; resident and intra-African migrant. Solitary or in pairs, seldom in flocks. **Voice:** Seldom heard; harsh croak. [C5.11b, G1.9.6]

3 BLACK STORK *Ciconia nigra* 95-100 cm
A large, glossy black stork with a white belly and undertail. Larger than Abdim's Stork, with black (not white) rump and lower back, red (not greenish) bill, and red face and legs. Juv. is browner, with olive-yellow bill and legs. **Habitat:** Lakes and rivers; also estuaries and lagoons. **Status:** Uncommon; a small population breeds on cliffs in S Africa; Palearctic migrant further N, mostly Oct-Apr. **Voice:** Silent except on nest, when loud whining and bill clapping are given. [C1.32, G1.9.4]

4 ABDIM'S (WHITE-BELLIED) STORK *Ciconia abdimii* 76-81 cm
A rather small, black stork with a white belly and undertail. Smaller than Black Stork, with white (not black) lower back and rump and greenish (not red) bill. Face is blue; legs are grey-green, with pink ankles and feet. In flight, legs do not project as far beyond tail as they do in Black Stork. Juv. is duller. **Habitat:** Grassland and fields, often in company of White Storks. **Status:** Common intra-African migrant. Breeds colonially in trees in N (Apr-Oct), moving S mostly Oct-Apr. Often in large flocks. **Voice:** Usually silent; weak, 2-note whistle at nests and roosts. [C5.1a, G1.9.5]

5 WHITE STORK *Ciconia ciconia* 102-120 cm
A large, mostly white stork. Structure is similar to Black Stork's, but head, neck, back and tail are white. Plumage superficially resembles Yellow-billed Stork's, but has red (not yellow) bill, white head, and all-white tail. Red legs often appear white because birds defecate on them to cool down. Juv. has darker bill and legs, and white plumage tinged brown. **Habitat:** Grassland and fields; occasionally at shallow wetlands. **Status:** Common Palearctic migrant, mostly Oct-Apr. A few pairs breed in W Cape, South Africa. **Voice:** Silent except on nest, when loud whining and bill clapping are given. [C1.33, G1.9.3]

6 YELLOW-BILLED STORK *Mycteria ibis* 95-105 cm
A mostly white stork with a long, slightly decurved, yellow bill. Breeding adult has naked red facial skin and pink-tinged wing coverts and back. In flight, differs from White Stork by having black tail. Juv. is brownish above and washed with grey-brown below, becoming whiter with age; head is mostly feathered, and facial skin, bill and legs are duller. **Habitat:** Lakes, rivers and estuaries. **Status:** Common resident and partial intra-African migrant. **Voice:** Normally silent except during breeding season, when it gives loud squeaks and hisses. [C5.10a, G1.9.10]

juv.

1

2

juv.

3

juv.

imm.

4

5

br.

6

juv.

Familiar waterbirds. Sexes differ in most species, but dimorphism is generally less marked in African species than in Palearctic migrants. Frequently kept in collections, so many out of range records are thought to be escapees.

1 FULVOUS DUCK *Dendrocygna bicolor*   43-53 cm
A long-legged, long-necked duck with a mostly golden-brown head and underparts. Has dark line from nape down back of neck, and conspicuous white flank stripes. In flight, pale uppertail coverts contrast with dark brown wings, rump and tail. **Habitat:** Freshwater lakes and dams. **Status:** Locally common, but generally less abundant than White-faced Duck. **Voice:** Soft, disyllabic whistle. [C5.16b, G1.10.10] **Similar species: Black-bellied Duck** *D. autumnalis* has similar structure, but is darker brown with a black belly, pink bill and grey face; Nearctic vagrant to Gambia, but could have been an escape.

2 WHITE-FACED DUCK *Dendrocygna viduata*   43-48 cm
A long-necked, dark brown duck with a diagnostic white face. Like Fulvous Duck, it stands erect, but is much darker chestnut-brown on breast, and has finely barred flanks. Apart from white face (which can be stained brown), appears all dark in flight. Juv. lacks white face. **Habitat:** Freshwater lakes and lagoons, and adjacent grasslands. **Status:** Common, often in large flocks. **Voice:** Characteristic, 3-note, whispy whistle, 'whit we-weeer'. [C5.17a, G1.10.9]

3 WHITE-BACKED DUCK *Thalassornis leuconotus*   38-40 cm
A small, rather grebe-like duck with a pale spot at base of bill, characteristic humped back and large head. Body is barred rufous and dark brown; white back is visible only in flight. An excellent diver, is seldom seen in flight, and spends much of day roosting with head tucked into scapulars. **Habitat:** Fresh water, typically among floating vegetation. **Status:** Locally common. **Voice:** Low-pitched whistle, rising on second syllable. [C5.17b, G1.11.1]

4 MACCOA DUCK *Oxyura maccoa*   48-51 cm
The only stiff-tailed duck in the region. Breeding male has chestnut body, black head and heavy blue bill. Female and eclipse male are dark brown, with pale stripe under eye and paler throat, giving head striped appearance (unlike female Southern Pochard, p. 70), which has a pale crescent behind the eye). Sits very low in water, with stiff tail often cocked at 45° angle. In flight, upperwing is uniform dark brown. **Habitat:** Freshwater lakes, dams and lagoons. **Status:** Locally common, but sparsely distributed. **Voice:** Peculiar, nasal trill. [C5.24, G1.12.7]

5 AFRICAN PYGMY GOOSE *Nettapus auritus*   30-33 cm
A tiny duck with diagnostic orange breast and flanks, white face and dark greenish upperparts. Male has bright yellow bill and lime-green neck patch, neatly bordered in black. Female and juv. are duller, with indistinct head markings. In flight, has large white patch formed by inner secondaries and greater coverts. Often sits motionless among floating vegetation. **Habitat:** Freshwater lakes with floating vegetation, especially *Nymphaea* lilies; nests in hole in tree. **Status:** Locally common. **Voice:** Soft, repeated 'tsui-tsui'. [C5.19b, G1.12.4]

6 HARTLAUB'S DUCK *Pteronetta hartlaubii*   56-58 cm
Africa's only true forest duck. Readily separated from all other ducks by its black head and upper neck, dark chestnut body and blue-grey upperwing coverts (mainly visible in flight). Extent of white on male's forehead is variable. Female duller; lacks any white on the head. **Habitat:** Rivers and streams in forest, marshy clearings and ponds inside forest or at forest edge. **Status:** Locally common. **Voice:** Varied whistles and quacks in flight. [C5.18b]

1 BLUE-WINGED GOOSE *Cyanochen cyanoptera*   50-75 cm
Endemic to Abyssinian highlands. Unmistakable: dull grey shelduck, with black legs and small black bill. Chalky-blue upperwing coverts are visible in flight; underwing coverts are white. Usually in pairs, but outside breeding season occurs in flocks of up to 100. **Habitat:** Pools, streams, marshes and adjacent grassland above 1 800 m. **Status:** Locally common. **Voice:** Soft, whistled 'whee-whu-whu-whu'; nasal 'penk, penk-penk' when taking to flight.

2 EGYPTIAN GOOSE *Alopochen aegyptiaca*   63-73 cm
A large, buff and brown duck with a dark brown face, neck ring and breast patch. Larger and longer-necked than shelducks, it stands more erect. In flight, white secondary coverts have thin black subterminal bar, unlike uniform white of South African and Ruddy shelducks. Juv. lacks brown mask and breast patch, and forewing is greyish. **Habitat:** Wetlands and adjacent grasslands and fields; also suburban areas and sheltered bays on coast. **Status:** Very common. **Voice:** Male hisses; female utters grunting honk; both honk repeatedly when alarmed or taking flight. [C1.46, G1.11.2]

3 SOUTH AFRICAN SHELDUCK *Tadorna cana*   60-65 cm
Endemic to S Africa. Smaller, with shorter neck and legs than Egyptian Goose, imparting more horizontal stance. Plumage is warm russet and brown. Male has grey head; female has variable white-and-grey head. In flight, both sexes have white forewings but no black dividing line as in Egyptian Goose. Juv. resembles male but is duller, with head suffused brown. **Habitat:** Freshwater lakes and dams in drier areas; nests in hole in ground. **Status:** Common, gathering in large flocks to moult after breeding. **Voice:** Various honks and hisses. [G1.11.3]

4 RUDDY SHELDUCK *Tadorna ferruginea*   60-64 cm
A richly coloured Eurasian shelduck. Male has distinctive creamy-buff head; female has white face. In flight, white upperwing and underwing coverts are conspicuous. **Habitat:** High-altitude marshes and lakes. **Status:** Uncommon; restricted to Ethiopian highlands, although may occur as vagrant in NW. **Voice:** Nasal honking; 2-note 'aah-wong'. [C1.47] **Similar species: Common Shelduck** *T. tadorna* has similar structure, but is bold black and white with a chestnut breast band and red bill; Palearctic vagrant to N.

5 SPUR-WINGED GOOSE *Plectropterus gambensis*   75-100 cm
A large, black goose with variable amounts of white on face, throat, belly and forewings. Bill, face and legs are pink-red. In flight, large size and white on forewing separate it from Comb Duck. Male is up to twice the size of female, and has a more extensive bare face with wattles. Juv. is browner. Grazes on grasses and other vegetable matter, often at night. **Habitat:** Wetlands and adjacent grasslands and fields. **Status:** Common. **Voice:** Feeble, wheezy whistle in flight. [C5.18a, G1.12.6] **Similar species: Bean Goose** *Anser fabilis*, **Greater White-fronted Goose** *A. albifrons* and **Brent Goose** *Branta bernicula* are rare Palearctic vagrants to N.

6 COMB (KNOB-BILLED) DUCK *Sarkidiornis melanotos*   56-76 cm
A large duck with a speckled head and contrasting blue-black and white plumage. In flight, wings are uniform black. Male has rounded knob on bill which enlarges during the breeding season. Female is smaller, with no bill knob and paler patch on lower back. Juv. is duller, with dark speckling on breast, belly and flanks; juv's head has pale supercilium and dark eye-line, and could be confused with female Garganey or Common Teal (p. 68), but is much larger and lacks scaled breast and flanks. **Habitat:** Pans and lakes in woodland and along larger rivers; nests in tree holes. **Status:** Locally common nomad and intra-African migrant. **Voice:** Whistles, but usually silent. [C5.19a, G1.12.5]

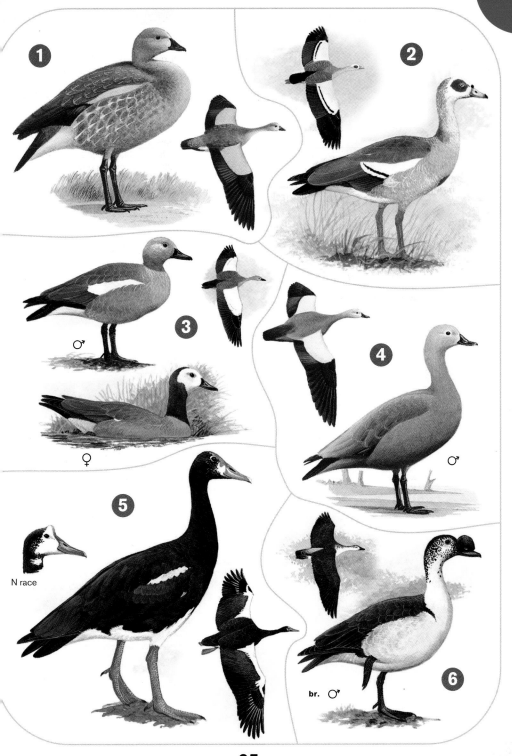

1

2

3

♂

♀

4

♂

5

N race

6

br. ♂

1 AFRICAN BLACK DUCK *Anas sparsa*   48-57 cm
A dark, sooty-coloured duck with white speckles on back, dark bill and orange legs. Sitting on water, it appears long-bodied. In flight, purple-blue speculum, bordered white, is bluer than that of Yellow-billed Duck, and underwing is whitish (not grey). Juv. is paler, with whitish belly and less brightly coloured legs. **Habitat:** Streams and rivers; less frequent on ponds and dams. Pairs defend territories along rivers, so seldom occurs in flocks. **Status:** Fairly common. **Voice:** 'Quack', especially in flight; male gives weak, high-pitched whistle. [C5.21b, G1.11.5]

2 YELLOW-BILLED DUCK *Anas undulata*   51-58 cm
The bright yellow bill with a black saddle is distinctive. Looks dark from a distance, but is browner than African Black Duck. At close range, pale feather edges give scaled appearance. In flight, has blue-green speculum narrowly edged with white, and grey underwing (not whitish, as in African Black Duck). **Habitat:** Freshwater lakes, ponds and flooded fields; also lagoons and estuaries. **Status:** Common; often occurs in flocks. **Voice:** Male gives rasping hiss; female quacks. [C5.21a, G1.11.4]

3 MALLARD *Anas platyrhynchos*   50-65 cm
Breeding-plumage male is unmistakable: bottle-green, glossy head, white ring around neck and chestnut breast. Female and eclipse male superficially resemble Yellow-billed Duck but are paler brown, with dark horn bill and dark line through eye. Domesticated form of Mallard looks similar to wild birds, but is much larger, with heavy 'bottom', and has khaki (not grey) back. **Habitat:** Wetlands. **Status:** Uncommon Palearctic migrant in N. Feral populations in South Africa are spreading and hybridising with local ducks (especially Yellow-billed Duck). **Voice:** Male gives rasping hiss; female quacks. [C1.52]

4 CAPE SHOVELLER *Anas smithii*   53 cm
Near-endemic to S Africa. Long, black, spatulate bill separates it from other ducks, except female Northern Shoveller. Both sexes have finely speckled grey-brown plumage. Male has paler, greyer head than female, with darker bill, paler yellow eyes, brighter orange legs, and more prominent blue-grey upperwing coverts. Female and juv. are darker and greyer than Northern Shoveller, especially around head and neck, and have smaller and darker slate-grey bill lacking any orange tinge along margins. **Habitat:** Freshwater lakes and ponds. **Status:** Common; vagrants wander as far as N Tanzania. **Voice:** 'Quack'; continuous rasping. [G1.12.2]

5 NORTHERN SHOVELLER *Anas clypeata*   44-52 cm
Breeding plumage of male is unmistakable: green head, white breast and chestnut belly and flanks. In flight, has powder-blue forewing. In both sexes, bill is heavier, longer and more spatulate than that of Cape Shoveller. Female and eclipse male are paler than Cape Shoveller, especially around head and neck. Female has white edges to tail and orange margins to bill. **Habitat:** Inland waterbodies. **Status:** Fairly common Palearctic migrant in N Oct-Apr; vagrant in S; most South African records probably are escapees. **Voice:** Male gives nasal 'crook, crook'; female quacks. [C1.55, G1.12.1]

6 NORTHERN PINTAIL *Anas acuta*   51-65 cm
Breeding-plumage male is striking, with dark, chocolate-brown head, white stripe running down side of neck to white breast, lanceolate back feathers and long central tail feathers. Female and eclipse male are speckled tan and brown, with blue-grey bill, long, slender neck, plain buffy face, and brown speculum with white trailing edge. Tail is pointed in both sexes. **Habitat:** Wetlands, including alkaline lakes and estuaries. **Status:** Common Palearctic migrant Nov-Apr; vagrant to S Africa. **Voice:** Male gives soft, nasal honk; female quacks. [C1.53, G1.11.9]

1 GADWALL *Anas strepera*   45-55 cm

Breeding-plumage male has fine grey vermiculations on breast and flanks, black rump and vent, and white inner secondaries visible on folded wing. Female and eclipse male have buffy body feathers with dark brown arrow markings; distinctive white patch in wing is duller, but still visible. Juv. male is brighter, with rufous-edged feathers. Wing patch of juv. female is very small and buffy. **Habitat:** Freshwater lakes and marshes; rarely estuaries. **Status:** Uncommon Palearctic migrant Oct-Apr. **Voice:** Mostly silent in Africa. [C1.50]

2 GARGANEY *Anas querquedula*   37-41 cm

Breeding-plumage male has large white eyebrow and black-and-white lanceolate back feathers. Brown breast is sharply demarcated from the white belly and pale grey flanks. Female and eclipse male have pale supercilium and dark eye-stripe. Shape differs from female Maccoa Duck (p. 62) and juv. Comb Duck (p. 64), with pale spot at base of bill (unlike female Common Teal). In flight, both sexes have pale blue forewings and green speculum, superficially similar to Cape and Northern shovellers (p. 66). **Habitat:** Lakes and marshes. **Status:** Common Palearctic migrant Oct-Apr. **Voice:** Nasal 'quack'; some harsh rattles. [C1.54, G1.11.10] **Similar species: Blue-winged Teal** *A. discors,* male has distinctive bluish head with white crescent in front of eye; female told from female Garganey by bluer upperwing coverts, fainter head stripes and white spots at base of bill. Nearctic vagrant to NW.

3 COMMON TEAL *Anas crecca*   34-38 cm

A small duck. Breeding-plumage male has chestnut head with bottle-green face patch and yellowish triangles on sides of vent. Female and eclipse male are relatively nondescript, with dark eye-line; best identified by small size and white-bordered green speculum. **Habitat:** Freshwater lakes and marshes; occasional at coastal wetlands. **Status:** Fairly common Palearctic migrant Oct-Mar. **Voice:** Male gives distinctive, soft, high-pitched 'preep-preep'; female is usually silent, but gives sharp 'quack' when flushed. [C1.51]

4 HOTTENTOT TEAL *Anas hottentota*   30-35 cm

A very small duck with a dark crown, cream cheeks and diagnostic darker smudges extending from ear coverts down neck. Much smaller than Red-billed Teal, with blue (not red) bill. In flight, has green speculum (brighter in male) with white trailing edge, and black and white underwing. **Habitat:** Freshwater wetlands, favouring areas with emergent or floating vegetation. **Status:** Locally common; typically in pairs or small flocks. **Voice:** Generally silent; utters high-pitched quacks on taking flight. [C5.22b, G1.11.7]

5 CAPE TEAL *Anas capensis*   44-48 cm

A pale grey duck with a rather plain, bulbous-looking head and pink bill. Sexes are alike. Differs from Red-billed Teal by uniformly coloured head. In flight, shows dark greenish speculum surrounded by white. Juv. is paler grey than adult. Usually occurs in mixed flocks. **Habitat:** Fresh or saline wetlands, especially alkaline lakes, salt pans, lagoons and sewage works. **Status:** Locally common. **Voice:** Thin whistle, usually in flight. [C5.20b, G1.11.6] **Similar species: Marbled Teal** *Marmaronetta angustirostris* has dark bill, dark eye patch, white-spotted plumage and a uniform grey wing in flight; rare vagrant to N.

6 RED-BILLED TEAL *Anas erythrorhyncha*   43-48 cm

Easily identified by its dark cap, pale cheeks and red bill. Larger than Hottentot Teal, with red (not blue) bill. Dark cap distinguishes it from Cape Teal. In flight, has diagnostic warm buff secondaries, lacking dark iridescent speculum of Cape and Hottentot teals. Female has smaller black bill saddle than male. **Habitat:** Freshwater wetlands. **Status:** Common. **Voice:** Male gives soft, nasal whistle; female quacks. [C5.22a, G1.11.8]

68

1 RED-CRESTED POCHARD *Netta rufina*   53-57 cm
A large pochard. Breeding-plumage male (not illustrated) has diagnostic orange head and pink bill, with white flanks contrasting with black breast, vent and rump. Female and eclipse male are dark sandy-brown, with chocolate cap and pale cheeks, throat and vent. Female's bill is dark grey, tipped pink. In flight, outer secondaries and inner primaries are white, and underwings are pale. **Habitat:** Large freshwater wetlands. **Status:** Rare Palearctic migrant, mostly Nov–Mar; popular ornamental bird and escapees frequently encountered outside normal range. **Voice:** Usually silent away from breeding grounds. [C1.57]

2 SOUTHERN POCHARD *Netta erythrophthalma*   48-51 cm
A fairly large, dark brown duck. Male is glossy, with paler, chestnut-brown flanks, pale blue bill and bright red eyes. Female is dark brown, with pale patch at bill base and pale crescent extending behind eye. Juv. lacks female's white facial crescent. Both have paler vents. In flight, has distinct white wing bar extending onto primaries. Very different in shape from Maccoa Duck (p. 62), with slender bill. Darker than female Common Pochard, and larger than Ferruginous and Tufted ducks. **Habitat:** Lakes and dams, including alkaline lakes. **Status:** Common. **Voice:** Male makes whining sound; female quacks. [C5.23, G1.12.3]

3 COMMON POCHARD *Aythya ferina*   42-49 cm
A medium-sized duck with an exaggerated 'ski-ramp' head silhouette. Breeding-plumage male has dark chestnut head, black breast, pale grey body and black rump and vent. Female and eclipse male are dull pale brown, with paler face and dark rump. In flight, has grey (not white) bar in flight feathers. Lacks white vent of Ferruginous Duck and pale cheeks of Red-crested Pochard. **Habitat:** Freshwater and alkaline lakes. **Status:** Fairly common Palearctic migrant Oct-Mar. **Voice:** Female gives harsh 'krrr' when flushed; males mostly silent. [C1.58]

4 FERRUGINOUS DUCK *Aythya nyroca*   38-42 cm
A medium-sized, dark chestnut-brown duck with a dark bill and conspicuous white vent. Male has white iris; iris is dark in female and juv. Female and juv. lack pale face markings of female and juv. Southern Pochard, and in flight have white (not dark) belly patch and underwings. Has less-rounded head than female Tufted Duck, and lacks that species' yellow eyes. **Habitat:** Freshwater wetlands. **Status:** Uncommon Palearctic migrant Nov-Mar; numbers possibly decreasing. **Voice:** Silent away from breeding grounds. [C1.59]

5 TUFTED DUCK *Aythya fuligula*   40-47 cm
Breeding-plumage male is glossy black, with bold white flanks and drooping head tuft. In eclipse plumage, flanks are grey. Female and juv. are darker, and could be confused with Ferruginous Duck, but are duller brown (not chestnut), with yellow eyes and much steeper forehead. More frequently swims with head raised (Ferruginous Duck usually carries head hunched on shoulders). **Habitat:** Open, freshwater bodies. **Status:** Locally common Palearctic migrant Oct-Apr; popular ornamental bird; escapees regularly encountered outside normal range. **Voice:** Female gives low grunt when flushed; males usually silent away from breeding grounds. [C1.60] **Similar species: Common Scoter** *Melanitta nigra* male is entirely black with yellow bill saddle; female dark brown with grey bill and pale cheeks and upper neck; Palearctic vagrant to NW coast.

6 EURASIAN WIDGEON *Anas penelope*   45-50 cm
A medium-sized, teal-shaped duck with a dark-tipped, dull blue bill. Breeding-plumage male has chestnut head, yellow forehead, pink breast and black-and-white vent. Female and eclipse male are much duller, with dull chestnut flanks and conspicuously white belly. In flight, male shows mostly white upperwing coverts and green speculum at base of secondaries. Female has narrow white trailing edge to otherwise black secondaries and dark, buff-edged coverts. Spends much time grazing out of water. **Habitat:** Freshwater ponds and lakes; rare on coast. **Status:** Uncommon Palearctic migrant Nov-Mar. **Voice:** Male gives penetrating 'wheeooo' whistle; female gives growling 'krrr', typically when flushed. [C1.49] **Similar species: American Widgeon** *A. americana* has speckled head and dark eye patch; Nearctic vagrant to NW.

ad. non-br.

71

Africa has a wealth of diurnal raptors, some of which are difficult to identify, given highly variable plumage sequences and polymorphisms. Many species are easier to identify in flight, where wing shape and profile are reliable characters. Sexes alike in most species, but females often larger than males.

1 BLACK-SHOULDERED KITE *Elanus caeruleus* 33 cm

A small, grey-and-white raptor with diagnostic black shoulder patches. Told from Scissor-tailed Kite by short, square (not forked) tail and black (not white) underwing tips. Hunts from perch or by hovering, dropping onto mouse prey with wings in deep 'V'. Pumps tail up and down when excited. Juv. is browner on back, with brown crown, grey tail and pale-edged upperpart feathers. **Habitat:** Savanna, grassland and agricultural areas; often perches on telephone poles and lines. **Status:** Common. **Voice:** High-pitched, whistled 'peeeu'; soft 'weep'; rasping 'wee-ah'. [C1.71, G1.13.7]

2 SCISSOR-TAILED (AFRICAN SWALLOW-TAILED) KITE
Chelictinia riocourii 30 cm

A small, graceful, tern-like kite with a deeply forked tail. Feeds largely on the wing. Smaller and longer-tailed than Black-shouldered Kite. Underwing has black carpal bars, but primaries are white (black in Black-shouldered Kite). Juv. has shorter tail and brown upperparts. **Habitat:** Arid savanna. **Status:** Localised resident and intra-African migrant, most moving south Aug-Jan. Roosts and breeds colonially. **Voice:** Twittering and rasping chattering when breeding, otherwise silent. [C5.27]

3 BLACK KITE *Milvus migrans* 51-60 cm

A long-winged hawk with a long, shallowly forked tail. Has diagnostic loose flight action, with long tail twisting incessantly. Wings are held level, not canted up as in harriers (p. 84), and are narrower than buzzards' (p. 96), with bent wrist. Bill is black, with yellow cere. Adult has grey ear coverts (brown in Yellow-billed Kite). Juv. has brown face, pale eye, slightly less forked tail and buffy feather margins. **Habitat:** Catholic, ranging from forest edge to semi-desert. Often found in flocks at termite emergences. **Status:** Common Palearctic migrant, mostly Oct-Apr. **Voice:** High-pitched, shrill whinnying. [C1.72, G1.13.5] **Similar species: Red Kite** *M. milvus* is larger, with longer tail, grey head and white primary bases on underwing; Palearctic vagrant to N.

4 YELLOW-BILLED KITE *Milvus aegyptius* 51-60 cm

Often treated as a race of Black Kite, but adult has a bright yellow (not black) bill, brown ear coverts and a more deeply forked tail. Juv. has black bill, less forked tail and buffy feather margins; often shows a more contrasting pale panel in inner primaries. **Habitat:** Woodland and open habitats; commonly in urban areas. **Status:** Common intra-African migrant. **Voice:** Similar to Black Kite's. [C5.28, G1.13.6]

juv.

juv.

1

juv.

2

3

juv.

juv.

4

juv.

73

1 OSPREY *Pandion haliaetus*   51-68 cm
A long, narrow-winged hawk with diagnostic bent wrists and a black carpal patch on an otherwise pale underwing. Upperparts are dark brown; underparts and crown are white. Much smaller than imm. African Fish-Eagle, from which it is easily separated by wing shape. Female has darker partial breast band. Juv. has pale-fringed upperpart feathers and dark-spotted crown. **Habitat:** Wetlands, estuaries and sheltered marine areas. **Status:** Fairly common; breeds along Red Sea coast; Palearctic migrant elsewhere. Scarce inland. **Voice:** Usually silent; shrill whistles. [C1.69, G2.2.10]

2 AFRICAN FISH-EAGLE *Haliaeetus vocifer*   63-73 cm
A large, broad-winged eagle with a short tail. Adult is unmistakable: black and chestnut plumage, with a white head, breast and tail. Juv. is dark brown, with white patches on head, belly, underwing coverts and primary bases; tail is white with brown tip; with age, head and breast gradually whiten. **Habitat:** Large rivers, lakes, estuaries and lagoons; occasionally hunts close inshore over sea. **Status:** Common. **Voice:** Ringing 'kyow-kow-kow' with head thrown back, from perches or in flight; male's call is higher pitched. [C5.29, G1.15.8]

3 PALM-NUT VULTURE *Gypohierax angolensis*   60 cm
A small, black-and-white vulture. Shape resembles that of African Fish-Eagle, but is smaller and has very different plumage pattern. Wings are broader than Egyptian Vulture's (p. 76), with mostly white (not black) primaries; tail is rounded, black tipped with white (not white and wedge-shaped). Juv. is brown; smaller than Hooded Vulture (p. 76), and with much heavier bill. **Habitat:** Forest, woodland and coastal areas, usually near oil or raffia palms; scavenges at fishing boats. **Status:** Locally common; juvs may disperse widely. **Voice:** Usually silent; 'kok-kok-kok' in flight. [C5.30, G1.15.7]

4 LAMMERGEIER (BEARDED VULTURE) *Gypaetus barbatus*   110 cm
A large vulture with a unique flight shape: long, pointed wings and a long, wedge-shaped tail. Adult is mainly dark, with rufous head and underparts. Black face mask has black 'beard', but this is visible only at close range. Juv. is dark brown; underparts gradually lighten with age. **Habitat:** Remote, mountainous areas; nests on cliff ledges. **Status:** Uncommon; range has contracted in S and E Africa; solitary. **Voice:** Silent except for high-pitched whistling display. [C1.75, G1.12.9]

1

imm.

♀   ♂

2

sub-ad.

♀   ♂

3

juv.

juv.

4

imm.

imm.

Large scavengers with long, broad wings and deeply slotted primaries. Use thermals to soar effortlessly while searching for carrion. Some species gregarious, others solitary. Sexes alike in most species; juvs differ.

1 EGYPTIAN VULTURE *Neophron percnopterus* 58-71 cm
A small, slender-billed vulture with a bare face and throat. Adult is white, with black flight feathers. In flight, has wedge-shaped tail and rather narrow wings, bent at wrist. Juv. is dark brown; wedge-shaped tail and long, very slender bill separates from juv. Palm-nut (p. 74) and Hooded vultures. Disjunct S African population is genetically distinct. **Habitat:** Grassland, savanna and semi-desert. **Status:** Uncommon to locally common (Chad) resident, Palearctic and intra-African migrant and nomad. Endemic S African race is very rare; genetically distinct from other races. **Voice:** Soft grunts and hisses when excited. [C1.76, G1.12.10]

2 HOODED VULTURE *Necrosyrtes monachus* 65-75 cm
A small, brown vulture with a slender bill. Larger than Palm-nut Vulture (p. 74), with down (not feathers) on head and neck. In flight, wings are broad and tail is rounded (not wedge-shaped, as in Egyptian Vulture). Adult has mostly bare, pink head. Juv. is darker brown, with blackish-brown head and mostly pale bill. **Habitat:** Savanna, woodland and urban areas; often commensal with humans. **Status:** Uncommon to abundant. **Voice:** Normally silent; soft whistling calls at nest. [C5.31, G1.13.1]

3 LAPPET-FACED VULTURE *Torgos tracheliotus* 78-115 cm
A large, blackish vulture with deeply slotted primaries and a short, wedge-shaped tail. Adults have conspicuous white thighs and forearm bar. At close range, horn-coloured bill and wrinkled red face and throat are diagnostic. Juv. is dark brown, with paler head and conspicuous white streaks on mantle; is much larger than Hooded Vulture. **Habitat:** Savannas, especially in more arid areas; nests and roosts on trees. **Status:** Vulnerable. Locally fairly common. Solitary or in loose colonies. **Voice:** High-pitched whistling display. [C1.79, G1.13.4] **Similar species: Cinereous (Black) Vulture** *Aegypius monachus* is all dark, with pale feet and cere; Palearctic vagrant to N.

4 WHITE-HEADED VULTURE *Trigonoceps occipitalis* 78-84 cm
White belly of adult is diagnostic; extends as white line along trailing edge of underwing coverts. Adult female also has white inner secondaries and tertials (greyish in male). Angular head is white, with naked pink face. Bill is orange-red, with blue cere. Juv. is dark brown, with narrow white line between flight feathers and underwing coverts. **Habitat:** Open savannas; roosts and nests on trees. **Status:** Uncommon to locally common; solitary; pairs sedentary and may be territorial. **Voice:** High-pitched chittering.

juv.

juv.

1

2

juv.

juv.

3

juv.

juv.

juv.

4

♀

♂

♂

♀

1 WHITE-BACKED VULTURE *Gyps africanus*   95 cm
A relatively small *Gyps* vulture. Adult's white lower back and pale brown upperwing coverts contrast with dark flight and tail feathers. Underwing coverts are white. Body is slightly streaked (not scaled as in Rüppell's Vulture). Eye and bill are dark. Juv. is dark brown, with only thin pale line on otherwise uniform underwing; coverts gradually whiten with age. **Habitat:** Savanna and open woodland, nesting and roosting on trees. **Status:** Common; usually most abundant vulture away from human habitation. **Voice:** Harsh cackles and hisses. [C5.32, G1.13.3]

2 RÜPPELL'S VULTURE *Gyps rueppellii*   95-107 cm
Intermediate in size between Cape and White-backed vultures. Cream-edged contour feathers give adults diagnostic scaled appearance. Bill and eye are yellow. In flight from below, differs from juv. White-backed Vulture by scaled body and underwing coverts; juv's bill and eye are dark, and has much narrower, buff feather edges, appearing darker and streaked (not scaled) below. Underwing is uniform (not two-tone like Cape Vulture). Bill is black; neck is reddish-pink. **Habitat:** Savanna, grassland and semi-arid areas; breeds and roosts on cliffs. **Status:** Locally common; rare in S Africa. **Voice:** Noisy hissing and cackling. [C5.33]

3 EURASIAN GRIFFON *Gyps fulvus*   95-110 cm
Differs from similar-sized Rüppell's Vulture by uniform (not scaled), warm brown body feathers. Bill and eye are black. Adult has grey head and white neck ruff; juv. and imm. show less contrast between head, neck and body. Flight feathers are darker, contrasting with paler body and wing coverts. Greater upperwing coverts have dark centres. **Habitat:** Favours mountainous areas but forages over lowlands; roosts on cliffs. **Status:** Uncommon Palearctic migrant, mostly Sep-Apr; numbers probably decreasing. Usually imms, singly or in flocks of Rüppell's Vultures. **Voice:** Hisses and croaks. [C1.77]

4 CAPE VULTURE *Gyps coprotheres*   100-115 cm
Endemic to S Africa. Larger than White-backed Vulture; adult has much paler, cream body and wing coverts, contrasting strongly with dark tail and flight feathers. At close range, adult's bill and eye are yellow, with two patches of blue skin at base of neck. Greater upperwing coverts have dark centres (more obvious in adults). Juv. has dark eye and neck skin flushed pink; body and wing coverts are darker brown, but shows more contrast with dark flight feathers than White-backed Vulture. **Habitat:** Grassland and arid savanna; scarce in well-wooded savanna; roosts and nests on cliffs. **Status:** Vulnerable. Range has contracted, but remains locally common in core of range. **Voice:** Cackling and hissing. [G1.13.2]

juv.

juv.

1

2

juv.

juv.

juv.

3

juv.

juv.

4

juv.

juv.

Small, large-headed eagles with large pale eyes and bare legs. Sexes alike; juvs differ.

1 SHORT-TOED SNAKE-EAGLE *Circaetus gallicus* 62-67 cm

Generally paler than Beaudouin's Snake-Eagle, with more boldly marked underwing coverts and belly. Pale birds with poorly marked wing coverts and belly (similar to Beaudouin's Snake-Eagle) have a less defined dark terminal band on the flight feathers. Upperwing coverts are paler than flight feathers (uniform in Beaudouin's Snake-Eagle). Male often has some white streaking on the breast. Juv. is paler below than adult, with pale (not brown) underwing coverts, and is darker and less rufous than juv. Beaudouin's Snake-Eagle; inseparable in the field from juv. Black-chested Snake-Eagle. Often hunts on the wing, hovering awkwardly into the wind. **Habitat:** Arid savanna and semi-desert. **Status:** Uncommon Palearctic migrant, mostly Sep-Mar. **Voice:** Silent in Africa. [C1.80]

2 BEAUDOUIN'S SNAKE-EAGLE *Circaetus beaudouini* 60-65 cm

Endemic to Sahel. Often treated as a race of Short-toed Snake-Eagle, but adult has a more extensive brown breast and pale (not dark) chin. In flight, underwing coverts are finely vermiculated, appearing white at a distance (not barred), and flight feathers have an obvious dark subterminal band (dusky in Short-toed Snake-Eagle). Upperwing is uniform. Juv. is darker, less rufous-brown than juv. Black-chested Snake-Eagle, but ranges rarely overlap. **Habitat:** Savanna, preferring moister areas than Short-toed Snake-Eagle; more often hunts from perches. **Status:** Uncommon, local nomad. **Voice:** Whistled 'kweeu', similar to Black-chested Snake-Eagle. [C5.34]

3 BLACK-CHESTED SNAKE-EAGLE *Circaetus pectoralis* 63-68 cm

Forms a superspecies with Beaudouin's and Short-toed snake-eagles, but adults are cleaner black and white, with white (not barred) belly and underwing coverts. Throughout most of range most likely confused with Martial Eagle (p. 106), but is much smaller with plain (not spotted) belly and mostly pale (not dark) flight feathers from below. Juv. is rich rufous, becoming pale brown below, with pale, lightly barred underwings and undertail. Imm. has large blotches on the belly and variable pale markings on the dark head; could be confused with Short-toed Snake-Eagle in NE. **Habitat:** Ranges from desert to savanna and woodland. **Status:** Uncommon to locally common nomad and possible intra-African migrant. **Voice:** Rarely calls; melodious, whistled 'kwo-kwo-kwo-kweeu'. [C5.35, G1.15.3]

4 BROWN SNAKE-EAGLE *Circaetus cinereus* 68-75 cm

Differs from other brown eagles by its large head, prominent yellow eyes and pale legs. In flight, dark brown underwing coverts contrast with pale flight feathers. Tail is barred. Juv. is sometimes paler, with a slightly scaled appearance. **Habitat:** Savanna and woodland. **Status:** Locally common; nomadic. **Voice:** Croaking 'hok-hok-hok-hok' flight call; generally silent. [C5.36, G1.15.2]

1

juv.

2

juv.

3

juv.

juv.

4

juv.

1 SOUTHERN BANDED SNAKE-EAGLE *Circaetus fasciolatus*   55-60 cm
Grey head and breast and rufous-barred belly similar to that of African Cuckoo Hawk (p. 86), but is much larger, with a large, rounded head. Barred belly, underwing coverts and tail pattern distinguish it from stockier Western Banded Snake-Eagle, which is smaller than African Crowned Eagle (p. 106), lacking chestnut underwing coverts. Juv. is dark brown above and pale below, with dark streaks on the head, neck and upper breast; tail is barred, like adult's. **Habitat:** Forests, woodland and plantations, often near water. **Status:** Uncommon to locally common; easily overlooked. **Voice:** Often calls, especially in early morning: harsh 'crok-crok-crok' and high-pitched 'ko-ko-ko-ko-keear'. [G1.15.4]

2 WESTERN BANDED SNAKE-EAGLE *Circaetus cinerascens*   55-60 cm
Stockier than Southern Banded Snake-Eagle, with a darker belly and underwing coverts. Tail is shorter, with a diagnostic broad white band across the middle, visible both in flight and at rest. Juv. is pale below, with a dark-streaked head, neck and breast; best told from juv. Southern Banded Snake-Eagle by broad grey tail band. Imm. is dark brown, with a broad grey tail band. **Habitat:** Woodland, especially along rivers; avoids dense forest. **Status:** Locally common. **Voice:** High-pitched 'kok-kok-kok-kok-kok'. [C5.37, G1.15.5]

3 BATELEUR *Terathopius ecaudatus*   55-70 cm
The broad secondaries, very short tail, and bold black, white and chestnut plumage are diagnostic. In flight, long wings are held in shallow 'V'; rarely flaps, but regularly rocks from side to side. Male has black secondaries and inner primaries; only tips are black in female. Juv. and imm. are uniform brown; differ from other brown eagles by flight action and shape; at rest, has loose ruff and noticeably short tail. **Habitat:** Savanna. Often seen on ground at waterholes. **Status:** Common, but has disappeared in some areas due to poisoning. **Voice:** Loud bark 'kow-wah'. [C5.38, G1.15.6]

4 BAT HAWK *Macheiramphus alcinus*   45 cm
A sooty brown raptor, appearing black in the field, with variable amounts of white on the throat and belly. In flight, has pointed, broad-based wings; resembles large falcon or even jaeger. At close quarters, white legs, eyelids and nape patches are distinctive. Juv. is paler brown with pale-spotted underwing and tail; more white on underparts than most adults. **Habitat:** Woodland, including plantations, and forest edge. **Status:** Uncommon. Easily overlooked; crepuscular and nocturnal, roosting in thick foliage during day. **Voice:** High-pitched whistling, similar to that of thick-knee. [C5.26, G1.13.9]

juv.

juv.

♀

♂

♀

♂

juv.

juv.

juv.

juv.

1

2

3

4

Large-tailed raptors, told from accipiters by long, narrow wings and loose, buoyant flight; wings usually held in shallow 'V' above body. Occur in open habitats. Typically fly low over the ground when searching for prey, but fly higher when commuting or displaying. Sexes and juvs differ in most species.

1 WESTERN (EURASIAN) MARSH-HARRIER *Circus aeruginosus*   48-56 cm
A large harrier. Male has a brown body and forewings contrasting with the grey-and-black wings and grey, unbarred tail. Underwing has rufous coverts, pale flight feathers and black primary tips. Female is dark brown, with a creamy white cap and throat, and usually has white-edged forewings. Unbarred brown tail separates it from African Marsh-Harrier, which can show a pale forehead and leading edge to the wings in worn juv. plumage. Juv. resembles female, but can lack the white on the crown and forewings. Differs from rare dark-morph Montagu's Harrier by larger size and uniform tail. **Habitat:** Marshes and adjoining grasslands and fields. **Status:** Fairly common Palearctic migrant, mostly Oct-Apr. **Voice:** Silent in Africa. [C1.84, G2.2.4]

2 AFRICAN MARSH-HARRIER *Circus ranivorus*   45-50 cm
Resembles Western Marsh-Harrier in size and shape, but flight feathers and tail are barred at all ages (not always visible from a distance, especially in juvs). Lacks marked sexual dimorphism, adults often paler and more mottled than female or juv. Western Marsh-Harrier, but individual variation is great. Larger and broader-winged than female Pallid and Montagu's harriers; rump is dark (not white). Juv. has a pale head and leading edge to the upperwing, like female Western Marsh-Harrier, but shows a prominent pale breast bar. **Habitat:** Marshes, reedbeds and adjacent grassland. **Status:** Locally common to scarce. **Voice:** Mainly silent; display call high-pitched 'fee-ooo'. [C5.41, G2.2.5]

3 PALLID HARRIER *Circus macrourus*   40-48 cm
A small, slender harrier. Male is paler grey than male Montagu's Harrier, with only a small black primary patch; underparts are plain. Female is brown above, with buff feather edges, and paler below, with dark streaking. Rump is white. Facial mask is slightly more distinct than that of female Montagu's Harrier, with a paler collar around the dark ear coverts. In flight from below, barring on secondaries is less distinct, with darker ground colour. Tail often has four (not five) dark bars. Juv. resembles female, but is more rufous and unstreaked below, and has dark secondaries from below in flight; has a pronounced white collar around the ear coverts. **Habitat:** Grassland and open savanna. **Status:** Uncommon Palearctic migrant, mostly Oct-Apr. **Voice:** Silent in Africa. [C1.82, G2.2.7]

4 MONTAGU'S HARRIER *Circus pygargus*   43-50 cm
Slightly larger and bulkier than Pallid Harrier. Male has a grey throat and upper breast, chestnut-streaked flanks, more black on the primaries and a conspicuous black bar on the upperwing. Secondaries are lightly barred below. Female and juv. are similar to female and juv. Pallid Harrier, but lack a pale collar behind the ear coverts. **Habitat:** Grassland and open savanna. **Status:** Locally common Palearctic migrant, mostly Oct-Apr. **Voice:** Silent in Africa. [C1.83, G2.2.6] **Similar species: Hen Harrier** *C. cyaneus* is larger, with broader wings; male has a white rump and lacks black line in upperwing; Palearctic vagrant to N.

1

♀

♀

♂

♂

2

juv.

juv.

juv.

3

♂

♂

juv.

sub-ad.

♀

♂

4

♂

♂

juv.

♀

♂

sub-ad.

85

1 BLACK HARRIER *Circus maurus*   48-53 cm
Endemic to S Africa. Adult mostly black or dark slate grey, with a large white rump, banded tail and pale wing panels. Differs from rare dark-morph Montagu's Harrier by white rump. Sexes alike. Juv. differs from female Pallid and Montagu's harriers (p. 84) by more rufous underparts, heavily streaked dark brown on the breast and flanks, and by paler ground colour to the barred flight feathers. Imm. has a black-and-grey barred tail. **Habitat:** Grassland and scrub, often near water, but forages over dry land. **Status:** Vulnerable. Uncommon resident in SW, nomadic elsewhere. **Voice:** Generally silent; 'pee-pee-pee-pee' display call; harsh 'chak-chak-chak' when alarmed. [G2.2.8]

2 AFRICAN HARRIER HAWK (GYMNOGENE) *Polyboroides typus*   60-66 cm
A large, broad-winged hawk with a small head, long legs, and loose, floppy flight action. Adult is grey above and finely barred below, with a bare yellow face (red when agitated) extending around the eye. In flight, broad black tips to flight feathers and single, central white tail band are distinctive. Juv. and imm. are brown, variably streaked and mottled; at a distance could be confused with brown eagles (p. 100), but show only 4-5 (not 6-7) primary 'fingers' in flight. Juv. has a bare, greyish face. Uses long, double-jointed legs to extract prey from crevices and weaver nests. **Habitat:** Woodland and forests; also more open, scrubby habitats. **Status:** Fairly common. **Voice:** During breeding season, whistled 'suuu-eeee-ooo'. [C5.40, G2.2.9]

3 LIZARD BUZZARD *Kaupifalco monogrammicus*   35-37 cm
A small, compact hawk, intermediate in size and shape between buzzards and accipiters. White throat with black central stripe is diagnostic at all ages. Adult has red cere and legs, and dark red eyes. In flight, shows white rump and one (rarely two) broad white tail bar(s). Larger and bulkier than Gabar Goshawk (p. 88). Juv. has paler cere and legs and pale fringes to upperpart feathers. **Habitat:** Woodland, well-wooded savanna and forest clearings. **Status:** Locally common resident; nomadic in drier areas. **Voice:** Noisy in breeding season: whistled 'peoo-peoo'; melodious 'klioo-klu-klu-klu-klu'. [C5.54, G2.1.4]

4 AFRICAN CUCKOO HAWK *Aviceda cuculoides*   40 cm
The long, rather broad wings and slow, relaxed flight separate this species from accipiters. At rest, wings reach almost to tail tip. Plumage is similar to that of African Goshawk (p. 90), but has small crest, short legs and much broader barring on belly and underwing coverts. Male's eyes are red-brown; female's yellow. Juv. is brown above and white below, with brown-streaked breast and larger spots on belly; best told from juv. African Goshawk by its larger size and shape. Imm. is browner above than adult, with mottled brown (not grey) breast. **Habitat:** Dense woodland and forest fringes. **Status:** Uncommon to locally fairly common; unobtrusive. **Voice:** Loud, far-carrying 'teee-oooo' whistle; shorter 'tittit-eoo'. [C5.25, G1.13.8]

1

2

juv.

juv.

3

juv.

4

juv.

juv.

Mostly fairly large, accipiter-like raptors with rather long, red legs. The three large species have loud, cuckoo-like calls, hence the common name. The smaller Gabar Goshawk is rather different and sometimes placed in its own genus *Micronisus*. Sexes alike; juvs differ.

1 GABAR GOSHAWK *Melierax gabar* 28-36 cm
A medium-small accipiter with a red cere and legs, prominent white rump, and plain grey (not finely barred) throat and upper breast, which distinguishes it from Ovambo Sparrowhawk (p. 92). Resembles Dark Chanting Goshawk, but is much smaller and has shorter legs. All-black melanistic form (5-25% of population) is more common in arid areas; smaller than melanistic Ovambo or Black (p. 90) sparrowhawks, with red (not yellow or orange) legs and cere. Juv. is brown above, with yellow eyes and orange legs; is only juv. accipiter with white rump. Breast is rufous-streaked; belly and underwing coverts are barred rufous. **Habitat:** Savanna and semi-arid scrub with at least some trees. **Status:** Locally common. **Voice:** High-pitched, whistling 'kik-kik-kik-kik-kik'. [C5.42, G2.2.1]

2 DARK CHANTING GOSHAWK *Melierax metabates* 43-56 cm
A large, long-legged goshawk with red legs and cere. Adult is darker grey than Eastern and Pale chanting goshawks, with a grey (not white) rump and dark lesser upperwing coverts contrasting with paler median and greater coverts. Much larger than Gabar Goshawk (which also has a white rump) or Ovambo Sparrowhawk (which has a barred breast, p. 92). Lacks throat stripe of smaller, more compact Lizard Buzzard (p. 86). Juv. has orange legs and cere and yellow eyes. Plumage is brown above, barred and streaked below; superficially harrier or *Buteo*-like. Best told from other juv. chanting goshawks by darker, barred rump. **Habitat:** Savanna and open woodland. **Status:** Uncommon; less obtrusive than other chanting goshawks. **Voice:** Piping 'kleeu-kleeu-klu-klu-klu'. [C1.85, G2.2.3]

3 EASTERN CHANTING GOSHAWK *Melierax poliopterus* 45-50 cm
Endemic to NE Africa. Paler and slightly larger and longer-legged than Dark Chanting Goshawk, with a white (or lightly barred) rump at all ages. Adult has a yellow cere, orange legs and uniform grey (not two-toned) upperwing coverts. In flight, barred underwing coverts are uniform with the belly (not paler). Juv. and imm. are brown, with yellow legs. **Habitat:** Arid savanna and semi-desert; more open habitats than Dark Chanting Goshawk. **Status:** Locally common. **Voice:** Slightly lower pitched than Dark Chanting Goshawk's.

4 PALE CHANTING GOSHAWK *Melierax canorus* 48-54 cm
Endemic to SW Africa. Paler and larger than Dark Chanting Goshawk, with a white rump and very pale grey secondaries contrasting strongly with the dark primaries. Juv. is paler than juv. Dark Chanting Goshawk and has a white (not barred) rump. Often treated as a race of Eastern Chanting Goshawk, but is much paler, especially on secondaries; ranges do not overlap. **Habitat:** Arid savanna, semi-desert and karoo scrub. **Status:** Common; three adults often breed together. **Voice:** Piping 'kleeu-kleeu-klu-klu-klu', usually uttered at dawn. [G2.2.2]

black morph

juv.

juv.

1

imm.

juv.

juv.

2

juv.

3

juv.

juv.

4

juv.

Long-tailed hawks with fairly short, rounded wings that do not reach the tail tip when folded. Flight rapid, direct and highly manoeuvrable when hunting, but frequently soar with wings held level or slightly depressed below body. Typically occur in wooded or forest habitats. Plumages vary with age, sex and between morphs; identification of juvs and imms very tricky. Females usually much larger than males.

1 LONG-TAILED HAWK *Urotriorchis macrourus*   65-70 cm
A large accipiter with a diagnostic long, rather wedge-shaped tail. Adult has rich chestnut breast and belly, contrasting with pale throat and vent. Rare grey phase has dark grey underparts and paler grey throat. In flight, has white rump, black-and-white barred tail, and barred underwings with chestnut underwing coverts. Eye, cere and legs are yellow. Juv. is brown above, with black-and-brown barred upperwing and tail; underwing is pale, with barred flight feathers. Underparts are either plain white or spotted and barred. **Habitat:** Forest and riparian woodland, including secondary growth; often quite low in canopy, as it hunts forest squirrels. **Status:** Locally common. **Voice:** Long, drawn-out cry; vocal, often located by call. [C5.52]

2 BLACK (GREAT) SPARROWHAWK *Accipiter melanoleucus*   46-58 cm
A large, black-and-white accipiter. Underparts vary from mostly white to black, but usually with a white throat. Larger than dark-morph Ovambo Sparrowhawk (p. 92) or Gabar Goshawk (p. 88), with yellow (not red or orange) legs and cere, and at least some white on underparts. Juv. is brown above and varies from pale to rufous below. Pale birds are much larger than juv. African Goshawk and are streaked (not spotted) below. Rufous birds resemble juv. African Hawk Eagle (p. 104), but are more heavily streaked, with unfeathered tarsi and a different shape and flight action. **Habitat:** Forests, woodland and plantations; sometimes forages far from cover. **Status:** Locally fairly common. **Voice:** Normally silent except when breeding. Male 'kee-yip'; female loud 'kek-kek-kek-kek'. [C5.51, G2.1.8]

3 AFRICAN GOSHAWK *Accipiter tachiro*   36-44 cm
A medium-sized accipiter with a pale grey cere and yellow legs and eyes; rump is dark. Adult is finely barred below. Smaller male is bluish-grey above, with two white spots on upertail, and barred rufous below (can appear uniform from a distance like Rufous-chested Sparrowhawk, p. 92). Female is brown above and barred brown below, with a brown-and-black barred tail. Juv. has bold tear-shaped spots on breast and belly. E African race has entirely black morph which is smaller than Black Sparrowhawk and told from Ovambo Sparrowhawk (p. 92) by paler yellow eye, cere and legs and lack of white flecks in tail. **Habitat:** Forest and dense woodland; often forages far from cover. **Status:** Common. **Voice:** Noisy; repetitive 'whit' or 'quick' every 1-2 seconds from perch or in aerial display; female mewing 'keeuuu'. [G2.1.10]

4 RED-CHESTED GOSHAWK *Accipiter toussenelii*   35-40 cm
Often treated as a race of African Goshawk but is slightly smaller and darker above, with broader white tail spots and more uniformly rufous breast and flanks (although W *macroscelides* is more barred below). Palest rainforest accipiter. Adult differs from Chestnut-flanked Sparrowhawk (p. 92) by pale (not dark grey) head (including throat), and by pale and dull (not rich orange-rufous) breast. Eye is orange. In flight, looks much paler than Chestnut-flanked Goshawk, and typically shows two (not three) broad white tail bars. Imm. is dark brown above, spotted and barred on sides of breast and flanks. **Habitat:** Rainforest, gallery forest and secondary growth. **Status:** Locally common. **Voice:** Similar to African Goshawk's but longer, 2-note 'chewit' call. [C5.44]

juv.

1

juv.

juv.

2

juv.

juv.

3

sub-ad.

juv.

♂

♀

juv.

♂

4

♂

♀

1 CHESTNUT-FLANKED SPARROWHAWK *Accipiter castanilius*   30-36 cm
A medium-sized, dark-backed rainforest accipiter with a yellow eye, cere and legs. Smaller than Red-chested Goshawk (p. 90), with much darker, slaty upperparts and three (not two) white tail spots. Larger than Red-thighed Sparrowhawk (p. 94) with dark (not white) rump and yellow (not orange-red) eye and cere. Throat is white, lightly barred rufous in female. Breast and belly are barred rufous, merging into chestnut flanks; vent is white. Juv. resembles juv. Red-chested Goshawk, but has paler, less heavily barred underwings; eye and cere yellow. **Habitat:** Closed-canopy rainforest, where it hunts in understorey. **Status:** Uncommon. **Voice:** Not known.

2 RUFOUS-CHESTED (RED-BREASTED) SPARROWHAWK
Accipiter rufiventris   33-40 cm
A fairly small accipiter with uniform upperparts and no white in the rump or white spots on tail. Adult has pale throat, rather dark, slate-grey upperparts (browner in female), and plain rufous underparts (darker in female); rufous extends up side of neck onto lower cheek, giving dark-capped appearance, quite unlike uniform head of African Goshawk (p. 90). Structure recalls Eurasian Sparrowhawk (p. 94), but is slightly larger and darker above, with more uniform rufous underparts. Eye, cere and legs are yellow. Juv. is brown above, with slight pale eyebrow and mottled rufous underparts. **Habitat:** Montane forest patches and plantations; often forages far from cover. **Status:** Locally common in S; scarce in N. **Voice:** Sharp, staccato 'kee-kee-kee-kee-kee' during display. [C5.50, G2.1.5]

3 OVAMBO SPARROWHAWK *Accipiter ovampensis*   32-40 cm
A medium-sized accipiter with yellow-orange legs, orange (rarely red) cere and dark red eyes. Adult is uniform grey above with darker bars in tail; rump is grey. Larger than Shikra, with dark (not bright) red eye, grey- (not rufous-) barred underparts, and white vertical flecks on tail. Rare melanistic form has diagnostic white vertical flecks in tail; larger than melanistic Gabar Goshawk (p. 88), with paler legs and cere; smaller than black morph African Goshawk or Black Sparrowhawk (p. 90) with richer orange bare parts. Juv. is variable, being brown above with white or rufous underparts; typically shows pale eyebrow (crown and nape are also pale in some birds). **Habitat:** Savanna, tall woodland and plantations, especially poplars. **Status:** Generally uncommon. **Voice:** Soft 'keeep-keeep-keeep' when breeding. [C5.49, G2.1.6]

4 SHIKRA (LITTLE BANDED GOSHAWK) *Accipiter badius*   28-30 cm
A small accipiter with uniform grey upperparts; lacks the white rump and tail spots of Little Sparrowhawk (p. 94). Smaller than Ovambo Sparrowhawk with rufous (not grey) barring below, bright cherry-red (not dark red) eye, yellow (not orange) cere, and unbarred central tail feathers. Paler above than male Levant Sparrowhawk (p. 94), with shorter wings, less rufous underparts and more barred underwing. Legs are orange-yellow. Juv. is brown, with streaked breast and barred belly like juv. Gabar Goshawk (p. 88), but its rump is dark (not white). **Habitat:** Savanna and tall woodland. **Status:** Common resident and local nomad. **Voice:** Male high-pitched 'keewik-keewik-keewik'; female softer 'kee-uuu'. [C5.46, G2.1.9]

1

♂ ♀

♂ juv.

2

juv.

♀ juv.

♀

black morph

3

juv.

juv.

juv.

♂

4

juv.

juv.

1 LEVANT SPARROWHAWK *Accipiter brevipes*   32-38 cm
Slightly larger and longer-winged than Eurasian Sparrowhawk; appears more falcon-like in flight. Adult has dark tips to outer primaries and relatively plain, unbarred underwing. Tail has 6+ bars (4-5 in Eurasian Sparrowhawk), and appears plain from above. Adult male resembles Shikra (p. 92), but is darker above with richer rufous underparts and paler underwing. Wings also distinctly longer and more pointed. At close range, has characteristic dark central throat stripe. Eyes are dark red (not yellow, as Eurasian Sparrowhawk or bright red, as Shikra). Juv. is browner above, with large spots on underparts and more heavily marked underwings. **Habitat:** Savanna and open woodland. **Status:** Scarce Palearctic migrant, mostly Nov-Mar; probably overlooked. **Voice:** Silent in Africa.

2 RED-THIGHED SPARROWHAWK *Accipiter erythropus*   25-30 cm
Rainforest form of Little Sparrowhawk, with dark grey, almost black, upperparts. Black face contrasts strongly with white throat. Eye and cere are orange-red; legs are yellow-orange. In flight, small size and black upperparts with white rump and tail spots are diagnostic. Smaller than Chestnut-flanked Sparrowhawk (p. 92) with white (not dark) rump. Male is pale grey below, with rufous-washed flanks; W birds are often more barred. Female is browner above, and usually has barred breast. Juv. is brown above, with dark rump; most are barred brown below, but some are white with only a few dark spots. Eye is yellow. **Habitat:** Rainforest and secondary growth. **Status:** Locally common. **Voice:** Sharp, repeated, high-pitched 'kik' or 'keek'. [C5.47]

3 LITTLE SPARROWHAWK *Accipiter minullus*   23-28 cm
The smallest accipiter. Adult is distinguished from Shikra (p. 92) by its white rump and the two white spots on the uppertail. Plumage is similar to male African Goshawk's (p. 90), but is much smaller, with white rump and yellow (not grey) cere. Smaller than Gabar Goshawk (p. 88) with white tail spots and yellow (not red) legs and cere. Breast is barred rufous or grey, with rufous-washed flanks. Juv. is brown above, with dark rump, and white below, with large spots on breast and belly. **Habitat:** Forest, woodland and plantations. **Status:** Locally common; secretive. **Voice:** Male high-pitched 'tu-tu-tu-tu-tu' during breeding season; female softer 'kew-kew-kew'. [C5.48, G2.1.7]

4 EURASIAN SPARROWHAWK *Accipiter nisus*   28-38 cm
Similar to Rufous-chested Sparrowhawk (p. 92), but underparts are whitish (not rufous), with throat heavily streaked and breast and belly barred rufous (in male) or greyish-brown (in female); upperparts are generally paler, and underwings are less heavily barred. Shorter winged than Levant Sparrowhawk, with more heavily barred underwing and fewer, broader tail bars. Legs and cere are yellow; eye is orange (in male) or yellow (in female). Juv. resembles female but is browner above, and has white-streaked eyebrow. **Habitat:** Savanna and woodland, mostly in more arid areas than Rufous-chested Sparrowhawk. **Status:** Uncommon Palearctic migrant Sep-May. **Voice:** Chattering 'kek kek kek'; seldom calls in Africa. [C1.86]

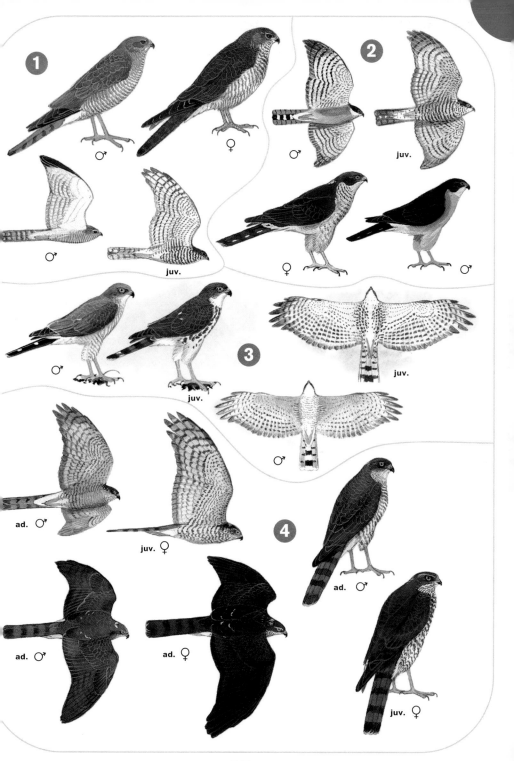

95

Medium-sized hawks wih fairly broad wings and rounded tails. Honey buzzards are related to kites, but superficially resemble true buzzards. Sexes alike, but plumages are highly variable.

1 EUROPEAN HONEY BUZZARD *Pernis apivorus*   52-60 cm

A small-headed, buzzard-like raptor; appears rather kite-like when perched. Plumage is variable, body ranging from white through barred to almost black, but adult has broad, dark subterminal tail band and two narrow bars (not easily seen) at base of tail; at close range, has scaly face feathers. In flight, wings are slightly narrower at body; wrists are held slightly bent and wings are bowed when gliding. Juv. has indistinctly barred tail; best told from Common Buzzard by shape. Adult eyes pale; juv's dark. **Habitat:** Woodland, forest edge and plantations; attracted to wasp nests. **Status:** Uncommon Palearctic migrant, mostly Oct-Apr. **Voice:** Generally silent; occasionally gives high-pitched 'meeuu'. [C1.70, G1.13.10]

2 COMMON & STEPPE BUZZARDS *Buteo buteo & B. vulpinus*   46-58 cm

Plumage extremely variable, from pale brown to almost black. Common Buzzard is typically darker, with more barred tail; Steppe Buzzard *vulpinus* has more rufous, less barred tail and longer, less rounded wings; recent evidence suggests they are best treated as separate species. Generally darker below than Forest and Mountain buzzards, with brown or barred flanks; occurs in more open habitats and frequently perches on telephone poles. Juv. has yellow eyes (not brown, as in Forest and Mountain buzzards) and narrower terminal tail bar. **Habitat:** Open country, avoiding very arid and forested areas. **Status:** Abundant Palearctic migrant, mostly Oct–Mar; Steppe Buzzard is common in E and S Africa; Common Buzzard is uncommon in W Africa. **Voice:** Gull-like 'pee-ooo'; seldom calls in Africa. [C1.88, G1.15.9]

3 MOUNTAIN BUZZARD *Buteo oreophilus*   45-50 cm

Endemic to NE Africa. Often treated as race of Forest Buzzard, but is typically browner above with darker underwing coverts; ranges do not overlap. Smaller than Steppe Buzzard; darker brown, less rufous above, with white underparts, heavily blotched dark brown. In flight, wing is relatively short and broad; underwing coverts are dark. Juv. is less spotted below. **Habitat:** Montane forests and adjacent grasslands. **Status:** Locally common. **Voice:** Typical buzzard 'peeuu', slightly higher pitched than Steppe Buzzard's. [C5.55]

4 FOREST BUZZARD *Buteo trizonatus*   45-50 cm

Endemic to S Africa. Very similar to Mountain Buzzard, but has diffuse white breast band, smaller underpart spots, paler underwing coverts, and is more rufous above; ranges do not overlap. Slightly smaller than Steppe Buzzard; whiter below, and lacks barred flanks. Juv. told from juv. Steppe Buzzard by its mostly white (not mottled) front and the tear-shaped flank streaks. However, some juvs are entirely brown below. **Habitat:** Forests and plantations, usually foraging along forest edges. **Status:** Locally common. **Voice:** Typical buzzard 'peeuu', slightly higher pitched than Steppe Buzzard's. [G1.15.10]

5 LONG-LEGGED BUZZARD *Buteo rufinus*   52-65 cm

A large, bulky eagle-like buzzard, with long, broad wings. Plumage is variable, but typically has dark belly, pale head and dark carpal patches on underwing. Adult has plain rufous tail that appears almost translucent but rufous-morph Steppe Buzzard also has pale rufous tail with only indistinct barring. Often confused with juv. Augur or Jackal buzzards (p. 98). In flight, has white, unmarked primaries with black tips and trailing edge. Wingbeats are slow and deep; hovers more often than Common or Steppe buzzards. Juv's tail is lightly barred; very hard to separate from other buzzards without direct comparison of size and shape. **Habitat:** Open grassland and semi-desert. **Status:** Uncommon Palearctic migrant Oct-Apr. **Voice:** Silent in Africa. [C1.90, G2.1.1]

soaring

gliding

rufous morph

dark morph

grey morph

pale morph

1

dark morph

pale morph

dark morph

pale morph

dark morph

2

dark morph

medium morph

3

4

dark morph

pale morph

gliding

5

soaring

juv.

1 RED-NECKED BUZZARD *Buteo auguralis*   36-40 cm

The common buzzard of W and C Africa with a rufous-brown head and neck. Adult has rufous tail with narrow dark subterminal band, dark chest, and white belly with dark spots. Smaller than Augur Buzzard, with longer tail and shorter secondaries. Underwing is mostly white, with broad black tip and trailing edge. Juv. has whitish underparts, with few dark spots on belly and flanks; tail is finely barred grey-brown. **Habitat:** Woodland and forest clearings. **Status:** Common resident and local nomad. **Voice:** Shrill, mewing calls while breeding. [C5.56]

2 AUGUR BUZZARD *Buteo augur*   48-55 cm

A large buzzard with a short, rounded tail and broad wings, broader on secondaries. Adult is dark grey-black above and white below. Underwing is mostly white (lacks dark coverts of Jackal Buzzard), with blackish tips to flight feathers and primary coverts; tail rufous with faint subterminal dark bar. Dark morph in moist habitats in N has black body and underwing coverts. Female has black throat or partial neck collar. Juv. is brown above and creamy-buff below, with dark streaking on sides of breast; tail rufous-brown, finely barred darker brown. N Somalia form *archeri* sometimes considered a separate species, Archer's Buzzard; typically browner above, with rufous underparts and underwing coverts, but highly variable; juv. darker buff below. **Habitat:** Mountain ranges and hilly country in woodland, savanna and desert. **Status:** Common. **Voice:** Harsh 'kow-kow-kow-kow' display call. [C5.57, G2.1.3].

3 JACKAL BUZZARD *Buteo rufofuscus*   48-55 cm

Endemic to S Africa. Similar to Augur Buzzard but has dark chestnut (not white) breast and barred black-and-white (not white) belly. Some birds have white breast, but differ from Augur Buzzard by black (not white) underwing coverts. Juv. is mostly brown, with slightly longer, finely-barred brown tail tail; can be confused with Steppe Buzzard but is larger, with broader wings and more aquiline head; often confused with Long-legged Buzzard (p. 96). Differs from brown *Aquila* eagles by bare tarsi. **Habitat:** Karoo scrub, grassland and agricultural lands; usually breeds on cliffs. **Status:** Locally common. **Voice:** Loud, drawn-out 'weeaah-ka-ka-ka', similar to call of Black-backed Jackal; male's call is higher pitched than female's. [G2.1.2]

4 GRASSHOPPER BUZZARD *Butastur rufipennis*   36-44 cm

A slender, long-winged, long-tailed buzzard with diagnostic rufous panels in outer upperwing (not visible in closed wings). Dark grey-brown upperparts contrast with chestnut-streaked, rufous underparts. Eye is yellow. White throat has central black stripe. Flight is buoyant, often low over ground; underwing is mostly white. Juv. is browner above, with less well-defined pale throat. **Habitat:** Savannas and other open habitats; often near grass fires. **Status:** Common intra-African migrant. **Voice:** Loud 'ki-ki-ki-keee' when breeding. [C5.53]

juv.

archeri

juv.

1

archeri

2

juv.

juv.

white-breasted
morph

juv.

juv.

3

4

juv.

juv.

Large raptors with long, fairly broad wings, deeply slotted primaries and feathered legs. Flight powerful and majestic, often soaring on thermals. Sexes alike, but the complex series of juv. and imm. plumages, plus colour morphs, complicates identification, especially among the large brown eagles. Smaller species formerly placed in *Hieraaetus*.

1 GREATER SPOTTED EAGLE *Aquila clanga*   65-72 cm

A broad-winged, relatively long-legged eagle, with tightly feathered tarsi. Darker than other brown eagles. In flight, upperwings, back and tail appear uniformly blackish-brown, with narrow white crescent on uppertail coverts; underwing is uniform. Broad wings appear square-ended and make the tail look short. Gape extends to below middle (not rear, as in Lesser Spotted and Steppe eagles) of eye. Adult eye dark brown (not yellow, as in Lesser Spotted Eagle). Juv. is heavily cream-spotted above; underparts are streaked buff. Scarce pale morph juv. is creamy-buff with dark flight feathers. **Habitat:** Savanna and open woodland. **Status:** Vulnerable. Scarce Palearctic migrant Oct-Mar, possibly under-recorded. **Voice:** Silent in Africa.

2 LESSER SPOTTED EAGLE *Aquila pomarina*   58-65 cm

A brown eagle with thin, tightly feathered tarsi; could be confused with large buzzards. Smaller and paler than Greater Spotted Eagle, with narrower wings and longer gape; dark flight feathers contrast with paler coverts and body (not uniform as Greater Spotted Eagle). Bill is relatively small (unlike large, bulky bill of Steppe Eagle), with yellow gape extending to rear of eye. In flight has long, broad wings and short, rounded tail (shorter than Steppe Eagle's). Juv. has white bar along edge of upper- and underwing coverts, like juv. Steppe Eagle's, but narrower; U-shaped white rump is also narrower than juv. Steppe Eagle's. **Habitat:** Savanna and woodland; often with Steppe Eagle in savanna. **Status:** Uncommon Palearctic migrant, mostly Oct-Apr. **Voice:** Silent in Africa. [G1.14.4]

3 STEPPE EAGLE *Aquila nipalensis*   67-82 cm

A large, brown eagle with a heavy bill and long, broad wings. Yellow gape extends to back (not middle, as in Tawny Eagle) of eye. Colour is variable, but adult's tail is barred and eye is brown (yellow in Tawny Eagle). Adult is usually uniform dark brown. More common juv. is lighter brown, with prominent pale bars along edge of upper- and underwing coverts, pale trailing edge to wing, and pale, U-shaped rump patch. White lines on wing coverts are broader than in Lesser Spotted Eagle, and it appears longer winged. Most birds are *orientalis*; vagrant *nipalensis* is larger, darker and has an even longer gape and heavier bill. **Habitat:** Savanna and open woodland. **Status:** Common Palearctic migrant Oct-Mar; *nipalensis* is rare migrant. **Voice:** Silent in Africa. [G1.14.3]

4 TAWNY EAGLE *Aquila rapax*   65-76 cm

Very similar to migrant Steppe Eagle. At close range, has shorter gape, extending only to below middle of eye (not to back, as in Steppe Eagle). Tail is unbarred or faintly barred (not heavily barred as adult Steppe Eagle's). Colour is variable: most birds are uniformly tawny, but range from streaked dark brown to pale buff. Female is usually darker than male. Adult has pale yellow (not brown) eye. Juv. is rufous brown, fading to buff with age; lacks pale wing bars and rump of juv. Steppe Eagle. **Habitat:** Savanna and woodland. **Status:** Common resident and local migrant. **Voice:** Seldom calls; sharp bark, 'kyow'. [C1.91, G1.14.2]

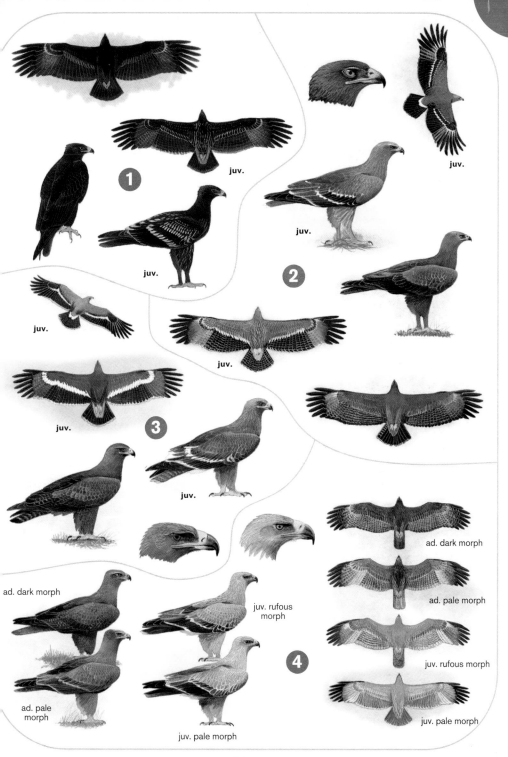

juv.

juv.

1

juv.

juv.

juv.

2

juv.

juv.

3

juv.

ad. dark morph

ad. dark morph

ad. pale morph

ad. pale
morph

juv. rufous
morph

juv. rufous morph

juv. pale morph

juv. pale morph

101

1 EASTERN IMPERIAL EAGLE *Aquila heliaca*   72-84 cm
Similar to Steppe Eagle (p. 100), but is slightly longer-tailed and has a larger bill. Adult is blackish-brown, with rufous hindcrown and nape, and white shoulder epaulettes. Rounded tail is grey, with broad black terminal band. Juv. is variable, but typically paler, often with large white rump, conspicuously pale inner primaries (much more distinct than Steppe Eagle's) and blackish tail with narrow white tip; streaked below, especially across breast. **Habitat:** Lowland grasslands. **Status:** Vulnerable. Rare Palearctic migrant Oct-March; possibly underrecorded. **Voice:** Silent in Africa.

2 GOLDEN EAGLE *Aquila chrysaetos*   75-90 cm
A large, long-tailed eagle; appears long and slender when perched. Adult is rich brown, with golden nape and gold wash on upperwing coverts. Head is smaller than Eastern Imperial Eagle's, and lacks white epaulettes. In flight has longer tail and characteristic narrow inner secondaries, giving a wing shape similar to Verreaux's Eagle. Juv. lacks obvious golden nape, but has diagnostic white tail with broad black terminal band and conspicuous white wing panels. **Habitat:** Mountainous areas. **Status:** Rare Palearctic migrant; small population may breed in Ethiopian highlands. **Voice:** Generally silent; sharp, dog-like yelping. [C1.94]

3 VERREAUX'S (BLACK) EAGLE *Aquila verreauxii*   80-95 cm
A large, long-tailed eagle with characteristic narrow wings at the base, bulging out in middle of wing due to long central and outer secondaries. Black-and-white adult is unmistakable. Female has larger white back patches. Juv. is best recognised by characteristic flight shape, as well as mottled light and dark brown plumage, with diagnostic rufous crown and nape contrasting with darker face and throat. **Habitat:** Mountainous areas. **Status:** Locally common. **Voice:** Rarely calls; melodious 'keee-uup'. [C5.59, G1.14.1]

4 WAHLBERG'S EAGLE *Aquila wahlbergi*   55-60 cm
A relatively small, slender eagle with a small, pointed crest on the hindcrown. Usually dark brown, but has pale and intermediate colour morphs. Pale morph has mostly white head (unlike dark cap and face of pale Booted Eagle, p. 104). In flight, has diagnostic long, narrow, square-ended tail, and slender, straight-edged wings. **Habitat:** Woodland and savanna. **Status:** Common intra-African migrant. **Voice:** Drawn-out whistle while soaring; yelping 'kop-yop-yip-yip-yip' when perched. [C5.58, G1.14.5]

juv.

juv.

①

juv.

②

juv.

③

juv.

juv.

④

juv.

dark morph

brown morph

pale morph

103

1 BOOTED EAGLE *Aquila pennatus*   45-55 cm
A small eagle with a relatively long, square-tipped tail, but tail is shorter and broader than that of Wahlberg's Eagle (p. 102), wings broader and usually held more angled at the wrist. Both pale and dark morphs have diagnostic 'landing lights' on leading edge of upperwing against body. Commoner pale morph shows strong contrast between whitish underwing coverts and dark flight feathers, superficially recalling Egyptian Vulture (p. 76), but tail shape and jizz quite different. Face is mostly brown, contrasting with white throat (unlike all-pale head of pale Wahlberg's Eagle). Dark morph is uniformly dark brown, apart from white 'landing lights', pale inner primaries and buffy bar across the upperwing coverts. Also rare rufous morph. **Habitat:** Virtually any habitat, but avoids extensive forests; breeds on cliffs. **Status:** Uncommon; breeds in extreme SW; elsewhere uncommon Palearctic migrant, mostly Oct-Apr. **Voice:** High-pitched 'kee-keeee' or 'pee-pee-pee-pee'. [C1.96, G1.14.6]

2 AFRICAN HAWK-EAGLE *Aquila spilogaster*   60-68 cm
A medium-sized, black-and-white eagle. Larger and longer-winged than Ayres' and Cassin's hawk-eagles. In flight, upperwing has distinctive white panels at base of primaries; tail is paler and barred, with broader terminal bar. From below, flight feathers are mainly white and tail has broad terminal bar. Juv. has rufous underparts and underwing coverts, becoming black-streaked with age. Upperparts with juv. lacking conspicuous terminal tail bar. Easily confused with Black Sparrowhawk (p. 90), but has feathered (not bare) legs. **Habitat:** Woodland and savanna; also arid areas with some trees. **Status:** Uncommon. **Voice:** Seldom calls; whistled, musical 'klee-klee-klee'. [C5.60, G1.14.7]

3 AYRES' HAWK-EAGLE *Aquila ayresii*   45-61 cm
A small, compact eagle. Differs from similar Cassin's Hawk-Eagle by bold, black-spotted (not plain) underparts and heavily barred underwing with blotched (not black) underwing coverts. Has small white 'landing lights' like Booted Eagle. Underparts vary from mostly white with black streaks to almost all black. Head is usually dark, but is pale in some birds. Smaller than African Hawk-Eagle, with uniform dark upperparts and more heavily marked underparts. Juv. is rufous below, with more heavily barred underwing than juv. African Hawk-Eagle. **Habitat:** Woodland and forest. **Status:** Uncommon resident and intra-African migrant. **Voice:** Normally silent; shrill 'pueep-pip-pip-pueep' when displaying. [C5.61, G1.14.8]

4 CASSIN'S HAWK-EAGLE *Spizaetus africanus*   50-61 cm
Similar to Ayres' Hawk-Eagle, but has black (not blotched) underwing coverts and mostly white (not spotted) underparts. Narrow wing base is more pronounced, and lacks white 'landing lights'. Is always more contrasting black and white than Ayres' Hawk-Eagle. Perched birds have feathered legs and very different shape from Black Sparrowhawk (p. 90). Juv. is dark brown above, with rufous-brown head, and white below, with breast, flanks and underwing coverts dark-spotted (not rufous, as in Ayres' Hawk-Eagle). **Habitat:** Forest canopy, edge of forest and secondary growth. **Status:** Uncommon. **Voice:** High-pitched scream. [C5.63]

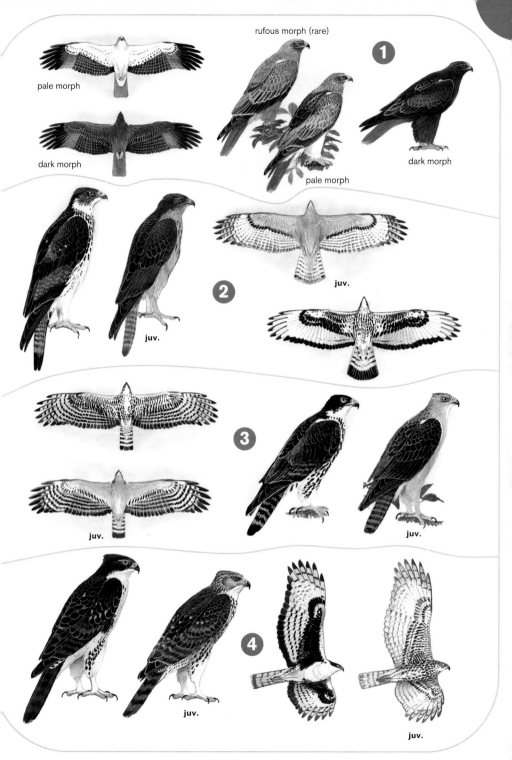

pale morph

dark morph

rufous morph (rare)

1

pale morph

dark morph

2

juv.

juv.

3

juv.

juv.

juv.

4

juv.

juv.

1 LONG-CRESTED EAGLE *Lophaetus occipitalis* 52-58 cm
The dull black plumage and long, floppy crest are diagnostic. In flight, has conspicuous white bases to primaries, and black-and-white barred secondaries and tail. Flight action is fast and direct, on stiffly held wings, with shallow wing beats. Male has white leggings and longer crest than female, which has brown or brown-and-white mottled leggings. Juv. has short crest and grey (not yellow) eyes. **Habitat:** Woodland, plantations and forest edges, especially near water. **Status:** Common resident and local nomad. **Voice:** High-pitched, screamed 'kee-ah' during display or when perched. [C5.62, G1.14.9]

2 CONGO SERPENT-EAGLE *Dryotriorchis spectabilis* 46-52 cm
Structure resembles that of a snake eagle (p. 80), with rounded head and large eyes (yellow in male, brown in female). Adult is dark above and white below. W African *batesi* is more heavily marked below, with dark spots on breast. White throat with central black stripe is sharply demarcated from grey cheeks by black lateral lines. In flight from below, appears mostly white, with boldly black-barred flight feathers; most likely to be confused with Ayres's Hawk-Eagle (p. 104). Juv. is browner, with scaled back, pale head and spotted underparts. **Habitat:** Forest, plantations and secondary growth. **Status:** Locally common. Unobtrusive in closed-canopy forest, but easily seen at edge of forest and in degraded areas. **Voice:** Regular, nasal 'caw' notes, or longer, wailing call; similar to Western Banded Snake Eagle's. [C5.39]

3 AFRICAN CROWNED EAGLE (CROWNED HAWK-EAGLE)
Stephanoaetus coronatus 80-98 cm
A huge, crested eagle with rounded, very broad wings and a long, broad tail. Adult is dark grey above, with breast and belly heavily mottled black. Underwing coverts, breast and neck are suffused rufous. In flight, flight feathers and tail are heavily barred black. Female has fewer wing bars than male. Juv. has creamy white head and underparts; similar to juv. Martial Eagle, but has dark speckling on flanks and legs, and broadly barred tail and underwing. **Habitat:** Forest and dense woodland. **Status:** Locally fairly common. **Voice:** Very vocal; flight call is ringing 'kewee-kewee-kewee'; male's call is higher pitched than female's. [C5.64, G1.15.1]

4 MARTIAL EAGLE *Polemaetus bellicosus* 78-86 cm
A huge eagle with a short crest, dark brown head and upper breast, and a white, lightly spotted belly. In flight, has dark (not pale, as in adult Black-breasted Snake-Eagle, p. 80) underwings. Juv. is longer winged and whiter than juv. Crowned Eagle, with darker, finely barred flight feathers and tail, and unspotted flanks. **Habitat:** Mainly savanna but frequents wide range of habitats, from desert to forest edge. **Status:** Locally common. **Voice:** Rapid 'klooee-klooee-klooee' in display. [C5.65, G1.14.10]

1

2

♀

♂

juv.

♂

imm.

3

juv.

♀

juv.

4

juv.

Small to medium-sized raptors with long pointed wings. Flight typically fast and direct, although smaller species often hover. Sexes differ in most species, with females often much larger than males.

1 COMMON KESTREL *Falco tinnunculus*   30-36 cm
Male has grey head and chestnut back with dark spots; upperwing rufous, lacking grey greater coverts of male Lesser Kestrel. Tail is grey, with broad black subterminal bar and whitish tip. Female typically has rufous head with faint malar stripes and rufous, barred tail; darker than female Lesser Kestrel with rufous (not grey) rump. Juv more heavily barred with pale tips to flight feathers. Resident *rufescens* (W and E Africa) is smaller and darker above with heavier barring and spotting, including barred tail; female has grey head, similar to Rock Kestrel, but genetic evidence places it closer to Common Kestrel; sometimes treated as a separate species, Mountain Kestrel. Somalia and Socotra *archeri* closer to *tinnunculus*. **Habitat:** Open areas. Typically breeds on cliffs. **Status:** Palearctic migrants are fairly common S to Tanzania and Angola, mostly Oct–Mar; resident races uncommon. **Voice:** High-pitched 'kik-kik-kik'; migrants seldom call. [C2.1b]

2 ROCK KESTREL *Falco rupicolus*   30-34 cm
Often treated as a race of Common Kestrel, but genetically distinct and lacks marked sexual dimorphism, with less streaked underparts and whiter underwing, recalling Lesser Kestrel (p. 110). Range not known to overlap with resident *rufescens*, but Palearctic migrant Common Kestrels probably reach its range. Male and female similar with greyish head, rump and grey barred tail (usually less barred in male). Juv. has rufous head, streaked darker; tail buffy-grey. **Habitat:** Grassland, scrub and open woodland, usually near rocky areas. Breeds on cliffs or buildings; sometimes uses nests of other birds. **Status:** Common, especially in S. **Voice:** High-pitched 'kik-ki-ki'. [G2.4.1]

3 GREATER KESTREL *Falco rupicoloides*   34-38 cm
A rather large, pale kestrel with dense uniform barring on the back, and little contrast between the pale rufous upper- and underparts. Plain head lacks malar stripe. In flight, flight feathers are barred from above, and whitish underwing contrasts with rufous body. Adult has grey-and-black barred tail with white tip and diagnostic whitish eyes. Juv. has rufous, barred tail, dark eyes and streaked (not barred) flanks. **Habitat:** Arid savanna and semi-desert. **Status:** Locally common. **Voice:** Shrill, repeated 'kee-ker-rik'. [G2.4.2]

4 FOX KESTREL *Falco alopex*   35-39 cm
A rather large, dark kestrel with a long, graduated tail. Like Greater Kestrel, has little contrast between upper- and underparts, but is darker rufous, with only small dark streaks (not barred) above. In flight, dark, unbarred flight feathers contrast with rufous upperwing coverts. Underwing is pale rufous, contrasting less with body than in Greater Kestrel. Adult has tail finely barred black; eye is dark. Juv. has clearer barring in tail and wings. Typically hunts from perch; rarely hovers. **Habitat:** Arid savanna, often near hills. **Status:** Uncommon to locally common, with local movements. **Voice:** High-pitched 'keek keek keek'; very vocal during breeding season (May-Sep). [C5.67]

1 ♂ ♀ juv. *archeri* ♂

♂ juv. 2 ♀

juv. 3

4 juv.

1 LESSER KESTREL *Falco naumanni* 29-32 cm

A slender kestrel with a slightly wedge-shaped tail. Male told from other kestrels by its plain chestnut back (no spots or barring), grey greater coverts, rather plain, buff underparts and unmarked underwing. Female is pale rufous above, densely barred; much paler than Common Kestrel (p. 108) with grey (not rufous) rump; smaller than Greater Kestrel (p. 108) with greater contrast between upper- and underparts. Cream underparts have dark spots; face is rather pale, with dark malar stripes. Juv. is slightly more rufous, with less well-defined malar stripe and rufous rump. At very close range has white claws. **Habitat:** Arid shrubland, grassland and fields. Roosts communally in tall trees. **Status:** Vulnerable. Locally abundant Palearctic migrant, mostly Oct-May. **Voice:** Silent during day, but noisy at roosts; high-pitched 'kiri-ri-ri-ri'. [C2.1a, G2.4.3]

2 RED-NECKED FALCON *Falco chicquera* 30-36 cm

A small, dashing, long-tailed falcon. Adult has chestnut crown and nape, uniformly barred, slate-grey upperparts, and broad subterminal tail band. Throat and upper breast are creamy buff, sometimes with indistinct rufous breast band. Lower breast and belly are finely barred. Smaller than adult Lanner Falcon (p. 116), with barred upperparts, belly and broad tail band. Head usually appears clean-cut, with narrow, dark brown moustachial stripes on white cheeks. Juv. is duller, with dark brown head, two buff patches on nape, and pale rufous underparts, finely barred brown; could be confused with Taita Falcon (p. 114), but tail is much longer. **Habitat:** Arid savanna, often near *Borassus* palms; usually perches within tree canopy. **Status:** Locally fairly common. **Voice:** Shrill 'ki-ki-ki-ki-ki' during breeding season. [C5.70, G2.3.8]

3 AMUR (EASTERN RED-FOOTED) FALCON *Falco amurensis* 28-30 cm

Similar to Red-footed Falcon. Male has diagnostic white (not slate grey) underwing coverts. Female is whitish (not rufous) below, with extensive spotting; vent is buffy and unmarked. Superficially resembles Eurasian Hobby (p. 114) but has a white (not dark) forehead, pale grey (not dark) crown, and paler underwing. Juv. resembles female, but is streaked below and has buffy edges to upperpart feathers. **Habitat:** Open grassland. Roosts communally in tall trees. **Status:** Common Palearctic migrant, mostly Nov-May. Winters mostly in S Africa; passage migrant further N. **Voice:** Shrill chattering at roosts. [G2.3.10]

4 (WESTERN) RED-FOOTED FALCON *Falco vespertinus* 28-31 cm

A small, kestrel-like falcon. Male is dark slate-grey, with chestnut vent (often not visible at a distance); lacks white underwing coverts of Amur Falcon. Female has rufous head with small dark mask around eye, and lightly streaked, buffy underparts; in flight, has rufous underwing coverts. From above, superficially resembles Red-necked Falcon, but the narrower dark subterminal tail bar and different shape and flight action are diagnostic. Juv. has off-white underparts, more heavily streaked than female's. Head is whitish, with dark face mask and indistinct cap; paler than female or juv. Amur Falcon. Underwing is much paler than Eurasian Hobby's (p. 114), with dark trailing edge. **Habitat:** Grassland and arid savanna. Roosts communally in tall trees, sometimes with Lesser Kestrels and Amur Falcons. **Status:** Fairly common Palearctic migrant, mostly Nov-May. Winters mostly in S Africa; passage migrant further N. **Voice:** Shrill chattering at roosts. [C2.2a, G2.3.9]

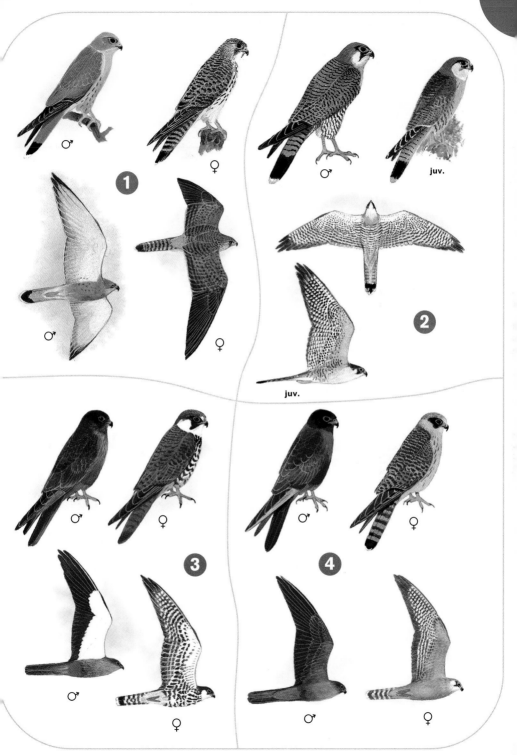

♂

♀

1

♂

♀

♂

juv.

2

juv.

♂

♀

3

4

♂

♀

♂

♀

♂

♀

1 AFRICAN PYGMY FALCON *Polihierax semitorquatus* 18-20 cm
A tiny, shrike-like falcon with an undulating, rapid flight. In flight, white-spotted black flight feathers and tail contrast with white rump. Male is grey above and white below. Female has chestnut back. Juv. has dull brown back. Sits upright on exposed perches. **Habitat:** Arid savanna. Breeds in nests of Sociable Weavers and buffalo-weavers, leaving distinctive, white-washed rim around nest entrance. **Status:** Uncommon to locally common. **Voice:** Noisy; high-pitched 'chip-chip' and 'kik-kik-kik-kik'. [G2.4.6]

2 GREY KESTREL *Falco ardosiaceus* 30-36 cm
A small, compact, uniform grey falcon. Has shorter, broader wings than Sooty Falcon; at rest, wings do not reach tip of square tail. Flat crown gives rather square-headed look (rounded in Sooty Falcon), and has more extensive yellow skin around eye. Juv. is lightly washed brown; facial skin is greenish. **Habitat:** Savanna and open woodland, often around palms. **Status:** Common. **Voice:** High-pitched, rasping trill. [C5.68, G2.4.4]

3 DICKINSON'S KESTREL *Falco dickinsoni* 28-30 cm
A grey kestrel with contrasting pale grey head and rump. Tail is strongly barred grey and black, with broader subterminal bar. From beneath, flight feathers are also conspicuously barred. Head is square, with flat crown; appears large-headed (unlike dark, small-headed Sooty Falcon). Adult has extensive bare yellow skin around eye, joining with cere. Juv. is lightly washed brown, with small, greenish eye-ring and cere. Head and rump are darker than adult's, similar to Grey Kestrel, but is easily separated from that species by barred tail and wings. **Habitat:** Palm savanna and open woodland, often near baobab trees. **Status:** Uncommon. **Voice:** High-pitched 'keee-keee-keee'. [C5.69, G2.4.5]

4 SOOTY FALCON *Falco concolor* 32-36 cm
A sleek, long-winged falcon, with folded wings extending beyond tail tip (unlike shorter, broader wings of Grey Kestrel). Adult is plain slate grey; lacks chestnut vent of Red-footed and Amur falcons (p. 110), and has yellow (not orange-red) legs and cere. In flight, resembles long-winged Eurasian Hobby (p. 114). Juv. is darker grey above, with narrow pale feather margins; throat is creamy; rest of underparts are buffy, streaked rather soft grey. Moustachial streak is narrower than in Eurasian Hobby, and breast streaking is paler. **Habitat:** Winters in savanna and woodland; breeds on arid cliffs and islands. **Status:** Uncommon; breeds in loose colonies at islands in Red Sea. **Voice:** Mostly silent; high-pitched shrieks at nest. [G2.3.5]

♂

♀

♂

♀

1

2

juv.

3

juv.

juv.

4

juv.

juv.

1 ELEONORA'S FALCON *Falco eleonorae*   36-42 cm
A large, slender falcon with very long, rather broad-based wings and long tail; has darker underwings than other falcons. Adult is dark sooty-brown above. Pale morph has clean white face and throat contrasting with dark-streaked rufous breast and belly. Larger than hobbies, with broader, darker wings. Dark morph is almost black; much darker amd larger than Sooty Falcon (p. 112). Legs are greenish-yellow; cere is yellow (in male) or blue (in female). Juv. has buffy fringes to upperpart feathers, appearing scaled at close range. **Habitat:** Savanna, woodland and forest. **Status:** Uncommon Palearctic migrant Oct-Nov and Apr-May. Most migrate to Madagascar, but some may remain along E coast Dec-Mar. **Voice:** Silent in Africa. [C2.2b, G2.3.7]

2 EURASIAN HOBBY *Falco subbuteo*   28-36 cm
A long-winged, relatively short-tailed falcon. In flight, appears almost swift-like. Adult has creamy (not rusty, as in African Hobby) underparts, with heavy streaking on breast and belly, and rufous leggings and vent. Larger, darker-backed and more heavily streaked below than juv. Amur and Red-footed falcons (p. 110). Juv. lacks rufous vent and leggings. In fresh plumage, has pale fringes to back and crown feathers, appearing scaled at close range. Feeds on the wing; often active at dawn and dusk. **Habitat:** Woodland, savanna, and other habitats on passage. **Status:** Fairly common Palearctic migrant Oct-May. **Voice:** Silent in Africa. [C2.3b, G2.3.3] **Similar species: Merlin** *F. columbarius* is much smaller with a pale supercilium and only a faint dark malar stripe; Palearctic vagrant to NW.

3 AFRICAN HOBBY *Falco cuvierii*   28-30 cm
Smaller and more compact than Eurasian Hobby, with unstreaked, rufous underparts (including throat and face). More slender than Taita Falcon, with a longer tail and dark head lacking rufous patches. Can appear all-dark in poor light. Juv. has dark-streaked, rufous breast and belly; head and throat colour vary from rufous to white. White-throated bird resembles pale-morph Eleonora's Falcon, but is much smaller and shorter tailed. Often forages at dawn and dusk. **Habitat:** Woodland, forests and adjoining open country. **Status:** Uncommon resident and intra-African migrant. **Voice:** High-pitched 'kik-kik-kik-kik' display call. [C5.71, G2.3.4]

4 TAITA FALCON *Falco fasciinucha*   28-30 cm
A small, compact falcon with a short tail, broad shoulders and large head. Flight resembles that of Peregrine Falcon (p. 116), but this species is much smaller, with more rapid wingbeats and more rounded-looking wings. Plumage resembles African Hobby's, but has rufous patches on nape, and white throat that contrasts with black moustachial stripe. Could be confused with juv. Red-necked Falcon (p.110), which also has rufous nape patches, but is much stockier and shorter-tailed. Juv. has buff fringes to back feathers, rufous face and throat, and is lightly streaked below. **Habitat:** Cliffs and gorges. **Status:** Rare and localised. **Voice:** High-pitched 'kree-kree-kree' and 'kek-kek-kek'. [G2.3.6]

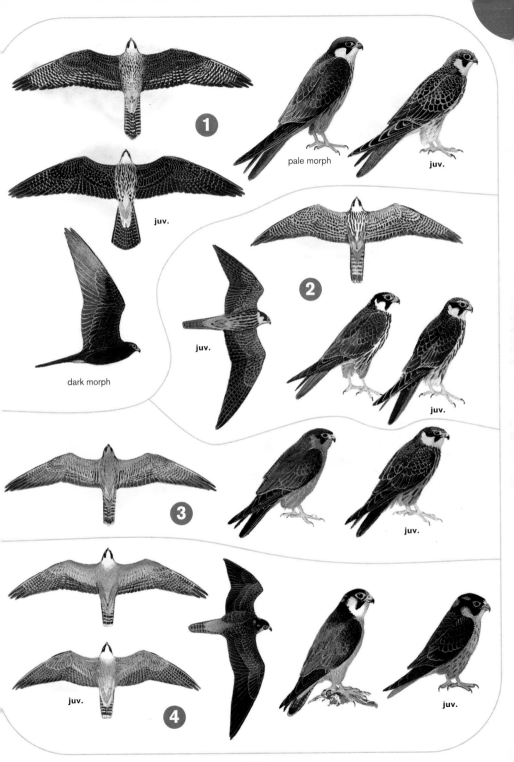

pale morph

juv.

juv.

1

juv.

dark morph

juv.

2

juv.

juv.

3

juv.

juv.

juv.

4

115

1 LANNER FALCON *Falco biarmicus* 36-48 cm
A large, broad-winged falcon with diagnostic rufous hind-crown and nape. Often soars with rounded wings and fanned tail. Adult *biarmicus* (S and E Africa) has rather plain, pinkish-cream underparts and pale, blue-grey upperparts. N African *abyssinicus* is darker slate-grey above, with spotted breast and barred belly. Juv. is dark grey-brown above, with creamy-brown crown and nape, and heavy brown streaking on breast and belly (juv. Peregrine Falcon has finer breast streaking). **Habitat:** Wide range, from mountains to deserts and open grassland; avoids forests. **Status:** Common to scarce resident. **Voice:** Harsh 'kak-kak-kak-kak-kak', similar to call of Peregrine Falcon; also whining and chopping notes. [C2.4a, G2.3.2]

2 SAKER FALCON *Falco cherrug* 42-52 cm
The largest African falcon. Appears small-headed, long-winged and long-tailed. Wings are even broader than Lanner Falcon's, and flight is looser. Plumage is highly variable, but generally is pale-headed (especially juv.), with narrow moustachial stripe. Upperwing and back are dark brown, contrasting with paler, barred tail in adult (juv's tail is dark, with tiny pale spots). Underwing coverts are streaked, contrasting with paler flight feathers, sometimes forming dark bar on midwing. Differs from Lanner Falcon in having dark trailing edges to underwing, and white-streaked (not rufous-brown) hindcrown and nape. **Habitat:** Arid savanna and semi-desert, often around wetlands. **Status:** Rare Palearctic migrant, mostly Oct-Mar. **Voice:** Silent in Africa. [C2.4b]

3 PEREGRINE FALCON *Falco peregrinus* 34-44 cm
A large, chunky falcon with pointed wings and a relatively short tail. Smaller and more compact than Lanner Falcon, with dark cap and broad moustachial stripes. Flight is dashing and direct. Adult of resident *minor* has dark slate-grey upperparts, mostly white breast and finely barred belly. Palearctic *calidus* is larger and paler above, with spotted breast and narrower moustachial stripes. Juv. is dark brown above; has variable paler streaking on crown, with paler patches on nape. **Habitat:** Migrant birds occur in wide range of open habitats; often forage at wetlands. Breeding birds require high cliffs and gorges. **Status:** Uncommon resident and Palearctic migrant Oct-Mar. **Voice:** Raucous 'kak-kak-kak-kak-kak' around nesting cliff; also whining and chopping notes. [C2.5a, G2.3.1]

4 BARBARY FALCON *Falco pelegrinoides* 34-40 cm
Sometimes treated as a race of Peregrine Falcon, but is smaller and paler. Adult has distinctive rufous hindcrown and nape, similar to Lanner Falcon, but has dark line behind eye, forming boundary between pale cheek and rufous crown and nape; structure is also different from Lanner Falcon's, with shorter tail and more pointed wings. Dark moustachial stripes are fairly narrow compared with Peregrine Falcon's. Creamy underparts have faint narrow barring on flanks and leg feathers. Juv. is dark brown above, with pale nuchal collar; less streaked below than juv. Peregrine Falcon. **Habitat:** Semi-desert to desert. **Status:** Uncertain; probably rare resident N Somalia, uncommon Palearctic migrant elsewhere. **Voice:** Similar to Peregrine Falcon's. [C2.5b]

biarmicus

1

juv.

juv.

2

juv.

juv.

3

minor

juv.
calidus

juv.

4

juv.

Large gamebirds. Conspicuous in open habitat but forest species secretive. Sexes differ in peacocks; sexes alike in most guineafowls.

1 CONGO PEACOCK *Afropavo congensis*   60-70 cm
Endemic to DRC. Larger and much more brightly coloured than Black and Crested guineafowls. Male is deep violet-green, with red throat and bizarre black-and-white crown tuft. Female is duller, with greenish back, rufous head and underparts, and green-barred rufous wings. **Habitat:** Undisturbed primary rainforest; forages on forest floor. **Status:** Vulnerable. Poorly known; secretive, but may be locally common in remote areas. Occurs in pairs. **Voice:** Repeated duet 'goway-gowaa', with male first and higher-pitched than female. [C5.76]

2 WHITE-BREASTED GUINEAFOWL *Agelastes meleagrides*   40-45 cm
Endemic to upper Guinea forests. Easily identified by its bare red head, white neck and breast, and otherwise black body. Juv. is brownish-black, with white belly. Occurs in groups of up to 20 birds; inquisitive and generally unafraid of man. **Habitat:** Primary rainforest with open understorey. **Status:** Vulnerable. Uncommon to locally common. **Voice:** Metallic twitter when foraging; loud, even-pitched whistle to muster flock; descending, flute-like whistle by isolated individuals. [C5.72]

3 BLACK GUINEAFOWL *Agelastes niger*   40-44 cm
Endemic to C Africa. A small, plain black guineafowl with a bare red head and neck. Juv. has feathered neck, dull brown head and grey belly. **Habitat:** Chiefly dense primary rainforest; also forest edge and old, overgrown fields. Small groups forage over forest floor and rapidly run to thickets for cover. **Status:** Locally common, but seldom seen. **Voice:** 'Keet keet' contact call; resonant 'huhuhuhuhu' crowing. [C5.73]

4 HELMETED GUINEAFOWL *Numida meleagris*   58-64 cm
A large, well-known gamebird. Plumage is blue-grey, with white spots. Head varies geographically, but generally is naked blue and red, with cheek wattles and pale casque on crown. Male has larger casque than female. Juv. has browner plumage. **Habitat:** Catholic; grassland, woodland, savanna and fields. **Status:** Common; may flock in hundreds. **Voice:** Loud 'kek kek kaaa, ke kaaa, ke kaaa'; monotonous, repeated 'krrdii-krrdii'; alarm note 'kek-kek-kek'. [C2.6a, G2.6.3]

5 CRESTED GUINEAFOWL *Guttera pucherani*   46-51 cm
A black guineafowl, finely spotted with pale blue. Naked face and upper neck are blue-grey, with varying amount of red skin (none in South and C Africa; throat red in W and C Africa; face and throat red in E Africa). Crown has tuft of curly black feathers, shape of which varies geographically. Outer secondaries have white outer webs, producing white wing panel in flight. **Habitat:** Forest edge, thickets and dense woodland. **Status:** Locally common. **Voice:** 'Chik-chik-chil-urrrrr'; soft 'keet-keet-keet' contact call. [C5.75, G2.6.4]

6 PLUMED GUINEAFOWL *Guttera plumifera*   44-48 cm
Endemic to C Africa. Slightly smaller than Crested Guineafowl, with long and erect (not curly) crest, dark grey (not blue-grey) face and white (not light blue) spotting. Adults have black facial wattles and no red throat. Juv. lacks spots; faintly scaled on underparts. Non-breeding birds gather in flocks of up to 50 birds. **Habitat:** Primary rainforest. **Status:** Locally common but rarely seen. **Voice:** Far-carrying 'kow kow kow'; sharp 'chik chik' contact call. [C5.74]

7 VULTURINE GUINEAFOWL *Acryllium vulturinum*   60-72 cm
A very distinctive and beautiful guineafowl with a long, thin neck and long, pointed tail. Breast and back are bright cobalt-blue, overlaid with spectacular black and white lanceolate feathers. Wings and remainder of body are black, spotted white; secondaries are edged lilac. Juv. is duller greyish-brown, barred and spotted black, brown and rufous. Occurs in small flocks outside breeding season. **Habitat:** Arid scrub and savanna. **Status:** Locally common. **Voice:** High-pitched, metallic 'chink-chink-chink-cheenk-cheek krrrrrrr'.

1 ♀

2 ♂

♀

3

4

5

E Africa

W Africa

imm.

imm.

S Africa

6

7

Gamebirds that forage on the ground, but some roost in trees. Can be secretive, especially if hunted. Often located by distinctive calls. Sexes usually alike.

1 STONE PARTRIDGE *Ptilopachus petrosus*   24-29 cm
A small, dark, bantam-like partridge with dull red legs and facial skin. At close range, shows barred flanks and creamy-white belly patch (paler in female). Cocks and fans its tail as it moves; seldom flushes. **Habitat:** Dry, stony hillsides, river courses and lightly wooded areas. **Status:** Locally common. **Voice:** Small groups call together, with some duetting at dawn and dusk; continuous, rolled-together 'weet-weet'. [C5.79]

2 UDZUNGWA FOREST PARTRIDGE *Xenoperdix udzungwensis*   29 cm
Endemic to C Tanzania; only discovered in 1991. Bright red bill, rufous throat and heavily black-scaled underparts are diagnostic. Related to Asian hill partridges. **Habitat:** Heavily forested mountain slopes and more even terrain with thick understorey. Occurs in small groups, foraging together over leaf litter in dense tangles and forest trails; roosts singly or in small groups in mid-storey. **Status:** Vulnerable. Known only from two montane forests. **Voice:** Reported to have a whistled song and high, peeping calls.

3 COQUI FRANCOLIN *Peliperdix coqui*   21-26 cm
A small, petite francolin with a black bill and yellow legs. Male has plain, buffy head with darker crown, and heavily barred breast. Female has neatly defined pale throat and supercilium, and plain buffy breast. S nominate-race birds have belly completely barred, but N races have plain belly. Difficult to flush; shows chestnut wings and outer-tail in flight. **Habitat:** Woodland and savanna, especially on sandy soils. **Status:** Common to locally common. **Voice:** Distinctive, disyllabic 'co-qui'; territorial 'ker-aak, aak, kara-kara-kara', with last notes fading away. [C5.81, G2.4.8]

4 WHITE-THROATED FRANCOLIN *Peliperdix albogularis*   22-25 cm
Similar to Coqui Francolin, but with a pale throat and no black barring on hindneck and underparts of male. Best identified by small size and buffy head, with grey crown and ear coverts, and plain buff underparts. S males (*dewittei*) have chestnut breast band. Female is duller, with fine dark bars on breast and flanks. Chestnut wings and tail are conspicuous in flight. **Habitat:** Grassy savanna, often in recently burned areas. **Status:** Uncommon to locally common. **Voice:** Similar to Coqui Francolin, but territorial song faster and slightly higher pitched, with up to 10 notes (not 4-6). [C5.82]

5 RING-NECKED FRANCOLIN *Scleroptila streptophorus*   33 cm
A distinctive member of the Red-winged Francolin group (p. 122), distinguished by its dark cap, broad white supercilium, chestnut face and neck, contrasting white throat and finely barred black-and-white collar. Keeps well hidden in grass and runs rapidly between and over rocks. **Habitat:** Open grasslands and lightly wooded areas on rocky hillsides. **Status:** Uncommon to locally common; usually in pairs or small family groups. **Voice:** Dove-like cooing call, followed by piping trill; raucous alarm call in flight. [C5.84]

6 SCHLEGEL'S FRANCOLIN *Peliperdix schlegelii*   22-25 cm
C African counterpart of White-throated Francolin, but both sexes look more like male Coqui Francolin. Differs from male Coqui Francolin by having grey-brown line from lores to ear coverts, and no barring on chestnut upperparts. Underparts are distinctly barred black on buff-white. Female's upperparts are browner, less rich than male's and belly is less heavily barred. **Habitat:** Grassland in well-wooded savanna. **Status:** Local and uncommon. **Voice:** Similar to Coqui and White-throated francolins, but faster and slightly lower pitched. [C5.83]

7 CHUKAR PARTRIDGE *Alectoris chukar*   33 cm
Introduced to Robben Island. Readily identified by its boldly-barred flanks and black face band. Juv. duller. **Habitat:** Scrubby thickets. **Status:** Fairly common. **Voice:** 'Chuk-chuk-chuk-chukar'. **Similar species: Barbary Partridge** *A. barbara* lacks black face band; rare in N Mauritania; **Sand Partridge** *Ammoperdix heyi* male has plain face and throat with white ear patch and chestnut flank stripes; female is paler and finely barred; localised resident in NE Sudan.

A rather uniform group of grassland francolins with variable amounts of rufous in the flight feathers. Identification based on head, neck and belly pattern, as well as range. All have similar piping, whistled calls, and occur in pairs or small coveys. Sexes alike.

1 GREY-WINGED FRANCOLIN *Scleroptila africanus* 33-35 cm
Endemic to S Africa. A well-marked, smallish francolin, easily identified by its grey-speckled (not white or buff) throat. When flushed, only bases of primaries are barred rufous. **Habitat:** Sand plain and mountain fynbos, S Karoo and montane grassland. **Status:** Fairly common to common; usually in coveys of 3-8 birds. **Voice:** Whistling, rather variable 'wip wip wip kipeeo, wip kipeeoo'. [G2.4.10]

2 RED-WINGED FRANCOLIN *Scleroptila levaillantii* 36 cm
A smallish, well-marked francolin. Broad, black-speckled necklace forms distinct breast band separated from pale throat by rufous collar. In addition to primaries, primary coverts and most secondaries are rufous in flight. **Habitat:** Grassland and fields in mountainous terrain, usually on lower slopes and in valleys. **Status:** Scarce to locally common; several populations have become rare due to unfavourable agricultural practices. **Voice:** Piping 'wip-tilleee', sometimes preceded by several short 'wip' notes. [C5.85, G2.5.2]

3 SHELLEY'S FRANCOLIN *Scleroptila shelleyi* 28-31 cm
Superficially resembles Red-winged Francolin, but chestnut-striped breast and flanks and black-and-white barred belly are diagnostic. Throat is white, edged with black. In flight, only primaries are rufous. **Habitat:** Savanna and open woodland, especially associated with rocky ground. **Status:** Locally common. **Voice:** Rhythmic, repeated 'til-it, til-leoo' ('I'll drink yer beer'); slower and less varied than other red-winged species. [C5.87, G2.5.1]

4 FINSCH'S FRANCOLIN *Scleroptila finschi* 36-38 cm
Localised counterpart of Red-winged Francolin, with duller, less patterned plumage. Distinguished from Coqui Francolin (p. 120) by its larger size, and from other grassland francolins by its yellowish legs and black bill. Primaries and outer secondaries are rufous in flight. **Habitat:** Mainly short-grass savannas in hilly country. **Status:** Locally common. **Voice:** Loud 'wit-u-wit'. [C5.86]

5 ARCHER'S FRANCOLIN *Scleroptila lorti* 35 cm
Endemic to NE Africa; formerly considered a race of Orange River Francolin. Darker than Moorland Francolin, lacking streaking on white throat, and has paler, less rufous underparts. Buff (not white) throat and pale underparts, lightly streaked black, separate it from Shelley's Francolin. **Habitat:** Open and slightly wooded grasslands and boulder-strewn hill slopes. **Status:** Locally common. **Voice:** Similar crowing to that of Shelley's Francolin but shorter and more abrupt; high-pitched, squealing flight call.

6 MOORLAND FRANCOLIN *Scleroptila psilolaemus* 34-36 cm
Endemic to NE Africa. Larger and darker than Archer's Francolin, with variably streaked (not white) throat and more rufous underparts. Has rather plain, buffy belly (not barred like Shelley's Francolin). Fairly extensive rufous in wing in flight, approaching Red-winged Francolin. **Habitat:** Montane heath and adjacent pastures; rarely found below 2 500 m. **Status:** Locally common. **Voice:** Very similar crowing to that of Shelley's Francolin; high-pitched squealing when flushed.

7 ORANGE RIVER FRANCOLIN *Scleroptila levaillantoides* 35 cm
Endemic to S Africa, with considerable geographic variation in coloration. Slightly smaller than Red-winged Francolin, with thin, dark necklace which never broadens to form dark breast band. Differs from Shelley's Francolin by lack of black markings on belly, and from Grey-winged Francolin by white (not grey-speckled) throat. **Habitat:** Grassland and semi-arid savanna. **Status:** Locally common. **Voice:** Rather strident 'kibitele', faster and higher-pitched than that of Shelley's Francolin, mostly at dawn. [G2.5.2]

levaillantoides
South Africa

langi
Kalahari

jugularis
Angola & Namibia

123

1 CRESTED FRANCOLIN *Dendroperdix sephaena*   33-35 cm
A distinctive spurfowl that frequently holds its tail cocked at a 45° angle, imparting a bantam-like appearance. Dark cap contrasts with broad white supercilium and dark-striped breast. Black tail is obvious in flight. Female more heavily barred above. Coastal SE Africa *rovuma* lacks dark moustache and has fine dark streaking on belly and flanks; sometimes considered a separate species, Kirk's Francolin. **Habitat:** Woodland and well-wooded savanna. **Status:** Common. **Voice:** Rattling duet, 'chee-chakla, chee-chakla'. [C5.88, G2.4.9]

2 FOREST (LATHAM'S) FRANCOLIN *Peliperdix lathami*   27 cm
A small, dark forest spurfowl. Best told from Nahan's Spurfowl by its pale grey (not black) ear coverts and yellow (not red) legs. Upperparts are dark brown with fine pale streaks; underparts are black with white spots. Female paler brown above, with buffy cheeks and supercilium, and pale brown underparts with cream spots. **Habitat:** Forest undergrowth. **Status:** Locally common, but difficult to observe in its dense habitat. **Voice:** 3-noted, dove-like cooing, often repeated; various whistles and clucking contact calls. [C5.80]

SPURFOWL
Superficially similar to francolins, but not closely related. Calls harsher. Sexes similar in most species.

3 GREY-STRIPED SPURFOWL (FRANCOLIN) *Pternistes griseostriatus*   33 cm
Endemic to Angola, where it replaces Scaly Spurfowl, but is paler. Told from Red-necked Spurfowl (p. 128) by lacking bold black-and-white underparts and bare red face and throat. **Habitat:** Thickets in riverine forest and secondary growth. **Status:** Vulnerable. Little known, but locally common. **Voice:** Flight and alarm call are raspy 'kerak kerak'; softer 'fififif', repeated rapidly towards a crescendo.

4 NAHAN'S SPURFOWL (FRANCOLIN) *Pternistes nahani*   23-26 cm
A small, localised forest spurfowl. Differs from Forest Francolin by red (not yellow) legs, bare red face and black (not pale grey) ear coverts. Much smaller and darker than Scaly Spurfowl, with bold black-and-white underparts. **Habitat:** Thick ground cover in dense primary rainforest; rarely ventures onto forest tracks or open spaces. **Status:** Endangered. Uncommon and difficult to see in its dense habitat. **Voice:** Soft 'keh keh' crowing in early morning. [C5.91]

5 SCALY SPURFOWL (FRANCOLIN) *Pternistes squamatus*   32 cm
A rather drab brown spurfowl, with pale feather edges that appear scaled at close range. Bill and legs are red. Told from Red-necked Spurfowl (p. 128) by lack of red skin around eyes and on throat and by its more forested habitat. Juv. warmer brown above with fine black streaks; underparts feintly barred black and white. **Habitat:** Dense vegetation along forest roads and tracks, forest edge, village plantations and secondary growth. **Status:** Locally common. **Voice:** Loud, high-pitched 'ker-ack ker-ack' repeated 5-10 times. [C5.89]

6 AHANTA SPURFOWL (FRANCOLIN) *Pternistes ahantensis*   33 cm
Endemic to W Africa, where it replaces Scaly Spurfowl; is the only orange-billed spurfowl in its range. A large, dark brown forest-edge spurfowl, with orange-red bill and feet. Has white edges to feathers of back and underparts, appearing streaked at close range. Juv. has black streaks above. **Habitat:** Dense vegetation at forest edge, in gallery forest and old plantations. **Status:** Common. **Voice:** Raucous, squealing 'kee-kee-keree', higher pitched than Scaly Francolin's. [C5.90]

7 MOUNT CAMEROON SPURFOWL (FRANCOLIN) *Pternistes camerunensis*   33 cm
Endemic to Mt Cameroon. A dark brown spurfowl with red bill, face and legs. Darker than Scaly Spurfowl, with bare red eye patch. Male has grey-edged feathers, especially on the underparts; female's feathers are buff-edged. Juv. similar to female, with underparts finely barred black and white. **Habitat:** Forested slopes on SE and NE Mt Cameroon; occurs along forest edge and in old fields adjacent to forest. **Status:** Endangered. Mostly in pairs, foraging among leaf litter. **Voice:** High-pitched, 3-noted whistle. [C5.95]

rovuma

sephaena

SPURFOWL (FRANCOLINS)

1 DOUBLE-SPURRED SPURFOWL (FRANCOLIN) *Pternistes bicalcaratus* 30-34 cm
Endemic to W Africa. Olive-green bill and legs and absence of bare facial skin are diagnostic. A handsome spurfowl with chestnut nape, black frons and eye-stripe, white supercilium, streaked back, and chestnut, black and white underparts. Female has smaller spurs. Juv. duller. **Habitat:** Open grasslands, fields and lightly wooded savannas. **Status:** Common in drier areas of W Africa. **Voice:** Raucous 'ke-raak, ke-raak' crowing, mostly at dawn and dusk. [C2.7b]

2 HEUGLIN'S SPURFOWL (FRANCOLIN) *Pternistes icterorhynchus* 30-34 cm
Part of the Double-spurred-Clapperton's Spurfowl superspecies. Easily identified by yellow-orange bill, facial skin and legs. Has chestnut crown, brown back and pale cream underparts heavily marked with black chevrons. Female slightly smaller; juv. more heavily barred above. **Habitat:** Grasslands, open woodland and adjacent fields. **Status:** Common; usually in pairs or small groups. **Voice:** Crowing similar to Double-spurred and Clapperton's francolins. [C5.93]

3 CLAPPERTON'S SPURFOWL (FRANCOLIN) *Pternistes clappertoni* 32 cm
Easily separated from Heuglin's and Double-spurred spurfowls by its red facial skin, black bill and red legs. Often has fairly extensive white neck, and white edges to feathers give strongly scaled appearance to back and underparts. Differs from Harwood's Spurfowl by having white supercilium, mostly black (not red) bill and variable black moustachial stripe. Juv. duller. **Habitat:** Semi-arid savanna and adjacent fields, often near water. **Status:** Locally common. **Voice:** Loud, raucous crowing at dawn and dusk. [C5.94]

4 HARWOOD'S SPURFOWL (FRANCOLIN) *Pternistes harwoodi* 30-32 cm
Localised endemic to Ethiopia. Darker than Clapperton's Spurfowl, with less red skin around eye and largely red (not mostly black) bill. Breast is vermiculated black and pale buff. Female is slightly paler. Easily told from Erckel's Spurfowl (p. 130) by its reddish (not black) bill, red (not yellow) legs and vermiculated (not streaked) underparts. **Habitat:** Semi-arid scrub along rivers and on hill slopes, foraging on adjacent fields; often near reeds. **Status:** Vulnerable. Locally common at several sites. **Voice:** Harsh, raucous 'ko reek' crowing at dawn and dusk.

5 HILDEBRANDT'S SPURFOWL (FRANCOLIN) *Pternistes hildebranti* 32-40 cm
Endemic to E Africa. Male is similar to Natal Spurfowl, but has much paler underparts, clearly marked with large black spots; ranges barely overlap. Female has distinctive plain, rusty underparts. Lacks red face and obvious white supercilium of Clapperton's Spurfowl. Juv. like female, but more heavily barred blackish above and below. **Habitat:** Thickets, scrub on grassy hill slopes, bracken and montane heath. **Status:** Thinly distributed in E Africa; in pairs or small groups. **Voice:** Raucous crowing 'kek kek kek kerak', similar to Natal Francolin's. [C5.92]

6 NATAL SPURFOWL (FRANCOLIN) *Pternistes natalensis* 35 cm
Near-endemic to S Africa. Forms a superspecies with Hildebrandt's Spurfowl, but is not sexually dimorphic; rarely hybridises with Swainson's Spurfowl (p. 128). A medium-sized brown spurfowl, vermiculated black and underwhite below. Smaller than Red-necked Spurfowl (p. 128), and lacks bare red face and throat. Base of upper mandible is yellow-green. Juv. has less speckling below and is darker brown on breast and back. **Habitat:** Woodland, especially riparian thickets. **Status:** Common. **Voice:** Raucous, screeching 'krr kik-ik-ik'. [G2.5.6]

7 RED-BILLED SPURFOWL (FRANCOLIN) *Pternistes adspersus* 35-38 cm
Endemic to S Africa. Combination of dull red bill and legs and yellow eye-ring is diagnostic. A medium-large, dark brown spurfowl with finely barred neck and underparts. Juv. lacks yellow around eye. **Habitat:** Arid savanna and open, broadleafed woodland, often in thickets along watercourses. **Status:** Locally common; easily observed; less skulking than other francolins. **Voice:** Loud, harsh 'chaa-chaa-chek-chek' at dawn and dusk. [G2.5.4]

127

1 YELLOW-NECKED SPURFOWL *Pternistes leucoscepus* 36-43 cm
Endemic to NE Africa. A large, dark brown spurfowl with a diagnostic bright yellow throat patch, red face and black bill and legs. Range overlaps slightly with that of Grey-breasted Spurfowl, where the two species hybridise. Juv. has paler yellow throat. In flight shows pale bases to primaries. **Habitat:** Open savanna, scrub areas and adjacent fields. **Status:** Common; in small groups and pairs, often on tracks. **Voice:** Raucous, repeated 'kerak' at dawn and dusk.

2 SWAINSON'S SPURFOWL *Pternistes swainsonii* 38 cm
Near-endemic to S Africa. A large, dark brown spurfowl with black legs and bill and red face and throat. Lacks white streaked underparts diagnostic of Red-necked Spurfowl or fine barring of Red-billed Spurfowl (p. 126). Juv. has less extensive and paler red face. **Habitat:** Dry savanna and fields. **Status:** Common; usually in groups of 3-6 birds. **Voice:** Raucous 'krraae-krraae-krraae' by males at dawn and dusk. [G2.5.9]

3 CAPE SPURFOWL (FRANCOLIN) *Pternistes capensis* 42 cm
Endemic to South Africa. A large, dark brown spurfowl with plain dark cap that contrasts with paler cheeks. Bill and legs are dull red, but lacks bare face or throat of Red-necked Spurfowl. At close range, fine vermiculation on body feathers is visible, with bolder white stripes on flanks. **Habitat:** Lowland fynbos, pastures, fields, large gardens and riparian thickets in Karoo. **Status:** Common; often confiding. **Voice:** Loud, ringing 'cackalac-cackalac-cackalac'. [G2.5.5]

4 RED-NECKED SPURFOWL *Pternistes afer* 36-41 cm
A large, brown-backed spurfowl with red bill, legs, face and throat. Underparts vary regionally: blackish with two white streaks on each feather (in South African *castaneiventer* and *notatus*), pale grey with black streaking (in W Angolan and NW Namibian *afer),* pale grey streaked black, with black belly patch (in Zimbabwean-coastal Kenyan *swynnertoni, melanogaster* and *leucopareus*), and rather plain grey with rufous belly streaks (in C African *cranchii* and *harterti*). **Habitat:** Forest edges, thickets, riparian scrub and adjoining grassland. **Status:** Common. **Voice:** Loud 'kwoor-kwoor-kwoor-kwaaa' at dusk and dawn. [C5.97, G2.5.8]

5 GREY-BREASTED SPURFOWL *Pternistes rufopictus* 34-40 cm
Endemic to N Tanzania. A dark brown spurfowl with broad chestnut streaks on back. Differs from Red-necked Spurfowl by having grey-brown (not red) legs, orange-pink (not red) throat, and white moustachial stripe. Has pale primary bases in flight. Hybridises with Yellow-necked Spurfowl in E. **Habitat:** Riverine thickets and acacia scrub and woodland, from S Serengeti, W to Mwanza. **Status:** Uncommon; in pairs and small groups. **Voice:** Crowing very similar to Yellow-necked Spurfowl's.

6 HARTLAUB'S SPURFOWL (FRANCOLIN) *Pternistes hartlaubi* 26 cm
Endemic to Namibia and SW Angola. A small spurfowl with a heavy, decurved yellow-horn bill and yellow legs. Male's dark cap contrasts with distinct white eyebrow; pale underparts are heavily streaked brown. Female is dull orange-brown. Juv. male resembles female but has white eyebrow. **Habitat:** Boulder-strewn slopes and rocky outcrops. **Status:** Uncommon and localised; pairs remain together throughout year. **Voice:** Distinctive duet, 'ke-rak, keer-a keer-a kew', led by female, mostly at dawn. [G2.5.7]

1

2

3

canstaneiventer

notatus

swynnertoni

4

afer

5

6

♂

♀

129

1 ERCKEL'S SPURFOWL (FRANCOLIN) *Pternistes erckelii*　　　39-43 cm
Endemic to NE Africa. A large, grey-and-chestnut-striped spurfowl with a striking head pattern: black frons and supercilium, chestnut crown, grey ear coverts and white throat. Differs from Chestnut-naped Francolin by black (not red) bill and yellowish (not red) legs. **Habitat:** Scrub-covered hill slopes, forest edge and cliffs above 2 000 m. **Status:** Locally common; mostly in pairs or small groups. **Voice:** Harsh cackling crow ending in chuckle-like rattle.

2 DJIBOUTI (OCHRE-BREASTED) SPURFOWL *Pternistes ochropectus*　　33 cm
Endemic to Djibouti. Resembles a small, drab Erckel's Francolin, but ranges do not overlap. **Habitat:** Juniper forests, acacia woodland and river courses. **Status:** Critically threatened. Fewer than 1 000 birds, confined to small area around Forêt du Day and nearby Mabla Mountains, between 700 and 1 800 m. Occurs in pairs and family groups. **Voice:** Rattling 'erk-erk-erk-krrrr' similar to Erckel's Francolin's.

3 CHESTNUT-NAPED SPURFOWL (FRANCOLIN) *Pternistes casteincollis* 33-37 cm
Endemic to NE Africa. A large, richly-coloured spurfowl. Red bill and legs separate it from Erckel's Francolin. Lacks bare red face of Harwood's Francolin (p. 126) and further differs by its rusty colour and white belly and vent. S race *atrifrons* is smaller and paler; lacks red face of similar Clapperton's Francolin (p. 126). **Habitat:** Montane heath, forest edge and scrubby areas at lower altitudes. **Status:** Common to abundant; in small groups or pairs. **Voice:** Noisy 'kek kek keraak' crowing, mostly at dawn and dusk.

4 HANDSOME SPURFOWL (FRANCOLIN) *Pternistes nobilis*　　　34-36 cm
Endemic to Albertine Rift. A large, rather plain rufous spurfowl with greyish head and rump. Larger and more rufous than Scaly Francolin (p. 124), with red eye patch. Bill and legs are red. Female is smaller and duller than male. Most easily seen in early morning, in clearings and on tracks. **Habitat:** Montane forest and forest edge, bamboo thickets and adjacent heaths. **Status:** Locally common; in small groups or pairs. **Voice:** Noisy; repeated 'chuk ker-ack' or 'ker-ack' crowing at dawn and dusk. [C5.96]

5 JACKSON'S SPURFOWL (FRANCOLIN) *Pternistes jacksoni*　　　38-44 cm
Endemic to E Africa. A large, rufous spurfowl with red legs and bill and narrow red eye-ring. Larger and more rufous than Scaly Francolin (p. 124). Juv. duller, with dark barring above and on belly. **Habitat:** Montane grasslands, heath and forest edge from 2 200 to 3 700 m; often dust-bathes on sandy roads. **Status:** Common in W and C Kenyan mountains, especially Aberdare range. **Voice:** Typical raucous crowing at dawn and dusk, reminiscent of Scaly Francolin's.

6 SWIERSTRA'S SPURFOWL (FRANCOLIN) *Pternistes swierstrai*　　　33 cm
Endemic to Angola. A large, brown-backed spurfowl with diagnostic black breast band, white throat and supercilium, and black-striped belly. Female is more marked above. **Habitat:** Montane forest, forest edge and adjacent grasslands and shrubby gullies. **Status:** Vulnerable. Restricted to a few montane forest patches; not seen in over 40 years. **Voice:** Harsh call, apparently similar to Jackson's Francolin's.

QUAILS
Small, sexually dimorphic gamebirds. Fly more strongly than buttonquails.

1 COMMON QUAIL *Coturnix coturnix*   17-20 cm
A small, rather pale buff gamebird, streaked black and white above. Usually seen when flushed; flight action is very rapid. On ground, runs swiftly through grass in hunched position. Underparts are buffy, streaked brown on breast; always much paler than Harlequin Quail. Male has variable black or russet throat. **Habitat:** Grassland, fields and croplands. **Status:** Locally abundant. African *erlangeri* is summer-breeding intra-African migrant in S, resident in E Africa; nominate race is non-breeding Palearctic migrant wintering across Sahel, S to Kenya. **Voice:** Repeated, high-pitched 'whit wit-wit' ('wet my lips'), slower and deeper than Harlequin Quail's; shrill 'crwee-crwee' in flight. [C2.6b, G2.5.10]

2 HARLEQUIN QUAIL *Coturnix delegorguei*   14-15 cm
Male is much darker than Common Quail, with chestnut-and-black underparts. Female and juv. have rufous underparts, darker than Common Quail's, but are hard to differentiate in flight. **Habitat:** Grassland, damp fields and savanna, often in moister areas than Common Quail. **Status:** Locally abundant nomad and intra-African migrant. **Voice:** High-pitched 'whit, wit-wit', more metallic than Common Quail's; squeaky 'kree-kree' in flight. [C5.78, G2.6.1]

3 BLUE QUAIL *Coturnix adansonii*   12-14 cm
A small quail, similar in size to buttonquails. At rest, male is unmistakable: black-and-white face pattern, chestnut upperparts and blue underparts. In flight, small size and chestnut wing coverts separate it from male Harlequin Quail; blue underparts appear black. On ground, female and juv. have barred underparts; in flight, appear small and dark. **Habitat:** Damp and flooded grassland. **Status:** Nomadic resident; local and generally uncommon. **Voice:** High-pitched whistle 'teee-ti-ti'; much less vocal than other quails. [C5.77, G2.6.2]

BUTTONQUAILS
Small, quail-like gamebirds. Usually seen when flushed; flight is weaker than quails'. Sexes differ; duller males raise the young.

4 KURRICHANE (SMALL) BUTTONQUAIL *Turnix sylvaticus*   14-15 cm
A small, rather pale buttonquail. Noticeably smaller than Common or Harlequin quails in flight, with longer neck and more rapid, almost frantic wing beats. Best told from Black-rumped Buttonquail in flight by lack of dark rump and back. On ground, black flecks on sides of breast and absence of chestnut on face are diagnostic. Female is larger and more boldly marked than male. **Habitat:** Tall grassland, old fields and open savanna. **Status:** Locally common. **Voice:** Repeated, low-pitched hoot, 'hmmmm'. [C2.8a, G2.6.5]

5 BLACK-RUMPED BUTTONQUAIL *Turnix nanus*   14-16 cm
Larger and more richly coloured than Kurrichane Buttonquail, with plain ginger face and throat. In flight, shows diagnostic dark back and rump which contrast with paler wings. Best separated from female Blue Quail by flight action and contrast between rump and wings. Not known to overlap with Hottentot Buttonquail; differs by flesh-white (not yellow) legs and unmarked belly, and female is less barred on breast and flanks. Juv. is spotted across breast. **Habitat:** Moist grassland, often around temporary wetlands; also damp areas in hilly and mountainous areas. **Status:** Scarce to locally common; apparently moves in relation to rainfall, but resident in some areas. **Voice:** Flufftail-like 'ooooop-oooooop'. [C6.1a, G2.6.6]

6 HOTTENTOT BUTTONQUAIL *Turnix hottentottus*   14-16 cm
Endemic to South Africa. Similar to Black-rumped Buttonquail, but lacks clearly defined dark back and has more extensive black spotting on neck, breast and belly. Legs are yellow (bright chrome-yellow in female), not flesh-white. Female less richly coloured on the breast than female Black-rumped Buttonquail; male duller. **Habitat:** Fynbos and strandveld, usually in fairly open areas dominated by restios. **Status:** Locally common, preferring areas 2–4 years after fires. **Voice:** Low, flufftail-like booming.

1 QUAIL PLOVER *Ortyxelos meiffrenii* 12-13 cm
A peculiar small gamebird related to buttonquails with diagnostic black-and-white wings that are conspicuous in flight. At rest, resembles diminutive courser rather than buttonquail. Differs from buttonquails by having longer legs, dark eyes and no black spotting on sides of breast and flanks. Most often seen when flushed. **Habitat:** Arid and semi-arid savanna and grassland. **Status:** Uncommon and thinly distributed resident and nomad. **Voice:** Soft, low whistle.

FLUFFTAILS
Tiny rails, renowned for their secretive behaviour, that are best located by their hooting or rattling calls. Hooting calls could be confused with buttonquails. Many species are crepuscular and call at night. All are strongly sexually dimorphic; females are difficult to identify unless a good view is obtained.

2 WHITE-WINGED FLUFFTAIL *Sarothrura ayresi* 14 cm
Both sexes show diagnostic white secondaries in flight. Outer web of outer primary is also white, forming thin white line on folded wing. Flight is fast and direct, with whirring wing beats. Both sexes have black-and-chestnut-barred tail and white belly. Female differs from female Striped Flufftail (p.136) by chestnut wash on neck and barred (not plain) tail. **Habitat:** Upland marshes and vleis. **Status:** Endangered. Rare and localised; apparently migratory. Breeding only confirmed in Ethiopia, but is regular in E South Africa. **Voice:** Low, deep hoot, repeated in duet. [G2.8.2]

3 WHITE-SPOTTED FLUFFTAIL *Sarothrura pulchra* 17 cm
Male differs from similar Buff-spotted Flufftail by white (not buff) spotting on body, all-rufous (not barred) tail, and call. Female is the only female flufftail with red head and breast; body is dark brown, barred buff. **Habitat:** Dense tangles in lowland rainforest and secondary scrub, often near streams. **Status:** Locally common; less retiring than other flufftails. **Voice:** Often-repeated, far-carrying series of ringing notes recalling bell-like 'tinking' of tinkerbird. [C6.2b]

4 BUFF-SPOTTED FLUFFTAIL *Sarothrura elegans* 17 cm
Male's back has large buff (not white) spots and black-and-rufous barred (not all-rufous) tail, but is best told from White-spotted Flufftail by call. Red head extends only onto upper breast, not onto lower breast and back as in Red-chested Flufftail (p. 136). Female is dark brown above, with buff breast and paler, barred belly. **Habitat:** Dense forest understorey, adjacent scrub and well-wooded gardens. **Status:** Locally common. **Voice:** Low, foghorn-like 'doooooooooooo', mainly at night and on overcast and rainy days. Calls from elevated perches at night; on or near the ground during the day. [C6.3a, G2.7.8]

1 RED-CHESTED FLUFFTAIL *Sarothrura rufa* 16 cm
Male is distinguished by red of head extending to lower breast and by dark tail. Belly and back are uniformly dark with small white speckles. Darker overall and lacks streaking on breast and belly of Streaky-breasted Flufftail, with more extensive red on throat. Female is darker than other female flufftails, especially on throat and upper breast. **Habitat:** Dense reeds and sedges around marshes and streams; also dry grassland near forest in W Africa. **Status:** Common resident. **Voice:** Low hoot, 'woop', repeated at intervals of about one second; more rapid 'gu-duk, gu-duk, gu-duk'; ringing 'tuwi-tuwi-tuwi'. [C6.3b, G2.7.7]

2 CHESTNUT-HEADED (LONG-TOED) FLUFFTAIL *Sarothrura lugens* 16 cm
Male has red confined to head and a dark tail. Easily confused with Streaky-breasted and Red-chested flufftails; best told apart by call. Lacks bold stripes of Striped Flufftail. Female differs from female Streaky-breasted Flufftail by chestnut wash on head, but this is seldom visible in the field. **Habitat:** Rank growth in damp areas at forest edge and marshes. **Status:** Uncommon and localised. **Voice:** Series of moaning notes increasing in intensity in middle and trailing off with a grunt. [C6.4a]

3 STREAKY-BREASTED FLUFFTAIL *Sarothrura boehmi* 16 cm
Male differs from Red-chested Flufftail by paler throat and streaked lower breast and belly, with less extensive red on breast; when flushed, appears much paler. Red breast separates it from Chestnut-headed Flufftail. Female is paler below than female Red-chested and Chestnut-headed flufftails. **Habitat:** Breeds in rank, seasonally flooded grassland, but occurs in dry grassland at other times. **Status:** Uncommon intra-African migrant; breeds in S and E Africa, wintering in C Africa. **Voice:** Low hoot, 'gawooo', repeated 20-30 times at half-second intervals. [C6.4b, G2.7.9]

4 STRIPED FLUFFTAIL *Sarothrura affinis* 15 cm
Male is distinguished by its plain red tail and black body boldly striped with white. Red is confined to head in S Africa; extends onto breast further N. Female and juv. are smaller than female Red-chested Flufftail and have chestnut-washed tail. **Habitat:** Montane grassland, fynbos and wetlands. **Status:** Locally common. **Voice:** Low, one-second 'oooooop' hoot, repeated at two-second intervals; also high-pitched, chattering trill. [G2.8.1]

RAILS
Rather secretive birds, mostly associated with marshes and reedbeds, but also found in rainforest and even montane heathlands. Feed on ground, but some species call from trees. Sexes alike; juvs duller.

5 ROUGET'S RAIL *Rougetius rougetti* 30 cm
Endemic to Abyssinian highlands. Plain, dull, dark olive upperparts and cinnamon underparts are diagnostic. Imm. is paler, with dull brown eye and bill, and dark brown cap. **Habitat:** Damp grassland and moorland, 1 500-4 100 m; also wetlands in forests and man-made habitats, including lawns. **Status:** Locally common, but threatened by grazing pressure. **Voice:** Ringing 'wrreeee-crreeeeuw'; alarm call is shrill 'dideet'.

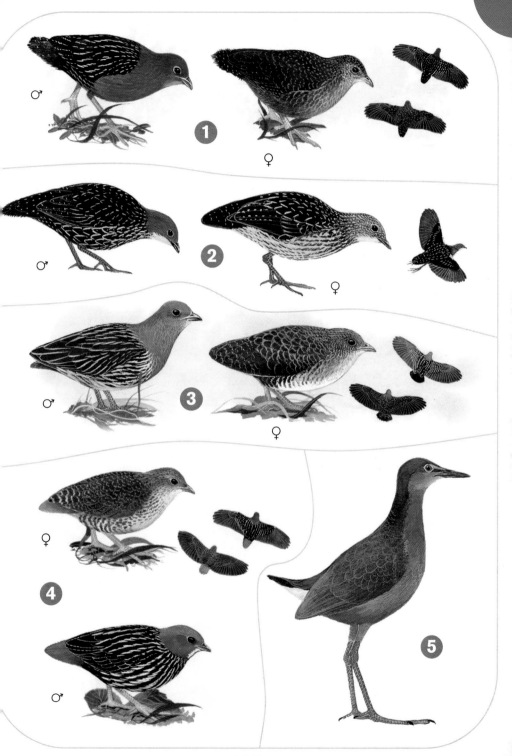

1 AFRICAN RAIL *Rallus caerulescens*   28-30 cm
Easily identified by the long, decurved, red bill and red legs, grey breast, and black-and-white-barred flanks. Juv. has brown bill and buff breast. **Habitat:** Marshes, reedbeds and flooded grassland, usually in areas with standing water. **Status:** Common; often ventures into open, especially in early morning. **Voice:** Explosive, high-pitched trill, 'trrreee-tee-tee-tee-tee-tee'. [C5.5b, G2.6.10] **Similar species: Water Rail** *R. aquaticus* differs by having streaked (not plain) brown underparts; potential vagrant in N.

2 CORNCRAKE *Crex crex*   25-30 cm
A large, pale sandy crake with conspicuous chestnut-orange wing coverts in flight. Much paler than smaller African Crake. Rarely seen except when flushed, when it flies with whirring wings and dangling legs. **Habitat:** Rank grassland and open savanna; occurs around edges of marshes, but seldom in areas with standing water. **Status:** Vulnerable. Uncommon Palearctic migrant Sep-Mar. **Voice:** Silent in Africa. [C2.8b, G2.7.1]

3 NKULENGU RAIL *Himantornis haematopus*   45 cm
A large forest rail with a heavy bill; looks like a slim, tall, long-legged francolin. Much taller than Grey-throated Rail, with conspicuous long red legs and upright stance. Very difficult to see but easy to locate at dusk by its powerful call. **Habitat:** Forest and gallery forest, not necessarily close to water; roosts in trees. **Status:** Common. **Voice:** Loud, far-carrying 'koKOW-koKAW-OOO', as well as owl-like 'hu-HOO'. Calls at night from elevated perches; from on or near ground during day. [C6.1b]

4 GREY-THROATED RAIL *Canirallus oculeus*   30 cm
Rich chestnut breast and conspicuous white wing bars are diagnostic; the grey face and throat are not a field identification mark. Imm. is duller below, with pale (not red, as in adult) eye. **Habitat:** Forest, near water; restricted to damp areas. **Status:** Generally uncommon. **Voice:** A long series of rather hoarse, raptor-like screams 'kree kree keree kee kee kee kee', given day and night. [C6.2a]

5 AFRICAN FINFOOT *Podica senegalensis*   52-65 cm
A large, peculiar waterbird, vaguely intermediate between cormorants and ducks. Swims low in the water; superficially resembles African Darter (p. 44), but has shorter, thicker neck and heavy red (not grey) bill. Out of water, bright red-orange legs and feet are conspicuous. Male is greyer, with plain dark face; female is browner, with boldly patterned brown-and-white face. Juv. has dark bill and pale belly. **Habitat:** Densely vegetated rivers and streams with well-vegetated banks. **Status:** Uncommon; a shy, furtive species. **Voice:** Normally silent; occasionally gives short, frog-like 'krork'. [C6.13, G2.8.9]

138

juv.

1

2

3

4

5

juv.

♀

♂

Small to medium-sized rails with relatively short, heavy bills. Several species rather similar, and hard to identify given typically fleeting views. Sexes alike in most species; juvs duller.

1 AFRICAN CRAKE *Crecopsis egregia* — 19-23 cm

A medium-sized crake, smaller and darker than Corncrake (p. 138). Differs from African Rail (p. 138) by its short, stubby bill. Flanks and belly are boldly barred black and white. When flushed, it flies a short distance with legs dangling, showing brown, mottled upperparts and barred flanks. Juv. is browner, with less boldly barred flanks. **Habitat:** Damp grassland and seasonal wetlands. **Status:** Uncommon to locally common. Resident in C and W, but many birds disperse N and S to breed during summer rainy seasons. **Voice:** Monotonous, hollow-sounding series of notes, 'krrr-krrr-krrr'. [G6.5a, G2.7.1]

2 BLACK CRAKE *Amaurornis flavirostris* — 18-20 cm

A small, uniformly black crake, with red legs, eyes and yellow bill. Breeding birds have much brighter legs and bill. Juv. is greyer, with darker bill and legs. **Habitat:** Marshes with dense reedbeds; sometimes at small ponds. **Status:** Common. Often bold, foraging out in open. Sometimes gleans prey from hippos and warthogs. **Voice:** Throaty 'chrrooo'; hysterical, bubbling, wheezy duet. [G6.7, G2.7.2]

3 LITTLE CRAKE *Porzana parva* — 18-20 cm

A small crake with a red spot at the base of the bill. Male is grey below and brown above, female is brown all over. Differs from larger Spotted and Striped crakes by barred undertail coverts. Most similar to Baillon's Crake, best told by bill and more boldly patterned back with pale brown stripes along the scapulars and tertials. Also appears more slender, with longer wings (tips extending almost to tail tip), and is duller and more uniform above. **Habitat:** Freshwater wetlands, including flooded grasslands and rice paddies. **Status:** Uncommon Palearctic migrant, mostly Sep-Apr. **Voice:** Largely silent in Africa; alarm call is sharp 'tyicuk'; contact calls include soft, rhythmic tapping. [C2.9b]

4 BAILLON'S CRAKE *Porzana pusilla* — 16-18 cm

The smallest African crake. Sexes are alike. Much smaller than African Crake, with white-spotted upperparts and less contrasting black-and-white barring on flanks and undertail. Darker and more richly coloured than Spotted Crake. Most similar to Little Crake, differs by lacking red base to bill and having a less boldly patterned back. Juv. is paler, mottled and barred below. **Habitat:** Wetlands, reedbeds and flooded grassland; rarely seen in open except at dawn or dusk. **Status:** Uncommon to locally common resident, but subject to local movements. **Voice:** Soft 'qurrr-qurrr'; various frog-like croaks. [C2.10a, G2.7.5]

5 SPOTTED CRAKE *Porzana porzana* — 21-24 cm

The white spots and stripes on the upperparts are diagnostic. Bill is mostly yellow. Flanks are barred, but finer and less boldly marked than African Crake's. In flight, shows distinctive white leading edge to wing and diagnostic pale greenish legs. On ground, often flicks its tail, showing buffy undertail coverts. **Habitat:** Flooded grassland and wetlands. **Status:** Uncommon Palearctic migrant Oct-Apr. **Voice:** Generally silent in Africa; short 'kreck' when alarmed. [C6.6, G2.7.6]

6 STRIPED CRAKE *Aenigmatolimnas marginalis* — 20-22 cm

A rather plain, medium-sized crake, identified by buffy upperparts with long white stripes, plain flanks and russet vent. Female is dominant sex and is more strikingly marked, with blue-grey breast and belly. Juv. resembles male, but with reduced stripes. **Habitat:** Seasonally flooded grassland and marshes. **Status:** Uncommon; apparently resident in parts of W and C Africa, but erratic summer-breeding visitor in S and E. **Voice:** Rapid 'tik-tik-tik-tik-tik...' which may continue for a minute or more. [C6.6, G2.7.6]

juv.

1

2

3

4

juv.

5

6

♂

♀

juv.

141

Large rallids associated with wetlands and adjacent vegetation. Sexes alike.

1 AFRICAN PURPLE SWAMPHEN (PURPLE GALLINULE)
Porphyrio madagascariensis   38-46 cm
A large gallinule, easily identified by its massive red bill, long red legs, and purplish coloration, with turquoise neck and breast and metallic back. Juv. is dull brown above and grey below, and has large, reddish-brown bill. **Habitat:** Reedbeds, marshes and flooded grassland. **Status:** Common. **Voice:** Variety of harsh shrieks, wails and booming notes. [C2.11a, G2.8.3]

2 ALLEN'S (LESSER) GALLINULE *Porphyrula alleni*   26-30 cm
Smaller and darker than African Purple Swamphen, with blue (in breeding male) or green (in breeding female) frontal shield. Non-breeding birds have dull brown shield. Adult differs from American Purple Gallinule by red (not yellow) legs and lack of yellow tip to bill. Juv. is pale buff-brown, lacks white flank stripes of juv. Common Moorhen and has pale, fleshy (not greenish-brown as in juv Common Moorhen or olive as in juv. American Purple Gallinule) legs. **Habitat:** Flooded grassland. **Status:** Locally common resident and summer visitor in N and S. **Voice:** 6 or more rapidly uttered, sharp clicks, 'duk duk duk duk duk duk'. [C6.8, G2.8.4]

3 AMERICAN PURPLE GALLINULE *Porphyrula martinicus*   33 cm
Smaller than African Purple Swamphen, with bright yellowish-green (not red) legs and yellow tip to bill. Adult's frontal shield is pale blue. Most records are juvs, which are very similar to juv. Allen's Gallinule but have olive (not flesh-coloured) legs; differ from juv. Common Moorhen by lack of white stripes on flanks. **Habitat:** Usually in reedbeds, but recent arrivals may occur virtually anywhere; several records from ships at sea. **Status:** Vagrant from Americas, mostly Apr-Jun, but some remain for many months. **Voice:** Silent in Africa. [G2.8.5]

4 COMMON MOORHEN *Gallinula chloropus*   30-36 cm
A dull, sooty-black gallinule with greenish-yellow legs and red frontal shield. Most similar to Lesser Moorhen, but is larger and darker, with mostly red (not yellow) bill. Juv. is larger and greyer than brown-washed juv. Lesser Moorhen. **Habitat:** Most wetlands with fringing vegetation; bolder than other gallinules, often swimming in open water. **Status:** Common to abundant. **Voice:** Sharp 'krrik'. [C2.11b, G2.8.6]

5 LESSER MOORHEN *Gallinula angulata*   23-27 cm
Smaller and more secretive than Common Moorhen, with less conspicuous white flank feathers and mainly yellow (not red) bill. Juv. is sandy-buff (not grey as juv. Common Moorhen) with dull, yellowish-green bill and legs. Skulking; usually heard rather than seen. **Habitat:** Flooded grassland and small, secluded ponds. **Status:** Locally common resident and intra-African migrant. **Voice:** Series of hollow notes, 'do do do do do do do'. [C6.9, G2.8.7]

6 RED-KNOBBED (CRESTED) COOT *Fulica cristata*   41-46 cm
A black, duck-like bird with a white bill and frontal shield. Most similar to Common Coot in N, from which it can be told by having red knobs at top of frontal shield which swell markedly during breeding season. Juv. is dull brown and lacks white undertail coverts of smaller juv Common Moorhen. **Habitat:** Dams, lakes and virtually any wetland except fast-flowing rivers. **Status:** Common to abundant. **Voice:** Harsh, metallic 'claak'. [C2.12b, G2.8.8.]

7 EURASIAN (COMMON) COOT *Fulica atra*   38-40 cm
Adult differs from Red-knobbed Coot by narrow white trailing edge to secondaries in flight. Lacks red knobs on frontal shield, but these are very small and difficult to see in non-breeding Red-knobbed Coot. Also subtle difference in face pattern: black feathers project forward in spur between bill and shield (rounded and less marked in Red-knobbed Coot). Juvs and imms probably inseparable from Red-knobbed Coot. **Habitat:** Open wetlands. **Status:** Uncommon and localised Palearctic migrant, mostly Oct-Mar. **Voice:** 1- or 2-note 'kowp' or 'kup' contact call, deeper-pitched than Red-knobbed Coot's. [C2.12a]

sub-ad.

imm.

juv.

juv.

br.

juv.

juv.

juv.

juv.

imm.

juv.

chick

imm.

1

2

3

4

5

6

7

143

Tall, stately birds of open grasslands and wetlands. Could possibly be confused with herons (e.g. Black-headed Heron, p. 46). Often gather in large flocks when not breeding, and roost communally, often at wetlands. Sexes alike.

1 COMMON (EURASIAN) CRANE *Grus grus* 115 cm
A large grey crane with a red mid-crown and white cheek patch extending down the neck. Only upper neck is black (black extends to breast in Demoiselle Crane). Juv. has brownish head and neck. **Habitat:** Grassland and agricultural lands. **Status:** Locally abundant Palearctic migrant Oct-Mar, often in large flocks; migrates in 'V'-formation. **Voice:** Low, purring contact call while feeding; flight call is loud and broken, lower pitched than Demoiselle Crane's. [C2.13a]

2 DEMOISELLE CRANE *Anthropoides virgo* 90 cm
Smaller than Common Crane, with a prominent white ear tuft and black neck extending in large 'bib' onto breast. Juv. is duller grey, lacks brownish neck of juv. Common Crane. **Habitat:** Grassland and open savanna, usually roosting at wetlands. **Status:** Rare to locally abundant Palearctic migrant Sep-Mar. **Voice:** Low, purring contact call when feeding; flight call is broken and raspy, higher pitched than Common Crane's. [C2.13b]

3 BLACK (NORTHERN) CROWNED CRANE *Balearica pavonina* 95-100 cm
A distinctive crane with a large gold crown, white wing coverts, black primaries and chestnut secondaries. Much darker than larger Grey Crowned Crane, appearing sooty black at a distance. Face patch is pink below with white top. Juv. has rufous edges to upperpart feathers, rufous head and neck and small crest; is darker than juv. Grey Crowned Crane. **Habitat:** Shallow wetlands (including rice paddies) and adjacent agricultural land. **Status:** Locally common in E, scarce in W. **Voice:** Loud, honking 'ka-wonk' or 'wonk'. [C6.11]

4 GREY CROWNED CRANE *Balearica regulorum* 105-110 cm
Similar to Black Crowned Crane, but has a paler grey body. Neck is especially pale and contrasts with darker back. Cheek patch is white, with red top. Juv. lacks unfeathered cheek patch, and has smaller crown. **Habitat:** Shallow wetlands, grassland and agricultural lands; commutes to wetlands to roost. **Status:** Locally common. **Voice:** Trumpeting flight call, 'may hem'; deep 'huum huum' when breeding. [C6.12, G2.6.9]

5 WATTLED CRANE *Grus carunculatus* 120 cm
A very large crane with a white neck and long wattles. Identified even at long range by white neck and upper breast contrasting with black underparts and dark back. Juv. has pale crown. **Habitat:** Shallow wetlands and adjoining grassland. **Status:** Vulnerable. Uncommon and localised. Usually in pairs or small groups, but non-breeding birds gather in flocks of up to 50. **Voice:** Loud 'kwaarnk'; seldom calls. [C6.10, G2.6.7]

6 BLUE CRANE *Anthropoides paradiseus* 100 cm
Endemic to S Africa. An all-grey crane with a bulbous head and long, trailing 'tail' (actually inner secondaries and tertials). In flight, shows less contrast between flight feathers and coverts than other cranes. Juv. lacks long 'tail' and is paler grey, especially on head. **Habitat:** Grassland and agricultural lands. **Status:** Vulnerable. Locally common in SW, but decreasing in E grasslands. In small pairs or family groups while breeding, but non-breeding flocks contain hundreds of birds. **Voice:** Loud, nasal 'kraaaank'. [G2.6.8]

juv.

1

juv.

2

3

4

5

juv.

juv.

6

Very large cursorial birds of open country. Males are much larger than females, and have inflatable throat pouches that create spectacular 'balloon' displays. Some species roost communally, and are often seen flying to and from roost sites.

1 DENHAM'S (STANLEY'S) BUSTARD *Neotis denhami*　　　　85-115 cm
The pale grey foreneck and black-striped head with pale crown stripe are diagnostic. Orange hindneck separates this from all bustards except Ludwig's Bustard, but Denham's Bustard has pale (not dark) foreneck and generally shows more white in folded wing. Female is smaller, with paler, more marked back and less white in wings. Displaying male inflates throat to form conspicuous balloon of white feathers. **Habitat:** Open grassland and agricultural land. **Status:** Uncommon to locally common. **Voice:** Deep booming by displaying male.

2 LUDWIG'S BUSTARD *Neotis ludwigii*　　　　85-100 cm
Endemic to SW Africa. Differs from Denham's Bustard in having dark grey-brown (not pale grey) foreneck and largely uniform, dark head. Normally shows less white in folded wing, but amount of white on wings of both species is variable. Male display 'balloon' is pale grey (not white). Female is markedly smaller. Juv. is paler on head and neck. **Habitat:** Karoo scrub and arid savannas; frequents drier areas than Denham's Bustard. **Status:** Uncommon to locally common resident and migrant. **Voice:** Displaying male gives explosive, deep 'woodoomp' every 15-30 seconds. [G2.9.1]

3 HEUGLIN'S BUSTARD *Neotis heuglinii*　　　　66-88 cm
Endemic to NE Africa. Told from Nubian Bustard by its greyish (not sandy) upperparts and dark (not rufous) crown; ranges not known to overlap. Differs from Denham's Bustard by having chestnut breast band, no rufous on hindneck and black-and-white-chequered forewing, especially obvious in flight. Male has diagnostic black face. Smaller than Arabian and Kori bustards and lacks crest. **Habitat:** Open gravel desert plains and semi-arid scrub. **Status:** Poorly known; locally fairly common. Usually in pairs; sometimes in flocks after rains. **Voice:** Unknown.

4 NUBIAN BUSTARD *Neotis nuba*　　　　62-70 cm
Endemic to Sahel. Larger than White-bellied Bustard (p. 150), with a darker head and rusty crown. In flight, differs from Arabian, Houbara and Denham's bustards by having white underwings and unbarred tail with white basal patches. Imm. is darker overall, with black throat reduced to thin stripe. **Habitat:** Arid to semi-arid scrub and savanna and desert edges. **Status:** Uncommon resident and nomad; occurs singly, in pairs or small groups. **Voice:** Shrill 'maqua'; shorter, grunted 'wurk'. **Similar species:** Houbara Bustard *Chlamydotis undulata* has shaggy, pale neck with diagnostic black breast band extending up side of neck; may stray into extreme N.

5 ARABIAN BUSTARD *Ardeotis arabs*　　　　85-100 cm
A large bustard with a hindcrown crest. Smaller and paler than Kori Bustard with no black on forewing and no black bar at base of neck. Back colour varies from grey in E to sandy-buff in W. **Habitat:** Semi-arid plains, scrub and savanna. **Status:** Locally fairly common; usually solitary or in pairs and in loose gatherings on freshly grassed areas. **Voice:** 'Wooomp' or 'paaah' display call. [C2.15b]

6 KORI BUSTARD *Ardeotis kori*　　　　105-130 cm
The largest bustard. Similar to Arabian Bustard, but has black at base of neck and in wing coverts. Neck is finely barred grey. Flight is heavy and laboured. Displaying male has raised crest, white throat 'balloon', and throws tail forward onto its back, showing white undertail coverts. **Habitat:** Semi-arid savanna and grassland, usually near cover of trees. **Status:** Generally scarce, but locally fairly common in protected areas. **Voice:** Deep, resonant 'oom-oom-oom' by male during breeding season. [G2.8.10]

Strongly sexually dimorphic species; males have loud, distinctive calls and displays.

1 SOUTHERN BLACK KORHAAN *Eupodotis afra*   52 cm
Endemic to South Africa. On ground, very similar to Northern Black Korhaan; best identified in flight by all-dark flight feathers. Female and imm. lack bold black-and-white head and neck. In display flight, male dangles legs as it 'parachutes' slowly to ground, calling continually. **Habitat:** Coastal fynbos and Karoo scrub. **Status:** Common; singly or in pairs. **Voice:** Male gives raucous 'kerrrak-kerrrak-kerrrak' in flight and on ground. [G2.9.8]

2 NORTHERN BLACK KORHAAN *Eupodotis afraoides*   52 cm
Near-endemic to S Africa. Differs from Southern Black Korhaan by white inner webs to primaries, forming conspicuous white window in flight. Female and imm. differ from female Red-crested Korhaan by black barring (not chevrons) on upperparts. **Habitat:** Karoo grasslands and arid savannas. **Status:** Common; singly or in pairs. **Voice:** Similar to that of Southern Black Korhaan. [G2.9.9]

3 BUFF-CRESTED BUSTARD *Eupodotis gindiana*   46-53 cm
Endemic to NE Africa. Smaller than Black-bellied and Hartlaub's bustards; has shorter, thicker neck and no white in wings; does not occur in open grasslands. Black belly separates it from Little Brown Bustard (p. 150). Slightly darker above than Savile's Bustard, with less extensive black below. Buff crest is seen only when calling. **Habitat:** Dry acacia scrub and woodland; rarely in open grasslands. **Status:** Fairly common to common; singly or in pairs. **Voice:** Piercing series of whistles and clicks preceding display flight.

4 RED-CRESTED KORHAAN *Eupodotis ruficrista*   50 cm
Endemic to SW Africa. Both sexes have black belly. Female has mottled brown crown and neck, and differs from female Northern Black Korhaan by black belly extending onto lower breast and by chevrons (not barring) on back. Male has aerial display: flies straight up, then suddenly tumbles to ground as though shot, before gliding to land. Bushy red crest is seen only during display. **Habitat:** Dry woodland and semi-desert grassland. **Status:** Common; singly or in pairs. **Voice:** Song is protracted; starts with series of clicks, 'tic-tic-tic', switching to extended series of loud, piping whistles, 'pi-pi-pi... pipity-pipity'. [G2.9.6]

5 SAVILE'S BUSTARD *Eupodotis savilei*   46-53 cm
Sahel form of Red-crested Korhaan. Range not known to overlap with very similar Buff-crested Bustard; differs by black on belly extending onto lower breast and more sandy upperparts. Female lacks grey on head. **Habitat:** Arid scrub and savanna, frequently near water. **Status:** Thinly distributed but locally common. **Voice:** Long, single whistled note followed by shorter, lower-pitched notes. [C6.14]

6 BLACK-BELLIED BUSTARD *Eupodotis melanogaster*   58-63 cm
Long, thin-necked bustard with a boldly mottled back. In E Africa, confusion possible with Hartlaub's Bustard; differs chiefly by having brown (not black) rump, lower back and tail. Underwings are dark, appearing black, with white patch in primaries. Male has black belly, extending as thin line up front of neck to throat. In slow display flight, male upperwing shows striking white primaries and outer secondaries. Female is nondescript, off-white below with brown wings; best separated from other small bustards by long, thin neck and dark underwing contrasting with white underparts. **Habitat:** Woodland and tall, open grassland. **Status:** Fairly common. **Voice:** Short, sharp 'chikk', followed by 'pop'. [C6.16, G2.9.7]

7 HARTLAUB'S BUSTARD *Eupodotis hartaubii*   61-71 cm
Endemic to NE Africa. Very similar to Black-bellied Bustard, but heavier billed, with more strikingly patterned face and neck; sides of neck are greyer and wings show more white. Main difference is dark, almost black lower back, rump and tail, best seen in flight. Female is darker than female Black-bellied Bustard with a whitish-buff line down throat and front of neck, and much more conspicuous dark barring on breast. **Habitat:** Drier, more open grassland than Black-bellied Bustard. **Status:** Uncommon. **Voice:** Clicking and popping sounds similar to Black-bellied Bustard; also soft, airy 'wooomp' booming, ending 'click-and-pop' call.

display

149

Species with limited sexual dimorphism; both sexes call together. Occur in pairs or family groups throughout the year.

1 KAROO KORHAAN *Eupodotis vigorsii* 58 cm

Endemic to S Africa. Rather drab, grey-brown korhaan with black throat and nape patch, and contrasting buff and black wings in flight. May overlap with similar Rüppell's Korhaan in S Namibia; differs by being darker on back and lacking bold face pattern, black line down throat front and bluish neck. Female has smaller, less defined throat and nape patches. **Habitat:** Karoo scrub; also croplands in S Cape. **Status:** Common; usually in groups of 2-3 birds. **Voice:** Deep, frog-like duet, 'wrok-rak' or 'wrok-rak-rak', mostly at dawn and dusk; male utters deeper first syllable, female responds. [G2.9.4]

2 RÜPPELL'S KORHAAN *Eupodotis rueppellii* 58 cm

Endemic to Namibia and Angola. Differs from similar Karoo Korhaan by paler, warmer brown back, conspicuous black line down foreneck, blue-tinged neck and contrasting facial pattern. Male is more boldly marked than female, especially on head and throat. **Habitat:** Gravel plains and arid scrub. **Status:** Common; usually in pairs or family groups. **Voice:** Similar to Karoo Korhaan's, but slightly higher pitched. [G2.9.5]

3 BLUE KORHAAN *Eupodotis caerulescens* 56 cm

Endemic to South Africa. Overlaps with closely related Karoo Korhaan in W. Blue-grey underparts, neck and wing (in flight) contrasting with chestnut back are diagnostic. Male has white face with pale-grey ear-coverts. Female is less brightly coloured, with brown ear-coverts. Juv's ear-coverts are blackish. **Habitat:** High elevation grasslands and eastern Karoo. **Status:** Locally common; usually in groups of 3-5 birds. **Voice:** Deep, discordant 'krok-kaa-krow', generally at dawn and dusk. [G2.9.2]

4 BARROW'S (SOUTHERN WHITE-BELLIED) KORHAAN

Eupodotis barrowii 52-61 cm

Endemic to S Africa. Often treated as a race of White-bellied Bustard, but male has rufous (not blue) hindneck, and lacks buff breast band between blue neck and white belly. Female and juv. have brown neck and superficially resemble female Black-bellied Bustard (p. 148), but have shorter neck and legs, and pale underwing coverts. Differ from female White-bellied Bustard by having more buffy (not whitish) face and darker upperparts. **Habitat:** Open grassland and lightly wooded savanna; prefers taller grass than most other korhaans. **Status:** Uncommon. **Voice:** Rhythmic, crowing 'takwarat' repeatedly at dawn and dusk. [G2.9.2]

5 (NORTHERN) WHITE-BELLIED BUSTARD *Eupodotis senegalensis* 48-61 cm

Resembles much larger Nubian Bustard (p. 146), but has whiter face and less black on chin. Darker than Little Brown Bustard with bold black-and-white markings on head and no pale wing bar in flight. Male differs from Barrow's Korhaan by blue (not rufous) hindneck. Female and juv. have less marking on head and neck; face whiter than female Barrow's Korhaan. **Habitat:** Lightly wooded savanna, semi-arid scrub and farmlands. **Status:** Sparsely distributed, with disjunct distribution; usually in groups of 2 or 3, rarely 4. **Voice:** Harsh and guttural, frog-like 'wakka waak'. [C6.15]

6 LITTLE BROWN BUSTARD *Eupodotis humilis* 45 cm

Endemic to Ethiopia and Somalia. Paler than White-bellied Bustard, with a more uniformly coloured head and pale wing bar in flight. Told from Buff-crested Bustard (p.148) by its whitish (not black) belly. Female duller. **Habitat:** Semi-arid scrub and desert edge. **Status:** Little known. **Voice:** Described as a rattle, usually given in evening.

1 CRAB PLOVER *Dromas ardeola*　　　　　　　　　38-41 cm
A large, predominantly white wader with a black back and flight feathers. Superficially recalls Pied Avocet (p. 172), but large, black, dagger-shaped bill is diagnostic. Long, greyish legs extend well beyond white tail in flight. Imm. has greyer wings and tail, with grey back and streaked hindcrown. Juv. is mottled brown above. **Habitat:** Coastal flats and estuaries, especially mangroves rich in crabs. **Status:** Common migrant to E coast; perhaps resident in NE; breeds in Somalia and probably Eritrea. **Voice:** Range of metallic calls: 'kwa-daaa-dak', 'kwa-da-dak' or 'grr-kwo-kwo-kwo'; flight call is 'kwa-da'. [G2.15.6]

OYSTERCATCHERS
Large coastal waders with distinctive reddish bills and legs. Sexes alike.

2 AFRICAN BLACK OYSTERCATCHER *Haematopus moquini*　　　　44 cm
Endemic to S Africa. A large, all-black wader with a bright orange bill and eye-ring and dull pink legs. Some adults have small white patches on underparts. Juv. is browner, with dark-tipped bill and grey-pink legs. **Habitat:** Coastline, estuaries and lagoons. **Status:** Common from C Namibia to E Cape; locally common in S Angola; vagrant to S Mozambique. **Voice:** 'Klee-kleeep'; fast 'peeka-peeka-peeka' alarm call. [G2.10.4]

3 EURASIAN OYSTERCATCHER *Haematopus ostralegus*　　　　40-43 cm
A large, pied wader with white underparts, and a bold white wing bar, back and rump. Smaller and more slender than African Black Oystercatcher. Has long orange bill and pink legs; non-breeding and young birds have white throat collar. Juv. has brown-tinged back and duller bill and legs. **Habitat:** Open coast and estuaries; vagrant at Rift Valley lakes. **Status:** Uncommon Palearctic migrant; locally common in NW. **Voice:** Sharp, high-pitched 'klee-kleep'. [C2.16b, G2.10.3]

JACANAS
Distinctive waders with extremely long toes to walk on floating vegetation. Sexes alike, but females larger in most species and are the dominant sex.

4 AFRICAN JACANA *Actophilornis africanus*　　　　　　28-31 cm
Unmistakable: a rich chestnut bird with a white neck and yellow upper breast, and a contrasting black-and-white head which highlights the blue frontal shield. Legs are long, with extremely long toes and nails that enable it to walk on floating vegetation. Female is larger and dominant sex; males incubate and care for young. Juv. is paler, with white belly, and lacks frontal shield. Can be confused with Lesser Jacana, but is much larger and lacks white trailing edge to wing in flight. **Habitat:** Wetlands with floating vegetation, especially water lilies. **Status:** Common. **Voice:** Noisy; sharp, ringing 'krrrek', rasping 'krrrrrrk' and barking 'yowk-yowk'. [C6.17, G2.9.10]

5 LESSER JACANA *Microparra capensis*　　　　　　　15-17 cm
Much smaller than African Jacana, with white underparts and eyebrow; upperparts are pale buffy-grey brown. Resembles juv. African Jacana but is much smaller and in flight shows white on trailing edges of secondaries and pale upperwing coverts that contrast with dark flight feathers. Underwing is dark. Juv. is less rufous above. Unique among jacanas in sharing parental duties. **Habitat:** River floodplains, lagoons and bays in wetlands with emergent grass and sedge. **Status:** Uncommon resident and local nomad. **Voice:** Soft, flufftail-like 'poop-oop-oop-oop'; scolding 'ksh-ksh-ksh'; high-pitched 'titititititi'. [C6.18, G2.10.1]

imm.

imm.

1

imm.

2

imm.

3

non-br.

4

juv.

5

juv.

THICK-KNEES (DIKKOPS)
Large, well-camouflaged waders of open country or wetland margins. They usually roost during the day and are active at night, when their ringing calls are frequently heard. Sexes alike.

1 EURASIAN THICK-KNEE (STONE CURLEW) *Burhinus oedicnemus* 40-44 cm
A large thick-knee with a pale grey wing panel at rest. Differs from other thick-knees by having white line along top of wing panel (lesser coverts) bordered with black below; lower black bar is less conspicuous in juvs. Basal third of bill is yellow. In flight, two white primary patches are small. Nominate race and the smaller, paler *saharae* occur in region. **Habitat:** Open country; not normally associated with water. **Status:** Uncommon Palearctic migrant Oct-Mar. **Voice:** Silent on non-breeding grounds. [C2.18a]

2 SENEGAL THICK-KNEE *Burhinus senegalensis* 32-38 cm
A small thick-knee with a pale grey wing panel at rest. Wing panel has dark border above and below but lacks white bar of both Water and Eurasian thick-knees. Large billed, with dark tip extending to base of bill along top of upper mandible. In flight, has large white panels in primaries. **Habitat:** Sandy areas, usually near water. **Status:** Common resident and intra-African migrant. **Voice:** Loud wailing 'pi pi pi-pi-pi-pi-PII-PII-PIIPII-pii-pii-pii'; also 'piLI piLI', usually at night. [C6.20]

3 WATER THICK-KNEE (DIKKOP) *Burhinus vermiculatus* 38-41 cm
A medium-sized thick-knee with a grey wing panel at rest. Told from Eurasian Thick-knee by white line along top of wing panel lacking black line below; also, has much less yellow at base of bill, with black cutting edges and dorsal ridge. White panel in outer primaries is smaller than Senegal Thick-knee's. **Habitat:** River and lake shores with suitable cover. **Status:** Common resident; usually in pairs. **Voice:** Rather mournful 'ti-ti-ti-tee-teee-tooo', slowing and dropping in pitch at end, usually at night. [C6.21, G2.15.8]

4 SPOTTED THICK-KNEE (DIKKOP) *Burhinus capensis* 43 cm
A large thick-knee with unique spotted upperparts and no pale wing bar at rest. In flight, has two small white patches at base of primaries. Roosts under cover during day; active primarily at night. **Habitat:** Virtually any open country, including fields and parks. **Status:** Common resident; often in pairs. **Voice:** Rising then falling 'whi-whi-whi-WHI-WHI-WHI-whi-whi', usually at night. [G6.22, G2.15.7]

SHEATHBILLS
Peculiar Antarctic waders that breed in association with seabird colonies, stealing food to rear their chicks. Sexes alike.

5 GREATER SHEATHBILL *Chionis albus* 40 cm
A large, white, plump, pigeon-like bird with a bare pink face and a short, stout, yellowish bill. Legs are thick and scaly. Juv. has smaller facial patch. **Habitat:** Coastal areas, especially seabird roosts and harbours. **Status:** Vagrant to South Africa, mostly Apr-Jun. Birds migrating north from Antarctic Peninsula to South America presumably land on ships and are carried across S Atlantic. **Voice:** Silent in Africa. [G6.15.10]

Mostly aerial-feeding waders, with long, rakish wings. Appear tern-like in flight, but can also run rapidly. Sexes alike; some species have distinct breeding plumages.

1 COLLARED (RED-WINGED) PRATINCOLE *Glareola pratincola* 24-25 cm
A large, long-winged pratincole. Pale buff throat separates it from all other species except Black-winged Pratincole; differs by being paler above, with dark rufous (not black) under-wing coverts and pale trailing edge to secondaries. In poor light, underwing can appear all dark. Throat patch is edged with a thin black collar in breeding plumage; incomplete or absent in non-breeding birds. Flight is light and graceful, showing conspicuous white rump and deeply forked tail. Juv. lacks clearly defined throat markings and has buff edges to mantle feathers. **Habitat:** Wetland margins and open areas near water. **Status:** Locally common intra-African and Palearctic migrant. **Voice:** 'Kik-kik', especially in flight. [C2.19a, G3.1.4]

2 BLACK-WINGED PRATINCOLE *Glareola nordmanni* 23-25 cm
Slightly darker than Collared Pratincole. Best distinguished in flight, when white rump con-trasts sharply with rest of upperparts, and it lacks white trailing edge to secondaries and has black (not rufous) underwing coverts. At close range has less red at base of bill and more extensive black lores, reaching to forehead. Juv. is drabber, with scalloped upperparts, and sometimes has rufous flecking on underwing coverts. **Habitat:** Grassland, fallow lands and edges of wetlands. **Status:** Locally common Palearctic migrant; usually in large, nomadic flocks. **Voice:** Often-repeated, single- or double-noted 'pik'. [C2.19b, G3.1.5]

3 MADAGASCAR PRATINCOLE *Glareola ocularis* 23-25 cm
A dark pratincole with a chestnut belly and a narrow white stripe below and behind the eye; lacks the pale throat of other large pratincoles. Larger than Rock Pratincole, with chestnut belly patch and underwing coverts. Juv. lacks white eye-stripe and has buff-fringed upper-parts and rufous-streaked breast. **Habitat:** Mostly estuaries and coastal-plain wetlands. **Status:** Locally abundant non-breeding migrant to E Africa from Madagascar, Mar-Sept. **Voice:** Sharp 'wick-we-wick'.

4 ROCK PRATINCOLE *Glareola nuchalis* 17-20 cm
A small, dark pratincole with relatively short wings and tail. Head has white stripe behind eye; in nominate race this extends onto nape, forming nuchal collar. W African *liberiae* has chestnut nape and no nuchal collar. Legs and bill base are red. White rump is conspicuous in flight. Juv. is duller; lacks white eye-stripe, and is lightly speckled buff above and on breast. **Habitat:** Rocky areas on large rivers; occasionally on sandbars. **Status:** Locally common resident and intra-African migrant. **Voice:** Loud, plover-like 'kik-kik'. [C6.26, G3.1.6]

5 GREY PRATINCOLE *Glareola cinerea* 18-20 cm
A small, compact pratincole. Mostly pale grey above and white below, with pale chestnut nape and buff breast. Legs and bill base are red. In flight, upperwing has bold black, white and grey pattern (recalls Sabine's Gull, p. 188). Underwings are white, with outerwing ringed black. Short, shallow-forked tail is white, with black subterminal bar. **Habitat:** Sandbanks of slow-flowing rivers, moving to coast and other wetlands when sandbanks are flooded. **Status:** Common resident and local migrant. **Voice:** Accelerating series of 'zi' notes. [C6.27]

6 EGYPTIAN PLOVER *Pluvianus aegyptius* 19-21 cm
Unmistakable: blue-grey upperparts, salmon-coloured underparts, a black breast band and a black-and-white head. In flight, upper- and underwings are largely white, with striking black bars. Tail is grey, with white tip. Juv. is duller, with rufous on black head and back. Affinities uncertain; close to pratincoles, but sometimes placed in its own sub-family. **Habitat:** Slow-flowing rivers with sandbars. **Status:** Locally common, moving in response to changing water levels; often tame close to human settlements. **Voice:** Rapid series of loud 'chersk' notes. [C6.23]

br.

non-br.

non-br.

br.

juv.

br.

non-br.

juv.

non-br.

1

2

3

juv.

4

5

6

Dry country waders with spindly legs and upright stance. Flight swift, but prefer to run when disturbed. Most species partly nocturnal. Sexes alike.

1 CREAM-COLOURED COURSER *Cursorius cursor*   21-24 cm
Larger, paler and less grey than Somali Courser. Best identified by dark underwing, with only narrow pale trailing edge to secondaries. Juv. is lightly mottled above, told from juv. Somali Courser by pale (not barred) tail with incomplete subterminal bar. **Habitat:** Desert and semi-desert plains, including dune slacks. **Status:** Locally common resident and intra-African migrant; resident on Socotra. **Voice:** Usually silent; sometimes gives sharp 'whit' or 'whit krit'. [C2.18b]

2 SOMALI COURSER *Cursorius somalensis*   20-22 cm
Endemic to NE Africa. Told from Temminck's Courser by its grey (not rufous) hindcrown and pale (not dark) belly. Smaller, paler and greyer than Cream-coloured Courser, with pale underwing; only primaries and primary coverts are dark; inner wing is pale grey, with conspicuous white trailing edge to secondaries. Juv. is mottled above with a barred tail. **Habitat:** Semi-arid grassy plains. **Status:** Locally common nomad. **Voice:** Sharp 'whit-whit'.

3 BURCHELL'S COURSER *Cursorius rufus*   21-23 cm
Endemic to SW Africa. Paler than Temminck's Courser, with blue-grey hindcrown and nape and less contrast between upperparts and breast. Black band separates rufous forebelly from white vent. In flight, has broad white trailing edge to secondaries. Underwing coverts are rufous, secondaries are mostly white and primaries are black. Juv. is mottled above, with barred tail tip and poorly defined black belly band. **Habitat:** Dry, sparsely grassed plains and open fields. **Status:** Uncommon nomad and intra-African migrant. **Voice:** Harsh, repeated 'wark'. [G2.15.9]

4 TEMMINCK'S COURSER *Cursorius temminckii*   19-21 cm
A small, plain rufous courser with a broad black patch behind the eye. Differs from other African *Cursorius* by having rufous (not grey) hindcrown; belly has black patch (not bar) between and in front of legs. In flight, flight feathers are black above. Underwing is black, with narrow white trailing edge to secondaries. Juv. is duller, with lightly speckled underparts and scalloped upperparts. **Habitat:** Dry, sparsely grassed and recently burned areas. **Status:** Locally common nomad and intra-African migrant. **Voice:** Grating 'keerkeer'. [C6.24, G2.15.10]

5 DOUBLE-BANDED COURSER *Rhinoptilus africanus*   20-24 cm
A small, pale courser with two narrow black breast bands. Head is plain, with creamy eye-stripe. Upperparts are scaled; dark back and wing coverts have broad creamy-buff edges. In flight, has white rump, and conspicuous chestnut secondaries and inner primaries contrasting with dark outer primaries. Juv. has chestnut breast bands. **Habitat:** Semi-arid and desert plains, usually in stony areas. **Status:** Common resident. **Voice:** Thin, falling and rising 'teeu-wee' whistle; repeated 'kee-kee', mostly at night. [G3.1.11]

6 THREE-BANDED (HEUGLIN'S) COURSER *Rhinoptilus cinctus*   25-27 cm
Larger than Double-banded Courser, with rufous, black and white bands on breast and neck. White eye-stripe forks behind eye and extends into hindcollar. In flight, has white rump, but upperwings are relatively uniform, with darker brown flight feathers than Double-banded Courser's. **Habitat:** Arid and semi-arid savanna. Largely nocturnal; roosts under bushes during day. **Status:** Uncommon to locally common. **Voice:** Repeated 'kika-kika-kika' at night. [G3.1.2]

7 BRONZE-WINGED (VIOLET-TIPPED) COURSER
Rhinoptilus chalcopterus   26-28 cm
A large, rather robust courser with distinctive head and breast markings. Violet-tipped primaries are not a field character. In flight, white uppertail coverts and wing bars contrast with dark upperparts. Juv. has rufous-tipped feathers on upperparts. **Habitat:** Woodland and savanna. Largely nocturnal; roosts under bushes during the day. **Status:** Fairly common resident and intra-African migrant. **Voice:** Ringing 'ki-kooi' at night. [C6.25, G3.1.3]

Familiar waders that hunt primarily by sight, alternating standing and running. Seldom forage in flocks. Sexes alike, but migrant species have distinct breeding plumages.

1 MONGOLIAN PLOVER *Charadrius mongolus* 19-21 cm
Smaller than Greater Sand Plover, with shorter legs and a shorter, less robust bill; legs are almost always very dark grey or black (not grey-green); in breeding plumage, rufous breast band is more extensive than Greater Sand Plover's. Lacks pale collar of White-fronted Plover. In flight, there is little colour contrast between tail, rump and back. Juv. has buff-fringed upperparts. **Habitat:** Coastal wetlands and Rift Valley lakes. **Status:** Locally common Palearctic migrant to E coast, mostly Aug-May. **Voice:** Hard 'chittick'. [G2.10.10]

2 GREATER SAND PLOVER *Charadrius leschenaultii* 22-25 cm
Slightly larger than Mongolian Plover, with a bigger body, longer legs and a longer, more robust bill; in breeding plumage, rufous breast band is less extensive; in flight, white sides of rump are more extensive. Leg colour is variable but usually grey-green (very rarely black). Caspian Plover has smaller bill and lacks extensive white-sided rump. Juv. has buff-fringed upperparts. **Habitat:** Coastal wetlands and Rift Valley lakes. **Status:** Locally common Palearctic migrant to E coast, mostly Aug-May. **Voice:** Soft trilled 'tirrrri'. [C2.23, G2.11.1]

3 CASPIAN PLOVER *Charadrius asiaticus* 18-22 cm
Non-breeding birds have a complete (or virtually complete) grey-brown wash across breast, and a broad, buffy supercilium. Bill is smaller and thinner than either Greater Sand or Mongolian plovers'. In flight, upperparts are uniform, apart from pale bases to inner primaries. In breeding plumage, has a black lower border to chestnut breast band, pale eyebrow and throat, and no dark eye patch. Juv. appears buffy-scaled. **Habitat:** Short grasslands, bare fields and wetland fringes. **Status:** Locally common Palearctic migrant, mostly Aug-Apr; usually in flocks. **Voice:** Clear, whistled 'tooeet'. [G2.11.2] **Similar species: Eurasian Dotterel** *Eudromius morinellus* has large buffy eye-stripe meeting on nape and narrow pale band across buffy breast. Palearctic vagrant in N.

4 KITTLITZ'S PLOVER *Charadrius pecuarius* 14-16 cm
Boldly patterned head is diagnostic in breeding adult. Head is less well marked in non-breeding plumage, but has pale buffy ring around crown extending to nape, and dark eye patch in all plumages. Breast is variably creamy buff to chestnut. **Habitat:** Fields, short grasslands and fringes of wetlands. **Status:** Common resident and local nomad. **Voice:** Short, clipped trill, 'kittip'. [C6.28, G2.10.8]

5 KENTISH PLOVER *Charadrius alexandrinus* 15-17 cm
A pale brown plover. In breeding plumage, differs from White-fronted Plover by having distinctive small black patches on sides of breast; crown and nape chestnut, but some races of White-fronted Plover also have rufous crowns. Non-breeding and imm. birds are very hard to separate from White-fronted Plover, but tend to have longer, darker legs and shorter tail, with wings reaching to tail tip, giving more slender and attenuated appearance. **Habitat:** Coastal wetlands and sandy beaches; large inland lakes and rivers. **Status:** Locally common Palearctic migrant. **Voice:** Short, sharp 'wiiit'. [C2.22]

6 WHITE-FRONTED PLOVER *Charadrius marginatus* 16 cm
A pale brownish plover, very similar to Kentish Plover (especially N races with rufous wash on crown). Tail is rather long, extending beyond folded wings. Breast varies from white to rich buff, but head pattern and paler upperparts distinguish it from Kittlitz's Plover. White collar separates it from larger Mongolian Plover. Larger than juv. Chestnut-banded Plover (p. 162), with longer tail and darker, browner upperparts. Non-breeding and imm. birds lack black markings on head, and are usually white below, with small, dusky breast patches. **Habitat:** Coastline, estuaries and larger inland rivers and pans. **Status:** Common. **Voice:** Clear 'wiiit'; 'tukut' alarm call. [C6.31, G2.10.6]

br.

non-br.

1

non-br.

non-br.

non-br.

2

non-br.

non-br.

br.

3

non-br.

br.

br.

4

non-br.

juv.

br.

5

non-br.

non-br.

non-br.

non-br.

br.

6

non-br.

juv.

br.

161

1 COMMON RINGED PLOVER *Charadrius hiaticula*   18-20 cm
A short-legged, dark plover with a white collar above a blackish-brown breast band which is often incomplete in non-breeding plumage. Yellow-orange legs separate it from other small plovers. Lacks bold yellow eye-ring of Little Ringed Plover, with orange (not pinkish-grey) legs and prominent white wing bar. Bill is usually orange at base. **Habitat:** Coastal and inland wetlands, preferring patches of soft, fine mud. **Status:** Common Palearctic migrant, mostly Sep-May. **Voice:** Fluty, rising 'too-li'. [C2.21, G2.10.5]

2 LITTLE RINGED PLOVER *Charadrius dubius*   15-17 cm
Smaller than Common Ringed Plover, with a conspicuous yellow eye-ring, pinkish-grey (not orange) legs and no obvious white wing bar. Juv. differs from other small plovers by its uniform upperwings. **Habitat:** Usually close to fresh water, favouring shores of lakes and rivers; occasionally on coast. **Status:** Uncommon to locally common Palearctic migrant, mostly Sep–Apr. **Voice:** Descending 'pee-oo'. [C2.20b]

3 THREE-BANDED PLOVER *Charadrius tricollaris*   18 cm
A small, dark, long-tailed plover with a distinctive double black breast band, grey cheeks and conspicuous red eye-ring and bill base. Slightly smaller than Forbes's Plover, with a white (not dark) forehead. In flight, has more extensive white in outer-tail and tail tips, and has narrow white wing bar. Juv. is duller and slightly scaled above. **Habitat:** Wetland fringes, preferring fresh water. **Status:** Common. **Voice:** Penetrating, high-pitched 'weee-weet' whistle. [C6.29, G2.10.9]

4 FORBES'S PLOVER *Charadrius forbesi*   18-20 cm
W African form of Three-banded Plover. Slightly larger and darker, with dark (not white) forehead and darker, browner face. In flight, lacks white wing bar and has less white in tail. Juv. is duller and slightly scaled above. **Habitat:** Short grasslands, wetland fringes, lawns and airstrips; often breeds on rocky hills. **Status:** Uncommon to locally common intra-African migrant. **Voice:** Single-note 'pleeuw'; flight display 'pleuw-pleuw-pleuw'. [C6.30]

5 CHESTNUT-BANDED PLOVER *Charadrius pallidus*   15 cm
The smallest, palest African plover, restricted to S and E Africa. Thin chestnut breast band is diagnostic in adults, but some White-fronted Plovers (p. 160) can show diffuse buff breast band. Adult male has darker band and neat black forehead and lores. Juv. has incomplete grey breast band; best told from larger White-fronted Plover by lack of white neck collar, paler and greyer upperparts, and short-tailed appearance. **Habitat:** Salt pans and soda lakes, estuaries and coastal wetlands. **Status:** Fairly common resident and local nomad. **Voice:** Single 'prrp' or 'tooit'. [G2.10.7]

br.

non-br.

juv.

br.

1

br.

br.

br.

juv.

2

3

4

♂

♀

juv.

5

♂

1 PACIFIC GOLDEN PLOVER *Pluvialis fulva*   23-26 cm
Very similar to American Golden Plover, but is more spangled gold above and its feet project slightly beyond its tail in flight; eyebrow is smaller and more buffy, and breast is suffused with buff. In breeding plumage, white neck stripe extends down flanks to vent. Juv. has yellower upperparts and breast. **Habitat:** Coastal mudflats and sandflats; also on inland grassland. **Status:** Uncommon Palearctic migrant to NE, vagrant elsewhere. **Voice:** Similar to American Golden Plover's. [G2.11.3] **Similar species: Eurasian Golden Plover** *P. apricaria* is larger with a white underwing and weak or absent eye-stripe; Palearctic vagrant to N.

2 AMERICAN GOLDEN PLOVER *Pluvialis dominica*   26 cm
Slightly smaller and more slender than Grey Plover, with a more upright stance. In non-breeding plumage, whitish eyebrow is more pronounced than in Grey or Pacific Golden plovers. In flight, rump is brown and underwing is grey, and feet don't project beyond last. Bulkier than Pacific Golden Plover, and has no buff on breast. In breeding plumage, has golden spangling on upperparts, and black underparts extend to undertail; it lacks white flank line of Pacific Golden Plover. Juv. has more scalloped and yellow upperparts. **Habitat:** Typically short grassland; less coastal than Pacific Golden Plover. **Status:** Nearctic vagrant. **Voice:** Variable; usually single- or double-noted whistle, 'oodle-oo'. [C2.25]

3 GREY (BLACK-BELLIED) PLOVER *Pluvialis squatarola*   28-31 cm
A large, stubby-billed plover. Larger than American and Pacific Golden plovers with black axillaries contrasting with whitish underwings, white (not grey-brown) rump and grey (not buff) speckling on upperparts. Underparts are black in breeding plumage with white (not golden) speckling on upperparts. Juv. has buffy-yellow markings on upperparts. **Habitat:** Coast and adjacent wetlands and Rift Valley lakes; elsewhere occurs inland only during migration. **Status:** Common Palearctic migrant, mostly Aug-Apr, but many year round. **Voice:** Clear 'tluuii'. [C2.27, G2.11.4]

LAPWINGS
Large, boldly patterned plovers. Often noisy, occurring at wetlands and in open country. Most species are resident or local migrants that retain the same plumage year round. Sexes alike.

4 WHITE-TAILED LAPWING (PLOVER) *Vanellus leucurus*   29 cm
A slender, long-legged, rather plain grey-brown lapwing. Yellow legs and uniform head separate it from Sociable Lapwing; also has all-white tail in flight. Juv. has slightly darker crown, but lacks prominent supercilium of Sociable and Caspian (p. 160) plovers; most have lost juv. plumage before arriving in Africa. **Habitat:** Along river banks and on open ground near wetlands. **Status:** Rare Palearctic migrant Oct-Mar. **Voice:** Whistled 'wee wik' and 'wee wee-ik'. [C2.28]

5 SOCIABLE LAPWING (PLOVER) *Vanellus gregarius*   27-30 cm
A short-legged, rather dumpy lapwing. Legs are black. Breeding adult has black cap above white head band. Upperparts and breast are sandy-buff, with dark black and chestnut belly. Non-breeding bird has white belly. In flight, has white secondaries and large black tail spot. Juv. has brown crown, buff head band, dark streaks on buff breast, and buff-fringed upperparts. **Habitat:** Arid plains, damp fields and highland grasslands. **Status:** Vulnerable. Increasingly rare Palearctic migrant Oct-Mar. **Voice:** Mostly silent in Africa; occasionally gives shrill whistle.

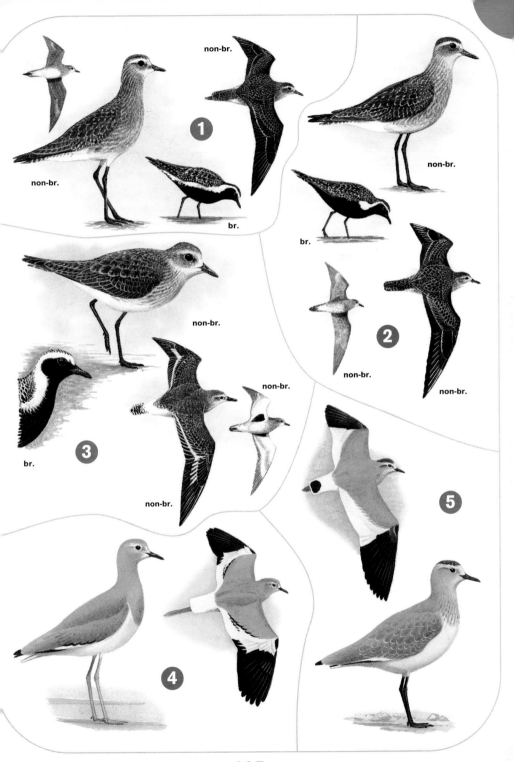

non-br.

non-br.

1

br.

non-br.

non-br.

br.

2

non-br.

non-br.

non-br.

non-br.

br.

3

non-br.

5

4

1 LONG-TOED LAPWING (PLOVER) *Vanellus crassirostris*   31 cm
The white face, throat and foreneck are diagnostic. Black nape extends down sides of neck
to form broad breast band. Legs and base of bill are reddish. Strikingly black and white in
flight, with grey-brown back. N nominate race has black flight feathers and white coverts;
leucoptera in S has all-white wings except for black outer primaries. Black tail contrasts with
white rump in all races. Juv. is slightly mottled above. **Habitat:** Marshes and floodplains; its
long toes aid walking on floating vegetation. **Status:** Locally common. **Voice:** Repeated,
high-pitched 'pink-pink'. [C6.41, G2.12.1]

2 BLACKSMITH LAPWING (PLOVER) *Vanellus armatus*   31 cm
This boldly marked, black, white and grey lapwing is easy to identify. Legs are blackish and
eye is dark red. Flight feathers are black, with grey upperwing coverts; there is no white wing
bar. Juv. is duller, with greyish-brown upperparts, and mottled brown head and neck; has
been confused with Spur-winged Lapwing. **Habitat:** Wetland margins and adjoining grassland and fields. **Status:** Common; often in flocks when not breeding. **Voice:** Very vocal; loud,
ringing 'tink, tink, tink' alarm call. [C6.36, G2.11.8]

3 SPUR-WINGED LAPWING (PLOVER) *Vanellus spinosus*   25-28 cm
A small lapwing with a pale brown mantle, white neck, and black breast, crown and throat
stripe. Juv. has browner crown with fine white spotting, and back feathers edged buff.
Habitat: Rivers, wetland margins and adjacent grasslands. **Status:** Common resident; often
in flocks and sometimes breeds in loose colonies. **Voice:** Loud, screeching, 3-4 note 'ti-ti-
tirri-ti'. [C6.37]

4 BLACK-HEADED LAPWING (PLOVER) *Vanellus tectus*   25 cm
The black-and-white patterned head with a wispy crest and small red face wattle are diagnostic. In flight, is similar to Crowned Lapwing (p. 168), but has white extending onto
primaries. Juv. is buff-fringed above, with smaller wattle. **Habitat:** Open, dry ground in arid
areas. **Status:** Common. **Voice:** Short, whistled 'kir-kir-kir-kir' when disturbed; mobbing call
is shrill 'kwairrr'. [C6.35] **Similar species: Northern Lapwing** *V. vanellus* also has long crest,
but upperparts are dark green with no white in wings. Rare Palearctic migrant to N.

5 WHITE-HEADED (WHITE-CROWNED) LAPWING (PLOVER)
Vanellus albiceps   30 cm
A boldly patterned lapwing with large, pendulous, yellow wattles and yellow legs. White (not
brown) breast separates it from African Wattled Lapwing. In flight, wings are mostly white,
with only outer primaries and inner coverts black. Juv. has brownish crown, smaller wattles
and barred upperparts. **Habitat:** Sandbanks on large rivers. **Status:** Locally common. **Voice:**
Repeated, ringing 'peek-peek'. [C6.34, G2.11.9]

6 AFRICAN WATTLED LAPWING (PLOVER) *Vanellus senegallus*   35 cm
The largest African lapwing. At rest, appears mostly brown, with black-and-white forehead,
streaked head and neck, and fairly large yellow face wattle. Races N of equator have pale
belly and bill is almost entirely yellow; *lateralis* in S has dark brown-black band across belly
and white vent; bill tip is black. In flight, has pale wing bar that does not extend to primary
coverts as in other large plovers. Juv. has small wattles and streaked forehead. **Habitat:**
Wetland margins and adjacent grasslands. **Status:** Fairly common. **Voice:** High-pitched,
ringing 'keep-keep'; regularly calls at night. [C6.36, G2.11.10]

leucoptera

1

juv.

2

3

4

5

6

1 SENEGAL (LESSER BLACK-WINGED) LAPWING (PLOVER)
Vanellus lugubris   22-26 cm
Smaller than Black-winged Lapwing, with a narrow black border to the grey breast, less
white on the forehead and a slight greenish tinge to the upperparts. Legs are dull red-brown.
In flight, white secondaries are diagnostic. Juv. is paler above, spotted with buff. **Habitat:**
Open, short-grass savanna, often in recently burned areas. **Status:** Uncommon resident and
local migrant. **Voice:** Clear, double-noted 'tee-yoo, tee-yoo'. [C6.39, G2.11.6]

2 BLACK-WINGED LAPWING (PLOVER) *Vanellus melanopterus*   26-27 cm
Larger than Senegal Lapwing, with more extensive white on the forehead (almost reaching
to the eye), redder legs and a broader black border separating the breast from the belly. In
flight, has broad white wing bar and black secondaries. Female has narrower breast band and
less white on forehead. Juv. is browner, with buff edges to upperparts. **Habitat:** Grassland;
restricted to high elevations in E Africa, but down to sea level in S. **Status:** Fairly common
resident and local migrant. **Voice:** Shrill, piping 'ti-tirree', higher pitched than Senegal
Lapwing's. [G2.11.7]

3 CROWNED LAPWING (PLOVER) *Vanellus coronatus*   29-31 cm
A mostly brown lapwing, with a black cap interrupted by a white 'halo'. Legs and bill base are
bright pink-red. Sandy brown breast is separated from white belly by black band. Juv. has
scalloped upperparts, buff-barred crown and pale yellowish legs and bill base. **Habitat:** Open
country; not associated with water. Favours short grassland, fields and fallow land. **Status:**
Common; regularly found with Black-winged Lapwing. **Voice:** Noisy; loud, grating 'kreep', day
and night. [C6.40, G2.11.5]

4 BROWN-CHESTED LAPWING (PLOVER) *Vanellus superciliosus*   23 cm
A small, dark-legged lapwing with a dark cap, grey face, neck and upper breast, and a diagnostic broad chestnut breast band. Adult has small yellow wattle at base of bill. Juv. is
duller, lacking black crown and white eye-stripe, and brown upperparts are fringed with
rufous. **Habitat:** Short grassland and parks. **Status:** Uncommon resident and intra-African
migrant. **Voice:** Rapid, harsh, 'chi-chi-chi' in flight. [C6.38]

5 SPOT-BREASTED LAPWING (PLOVER) *Vanellus melanocephalus*   34 cm
Endemic to Ethiopian highlands. Easily identified by black crown, throat and foreneck, and
black-speckled upper breast. Legs are yellow. Similar to Black-winged Lapwing in flight, but
head pattern is diagnostic. Juv. is undescribed. **Habitat:** Moorland, grassland and marshes
above 1 800 m. **Status:** Locally common; flocks of up to 40 birds form outside breeding
season; may be some altitudinal movement. **Voice:** 2-note 'pew-eep'; longer 'kree kree kre
krep kreep kreep'.

juv.

juv.

juv.

Cryptic waders that favour muddy wetlands with emergent vegetation. Identification extremely tricky. Sexes differ in painted snipes; alike in true snipes.

1 GREATER PAINTED SNIPE *Rostratula benghalensis*   24-28 cm
Differs from true snipes by having white eye-ring extending onto ear coverts, dark breast band and obvious white breast extending up onto shoulder. Bill is shorter and slightly decurved, and legs are longer than those of the snipes. Female is dominant sex and is more strikingly marked, with rich chestnut neck and breast and uniform upperparts. Male and juv. are more cryptic, with buff spotting on upperparts and conspicuous golden 'V' on back. Flight is slow, on large, broad wings, with legs often trailing. **Habitat:** Marshes and flooded grassland. **Status:** Uncommon resident and local nomad. **Voice:** Silent when flushed; female gives soft 'wuk-oooooo', repeated monotonously, often at night. [C6.19, G2.10.2]

2 GREAT SNIPE *Gallinago media*   28-30 cm
A large, chunky snipe with a relatively short, heavy bill. Told from other African snipes by its boldly barred flanks and vent. When flushed, tends to fly directly away, not jinking like African and Common snipes. Bill is held more level in flight. Adult has large white tips to upperwing coverts forming prominent white wing bars and white outer-tail feathers. Juv. is more heavily barred below, has reduced white spots on wing coverts, and has barred outer-tail. **Habitat:** Marshes and flooded grassland. **Status:** Uncommon Palearctic migrant Oct-May. **Voice:** Generally silent; occasionally utters one or two short croaks deeper than African Snipe's when flushed. [C2.43, G2.14.4]

3 COMMON SNIPE *Gallinago gallinago*   25-27 cm
Similar to African Snipe, but is slightly paler above and has much less white in outer-tail (white confined to tail tips and outer margin of outer-tail feather). Bill is slightly shorter and wings are longer and more pointed. Has explosive, zig-zag flight when flushed. **Habitat:** Swamps, marshes and seasonally flooded grasslands. **Status:** Common Palearctic migrant Oct-Mar. **Voice:** Loud 'scraap' on flushing; more rasping than African Snipe's. [C2.42] **Similar species: Pintail Snipe** *G. stenura* has a narrow, pale grey trailing edge to secondaries in flight (obvious and white in Common Snipe) and toes project slightly beyond tail tip; at rest is slightly paler and has broader pale eye-stripe at base of bill. Rare vagrant to E Africa.

4 AFRICAN (ETHIOPIAN) SNIPE *Gallinago nigripennis*   28-30 cm
Darker above than Common Snipe, and having heavily streaked neck and breast more contrasting with white belly. In flight, shows more white in outer-tail (five outer-tail feathers barred black and white), and pale fringes to greater coverts contrast more with darker wings. Wings are shorter and broader and bill is slightly longer. When flushed flight is more erratic than Great Snipe. **Habitat:** Marshes and flooded grassland, usually in muddy areas with short vegetation. **Status:** Common resident and local nomad. **Voice:** Sucking 'scaap' when flushed; males produce whirring, drumming sound with their stiffened outer-tail feathers during aerial display flights. [C6.42, G2.14.5]

5 JACK SNIPE *Lymnocryptes minimus*   19 cm
A small, relatively short-billed, narrow-winged snipe. Unlike other African snipes, its crown lacks a pale central stripe and it has a double pale supercilium above eye. Uppertail is wholly dark. Flushes less readily than other snipes, preferring to freeze and rely on camouflage. Flight is relatively slow and weak. **Habitat:** Waterlogged areas with short grass or sedges. **Status:** Uncommon Palearctic migrant, mostly Oct-Mar. **Voice:** Generally silent; faint 'gah' sometimes given on flushing. [C2.41]

A diverse group of long-legged and long-billed shorebirds. Often occur in large, mixed-species flocks. Smaller species require careful attention to plumage characters and jizz. Sexes alike, but migrant species have distinct breeding plumages; female's bills longer in many species. Juvs distinctive, usually with buff-fringed upperpart feathers.

1 BLACK-WINGED STILT Himantopus himantopus   38 cm
A black-and-white wader with very long red legs and a very thin, pointed, black bill. In flight, black underwings contrast with white underparts, and long legs trail conspicuously. Head and neck vary from pure white to predominantly dusky. Juv. has greyish nape, grey-pink legs and brownish wings with pale trailing edge. **Habitat:** Most wetlands, both fresh and salt water. **Status:** Common nomadic resident. **Voice:** Harsh, short 'kik-kik', especially when alarmed; very vocal in defence of nest and young. [C2.17a, G2.15.5]

2 PIED AVOCET Recurvirostra avosetta   43 cm
Large white-and-black wader; superficially resembles Crab Plover (p. 152), but long, very thin, upturned bill is unmistakable. In flight, long, bluish-grey legs extend beyond tail. Underwing is black only at tip. Juv. has mottled brown back. Feeds by sweeping bill from side to side; often swims, upending duck-like, in deeper water. **Habitat:** Most wetlands and occasionally along coast. **Status:** Common nomadic resident and Palearctic migrant in N; usually in small flocks. **Voice:** Clear 'kooit'; 'kik-kik' alarm call. [C2.17b, G2.15.4]

3 BLACK-TAILED GODWIT Limosa limosa   40 cm
A large, long-legged godwit with a plain back and a relatively long, almost straight, pink-based bill. Differs from Bar-tailed Godwit by having black (not barred) tail and obvious white wing bar. In breeding plumage, neck and upper breast are chestnut and belly is barred. Juv. is buffy below. **Habitat:** Lakes, estuaries and rice paddies; regularly forages in deep water. **Status:** Common Palearctic migrant in N, scarce in S, mostly Sep-Apr. **Voice:** Repeated 'weeka-weeka', given especially in flight. [C2.45, G2.14.6] **Similar species: Hudsonian Godwit** L. haemastica has similar flight pattern but white wing bar is smaller and underwing coverts are black; Nearctic vagrant.

4 BAR-TAILED GODWIT Limosa lapponica   38 cm
Slightly smaller than Black-tailed Godwit, with a shorter, upturned bill and appreciably shorter legs. Back and wing coverts have distinct pale fringes, making upperparts appear streaked. In flight, shows thin brown tail bars and white rump extending up back, and lacks bold white wing bar of Black-tailed Godwit. In breeding plumage, head, neck and underparts are deep chestnut. Juv. is buffy below. **Habitat:** Estuaries and coastal lagoons; rare inland. **Status:** Fairly common Palearctic migrant, especially along the W coast, mostly Aug-Apr. **Voice:** 'Wik-wik' or 'kirrik' call, often given in flight. [C2.46, G2.14.7]

5 EURASIAN CURLEW Numenius arquata   53-59 cm
The largest wader, with a long, decurved bill. Paler than Whimbrel, with much longer bill and plain (not striped) head. In flight, shows conspicuous white rump which extends up back, and pale inner wing contrasting with darker outer wing. **Habitat:** Large estuaries and lagoons; scarce inland but regular at Rift Valley lakes. **Status:** Fairly common Palearctic migrant, mostly Aug-Apr; numbers have decreased in S of range. **Voice:** Loud 'cur-lew'. [C2.49, G2.14.9]

6 WHIMBREL Numenius phaeopus   40-43 cm
A large wader with a strongly decurved bill. Told from Eurasian Curlew by shorter bill (which is decurved along full length, not only towards tip), darker coloration and striped (not uniform) head. In flight, shows white rump and back, and more uniform upperwing than Eurasian Curlew. Juv. has scalloped upperparts. **Habitat:** Coastal wetlands and, to lesser extent, open shores; scarce inland. **Status:** Common Palearctic migrant, mostly Aug-Apr, but many year round. **Voice:** Bubbling, whistled 'whiri-iri-iri-iri-iri'; highly vocal in non-breeding season. [C2.47, G2.14.10] **Similar species: Upland Sandpiper** Bartramia longicauda is smaller with yellowish legs and a much shorter bill; superficially Ruff-like, but behaviour plover-like. Nearctic vagrant.

head pattern varies

1

juv.

2

juv.

non-br.

non-br.

br.

3

non-br.

br.

non-br.

4

non-br.

6

5

juv.

1 SPOTTED REDSHANK *Tringa erythropus* 29-32 cm
A large, long-billed wader with long red legs. Larger and paler than Common Redshank, with uniform upperwing and longer bill, with only the base of the lower mandible red. Head has distinct black line from bill to eye and pale supercilium. In flight, has white back and finely barred rump. In breeding plumage, body is black, finely spotted and scalloped with white. Juv. is more extensively barred grey below. **Habitat:** Wetlands and sheltered coastal sites. **Status:** Common Palearctic migrant in N, vagrant in S; mostly Oct-May. **Voice:** Clear, double-noted 'tu wik'. [C2.51, G2.12.7]

2 COMMON REDSHANK *Tringa totanus* 27-29 cm
Smaller and darker than Spotted Redshank, with a shorter bill, brighter orange-red legs and diagnostic white secondaries and outer primaries; also, base of both mandibles red, and face is less marked. In flight, has white back and finely barred rump. Underparts are boldly streaked in breeding plumage. Juv. is browner, with duller red legs and bill base. **Habitat:** Freshwater and coastal wetlands. **Status:** Fairly common Palearctic migrant, mainly along the coast and Rift Valley lakes. **Voice:** 'Teu-hu-hu', first syllable higher pitched. [C2.52, G2.12.8]

3 MARSH SANDPIPER *Tringa stagnatilis* 22-25 cm
A medium-sized, pale grey wader. Smaller and more slender than Common Greenshank, with much thinner, straight, black bill, and proportionally longer legs. White back and rump are conspicuous in flight. Non-breeding Wilson's Phalarope (p.180) has much shorter, yellow (not grey-green) legs and dark back in flight. **Habitat:** Wetlands. **Status:** Common Palearctic migrant, mostly Aug-Apr. **Voice:** High-pitched 'yeup', often repeated; higher-pitched and less strident than Common Greenshank's. [C2.53, G2.12.9] **Similar species: Lesser Yellowlegs** *T. flavipes* has orange-yellow legs, heavier bill with pale base and dark back in flight; Nearctic vagrant.

4 COMMON GREENSHANK *Tringa nebularia* 30-35 cm
A large wader with greenish legs. Larger than Marsh Sandpiper, with a heavier, slightly upturned bill with grey-green base. In flight, shows white rump and back. Juv. is darker above. **Habitat:** Coastal and freshwater wetlands. **Status:** Common Palearctic migrant, mostly Aug-Apr, but many year round. **Voice:** Loud, slightly rasping 'chew-chew-chew'. [C2.54, G2.12.10] **Similar species: Greater Yellowlegs** *T. melanoleuca* has orange-yellow legs and dark back in flight; Nearctic vagrant.

5 RUFF *Philomachus pugnax* m. 30 cm, f. 24 cm
A medium to large wader with conspicuous scaling on the upperparts. Leg colour varies from greenish-yellow to orange-red. Black, slightly decurved bill may show orange or reddish base, leading to possible confusion with redshanks, but these have white backs in flight and straight, longer bills. In flight, has dark back and distinctive white oval patches on either side of dark rump. Males sometime have white head and neck during non-breeding season. Juv. is buffier. **Habitat:** Most wetlands; also forages in dry fields. Often swims in deep water. **Status:** Common Palearctic migrant, mostly Aug-May. **Voice:** Generally silent; occasional 'tooi' flight note. [C2.40, G2.14.3] **Similar species: Buff-breasted Sandpiper** *Tryngites subruficollis* is smaller, with buffy underparts and bright yellow legs; Nearctic vagrant.

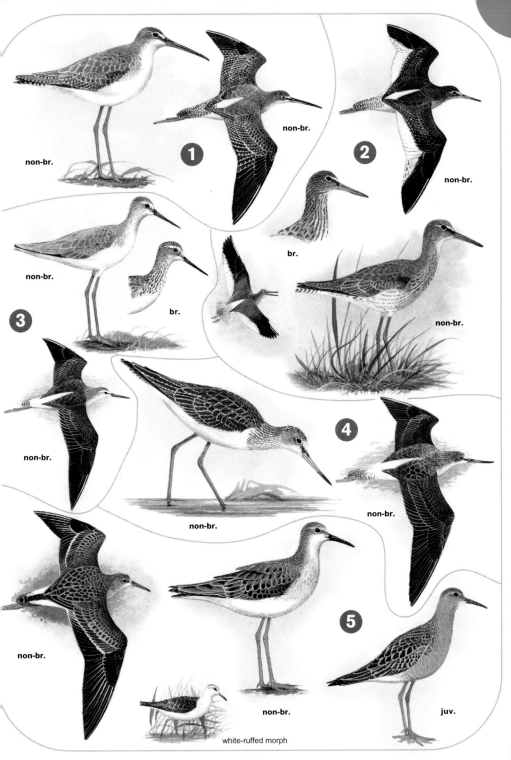

non-br.

1

non-br.

2

non-br.

non-br.

br.

3

br.

br.

non-br.

non-br.

4

non-br.

non-br.

non-br.

non-br.

5

non-br.

white-ruffed morph

juv.

1 GREEN SANDPIPER *Tringa ochropus* 21-24 cm

Larger than Wood and Common sandpipers, with blackish underwings and darker greenish upperparts, with fine pale spots. In flight, dark back contrasts with white rump, and tail barring is broader than Wood Sandpiper's. Juv. is browner above. **Habitat:** Mostly freshwater wetlands, but also sheltered coastal sites and mangroves. **Status:** Fairly common Palearctic migrant, mostly Aug-Apr. Scarce in S Africa. **Voice:** 3-note whistle, 'tew-a-tew'. [C2.55, G2.12.5] **Similar species: Solitary Sandpiper** *T. solitaria* has dark rump and barred undertail; Nearctic vagrant.

2 WOOD SANDPIPER *Tringa glareola* 20-22 cm

Intermediate in size between Common and Green sandpipers. Paler above than Green Sandpiper, with larger pale flecking; also, underwings are grey (not blackish), legs are yellower and pale supercilium extends behind eye. In flight, has dark back, white rump and finely barred tail. Juv. is warmer brown above. **Habitat:** Freshwater wetlands. **Status:** Common Palearctic migrant, mostly Aug-May. **Voice:** Highly vocal; high-pitched, slightly descending 'chiff-iff-iff'. [C2.56, G2.12.6]

3 COMMON SANDPIPER *Actitis hypoleucos* 18-20 cm

A fairly small, dark-backed wader with an obvious white shoulder in front of the closed wing. Smaller and shorter legged than Wood and Green sandpipers, with no pale spotting above. In flight, has prominent white wing bar, dark rump and barred sides to dark tail. Regularly bobs tail. Flight comprises rapid bursts of shallow wing beats interspersed with short glides on slightly bowed wings. **Habitat:** Wetlands and along coast. **Status:** Common Palearctic migrant, mostly Aug-Apr. **Voice:** Shrill 'ti-ti-ti', higher-pitched and thinner than Wood Sandpiper's. [C2.58, G2.12.4] **Similar species: Spotted Sandpiper** *A. macularia* is shorter tailed and slightly smaller and paler; Nearctic vagrant to W Africa.

4 TEREK SANDPIPER *Xenus cinerea* 22-25 cm

A medium-small wader with short yellow-orange legs and a long, upturned bill with an orange base. In flight, has white trailing edge to secondaries. Juv. is buffier above. **Habitat:** Muddy estuaries and lagoons, especially mangroves and areas with eel-grass (*Zostera*). **Status:** Common Palearctic migrant, mostly Aug-Apr. **Voice:** Series of fluty, uniformly pitched 'weet-weet-weet' notes. [C2.57, G2.12.3]

5 PECTORAL SANDPIPER *Calidris melanotos* 18-20 cm

A dark, medium to small wader, slightly smaller than Curlew Sandpiper (p. 178), with greenish-yellow (not dark grey) legs and yellow base to slightly decurved bill. Abrupt division between streaked breast and white belly is distinctive. Larger and longer-necked than the stints (p. 178), with dark-capped appearance. In flight, shows dark-centred rump with white sides. **Habitat:** Muddy fringes of wetlands. **Status:** Holarctic vagrant. **Voice:** Low trill, 'prrt'. [C2.35, G2.13.9]

6 RED KNOT *Calidris canutus* 23-25 cm

A short-legged, dumpy, rather plain wader. Larger than Curlew Sandpiper (p. 178), with shorter, straighter bill and greenish (not dark grey) legs. Smaller than Grey Plover (p. 164), with uniform grey (not speckled) back and longer bill. In flight, shows pale wing bar and rump is lightly barred grey. In breeding plumage, underparts are deep chestnut and upperparts are spangled with gold and black. **Habitat:** Estuaries and coastal lagoons; occasionally inland. **Status:** Locally common Palearctic migrant to W and S coast, mostly Aug-May; vagrant elsewhere. **Voice:** Soft 'knut'. [C2.30, G2.13.1] **Similar species: Great Knot** *C. tenuirostris* is larger with a much longer, heavier bill; Palearctic vagrant to W coast.

1

2

3

4

5

6

br.

br.

non-br.

br.

non-br.

1 CURLEW SANDPIPER *Calidris ferruginea*   19-23 cm
An abundant, small to medium wader with an obviously decurved bill. In flight, shows square white rump. In breeding plumage, underparts and face are chestnut-red. Juv. has buffy edgings to upperpart feathers. **Habitat:** Coastal and freshwater wetlands, usually in flocks. **Status:** Abundant Palearctic migrant, mostly Aug-May; many young birds remain year round. **Voice:** Short trill, 'chirrup'. [C2.36, G2.13.2] **Similar species: White-rumped Sandpiper** *C. fuscicollis* and **Baird's Sandpiper** *C. bairdii* are both smaller, with long wings extending well beyond tail tip at rest; former has white rump, latter dark rump with white sides; Nearctic vagrants.

2 DUNLIN *Calidris alpina*   15-22 cm
Larger than the stints, with a longer, more decurved bill. Best separated from Curlew Sandpiper by dark stripe down centre of rump. Bill is generally shorter and less curved, but this is variable: females have longer bill in both species. Pale eye-stripe is less marked than Curlew Sandpiper's, and it lacks striped head of Broad-billed Sandpiper (p. 180). In breeding plumage, has black belly patch and chestnut back. **Habitat:** Coastal wetlands and large inland lakes and rivers. **Status:** Common Palearctic migrant in NW and along Nile River; uncommon elsewhere. **Voice:** Weak 'treep'. [C2.38, G2.13.3]

3 LITTLE STINT *Calidris minuta*   13-15 cm
The most abundant stint. Very similar to Red-necked Stint, but with longer, less stubby bill and broader dark centres to upperpart feathers; in breeding plumage, has pale (not rufous) throat with vertical dark streaking. Legs are black (greenish in Temminck's and Long-toed stints). In flight, has narrow white wing bar and white sides to rump. **Habitat:** Estuaries, lagoons and freshwater wetlands. **Status:** Common Palearctic migrant, mostly Aug–May. **Voice:** Short, sharp 'schit'. [C2.32, G2.13.4]

4 RED-NECKED STINT *Calidris ruficollis*   13-16 cm
Very difficult to separate from Little Stint, except in breeding plumage, when throat, neck and cheeks are rufous and lack vertical dark streaking. In non-breeding plumage, upperparts are pale grey, with narrow dark feather shafts. Bill is shorter and stubbier than Little Stint's, and wings are slightly longer. Often appears more chunky due to crouched posture. Legs are black. **Habitat:** Muddy fringes of wetlands and saltpans. **Status:** Very rare Palearctic migrant, mostly Oct-Apr. **Voice:** Short 'chit' or 'prrp'. [G2.13.6]

5 TEMMINCK'S STINT *Calidris temminckii*   13-15 cm
A plain-backed stint with greenish legs and a diagnostic white outer-tail. Appears more elongate than Little Stint, and is paler above than Long-toed Stint. Bill has slight droop at tip. Juv's upperpart feathers are edged with buff. **Habitat:** Muddy edges of freshwater wetlands, often in small openings among vegetation. **Status:** Uncommon Palearctic migrant. **Voice:** Shrill 'prrrtt'. [C2.33, G2.13.10]

6 LONG-TOED STINT *Calidris subminuta*   14 cm
Yellowish (not dark grey) legs separate this species from all stints except Temminck's. Upperpart feathers have broad dark centres (in non-breeding plumage) or are broadly edged rufous (in breeding plumage), giving much more marked back than Temminck's Stint; also, outer-tail is dark (not white). Legs and neck are relatively long. **Habitat:** Muddy fringes of wetlands. **Status:** Very rare Palearctic migrant. **Voice:** Soft 'chirrup'; sharp 'tik-ik-ik'. [G2.13.5]

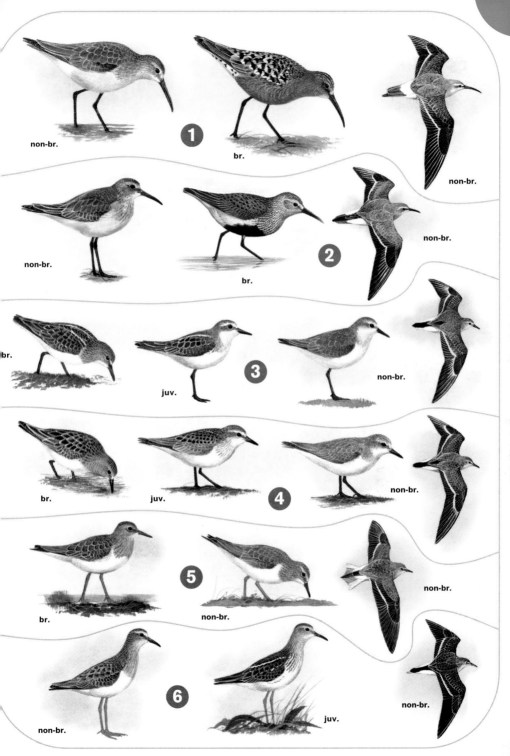

non-br.

br.

non-br.

①

non-br.

non-br.

②

br.

br.

juv.

③

non-br.

br.

juv.

④

non-br.

br.

non-br.

⑤

non-br.

non-br.

⑥

juv.

non-br.

179

1 SANDERLING *Calidris alba* 19-21 cm
A fairly small wader with a short, stubby, black bill and a dark carpal patch. Larger than Broad-billed Sandpiper, with shorter bill, and no head stripes. In non-breeding plumage is pale grey above and white below. In breeding plumage, upperparts and breast are chestnut and black. In flight, shows distinct white wing bar and darker line through white rump. **Habitat:** Mainly sandy beaches, also rocky shores and coastal wetlands; rare inland. **Status:** Common Palearctic migrant, mostly Aug-Apr. **Voice:** Single, decisive 'wick'. [C2.31, G2.14.1]

2 BROAD-BILLED SANDPIPER *Limicola falcinellus* 17 cm
A small, short-legged wader, slightly larger than the stints (p. 178), with a diagnostic pale double supercilium. Bill is relatively long and broad, with drooped, flattened tip. Legs are dark greenish-grey. In non-breeding plumage, is pale grey above, with dark shoulder patch (less pronounced than in Sanderling). In breeding plumage, upperparts are blackish with rufous feather margins. Juv. is darker and browner above than non-breeding ad. **Habitat:** Estuaries and muddy lake shores. **Status:** Uncommon Palearctic migrant, mostly Aug-Apr. **Voice:** Low-pitched, short trill, 'drrrt'. [C2.39, G2.14.2]

3 WILSON'S PHALAROPE *Steganopus tricolor* 22-24 cm
Larger than other phalaropes, with a longer bill and yellow legs. In non-breeding plumage, lacks distinct black eye patch; superficially resembles Marsh Sandpiper (p. 174) but has much shorter, yellow legs. In flight, white rump contrasts with grey tail and back; has no wing bar. In breeding plumage, sides of breast and mantle are washed rufous; female is more brightly coloured than male. Juv. has darker and more scalloped upperparts. **Habitat:** Coastal wetlands; swims less than other phalaropes. **Status:** Nearctic vagrant. **Voice:** Short, grunting 'grrg'. [C2.60, G2.15.3]

4 RED-NECKED (NORTHERN) PHALAROPE *Phalaropus lobatus* 18-20 cm
Slightly smaller than Red Phalarope, with a darker grey back streaked with white, and a longer, thinner, all-black (not yellow-based) bill. In flight, rump is black, fringed with white (not grey). Body is dark grey in breeding plumage, with rufous neck band; female is more brightly coloured than male. Juv. is browner, with more scalloped upperparts. **Habitat:** At sea off E Africa; also lakes, saltpans and sewage works. **Status:** Common Palearctic migrant to E Africa, mostly Oct-Apr; scarce elsewhere. **Voice:** Low 'tchick' in flight. [C2.61, G2.15.2]

5 RED (GREY) PHALAROPE *Phalaropus fulicarius* 18-20 cm
Larger and paler than Red-necked Phalarope, with a shorter, thicker bill that is broad to the tip and may show a yellow base. Back and rump are grey, but can look mottled in moulting birds. In breeding plumage, has chestnut underparts and white face; female is more brightly coloured than male. Juv. is browner, with more scalloped upperparts. **Habitat:** At sea off W coast; stragglers occur on lakes. **Status:** Fairly common Palearctic migrant to W coast, mostly Oct-Apr; vagrant elsewhere. **Voice:** Soft, low 'wiit'. [C2.62, G2.15.1]

6 RUDDY TURNSTONE *Arenaria interpres* 23 cm
A stocky, short-billed wader with orange legs. White belly and lower breast contrast with blackish patches on upper breast. In breeding plumage, has rich chestnut back and striking black-and-white patterned head and neck. In flight, appears boldly black and white above, with strong white wing bar, white back stripes and rump, and black tail with narrow white tip. **Habitat:** Rocky shores and estuaries, occasionally on sandy shores and coastal lagoons; rare inland. **Status:** Common Palearctic migrant, mostly Aug-Apr. **Voice:** Hard 'kttuck', especially in flight. [C2.59, G2.12.2]

non-br.

1

br.

non-br.

non-br.

2

br.

non-br.

non-br.

juv.

3

non-br.

br. ♀

br. ♀

4

non-br.

non-br.

non-br.

non-br.

♂

br.

♀

5

non-br.

non-br.

non-br.

non-br.

6

br.

non-br.

Pelagic, gull-like seabirds; often steal food from other seabirds. Smaller jaegers have pale and dark morphs as well as distinctive breeding, non-breeding and juv. plumages. Larger skuas less varied, but species differences subtle. Sexes alike.

1 SUBANTARCTIC (BROWN) SKUA *Catharacta antarctica*   60-64 cm
A large, heavy-bodied skua with large white wing flashes (reduced in juv.). Generally lacks dark cap of very similar Great Skua. Short, broad wings and short rump and tail distinguish it from jaegers. Upperparts are variably streaked and blotched buff; plainer in juv. Larger, chunkier and heavier-billed than rare dark-morph South Polar Skua, which has only sparse, fine pale streaking on upperparts. Race *lonnbergi* is most frequent visitor but at least some *antarctica/hamiltoni* occur; separation in the field is obscure. **Habitat:** Open ocean; regularly scavenges at trawlers. **Status:** Common migrant in S, most abundant Apr-Sep. Status in N Atlantic uncertain, but probably regular off Senegal. **Voice:** Generally silent. [G3.1.10]

2 GREAT SKUA *Catharacta skua*   53-58 cm
Apparently restricted to N Atlantic. A large, dark brown skua, typically with a dark cap; is often more streaked and blotched above than Subantarctic Skua, but juvs probably inseparable in the field. Dark cap, straw-coloured hackles, broad rufous streaking and bulky build separate it from dark-morph South Polar Skua. Juv. is plainer, with less white in wing; best told from dark-morph South Polar Skua by its heavier bill and shape. **Habitat:** Open ocean; follows ships. **Status:** Fairly common Palearctic migrant Oct-Mar. **Voice:** Silent away from breeding grounds. [C2.66]

3 SOUTH POLAR SKUA *Catharacta maccormicki*   52-54 cm
Smaller and more slender than other *Catharacta* skuas; body shape recalls Pomarine Jaeger. Pale streaks on neck and back are fine and sparse compared to adults of other skuas. Head, neck and breast colour varies from ash (pale morph) to dark brown (dark morph). Pale morph is identified by contrast between dark wings and pale head and body. Dark morph differs from juv. skuas by smaller bill and plain plumage; often has paler, greyish feathers at base of bill. Intermediate birds are variable, but often show pale hindneck. Sits more upright on water than other large skuas. **Habitat:** Open sea; more pugnacious than other skuas. **Status:** Rare passage migrant. **Voice:** Silent in Africa. [G3.2.1]

4 POMARINE JAEGER (SKUA) *Stercorarius pomarinus*   48 cm (+8 cm tail)
Larger and more barrel-chested than other jaegers; wings are relatively broad, with large white wing flashes. Bill is stout. Flight is direct and powerful. Breeding adult is identified by spoon-shaped (not pointed) central tail feathers. Pale morph is much more common; has darker back than other pale-morph jaegers. Non-breeding birds are often barred on belly, flanks and rump. Juv. and imm. have boldly barred underwing. Steals food from gannets, terns and other seabirds, but also scavenges. **Habitat:** Coastal waters; rarely far from land; occasionally roosts ashore. **Status:** Common Palearctic migrant to W coast, mostly Oct-Apr; scarce off E coast; vagrant to Rift Valley lakes. **Voice:** Silent in Africa. [C2.63, G3.1.9]

5 PARASITIC JAEGER (ARCTIC SKUA) *Stercorarius parasiticus*   46-67 cm
A medium-sized jaeger with white wing flashes, intermediate in shape and jizz between larger, darker Pomarine Jaeger and smaller, paler Long-tailed Jaeger (which lacks prominent wing flashes). If present, central tail feathers are relatively short and straight. Pale, dark and intermediate colour morphs occur. Juv. has browner underwing, less strongly barred than other jaegers. Steals food from terns and gulls. **Habitat:** Coastal waters; occasionally roosts ashore. **Status:** Common Palearctic migrant, mostly Oct-Apr. **Voice:** Silent in Africa. [C2.64, G3.1.7]

6 LONG-TAILED JAEGER (SKUA) *Stercorarius longicaudus* 38 cm (+20 cm tail)
A small, short-necked, round-headed jaeger. Almost all birds are pale morphs. Adults are plain, cold greyish above. Elongated central tail feathers are diagnostic in breeding plumage. Flight is buoyant and tern-like on long, slender wings. From above, only shafts of outer two primaries are white. Bill is short; at close range, nail (upper mandible tip) comprises roughly half bill length (less than a third in other jaegers). Juv. has boldly barred uppertail coverts and underwing. Scavenges at trawlers; seldom harries other seabirds. **Habitat:** Oceanic waters; scarce close to land. **Status:** Fairly common Palearctic migrant to oceanic waters off S Africa, mostly Nov-Apr; scarce further N off Africa; migration route unknown. **Voice:** Silent in Africa. [C2.65, G3.1.8]

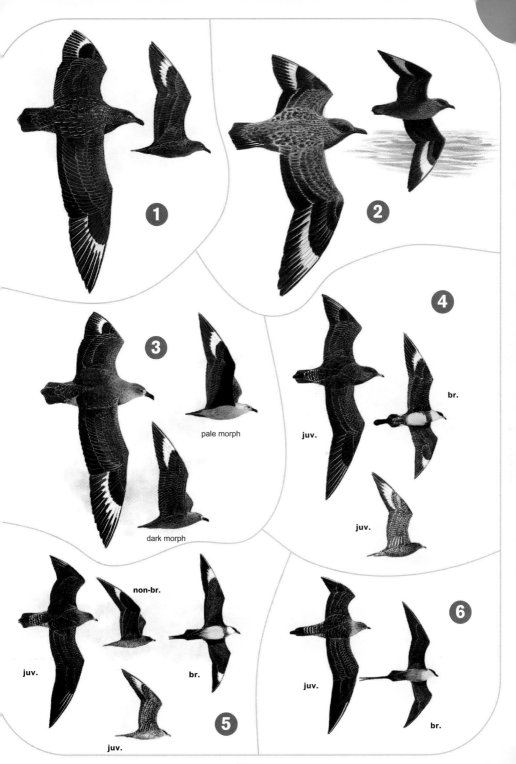

1

2

3

pale morph

dark morph

4

juv.

br.

juv.

non-br.

juv.

br.

juv.

5

6

juv.

br.

juv.

183

Familiar coastal birds. Relatively few species breed in Africa, but many Palearctic species winter in the region. Taxonomy of some groups in flux. Sexes alike; large species have complex juv. and imm. plumages.

1 CAPE GULL Larus vetula   55-65 cm

A large, black-backed gull. Body is heavier and wings are shorter than Lesser Black-backed Gull's. Bill is large. Adult's eye is dark grey-brown (rarely yellow or silver-grey); legs are olive-grey. Imm. and juv. are heavily streaked dark brown; legs are brownish-pink. Dark wings and pale, barred rump separates it from skuas. Takes approximately three years to reach adult plumage. **Habitat:** Coast and adjacent wetlands; follows trawlers up to 100 km from shore. Increasingly found on fields up to 50 km inland. **Status:** Common in S Africa; isolated population in W Africa. **Voice:** Loud 'ki-ok'; short, repeated alarm call, 'kwok'. [C6.46, G3.2.2] **Similar species: Kelp Gull** L. dominicanus has pale eye, smaller bill, steeper forehead and flat crown; rare winter vagrant to S Africa from sub-Antarctic islands.

2 HEUGLIN'S GULL Larus heuglini   58-65 cm

Often treated as a race of Lesser Black-backed Gull, but is larger and adults have a paler back (especially than nominate fuscus, with which its range mostly overlaps). Also has a longer bill and shallower forehead, giving a rakish appearance to the head. Adult's back is darker than Yellow-legged Gull's. Longer winged than Kelp Gull, appearing more attenuated; adults have bright yellow (not olive) legs and feet. Juvs and imms hard to differentiate: averages larger than Lesser Black-backed Gull and longer-winged than Cape Gull, with paler, flesh-coloured (not brownish) legs. **Habitat:** Coast and inland waterbodies. **Status:** Fairly common Palearctic migrant, mostly Oct-Apr. **Voice:** Similar to Lesser Black-backed Gull's.

3 LESSER BLACK-BACKED GULL Larus fuscus   51-61 cm

Large Palearctic migrant gull. Smaller than Cape Gull with a less robust bill and more slender appearance, with the wings projecting well beyond the tail at rest; adults have bright yellow (not olive-grey) legs and feet. Two races occur: fuscus is slightly smaller and adults have a very dark grey or black back; they mostly migrate down the east coast and Rift Valley, whereas graellsii is slightly larger, with dark slate-grey adults that mostly winter in W Africa (rarely to Rift Valley). Very similar to Heuglin's Gull in E Africa, but is slightly smaller, with adults having a darker back, shorter bill and less rakish head shape. Juvs and imms hard to differentiate, although averages smaller than Heuglin's and Yellow-legged gulls and longer-winged than Cape Gull with paler, flesh-coloured (not brownish) legs. **Habitat:** Coast and inland waterbodies. **Status:** Fairly common Palearctic migrant, mostly Oct-Apr. **Voice:** Typical, large-gull 'kow-kow'; shorter 'kop'. [C2.74, G3.2.3]

4 YELLOW-LEGGED GULL Larus cachinnans   59-68 cm

A large, fairly long-winged gull. Adult pale grey above, paler than Heuglin's Gull, with yellow legs. Non-breeding adults have much less head and neck streaking than Heuglin's and Lesser Black-backed gulls. Juvs and imms similar to Heuglin's and Lesser Black-backed gulls; identification characters unresolved. Recently split from Herring Gull L. argentatus, but probably closer to Lesser Black-backed Gull. Herring Gull formerly listed in error from S Africa. **Habitat:** Coast and estuaries. **Status:** Palearctic migrant, mostly Oct-Mar; western michahellis regular in small numbers in NW; eastern cachinnans (sometimes treated as a separate species, Pontic Gull) likely to occur along the Red Sea coast and possibly farther S on the E coast. **Voice:** Loud, yelping 'kleeuw' and 'kyi-ki-ki-ki-ki'. [C2.76]

5 GREAT BLACK-HEADED GULL Larus ichthyaetus   57-61 cm

A large, long-winged gull with a 'long-bodied' appearance. Much larger than Sooty Gull (p. 188) with paler upperparts. Bill is very large, with dark subterminal bar at all ages. Head profile is diagnostic: flat crown, shallow forehead with a slight bump, and feathering extending far down bill. All ages show incomplete white eye-ring. **Habitat:** Open coast and lake shores. **Status:** Uncommon Palearctic migrant, mostly Dec-Mar. **Voice:** Deep, croaking 'kuraaak'.

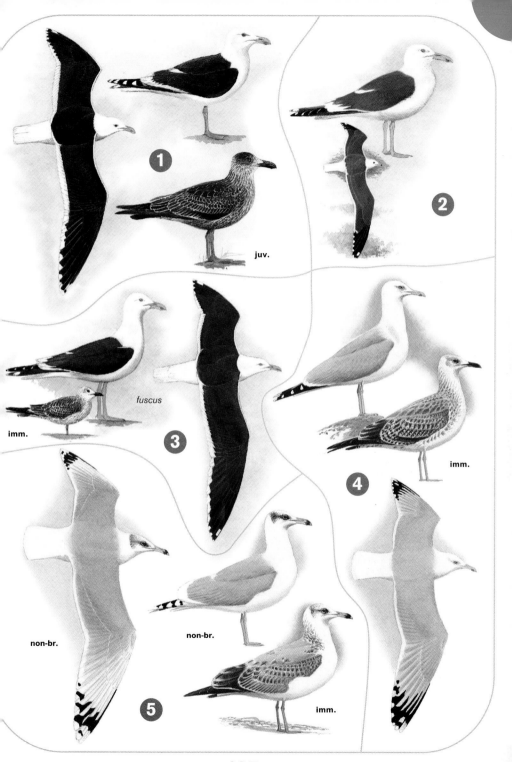

1

juv.

2

fuscus

imm.

3

imm.

4

non-br.

non-br.

5

imm.

1 GREY-HEADED GULL *Larus cirrocephalus*   40-42 cm
Adult has diagnostic pale grey head (darker in breeding season). Larger than Hartlaub's Gull, with longer and brighter red bill and legs. Eyes are pale silver-yellow, with narrow red outer ring. In flight, outer primaries are mostly black and underwing is grey. Imm. has extensive dark-smudged ear coverts and dark-tipped, pink-orange bill. Juv. is heavily mottled brown above. **Habitat:** Open coast, and coastal and freshwater wetlands. **Status:** Locally common. **Voice:** Typical 'karrh' and 'pok-pok'. [C2.69, G3.2.5]

2 HARTLAUB'S GULL *Larus hartlaubii*   36-38 cm
Endemic to S Africa. Slightly smaller than Grey-headed Gull, with a shorter, thinner and darker bill and deeper red legs. In flight, outer primaries are mostly black and underwing is grey. Eye is dark at all ages; rare birds with pale eyes may be hybrids with Grey-headed Gull. Breeding birds have slight lavender shadow line demarcating hood; non-breeding birds have plain white head. Imm. has uniform dark bill and darker legs; sometimes shows small dark patches on ear coverts. Juv. is mottled brown above, but less so than Grey-headed Gull. Active at night. **Habitat:** Inshore waters, coastline, estuaries, urban areas and flooded fields. **Status:** Common. **Voice:** Drawn-out, rattling 'kaaarrh' and 'pok-pok'. [G3.2.6]

3 COMMON BLACK-HEADED GULL *Larus ridibundus*   38-44 cm
Paler grey above than Grey-headed Gull; in flight, has mostly white outer primaries (but aberrant Hartlaub's and Grey-headed gulls can also show this) and whitish (not grey) underwings. Breeding adult has dark brown hood and partial white eye-ring; bill is dark red. Non-breeding birds have dark smudges on head and paler red bill with dark tip. Franklin's Gull is darker grey above, with distinct wing pattern. Juv. has mottled brown wing coverts, dark subterminal tail band and dark trailing edges to wing. **Habitat:** Coasts and inland waters. **Status:** Locally common Palearctic migrant. **Voice:** Typical, small-gull 'kraah'. [C2.70, G3.2.9] **Similar species: Mediterranean Gull** *L. melanocephalus* is paler, with heavier bill; Palearctic vagrant. **Bonaparte's Gull** *L. philadelphia* is smaller with a black head and mostly black bill; Nearctic vagrant to NW Africa.

4 SLENDER-BILLED GULL *Larus genei*   36-46 cm
A small, white-headed gull. Head and bill profile are distinctive: shallow sloping forehead and long, red bill that droops slightly at the tip. Slightly larger than Hartlaub's Gull, with pale (not dark) eye. Washed pink below in breeding plumage. In flight, wing pattern resembles Common Black-headed Gull's, but body appears longer. Imm. has paler smudge behind eye than imm. Grey-headed and Common Black-headed gulls, and bill is uniform red. **Habitat:** Open coast and lakes in E African Rift Valley. **Status:** Locally common resident in W; uncommon Palearctic migrant in E. **Voice:** Repeated 'ka' or 'kra', deeper than Common Black-headed Gull's. [C2.71] **Similar species: Audouin's Gull** *L. audouinii* is much larger, with heavy red bill; Palearctic vagrant to NW coast.

5 FRANKLIN'S GULL *Larus pipixcan*   32-36 cm
A small, black-headed gull with a rather short, stubby bill. Always has at least partial black hood and white crescents above and below eye. Darker grey above than other small gulls. In flight, has broad white trailing edge to secondaries, and black subterminal band on primaries is separated from grey inner wing by white band. Underwings are whitish. Juv. has broad subterminal tail band and much darker wings, but still has broad white trailing edge to secondaries. **Habitat:** Coast, estuaries and inland waterbodies. **Status:** Nearctic vagrant. **Voice:** Silent in Africa. [C6.46] **Similar species: Laughing Gull** *L. atricilla* is larger, with longer bill and no white in outer primaries; Nearctic vagrant to NW African coast.

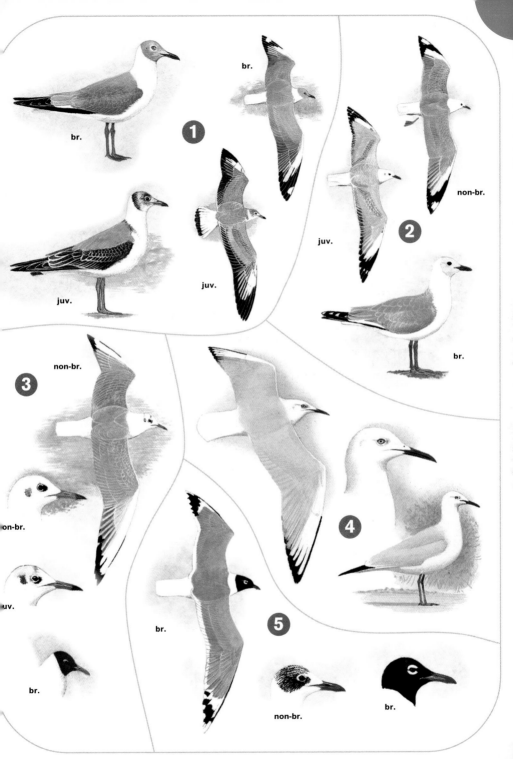

br.

br.

juv.

juv.

juv.

1

non-br.

juv.

2

br.

3

non-br.

non-br.

uv.

br.

br.

4

5

non-br.

br.

1 SABINE'S GULL *Xema sabini* 27-32 cm
A small, oceanic gull with a shallow-forked tail and buoyant, tern-like flight. In flight, boldly tri-coloured upperwing is diagnostic. Breeding adult has dark grey hood and yellow-tipped, black bill. Legs are black. Juv. has brownish upperparts, scaled white; in flight, shows darker upperwing coverts. Bill is black; legs are grey-pink. **Habitat:** Coastal waters, including large, sheltered bays. **Status:** Common Palearctic migrant, often in flocks. **Voice:** Silent in region. [G3.2.8] **Similar species: Black-legged Kittiwake** *Rissa tridactyla* is larger with only tips of primaries black; imm. has black 'M' across upperwing and black hindcollar; Palearctic vagrant to W coast. **Little Gull** *Larus minutus* is very small, with dark head, red legs, plain upperwing and dark underwing; imm. has dark 'M' on upperwing and dark head; Palearctic vagrant to W Africa. **Common Gull** *Larus canus* is larger, with pink legs, small bill and rounded head; Palearctic vagrant to W Africa.

2 WHITE-EYED GULL *Larus leucophthalmus* 39-43 cm
A dark, long-winged gull with a very long, slender, slightly downcurved bill; unique bill shape separates it from larger Sooty Gull at all ages. Adult has black hood, grey-smudged breast, large white crescents above and below eye, and dark red bill with black tip. Juv. has dull brown bill, dark subterminal tail band, and is browner above, slightly mottled on breast and upperparts. White eye crescents are visible at all ages. Typically forages at sea, and follows ships. **Habitat:** Breeds on islands in Red Sea, dispersing along E coast. **Status:** Locally common resident and short-distance migrant. **Voice:** Long, screaming 'kiooow'.

3 SOOTY (HEMPRICH'S) GULL *Larus hemprichii* 44-47 cm
A dark, long-winged gull. Larger than White-eyed Gull, but best separated by its much heavier bill. Basal two thirds of bill is yellow (in breeding adults) or pale grey, with dark subterminal band and reddish tip. Juv. is paler above than White-eyed Gull, with obviously two-tone bill and less obvious pale eye crescents. Smaller than imms of Herring/Lesser Black-backed Gull complex (p. 184), with grey legs and very long primary extension beyond tail tip. **Habitat:** Coast and inshore waters. **Status:** Common resident and partial migrant, commonest in S of range Oct-May. **Voice:** Drawn-out, screaming 'kleeeeeow'.

4 AFRICAN SKIMMER *Rynchops flavirostris* 38-40 cm
A long-winged, tern-like bird with a peculiar bill shape: lower mandible is much longer than upper; feeds by flying with lower mandible trailing in water. In flight, white trailing edge contrasts with dark upperwing and narrow white outer-tail. Juv. is browner above, with pale feather fringes; bill is blackish, gradually turning red. **Habitat:** Large rivers, bays and lakes with sandbanks for roosting and breeding. **Status:** Locally common resident and local migrant. **Voice:** Harsh 'rak-rak'. [C6.50, G3.5.3]

TERNS
Long-winged seabirds with loose, buoyant flight; feed by plunge-diving or surface seizing; also occasionally hawk insects in the air. Some species occur on freshwater wetlands. Sexes alike, but most species have distinct breeding, non-breeding and juv. plumages. Identified chiefly by size, structure and bill colour.

5 GULL-BILLED TERN *Sterna nilotica* 35-38 cm
A very pale, relatively long-legged tern with a short, stubby, black bill. Similar in size to Sandwich Tern (p. 190), but is heavier-bodied and broader-winged, with shorter, shallow-forked tail and all-black (not yellow-tipped) bill. Has full black cap in breeding plumage; non-breeding birds have only black smudge behind eye and crown is entirely white. Juv. is mottled brown above. **Habitat:** Coastal lagoons and wetlands; sometimes forages over adjacent fields and reedbeds. **Status:** Locally common breeding resident in NW Africa; fairly common Palearctic migrant elsewhere, mostly Aug-Apr. **Voice:** 'Kaak' and 'kek-kek'. [C2.82, G3.3.1]

non-br.

juv.

juv.

br.

br.

sub-ad.

juv.

juv.

non-br.

br.

br.

br.

1

2

3

4

5

1 CASPIAN TERN *Sterna caspia* 47-54 cm
The largest tern, with very heavy red or orange-red bill with black tip. In flight, dark primaries form large black tip to underwing. Cap is black in breeding plumage, variably streaked white in non-breeding plumage. Larger and darker above than Royal Tern, with heavier, redder bill and less deeply forked tail. Juv. has brown fringes to wing coverts, more grey in tail, and more extensive black tip to bill. **Habitat.** Virtually any large wetland and sheltered coastal waters. **Status:** Locally common breeding resident in W and S; Palearctic migrant elsewhere. **Voice:** Deep, harsh 'kraaak'. [C2.83, G3.3.2]

2 ROYAL TERN *Sterna maxima* 48 cm
A pale tern with an orange bill. Smaller than Caspian Tern, with more slender, relatively longer bill that lacks dark tip; in flight, primaries are greyish (not black) on underwing. Breeding birds have full black crown with shaggy crest; non-breeding birds have more extensive white forehead and crown than Caspian Tern. Paler upperparts and orange (not greenish-yellow) bill separate it from Swift Tern. Lesser Crested Tern is much smaller and has more slender bill. Juv. is mottled above. Imm. has dark carpal bar. **Habitat.** Coasts, bays and estuaries. **Status:** Breeding resident in W Africa, dispersing S to Angola. **Voice:** Loud, harsh 'ree-ack'. [C2.84, G3.3.3]

3 LESSER CRESTED TERN *Sterna bengalensis* 35-37 cm
A medium-sized tern (slightly smaller than Sandwich Tern), with a slender, orange-yellow bill. Smaller, more graceful and generally paler above than Swift Tern. Much smaller than Royal Tern, and bill is more slender and less orange. Juv. is mottled blackish-brown above. **Habitat.** Inshore waters, bays and estuaries. **Status:** Breeding resident Red Sea to Somalia; migrant along E coast and NW Africa. **Voice:** Hoarse 'kreck'. [C2.85, G3.3.5]

4 SWIFT (GREATER CRESTED) TERN *Sterna bergii* 46-49 cm
A large tern, similar in size to Royal Tern, but with a long, slightly drooped yellow or greenish-yellow (not orange) bill, and white frons in breeding plumage. Larger than Lesser Crested Tern, which also has orange-yellow bill. Non-breeding birds have white forecrown. Back colour varies from pale grey in S and SE to fairly dark grey in NE (*velox*). Juv. is mottled dark blackish-brown above and has dusky yellow-olive bill. Adult's legs are black; some juvs have yellow-orange legs. **Habitat.** Coastal waters, estuaries and coastal wetlands. **Status:** Common resident and local migrant. **Voice:** Adult's call is harsh 'kree-eck'; juv. gives thin, vibrating whistle. [G3.3.4]

5 SANDWICH TERN *Sterna sandvicensis* 36-41 cm
A very pale, medium to large tern, with long black bill with yellow tip. In flight, told from Gull-billed Tern (p. 188) by white (not grey) rump and more forked tail. In breeding plumage has black cap, and breast often has faint pinkish wash; non-breeding birds have white forecrown. Juv. is mottled above. **Habitat.** Coastal waters, estuaries and bays. **Status:** Common Palearctic migrant along W and S coasts, uncommon on central E coast, vagrant inland; breeds Red Sea to Somalia. **Voice:** 'Kirik'. [C2.86, G3.3.6]

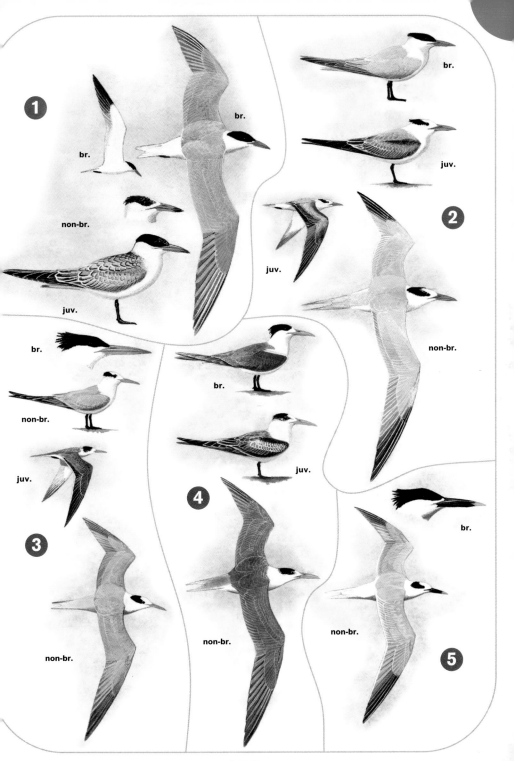

1

br.

br.

non-br.

juv.

br.

2

br.

juv.

juv.

non-br.

3

br.

non-br.

juv.

non-br.

br.

juv.

4

non-br.

br.

non-br.

5

1 ROSEATE TERN *Sterna dougallii* 33-38 cm
A very pale, medium-sized tern with a long, blackish, slightly drooped bill. Legs are slightly longer than Common Tern's. Underwing appears all white in flight. Breeding birds have full black cap, pink wash to breast, crimson legs, red bill base and long white outer-tail feathers projecting well beyond wings at rest. Non-breeding birds have white forecrown; best identified by long bill and pale colour. Juv. can be told from juv. Antarctic Tern by blacker cap, longer bill, greyer wings and more slender body. **Habitat.** Coastal waters. **Status:** Breeds Somalia to Tanzania and S Africa (rare); fairly common Palearctic migrant to W Africa. **Voice:** Grating 'aarh'. [C2.87, G3.3.10]

2 COMMON TERN *Sterna hirundo* 31-35 cm
The commonest medium-sized tern. Differs from Arctic and Antarctic terns by its longer bill and legs; non-breeding birds have greyish (not white) rump and tail; rump and tail contrast with darker grey back (White-cheeked Tern has uniform grey back and rump). Primaries have broader black webs than in Arctic and Antarctic terns, visible in flight as darker panel on upper- and underwing. In breeding plumage has black-tipped, red bill, light grey wash to breast and short tail streamers (level with folded wing tips). Bill is not as long or drooped as Roseate Tern's. Juv. is mottled brown above. Imm. retains conspicuous dark carpal bars. Orange-billed morph rare along E coast. **Habitat.** Coastal waters, adjacent wetlands and Rift Valley lakes; peculiar tropical W African population resident on large rivers. **Status:** Abundant Palearctic migrant, mostly Aug-Apr, but some imms year round. Breeds Mauretania and W African rivers. **Voice:** 'Kik-kik' and 'kee-arh'. [C2.88, G3.3.7]

3 ARCTIC TERN *Sterna paradisaea* 33-35 cm
Similar to Common Tern, but with a shorter bill and legs, white (not pale grey) rump and tail, and paler wing tips in flight. In breeding plumage, bill and legs are dark red and tail streamers extend beyond folded wing (but growing feathers are shorter). In non-breeding plumage, differs from Antarctic Tern by shorter, more delicate, black bill and black legs. Imm. lacks bold carpal bar, pale secondaries, and marked contrast between grey back and white rump, avoiding confusion with imm. Common Tern. **Habitat.** Pelagic; sometimes roosts ashore, usually with Common Terns. **Status:** Fairly common passage migrant along W coast, rare on E coast and vagrant inland. **Voice:** Short 'kik-kik' in flight. [C2.89, G3.3.8]

4 ANTARCTIC TERN *Sterna vittata* 34-36 cm
Dumpier than Arctic and Common terns, with a heavier bill. Rump is white (not grey as in White-cheeked Tern). Leg length varies among races but typically rather short. In breeding plumage, has full black cap, grey underparts and white cheek stripe; bill and legs are crimson. Non-breeding adults are paler grey below, with conspicuously white forecrown, but retain red bill (unlike black bill of non-breeding Common and Arctic terns; Imm. has black bill and legs; best told by heavy bill and dumpy body. Juv. has chequered brown, grey and white upperparts; differs from juv. Roseate Tern by its shorter, heavier bill and paler cap. **Habitat.** Coastal waters to shelf-break; often roosts ashore. **Status:** Fairly common migrant from Antarctica and the sub-Antarctic, mostly Apr-Oct. **Voice:** Sharp, high-pitched 'kik-kik'. [G3.3.9]

5 WHITE-CHEEKED TERN *Sterna repressa* 32-35 cm
A medium-sized tern, resembling a dark Common Tern. Uniform grey back, rump and tail distinguish it from Common, Arctic and Antarctic terns. In breeding plumage, is dark grey below, almost as dark as Whiskered Tern (p. 196), but is larger, with deeply forked tail and dusky grey (not white) vent. Imm. has very large dark carpal bar. **Habitat.** Coastal waters and islands; breeds Red Sea to Kenya; rarely occurs further S. **Status:** Locally common. **Voice:** Ringing 'kee-leck'.

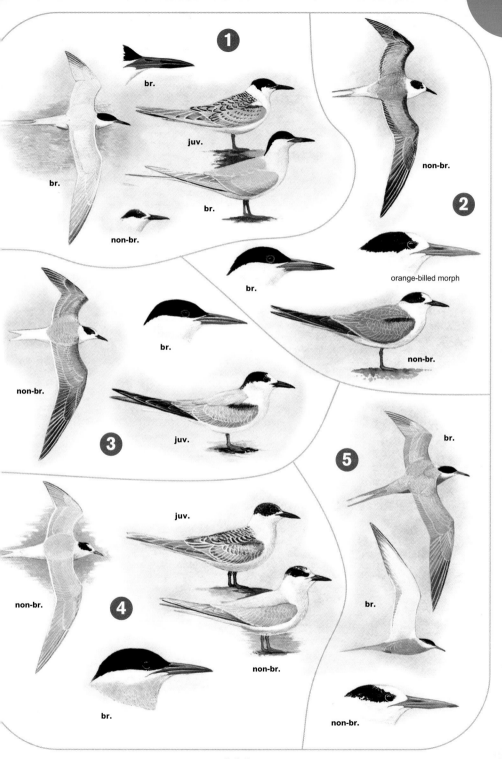

1

br.

juv.

br.

br.

non-br.

2

non-br.

orange-billed morph

br.

non-br.

3

non-br.

br.

juv.

4

juv.

non-br.

non-br.

br.

5

br.

br.

non-br.

1 BLACK-NAPED TERN *Sterna sumatrana* 30 cm
A small, very pale tern, superficially resembling a miniature Sandwich Tern (p. 190). Adult has black band extending behind eye, broadening across nape; crown is pure white. Bill and legs are black. In flight, only outer primaries are black. Juv. has crown feathers tipped with black, and is mottled brown above. Imm. has dusky carpal bar. **Habitat.** Coastal waters, sometimes roosting at estuaries. **Status:** Vagrant to SE coast. **Voice:** Clipped, repeated 'ki-ki'. [G3.4.1]

2 LITTLE TERN *Sterna albifrons* 22-24 cm
A very small tern with narrow wings and rapid wing beats. Inseparable from Saunders' Tern in non-breeding plumage; in breeding plumage, has larger area of white on forehead which extends to behind eye. Bill is shorter and straighter than Damara Tern's, with rump and tail paler grey than back, and more constrast between dark outer primaries and rest of upperwing. In breeding plumage, has white frons, yellow legs, and yellow bill with small black tip (absent in some W African birds). Non-breeding birds have brownish-yellow legs and bill shows varying amounts of yellow at base, often appearing all dark. Juv. is lightly mottled brown above. Juv. and imm. show indistinct darker carpal bar. **Habitat.** Shallow coastal waters, estuaries, lakes and large rivers; breeds W African coast and along major rivers; also Lake Turkana. **Status:** Fairly common migrant. **Voice:** Slightly rasping 'ket-ket'. [C2.92]

3 SAUNDERS' TERN *Sterna saundersi* 22-24 cm
Very similar to Little Tern. In breeding plumage has smaller white frons, which barely reaches eye and is squared off (pointed in Little Tern, extending to back of eye). Non-breeding birds are very difficult to identify; no reliable features known; grey rump is not good separation character. Best feature may be upperwing pattern: outer three primaries are uniformly dark, with black feather shafts (Little Tern has pale inner webs and ivory or brownish shafts). Imm. is probably indistinguishable from imm. Little Tern. **Habitat.** Known from coast, but may occur along Nile to Rift Valley lakes; breeds on coast S to Somalia. **Status:** Poorly known; non-breeding visitor further S, Sep-Apr. **Voice:** 'Kit-kit' or 'kit-ir-kit', similar to Little Tern.

4 DAMARA TERN *Sterna balaenarum* 23 cm
A very small, rather uniform pale grey tern. In breeding plumage has diagnostic full black cap, lacking white forehead of similar-sized Little Tern; further differs by its longer, slightly droop-tipped bill, more uniform upperwing, and uniform grey rump and back. Frons is white in non-breeding plumage. Bill black; legs black or yellow. Juv. has some brown barring on upper-parts, and horn-coloured bill base. **Habitat.** Sheltered coastlines, bays and lagoons; breeds South Africa (scarce) to Namibia. **Status:** Locally common intra-African migrant. **Voice:** Far-carrying, rapid 'chit-ick', higher-pitched than Little Tern's. [C6.47, G3.4.4]

5 BRIDLED TERN *Sterna anaethetus* 30-32 cm
An elegant, dark-backed tern. Smaller than Sooty Tern, with paler, brown-grey upperparts; white frons narrower and extends behind eye. Dark crown contrasts with paler back. Juv. and imm. have wing coverts finely edged buffy white, and white (not blackish, as in juv. and imm. Sooty Tern) underparts. **Habitat.** Open ocean and offshore islands; occasionally roosts ashore; breeds locally in W and E Africa. **Status:** Fairly common but less abundant than Sooty Tern. **Voice:** 'Wup-wup'. [C2.90, G3.4.3]

6 SOOTY TERN *Sterna fuscata* 40-44 cm
A long-winged, dark-backed tern. Larger than Bridled Tern, with broader white frons that does not extend behind eye, and black crown does not contrast with blackish back. In flight, both Sooty and Bridled terns have bold white leading edge to upperwing. Juv. and imm. have blackish throat and breast (juv. and imm. Bridled Tern are white below); differ from noddies by black crown, white belly and pale underwing coverts. **Habitat.** Open ocean and offshore islands; rarely roosts ashore; breeds at islands off W and E Africa. **Status:** Common; in non-breeding season disperses widely in tropical waters and in subtropical waters in SE. **Voice:** Variations on 'wick-a-wick'. [C2.91, G3.4.2]

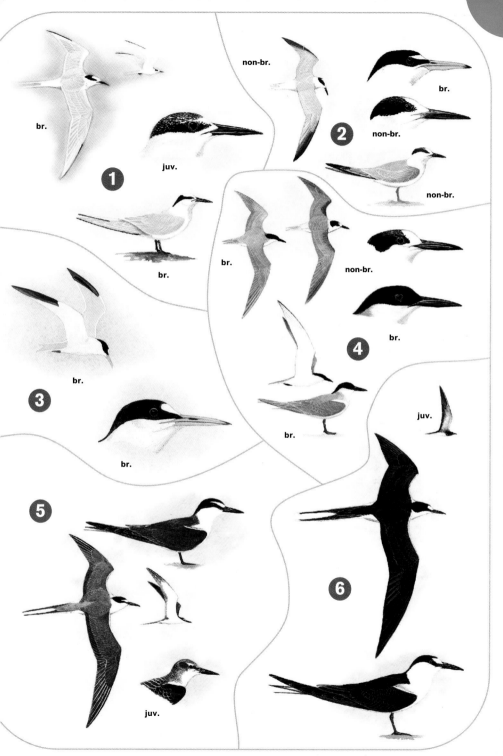

br.

juv.

1

br.

non-br.

br.

2

non-br.

non-br.

br.

non-br.

br.

4

br.

br.

br.

3

br.

5

juv.

6

juv.

NODDIES
Dark tropical terns with long, wedge-shaped tails. Flight loose and buoyant. Seldom come to land away from breeding colonies. Could be confused with imm. Sooty Tern (p. 194); dark-phase jaegers (p. 182) lack white in wing. Juvs have smaller pale crowns.

1 BROWN (COMMON) NODDY *Anous stolidus* 36-45 cm
Slightly larger and browner than other noddies, with paler centre to underwing and paler greater upperwing coverts contrasting with almost-black flight feathers. Bill is rather heavy, and pale crown does not extend onto nape as in Lesser Noddy; white frons contrasts sharply with brown lores (not diffuse). **Habitat.** Open ocean and offshore islands. **Status:** Common at breeding islands (Gulf of Guinea, Red Sea to Tanzania); uncommon elsewhere. **Voice:** Hoarse 'kark'. [C6.49, G3.4.10]

2 BLACK NODDY *Anous minutus* 34 cm
In the region, found only in W Africa. Slightly smaller than Brown Noddy, with relatively longer, more slender bill, uniform wings and whitish crown extending further down nape. **Habitat.** Open ocean and offshore islands. **Status:** Common near breeding islands (Prìncipé, Pagalu); uncommon elsewhere. **Voice:** Generally silent at sea; flight call is 'krik-rik-rik'. [C6.48]

3 LESSER NODDY *Anous tenuirostris* 30-34 cm
In the region, found only along E coast. Slightly smaller than Brown Noddy, with relatively longer, more slender bill. Whitish forehead merges with brown lores and ashy-grey crown extends further back onto nape than in Brown Noddy, and underwing is dark brown (not pale and dark-rimmed). **Habitat.** Open ocean, but occasionally roosts ashore. **Status:** Uncommon non-breeding visitor to E African coast. **Voice:** Generally silent at sea; short, rattling 'churrr'. [G3.5.1]

LAKE TERNS
Small, mostly fresh-water, terns. Breeding plumages distinctive, but non-breeding birds harder to separate. Typically pick prey from the water surface. Sexes alike.

4 WHISKERED TERN *Chlidonias hybrida* 25-26 cm
Dark grey underparts in breeding plumage are diagnostic; smaller than White-cheeked Tern (p. 192), with white (not dusky grey) vent and less deeply forked tail. Non-breeding birds are larger than other lake terns, with *Sterna*-type head pattern (lacks dark cheek patch extending below eye). Rump is pale grey (not white, as in White-winged Tern), and is paler overall than Black Tern, lacking dark shoulder smudge. Juv. is mottled brown on back. **Habitat.** Most wetlands and marshes, but requires floating vegetation to breed. **Status:** Fairly common resident and Palearctic migrant; breeds S and E Africa; migrant elsewhere. **Voice:** Repeated, hard 'zizz'. [C2.93, G3.4.7]

5 WHITE-WINGED TERN *Chlidonias leucopterus* 20-23 cm
The smallest lake tern. Striking black and white in breeding plumage; differs from Black Tern by pale (not dark) upperwings, black (not white) underwing coverts, paler rump and tail, and bright red (not dark) legs. Non-breeding birds differ from other lake terns by white rump. Much paler above than Black Tern, with less black on head, and no black shoulder smudge. Juv. has slight brown tips to upperpart feathers. **Habitat.** Lakes, estuaries and marshes; occasionally forages in sheltered bays on coast and over open country. **Status:** Common Palearctic migrant, mostly Aug-Apr. **Voice:** Short 'kek-kek'. [C2.95, G3.4.8]

6 BLACK TERN *Chlidonias niger* 22-24 cm
A dark-backed lake tern. In breeding plumage, black head, breast and belly merge into dark grey back and wings; lacks contrast of White-winged Tern. Non-breeding birds have diagnostic dark shoulder smudges (as do some transitional White-winged Terns), more black on head than White-winged Tern, and no contrast between back, rump and tail. Darker than Whiskered Tern, with different head pattern. Juv. is slightly darker and less uniform above. **Habitat.** Open ocean, bays and coastal wetlands; usually forages at sea, but many roost ashore. **Status:** Common Palearctic migrant along W coast, mostly Aug-Apr; scarce on E coast; vagrant inland. **Voice:** Usually silent in Africa; quiet 'kik-kik' flight call. [C2.94, G3.4.6]

1

2

3

non-br.

br.

4

juv.

non-br.

br.

5

non-br.

non-br.

br.

non-br.

6

br.

non-br.

non-br.

non-br.

Short-legged, cursorial birds of arid or semi-arid grassland and savanna. Flocks fly to water at fixed times every day. Flight fast on narrow, pointed wings; usually calls in flight. Sexes differ.

1 CHESTNUT-BELLIED SANDGROUSE *Pterocles exustus* 28-33 cm
A fairly small, long-tailed sandgrouse. Male differs from male Spotted Sandgrouse by its dark underwing coverts, uniform face and throat, narrow black breast band and extensive dark underparts. Female has elongated central tail feathers, heavy barring above, a streaked neck and breast with a broad buff breast band, and a dark brown belly with fine buff barring. In flight, dark underwing coverts are contiguous with dark underparts in both sexes. Associates with larger, shorter-tailed Yellow-throated Sandgrouse (p. 200) in E of range. **Habitat.** Open semi-deserts, cultivated fields and grasslands. **Status:** Fairly common to abundant nomad; drinks 2-3 hours after dawn. **Voice:** Deep, musical 'gutter-gutter', creating a soft murmuring by flocks at waterholes. [C6.51]

2 SPOTTED SANDGROUSE *Pterocles senegallus* 30-35 cm
A pale, buffy, long-tailed sandgrouse with pale underwing coverts. Male has a contrasting face pattern and only a narrow, dark stripe on the belly (not dark belly of Chestnut-bellied Sandgrouse). Female lacks a breast band and has a buffy-orange face and throat, which separate it from other species except Crowned Sandgrouse, from which it can be told by its longer tail and dark spotted (not barred) neck and breast. Juv. resembles female but has a shorter tail. **Habitat.** Open, flat, stony deserts with scattered patches of short vegetation. **Status:** Fairly common nomad; drinks 2-3 hours after dawn. **Voice:** Liquid 'wittu wittu'. [C3.2a]

3 CROWNED SANDGROUSE *Pterocles coronatus* 27-30 cm
A pale sandgrouse lacking obvious breast bands. Male lacks long central tail feathers, and has a black face mask that extends to the chin and a pale belly. Female has a well-defined yellowish throat patch; differs from similar Spotted Sandgrouse in having shorter tail feathers and a barred (not spotted) neck and breast. Underwing is off-white with a brownish-grey trailing edge to the underwing coverts. **Habitat.** Desert and semi-desert, including mountainous areas (Tibetsi Massif, Chad). **Status:** Uncommon to locally common nomad; drinks 1-3 hours after dawn. **Voice:** Soft, staccato 'kla kla kla', quite unlike other sandgrouses'. [C3.2b]

4 BLACK-FACED SANDGROUSE *Pterocles decoratus* 25-28 cm
Endemic to NE Africa. A small sandgrouse with a short tail and pale underwing coverts. Male has a distinctive face pattern, black-and-white breast bands, and a black belly with a pale vent. Female differs from all co-occurring sandgrouse by having a broad white breast band. **Habitat.** Semi-desert scrub and arid savanna, often on bare ground. **Status:** Common; drinks 1-4 hours after dawn and at dusk. **Voice:** Low 'chuck-chuck-chuck'; on flushing, gives a whispy 'tseeoo whit-i-weeer whit-i-weeer'.

5 LICHTENSTEIN'S SANDGROUSE *Pterocles lichtensteinii* 25-28 cm
A heavily barred, short-tailed sandgrouse with pale underwing coverts. Male has a well-marked breast band and a barred belly, like male Four-banded Sandgrouse (p. 200), but differs in having a heavily barred neck and wing coverts. Female is almost entirely narrowly barred dark brown above and below; smaller than female Yellow-throated Sandgrouse (p. 200) with barred (not mottled) plumage. **Habitat.** Semi-desert, often in stony and hilly habitats with scattered bush. **Status:** Uncommon to locally common nomad; active mostly at night; drinks after dusk and before dawn. **Voice:** Liquid, whistled 'kweetoo-kweetoo, kweetoo-kweetoo'. [C3.3a]

SANDGROUSE

1 YELLOW-THROATED SANDGROUSE *Pterocles gutturalis*　　28-30 cm
The largest African sandgrouse, identified in flight by its short tail and dark brown belly and underwings. Male has a creamy yellow face and throat, with a broad black neck collar. Female is heavily mottled on the neck, breast and upperparts; lacks the breast band of female Chestnut-bellied Sandgrouse (p. 198), and is larger, with a shorter tail. **Habitat.** Grassland and arid savanna; drinks during the morning. **Status:** Locally common. **Voice:** Flight call a deep, far-carrying bisyllabic 'aw-aw', the first higher pitched; sometimes preceded by 'ipi'. [G3.5.6]

2 DOUBLE-BANDED SANDGROUSE *Pterocles bicinctus*　　25-28 cm
Near-endemic to S Africa. A small, short-tailed sandgrouse similar to Four-banded Sandgrouse, but ranges do not overlap. Male has diagnostic head pattern, black-and-white breast bands and a barred belly. Female is rather uniformly barred; differs from female Namaqua Sandgrouse by its darker, streaked crown, barred (not streaked) upper breast, and short tail. **Habitat.** Woodland and savanna, but also arid Karoo grassland in SW. **Status:** Locally common; drinks at dusk, often after dark. **Voice:** Whistling 'chwee-chee-chee' and soft 'wee-chee-choo-chip-chip' flight call. [G3.5.7]

3 FOUR-BANDED SANDGROUSE *Pterocles quadricinctus*　　25-28 cm
A small, short-tailed sandgrouse similar to Double-banded Sandgrouse, but ranges do not overlap. Male has a buff-and-black breast band and a barred belly; differs from Lichtenstein's Sandgrouse (p. 198) by its plain (not barred) neck and wing coverts. Female differs from all co-occurring sandgrouse by its rich buffy-brown neck contrasting with the barred lower breast. Both sexes have pale underwing coverts. **Habitat.** Dry savannas and cultivated areas. **Status:** Common resident and intra-African migrant; drinks soon after dusk; may be largely nocturnal. **Voice:** Whistled 'wurr wulli' or 'pirrou-ee'. [C6.52]

4 NAMAQUA SANDGROUSE *Pterocles namaqua*　　25 cm
Endemic to SW Africa, where it is the only sandgrouse with a long, pointed tail. Male has a double breast band but lacks the black-and-white head bands of male Double-banded Sandgrouse and has a plain (not barred) lower breast and belly. Female has a more buffy yellow throat and streaked (not barred) breast than female Double-banded Sandgrouse, and has a pointed (not rounded) tail. **Habitat.** Grassland, semi-desert and desert. **Status:** Common nomad and resident; drinks 1-4 hours after dawn. **Voice:** Flight call a nasal 'kelkie-vein'. [G3.5.4]

5 BURCHELL'S SANDGROUSE *Pterocles burchelli*　　25 cm
Endemic to S Africa. A small, compact sandgrouse easily identified by its white-spotted, cinnamon breast and belly. Female resembles a drab male but has a buffy (not blue-grey) face and throat. **Habitat.** Semi-arid savanna; particularly common on Kalahari sands. **Status:** Scarce to locally common; drinks 3-5 hours after dawn, generally later in the day than Namaqua Sandgrouse. **Voice:** Flight call a soft, mellow 'chup-chup, choop-choop'. [G3.5.5]

Common, familiar group of birds. Sexes alike in most species.

1 ROCK DOVE (FERAL PIGEON) *Columba livia*   32-33 cm

A large, bluish-grey pigeon with black bars on the wings and tail, a white rump patch, and glossy green and purple on the sides of the neck. W birds are darker, with pale eyes (eyes are red in E birds). Female and juv. are duller. Feral populations of domesticated Rock Doves are more variable, with black, white and reddish forms in addition to more typical grey birds. **Habitat:** Cliffs, wadis and old buildings, primarily in arid and semi-arid areas; feral populations mostly in urban areas. **Status:** Wild populations breed in Sahara and Sahel; feral populations are common in many urban areas (not mapped). **Voice:** Deep, rolling 'coo-roo-coo'. [C3.6, G3.5.8] **Similar species. Common Wood Pigeon** *C. palumbus* is larger, with white bar on wing coverts; Palearctic vagrant to N.

2 SPECKLED PIGEON *Columba guinea*   32-34 cm

A large red-and-grey pigeon. Reddish back and wings, white-spotted wing coverts and bare red skin around eyes are diagnostic. Legs are red; bill is black. In flight, has two dark bars across tail. N race has pale rump; rump is darker in S. Most similar to Rock Dove. Occasionally hybridises with Feral Pigeons. Juv. lacks red on face. **Habitat:** Rocky areas, coastal cliffs and cities, ranging into fields and grassland to feed. **Status:** Common. **Voice:** Deep, booming 'hooo-hooo-hooo'; softer 'coocoo-coocoo'. [C6.68, G3.5.9]

3 WHITE-COLLARED PIGEON *Columba albitorques*   32 cm

Endemic to Abyssinian highlands. A large grey-brown pigeon with an obvious white hindcollar contrasting with dark slate head. In flight, has prominent white wing patches formed by white inner primary coverts. White collar separates it from Feral Pigeon, which occurs in towns and villages within its range. **Habitat:** Rocky cliffs and gorges and surrounding countryside; also common in urban areas. **Status:** Common; often in large flocks. **Voice:** Rather soft, deep cooing.

4 SOMALI PIGEON (SOMALI STOCK DOVE) *Columba oliviae*   30 cm

Endemic to N Somalia. A plain grey pigeon with a brownish back and diagnostic purplish crown and rufous nape. In flight, appears to have dark cap, black-tipped tail and dark trailing edge to wings. At close range, has red eye-ring, yellowish eye and pink legs. **Habitat:** Arid hillsides, from coast to 800 m. **Status:** Uncommon; forages in small groups; flocks gather to drink. Absent from known range May-Sep; suspected to range to E. **Voice:** Typical cooing and 'tok' calls of pigeons.

5 AFEP PIGEON *Columba unicincta*   31 cm

A large, pale grey forest pigeon. Much paler than other large forest pigeons; in bright sunlight, can appear almost white on head and underparts. In flight, grey tail with black tip and broad subterminal pale grey bar is diagnostic. Back and wings are slate-grey edged with pale grey, appearing scaled at close range. Males have pink wash on breast; females are greyer. Juv. is darker above, with brown wash on underparts. **Habitat:** Forest canopy, gallery forest and tall trees in secondary growth. **Status:** Common, but often hard to locate in canopy. **Voice:** Slow, regular 'hooo' calls of even pitch. [C6.67]

6 LEMON (CINNAMON) DOVE *Aplopelia larvata*   24-26 cm

A medium-sized, dark-backed dove of the forest floor and understorey; sometimes placed in *Columba.* Larger and darker than wood-doves; pale face and habitat separate it from bronze-naped pigeons. In flight, appears all dark, with slightly paler outer-tail tips. Pale forehead and face contrast with darker, iridescent greeny-bronze hindcrown, nape and mantle. Eye-ring is usually red. Rest of plumage varies geographically: most E and S African birds have dark brown upperparts and rich cinnamon underparts, but *jacksoni* (Albertine Rift to NW Zambia) is paler grey underneath and has grey eye-ring; W African *inornata* is dark grey above and pale grey below, and São Tomé and Prìncipé each have distinct forms. São Tomé *simplex* is quite different call; sometimes treated as a separate species, São Tomé Lemon Dove. Female and juv. duller; juv. has buff barring on mantle. **Habitat:** Forest floor and understorey. **Status:** Fairly common. **Voice:** Deep-based, somewhat raspy 'hooo-oooo'. [C6.63, G3.6.10]

larvata

inornata

1 AFRICAN OLIVE-PIGEON (RAMERON PIGEON) *Columba arquatrix* 37-39 cm
A large pigeon, easily identified by its dark, purplish plumage, paler grey nape and breast band, and conspicuous bare yellow face, bill and legs. Wing coverts and belly are finely spotted white. Bright yellow feet and face separate it from Cameroon and São Tomé olive-pigeons. In flight against a pale sky, appears all dark with pale legs. Juv. has duller yellow face patches, bill and legs. **Habitat:** Forest, thickets and plantations. **Status:** Common. **Voice:** Low, raucous 'coo'. [C6.65, G3.5.10]

2 SÃO TOMÉ OLIVE-PIGEON (MAROON PIGEON) *Columba thomensis* 38-40 cm
Endemic to São Tomé, where it is the largest pigeon. Grey head contrasts with maroon breast and back. In flight, appears distinctly longer tailed than São Tomé Bronze-naped Pigeon, with pale bill and fine white spotting on belly and wing coverts. **Habitat:** Forest and old secondary growth, from sea level to mountain summit. **Status:** Vulnerable. Fairly common in primary forest. **Voice:** Similar to African Olive-Pigeon's. [C6.66]

3 CAMEROON OLIVE-PIGEON *Columba sjostedti* 36-38 cm
Endemic to SW Cameroon highlands and Bioko. Slightly smaller than African Olive-Pigeon, with purple legs, red base to bill and no bare skin around eye. Uniform grey head contrasts with rich maroon body, which is more extensively spotted white than African Olive-Pigeon's. White spotting on wing coverts and dark tail lacking paler terminal band separate it from White-naped and Western Bronze-naped pigeons. **Habitat:** Montane forest and forest edge. **Status:** Locally common. **Voice:** Undescribed, but probably similar to African Olive-Pigeon's. [C6.64]

4 WHITE-NAPED PIGEON *Columba albinucha* 34 cm
A fairly large, dark forest pigeon. Smaller than olive-pigeons, with an obvious white (in male) or grey (in female) nape. Lacks white spotting on wings of olive-pigeons, and in flight has broad, paler tip to tail. Larger than Western Bronze-naped Pigeon; male's white nape distinctive. Juv. is darker above. **Habitat:** Primary forest to 1 500 m. **Status:** Little known; apparently uncommon in Albertine Rift; very rare in SW Cameroon. **Voice:** Deep, resonant 'tuuu tuuu'.

5 WESTERN BRONZE-NAPED PIGEON *Columba iriditorques* 24 cm
A rather small, dark, short-tailed pigeon of the forest canopy. Smaller than Eastern Bronze-naped Pigeon, with broad buffy tip to tail; male has cinnamon (not white) collar on hindneck. Dark face and canopy (not understorey) habitat separate it from Lemon Dove (p. 202). Green iridescence on nape and mantle are visible only at close range. Underparts vary from grey to dark wine-red. Female is browner on head and upperparts. **Habitat:** Forest canopy, gallery forest, patches of woodland and secondary growth. **Status:** Fairly common in some areas, but easily overlooked. **Voice:** Series of quiet, low notes, followed by 4-5 loud coos, 'oo oo oo oo COO COO COO COO oo oo'. [C6.61]

6 EASTERN BRONZE-NAPED PIGEON *Columba delegorguei* 26-28 cm
Larger than Western Bronze-naped Pigeon, but smaller and shorter-tailed than African Olive-Pigeon. Male has greyish head and diagnostic pale, crescent-shaped hindneck collar. Iridescent green neck is visible only at close range. Female and juv. lack pale hindcollar; dark face and canopy (not understorey) habitat separate it from Lemon Dove (p. 202). **Habitat:** Forest canopy. **Status:** Uncommon and localised. **Voice:** Similar to Western Bronze-naped Pigeon's, but with a longer series of fast notes at the end, descending in pitch, 'oo oo oo COO COO COO cu-cu-cu-cu-cu'. [G3.6.1]

7 SÃO TOMÉ (GULF OF GUINEA) BRONZE-NAPED PIGEON
Columba malherbii 26 cm
Endemic to São Tomé, Prìncipé and Annobon. Male lacks distinct hindneck collar, and has grey underparts with rich buff undertail coverts; appears dark grey in flight, except for buff undertail coverts. Dark face and canopy (not understorey) habitat separates it from Lemon Dove (p. 202). Female is slightly browner below and less glossy above. **Habitat:** Forest , from secondary growth and plantations; feeds on ground in open areas, even on rocky beaches. **Status:** Common. **Voice:** Lacks the leading notes of other bronze-naped pigeons: 'CROO CROO CROO cuu cuu cuu cucucucucucucu'. [C6.62]

1 RED-EYED DOVE *Streptopelia semitorquata* 30-33 cm
Larger and darker than other collared doves, with a pale face and pinkish head and breast. In flight, has diagnostic broad buffy band at tip of tail. Similar in size to Dusky and Adamawa (p. 208) turtle-doves, but is paler and warmer coloured with complete neck collar and broader pale tail tip. Dull red eye-ring is less prominent than that of African Mourning Dove. Juv. is browner, with smaller collar. **Habitat:** Woodland, forest and gardens. **Status:** Common. **Voice:** Typical call, 'coo coo, co-kuk coo coo', is diagnostic; harsh 'chwaa' alarm call. [C6.69]

2 AFRICAN MOURNING DOVE *Streptopelia decipiens* 28-30 cm
Plain grey head and broad red eye-ring are diagnostic; eye varies from pale yellow (in E and S) to orange-red (in W). Smaller and paler than Red-eyed Dove, but is larger than all other collared doves. In flight, has white in outer-tail. Juv. is browner. **Habitat:** Woodland, riverine forests, thickets and gardens in semi-arid savanna. **Status:** Locally common. **Voice:** Distinctive series of coos, alternating in intensity; grating trills, 'currrrrrrow'; throaty 'aaooow' on landing. [C6.70, G3.6.3]

3 CAPE TURTLE (RING-NECKED) DOVE *Streptopelia capicola* 25-27 cm
A small, pale, collared dove, abundant in S and E. Forms a superspecies with very similar Vinaceous Dove, overlapping in NE; best told by call, but has grey (not pink) forehead and paler grey underwings. Overlaps with African Collared Dove in extreme N; again, call is best feature, but is also distinguished by dark base to uppertail and flight feathers being darker than upperwing coverts. Smaller and paler than Red-eyed and African Mourning doves, with dark eye lacking red eye-ring. In flight, has conspicuous white tips to all but central tail feathers, contrasting with their blackish bases. Juv. is duller, with some buff edgings to feathers. **Habitat:** Almost all, except forest. **Status:** Abundant. **Voice:** Well-known 'kuk-coorrrr-uk' ('how's father?'), middle note descending and trilled; harsh 'kurrrr' alarm call. [C6.72, G3.6.4]

4 VINACEOUS DOVE *Streptopelia vinacea* 24-26 cm
NW counterpart of Cape Turtle-Dove, with which it overlaps in NE; best told by call, but has pink (not grey) forehead and darker grey underwings. Smaller than African Collared Dove, with darker base to uppertail, flight feathers darker than upperwing coverts, and darker underwings. Smaller and paler than Red-eyed and African Mourning doves, with dark eye lacking red eye-ring. **Habitat:** Dry woodland, scrub and farmland. **Status:** Common to abundant. **Voice:** High-pitched series of coos, repeated monotonously, 'coo oo oo oo...'. [C6.71]

5 AFRICAN COLLARED (ROSE-GREY) DOVE *Streptopelia roseogrisea* 27-28 cm
A pale, sandy-coloured dove of arid areas. Slightly larger than Vinaceous and Cape turtle-doves. In flight, shows little if any contrast between flight feathers and upperwing coverts, and no black in base of tail. Underwing is pale. At close range, has narrow, pale eye-ring. **Habitat:** Arid and semi-arid areas, dry river courses and scrub. **Status:** Fairly common resident and local migrant. **Voice:** 2-note 'coo currroo', second note deeper and longer. [C6.73]

6 LAUGHING (PALM) DOVE *Streptopelia senegalensis* 22-24 cm
A small, distinctively plumaged dove of open country. Speckled, rufous breast band and blue-grey greater and median coverts and rump are diagnostic. Lacks black neck collar. Smaller than European Turtle-Dove (p. 208), with plain wing coverts and no neck patch. In flight, cinnamon-coloured back contrasts with blue-grey forewings; outer-tail tips are white. Female and juv. are duller. **Habitat:** Wide range, including urban areas, but avoids forests; found near water only in very arid areas. **Status:** Abundant. **Voice:** Distinctive, rising and falling 'uh hu hu huu hu', rather like subdued laugh, hence common name. [C3.9, G3.6.5]

7 AFRICAN WHITE-WINGED DOVE *Streptopelia reichenowi* 26 cm
Localised endemic to NE Africa. In flight, obvious white crescent across upperwing coverts is diagnostic; outer-tail tipped white. At rest, white wing bar is not conspicuous and it could be confused with Cape Turtle-Dove, but is much greyer on head and underparts. Bright yellow eye surrounded by white feathered eye-ring is striking at close range. **Habitat:** Dry river courses with palms and large trees; also adjacent farmlands. **Status:** Common within its restricted range; occurs in small groups and flies to water in mornings and evenings. **Voice:** Deep cooing.

1 EUROPEAN TURTLE-DOVE *Streptopelia turtur*   26-28 cm
A richly coloured dove with a diagnostic black-and-white neck patch and strongly patterned wing coverts, with dark feather centres contrasting with broad chestnut margins. Larger than Laughing Dove (p. 206), and lacks rufous breast. In flight, has broad white tips to outer-tail, contrasting with blackish subterminal band. Juv. lacks neck patch and has barred and mottled upperparts. **Habitat:** Semi-arid savannas, woodland and fields. **Status:** Localised resident at oases in N; common Palearctic migrant Nov-May. **Voice:** Soft, purring 'crrrr roorrrrrrr'. [C3.8]

2 DUSKY (PINK-BREASTED) TURTLE-DOVE *Streptopelia lugens*   28-30 cm
A dark, slate-grey turtle-dove with diagnostic black patches on the side of the neck. Forms a superspecies with Adamawa Turtle-Dove, but is much darker, with grey (not dark pink) flanks. Wing coverts have grey margins, forming greyish band along wrist of folded wing; secondaries have tawny margins. Eye is orange-yellow, contrasting with purplish eye-ring. In flight, has only rather narrow dusky tips to tail (not broad, as in Red-eyed Dove, p. 206). Juv. is paler and browner. **Habitat:** Wide variety of montane habitats, 1 800-3 200 m, including forest edge, open woodland, pine plantations, bamboo, cultivated areas and gardens. **Status:** Locally common. **Voice:** Deep, slow 'cuu-or, coo-or'; growling 'ooooh'. [C6.75]

3 ADAMAWA TURTLE-DOVE *Streptopelia hypopyrrha*   29 cm
Localised endemic to WC Africa. Forms a superspecies with Dusky Turtle-Dove, but has paler, silver-grey head and chest, and dark pink (not grey) belly. Wing coverts have dark centres with broad tawny (not grey) edges, recalling European Turtle-Dove. **Habitat:** Riverine woodland and hilly country with wooded galleries and adjacent scrub. **Status:** Locally common. **Voice:** Similar to Dusky Turtle-Dove's; deeper than European Turtle-Dove's, with 3-4 (not 2) notes. [C6.74]

4 AFRICAN GREEN PIGEON *Treron calvus*   25-28 cm
A parrot-like pigeon, often seen in small groups clambering around canopy of fruiting trees. Grey-green head and breast, and small (not extensive) yellow belly separate it from Bruce's Green Pigeon. Bill is pale, with red cere. Legs are yellow (in W) or red (in E and S). In flight, has dark flight feathers and greater coverts contrasting with paler green forewing; broad grey tip to tail. Secondaries and greater coverts have yellow margins. Adult has mauve shoulder patches; juv's are olive-yellow. **Habitat:** Forests, woodland and savanna; always associated with fruiting trees, especially figs. **Status:** Common, subject to local movements. **Voice:** Distinctive series of un-pigeon-like croaks, wails and whinnying calls. [C6.53, G3.7.1]

5 BRUCE'S GREEN PIGEON *Treron waalia*   28-30 cm
Arid-country counterpart of African Green Pigeon in N Africa. Head and upper breast are much greyer than African Green Pigeon's, and sharply demarcated from lemon-yellow lower breast and belly (only centre of lower belly is yellow in African Green Pigeon). Legs are orange. Juv. is duller, with less distinct mauve carpal patch. **Habitat:** Arid savannas, lowland riverine and podocarp forests; often associated with human habitation. **Status:** Locally common resident and nomad. **Voice:** Complex song that starts with slow creaking, followed by whistles, a growl and a series of sharp yaps. [C6.55]

6 SÃO TOMÉ GREEN PIGEON *Treron sanctithomae*   26 cm
Endemic to São Tomé, where it is the only green pigeon (but African Green Pigeon occurs on Prìncipé). Differs from African Green Pigeon by greyer head and underparts and thick, relatively short bill. Juv. duller and greyer. **Habitat:** Forest canopy, plantations and secondary growth. **Status:** Common. **Voice:** Similar to African Green Pigeon's, but longer and more complex. [C6.54]

7 PEMBA GREEN PIGEON *Treron pembaensis*   25 cm
Endemic to Pemba Island, where it is the only green pigeon. Head, neck and underparts are predominantly grey, apart from yellow leggings and yellow-and-chestnut vent. Told from African Green Pigeon by its greyer underparts. **Habitat:** Forest, clove plantations, parks and gardens; favours large trees. **Status:** Uncommon to locally common. **Voice:** Muted 'kiu, kiuri-uu', less grating than African Green Pigeon's.

1 BLACK-BILLED WOOD-DOVE *Turtur abyssinicus*   20 cm
A small dove with iridescent greenish wing spots. In flight, has two black bars across lower back and rufous flight feathers. Forms a superspecies with Emerald-spotted Wood-Dove; in limited area of overlap in NE, can be told by black (not reddish) bill, paler, greyer plumage and denser woodland habitat. Overlaps broadly with Blue-spotted Wood-Dove, from which it is separated by black bill and paler, greyer plumage with whiter undertail coverts. Juv. is barred buff above. **Habitat:** Savannas, typically in drier areas than Blue-spotted Wood-Dove, but in denser woodland and even forest in area of overlap with Emerald-spotted Wood-Dove. **Status:** Common resident, with some local movement. **Voice:** Series of about 25 deep coos, starting hesitantly, then accelerating and descending in pitch, 'duu, duu, du-du, du-du du du du-du-du-dudududu...'; series lasts more than 15 seconds; is higher pitched than calls of Blue-spotted and Tambourine doves. [C6.60]

2 EMERALD-SPOTTED WOOD-DOVE *Turtur chalcospilos*   17-20 cm
S counterpart of Black-billed Wood-Dove; in area of overlap in NE, can be told by darker, browner plumage and dull reddish (not black) bill (but bill can appear all-black from a distance). Plumage is paler than Blue-spotted Wood-Dove's, and has green (not blue) wing spots. Juv. is browner, barred buff above; paler, less rufous than juv. Blue-spotted Wood-Dove. **Habitat:** Woodland and savanna; generally drier habitats than Blue-spotted Wood-Dove. **Status:** Common. **Voice:** Similar to Black-billed Wood-Dove's, but shorter, only some 15 notes and lasting less than 15 seconds. [C6.59, G3.6.8]

3 BLUE-SPOTTED WOOD-DOVE *Turtur afer*   18-21 cm
Similar to Black-billed and Emerald-spotted wood-doves, but is richer brown, with blue (not green) wing spots and a yellow-tipped, red bill (only visible at close range). In flight, back and rump appear more rufous. Juv's bill is brown. Juv. has reduced wing spots; told from other juv. wood-doves by more rufous plumage. **Habitat:** Moist, broadleafed woodland, riparian woodland, forest and thickets. **Status:** Fairly common resident and local migrant in N. **Voice:** Series of muffled coos, like calls of Black-billed and Emerald-spotted wood-doves, but shorter (8-12 notes) and deeper in pitch. [C6.58, G3.6.7]

4 TAMBOURINE DOVE *Turtur tympanistria*   20-22 cm
Much darker above than other wood-doves; at close range, has metallic-green wing patches, but these are hard to see against dark upperparts. Male has diagnostic white face and underparts. In flight, chestnut underwings contrast strongly with white belly. Female and juv. are greyer below, but still have paler face and underparts than all other wood-doves. **Habitat:** Forest, secondary forest, thickets and tropical plantations; feeds on ground. **Status:** Common. **Voice:** Series of 20-40 'du-du-du' notes, similar to other wood-doves', but not changing intensity or pitch at end. [C6.57, G3.6.9]

5 BLUE-HEADED WOOD-DOVE *Turtur brehmeri*   25-27 cm
A richly coloured rufous forest dove with a diagnostic, contrasting pale blue-grey head. Larger than other wood-doves and, in flight, appears longer-tailed; dark bars on lower back are indistinct. Adult has iridescent green wing spots. Juv. has buffy face and dark barring on upperparts. **Habitat:** Closed-canopy forest understorey and gallery forest, often on ground; can be seen on forest tracks and edges of forest roads. **Status:** Locally common. **Voice:** Very similar to Tambourine Dove's. [C6.56]

6 NAMAQUA DOVE *Oena capensis*   28 cm
Resembles a wood-dove (small size, rufous wings, wing spots, and 2 barred bars on back) with a long, pointed tail. Male has diagnostic black face and throat, and yellow-tipped red bill. Female and juv. lack black face; have slightly shorter tail and brown bill. Juv. has black-and-white-spotted wing coverts and dark-barred crown and rump. **Habitat:** Arid and semi-arid savannas and open woodland. **Status:** Common resident and local migrant. **Voice:** Deep, soft 'hoo huuuu', first note sharp, second longer. [C3.3b, G3.6.6]

♀

♂

♀

♂

juv.

211

Noisy, colourful birds, often seen as they fly to and from their roosts. Some lovebirds and *Poicephalus* parrots require careful observation before they can be identified. Sexes alike in most species. Due to their popularity as cage birds, many non-African species are occasionally seen, but usually in towns.

1 GREY PARROT *Psittacus erithacus* 30 cm

A large grey parrot with a red tail, whitish face and dark bill. Some birds show more extensive red, especially on belly and thighs. Upper Guinea *timneh* is slightly smaller and darker, with darker red tail and dull reddish bill; Prìncipé population closer to *timneh*. Juv's tail is darker red; eye is grey (yellow in adult). **Habitat:** Primary forest and secondary growth with tall fruiting trees, gallery forest, and areas rich in palm trees including oil palms. **Status:** Locally common. **Voice:** Variety of loud screeches and clear whistles. [C6.76]

2 CAPE PARROT *Poicephalus robustus* 35 cm

Endemic to South Africa. A large green parrot with a characteristic brown head and red wrists and legs. Much larger than Brown-headed Parrot (p. 214), with much more massive, pale bill; typically occurs in forest (not woodland habitat). Female usually has red forehead. Juv. lacks red wrists and thighs, but is readily identified by large size and massive bill. **Habitat:** Forest and plantations; also commutes to orchards to feed. **Status:** Uncommon; usually in pairs or small flocks, often moving large distances to feed. **Voice:** Various loud, harsh screeches and squawks. [G3.7.2]

3 GREY-HEADED PARROT *Poicephalus suahelicus* 36 cm

Often considered a race of Cape and Brown-necked parrots, but is slightly larger than both and has distinctly greyish (not brown) head; ranges do not overlap. **Habitat:** Broadleafed woodland with large, emergent trees and riverine forests. **Status:** Locally common; usually in pairs or small groups, but large flocks gather at fruiting trees. **Voice:** Harsh shrieks and whistles, similar to Cape Parrot's. [G3.7.3]

4 BROWN-NECKED PARROT *Poicephalus fuscicollis* 34 cm

Endemic to W Africa. Often considered a race of Cape and Grey-headed parrots, but is smaller, with larger bill and bluer plumage; ranges do not overlap. Larger than Senegal Parrot (p. 214), with blue-green (not orange-yellow) belly. **Habitat:** Savanna, riverine forests and mangroves. **Status:** Locally common but thinly distributed. **Voice:** Similar to Cape Parrot's; flight call is double 'eee-shik'. [C6.77]

5 RED-FRONTED PARROT *Poicephalus gulielmi* 27 cm

A medium-large, green forest parrot with red frons, wrist and legs. Smaller than Grey-headed or Brown-necked parrots, with green (not grey or brown) head and less massive, bicoloured bill (pale upper mandible, dark lower mandible). Juv. lacks any red in plumage. **Habitat:** Forest canopy, edge of forest and gallery forest, old secondary growth with tall trees. **Status:** Locally common. **Voice:** Various screeches and squawks. [C6.78]

6 YELLOW-FRONTED PARROT *Poicephalus flavifrons* 25 cm

Endemic to Ethiopia. A medium-sized, green parrot with a distinctive bright yellow crown and face, sometimes tinged orange. Some birds have yellow leading edge to inner wing or yellow thighs. Juv's head olive-green suffused with yellow. **Habitat:** Forests, mostly 1 000-3 400 m. **Status:** Locally common; usually encountered in small flocks (3-8). **Voice:** Typical parrot-like shrieks.

7 ROSE-RINGED PARAKEET *Psittacula krameri* 40 cm

The only parakeet in Africa; easily identified by its extremely long, pointed tail. Bill is dark red. Adult male has black throat and distinctive neck collar (lacking in female). Juv. has shorter tail. **Habitat:** Woodland, savanna and semi-arid areas with scattered trees; also parks and gardens. **Status:** Common; often in large flocks; feral populations occur locally in South Africa, Kenya and Uganda. **Voice:** Various shrieks and screams; particularly vocal at roosts. [C6.84]

1 MEYER'S (BROWN) PARROT *Poicephalus meyeri*   23 cm
The most widespread of the brown parrot superspecies complex; overlaps with Senegal and Niam-Niam parrots in C, African Orange-bellied Parrot in E, Brown-headed Parrot in SE and Rüppell's Parrot in SW. A rather dark brown parrot with conspicuous blue-green rump, yellow wrists and green belly, with bluish vent. Bill and eye are dark; some birds have yellow bar across crown. Juv. is duller and lacks yellow on crown. **Habitat:** Broadleafed woodland and savanna. Flocks regularly congregate at waterholes. **Status:** Scarce to locally common. **Voice:** Loud, piercing 'chee-chee-chee-chee'; various other screeches and squawks. [C6.79, G3.7.5]

2 SENEGAL PARROT *Poicephalus senegalus*   25 cm
Endemic to W Africa. A small parrot with a grey head, green chest and yellow, orange-yellow or red lower breast, belly and vent. Eyes are pale yellow. S *versteri* tend to be redder. Juv. is duller, with browner head and greenish underparts; eyes are brown. Overlaps slightly with Niam-Niam and Meyer's parrots in E, where single juvs are hard to separate. **Habitat:** Mesic and semi-arid savannas. **Status:** Common. **Voice:** Similar to Meyer's Parrot. [C6.80]

3 NIAM-NIAM PARROT *Poicephalus crassus*   26 cm
Endemic to C Africa. At close range, bicoloured bill (dark upper mandible, paler lower mandible) is diagnostic. Slightly larger than Senegal and Meyer's parrots. Adult easily separated from Senegal Parrot by green (not orange-red) belly and brown (not grey) head. Told from Meyer's Parrot by its yellow-green (not blue-green) rump and green (not yellow) shoulders. Juv. has yellow on head and could be confused with Meyer's Parrot. **Habitat:** Well-wooded savanna, typically in denser woodland than Meyer's Parrot. **Status:** Local and uncommon. **Voice:** Similar to Meyer's Parrot. [C6.81]

4 AFRICAN ORANGE-BELLIED PARROT *Poicephalus rufiventris*   24 cm
Endemic to NE Africa. Adult male has diagnostic orange belly and underwing coverts. Female and juv. differ from Meyer's and Brown-headed parrots by lacking yellow shoulder and underwing, and having dark (not yellow) eye. **Habitat:** Dry woodland and riverine bush and adjacent farmlands. **Status:** Locally common; in small groups or pairs but never in flocks. **Voice:** Typical parrot-like shrieking.

5 BROWN-HEADED PARROT *Poicephalus cryptoxanthus*   25 cm
Endemic to SE Africa. A green and brown parrot with diagnostic pale yellow eyes and pale lower mandible. In flight, has distinctive yellow underwing coverts, but upperwings are olive-brown, lacking yellow shoulders or crown of Meyer's Parrot. Yellow (not brown) underwing separates it from female African Orange-bellied Parrot. Juv. is duller, with less vivid yellow underwings, and dark eyes. **Habitat:** Savanna, riverine forests and open woodland. **Status:** Locally common. **Voice:** Typically parrot-like, raucous shriek. [G3.7.4]

6 RÜPPELL'S PARROT *Poicephalus rueppellii*   22 cm
Endemic to SW Africa. Head and throat are greyer than Meyer's Parrot's, with blue (not green or turquoise) belly; never shows yellow on crown. In flight, is easily identified by blue-washed (not green) rump. Female is brighter than male, with more extensive blue on vent and rump. Juv. is duller. **Habitat:** Dry woodland, savanna and dry rivercourses. **Status:** Uncommon to locally common. **Voice:** Screeches and squawks similar to those of Meyer's Parrot. [G3.7.6]

1

juv.

2

3

4

5

juv.

6

♀

juv.

♀

1 RED-HEADED LOVEBIRD *Agapornis pullarius*   12 cm
A small lovebird of W and C Africa. Range overlaps with Black-collared Lovebird, but has reddish (not green) face and no black collar; also habitat differs. Overlaps with Rosy-faced Lovebird in N Angola, but is smaller, with less extensive red (not pink) on face, and has more prominent subterminal tail bar. **Habitat:** Riparian forest, secondary growth and moist savannas and farmlands; avoids primary forest. **Status:** Locally common to abundant. **Voice:** Usual lovebird-like squawks and shrill screeches. [C6.82]

2 BLACK-COLLARED LOVEBIRD *Agapornis swindernianus*   13 cm
A small forest lovebird. Green (not reddish) face with black neck collar separates it from Red-headed Lovebird. Black collar is bordered by yellow or orange-red band. Juv. is duller and lacks black collar. **Habitat:** Forest canopy and gallery forest, descending to lower levels at forest edge. **Status:** Locally common; most often seen flying high in groups above forest, and located by call. **Voice:** High-pitched lovebird-type shrieking. [C6.83]

3 BLACK-WINGED LOVEBIRD *Agapornis taranta*   15 cm
Endemic to Abyssinian highlands. A bright green lovebird with a red bill and red (in male) or green (in female) frons. Range overlaps with Red-headed Lovebird in SW, but has green (not blue) rump, dark brown primaries edged with green, and black secondaries. Male's under-wing coverts are black; female's green. **Habitat:** Savannas and woodland. **Status:** Common; usually in flocks of 5-10. **Voice:** Whistled 'tsweet' in flight.

4 FISCHER'S LOVEBIRD *Agapornis fischeri*   13 cm
Endemic to E Africa. A green lovebird with a reddish-brown head, broad pale eye-ring and bright yellow upper breast and wide nuchal collar. Resembles Lilian's Lovebird's but ranges do not overlap. Most easily confused with Yellow-collared Lovebird, which has much darker head and broader yellow collar and breast. The two species hybridise, producing intermediate individuals, and feral populations of hybrids are common in Kenya. Juv. is duller. **Habitat:** Woodland, savanna and adjacent fields. **Status:** Common. **Voice:** Shrill whistle.

5 YELLOW-COLLARED LOVEBIRD *Agapornis personatus*   13-15 cm
Endemic to E Africa. A bright green lovebird with a dark brown head (appearing black at a distance) with a broad white orbital ring. Breast and nuchal collar are golden-yellow; body and wings are green, with pale blue upertail coverts. Much more contrasting dark head and golden collar and breast separate it from Fischer's Lovebird, but hybrids of intermediate appearance are widespread, with many feral populations in Kenya. **Habitat:** Well-wooded savannas. **Status:** Locally common. **Voice:** Shrill screeching.

6 ROSY-FACED LOVEBIRD *Agapornis roseicollis*   16 cm
Endemic to SW Africa; range overlaps slightly with Red-headed Lovebird but has pinkish (not red) face. In flight, blue rump contrasts strongly with green back and pink face. Juv. is paler on face and upper breast. **Habitat:** Dry, broadleafed woodland, semi-desert and mountainous terrain; often breeds in Sociable Weaver nests. **Status:** Common. **Voice:** Typical parrot-like screeches and shrieks. [G3.7.8]

7 LILIAN'S (NYASA) LOVEBIRD *Agapornis lilianae*   14 cm
Endemic to SC Africa. The only lovebird in its range with a reddish face, prominent white eye-ring, pale bill and green rump. Female has paler pink face. Juv. lacks white eye-ring and has darker cheeks and a dark base to the upper mandible. Sometimes lumped with Black-cheeked Lovebird. **Habitat:** Broadleafed woodland, especially mopane. **Status:** Locally common. **Voice:** High-pitched, staccato shrieking. [G3.7.9]

8 BLACK-CHEEKED LOVEBIRD *Agapornis nigrigenis*   14 cm
Endemic to SW Zambia. Often considered a race of Lilian's Lovebird, but has dark brown (not orange) head contrasting with white eye-ring and reddish bill. **Habitat:** Tall mopane woodland, riparian woodland and adjacent fields. **Status:** Vulnerable. Locally common in its small range. A small population near Victoria Falls, Zimbabwe, apparently derives from escaped cage birds. **Voice:** Shrieking call, similar to other lovebirds'. [G3.7.10]

An endemic African order, with a single family. Large, long-tailed birds that bound adroitly through forest and woodland canopy. Flight quite weak; gliding between trees. Sexes usually alike. Many species quite similar, but ranges often don't overlap.

1 GREAT BLUE TURACO *Corythaeola cristata* 75 cm

A huge turquoise-blue turaco with a diagnostic large black crest and very long tail with a broad subterminal black band. Bill is yellow, with red tip. Wings are all blue (lacks crimson primaries of other turacos). Juv. is duller, with shorter crest and greyer breast. **Habitat:** Canopy of forest, gallery forest and tall trees in secondary growth. **Status:** Locally common. Usually in flocks of 5-8 birds. **Voice:** Loud series of deep, guttural 'caw' notes, sometimes preceded by bubbling trill. [C6.85]

2 RWENZORI TURACO *Gallirex johnstoni* 45 cm

Endemic to Albertine Rift Mts. Slightly larger than Purple-crested Turaco, with darker chin, pale (not dark) bill and reddish (not purple) nape; ranges are not known to overlap. Nominate N race has bare yellow and red face; S *kivuensis* has feathered face. **Habitat:** Montane forest and adjacent secondary growth. **Status:** Common within its restricted range. Usually in pairs, but groups gather at fruiting trees. **Voice:** Rapid series of clicks, unlike any other turaco's call. [C6.93]

3 PURPLE-CRESTED TURACO (LOURIE) *Gallirex porphyreolopha* 43 cm

A rather dark turaco with a purple-blue crown, which separates it from most other green turacos. Lacks white loral spot and cheek stripe of Hartlaub's Turaco (p. 220), and has green body washed rose-pink. Dark bill, purple (not blue-green) crest, blue-green (not yellow or green) face, and pale chin separate it from localised Rwenzori Turaco. Juv. is duller. **Habitat:** Coastal and riverine forests and broadleafed woodland. **Status:** Common. **Voice:** Loud series of hollow 'kok-kok-kok-kok', typically longer and faster than other green turacos'. [G3.8.1]

4 VIOLET TURACO *Musophaga violacea* 50 cm

Near-endemic to W Africa. A dark violet-blue turaco with a prominent yellow frontal shield, dark red crown and naked red face. Forms a superspecies with Ross's Turaco, but is easily distinguished by red bill tip and face, white cheek stripe and short (not erect) red crest; ranges may overlap in Cameroon and Central African Republic. Juv. has all-dark head and bill. **Habitat:** Gallery forest and woodland patches in savanna. **Status:** Locally common; escaped birds persist in some areas (e.g. Johannesburg). **Voice:** Similar to that of Ross's Turaco. [C6.94]

5 ROSS'S TURACO *Musophaga rossae* 52 cm

An entirely dark purple-blue turaco, with crimson primaries, a bizarre red crest and naked yellow face, bill and frontal shield. May overlap with Violet Turaco in Cameroon and Central African Republic; differs in having yellow (not red) face and erect, fez-like crest. Juv. is duller, with blackish bill and face; crest much shorter. **Habitat:** Riverine forest and dense woodland. **Status:** Locally common. **Voice:** Loud series of deep, guttural 'caws', often given by several birds at once, producing almost continuous cacophany. [C6.95, G3.8.2]

1 BANNERMAN'S TURACO *Tauraco bannermani* 40 cm
Endemic to Bamenda highlands of SW Cameroon. Easily identified by short, red-orange crest and plain grey face. Reddish ridge to upper mandible and grey (not whitish) face separate it from Red-crested Turaco; ranges do not overlap. **Habitat:** Montane forest. **Status:** Endangered. Still fairly common in its restricted range. **Voice:** Deep barking call, similar to other turacos'. [C6.91]

2 RED-CRESTED TURACO *Tauraco erythrolophus* 40 cm
Endemic to Angola. Reddish crest and nape (some crest feathers with white tips), yellow bill and whitish face are diagnostic. Told from Bannerman's Turaco by its whitish (not grey) face and entirely yellow bill; ranges do not overlap. **Habitat:** Forest, gallery forest and forest edge and miombo woodland. **Status:** Locally common, but probably decreasing due to forest clearing. **Voice:** Deep, barking call similar to other green turacos'. [C6.92]

3 HARTLAUB'S TURACO *Tauraco hartlaubi* 43 cm
Endemic to E Africa. A blue-backed turaco with a diagnostic metallic-blue crown. Conspicuous white spot in front of eye and narrow white line below eye separate it from Purple-crested Turaco (p. 218). Range also overlaps narrowly with Fischer's (W Usambaras), Schalow's (Loita Hills, Kenya), Black-billed (Kaimosi, Kenya), and White-crested (NW Kenya) turacos, but told from all by its blue crown. **Habitat:** Forest and well-treed gardens. **Status:** Common. **Voice:** Loud, guttural 'kwa, kak, kwak-kwak, kwak', harsher than other co-occurring green turacos'.

4 WHITE-CRESTED TURACO *Tauraco leucolophus* 40 cm
A distinctive turaco with a snow-white crest and a white head with a contrasting black forehead. Red eye-ring and green bill with yellow tip add to its striking head pattern. **Habitat:** Riverine forest and well-wooded hillsides; avoids dense forest. **Status:** Locally common. **Voice:** Long, hooted 'aaaaaah', followed by 10-20 rapid, raucous barks, 'kow-kow-kow-kow-kow-kow-kow'. [C6.90]

5 WHITE-CHEEKED TURACO *Tauraco leucotis* 43 cm
Endemic to Ethiopia; range overlaps only with very restricted Ruspoli's Turaco. Crescent-shaped white patch on side of neck is diagnostic, but extent varies, and may be almost absent in some areas. Green-blue crest and white face markings separate it from Ruspoli's Turaco. SC Ethiopian *donaldsoni* has reddish hindcrest. **Habitat:** Woodland and forest up to 3 200 m. **Status:** Common. **Voice:** Flight call is 'kek, kek, kek...'; male in breeding season has variable, cackling call, 'KUK kuk kuk KUK kuk kuk KUK kukukukukuk'.

6 RUSPOLI'S TURACO *Tauraco ruspolii* 40 cm
Endemic to S Ethiopia. A plain-faced turaco with a diagnostic pale creamy-pink crest and small red nape patch. Bill and eye-ring are red. Pale (not green-blue) crest and lack of white face markings separate it from White-cheeked Turaco. **Habitat:** Juniper forest. **Status:** Vulnerable. Locally fairly common. **Voice:** Deep barking; responds to tape-recording of call of Knysna Turaco.

1 GUINEA TURACO *Tauraco persa*   40 cm
The W form of the green turaco species complex. Easily told from other turacos in its range by its pronounced, plain green crest; red bill and bronze-violet wing coverts and tail also are diagnostic. In flight, shows conspicuous crimson patches on primaries. Overlaps extensively with Yellow-billed Turaco, from which it is easily told by its red (not yellow) bill. Extreme W *buffoni* has broader black line under eye and reduced or absent white cheek stripe. **Habitat:** Forest, gallery forest and secondary growth. **Status:** Common. **Voice:** Hoarse 'kow-kow-kow-kow'; quieter 'krrr' alarm note. [C6.86]

2 SCHALOW'S TURACO *Tauraco schalowi*   40 cm
The C African form of green turaco, found W of Rift Valley. Most closely resembles Livingstone's Turaco, but has longer crest (especially at front of crest), tail is dark blue or purple (not dark green), and is slightly paler green below. Long, pointed crest also separates it from other green turacos with which it overlaps (Hartlaub's, Black-billed and Purple-crested turacos). Juv. has shorter crest. **Habitat:** Forest and dense riparian woodland. **Status:** Common. **Voice:** Similar to Guinea Turaco's. [C6.87, G3.7.13]

3 LIVINGSTONE'S TURACO *Tauraco livingstonii*   40 cm
The form of green turaco found E of Rift Valley, apart from an isolated population in NW Tanzania and Burundi. Large, white-tipped crest is more rounded and less pointed in front than that of Schalow's Turaco; also, tail is dark green (not bluish), and is darker on breast. Range abuts Knysna Turaco's, but the two species are altitudinally segregated; differs in having longer, more pointed crest and slightly darker back. **Habitat:** Forest and dense, riparian woodland. **Status:** Common. **Voice:** Similar to Guinea Turaco's. [G3.7.12]

4 KNYSNA TURACO (LOURIE) *Tauraco corythaix*   40 cm
Endemic to S Africa. The rounded, green crest with a narrow white fringe is diagnostic. Altitudinally segregated from Livingstone's Turaco, with rounded (not pointed) crest. Body is much greener than Purple-crested Turaco's, with green (not purple) crest; also occurs in more forested habitat. Juv. has shorter crest which lacks white tips. Disjunct N *phoebus* is more blue above. **Habitat:** Afromontane forest, from sea level in W, but at higher elevations in E. **Status:** Common. **Voice:** Similar to Guinea Turaco's. [G3.7.11]

5 BLACK-BILLED TURACO *Tauraco schuettii*   40 cm
A green turaco of C Africa with a diagnostic black bill. Green crest is rounded (not pointed, as in Schalow's Turaco) and has white tips (not plain green, as in Guinea Turaco); ranges are not known to overlap. C African *schuetti* has bluer upperparts and black rump; E African *emini* is greener above with a green rump. **Habitat:** Forest and gallery forest. **Status:** Locally common. **Voice:** Similar to Guinea Turaco's. [C6.88]

6 FISCHER'S TURACO *Tauraco fischeri*   40 cm
Endemic to coastal E Africa. Range overlaps narrowly with Hartlaub's (p. 220) and Livingstone's turacos, but is easily identified by its relatively short green crest, which is tipped red and white, with red coloration extending onto nape. Endemic Zanzibar race is bluer above. **Habitat:** Coastal lowland forest. **Status:** Locally common. **Voice:** Starts with 2-3 fairly high-pitched notes, turning into series of harsh barks.

7 YELLOW-BILLED (VERREAUX'S/BLACK-TIP CRESTED) TURACO
Tauraco macrorhynchus   40 cm
Differs from Guinea Turaco by shorter rounded crest tipped with black and white (in W African nominate race) or with red (C African *verreauxii*) and by yellow (not red) bill with red spot at its base. Wing coverts are more dark blue than violet-purple. Genetic evidence groups it with *Musophaga.* **Habitat:** Forest and gallery forest. **Status:** Common. **Voice:** Long series of barking calls, slowing in pace. [C6.89]

macrorhynchus

verreauxii

1 GREY GO-AWAY-BIRD (LOURIE) *Corythaixoides concolor*　　　48 cm
An entirely ash-grey turaco with a long tail and pointed, loose crest similar to that of a mousebird. Lacks bare black face and white neck of Bare-faced Go-away-bird. Juv. is buffier and has shorter crest. **Habitat:** Acacia savanna and dry, open woodland; also gardens. **Status:** Common; vocal and conspicuous; often seen in small groups perched on top of acacia trees. **Voice:** Harsh, nasal 'waaaay' or 'kay-waaaay' (rendered 'go-away'). [C6.96, G3.8.3]

2 BARE-FACED GO-AWAY-BIRD *Coythaixoides personatus*　　　48 cm
Endemic to NE Africa. Forms a superspecies with Grey Go-away-bird, but has a diagnostic white neck and breast contrasting with a conspicuous bare, black face. In flight, has uniform grey wings and tail (not black-and-white, as in White-bellied Go-away-bird and Eastern Grey Plantain-eater). Flight is undulating. Juv. is slightly browner, with inconspicuously barred upperparts. **Habitat:** Open woodland, thickets and cultivated areas with scattered trees. **Status:** Uncommon to locally common; birds often travel in small groups. **Voice:** Deep 'kow kow'. [C6.97]

3 WHITE-BELLIED GO-AWAY-BIRD *Criniferoides leucogaster*　　　50 cm
Endemic to NE Africa. A boldly patterned grey turaco with a long, pointed crest. Dark grey breast sharply divided from white belly separates it from Bare-faced Go-away-bird and Eastern Grey Plantain-eater. Black tips to upperwing coverts form bars on closed wing. In flight, white bases to blackish primaries form prominent wing flashes; has white band in tail. Male's bill is black; female's is green. Juv. is browner and has less conspicuous wing bars. **Habitat:** Savanna and open woodland, especially acacia. **Status:** Common. **Voice:** Varied; usually nasal 'haa haa haa'.

4 EASTERN GREY PLANTAIN-EATER *Crinifer zonurus*　　　50 cm
A large, grey-brown turaco with a yellow-green bill and a shaggy nuchal collar. Lack of crest, streaked (not uniform) neck and underparts, and indistinct boundary between dark breast and pale belly distinguish it from White-bellied Go-away-bird. In W, range overlaps with Western Grey Plantain-eater; differs by having white panels in outer-tail and by being barred (not spotted) above. **Habitat:** Lightly wooded savannas, mostly below 1 500 m. **Status:** Common. **Voice:** Loud yelping and cackling, including 'kwow how-how-how'. [C6.99]

5 WESTERN GREY PLANTAIN-EATER *Crinifer piscator*　　　50 cm
The only grey turaco in W Africa. Range overlaps narrowly with Eastern Grey Plantain-eater in E; differs by having uniform grey tail (no pale panels in outer-tail), yellower bill, and spotted (not barred) upperparts. **Habitat:** Wooded savanna and gallery forest. **Status:** Common. **Voice:** Similar to Eastern Grey Plantain-eater's, but faster and higher pitched. [C6.98]

Obligate brood parasites; easily overlooked when not calling. Long-tailed and grey cuckoos pose significant identification problems. Sexes differ in most species.

1 DIDERICK CUCKOO *Chrysococcyx caprius* 17-19 cm
A small, glossy green cuckoo with diagnostic white wing spots, red eyes and broadly barred green flanks. In adult, white supercilium typically extends in front of reddish eye, and has green malar stripe. Female is duller, with barring extending up onto breast; throat is often buffy. Juv. has conspicuous red bill; occurs in green and rufous morphs. **Habitat:** Woodland, savanna, grassland and suburban gardens; often near reedbeds and weaver colonies. **Status:** Common resident and intra-African migrant. **Voice:** Clear, persistent 'dee-dee-deed-ereek'. [C7.16, G3.9.6]

2 KLAAS'S CUCKOO *Chrysococcyx klaas* 16-18 cm
A plain, glossy green cuckoo with a small white post-ocular eye-stripe; lacks white wing spots of Diderick Cuckoo. Male is white below, with green spurs extending onto sides of breast, and only few green bars on thighs. Female is bronzy brown above and finely barred below; extent of barring varies geographically: in S is densely barred, with breast almost all dark, but in N some resemble males. Juv. is barred bronze and green above, similar to female Emerald Cuckoo, but has diagnostic white post-ocular eye-stripe. **Habitat:** Forests, woodland, savanna and gardens. **Status:** Common resident and intra-African migrant. **Voice:** Far-carrying 'huee-jee' (rendered in Afrikaans as 'meitjie'), repeated 3-6 times. [C7.15, G3.9.5]

3 AFRICAN EMERALD CUCKOO *Chrysococcyx cupreus* 21-23 cm
A forest cuckoo; larger than other glossy green species. Male has sulphur-yellow lower breast and belly contrasting with brilliant emerald-green throat, upper breast and upperparts; vent is barred green and white. Female and juv. are finely barred green and brown above, and green and white below; lack white eye-stripe of Klaas's Cuckoo. **Habitat:** Evergreen forests. **Status:** Common resident and intra-African migrant. **Voice:** Loud, ringing whistle, 'wit-huu, orr-weee' (rendered 'pretty georg-eee'). [C7.13, G3.9.4]

4 YELLOW-THROATED CUCKOO *Chrysococcyx flavigularis* 15-16 cm
A tiny, rather dark forest cuckoo with plain bronze-brown upperparts with a green sheen if seen in good light. If seen from front, male's narrow yellow line from throat to centre of breast is diagnostic; lower breast and belly are finely barred green and light brown. Has distinct yellow eyes and feet. Female is duller, with underparts entirely densely barred, appearing dark at a distance. Juv. has tawny bars above. **Habitat:** Forest canopy, gallery forest and secondary growth in tall trees. **Status:** Locally common in C Africa; rare in W. **Voice:** Loud, far-carrying series of whistled notes on the same pitch, 'teuu teuu'; double-noted 'wee heeu'. [C7.14]

5 JACOBIN CUCKOO *Clamator jacobinus* 33-34 cm
A medium-sized, black-and-white, crested cuckoo. Smaller than Levaillant's Cuckoo, with no stripes on throat and breast. Dark-morph birds (mostly coastal in S) are all black except for white patch at base of primaries; smaller than dark-morph Levaillant's Cuckoo, with no white in tail. Crest and long, graduated tail easily separate it from Black Cuckoo (p. 230). Juv. is browner above, with creamy grey underparts; dark morph has dull black underparts. **Habitat:** Woodland, thickets and acacia savanna. **Status:** Common intra-African migrant, with some non-breeding migrants from India. **Voice:** Shrill, repeated 'klee-klee-kleeuu-kleeuu', very similar to start of call of Levaillant's Cuckoo. [C7.1, G3.9.2]

6 LEVAILLANT'S (AFRICAN STRIPED) CUCKOO *Clamator levaillantii* 38-40 cm
A large, black-and-white cuckoo with a long crest. Larger than Jacobin Cuckoo, with a distinctive striped throat and breast. Rare black morph (mostly coastal in NE) differs from dark morph Jacobin Cuckoo by having white tail tips. Both morphs have prominent white patches in primary bases. Juv. is browner above and buff below, but still shows diagnostic throat striping. **Habitat:** Savanna and woodland. **Status:** Locally common intra-African migrant. **Voice:** Loud 'klee-klee-kleeuu', followed by descending 'che-che-che-che'. [C7.2, G3.9.1]

1 GREAT SPOTTED CUCKOO *Clamator glandarius* 36-41 cm
A large cuckoo with a white-spotted grey back and wings, a long, wedge-shaped tail and a grey crest. Throat is buffy; rest of underparts are white. Juv. is also heavily spotted on back but has small, black crest, buffish underparts and rufous patches on primaries. **Habitat:** Woodland and savanna. **Status:** Fairly common intra-African migrant. **Voice:** Loud, far-carrying 'keeow-keeow-keeow'; shorter, crow-like 'kark'. [C3.10, G3.8.11]

2 THICK-BILLED CUCKOO *Pachycoccyx audeberti* 36 cm
A large, rather hawk-like cuckoo with a noticeably thick, heavy bill. Plain white underparts and lack of crest are diagnostic. Adult is dark grey above, with white underparts and broadly barred undertail. Juv. has striking white head flecked with black, and white-spotted upperparts similar to Great Spotted Cuckoo, but lacks crest and dark cap. **Habitat:** Riparian forests and woodland. **Status:** Uncommon resident; rare in W. **Voice:** Repeated, ringing 'weee we-wick', like a fast, harsh Klaas's Cuckoo. [C7.3, G3.9.3]

3 BARRED LONG-TAILED CUCKOO *Cercococcyx montanus* 33 cm
A small, dark cuckoo with a very long tail. Within most of its range, is easily identified by diagnostic shape, brownish, barred upperparts and broadly barred underparts. Overlaps with other long-tailed cuckoos in Albertine Rift but occurs at higher elevations (above 1 200 m); adults differ by having barred upperparts (although nominate race from that area is less barred, and juvs of other species are barred above); call is best feature. Juv. has more dusky underparts, with some streaking. **Habitat:** Forest, riparian thickets and mature miombo woodland. **Status:** Uncommon resident and intra-African migrant; seldom seen if not calling. **Voice:** Long series of 'cheee-phweew's, increasing in intensity, followed by ringing 'whit whew hew hew', recalling call of Red-chested Cuckoo but with 4-5 notes; shorter 'hwee-hooa' or 'hwee-hooo'; often calls at night. [C7.12, G3.8.10]

4 OLIVE LONG-TAILED CUCKOO *Cercococcyx olivinus* 33 cm
Forms a superspecies with Barred Long-tailed Cuckoo, overlapping with both other long-tailed cuckoos in Albertine Rift forests, where it only occurs up to 1 500 m (Barred Long-tailed Cuckoo occurs above 1 200 m). Differs in song and adults have rather plain (not barred) upperparts. Upperparts are paler bronzy-olive, underparts are more finely barred and undertail coverts are paler buff than Dusky Long-tailed Cuckoo's, but these features are hard to see on birds in canopy; best told apart by song. Juv. is browner above, barred blackish. **Habitat:** Forest canopy, gallery forest and patches of woodland. **Status:** Fairly common; most abundant long-tailed cuckoo of C Africa, easily located by call. **Voice:** 3-syllable call similar to Red-chested Cuckoo's, descending in pitch; long, monotonous series of 'doo you' calls, sometimes ending in ecstatic bubbling call; often calls in late afternoon. [C7.11]

5 DUSKY LONG-TAILED CUCKOO *Cercococcyx mechowi* 33 cm
A forest long-tailed cuckoo; very difficult to separate from Olive Long-tailed Cuckoo if not calling. Has darker, slate-grey upperparts, more heavily barred underparts and darker tawny vent and thighs, but these features are hard to observe in canopy birds. **Habitat:** Forest canopy, often near streams and rivers, also at forest edge. Typically in lowland forest, but up to 1 800 m in Albertine Rift forests. **Status:** Locally fairly common, but elusive; best located by call. **Voice:** In W Africa has sharp, high-pitched call, 'huit-huit-huit', increasing slightly in pitch; in C Africa, song is faster and more rapidly delivered (may be undescribed species, tentatively named *C. occidentalis* by C. Chappuis). [C7.9-10]

juv.

1

juv.

juv.

juv.

2

3

4

5

1 RED-CHESTED CUCKOO *Cuculus solitarius* 28-31 cm

Adult has a diagnostic rufous breast combined with a dark slate back (darker than African and Common cuckoos, but is paler than W form of Black Cuckoo). Rufous breast may be barred (in male) or paler in centre (in female). Best located by characteristic 3-note call. Juv. lacks rufous breast and is almost black above and on throat and breast (not barred, like juv. African and Common cuckoos), with pale feather edges; lower breast and belly are strongly barred black and white. **Habitat:** Forests, plantations, woodland and gardens. **Status:** Common resident and intra-African migrant. **Voice:** Male calls monotonous 'weet-weet-weeoo' (rendered 'piet my vrou' in Afrikaans); female gives shrill 'pipipipipi'. [C7.4, G3.8.8]

2 BLACK CUCKOO *Cuculus clamosus* 28-31 cm

The only all-black cuckoo. Lacks crest and white wing patches of dark-morph Jacobin and Levaillant's cuckoos (p. 226). At close range, has indistinct pale tips to tail feathers, and females have indistinct paler bars on belly. WC African *gabonensis* has rufous breast and throat, and buffy-barred belly; is always darker than Red-chested Cuckoo, with all-dark (not yellow-based) bill, and no yellow eye-ring. Intergrades occur in E Africa. Juv. is duller black, with no white tips to tail. **Habitat:** Woodland, forest, plantations and gardens. **Status:** Common resident and intra-African migrant. **Voice:** Male song is mournful 'hoo hooee' or 'hoo hoo hooeee' (rendered 'I'm so sick'), with last note rising in pitch, repeated monotonously and sometimes ending in excited, rattling 'whurri whurri whurri'; female gives fast 'yow-yow-yow-yow'. [C7.5, G3.8.9]

3 AFRICAN CUCKOO *Cuculus gularis* 32-34 cm

A large grey cuckoo, virtually identical in the field to Common Cuckoo. Adult typically has more extensive yellow base to bill, barred (not spotted) outer-tail, and vent and undertail coverts more finely barred, but call is most distinctive feature. Lacks hepatic morph. Juv. is barred black and white, with upperparts blackish, scalloped with white (rump is not plain, as in Common Cuckoo). **Habitat:** Woodland and savanna. **Status:** Locally common intra-African migrant. **Voice:** Similar to African Hoopoe's 'hoop-hoop' call, but slower; female utters fast 'kik-kik-kik'. [C7.6, G3.8.5]

4 COMMON (EURASIAN) CUCKOO *Cuculus canorus* 32-34 cm

Forms a superspecies with African Cuckoo. Differs in having spotted (not barred) outer-tail, more boldly barred vent and undertail coverts, and generally less yellow at base of bill. Female has rare hepatic morph, barred black-and-rufous above. Juv. may be brown, grey or chestnut; upperparts are usually barred, but with plain rump; underparts are heavily barred. **Habitat:** Woodland, savanna, riverine forests and plantations. **Status:** Scarce to locally common Palearctic migrant Aug-Apr. **Voice:** Generally silent in Africa. [C3.11, G3.8.4]

5 LESSER CUCKOO *Cuculus poliocephalus* 26-28 cm

A grey cuckoo, similar to African and Common cuckoos, but smaller, and with darker upperparts and more heavily barred underparts. Very similar to Madagascar Cuckoo, but typically occurs in different season, and has strongly barred (not plain or weakly barred) undertail coverts; rare hepatic morph is absent in Madagascar Cuckoo. In flight, dark tail and rump contrast with paler back; this feature is lacking in both African and Common cuckoos. Female's upper breast is barred buffy; male's upper breast is grey. Juv. is barred above. **Habitat:** Savanna and riparian forests. **Status:** Scarce Palearctic migrant Nov-Apr, but may be overlooked. **Voice:** Staccato, 5- to 6-note 'chok chok chi chi chu-chu', higher in middle. Usually silent in Africa.

6 MADAGASCAR CUCKOO *Cuculus rochii* 26-28 cm

Very similar to Lesser Cuckoo. Typically has plain or weakly barred (not strongly barred) undertail coverts, but best told by call and season of occurrence. Juv. is mottled with rufous on upperparts. **Habitat:** Riverine forests, woodland and dense savanna. **Status:** Scarce migrant from Madagascar, mostly Apr-Sep; may be overlooked. **Voice:** Similar to Red-chested Cuckoo's, but deeper in tone, and typically has 4 (not 3) notes ('piet-my-vrou-vrou'), last note being lower. [C7.7/8, G3.8.7]

1

juv.

2

gabonensis

clamosus

3

juv.

♀

4

♂

♀

hepatic morph

5

6

COUCALS & MALKOHAS

Large, rather lethargic cuckoo-like birds. Quite skulking, but often sun themselves out in the open in the early morning. Flight heavy. Sexes alike; juvs differ; some species have distinct breeding plumages. Unlike cuckoos, they are not brood parasites.

1 BLACK COUCAL *Centropus grillii*   38 cm
A small, dark coucal. Breeding adult has entirely black head, mantle and underparts, contrasting with plain chestnut wings. Non-breeding adult and juv. are buff all over, heavily barred blackish on wings, back and tail; crown and mantle are streaked tawny and brown, but lacks clear supercilium. Darker than juv. Senegal Coucal, with richer chestnut wings and streaked (not barred) head and mantle. **Habitat:** Moist grassland with rank vegetation. **Status:** Uncommon to locally common resident and intra-African migrant. **Voice:** Female gives monotonous, repeated 'poopoop'; also bubbling call, like White-browed Coucal's but faster and higher pitched. [C7.21, G3.9.8]

2 GREEN MALKOHA (COUCAL/YELLOWBILL) *Ceuthmochares australis* 33 cm
The large yellow bill, dull green upperparts and long tail are diagnostic. Differs from Blue Malkoha in green (not blue) plumage and distinctive call; ranges do not overlap. Juv. has duller, greenish bill. **Habitat:** Dense tangles at forest edge, riparian forest and thickets. **Status:** Scarce to locally common, but shy and easily overlooked if not calling. **Voice:** Clicking 'kik-kik-kik', winding up to loud 'cher-cher-cher-cher'. [G3.9.7]

3 BLUE MALKOHA (COUCAL/YELLOWBILL) *Ceuthmochares aereus*   30 cm
Often treated as a race of Green Malkoha, but has a blue (not green) wash over the back and tail; undertail has a purple (not green) sheen. Vocally quite different; ranges do not overlap. Juv. has duller, greenish bill. **Habitat:** Lowland and mid-altitude forest and secondary growth, favouring dense tangles in the mid-storey to canopy. **Status:** Locally common but secretive; often occurs with bird parties. **Voice:** Similar clicking start of Green Malkoha call but ends in a winding trill. [C7.17]

4 SENEGAL COUCAL *Centropus senegalensis*   38-40 cm
A small, black-headed coucal. Much smaller than Gabon, Blue-headed or Coppery-tailed coucals (p. 234), lacking bluish sheen to head (may appear greenish in W), and wings are richer chestnut. Slightly smaller than Burchell's Coucal, with plain (not barred) rump and uppertail. Dark morph found in W Africa has blackish throat and upper breast and rufous belly; smaller and belly much darker than Black-throated Coucal's (p. 234); could be confused with adult Black Coucal, but belly rufous (not black). Juv. is buffy, heavily barred above (not streaked on head and mantle, as in Black Coucal). **Habitat:** Tangled vegetation and long grass; less tied to water than most other coucals. **Status:** Uncommon to locally common resident or partial migrant. **Voice:** Bubbling call note, very similar to that of Burchell's Coucal. [C7.22, G3.9.10]

5 WHITE-BROWED COUCAL *Centropus superciliosus*   41 cm
A medium-sized coucal with a diagnostic white supercilium and heavily streaked nape and mantle in adult plumage. Adult is similar to juv. Burchell's Coucal, but has plain (not barred) wings and generally is whiter below. Juv. is buffier than adult, with less prominent buff supercilium and barred wings; probably not separable from juv. Burchell's Coucal in small area of overlap. **Habitat:** Reedbeds and thickets, usually close to water. **Status:** Common. **Voice:** Liquid, bubbling 'doo-doo-doo-doo', falling in pitch, then slowing and rising in pitch at end. [C7.25, G3.10.2]

6 BURCHELL'S COUCAL *Centropus burchelli*   40-41 cm
Often treated as a race of White-browed Coucal, but adult has a black (not streaked) cap and mantle. Slightly larger than Senegal Coucal with fine rufous barring (not plain) on rump and base of tail. Juv. has brown cap with strong supercilium and streaked mantle; buffy underparts and barred wings separate it from adult White-browed Coucal, but is virtually identical to juv. **Habitat:** Rank grass, riverine scrub, reedbeds, thickets and gardens. **Status:** Common. **Voice:** Bubbling song, similar to that of White-browed Coucal. [G3.10.1]

br.

juv.

1

2

3

4

5

6

juv.

1 BLACK-THROATED COUCAL *Centropus leucogaster* 48-50 cm

Endemic to W Africa. A large coucal with a diagnostic blue-black throat and upper breast. Much larger than dark-morph Senegal Coucal (p. 232), with white (not rufous) lower breast and belly. Juv. lacks blue gloss on head, and has buffy lower breast and barred back. **Habitat:** Dense vegetation in open-canopy forest, forest edge and gallery forest. **Status:** Locally common, but secretive. **Voice:** Deep, booming coucal call of 10-20 notes, slowing and falling in pitch, then rising and speeding up again, 'doo-doo-doo doo duuu duuu duuu duuu doo doo-doo'. [C7.18]

2 NEUMANN'S COUCAL *Centropus neumanni* 46-48 cm

Endemic to N DRC. Often considered a race of Black-throated Coucal, but is overall smaller; ranges do not overlap. Juv. resembles juv. Black-throated Coucal. **Habitat:** Thick tangles and vines at forest edge and along rivers in lowland forest. **Status:** Fairly common, but more often heard than seen. **Voice:** Deep, booming series of 'doo' notes, like Black-throated Coucal's.

3 GABON COUCAL *Centropus anselli* 48-50 cm

Endemic to W Africa. A large coucal, similar to Black-throated and Neumann's coucals, but with tawny rufous underparts (not pale belly and dark throat and breast). Juv. has dark mottling on sides of throat and breast, but underparts are more rufous than Black-throated Coucal's, and tail is more extensively barred. **Habitat:** Dense herbaceous vegetation along forest streams or at edge of forest, along forest trails and in gallery forest. **Status:** Common. **Voice:** Deep, booming series of 'doo' notes, like Black-throated Coucal's. [C7.19]

4 BLUE-HEADED COUCAL *Centropus monachus* 46 cm

Much larger and heavier than Senegal Coucal (p. 232), with less chestnut wings. In direct light, black crown and nape have distinct bluish-black iridescent tinge. Overlaps marginally with Coppery-tailed Coucal, but is smaller, and has unbarred uppertail coverts. Juv. is darker and duller, with barred wings. **Habitat:** Typically in swamps, swamp forest, forest edge and riverine forests; prefers thick cover, but perches openly when calling. **Status:** Common; single or in pairs. **Voice:** Series of 'doo doo' notes, slower and deeper than White-browed Coucal's. [C7.24]

5 COPPERY-TAILED COUCAL *Centropus cupreicaudus* 52-55 cm

Endemic to SC Africa. A very large coucal, similar to Blue-headed Coucal, but larger, with coppery (not bluish) sheen on head and finely barred (not plain) uppertail coverts. Much larger than Burchell's or Senegal coucal, and in flight has distinct brown trailing edge to wing. Juv. is duller and more barred above. **Habitat:** Marshlands, thick reedbeds and adjoining bush. **Status:** Common. **Voice:** Deep, loud, resonant series of 'doo' notes. [C7.20, G3.9.9]

1 BARN OWL *Tyto alba*   35 cm
A medium-sized, pale owl with golden buff and grey upperparts, a white, heart-shaped facial disc and off-white underparts. Much paler above than African Grass-Owl, with less contrast between upperparts and underparts. In flight, has distinctive large head and short tail. São Tomé and Prìncipé *thomensis* is darker, with buffy facial disc and underparts. **Habitat:** Open habitats, from woodland to desert; avoids dense forest. Often roosts in old buildings, but also in caves, hollow trees and mine shafts; doesn't roost on ground. **Status:** Common. **Voice:** Typical call is high-pitched 'shreeee'; hisses and bill-clicks when disturbed. [C3.12, G3.10.3]

2 AFRICAN GRASS-OWL *Tyto capensis*   38 cm
Slightly larger than Barn Owl, with much darker brown upperparts that contrast strongly with pale buff underparts; also habitat differs. Paler beneath than Marsh Owl, with pale (not dark) face. In flight, has longer, more slender wings than Marsh Owl, with darker coverts contrasting with paler flight feathers and only small buffy bases to primaries; outer-tail is white. Juv. has rufous facial disc and darker underparts. **Habitat:** Marshes and tall grassland; not in reedbeds. **Status:** Uncommon and local. **Voice:** Soft, cricket-like 'tk-tk-tk-tk...' in flight. [C7.26, G3.10.4]

3 MARSH OWL *Asio capensis*   35 cm
A plain brown, medium-sized owl with a buff-coloured face, small 'ear' tufts and dark brown eyes. Plain (not streaked) body and wing coverts separate it from Short-eared Owl. In flight, wings are broader than African Grass-Owl's, with much larger buff 'windows' at base of primaries, less contrast between coverts and flight feathers, and pale trailing edge to secondaries and outer primaries. Underwing has dark carpal marks; tail is barred (not white). Often circles overhead after flushing. Less nocturnal than most other owls. **Habitat:** Marshes and damp grassland. Sometimes roosts in flocks. **Status:** Common. **Voice:** Harsh, rasping 'krikkk-krikkk', like material being torn. [C3.19, G3.10.6]

4 CONGO BAY (ITOMBWE) OWL *Phodilus prigoginei*   24 cm
Endemic to Albertine Rift forests. Much smaller and more rufous than Barn and African grass-owls, with rich buff facial disc. Dark brown wing coverts contrast with rufous flight feathers, barred dark brown. Looks less big-headed than *Tyto* owls, with short horns formed by upperpart of facial disc. **Habitat:** Forest; recently found in degraded secondary forest. **Status:** Endangered. Very poorly known. **Voice:** Described as 'wok wok wok'.

5 SHORT-EARED OWL *Asio flammeus*   35 cm
Structure is similar to Marsh Owl's, but plumage is heavily streaked below and blotched above (not plain). Eyes are yellow (not brown). Ear tufts are small, centrally sited on head and usually invisible. In flight, is similar to Marsh Owl, but has blotched (not uniform) upperwing coverts. Underwings are pale, with dark tips and dark carpal bar. **Habitat:** Marshy areas, wetlands and saltmarshes. **Status:** Uncommon Palearctic migrant Nov-Apr. **Voice:** Usually silent in Africa; contact call is low 'gook'. [C3.18]

6 ABYSSINIAN LONG-EARED OWL *Asio abyssinicus*   43 cm
Endemic to E Africa; sometimes considered a race of Common Long-eared Owl *A. otus* (which does not occur in Africa). An obviously 'eared' owl; smaller and slimmer than eagle-owls, with a striking, tawny facial disc. Richly coloured, with heavily blotched breast and chequered belly, resulting from short, pale, transverse bars. **Habitat:** High-altitude forest and giant heaths; roosts in tall trees, including plantations. **Status:** Uncommon to rare. **Voice:** Male calls 'ooh-whoomm', rising in pitch.

7 AFRICAN WOOD-OWL *Strix woodfordii*   34 cm
A medium-sized owl with a rounded head lacking ear tufts, dark eyes and yellow bill. Facial disc is finely barred and paler than white-spotted brown head and upper breast; belly is barred brown and white. Larger than owlets, and lacks ear-tufts of eagle-owls or Maned Owl (p. 238). Plumage varies from very dark brown to russet. **Habitat:** Evergreen and riverine forests, mature woodland and exotic plantations. **Status:** Common. **Voice:** Female calls 'hu hu, hu whoo-oo', with male normally responding with low hoot; also gives high-pitched 'who-uuu'. [C7.44, G3.10.5]

1 MANED OWL *Jubula lettii*   35-37 cm
Slightly larger than African Wood-Owl (p. 236), with more rufous plumage, long ear tufts and diagnostic shaggy, elongated nape feathers, as well as long feathers of top of head, which give it very distinctive head shape. Eyes are yellow (not brown). Plain rufous chest and the buff belly with conspicuous dark streaks distinguish it from medium-sized forest eagle-owls. **Habitat:** Forest understorey, in dense clumps of vegetation. **Status:** Uncommon. **Voice:** Unknown.

2 PEL'S FISHING-OWL *Scotopelia peli*   56-62 cm
A large, ginger-coloured owl associated with rivers and other waterbodies. Larger than other fishing-owls, with spotted or lightly barred (not streaked) breast, and dark eyes and bill. Pale, unfeathered legs and feet are difficult to see in the field. When alarmed, it fluffs up head feathers, giving huge, round-headed appearance. Juv. is paler and more buffy coloured, with almost white head. **Habitat:** Large trees around lakes and slow-moving rivers. **Status:** Uncommon. **Voice:** Deep, booming 'hoo-huuuum'; jackal-like wailing. [C7.36, G3.11.3]

3 RUFOUS FISHING-OWL *Scotopelia ussheri*   43-51 cm
Endemic to W Africa. Smaller than Pel's Fishing-Owl, with streaked (not spotted) breast. Mainly rufous (paler on head and underparts), with rounded head, pale unmarked face, very large dark eyes and faint rufous streaks on fawn underparts. Juv. is paler. **Habitat:** Forest, along rivers and streams, and gallery forest. **Status:** Endangered. Scarce and uncommon. **Voice:** Soft, dove-like, low hoots at 1-minute intervals; long, drawn-out, wailing hoot. [C7.37]

4 VERMICULATED FISHING-OWL *Scotopelia bouvieri*   43-51 cm
Endemic to W Africa. Much smaller and paler than Pel's Fishing-Owl, with diagnostic, well-marked black streaks on white breast; streaks become narrower and fainter on belly. Bill is pale yellow tipped with black (not all-black). Juv. is almost white, with brown-barred flight feathers. **Habitat:** Forest rivers and streams, marsh forest and gallery forest. **Status:** Locally common. **Voice:** Single, drawn-out, harsh, wailing hoot; various 'kraak' and 'kok kok' calls; young has wailing call similar to that of young Pel's Fishing-Owl. [C7.38]

5 VERREAUX'S (GIANT) EAGLE-OWL *Bubo lacteus*   58-66 cm
A large woodland and savanna owl, easily identified by its size and finely vermiculated, pale grey plumage. At close range, pink eyelids and dark brown eyes are distinctive. Most other eagle-owls are smaller, with more boldly barred or blotched plumage; ear tufts are shorter than other species'. Juv. is paler grey, lacking white tips to greater coverts. **Habitat:** Broadleafed woodland, savanna, thornveld and riverine forests. **Status:** Uncommon to locally common resident. **Voice:** Grunting, pig-like 'unnh-unnh-unnh'. [C7.35, G3.11.2]

6 SHELLEY'S EAGLE-OWL *Bubo shelleyi*   54-61 cm
A large forest eagle-owl, very rarely seen. Similar in size to Verreaux's Eagle-Owl, but much darker, with densely barred black or dark brown upperparts, and regularly barred white and blackish-brown underparts; ear tufts are long. Dark brown (not yellow) eyes separate it from all forest eagle-owls except Fraser's (p. 240), from which it can be told by being much larger and less rufous, and having cream (not blue-grey) bill. Juv. is paler, with large white patches on plumage. **Habitat:** Forest. **Status:** Local and rare. **Voice:** Loud, far-carrying, single scream, 'wheeehaaaa'. [C7.34]

1 PHARAOH EAGLE-OWL *Bubo ascalaphus*　　　　　　　　45-50 cm
A large, pale eagle-owl of N African deserts. Much paler than Cape Eagle-Owl and less heavily marked below. Larger than Greyish Eagle-Owl, with orange (not brown) eyes and streaked (not barred) breast. **Habitat:** Arid country, from dry savannas to rocky deserts. Often roosts on ground among rocks. **Status:** Poorly known; probably uncommon to rare. **Voice:** 3-syllable 'hu-huh-ooh' during courtship; short 'huo', dropping in pitch at end. [C3.14]

2 CAPE EAGLE-OWL *Bubo capensis*　　　　　　　　　　48-54 cm
A large, heavily marked eagle-owl, typically in mountainous areas. Larger than Spotted Eagle-Owl, with black and chestnut blotching on breast, and bold (not fine) barring on belly and flanks. Feet are much larger, and has orange (not yellow) eyes (but rare rufous-morph Spotted Eagle-Owl has more orange eyes). Upperparts are mottled tawny and dark brown; is generally richer and more strongly marked than Spotted Eagle-Owl. **Habitat:** Rocky and mountainous terrain. **Status:** Generally uncommon. **Voice:** Deep, far-carrying 'hooooo' calls, sometimes 2-3 notes; dog-like bark, 'wak-wak-wak'; seldom duets. [G3.10.11]

3 SPOTTED EAGLE-OWL *Bubo africanus*　　　　　　　　43-50 cm
Most birds are greyish, and are easily told from Cape Eagle-Owl by their smaller size, lack of dark breast patches, finely (not boldly) barred belly and flanks, yellow (not orange) eyes, and smaller feet. Rare rufous morph is more heavily blotched and has orange-yellow eyes; is best distinguished from Cape Eagle-Owl by call, smaller size and smaller feet. Range is not known to overlap with very similar Greyish Eagle-Owl; differs in being greyer, with yellow (not brown) eyes. Juv. is browner. **Habitat:** All except forest, from desert to woodland and gardens. **Status:** Common. **Voice:** Male gives deep 'hoo-huuu', often followed by female's 'huu-ho-huuu', with second note higher-pitched. [G3.11.1]

4 GREYISH EAGLE-OWL *Bubo cinerascens*　　　　　　　　40-46 cm
Often considered a race of Spotted Eagle-Owl, but is smaller with shorter ear-tufts and dark brown (not yellow) eyes; has finer vermiculations on upperparts, with reduced spotting; underparts are more finely barred. At close range, bill has dark grey tip (not uniform horn); eyelids pink. Juv. is browner. **Habitat:** Dry woodland to semi-arid scrub and desert areas. **Status:** Uncommon to locally common. **Voice:** Similar to Spotted Eagle-Owl's. [C7.31]

5 FRASER'S EAGLE-OWL *Bubo poensis*　　　　　　　　　43 cm
A medium-sized forest eagle-owl. Separated from Akun Eagle-Owl by its brown (not yellow) eyes, rufous (not greyish) face, and uniformly barred (not blotched) underparts. Overall plumage is rufous-brown and buff, with long, buffy ear-tufts bordered with black. Much smaller and more rufous than Shelley's Eagle-Owl (p. 238). Bill is bluish grey; eyelids are pale blue. Juv. is much paler, almost white, with fine brown barring. **Habitat:** Forest, edge of forest and old secondary growth. **Status:** Locally common. **Voice:** Usual call is hooting 'hoohaa' and mechanical 'duka duka' staccato trill. [C7.33]

6 USAMBARA (NDUK) EAGLE-OWL *Bubo vosseleri*　　　　48 cm
Endemic to Tanzania's E Arc Mts. Often considered a race of Fraser's Eagle-Owl, but is larger, with heavy blotching (not barring) on upper breast and yellow-orange or orange-brown (not dark brown) eyes. Juv. is almost white, with narrow dark bars; facial disc is prominently ringed dark brown. **Habitat:** Evergreen forest and forest edge, 200-1 500 m. **Status:** Vulnerable. Rare and localised. **Voice:** Deep 'ub-a-wb-a-wb-wb-a', lasting several seconds; has been likened to noise made by displaying Common Snipe.

7 AKUN EAGLE-OWL *Bubo leucostictus*　　　　　　　　43 cm
Less rufous than Fraser's Eagle-Owl, with a greyish face, prominent whitish eyebrows and yellow (not dark brown) eyes; also lacks regularly barred underparts. Yellow eyes distinguish it from Shelley's (p. 238) and Greyish eagle-owls. Overall plumage is blackish brown above; upper breast is brown, with tawny bars and streaks; lower breast and belly are white, marked with irregular dark spots and bars. Juv. is much paler, almost white, with sparse darker barring. **Habitat:** Forest. **Status:** Uncommon. **Voice:** Grunting trill similar to Fraser's Eagle-Owl's, but has various hooting calls. [C7.32]

desertorum

ascalaphus

1 AFRICAN SCOPS-OWL *Otus senegalensis* 15-17 cm
A small, slender owl with fairly prominent ear tufts. Typically greyish, but some individuals are more rufous. Slightly smaller than European Scops-Owl (often considered conspecific), with more pronounced black edge to facial disc and heavier streaking, but there is much individual variation. Smaller than white-faced scops-owls, with grey (not white) face and yellow (not orange) eyes; range does not overlap with other scops-owls'. Isolated population on Pagalu (Annobon Island) is darker and more heavily streaked. **Habitat:** Savanna and dry, open woodland; avoids forests. Typically roosts on branch adjacent to tree trunk. **Status:** Common. **Voice:** Soft, frog-like 'prrrup', repeated every 5-8 seconds. [C7.28]

2 EUROPEAN SCOPS-OWL *Otus scops* 18 cm
Very similar to African Scops-Owl, with which range overlaps in N; both are variable in colour and markings. Black border to facial disc is slightly narrower. In the hand, may be told by longer primary 10; P8 and P9 are of equal length and P10 projects as far as P6 (in African Scops-Owl, P9 is shorter than P8 and P10 is level with P3). **Habitat:** Wooded savannas, mostly with open understorey. **Status:** Palearctic migrant Oct-Mar; apparently uncommon in W, becoming increasingly rare further E. **Voice:** Short, flute-like 'ciute' every 2 seconds; mostly silent in region. [C3.13]

3 SANDY SCOPS-OWL *Otus icterorhynchus* 17 cm
The only rainforest scops-owl in its range. More rufous than African Scops-Owl. Ear tufts and less strikingly marked plumage separate it from *Glaucidium* owlets (p. 244). Nominate race (W Africa) has brown upperparts spotted with tawny, and paler brown underparts spotted with white. C African *holerythrus* is more richly coloured, rufous and cinnamon. **Habitat:** Rainforest. **Status:** Uncommon; difficult to observe; best located by call. **Voice:** Long, whistled 'tweeooo', repeated every 3-4 seconds. [C7.27]

4 SOKOKE SCOPS-OWL *Otus ireneae* 16 cm
Endemic to E Africa. A small scops-owl of coastal forest and dense woodland; range is not known to overlap with other scops-owls'. Coloration ranges from pale grey through rufous to dark brown; all morphs have yellow eyes. Ear tufts are small, barely visible at night. Smaller than Barred Owlet (p. 244), and lacks bold white wing spots. **Habitat:** Coastal forest, rarely moving into adjacent miombo woodland. Normally roosts in lower canopy of trees. **Status:** Endangered. Locally common in Arabuko-Sokoke Forest, Kenya and foothills of E Usambara Mtns, Tanzania. **Voice:** Tinkerbird-like 'too-too-too-too', usually 5-10 notes per phrase.

5 SÃO TOMÉ SCOPS-OWL *Otus hartlaubi* 18 cm
Endemic to São Tomé; reports of a scops-owl on Prìncipé are unconfirmed, and may be a different species. Small size and behaviour distinguish it from Barn Owl (p. 236; the only other owl on São Tomé). Colour ranges from pale greyish brown to rich rufous. **Habitat:** Forest understorey, old secondary growth and edge of forest, from coast to about 1 600 m. **Status:** Common. **Voice:** Soft 'kwuh, kuwuh', repeated every 10-15 seconds. [C7.29]

6 PEMBA SCOPS-OWL *Otus pembaensis* 20 cm
Endemic to Pemba, where it is the only small owl. A rather plain scops-owl, varying from rufous and buff, with prominent whitish scapular line, to uniformly rich rufous. **Habitat:** Woodland and forest; also clove plantations. **Status:** Common. **Voice:** Resonant, single notes, spaced unevenly; during duets, higher pitched notes are made by female.

7 LITTLE OWL *Athene noctua* 20 cm
A small, long-legged owl. Lacks ear tufts of African and European scops-owls, and is browner. Whitish below, lightly streaked brown, and rufous-brown above, with irregular large white spots on coverts. Tail is brown, with three white bars. More diurnal than most other small owls. **Habitat:** Acacia savanna. **Status:** Common in NE, vagrant to W Africa. **Voice:** Whistled 'kieeeuw', rising in pitch; often calls during day. [C3.15]

rufous morph

grey morph

rufous morph

pale morph

rufous morph

1 NORTHERN WHITE-FACED SCOPS-OWL *Ptilopsus leucotis*   25-28 cm
A fairly small owl with ear tufts. Recently split from Southern White-faced Scops-Owl; differs by being paler, with less distinct black face and breast markings, but best told by different call; ranges are not known to overlap. Larger than other scops-owls, with prominent whitish face with a broad, black margin; eyes are orange-red (not yellow). Juv. is browner, with greyer face and yellow eyes. **Habitat:** Dry woodland and riverine forest in dry areas. **Status:** Local and thinly distributed. **Voice:** Fluty 'ploo pluuu' call. [C7.30]

2 SOUTHERN WHITE-FACED SCOPS-OWL *Ptilopsus granti*   25-28 cm
Often considered a race of Northern White-faced Scops-Owl; ranges are not known to overlap. Larger than other scops-owls, with bright orange (not yellow) eyes and prominent black-and-white facial disc. Juv. is browner, with yellow eyes. **Habitat:** Acacia savanna and dry, broadleafed woodland. **Status:** Common. **Voice:** Differs greatly from Northern White-faced Scops-Owl's: fast hooting, 'doo-doo-doo-doo-hohoo'. [G3.10.8]

3 PEARL-SPOTTED OWLET *Glaucidium perlatum*   18-19 cm
A small, long-tailed owl. Told from scops-owls by its rounded head, lack of ear tufts, and white spotting on back and tail. Smaller than Barred Owlet, with small white spots on upperparts. Has two black 'false eyes' on nape. Juv. is less spotted on crown and mantle. Often active during day. **Habitat:** Acacia savanna and woodland. **Status:** Common. **Voice:** Series of low hoots, rising in pitch, 'tu tu tu tu tu', then a brief pause following by piercing, downslurred whistles, 'tseuu tseuu tseuu'; sometimes calls during day. [C7.39, G3.10.9]

4 BARRED OWLET *Glaucidium capense*   21 cm
Slightly larger than Pearl-spotted Owlet, with faintly barred upperparts and tail, barred breast, and spotted (not streaked) belly; appears larger-headed and shorter-tailed. Large white tips to scapulars form conspicuous line of spots on back. Juv. is less distinctly spotted below. Albertine Rift *castaneum* has a plain brown back; told from Albertine Owlet by its white (not buffy) wing bar. Together with W African *etchecopari* is sometimes treated as a separate species, Chestnut Owlet. **Habitat:** Mature woodland, thickets, forest and forest edge. **Status:** Locally common. **Voice:** Series of 6-10 notes, starting softly and increasing in volume, 'kerrr-kerrr-kerrr-kerrr', often followed by series of purring whistles, 'trru-trrre, trru-trrre', second note higher pitched. [C7.41, G3.10.10]

5 ALBERTINE OWLET *Glaucidium albertinum*   20 cm
Endemic to Albertine Rift. Similar to Barred Owlet, but upperparts barred and spotted cream (not white); also has finely spotted (not barred) crown and nape, and uniform or finely barred back. Similar to *castaneum* race of Barred Owlet, but has buffy (not white) wing bar. **Habitat:** Montane forests. **Status:** Vulnerable. Known from only five specimens from E DRC and N Rwanda. **Voice:** Calls similar to Barred Owlet's recorded from its range, suggesting it may be race of Barred Owlet. [C7.42]

6 RED-CHESTED OWLET *Glaucidium tephronotum*   19 cm
A distinctive forest owlet. Smaller than Barred or Sjostedt's owlets, with unmarked grey head (not brown, spotted white), rufous sides of breast and flanks, and large blackish spots on whitish underparts (other two species show distinct barring on breast). In flight, white spots on tail are diagnostic. Juv. is undescribed. **Habitat:** Forest, from understorey to lower canopy. **Status:** Uncommon to locally common. **Voice:** Short, whistled 'duut duut' notes, uttered at varying rates. [C7.40]

7 SJOSTEDT'S (CHESTNUT-BACKED) OWLET *Glaucidium sjostedti*   24 cm
A rather large, richly coloured owlet with diagnostic tawny underparts barred with chestnut, and dark chestnut or rufous-brown upperparts. Head is finely spotted and barred. Wings and tail are black barred with white. Appreciably larger than Red-chested Owlet. Range does not overlap with Barred Owlet's. Juv. is paler and buffy below. **Habitat:** Forest understorey to lower canopy. **Status:** Locally common. **Voice:** Similar to Barred Owlet's but lower pitched and slower. [C7.43]

Nocturnal aerial feeders. Roost on ground or along branches during the day. Identification is very tricky, based on extent of white or cream in primaries and tail as well as general plumage colour. Sexes differ.

1 FIERY-NECKED NIGHTJAR *Caprimulgus pectoralis*   23-25 cm
Forms a superspecies with Black-shouldered, Rwenzori and Montane nightjars; ranges barely overlap. A heavily marked nightjar with a rich rufous collar (not orange-buff, as in Rufous-cheeked Nightjar; p. 248) and a white moustache and throat patch. In flight, male has broad white tips to outer-tail and white primary patches; these are buffy in female, and tail tips are smaller. Amount of rufous on face and breast varies considerably. **Habitat:** Woodland, savanna and plantations. **Status:** Common. **Voice:** Characteristic night sound of Africa: plaintive, whistled 'good lord, deliver us', descending in pitch, first note often repeated. [C7.51, G3.11.5]

2 BLACK-SHOULDERED NIGHTJAR *Caprimulgus nigroscapularis*   23-25 cm
Sometimes treated as a race of Fiery-necked Nightjar, but is generally more rufous, especially on underparts, with more brightly patterned wing coverts contrasting with dark shoulder patch. Also shows broader, more rufous collar and smaller white spots on primaries. **Habitat:** Very variable but chiefly in woodland or forest edge from 2 000 m to sea level. **Status:** Locally common. **Voice:** Higher pitched and faster delivered version of Fiery-necked Nightjar's, with sharper and faster 'werp werp' notes. [C7.52]

3 MONTANE (ABYSSINIAN) NIGHTJAR *Caprimulgus poliocephalus*   22-24 cm
Range is not known to overlap with similar Fiery-necked, Black-shouldered and Rwenzori nightjars; differs in having more extensive white in outer-tail (male's outer-tail is fully white; female's is mostly white). A dark brown nightjar; much darker and less spotted than Swamp Nightjar (p. 252). White in outer-tail is more extensive than in Square-tailed and Slender-tailed nightjars (p. 250). **Habitat:** Woodland, forest edge and scrub in heathland and grasslands; usually at higher elevations than other similar nightjars but descends to 1 000 m in some areas. **Status:** Locally common. **Voice:** High-pitched whistling similar to Black-shouldered and Rwenzori nightjars'; harsh 'kwa kwa' flight call. [C7.53]

4 RWENZORI (MONTANE) NIGHTJAR *Caprimulgus ruwenzorii*   22-24 cm
Very similar to Montane Nightjar, but has only distal half of outer-tail white (slightly less in female); ranges do not overlap. Darker than Fiery-necked and Black-shouldered nightjars, with more white in wing and tail; also occurs at higher elevations. E *guttifer* (Usambara Mts, Tanzania, NE Zambia and Malawi) has slightly less white in the outer-tail; sometimes treated as a separate species, Usambara Nightjar. **Habitat:** High- and mid-altitude forest edge, woodland and scrub on heathland and highland grasslands. **Status:** Locally common. **Voice:** High-pitched, whistling version of Fiery-necked Nightjar's, almost shrill in content, with 'kah' or 'kwa' notes. [C7.54]

5 SOMBRE (DUSKY) NIGHTJAR *Caprimulgus fraenatus*   23-25 cm
Endemic to NE Africa. Darker than Fiery-necked Nightjar, with less reddish brown on mantle, larger buffy spots on wing coverts and churring, not whistled, call. Differs from similar Montane Nightjar by having much smaller white tips to tail feathers. **Habitat:** Open bush and grasslands in dry areas; always roosts on the ground, not in trees. **Status:** Locally common. **Voice:** Rapid churring song, often beginning with 'woka woka' and interspersed with 'werk' notes.

6 PRIGOGINE'S (ITOMBWE) NIGHTJAR *Caprimulgus prigoginei*   19 cm
Known only from a single female specimen, collected in Itombwe Mts, DRC, in 1955. Field identification is uncertain; probably appears small, with short tail and largish head. Plumage is dark brown, with extensive speckling. Most closely resembles female Fiery-necked Nightjar. **Habitat:** Forest or forest edge. **Status:** Unknown; listed as Endangered. **Voice:** Unknown, although churring and chopping nightjar calls have been heard in area.

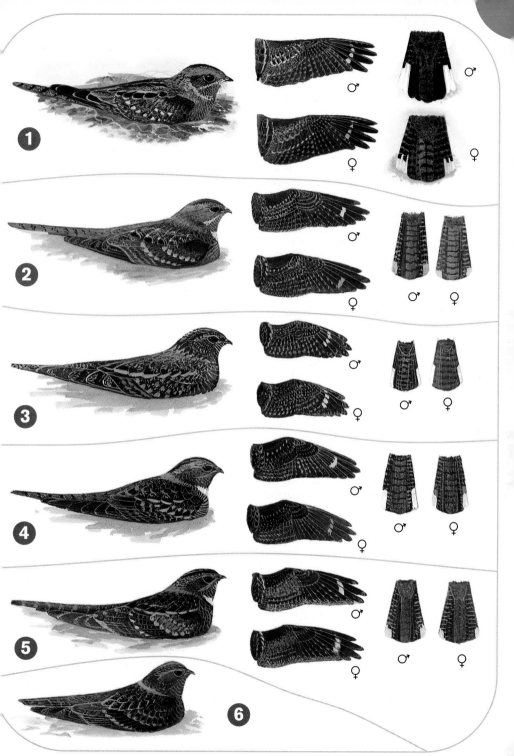

1 EURASIAN NIGHTJAR *Caprimulgus europaeus*   25-28 cm
A large, long-winged nightjar. At rest, appears rather pale grey, with buff bar across lesser coverts and pale moustachial streak. Lacks rufous nuchal collar. In flight, male has white tips to outer-tail and primary patches; these are lacking in female. Female is greyer than female Pennant-winged Nightjar (p. 254). Sometimes roosts lengthwise on branches. **Habitat:** Woodland, savanna, plantations and suburban areas. **Status:** Locally common Palearctic migrant Oct-Apr. **Voice:** Generally silent in Africa; occasionally utters nasal grunt on flushing. [C3.22, G3.11.4]

2 EGYPTIAN NIGHTJAR *Caprimulgus aegyptius*   24-26 cm
A fairly large, greyish-sandy nightjar with irregular black markings especially on scapulars. In flight, wings are broad and long; both sexes typically lack white in wing and tail. Wing beats are deep, interspersed with frequent glides. Colder grey plumage and lack of white in wings and tail separate it from Golden Nightjar. Larger and paler grey than female Plain Nightjar (p. 250). **Habitat:** Desert and semi-desert, especially near water. **Status:** Uncommon Palearctic migrant, mostly Oct-Apr. **Voice:** Rapid, purring 'powrr-powrr-powrr-powrr'. [C3.20]

3 NUBIAN NIGHTJAR *Caprimulgus nubius*   21-22 cm
A small, highly variable species. Grey or pale brown above, with buffy underparts barred brown. Larger and less richly coloured than Donaldson-Smith's Nightjar (p. 250); paler and more variegated than Star-spotted (p. 250) or Sombre (p. 246) nightjars. In flight, appears pale, with large buffy wing patches and small white tips to outer-tail. Male has white spots in outer primaries; these are buff in female. **Habitat:** Arid and semi-arid scrub and coastal dunes, often close to water. **Status:** Locally common resident and possibly intra-African migrant. **Voice:** Repeated 'ow-wow', similar to Freckled Nightjar's.

4 GOLDEN NIGHTJAR *Caprimulgus eximius*   23-25 cm
A medium-sized, tawny-coloured nightjar with fine black-and-white barring. Appears large-headed at rest. Has conspicuous white throat patch. In flight, extensive white panels in outer primaries are broadly bordered with black. Outer-tail is broadly tipped white (in male) or buff (in female). Does not flush easily. **Habitat:** Open, grassy, arid areas with scattered bush. **Status:** Locally common. **Voice:** Low-pitched churring, lasting up to several minutes.

5 RED-NECKED NIGHTJAR *Caprimulgus ruficollis*   30-32 cm
A large, noticeably large-headed nightjar. Generally greyish above, with prominently buff-spotted wing coverts. In flight, both sexes have white primary patches and outer-tail tips (off-white in female). Larger than Eurasian Nightjar, with rufous collar. Flight is slow and measured; appears long-winged and long-tailed. **Habitat:** Sparsely vegetated and semi-arid areas, hunting over open ground and wetlands. **Status:** Uncommon Palearctic migrant Oct-Apr. **Voice:** Repeated 'cut-ock' lasting 2 minutes or more, sometimes preceded by series of rapid single notes; seldom calls in region. [C3.21]

6 RUFOUS-CHEEKED NIGHTJAR *Caprimulgus rufigena*   23-24 cm
A fairly small, variegated nightjar. In its breeding range, is paler grey than Fiery-necked Nightjar (p. 246), with orange-buff (not rufous) collar; female has less buff in tail than female Fiery-necked Nightjar. Range is not known to overlap with much larger Red-necked Nightjar. **Habitat:** Dry thornveld, woodland and scrub desert. **Status:** Locally common intra-African migrant, breeding in S Oct-Apr. **Voice:** Prolonged churring, usually preceded by choking 'chukoo, chukoo'. [C7.57, G3.11.6]

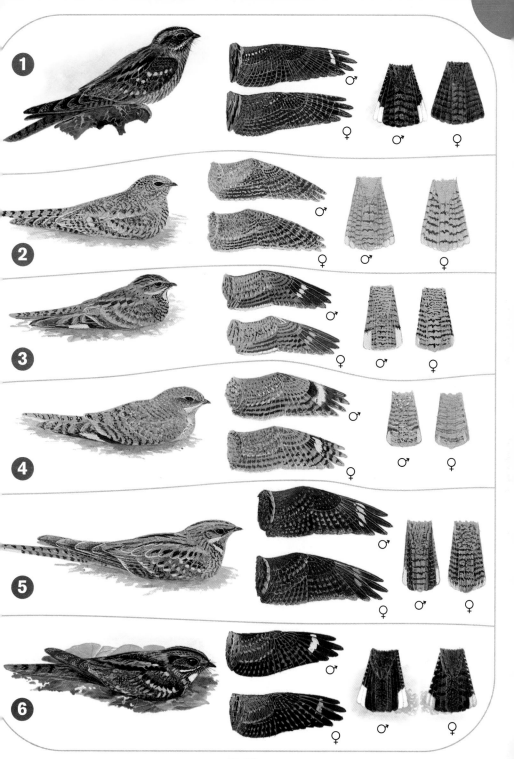

1 SQUARE-TAILED (MOZAMBIQUE) NIGHTJAR *Caprimulgus fossii*   23-24 cm
Square (not wedge-shaped) tail separates this species from Long-tailed and Slender-tailed nightjars. Resembles Swamp Nightjar (p. 252) in having white outer-tail feathers , but differs in being darker brown and less buff above, and by its larger size. Female has less white on tail than female Swamp Nightjar. **Habitat:** Coastal dune scrub and sandy woodland, often near water. **Status:** Common. **Voice:** Prolonged churring, changing in pitch at intervals ('changing gears'). [C7.49, G3.11.9]

2 LONG-TAILED NIGHTJAR *Caprimulgus climacurus*   28-43 cm (including tail)
A small-bodied nightjar. Breeding adult has longer tail than Slender-tailed Nightjar, with central feathers projecting well beyond rest of tail. Some resident populations have long tail all year; migrant populations lose long tail in wintering areas, but central tail feathers are always slightly longer than in Square-tailed Nightjar. E populations are more tawny-buff than greyer Slender-tailed Nightjar; *nigricans* from S Sudan is much darker, almost black above. **Habitat:** Semi-arid to wooded savannas; also clearings and villages in lowland forest. **Status:** Common. **Voice:** Rapid churring, much faster than other 'churring' nightjars'. [C7.48]

3 SLENDER-TAILED NIGHTJAR *Caprimulgus clarus*   25-28 cm
Endemic to NE Africa. Most similar to Square-tailed Nightjar, but tail is wedge-shaped (not square-ended), with central tail feathers projecting beyond rest of tail. Tail typically is shorter than Long-tailed Nightjar's, but can be confused with female and moulting male of this species; tends to be greyer, with more coarsely barred central tail feathers. **Habitat:** Dry woodlands and wooded grasslands and adjacent farmlands. **Status:** Common. **Voice:** Rattled churring similar to Square-tailed Nightjar's, with 'kwarr kwaar' ending to churring phrase. [C7.50]

4 DONALDSON-SMITH'S NIGHTJAR *Caprimulgus donaldsoni*   18-19 cm
Endemic to NE Africa. A very small nightjar, with richly coloured upperparts lacking greyish tones. Much smaller, darker and less grey than Nubian Nightjar (p. 248). Plumage is strongly marked and speckled, unlike in Plain and Star-spotted nightjars. Male has broad white tips to outer-tail and large white primary patch; these are smaller in female. Bases of outer-tail are brown (white in Swamp; p. 252, and Square-tailed nightjars). **Habitat:** Semi-arid acacia and broadleafed savannas. **Status:** Locally common. **Voice:** Diagnostic 3-note whistled phrase, 'tew wee pitee'.

5 PLAIN NIGHTJAR *Caprimulgus inornatus*   23 cm
A small savanna nightjar, relatively uniformly coloured above, lacking a nuchal collar and varying from pale rufous to light grey or dusky brown. Dark birds resemble Star-spotted Nightjar, but are longer tailed and lack any white on throat. In flight, male has extensive white tips to outer-tail feathers and white primary patches; female lacks white in tail and has buff primary patches. **Habitat:** Semi-arid areas in breeding grounds and to forest edge on migration. **Status:** Common intra-African migrant, breeding Mar-Aug in Sahel, then moving S. **Voice:** Long, monotonous, churring song, sometimes preceded by series of deep, short notes. [C7.55]

6 STAR-SPOTTED NIGHTJAR *Caprimulgus stellatus*   21-23 cm
Endemic to NE Africa. Mostly a uniform dark brown nightjar, although some individuals are paler buff and sandy. Diagnostic small white patches at sides of throat and tiny black dots on crown and mantle are visible only at very close range. Typically darker than Plain Nightjar; both sexes have white primary bars and narrow white edges to tail (male Plain Nightjar has broad white tail edges; female has plain tail and buff primary bar). Smaller and plainer than Nubian Nightjar (p. 248). **Habitat:** Open areas in dry scrubby woodland and grasslands. **Status:** Uncommon. **Voice:** Repeated, sharp 'cheuu cheuu' from ground and sometimes in flight.

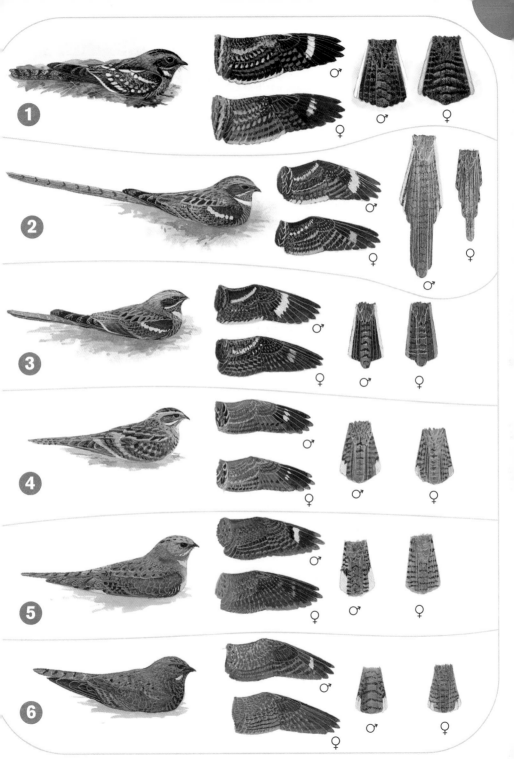

1 SWAMP (NATAL) NIGHTJAR *Caprimulgus natalensis*   20-22 cm
A heavily spotted and vermiculated nightjar; appears buffy-brown or grey-brown at rest. Outer-tail feathers are entirely white (in male) or buff (in female). Male has white spots in outer primaries; these are buff in female. Smaller and more uniformly spotted than Square-tailed Nightjar (p. 250). In E Africa, is paler and more marked than Montane Nightjar (p. 246). **Habitat:** Open grassland, often in damp areas, and palm savanna; roosts on ground. **Status:** Locally common. **Voice:** 'Chow-chow-chow' or 'chop-chop-chop'. [C7.47, G3.11.7]

2 FRECKLED NIGHTJAR *Caprimulgus tristigma*   26-28 cm
Differs from both Eurasian (p. 248) and Pennant-winged (p. 254) nightjars by its greyish upperparts, which blend well with the rocky terrain it frequents. In flight, may be distinguished from Eurasian Nightjar by outer-tail feathers, the tips of which show less white. Female and juv. lack white tail patches of male. **Habitat:** Rocky outcrops in woodland and hilly terrain; also found roosting on buildings in towns and cities. **Status:** Locally common. **Voice:** Yapping, double-noted 'kow-kow', sometimes extending to four syllables. [C7.56, G3.11.8]

3 BATES'S NIGHTJAR *Caprimulgus batesi*   28-30 cm
A large, forest nightjar unlikely to be confused with any other species in its habitat; larger and darker grey-brown (less rufous) than Brown Nightjar. Male has small white panels in outer primaries and broad white tips to outer-tail; female is all dark. Appears darker than female Pennant-winged Nightjar (p. 254), with more rounded wings. Flies low over grasslands and clearings in rainforest and calls from branches in unusual upright posture, not lying along branch. **Habitat:** Rainforests and secondary growth; roosts perching in forest and hunts in adjacent clearings and grasslands. **Status:** Locally common. **Voice:** Repeated, barking 'whow whoh'. [C7.45]

4 BROWN NIGHTJAR *Caprimulgus binotatus*   21-23 cm
A small forest nightjar, with rather uniform rufous-brown plumage. Sexes are alike, lacking any white on tail and wings. Much smaller than Bates's Nightjar. White throat patches are not a field character; located mostly by its fruit-bat-like song. **Habitat:** Forest, in dry-land forest and near rivers, and gallery forest. **Status:** Generally uncommon. **Voice:** Described as 'kiiuup' or 'yiiup' notes; calls from tree perches, rarely from ground or in flight. [C7.46]

5 NECHISAR NIGHTJAR *Caprimulgus solala*   approx. 28 cm
Known only from a road-kill specimen (sex unknown), from which only a wing was retained, on Nechisar Plains, Ethiopia, in September 1990. A large, reddish-brown nightjar with white tail corners. White patches in primaries are closer to base of primaries than in all other African nightjars, except distinctive male Pennant-winged Nightjar (p. 254). **Habitat:** Tall-grass savanna. **Status:** Vulnerable. Subsequent searches at Nechisar have failed to find the bird; it is thus either rare or its distribution is centred elsewhere. **Voice:** Unknown.

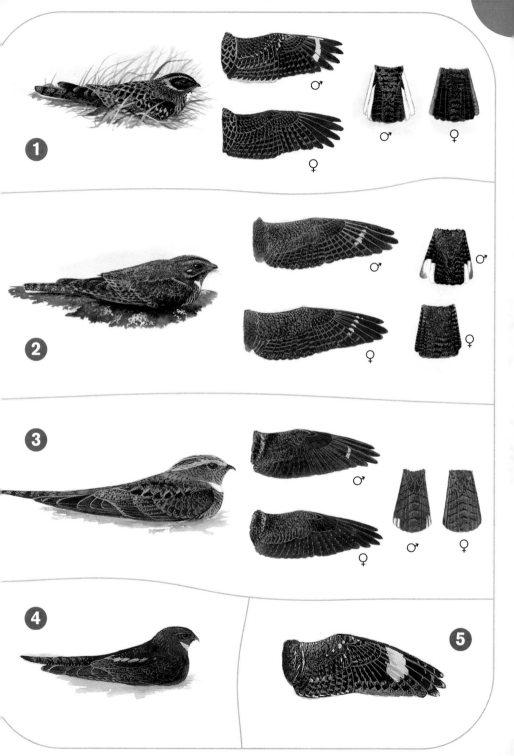

1 STANDARD-WINGED NIGHTJAR *Macrodipteryx longipennis*   21-22 cm
Breeding male has remarkable elongated inner primaries with narrow shafts and broad, ovate tips, which trail above the bird in flight. Female lacks standards. Both sexes have wings and tail barred rufous and brown, lacking any white. Smaller than female Pennant-winged Nightjar, with less boldly barred flight feathers. **Habitat:** Savannas, pastures and forest clearings. **Status:** Common intra-African migrant, breeding in savannas of W and C Africa Jan-Jun before migrating N to Sahel. **Voice:** Rapid series of single notes, very soft and high-pitched; male calls 'trrp' during aerial display. [C7.58]

2 PENNANT-WINGED NIGHTJAR *Macrodipteryx vexillarius*   23-26 cm
Male has a diagnostic broad white band across primaries, with longer inner primaries giving the wing a peculiar shape. Breeding male has long, white inner primaries which trail behind the bird. Female lacks any white on wings or tail; is larger than Standard-winged Nightjar, with more boldly barred flight feathers and more pointed wing appearance. **Habitat:** Wide variety of habitats when on migration; roosts on ground, but often perches on branches after flushing; breeds in broadleafed woodland. **Status:** Locally common intra-African migrant, breeding in S Aug-Feb, moving N Jan-Sep. **Voice:** Continuous, high-pitched twittering. [C7.59, G3.11.10]

RED-NECKED NIGHTJAR

GOLDEN NIGHTJAR

NUBIAN NIGHTJAR

EGYPTIAN NIGHTJAR

BROWN NIGHTJAR

PLAIN NIGHTJAR

LONG-TAILED NIGHTJAR

SLENDER-TAILED NIGHTJAR

DONALDSON-SMITH'S NIGHTJAR

PENNANT-WINGED
NIGHTJAR

♀

EURASIAN
NIGHTJAR

BATES'S
NIGHTJAR

FIERY-NECKED
NIGHTJAR

FRECKLED
NIGHTJAR

SQUARE-TAILED
NIGHTJAR

RUFOUS-
CHEEKED
NIGHTJAR

SWAMP
NIGHTJAR

257

Aerial feeders. Told from swallows (p. 358) by sombre plumage, scythe-shaped wings and distinctive flight action. Sexes alike.

1 SCARCE SWIFT *Schoutedenapus myoptilus* 17 cm
A fairly small, grey-brown swift with a long, deeply forked tail; its shape appears intermediate between White-rumped and African Palm swifts'. Flight action is rapid and slightly jerky; glides with wings angled down. Pale throat separates it from extremely restricted Schouteden's Swift; paler and longer-tailed than Bates's Swift. **Habitat:** Aerial, over cliffs and rocky bluffs in forested mountain areas. **Status:** Local but fairly common. **Voice:** Nasal twittering and a trill. [C7.65, G3.12.10]

2 SCHOUTEDEN'S SWIFT *Schoutedenapus schoutedeni* 17 cm
Apparently endemic to E DRC; known only from 5 specimens. Darker than Scarce Swift, with more deeply forked tail, and lacks pale throat. Paler than Bates's Swift, with longer, more deeply forked tail; flight action presumably is closer to Scarce Swift's. **Habitat:** Aerial, over forest, forest edge and clearings. **Status:** Vulnerable. Population assumed to be decreasing due to forest clearing. **Voice:** Unknown.

3 BATES'S SWIFT *Apus batesi* 14 cm
A small, slender, black swift, with a medium-long forked tail that is mostly held closed, appearing pointed. Blacker than Scarce and Schouteden's swifts. Best distinguished by flight action: rapid fluttering, interspersed by short glides, with only tips of wings appearing to flap. Wings are relatively straight, and posterior part of body with tail appears long for an *Apus* swift, but shorter than *Schoutedenapus* swifts. **Habitat:** Aerial, over rocky outcrops in forest and adjacent areas. **Status:** Uncommon to locally common. **Voice:** High-pitched trill.

4 AFRICAN PALM SWIFT *Cypsiurus parvus* 16 cm
A pale grey-brown, very slender, streamlined swift with long, thin wings and a long, deeply forked tail. Tail is longer than any other swift's. Juv. has shorter, less streamer-like tail, and could be confused with Scarce Swift. **Habitat:** Aerial, usually in vicinity of palm trees, including those in towns. **Status:** Common resident and local migrant. **Voice:** Soft, high-pitched scream. [C7.66, G3.13.1]

5 LITTLE SWIFT *Apus affinis* 12 cm
A small, square-tailed swift with a large, square, white rump patch which wraps around the flanks, and a large white throat. In flight, it seems squat and dumpy, with rounded wing tips. Smaller than Mottled Spinetail (p. 260), with no white stripe across belly, plain white throat (in most races) and very different flight action. **Habitat:** Aerial; the most common swift over towns, often seen wheeling in tight flocks during display flights. Usually nests in colonies, under eaves of buildings and rocky overhangs. **Status:** Common resident, but subject to some movements in S. **Voice:** Soft twittering; high-pitched screeching. [C3.26, G3.12.7]

6 HORUS SWIFT *Apus horus* 14 cm
A bulky version of Little Swift, with a shallow-forked tail, intermediate between Little and White-rumped swifts' tails. Large white rump and throat are as Little Swift's; has much more extensive white rump than White-rumped Swift. Brown-rumped 'Loanda' Swift of Angola appears to be a colour morph of Horus Swift. **Habitat:** Aerial; forages over variety of habitats, including grassland, woodland and semi-desert; breeds in holes made by bank-nesting birds. **Status:** Uncommon resident and intra-African migrant. **Voice:** Normally silent; occasionally screams at breeding sites. [C7.68, G3.12.6]

7 WHITE-RUMPED SWIFT *Apus caffer* 14 cm
A slender black swift with a fairly long, deeply forked tail and diagnostic narrow white 'U' on the rump. Tail is frequently held closed, appearing long and pointed. Has prominent white throat like Little and Horus swifts. **Habitat:** Aerial, over open country, often near water. Usually occupies red-rumped swallows' nests, and sometimes holes in buildings. **Status:** Common resident and intra-African migrant. **Voice:** Deeper screams than Little Swift's, and generally less vocal. [C3.25, G3.12.5]

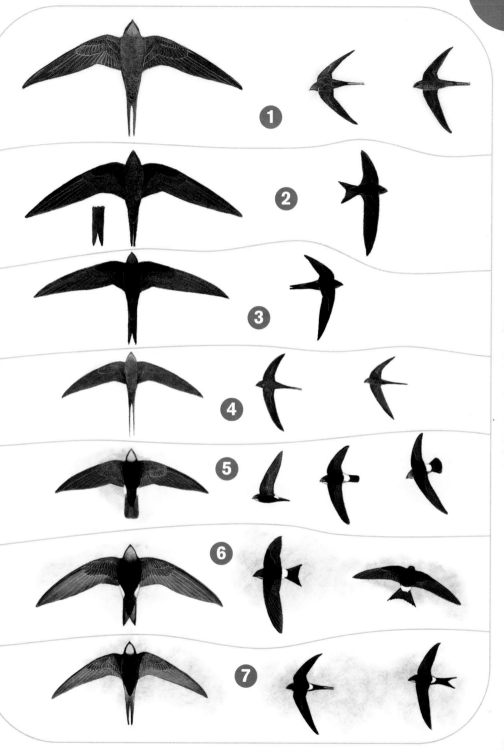

1 SÃO TOMÉ SPINETAIL *Zoonavena thomensis*   10 cm
Endemic to São Tomé and Príncipé. A small, square-tailed swift with a diagnostic dark head and throat, grading into a whitish breast, belly, undertail coverts and broad rump; these areas are streaked black. Smaller than Little Swift (p. 258), with white (not black) underparts. **Habitat:** Aerial, above forest and forest edge, secondary growth and plantations, from coast to mountain. **Status:** Common. **Voice:** High-pitched 'tsip, tsi-tsiiip'.

2 MOTTLED SPINETAIL *Telacanthura ussheri*   14 cm
A rather *Apus*-like spinetail, with a fairly long, broad tail, broad white rump, mottled throat and diagnostic white line across the vent. Predominantly dark belly separates it from all other African spinetails except Black Spinetail, which lacks white rump. Larger than Little Swift (p. 258), with different wing shape: narrow secondaries give wings a pinched look near body. **Habitat:** Aerial, over woodland and savanna, often along forested rivers. Breeds in hollow trees or vertical shafts; often associated with baobabs. **Status:** Locally common. **Voice:** Soft twittering. [C7.62, G3.13.2]

3 BLACK (CHAPIN'S) SPINETAIL *Telacanthura melanopygia*   16 cm
The largest African spinetail, with remarkably powerful and rapid flight. Black belly and upperparts separate it from all other spinetails. Throat is mottled, but often looks entirely black in the field. Narrow-based wings and erratic flight action of spinetails separate it from dark *Apus* swifts. **Habitat:** Aerial, above forest, often near rivers. **Status:** Uncommon and localised. **Voice:** Various harsh 'chzit' and 'chezroo' notes, but usually silent. [C7.61]

4 SABINE'S SPINETAIL *Rhaphidura sabini*   12 cm
A small, black-and-white spinetail with a crisp contrast between the blue-black breast and white belly. Longer-tailed than Cassin's Spinetail, with extensive white rump and uppertail coverts. In flight, wings are typically paddle-shaped. **Habitat:** Aerial, above forest, forest edge, adjacent savannas and forested rivers. **Status:** Common. **Voice:** High-pitched 'teet' and 'wiit' notes. [C7.60]

5 CASSIN'S SPINETAIL *Neafrapus cassini*   15 cm
Very short-tailed with broad wings. Much shorter-tailed than Sabine's Spinetail, with only very narrow white band on rump and less contrast between dark throat and pale belly. Larger than Böhm's Spinetail, with much less white on rump and more powerful flight; ranges don't overlap and habitats differ. **Habitat:** Aerial, above forest, adjacent savannas and forested rivers. **Status:** Common. **Voice:** Normally silent; harsh 'tchziit' calls. [C7.63]

6 BÖHM'S (BAT-LIKE) SPINETAIL *Neafrapus boehmi*   10 cm
A tiny, very short-tailed swift. Much smaller than Cassin's Spinetail, with broader white rump; occurs in woodland and savanna (not forest), and ranges are not known to overlap. Flight is very fast and erratic, almost bat-like. **Habitat:** Aerial, over savanna and woodland; often near baobab trees. Breeds in hollow trees or vertical shafts. **Status:** Locally common. **Voice:** Seldom calls; high-pitched 'tsit-tsit-tsee-tseeuu'. [C7.64, G3.13.3]

7 ALPINE SWIFT *Tachymarptis melba*   20-22 cm
A very large, brown swift with a diagnostic white belly and throat, separated by a dark breast band. Flight is swift and direct, with deep beats of long, scythe-like wings. Is often seen in mixed flocks with other swift species. **Habitat:** Aerial and wide ranging. Breeds on high inland cliffs with vertical cracks. **Status:** Common resident and intra-African migrant; scarce Palearctic migrant in W Africa. Often in large flocks. **Voice:** Shrill scream. [C3.27, G3.12.8]

8 MOTTLED SWIFT *Tachymarptis aequatorialis*   22 cm
Structure and flight action are similar to Alpine Swift's, but this species has a darker belly and slightly longer, more deeply forked tail. Throat is pale and underparts are scaled and mottled; belly is off-white (never white), with dark crescents in *furensis* of W Sudan. **Habitat:** Aerial; wide ranging, but usually around rocky areas. Breeds on cliffs. **Status:** Uncommon. **Voice:** Typical swift scream. [C7.69, G3.12.9]

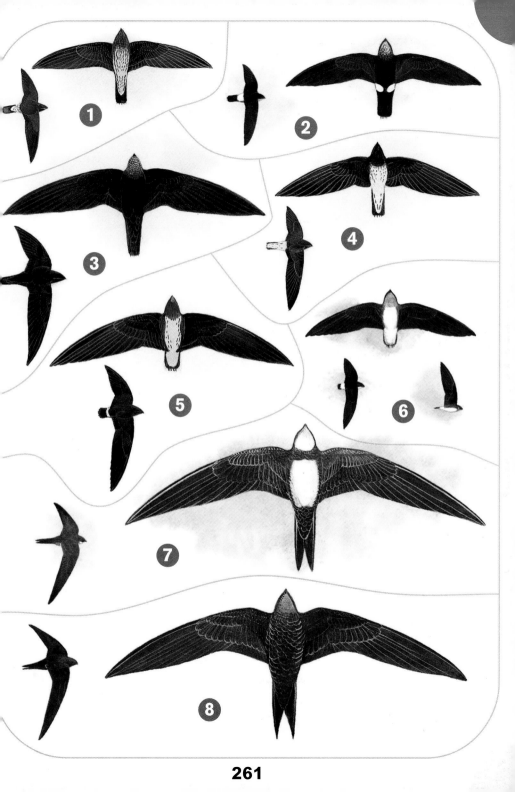

1 COMMON SWIFT *Apus apus*   16-17 cm
A fairly large, blackish-brown swift. Appears more sleek and rakish than African, Nyanza and Pallid swifts. Told from African and Nyanza swifts by its uniform secondaries and back. Asian birds are paler and greyer, with a larger throat patch, and could be confused with Pallid Swift. Juv's forehead is pale. **Habitat:** Aerial and wide ranging; often in large flocks; roosts on the wing. **Status:** Common Palearctic migrant, mostly Aug-Apr. **Voice:** Shrill scream. [C3.24, G3.12.1] **Similar species. Plain Swift** *A. unicolor* is slightly smaller, more uniformly coloured and more rakish; winter vagrant to Mauritania from Canary Islands.

2 AFRICAN (BLACK) SWIFT *Apus barbatus*   18 cm
Best told from Common Swift by the paler secondaries which contrast with the darker back when seen in good light. Also appears bulkier, with less sharply pointed tail and blunter wings. Larger than Nyanza Swift, with blacker plumage and typically more contrasting white throat. **Habitat:** Aerial. Breeds in crevices on inland cliffs. **Status:** Common resident and intra-African migrant; status in W Africa uncertain. **Voice:** High-pitched screaming. [C7.67, G3.12.2]

3 FERNANDO PO SWIFT *Apus sladeniae*   17 cm
Often considered a race of African Swift, but is blacker, with less grey on throat and forehead; ranges are unlikely to overlap. Like African Swift, pale inner secondaries contrasting with dark back separate it from Common Swift. Status of Sierra Leone records is uncertain; presumably they are of this species. **Habitat:** Aerial, over forests and grasslands. Nests on cliffs in highland areas; swifts breeding in buildings in Luanda may also be this species. **Status:** Local and uncommon; W African records may be African Swift. **Voice:** Unrecorded.

4 PALLID SWIFT *Apus pallidus*   16 cm
Paler than African and Common swifts, with more extensive white throat patch and paler forehead (but juvs of other species often have paler frons). Tail is less pointed and more shallow-forked than Common Swift's; closer to African Swift's. Shows some contrast between paler secondaries and back, but less than in African and especially Nyanza swifts. Lacks scaled underparts of Bradfield's Swift. In flight, appears rather robust, with broad wings (especially broad primaries) and slow, leisurely flight. **Habitat:** Aerial. **Status:** Probably breeds locally in N; scarce Palearctic migrant, mostly Oct-Mar. **Voice:** Typical swift scream, less shrill than Common Swift's. [C3.23, G3.12.4]

5 NYANZA SWIFT *Apus niansae*   15 cm
Endemic to NE Africa. Slightly smaller and browner than African Swift, showing even greater contrast between very pale brown secondaries and greater coverts, and darker back and outerwings. Appears brown rather than black, with distinctly pointed tail; jizz is closer to Common Swift's. Pale throat patch is poorly defined, but NE *somalicus* is paler, with larger throat patch; could be confused with Forbes-Watson's Swift in coastal Somalia and Kenya. **Habitat:** Aerial, over dry, rocky areas up to 2 800 m. **Status:** Locally common resident and intra-African migrant. **Voice:** Descending, twittering scream.

6 FORBES-WATSON'S SWIFT *Apus berliozi*   16 cm
A rather uniform brown swift with a large white throat patch and pale forehead; appears pale-headed when seen head-on. Inseparable in the field from Pallid Swift, but the two rarely, if ever, co-occur. Lacks strongly contrasting pale secondaries of African and Nyanza swifts. Flight is more leisurely than African or Common swifts'. **Habitat:** Aerial. Breeds in caves on Somalia coast, foraging over coastal dunes. Non-breeding migrants forage over coastal Kenyan forests. **Status:** Locally common resident and intra-African migrant. **Voice:** Poorly known; nasal 'dzhhh dzhhh' and more typical screams and chitters.

7 BRADFIELD'S SWIFT *Apus bradfieldi*   17 cm
Endemic to SW Africa. A pale grey-brown swift, paler than Common and African swifts. At close range and in good light, the scaled, mottled underparts are distinctive. Lacks contrasting secondaries of African Swift. Bulkier than Common Swift, appearing similar to vagrant Pallid Swifts. **Habitat:** Aerial. Breeds in cliff crevices; rarely on palm fronds. **Status:** Locally common. **Voice:** High-pitched screaming. [G312.3]

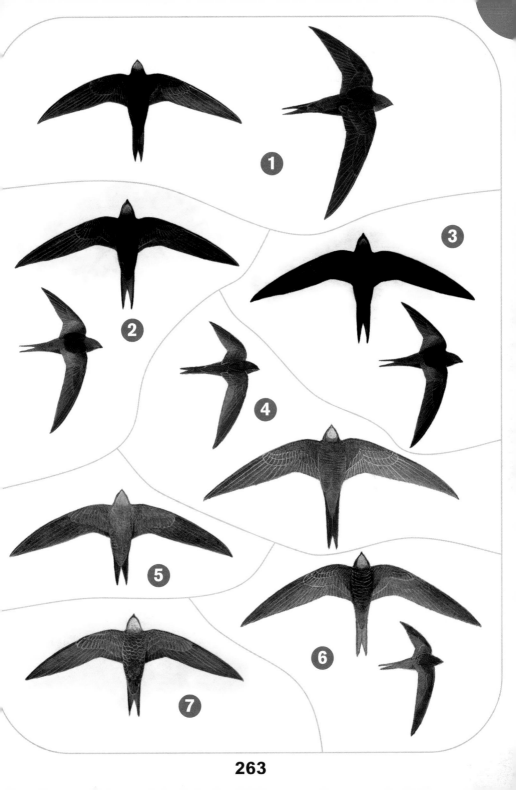

An endemic African order. Peculiar, long-tailed birds that creep mouse-like in bushes and trees. Flight fast and direct. Occur in small groups, roosting together and often sunning themselves. Sexes alike.

1 SPECKLED MOUSEBIRD *Colius striatus*   32 cm
A drab brown mousebird with a buffy belly and rather broad tail. Body and bare-part coloration varies geographically: in S, legs and eye are dark, upper bill is dark, lower bill is pale, crest is brown, and face and throat are blackish. Further N, legs are red or pink, upper bill has pale base, ear coverts are whitish and eye is often pale. W races have pale crest and ear coverts contrasting strongly with black face. Mantle and breast are barred in some races, plain in others. Darker and browner than Blue-naped and Red-faced mousebirds, with weaker flight. **Habitat:** Thick, tangled bush, and fruiting trees in gardens. **Status:** Common; usually in groups, often sunning after feeding or dashing between bushes in 'follow-my-leader' fashion. **Voice:** Harsh 'zhrrik-zhrrik'. [C7.72, G3.13.4]

2 RED-BACKED MOUSEBIRD *Colius castanotus*   32 cm
Endemic to Angola. Forms a superspecies with Speckled Mousebird, and their ranges overlap marginally in N; differs in having reddish (not brown) back, brown (not whitish) ear coverts and crest, and pale (not brown) eyes. Co-occurs with Red-faced Mousebird, but is much darker brown (not pale grey), and lacks red face patch; flight is weaker. **Habitat:** Riverine woodland, forest edge, *Euphorbia* scrub, farmlands and gardens. **Status:** Common. **Voice:** Whistled 'zweet', similar to White-backed Mousebird's, and harsher 'zhrrik'.

3 WHITE-BACKED MOUSEBIRD *Colius colius*   32 cm
Endemic to S Africa. Paler and greyer than Speckled Mousebird, with mostly white bill and coral-pink legs. In flight, central back is white, bordered by glossy violet stripes (appear black in the field). Paler and shorter-tailed than Red-faced Mousebird, with weaker flight. **Habitat:** Strandveld, fynbos and scrubby areas in semi-desert. **Status:** Common; usually in flocks of 3-10. **Voice:** Rather harsh, whistled 'zwee-wewit'. [G3.13.5]

4 WHITE-HEADED MOUSEBIRD *Colius leucocephalus*   31 cm
Endemic to NE Africa. Whitish crest (extending forward to base of bill) and black-and-white vermiculated neck, upper breast and back are diagnostic. Paler and greyer than Speckled Mousebird, with mostly white head (including face) and bill; does not overlap with white-crested races of Speckled Mousebird. Dark grey orbital skin appears as blackish mark. Whitish stripe down back is usually visible only in flight. Juv. has buffy throat and upper breast. **Habitat:** Dense bush and creepers in arid habitat up to 1 300 m. **Status:** Uncommon to locally common. **Voice:** Contact call is scratchy 'tsik tsik'; song is descending 'tsip-tsip tseeeer'.

5 RED-FACED MOUSEBIRD *Urocolius indicus*   34 cm
A pale grey mousebird with a bare red face. Red face and generally paler appearance separate it from Speckled and White-backed mousebirds. Lacks blue nape patch of Blue-naped Mousebird. In flight, grey rump contrasts with darker back and tail. Flight is direct, fast and powerful; usually more sustained than *Colius* mousebirds. Juv. has yellowish-green face. **Habitat:** Thornveld, open broadleafed woodland and suburban gardens. **Status:** Common resident. **Voice:** Clear, whistled 'chi vu vu', first note higher pitched. [C7.70, G3.13.6]

6 BLUE-NAPED MOUSEBIRD *Urocolius macrourus*   34 cm
N counterpart of Red-faced Mousebird, but easily separated by its bright turquoise-blue nape patch. Juv. lacks blue nape patch, and has pink facial skin and greenish bill, but usually occurs with adults. **Habitat:** Coastal scrub and arid savanna. **Status:** Locally common; in flocks of up to 50 birds. **Voice:** Far-carrying 'peeeeeeeee' whistle. [C7.71]

juv.

TROGONS
Distinctive, colourful birds of forest subcanopy. Often perch motionless for long periods; easily overlooked if not calling. Sexes differ.

1 NARINA TROGON *Apaloderma narina* 30-34 cm
A squat, long-tailed forest bird that often sits quietly in mid-storey and can be hard to locate if not calling. Plain white (not barred) undertail separates it from Bar-tailed Trogon. Song and blue-green (not bright yellow) facial patches separate it from localised Bare-cheeked Trogon. Female has rufous-brown forehead, face and throat, merging into greyer breast and dull crimson belly. Juv. is paler than female. **Habitat:** Forest, dense woodland and thickets. **Status:** Fairly common resident, with some local movements. **Voice:** Deep, hoarse 'hoo hook', with emphasis on second syllable, repeated 6-10 times; wags tail down slightly when calling. [C7.74, G3.13.7]

2 BARE-CHEEKED TROGON *Apaloderma aequatoriale* 34 cm
Endemic to C Africa. Best separated from Narina Trogon by song and bright yellow (not blue-green) patches of bare skin on face. Female has rufous-brown forehead, throat and breast, merging into reddish belly. **Habitat:** Closed-canopy forest, from understorey to below canopy, often along rivers and streams. **Status:** Locally common. **Voice:** Mournful series of 6-8 notes, descending in pitch, 'hoo hoo hoo huu huu…', similar to voice of wood doves. [C7.75]

3 BAR-TAILED TROGON *Apaloderma vittatum* 30 cm
A montane trogon with disjunct distribution. Smaller than Narina and Bare-cheeked trogons, with strikingly barred outer-tail feathers visible from below. Male has bluish breast band; female's head and crown are rufous-brown. Facial spots are orange-pink (not blue-green as Narina Trogon. **Habitat:** Evergreen forests, mostly montane, 900-3 000 m. **Status:** Locally common. **Voice:** Distinctive yelping call, 'yeeup', repeated 6-15 times, softly at first, then with increasing volume; wags tail down slightly when calling. [C7.73]

HOOPOES
Unmistakeable buff, black and white birds with long, decurved bills and long, erectile crests. Flight buoyant on broad, rounded wings. Sexes alike.

4 AFRICAN HOOPOE *Upupa africana* 25-28 cm
Often considered a race of Eurasian Hoopoe, but is richer, darker cinnamon with all-black primaries and more extensive white on secondaries; lacks white subterminal bar on crest feathers of Eurasian Hoopoe. Call also differs from that of Eurasian Hoopoe. Juv. is duller. **Habitat:** Savanna, broadleafed woodland, parks and gardens. **Status:** Common. **Voice:** 'Hoop-hoop-hoop', typically all notes at same pitch. [G4.1.1]

5 EURASIAN HOOPOE *Upupa epops* 25-28 cm
Has broad white subterminal band in primaries, more black bars in secondaries and is paler sandy-buff than the rich cinnamon of African Hoopoe, although this last character changes gradually from N to S. Central and rear crest feathers have white or buff subterminal spots and white tail band is typically broader. Resident N African *senegalensis* has more white in secondaries and is slightly darker then migrant *epops*. **Habitat:** Savannas with sparse or short-grass understorey. **Status:** Fairly common; breeds in Sahelian savannas, with population augmented by Palearctic migrants Sep-Apr. **Voice:** Deep, onomatopoeic 'hoo-poe', second note generally lower. [C3.32]

Endemic African family. Closely resemble scimitarbills, but occur in larger groups and are generally more colourful. Many species quite similar and require careful observation. Males slightly larger with obviously longer bills.

1 GREEN (RED-BILLED) WOOD-HOOPOE *Phoeniculus purpureus*   32-36 cm
A widespread African wood-hoopoe, with a long, decurved, red bill, red legs, white wing bars and long tail with white subterminal bars in outer feathers. In good light, bottle-green head and back distinguish it from Violet and Grant's wood-hoopoes. Male has longer and more decurved bill than female. Juv. has black bill; red legs and feet separate it from scimitarbills, but is hard to separate from Black-billed Wood-Hoopoe and juv. Violet or Grant's wood-hoopoes. Juv. male has brown throat patch; throat patch is black in juv. female. **Habitat:** Wide variety of woodland, thicket and forest edge. **Status:** Common. **Voice:** Harsh chattering and cackling, usually by groups. [C8.8b, G4.1.2]

2 VIOLET WOOD-HOOPOE *Phoeniculus damarensis*   36-40 cm
Endemic to Namibia and Angola. Larger than Green Wood-Hoopoe, and in good light the violet (not bottle-green) head, mantle and back can be seen; flight is loose and floppier. Female's bill is less decurved and shorter than male's. Juv. male has brown throat patch; throat patch is black in juv. female. Recent studies suggest some hybridisation with Green Wood-Hoopoe. **Habitat:** Dry thornveld, wooded, dry watercourses and mopane woodland. **Status:** Common. **Voice:** Harsh cackling, slightly slower than Green Wood-Hoopoe's. [G4.1.3]

3 BLACK-BILLED WOOD-HOOPOE *Phoeniculus somaliensis*   33-35 cm
Endemic to NE Africa. Slightly smaller and more slender than Green and Grant's wood-hoopoes, with black (not red) more deeply curved bill; some birds have red base to bill. Identification of single birds is problematic because of age and sex variation in bill colour and shape. Much larger than Black Scimitarbill (p. 270), with longer bill and longer, more graduated tail. **Habitat:** Dry acacia woodland and scrub, riverine forest and adjacent farmland. **Status:** Locally common; occurs in groups of 4-10 birds. **Voice:** Cackling calls similar to Green Wood-Hoopoe's.

4 GRANT'S WOOD-HOOPOE *Phoeniculus granti*   34-37 cm
Endemic to E Africa. Often treated as a race of Violet Wood-Hoopoe, but ranges do not overlap. Similar to Green Wood-Hoopoe, but is more uniformly violet on head, body and tail, and appears larger and bulkier. However, identification is complicated by racial variation in Green Wood-Hoopoes in its range. Juv. has black bill and unless accompanied by adults is unlikely to be separable from Black-billed Wood-Hoopoe or juv. Green Wood-Hoopoe. Some adults have black base to bill. **Habitat:** Various types of dry woodland, especially acacia and riverine woodland with doum palms. **Status:** Locally common, in small family groups. **Voice:** Cackling calls similar to Green Wood-Hoopoe's.

5 FOREST WOOD-HOOPOE *Phoeniculus castaneiceps*   26 cm
A dark, glossy-green forest wood-hoopoe, lacking any white in wings or tail. Smaller and more slender than White-headed Wood-Hoopoe, with black (not red) bill and legs. Bill is short and rather straight; tail appears long and narrow. W nominate race has head and upper breast chestnut in both sexes; head of C African *brunneiceps* is dark green (in male) or buffy-white (in male or female). Juv. is duller. **Habitat:** Open-canopy forest with tall trees, edge of forest. **Status:** Locally common. **Voice:** Plaintive 'whoi whoi whoi', repeated 10-20 times. [C8.7b]

6 WHITE-HEADED WOOD-HOOPOE *Phoeniculus bollei*   35 cm
A forest wood-hoopoe with a distinctive white or buffy face and throat. Much larger than Forest Wood-Hoopoe, with longer, more decurved red (not black) bill and red (not black) feet. Lack of white in wings and tail separates it from all other wood-hoopoes. Extent of white on head varies geographically, and is least in *okuensis* (SE Cameroon). Juv. has buffy head and duller plumage, with black bill, but red legs. **Habitat:** Open-canopy forest with tall trees, montane forest. **Status:** Locally common. **Voice:** High-pitched, chuckling call. [C8.8a]

1

♀

juv.

♂

2

♂

♀

juv.

3

4

5

castaneiceps

brunneiceps

♂

6

SCIMITARBILLS

Endemic African family. Closely resemble wood-hoopoes, but not social; usually seen in pairs. Sexes similar, although females less glossy.

1 ABYSSINIAN SCIMITARBILL *Rhinopomastus minor* 23-24 cm

Endemic to NE Africa. A small, glossy purplish-black scimitarbill with a short tail, easily separated from all other species by its strongly decurved, bright reddish-orange (not black) bill. Black legs and feet separate it from larger wood-hoopoes with red bills (p. 268). S *cabanisi* lacks any white in wings or tail, but N nominate race has white bar in central primaries. Juv. is duller and has dusky, blackish bill. **Habitat:** Arid and semi-arid scrub and woodland below 1 400 m. **Status:** Uncommon. **Voice:** Chattering 'kirrie-kirrie-kirrie-kirrie', each note rising then falling; repeated, yelping 'kweee-u'.

2 BLACK SCIMITARBILL *Rhinopomastus aterrimus* 26-28 cm

A small, glossy black scimitarbill, with a rather short, weakly graduated tail. Separated from other scimitarbills and especially Common Scimitarbill by its relatively straight, short, black bill and shorter tail. White primary coverts and bar across centre of primaries result in two white wing bars. Nominate race (W Africa to Chad) has all-dark tail; other races (from Sudan E and S) have white tips to outer-tail feathers. Juv. is browner, less glossy. **Habitat:** Wooded savanna. **Status:** Locally common. **Voice:** Plaintive 'poui poui poui', repeated monotonously. [C8.9b]

3 COMMON SCIMITARBILL *Rhinopomastus cyanomelas* 28-30 cm

A small, glossy black scimitarbill. Forms a superspecies with Black Scimitarbill, and the two forms intergrade from S Angola through Zambia to DRC. Differs in having longer, more graduated tail and longer, much more decurved bill. Smaller and more slender than wood-hoopoes, with black (not red) legs and feet. White bars on primaries, primary coverts and white tips to outer-tail feathers are visible in flight. Female and juv. have brownish (not glossy, as in male) head and shorter bill. **Habitat:** Dry savanna and open, broadleafed woodland. **Status:** Common. **Voice:** High-pitched, whistling 'sweep-sweep-sweep'; harsher chattering. [C8.9a, G4.1.4]

ALCEDO KINGFISHERS

Small, blue-and-orange kingfishers, identified by bill colour, head and belly plumage. Sexes alike, but juvs distinctive.

4 HALF-COLLARED KINGFISHER *Alcedo semitorquata* 18 cm

A black-billed, aquatic kingfisher with a brilliant blue back and rump. Very similar to Shining-blue Kingfisher, but with paler orange breast, large blue breast patches and off-white (not rufous) loral spot. Larger than Malachite Kingfisher (p. 272), with more subdued crest, blue (not white) cheeks and black (not red) bill (although juv. Malachite Kingfisher also has dark bill). Juv. has black-tipped breast feathers and appears barred. **Habitat:** Wooded streams, channels in large reedbeds and coastal lagoons. **Status:** Uncommon, with some local movement. **Voice:** High-pitched 'chreep' or softer 'peeek-peek'. [C7.85, G3.13.10] **Similar species: Common (European) Kingfisher** *A. atthis* is paler, with rufous (not blue) ear patch and no blue breast patches; Palearctic vagrant along Nile and Red Sea coast in Sudan.

5 SHINING-BLUE KINGFISHER *Alcedo quadribrachys* 16 cm

A black-billed kingfisher with brilliant cobalt-blue back and rump (less bright in W African birds). Wings and upperparts (excluding crest, back and rump) are darker blue (not tinged greenish) than those of Half-collared Kingfisher, with richer underparts contrasting more strongly with white throat. Also has smaller blue patches on sides of breast, and rufous (not pale) loral spot. Larger than Malachite Kingfisher (p. 272), with blue (not white) cheeks. Juv. is lightly barred on breast. **Habitat:** Rivers and streams in forest and mangroves. **Status:** Common. **Voice:** High-pitched 'cheep' in flight. [C7.86]

juv.

♂

♂

♀

1 MALACHITE KINGFISHER *Alcedo cristata*   13-14 cm
A small, aquatic kingfisher with a diagnostic turquoise-and-black barred crown extending down to eye. Adult has red bill, but is larger and has different habitat from African Pygmy- and Dwarf-Kingfishers. Pale-bellied individuals of Malachite Kingfisher can be confused with White-bellied Kingfisher; separated by banded crown extending to eye, paler back and lack of white belly. Juv. has black bill and is blackish on back, but is much smaller than Half-collared and Shining-blue kingfishers (p. 270), and has rufous (not blue) ear coverts and diagnostic barred crown. **Habitat:** Lakes and dams, and along streams and lagoons. **Status:** Common resident. **Voice:** High-pitched 'peep-peep' in flight. [C7.84, G3.14.1]

2 WHITE-BELLIED KINGFISHER *Alcedo leucogaster*   12 cm
A forest counterpart of Malachite Kingfisher, with white central belly, usually linking with white throat, crisply demarcated from rich rufous underparts. Crown is only subtly banded and does not reach down to eye (except in E race *leopoldi*). Adult's bill is bright red; juv's bill is black. **Habitat:** Streams and small rivers in forest. **Status:** Poorly known; secretive, but locally common. **Voice:** High-pitched call in flight.

3 SÃO TOMÉ KINGFISHER *Alcedo thomensis*   13-14 cm
Endemic to São Tomé Island. Sometimes considered a race of Malachite Kingfisher, but with short crown feathers. Juv. is very dark, almost black on back and cheeks, and dark rust on underparts, heavily blotched black. **Habitat:** Never far from water; mostly in lowlands, along rivers and streams, but also along coast in more sheltered areas. **Status:** Common. **Voice:** Sharp, high-pitched 'peep peep' flight call.

4 PRÌNCIPÉ KINGFISHER *Alcedo nais*   13-14 cm
Endemic to Prìncipé Island; the much larger Blue-breasted Kingfisher (p. 274) also occurs here but should not cause any confusion. Sometimes considered a race of White-bellied Kingfisher, but blue crown reaches to eye (not above eye), and has only weakly defined white belly, not linked to throat. Juv. is not as dark on underparts as São Tomé Kingfisher. **Habitat:** Usually associated with water in open woodland and also in tidal pools in sheltered bays; avoids dense forest. **Status:** Common in lowland areas near coast. **Voice:** High-pitched flight call.

5 AFRICAN PYGMY-KINGFISHER *Ispidina picta*   12 cm
A small, richly coloured, dry-land kingfisher. Adult's dark blue cap separates it from African Dwarf-Kingfisher. Smaller than Malachite Kingfisher, with finely barred blue (not uniform) crown that does not extend down to eye, and violet wash around ear coverts. Juv. has black-ish bill and diffuse, dark moustachial stripe. S race (*natalensis*) has paler underparts, smaller blue crown and blue spot above white neck patch. **Habitat:** Woodland, savanna and coastal forest; generally in more open habitats than African Dwarf-Kingfisher. **Status:** Common resident and intra-African migrant. **Voice:** High-pitched 'chip-chip' flight note. [C7.83, G3.14.2]

6 AFRICAN DWARF-KINGFISHER *Ispidina lecontei*   10 cm
A very small forest kingfisher. Adult lacks blue on crown of African Pygmy-Kingfisher, with only a narrow black bar across forehead. Red bill is broad, with square-ended tip. Juv. is similar to juv. African Pygmy-Kingfisher, with blue crown and black bill, but lacks mauve wash on ear coverts. **Habitat:** Forest understorey, sometimes at forest edge; usually seen in open under-storey of forest, near ground, and is not confined to water. **Status:** Locally common. **Voice:** Very high-pitched chipping call in flight. [C7.82]

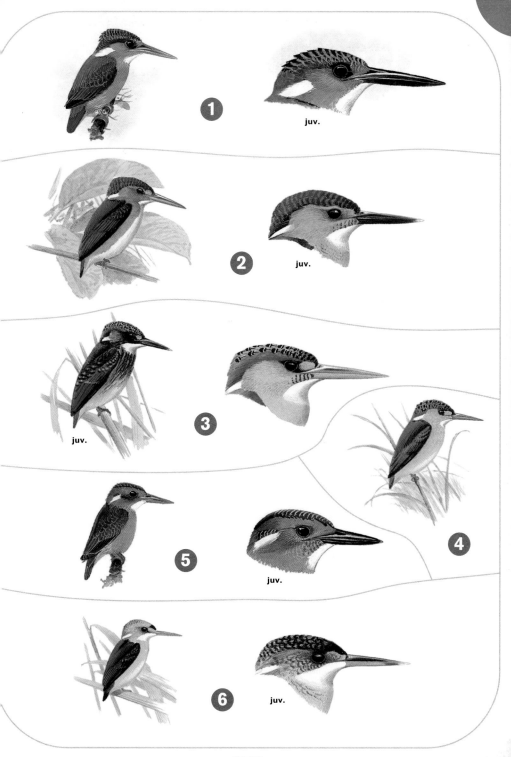

1

juv.

2

juv.

juv.

3

4

5

juv.

6

juv.

Medium-sized kingfishers with distinctive powder-blue flight feathers and loud, trilling calls. Sexes alike in most species.

1 CHOCOLATE-BACKED KINGFISHER *Halcyon badia*   20 cm
A medium-sized forest kingfisher, more often heard than seen. Unmistakable, with vivid red bill, rich chestnut head, back and wing coverts, azure wing panel and entirely white underparts. Juv. has buffy, lightly barred breast, and darker bill. **Habitat:** Confined to forest and gallery forest. **Status:** Common. **Voice:** High-pitched 'pee', followed by series of 10-15 descending whistles, 'tee tee tee', lasting 5-6 seconds. [C7.76]

2 GREY-HEADED KINGFISHER *Halcyon leucocephala*   20-21 cm
The grey head and chestnut belly are diagnostic. Lacks streaked head and flanks of Brown-hooded Kingfisher. Juv. has blackish bill, and dark barring on breast and neck. **Habitat:** Non-aquatic; broadleafed woodland and savanna. **Status:** Locally common resident and intra-African migrant. **Voice:** Whistled 'cheeo cheeo weecho-trrrrr', similar in pitch to Brown-hooded Kingfisher's, but much slower. [C7.78, G3.14.6]

3 BLUE-BREASTED KINGFISHER *Halcyon malimbica*   26 cm
A large kingfisher with a heavy red and black bill. Larger than Woodland Kingfisher, with blue wash on head and breast, and darker blue back and primary coverts. Habitat also differs. Black eye-stripe extends behind eye onto cheek, unlike in Woodland Kingfisher in areas of overlap. Juv. has darker bill, is washed green on head and breast, and has flanks lightly barred buffy. **Habitat:** Forest, gallery forest and mangroves. **Status:** Common. **Voice:** Loud 'chip, pu pu pu puu puu puu puu', with later notes longer and more emphatic. [C7.79]

4 WOODLAND KINGFISHER *Halcyon senegalensis*   20-22 cm
Smaller than Blue-breasted Kingfisher, with light (not dark blue) back and grey (not blue-washed) head and breast. Very similar to Mangrove Kingfisher, but there is little overlap in habitat and has black lower mandible (not all-red bill, although rare individuals do have red bill), much paler head, and all-white underwing. In S race *cyanoleuca*, black eye-stripe extends behind eye. Juv. has dusky reddish-brown bill and is lightly barred grey on sides of breast. **Habitat:** Woodland and savanna. **Status:** Common resident and intra-African migrant. **Voice:** Loud, piercing 'chip-cherrrrrrrrr', descending. [C7.80, G3.14.3]

5 MANGROVE KINGFISHER *Halcyon senegaloides*   21-23 cm
Differs from Woodland Kingfisher by all-red (not red-and-black) bill, black carpal patch on underwing, and darker grey head. Woodland Kingfishers occasionally have all-red bill, but habitat differs. Pale blue back separates it from other African *Halcyon* kingfishers. Juv. has brownish bill and dark scaling on breast. **Habitat:** Winters in mangrove swamps; breeds in coastal forest and riparian thickets. **Status:** Uncommon and local. **Voice:** Noisy: loud, ringing 'cheet choo-che che che', latter part ending in trill. [G3.14.4]

6 BROWN-HOODED KINGFISHER *Halcyon albiventris*   19-20 cm
Differs from other red-billed *Halcyon* kingfishers by its brownish head streaked with black, rufous patches on sides of breast, and streaked flanks. Larger than Striped Kingfisher, with all-red (not black-and-red) bill, and lacks white in upper- or underwing. Male back black; female and juv. brown. **Habitat:** Woodland, coastal forests, parks and gardens. **Status:** Common. **Voice:** Whistled 'tyi-ti-ti-ti'; harsher 'klee-klee-klee' alarm note. [C7.77, G3.14.5]

7 STRIPED KINGFISHER *Halcyon chelicuti*   16-18 cm
A small, dry-land kingfisher. Grey-streaked crown, black-and-red bill and white collar are diagnostic. Smaller than Brown-hooded Kingfisher, with darker cap and white collar. In flight, shows extensive white on underwing, white flash in upperwing, and blue rump. Male has black band across underwing, which female lacks. Juv. has dusky bill and blackish, scaled breast and flanks. **Habitat:** Woodland, savanna, and forest edge. **Status:** Common. **Voice:** High-pitched, piercing 'cheer-cherrrrrrrr'. [C781, G3.14.7]

1 WHITE-COLLARED KINGFISHER *Todirhamphus chloris*   23-25 cm
The combination of blue-green upperparts, pure white underparts and wide nuchal collar, and black bill (some show pale flesh colour towards base of lower mandible) distinguishes this species from all other African kingfishers. Juv. has dark mottling on nuchal collar and sides of breast. **Habitat:** Exclusively coastal: in dense mangrove stands, hunting along creeks and on adjacent mudflats. **Status:** Rare and highly localised; possibly non-breeding visitor in S. **Voice:** Loud, metallic, repeated 'kik', usually when taking flight.

CERYLID KINGFISHERS
Large, relatively uncolourful kingfishers. Sexes differ.

2 GIANT KINGFISHER *Megaceryle maximus*   38-43 cm
The largest kingfisher in the region. Easily identified by its long, heavy bill, dark grey, white-spotted upperparts and rufous underparts. Male has rufous breast and white underwing coverts; female has rufous belly and underwing coverts. Juv. male has black-speckled, chestnut breast; juv. female has white breast. Usually hunts from exposed perch, but occasionally hovers. **Habitat:** Wooded streams and dams, fast-flowing rivers and coastal lagoons. **Status:** Common. **Voice:** Loud, harsh 'kahk-kah-kahk'. [C7.87, G3.13.9]

3 PIED KINGFISHER *Ceryle rudis*   23-25 cm
The only black-and-white kingfisher in the region, with a long black bill and short crest. Male has double breast band; female and juv. have single, incomplete breast band. Frequently feeds by hovering, and forages up to 5 km from land over large lakes. **Habitat:** Any open stretch of fresh water, coastal lagoons and tidal pools. **Status:** Common. **Voice:** Rattling twitter; sharp, high-pitched 'chik-chik'. [C7.88, G3.13.8]

ROLLERS
Large, colourful birds of woodland and savanna. Hunt from perches, dropping to the ground to take prey. Named for their distinctive, rolling aerial displays. Sexes alike.

4 BROAD-BILLED ROLLER *Eurystomus glaucurus*   27-29 cm
A compact, dark roller with a bright yellow bill. Larger than similar Blue-throated Roller, with uniform lilac throat (lacks blue patch) and less extensive rufous on upperwing (greater coverts are blue, not rufous). Juv. is paler and slightly mottled, with duller yellow bill. Larger nominate race with greyer (not blue) vent is non-breeding visitor from Madagascar to E Africa. **Habitat:** Riverine forests and adjacent savanna. Often perches and breeds in dead trees. **Status:** Locally common resident and intra-African migrant. **Voice:** Harsh screams and cackles. [C8.7a, G3.15.10]

5 BLUE-THROATED ROLLER *Eurystomus gularis*   24-25 cm
A smaller, forest version of Broad-billed Roller, differing in having a blue throat patch (not uniform lilac throat) and mottled brown-and-rufous (not blue) vent and undertail coverts. The two species occur together when migrant Broad-billed Rollers visit equatorial forest. W African *gularis* has rufous breast and belly; C African *neglectus* has lilac wash over breast. Juv. is paler and mottled. **Habitat:** Forest canopy, edge of forest and gallery forest. **Status:** Common; often on tall dead trees. **Voice:** Rapid series of harsh squawks. [C8.6b]

1

2

♂

juv.

3

♂

♂   ♀

4

5

gularis

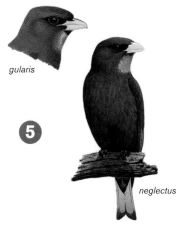

neglectus

1 EUROPEAN ROLLER *Coracias garrulus*   30-32 cm
A large, chunky roller. Differs from all African rollers by black (not blue) flight feathers from above. Easily separated from adults of African species, which have distinctive tail streamers, but juvs are problematic. Similar to streamer-less Racket-tailed Roller but has fairly sharp (not gradual) divide between bluish head and brown back. Larger than Abyssinian Roller, with black (not blue) flight feathers, greener wing coverts and less white on frons and chin. Juv. is more olive-green; best told from juv. Lilac-breasted and Abyssinian rollers by larger size and black (not dark blue) flight feathers. **Habitat:** Savanna. **Status:** Common Palearctic migrant Sep-Apr. **Voice:** Normally silent in Africa; 'krack-krack' call when alarmed. [C3.31, G3.15.6]

2 ABYSSINIAN ROLLER *Coracias abyssinicus* 29 cm (40 cm incl. tail streamers)
N counterpart of Lilac-breasted Roller, with some overlap in NE. Apart from whitish forehead and chin, adult's head and underparts are pale blue; lacks lilac face and throat of Lilac-breasted Roller, and tail streamers are much longer. Adult lacking tail streamers and juv. are smaller than European Roller, with ultramarine (not black) flight feathers and blue (not greenish) wing coverts. Juv. is very similar to juv. Lilac-breasted Roller, but has bluer face, paler throat and generally lacks black eye-stripe extending behind eye. **Habitat:** Arid savannas; also around human habitation. **Status:** Common resident and intra-African migrant. **Voice:** Raucous 'aaaarhh' when perched; 'rack' in flight; intensifying 'ga-ga-ga-ga-gaaaa-gaaaa-gaaaa' in aerial display. [C8.5a]

3 LILAC-BREASTED ROLLER *Coracias caudatus* 29 cm (37 cm incl. tail streamers)
S counterpart of Abyssinian Roller, with lilac throat and breast and shorter tail streamers. Pointed tail streamers separate it from Racket-tailed Roller. Adults lose elongated tail feathers during winter moult, when confusion can arise with lilac-breasted C African race of Racket-tailed Roller, but differs by having blue (not green) head. Juv. lacks elongated tail feathers and has faded lilac breast which separates it from juv. European Roller. Juv. differs from juv. Racket-tailed Roller by having blue (not brown) median wing coverts and uniform dark blue flight feathers (not with pale bases). NE race *lorti* has lilac confined to throat. **Habitat:** Savanna. Perches conspicuously, often along telephone lines. **Status:** Common resident and local migrant (NE). **Voice:** Harsh squawks and screams, like Abyssinian Roller's. [C8.5b, G3.15.7]

4 RACKET-TAILED ROLLER *Coracias spatulatus* 29 cm (36 cm incl. tail streamers)
Adult tail is diagnostic, but moulting adult (winter) and juv. lack diagnostic spatulate tail streamers. At all ages has brown back extending onto median coverts (blue in European and Lilac-breasted rollers) and pale blue wing bar formed by pale bases to flight feathers (uniformly black in European Roller, dark blue in Lilac-breasted Roller). Also lacks sharp demarcation between brownish back and greenish hindneck. Nominate race (S Africa) has blue face and breast, but *weigalli* (C Africa) has lilac face and breast, recalling adult Lilac-breasted Roller. **Habitat:** Tall woodland, especially miombo. **Status:** Uncommon; unobtrusive, as it perches just below canopy. **Voice:** Harsh 'chak'; raucous screams in aerial display. [C8.6a, G3.15.8]

5 PURPLE (RUFOUS-CROWNED) ROLLER *Coracias naevius*   34-38 cm
The largest roller; easily identified by its broad, pale supercilium and lilac- or pink-brown underparts streaked with white. Nominate race (Sahel S to Tanzania) has rufous crown and pinker underparts; *mosambica* (South Africa to Zambia) has greenish crown and lilac underparts. Juv. is duller. **Habitat:** Dry thornveld and open, broadleafed woodland. **Status:** Scarce to common resident and intra-African migrant. **Voice:** Harsh, repeated 'karaa-karaa' in display flight, accompanied by exaggerated, side-to-side, rocking motion. [C8.4a, G3.15.9]

6 BLUE-BELLIED ROLLER *Coracias cyanogaster* 29 cm (35 cm incl. tail streamers)
The creamy white head and breast, deep blue belly, wings and rump, paler blue tail with fairly short streamers and brownish-black back are diagnostic. In flight, wings have conspicuous pale blue bar at base of flight feathers. Juv. is duller, with shorter tail lacking streamers. **Habitat:** Savannas dominated by *Isoberlina* trees, forest edge and damp areas with scattered *Borassus* palms. **Status:** Resident and intra-African migrant; common in W, becoming increasingly scarce towards E. **Voice:** Rapid, clicking 'ga-ga-gaaa-ga', usually lasting 5 seconds.

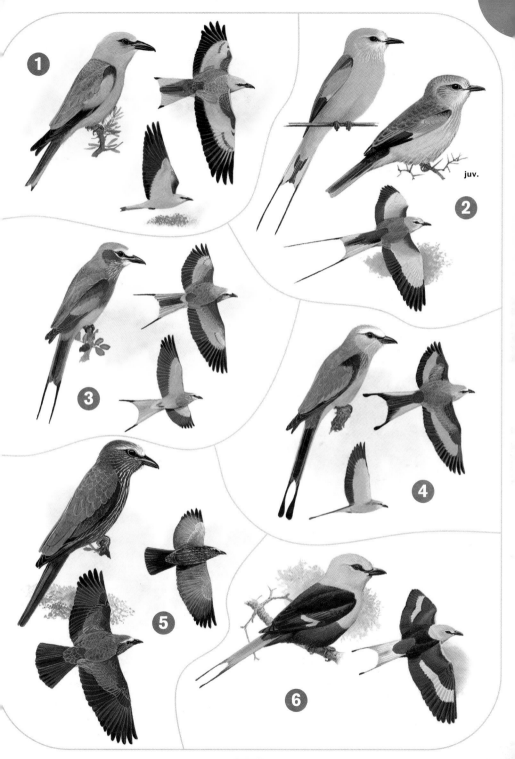

juv.

A rather uniform group of colourful, aerial insectivores that sally from perches or during longer flights. Sexes alike, but juvs and ads in worn plumage duller. Nest in burrows, sometimes in large colonies.

1 BLACK BEE-EATER *Merops gularis*   20 cm

A small, black-and-blue forest bee-eater with a red throat. Black (not russet) back, wing coverts and crown separate it from Blue-headed Bee-eater. Belly and undertail coverts are blue, with blue streaks extending onto breast; however, in poor light, can appear all-black. In flight, bright azure-blue rump and uppertail coverts are diagnostic. Juv. is duller. Nominate race (W Africa) has blue frons and supercilium (lacking in C African *australis*). **Habitat:** Forest, in canopy or at edge, riverbanks and secondary growth with tall dead trees. **Status:** Common; usually in pairs. **Voice:** Short, sharp 'tsit, tit' or 'psitt'. [C7.91]

2 BLUE-HEADED BEE-EATER *Merops muelleri*   19 cm

A small, dark, forest bee-eater, with dark russet back and wings, blue-and-black head, red throat, and dark blue underparts. Readily distinguished from Black Bee-eater by chestnut (not black) back and rump, and lack of blue stripes on underparts. Juv. is duller. W African *mentalis* has short central tail streamers (lacking in C African nominate race, which has whitish frons gradually merging into pale blue crown). **Habitat:** Forest canopy, where it lives in pairs on dead branches; edge of forest, along trails and roads. **Status:** Widespread, but generally uncommon. **Voice:** Soft 'chwer ter wer' interspersed with metallic notes. [C7.90]

3 ROSY BEE-EATER *Merops malimbicus*   24 cm (28 cm incl. tail streamers)

A fairly large, colonial bee-eater, identified by combination of dark slate-grey upperparts and rich pink underparts. Black facial stripe is bordered below by white moustache. Dark grey (not pinkish) upperparts prevent confusion with Northern Carmine Bee-eater. Juv. lacks tail streamers, and is paler above and duller below. **Habitat:** Breeds colonially on sandbanks in large rivers, then migrates to forage over lowland forest, mangroves and savannas. **Status:** Common, with local migrations. **Voice:** Similar to but more abrupt and harsher than European Bee-eater. [C8.2b]

4 SOUTHERN CARMINE BEE-EATER
Merops nubicoides   27 cm (36 cm incl. tail streamers)

A bright red bee-eater with blue rump and belly and elongated central tail feathers. Crown turquoise; eye-stripe black. Often treated as a race of Northern Carmine Bee-eater; slightly larger, with carmine (not turquoise) throat. Juv. lacks elongated central tail and is duller. **Habitat:** Woodland, savanna and floodplains. Breeds colonially in riverbanks. **Status:** Common resident and local migrant. **Voice:** Like Northern Carmine Bee-eater. [C8.3b, G3.15.1]

5 NORTHERN CARMINE BEE-EATER
Merops nubicus   24 cm (34 cm incl. tail streamers)

Often treated as a race of Southern Carmine Bee-eater; slightly smaller, with turquoise (not carmine) throat. Juv. lacks elongated central tail feathers, and has brown (not carmine, as in adult) back and less brightly coloured underparts. **Habitat:** Savannas, usually near water. Breeds colonially in riverbanks. **Status:** Locally common resident and local migrant. **Voice:** Deep 'terk, terk'. [C8.3a]

6 BLACK-HEADED BEE-EATER
Merops breweri   26 cm (34 cm incl. tail streamers)

Endemic to C Africa. A large bee-eater, easily identified by its black head, green upperparts and orange-brown underparts. Black head is separated from breast by narrow cinnamon band. Adult has green, elongated central tail feathers; other tail feathers are largely chestnut. Bill is stout, and feathers of head are often puffed out, giving big-headed appearance. Juv. lacks tail streamers, and head is blotched green and black. **Habitat:** Forest edge, clearings, gallery forest and riverbanks in forested areas with adjacent savanna. **Status:** Generally uncommon; occurs in pairs. **Voice:** Seldom calls; a soft 'chuk' or 'chiruk' in flight. [C7.89]

1 SWALLOW-TAILED BEE-EATER *Merops hirundineus* 20-22 cm
The only bee-eater with a deeply forked tail; blue belly is also diagnostic among small, green African bee-eaters. Juv. lacks adult's yellow throat and blue collar. W African *chrysolaimus* has green tail and blue frons and supercilium. **Habitat:** Wide range, from semi-desert scrub to forest margins. **Status:** Common resident with local movements. **Voice:** 'Kwit-kwit'; soft twittering. [C7.95, G3.15.5]

2 LITTLE BEE-EATER *Merops pusillus* 15-17 cm
A tiny bee-eater. Black (not blue) collar and lack of any white on sides of throat separate it from Blue-breasted Bee-eater. Appreciably smaller than Cinnamon-chested Bee-eater, with smaller black collar and conspicuous russet (not green) flight feathers with dark trailing edge; underwings entirely russet. Central tail is green; rest of tail is russet, with black tip. Juv. lacks black collar. Supercilium varies from green (W Africa) to blue (S and E Africa); NE African *cyanostictus* has extensive supercilium extending onto frons, and narrow blue line above collar. **Habitat:** Savanna, woodland, forest edge and around wetlands. **Status:** Common; usually in pairs or small groups. **Voice:** 'Zeet-zeet' or 'chip-chip'. [C7.92, G3.15.4]

3 BLUE-BREASTED BEE-EATER *Merops variegatus* 17-19 cm
Slightly larger than Little Bee-eater, with white patches on sides of neck, between green hindneck and yellow throat (visible only at close range). Yellow throat typically is bordered by dark blue band (only present in NE race of Little Bee-eater), but collar may be entirely blue (Ethiopian *lafresnayi*) or black (S *bangweoloensis*). Juv. lacks dark collar and has greenish, streaked breast. Ethiopian race has blue frons and supercilium. **Habitat:** Long-grass savannas and old fields, usually in more humid savannas than Little Bee-eater. Ethiopian race occupies montane forest edge up to 3 200 m. **Status:** Common; in pairs or small groups. **Voice:** Similar to Little Bee-eater. [C7.93]

4 CINNAMON-CHESTED BEE-EATER *Merops oreobates* 20-21 cm
Endemic to E Africa. Larger and more intensely coloured than Little and Blue-breasted bee-eaters, with greenish (not russet) flight feathers and tail, and large collar. Has white cheek patch, like Blue-breasted Bee-eater. Juv. lacks dark collar and has greenish breast, tinted cinnamon; belly and flanks are buffy, undertail coverts are pale green. **Habitat:** Wooded hillsides and forest edge, mostly 1 800-2 500 m. **Status:** Locally common resident and altitudinal migrant. **Voice:** High-pitched 'tseep'; song is 'siddip-siddip, tsip-tse-tsee'. [C7.94]

5 LITTLE GREEN BEE-EATER *Merops orientalis* 18-20 cm (25 cm incl. tail streamers)
A small, slender, green bee-eater with narrow black collar and conspicuous black eye-stripe. Central tail streamers are blackish and very long. In flight, wings are mostly green, with black trailing edge. Throat is usually green, but sometimes yellow (possibly when feathers are worn). Juv. is paler, especially below, and lacks black collar. Upperpart feathers are finely tipped whitish, giving lightly scalloped appearance. **Habitat:** Arid savannas and cultivated areas, often far from water. **Status:** Common to locally abundant. **Voice:** Rapid, buzzing, monotonous trill, 'tree-tree-tree-tree-tree'. [C8.1a]

6 BÖHM'S BEE-EATER *Merops boehmi* 16-18 cm (24 cm incl. tail streamers)
A small, slender bee-eater with chestnut crown and throat and very long central tail streamers. Smaller than Madagascar Bee-eater (p. 284), with neater head pattern, lacking white supercilium and cheek stripes, and has dark tip to tail. Juv. is duller, with shorter central tail feathers. **Habitat:** Open areas in broadleafed woodland, usually near water. **Status:** Fairly common but localised. **Voice:** Soft 'swee'. [C8.1b, G3.15.2]

7 SOMALI BEE-EATER *Merops revoilii* 15-16 cm
Endemic to E Africa. A small, pale bee-eater with white throat, black eye-stripe, buffy breast and belly, and buffy-green mantle. Wings and tail are pale green. Bright blue lower back, rump and uppertail coverts are conspicuous in flight. Undertail coverts are pale blue. Juv. is duller. Foraging behaviour recalls Little Bee-eater. **Habitat:** Open, arid and semi-arid country. **Status:** Common. **Voice:** Soft, warbled whistle, 'turee-turee-turee-turee'.

1 RED-THROATED BEE-EATER *Merops bulocki*   20-22 cm
Forms a superspecies with White-fronted Bee-eater, but lacks white frons and cheek stripe. A colonial bee-eater, green above and red and orange below, with a black facial mask and square tail. Red throat merges into cinnamon-brown breast and belly. Undertail coverts are dark blue. Juv. is duller, with green cheek stripe. E *frenatus* has blue supercilium and cheek stripe (absent in nominate race, W Africa to Chad). Rarely, some birds have yellow throat. **Habitat:** Savannas, often near water. **Status:** Common. **Voice:** Sharp 'wik', often repeated. [C7.96]

2 WHITE-FRONTED BEE-EATER *Merops bullockoides*   22-24 cm
The crimson throat, white cheek stripe and frons, and lack of elongated central tail streamers are diagnostic. Forms a superspecies with smaller Red-throated Bee-eater, but there is no overlap in range and is easily separated by white frons and cheek stripe, as well as blue uppertail coverts; tail is green (tail has chestnut windows in Red-throated Bee-eater). Juv. is duller. **Habitat:** Wide, slow-moving rivers with steep sandbanks, and other freshwater expanses. **Status:** Common. **Voice:** 'Qerrr', like that of Greater Blue-eared Starling; twittering noises when roosting. [C7.97, G3.15.3]

3 WHITE-THROATED BEE-EATER
Merops albicollis   20 cm (32 cm incl. tail streamers)
A rather small, slender bee-eater, easily identified by its diagnostic black-and-white striped head, black breast band and blue-green upperparts. Adult has very long central tail streamers; these are absent in juv., which is duller green and lightly scalloped above. **Habitat:** Semi-arid savannas when breeding, moister savannas on migration, even hunting over canopy of forest and gallery forest. **Status:** Common intra-African migrant; colonial and gregarious. **Voice:** Similar to but higher-pitched and more repetitive than that of European Bee-eater. [C7.98]

4 BLUE-CHEEKED BEE-EATER *Merops persicus*   25 cm (33 cm incl. tail streamers)
A large green bee-eater. Slightly larger than Madagascar Bee-eater, with green (not brown) crown, blue (not white) frons, supercilium and cheek stripe, and yellow (not rufous) chin. In worn plumage, blue facial stripes can appear white, causing potential confusion with Madagascar Bee-eater; in such birds, green (not brown) crown is key to identification. Juv. is duller and lacks tail streamers. **Habitat:** Floodplains and adjacent broadleafed woodland. **Status:** Local, fairly common breeding visitor in N Mar-Sep and common Palearctic migrant Sep-Apr. **Voice:** Liquid 'prrrup' and 'prrreo', less mellow than that of European Bee-eater. [C3.29, G3.14.10]

5 MADAGASCAR (OLIVE) BEE-EATER
Merops superciliosus   24 cm (30 cm incl. tail streamers)
Slightly smaller than Blue-cheeked Bee-eater, with white (not blue) supercilium and cheek stripe, rufous (not yellow) throat and paler green underparts. Crown usually brown, but green in some individuals of W race. Much larger than Böhm's Bee-eater (p. 282), with dull brown (not chestnut) cap and white (not blue) facial stripes. Juv. lacks tail streamers. **Habitat:** Broadleafed woodland near lakes, rivers and swamps. **Status:** Common resident and intra-African migrant. **Voice:** Metallic 'prrrup', higher and sharper than Blue-cheeked Bee-eater. [C8.2a, G3.14.9]

6 EUROPEAN BEE-EATER *Merops apiaster*   25 cm (28 cm incl. tail streamers)
The chestnut crown and back, golden mantle, yellow throat and blue breast and belly are diagnostic. Coloration of South African breeding birds is more intense. Juv. lacks elongate central tail, and has a green back and faded underparts. **Habitat:** Savanna, broadleafed woodland, fynbos and adjacent grassy areas. **Status:** Common Palearctic migrant Sep-Mar and intra-African migrant breeding in South Africa Aug-Feb. **Voice:** Far-carrying, frog-like flight call, 'prrrup'; 'krroop-krroop'. [C3.30, G3.14.8]

OSTRICHES
The largest birds; flightless. Sexes differ. Chicks are banded tan and brown, resembling small, downy bustards. Nest on the ground; several females often lay in the same nest.

1 COMMON OSTRICH *Struthio camelus*   200-240 cm
Male plumage is blackish, with white wings and tail (often stained chestnut). Typically shows white ring of feathers at base of grey or pink (in *massaicus*) neck. Female is grey-brown. In NE *massaicus* overlaps with Somali Ostrich; males differ by having pink (not blue-grey) necks. **Habitat:** Open country, arid savannas and semi-desert plains. **Status:** Wild populations restricted to large reserves and wilderness areas; often farmed; feral birds widespread in S Africa. **Voice:** Booming, leonine roar, mostly at night. [C5.1a, G1.1.1]

2 SOMALI OSTRICH *Struthio molybdophanes*   200-240 cm
Endemic to NE Africa. Male differs from Common Ostrich by lacking white neck ring (but there is some individual variation). Differs from Common Ostrich *massaicus* by its blue or blue-grey (not pink) neck and thighs (more pronounced when breeding). Black plumage appears more intensely black than that of Common Ostrich. Female and imm. are similar to Common Ostrich. Typically more solitary than Common Ostrich. **Habitat:** Arid and semi-arid grasslands and savanna. **Status:** Rare outside game parks. **Voice:** Similar booming call to that of Common Ostrich.

SECRETARYBIRD
Endemic, monotypic family. Unique, long-legged raptor that could possibly be mistaken for a crane (p. 144). Long legs and tail streamers trail behind in flight. Sexes alike.

3 SECRETARYBIRD *Sagittarius serpentarius*   140 cm
Long legs, head plumes and long central tail feathers, characteristic long-striding gait and horizontal body posture are diagnostic. In flight, the two central tail feathers project well beyond legs, and black flight feathers and thighs contrast with pale grey coverts and body. Juv. has shorter tail and yellow (not red) bare facial skin. **Habitat:** Savanna and open grassland. **Status:** Uncommon to locally common, usually singly or in pairs. **Voice:** Normally silent but utters deep croak during aerial display. [C5.66, G1.12.8]

GROUND-HORNBILLS
An endemic family. Huge, ground-dwelling hornbills with black plumage except for white primaries and primary coverts. Usually in pairs or small groups. Unlike other hornbills, female not confined to nest while breeding. Sexes differ.

4 NORTHERN (ABYSSINIAN) GROUND-HORNBILL
Bucorvus abyssinicus   90-100 cm
A large, turkey-sized black bird with a long, decurved bill and conspicuous blue face and white primaries in flight. Tall casque tilts upward at front. Male has bare red throat patch. Bill is less robust than that of Southern Ground-Hornbill, with yellow-orange patch at base of upper mandible. Imm. has dull greyish face and reduced casque. **Habitat:** Dry savanna and open grasslands. **Status:** Thinly and patchily distributed N of equator. **Voice:** Deep, booming call, faster and slightly higher pitched than that of Southern Ground-Hornbill. [C8.10a]

5 SOUTHERN GROUND-HORNBILL *Bucorvus leadbeateri*   90-100 cm
Similar to Northern Ground-Hornbill, but with heavier, all-black bill with much smaller casque. Adult has red (not blue-grey) facial skin. Adult female has small blue throat and extensive red neck pouches. Juv's face and throat are yellow (not red). **Habitat:** Savanna, woodland and grassland with adjoining forests. **Status:** Scarce; occurs in family groups. Now mainly confined to large reserves and national parks. **Voice:** Loud, booming 'ooomph ooomph' early in morning. [C8.10b, G4.2.3]

Noisy, large, long-tailed birds with characteristic long, heavy bills, often with casques. Most species have striking plumage, making identification easy. Sexes usually similar, although females have smaller casques. Nest in holes in trees; female cemented into nest and is entirely dependent on the male while she undergoes a flightless moult.

1 BLACK DWARF HORNBILL *Tockus hartlaubi* 38 cm
A rather indolent, small forest hornbill, relatively silent and easily overlooked. Identified by its small size, dark plumage (lighter on belly), and large whitish stripe above eye and along sides of crown. In flight has narrow pale tips to outer-tail. Male has dull red bill with small casque and bare pink throat patches; female and juv. are duller, with dark bill lacking casque. E *granti* has white tips to wing coverts and inner secondaries. **Habitat:** Forest understorey, mainly under canopy or at middle levels, gallery forest and forest edge. **Status:** Locally common. **Voice:** Usually silent; soft hissing; 'chwee-kee' notes; louder 'peep-pep'. [C8.11b]

2 RED-BILLED DWARF HORNBILL *Tockus camurus* 38 cm
A small, insectivorous forest hornbill, noisy, active, and easily located by its whistling call. Identified by red bill and rufous-brown plumage, with white belly, pale edges to wing feathers and white tips to outer-tail. Lacks white head stripe of Black Dwarf Hornbill. Male has small casque; female and juv. lack casque and have darker tip to bill. **Habitat:** Forest and gallery forest. **Status:** Common. **Voice:** A series of mournful, rising and falling, whistled notes. The far-carrying call is a useful indicator of rainforest canopy bird parties. [C8.12a]

3 WHITE-CRESTED HORNBILL *Tropicranus albocristatus* 75 cm
A black forest hornbill with a distinctive white crest. Tail is very long and graduated, with each feather tipped white. Bill is dark grey, with pink line along upper mandible and pink throat patch. Female has slightly smaller casque. W African races have grey or whitish face; C African *cassini* has dark face and white-tipped greater coverts and scapulars. Pairs associate with monkeys, catching large insects disturbed by them; also attend ant swarms. **Habitat:** Forest; rarely secondary growth. **Status:** Common. **Voice:** Hyaena-like wail, quite unlike any other hornbill's. [C8.11a]

4 EASTERN (NORTHERN) YELLOW-BILLED HORNBILL *Tockus flavirostris* 50 cm
Endemic to NE Africa. Yellow bill, spotted wing coverts and white underparts are diagnostic in its range; told from Southern Yellow-billed Hornbill by black (not pink) circum-orbital skin and less white in the wing. Shares white-spotted wing coverts with red-billed (p. 290) and Jackson's (p. 292) hornbills', but is distinguished from both by entirely yellow (not red and yellow) bill. Male has pink throat patches; female and juv. have smaller bill and shorter casque. **Habitat:** Savannas, especially with baobab and *Commiphora* trees. **Status:** Uncommon. **Voice:** Intensifying sequence of clucking notes, like red-billed hornbills', but deeper: 'wok-wok-wok-wok-WOK-WOK-WOK'.

5 SOUTHERN YELLOW-BILLED HORNBILL *Tockus leucomelas* 55 cm
Near-endemic to S Africa. Yellow bill, spotted wing coverts and pale underparts are diagnostic in its range; told from Eastern Yellow-billed Hornbill by pink (not black) circum-orbital skin and more white in the wing. Female and juv. have smaller bill and shorter casque. **Habitat:** Thornveld and dry, broadleafed woodland. **Status:** Common. **Voice:** Rapid, hollow-sounding 'tok tok tok tok tok tokatokatoka', uttered with head lowered and wings fanned. [G4.1.9]

1 hartlaubi ♂ ♀ juv. granti ♂ granti ♂

2 ♀ ♂

3 ♂

4 ♂ ♀

5 ♀ ♂

RED-BILLED HORNBILLS

Small, rather slender-billed hornbills of open savannas. Recent studies show that the five races of red-billed hornbills are genetically distinct and behave as good species. They differ primarily in facial pattern, with specific differences in facial feather colour, facial skin colour around the eye, and iris colour; displays and vocalisations also differ. Ranges may overlap narrowly, with hybrid zones between some species. Females smaller, with less extensive dark bases to their lower mandibles. Juvs have shorter, more orange bills and buff (not white) spotted wing coverts.

1 NORTHERN RED-BILLED HORNBILL *Tockus erythrorhynchus* 42-48 cm
The widespread red-billed hornbill of N Africa. Differs from adjacent Western and Tanzanian red-billed hornbills by having pale pink (not blackish) facial skin. Most likely to be confused with male Jackson's Hornbill (p. 292), but is appreciably smaller-billed, with a pale (not dark) face. Easily told from Von der Decken's Hornbill (p. 292) by its white spotted upperwing coverts. Red (not yellow) bill and pale face separate it from Eastern Yellow-billed Hornbill (p. 288). Eye usually dark brown, but some birds in N Kenya have pale eyes and may represent an undescribed taxon. **Habitat:** Savanna and semi-arid woodland. **Status:** Locally common. **Voice:** Apparently similar to Western Red-billed Hornbill's, although tends to have more single notes, and pitch is more varied.

2 DAMARA RED-BILLED HORNBILL *Tockus damarensis* 44-50 cm
Endemic to SW Africa. Slightly larger than Southern Red-billed Hornbill, with whiter head and neck, and typically has brown (not yellow) eyes. Wings are partly opened by male in display (not closed). White (not dark) face and breast, more boldly spotted upperwing coverts and relatively small bill separate it from Monteiro's Hornbill (p. 292). **Habitat:** Savanna and semi-arid woodland, often in hilly areas. **Status:** Locally common. **Voice:** Staccato 'kwa kwa kwa kokkok kokkok kokkok'.

3 SOUTHERN RED-BILLED HORNBILL *Tockus rufirostris* 40-47 cm
Endemic to SC Africa. Differs from Damara Red-billed Hornbill by having brown-streaked (not white) facial feathers and pale yellow (not brown) eye. Easily told from all other red-billed hornbills in S Africa (Monteiro's, Bradfield's and Crowned hornbills; p. 292) by its white (not brown) throat, smaller bill and boldly spotted upperwing coverts. Appreciably smaller than Southern Yellow-billed Hornbill (p. 288), with a red (not yellow) bill. **Habitat:** Savanna and semi-arid woodland. **Status:** Locally common. **Voice:** A long series of 'kuk kuk kuk' calls, becoming faster and louder, ending with double notes 'kuk-we kuk-we'. Apparently unique among red-billed hornbills in not raising its wings during its display. [G4.1.8]

4 TANZANIAN RED-BILLED HORNBILL *Tockus ruahae* 42-48 cm
Endemic to Tanzania. Differs from Northern and Southern red-billed hornbills by having black (not pale pink) facial skin. Further differs from Northern Red-billed Hornbill by its pale (not dark) eye (but beware pale-eyed Northerns in Kenya). Easily told from Von der Decken's Hornbill (p. 292) by its heavily spotted (not plain black) upperwing coverts and smaller bill, with a blackish base to the lower mandible and no yellow tip. **Habitat:** Savanna and acacia woodland; avoids broad-leafed miombo woodland. **Status:** Locally common. **Voice:** Similar to Nothern Red-billed Hornbill's.

5 WESTERN RED-BILLED HORNBILL *Tockus kempi* 40-47 cm
Endemic to W Africa. Similar to Northern Red-billed Hornbill, but has black (not pink) facial skin; ranges not known to overlap. Larger than Red-billed Dwarf Hornbill (p. 288), with more pied (not brown) plumage, and occurs in open savanna habitat (not forests). **Habitat:** Savanna and semi-arid woodland. **Status:** Locally common. **Voice:** A long series of rather dry, nasal notes, starting singly, then increasing in pace and becoming more complex 'who who who who-err-err, who-err-errr-errr, who-err-err-err...'. [C8.12b]

1 MONTEIRO'S HORNBILL *Tockus monteiri* 56 cm
Endemic to S Angola and N Namibia. A brown hornbill with a large red bill. White-spotted (not uniform) wing coverts, and white (not dark) secondaries and outer-tail separate it from Bradfield's Hornbill. Female has smaller bill and turquoise (not blackish, as in male) facial skin. **Habitat:** Dry thornveld and broadleafed woodland. **Status:** Common resident and local nomad. **Voice:** Hollow-sounding 'tooaak tooaak', uttered with head lowered and wings closed. [G4.2.2]

2 VON DER DECKEN'S HORNBILL *Tockus deckeni* 47 cm
Endemic to NE Africa. Differs from Jackson's Hornbill in lacking white spots on wing coverts. White (not greyish) breast and throat separate male from Crowned and Hemprich's hornbills. Female has black bill. Juv. has blackish-horn bill and faint spotting on wing coverts. **Habitat:** Dry, open savanna, bush and thorn scrub. **Status:** Fairly common resident. **Voice:** Low-pitched, monotonous 'wuk-wuk-wuk-wuk-wuk', deeper and quicker than that of Jackson's Hornbill.

3 JACKSON'S HORNBILL *Tockus jacksoni* 50 cm
Localised endemic to E Africa. Sometimes considered a race of Von der Decken's Hornbill, but has white-spotted (not uniform) wing coverts, and male's bill is less two-tone. Bill of male is more robust and more orange than that of Northern Red-billed Hornbill (p. 290), lacking dark base to lower mandible. Female's bill is black. Juv. male has black and dull orange-red bill. **Habitat:** Dry, open savanna, bush and thorn scrub. **Status:** Common. **Voice:** Monotonous 'wuk-wuk-wuk-wuk', higher pitched and slightly slower than that of Von der Decken's Hornbill.

4 CROWNED HORNBILL *Tockus alboterminatus* 54 cm
A dark brown hornbill with a white belly. In SW, is darker brown than Bradfield's Hornbill, with shorter, deeper red bill with yellow line at base and obvious casque (in male only); also has more extensive white tips to outer-tail. In NE, has brighter red bill than Hemprich's Hornbill, pale (not dark) eye and less white in tail. Female has turquoise facial skin (black in male). Juv. has orange bill and lacks casque. Flight is extremely undulating. **Habitat:** Inland, coastal and riverine forests. **Status:** Common resident and local nomad in dry season; often in flocks. **Voice:** Whistling 'chleeoo chleeoo'. [G4.1.10]

5 BRADFIELD'S HORNBILL *Tockus bradfieldi* 56 cm
Near-endemic to S Africa. Differs from Monteiro's Hornbill in having no white in wings and lacking white outer-tail feathers. Is paler brown than Crowned Hornbill, with longer, orange-red bill without distinct casque. Female has smaller bill, with turquoise (not black, as in male) facial skin. **Habitat:** Open mopane woodland and mixed thornveld. **Status:** Common. **Voice:** Rapidly repeated, whistling 'chleeoo' note, with bill raised vertically. [G4.2.1]

6 HEMPRICH'S HORNBILL *Tockus hemprichii* 56-58 cm
Endemic to NE Africa. A dark brown hornbill with a dull red bill darkening towards tip. Belly is white. Tail feathers 3 and 4 (of 5) are white. Wing coverts and secondaries are finely edged white. Slightly larger than Crowned Hornbill, with duller bill, dark (not pale) eye and more extensive white in tail and wing. **Habitat:** Rocky cliffs and gorges in semi-arid areas. **Status:** Uncommon and localised. **Voice:** High-pitched, whistling 'kweeo, pipipipipipipi', faster and higher-pitched than Crowned Hornbill's; bill is raised vertically and tail is raised and lowered.

1 AFRICAN GREY HORNBILL *Tockus nasutus*　　　　　46-51 cm
A drab brown hornbill with a pale eye-stripe and a paler stripe down back (visible in flight). Wings are brown, with narrow pale feather edges; outer-tail tips are white. Male has dark grey bill with creamy stripe at base; casque protrudes in S *epirhinus*, is smaller in N *nasutus*. Upper part of female's bill is pale yellow, tip is maroon. Juv. lacks casque; bill is all-grey (in nominate race) or has pale stripe (in *epirhinus*). **Habitat:** Acacia savanna and dry, broadleafed woodland. **Status:** Common. **Voice:** Plaintive, whistling 'phee pheeoo phee pheeoo', with bill held vertically and wings flicked open on each note. [C8.15, G4.1.7]

2 PALE-BILLED HORNBILL *Tockus pallidirostris*　　　　　49-51 cm
Paler than African Grey Hornbill, with less sooty face and less contrast between breast and paler belly. Lacks pale stripe on back. Main difference is pale, horn-coloured bill (not predominantly dark grey). Female and juv. have smaller casque. **Habitat:** Chiefly miombo woodland, where it rarely overlaps with African Grey Hornbill. **Status:** Uncommon; easily overlooked unless calling. **Voice:** Whistled piping, similar to African Grey Hornbill's but lower pitched and more mellow. [C8.14]

3 AFRICAN PIED HORNBILL *Tockus fasciatus*　　　　　53 cm
A noisy, demonstrative black forest hornbill with a white belly. Fully black (not pied) wings and exaggerated undulating flight separate it from Piping Hornbill (p. 296). C African *fasciatus* has tail feathers 3 and 4 (of 5) entirely white; W African *semifasciatus* has only ends of some rectrices white. Bill is pale yellow with reddish (in *fasciatus*) or black (in *semifasciatus*) tip. **Habitat:** Mature forest, secondary growth, gallery forest, well-wooded savanna, plantations and gardens. **Status:** Common. **Voice:** High pitched piping and yelping notes. [C8.13a]

WATTLED HORNBILLS
Huge hornbills of lowland rainforest canopy, with very heavy, noisy flight.

4 YELLOW-CASQUED WATTLED HORNBILL *Ceratogymna elata*　　　90 cm
Endemic to W Africa. Very similar to Black-casqued Wattled Hornbill, but has fully white outer-tail and pale (not dark) casque. Male has very tall, whitish casque that extends less than half way down bill, and cream-streaked neck. Female has chestnut crown, buff neck, and pale bill and casque. Juv. resembles female but has darker neck. **Habitat:** Forest and forest edge. **Status:** Locally common. **Voice:** Flight call is loud trumpeting; wings make loud whooshing noise. [C8.22]

5 BLACK-CASQUED WATTLED HORNBILL *Ceratogymna atrata*　　　90 cm
A huge, mostly forest hornbill with blue face and throat skin. Differs from Yellow-casqued Wattled Hornbill by its black (not yellow) casque, and by having only the final third of the outer-tail white (not all-white). Male has a black head with a huge casque extending two-thirds of the way along bill. Female has a chestnut-rufous head and smaller casque. Juv. lacks throat wattles, and has brownish head and olive bill with no casque. Flight is laboured and noisy. **Habitat:** Forest, secondary growth and gallery forest. **Status:** Locally common. **Voice:** Very vocal: calls are far-carrying wailing and trumpeting; wings make loud, whooshing noise. [C8.21]

FOREST HORNBILLS

Large black-and-white hornbills, differing in the extent of white on the wings and tail.

1 PIPING (WHITE-TAILED) HORNBILL *Bycanistes fistulator* 50 cm
A medium-sized, black-and-white hornbill with a dark bill and small casque. Extensive white underparts reaching lower breast separate it from other *Bycanistes* hornbills except Trumpeter Hornbill, from which it differs by having more white in wing and tail, smaller bill and different call. Flight is undulating and silent relative to larger congeners, but not as undulating as African Pied Hornbill's (p. 294). Nominate race (in W Africa) has white tips to central secondaries and white tips to outer-tail, but C African races are much whiter, with inner primaries, secondaries and full outer-tail white. Male has small yellow casque and yellow tip and base of bill. Female's bill is smaller and darker. Juv. lacks casque and bill is all-dark. **Habitat:** Mature forest to secondary growth, gallery forest. **Status:** Common; congregates in groups after breeding. **Voice:** Often noisy: cackling laugh; raucous 'kah-k-k-k-k'; piping 'peep-peep-peep'. [C8.17]

2 TRUMPETER HORNBILL *Bycanistes bucinator* 58-60 cm
A medium-large, black-and-white hornbill with extensive white underparts extending onto lower breast, separating it from all other congeners except Piping Hornbill, from which it differs by having only narrow white trailing edges to secondaries and inner primaries and only tips of outer-tail white. Smaller than Silvery-cheeked Hornbill, with smaller, darker casque and darker bill. In flight, has white in wing and white uppertail coverts, but black rump and back. At close range, has pinkish-red (not blue) eye skin. Female has smaller bill and casque. Juv. has almost no casque. **Habitat:** Lowland, coastal and riverine evergreen forests. **Status:** Common resident and local nomad. **Voice:** Wailing, plaintive 'waaaaa-weeeee-waaaaa'. [C8.16, G4.1.5]

3 SILVERY-CHEEKED HORNBILL *Bycanistes brevis* 75 cm
A large black-and-white hornbill with diagnostic black wings (underwing coverts are white). Belly, back and outer-tail tips are white. Male has huge, creamy casque; female and juv. have much reduced casque. Cheek feathers of adults have silvery tips, giving pale-faced appearance. Flight is heavy and noisy compared to Trumpeter Hornbill's. **Habitat:** Montane and coastal forests up to 2 600 m. **Status:** Fairly common resident and local nomad. **Voice:** Deep wail; harsh 'quark-quark'; nasal calls. [G4.1.6]

4 BLACK-AND-WHITE-CASQUED HORNBILL *Bycanistes subcylindricus* 75 cm
A large black-and-white hornbill, with extensive white wings. Differs from sympatric Brown-cheeked and White-thighed hornbills by having central tail black to tip (not mostly white tail). Male has large, bicoloured casque and dark bill. Female and juv. have much smaller casque; bill and casque are dark (not pale, as in Brown-cheeked and White-thighed hornbills). Laboured, noisy flight separates it from smaller Piping Hornbill. **Habitat:** Edge of forest, gallery forest and tall trees in secondary growth. **Status:** Locally common. **Voice:** Loud, nasal calls, similar to Trumpeter Hornbill's but more raucous. [C8.18]

5 WHITE-THIGHED HORNBILL *Bycanistes albotibialis* 75 cm
Sometimes considered a race of Brown-cheeked Hornbill, but has a narrower black band across white tail, darker bill, glossy black ear coverts, yellowish circum-orbital skin and a dark eye. Distinctive white tail with narrow central black band separates it from Black-and-white-casqued Hornbill. Male has long, protruding casque. Casque is smaller in female and juv., which have dark bill with pale tip. Noisy flight separates it from Piping Hornbill. **Habitat:** Forest, gallery forest, forest edge and old secondary growth with tall trees. **Status:** Locally common. **Voice:** Bark-like 'gah gah' and 'kek kek'. [C8.19]

6 BROWN-CHEEKED HORNBILL *Bycanistes cylindricus* 75 cm
Endemic to Upper Guinea forests. Pale yellow (not yellow and black) bill and casque, and broad white (not dark) tail tip separate it from Black-and-white-casqued Hornbill; white in flight feathers is not as extensive. Told from allopatric White-thighed Hornbill by broader black tail band, brownish ear-coverts and red circum-orbital skin and eye. Male has large casque and pale bill. Casque is reduced in female and juv., which also have pale bill. **Habitat:** Forest canopy. **Status:** Local and uncommon. **Voice:** Harsh 'klee klee' flight notes. [C8.20]

Compact, stout-bodied birds with heavy bills. Largely frugivorous; often gather at fruiting trees. Most are quite vocal. Sexes alike in most species.

1 NAKED-FACED BARBET *Gymnobucco calvus*   18 cm
The most widespread *Gymnobucco*, distinguished by lacking prominent nasal tufts. Differs from Grey-throated Barbet by dark bare skin on head (not feathered) and yellow (not black) bill. Has larger bill than Bristle-nosed Barbet, with greyer throat and darker brown rump. S races (Congo-Angola) have whitish throat. **Habitat:** Forest and secondary growth. Breeds colonially in tall dead trees, often with other *Gymnobucco* barbets. **Status:** Common. **Voice:** Sharp 'cheeup'; various rattles and trills. [C8.25]

2 BRISTLE-NOSED BARBET *Gymnobucco peli*   18 cm
Similar to Naked-faced Barbet; often occurs in the same colonies. Best told by prominent, pale yellow nasal tufts, smaller bill, paler rump and yellowish edges to feathers. These features often hard to see when birds are silhouetted against sky. **Habitat:** Forest and secondary growth. Breeds colonially in tall dead trees. **Status:** Locally common. **Voice:** Shorter and higher pitched than Naked-faced Barbet's. [C8.24]

3 SLADEN'S BARBET *Gymnobucco sladeni*   18 cm
Endemic to DRC. Forms a superspecies with Bristle-nosed Barbet, but has dark (not yellow) bill; ranges not known to overlap. Naked (not feathered) face separates it from Grey-throated Barbet, and also has more uniform (not streaked) plumage, paler nasal tufts and, in E, dark (not white) eye. **Habitat:** Lowland forest. Breeds in tall dead trees. **Status:** Less common than Grey-throated Barbet; occurs in mixed colonies. **Voice:** Unknown.

4 GREY-THROATED BARBET *Gymnobucco bonapartei*   17 cm
The only *Gymnobucco* with a fully feathered head, except for a small area of dark red-brown skin below eye, which is seldom visible. In W, is only species with black bill, but in E overlaps with Sladen's Barbet which also has black bill; differs by less prominent and darker nasal tufts, more extensive grey feathered (not naked) face and streaked plumage. E *cinereiceps* has white (not dark) eye. **Habitat:** Tall dead trees in forest and secondary growth, gallery forest. Occurs in same colonies as other *Gymnobucco* species. **Status:** Common. **Voice:** 'Chewp', buzzy and nasal notes. [C8.23]

5 WHITE-EARED BARBET *Stactolaema leucotis*   17-18 cm
A dark brown barbet with a black head and prominent white ear-stripes and belly. Tanzanian *leucogrammica* has more extensive white on head, extending from gape to around and above eye. Head of Kenyan *kilimensis* resembles nominate race, but bird has whitish rump. Juv. has paler base to bill. **Habitat:** Coastal forest and bush in S, up to 2 600 m in N Tanzania. Often near rivers. **Status:** Common; usually in groups. **Voice:** Loud, twittering 'treee treeetee teee-tree'; harsher 'waa waa' notes. [G4.2.6]

6 ANCHIETA'S BARBET *Stactolaema anchietae*   17-18 cm
Endemic to SC Africa. A brown barbet with distinctive yellow-streaked face, crown, throat and upper breast. Forms a superspecies with Whyte's Barbet; ranges overlap in Zambia, but has yellow extending onto throat and breast; white wing panel is not as prominent, and lacks white bases to primaries. Juv. has pale base to bill. **Habitat:** Miombo woodland, riverine forest and adjacent woodland. **Status:** Local and usually uncommon; sometimes joins bird parties. **Voice:** Soft 'coo', repeated once a second; 5-35 times.

7 WHYTE'S BARBET *Stactolaema whytii*   18 cm
Endemic to SC Africa. Extent of yellow on head varies geographically, but never extends onto throat or breast as in Anchieta's Barbet. White wing panel is more prominent and has white bases to outer primaries, giving second white panel in folded wing. Juv. has pale base to bill and less extensive yellow on face. **Habitat:** Miombo woodland and riverine forests, usually near fig trees. **Status:** Locally common. **Voice:** Faster and slightly higher pitched than Anchieta's Barbet. [C8.26, G4.2.7]

S races

1 GREEN BARBET *Stactolaema olivacea*   15-17 cm
A chunky, short-tailed, dark olive-green barbet, slightly paler below, with a darker head that varies geographically: Kenyan and N Tanzanian birds have uniform head; *rungweensis* (S Tanzania and N Malawi) has buffy ear coverts; *belcheri* (S Malawi and N Mozambique) has black head and breast with yellow-green ear coverts; and *woodwardi* (S Tanzania and South Africa) has yellow-green ear coverts. Underwing coverts in all races are yellowish white. In flight, has pale primary bases. Larger, darker and more heavily built than Green Tinkerbird. Juv. is duller than adult. **Habitat:** Lowland and montane forest to 2 000 m. Usually forages in canopy. **Status:** Localised, but fairly common in coastal and montane forests. **Voice:** Hollow, repetitive 'tjop tjop tjop'; regularly duets. [G4.2.8]

2 SPECKLED TINKERBIRD *Pogoniulus scolopaceus*   13 cm
A large tinkerbird with unusual spotted and speckled plumage. At a distance, can appear rather uniform, drab olive. Pale yellow eye and strong black bill are prominent at close range. W African birds are paler and less speckled below than C African *flavisquamatus* (from Cameroon E). **Habitat:** Forest, gallery forest and secondary growth. **Status:** Locally common. **Voice:** Series of ticking notes, increasing in number as series progresses; also more typical tinkerbird-like popping calls. [C8.28]

3 GREEN TINKERBIRD *Pogoniulus simplex*   9-10 cm
Endemic to SE Africa. A dull green tinkerbird with pale yellow wing bars and a yellow rump. Paler than Moustached Tinkerbird, and lacks that species' white moustache. Juv. has more extensive pale base to bill. **Habitat:** Canopy of coastal forests. **Status:** Local and uncommon in N; range poorly known in S. **Voice:** Fast trill, lasting up to 2 seconds, sometimes preceded by 'pop'; faster than call of *fischeri* Yellow-rumped Tinkerbird in coastal E Africa. [G4.3.2]

4 WESTERN TINKERBIRD *Pogoniulus coryphaeus*   10 cm
A small, montane forest tinkerbird distinguished by yellow crown stripe that extends down back to rump. Rest of upperparts are black, with prominent yellow wing bar and yellow edges to flight feathers and greater coverts. Grey-olive underparts are demarcated from black face by distinct white moustache. **Habitat:** Montane forest and forest edge. **Status:** Localised but fairly common. **Voice:** Very similar to Moustached Tinkerbird's. [C8.27]

5 MOUSTACHED TINKERBIRD *Pogoniulus leucomystax*   9-10 cm
A dull green tinkerbird with obvious white moustachial stripes, prominent yellow wing bars and a yellow rump. Plumage is darker and more contrasting than that of Green Tinkerbird; occurs at higher elevations. **Habitat:** Mid-level and montane forests, sometimes in small, isolated patches. **Status:** Locally common to common in some areas; seen mostly singly or in pairs; most often located by obvious song. **Voice:** Staccato trilling call, vaguely recalling an apalis (and will respond to playback of Bar-throated Apalis's song).

6 YELLOW-FRONTED TINKERBIRD *Pogoniulus chrysoconus*   10-11 cm
A distinctive tinkerbird with white-streaked black upperparts and yellow-washed underparts. Best told from Red-fronted Tinkerbird by yellow (not red) forehead, but is also larger, with heavier bill and yellower throat. Forehead colour varies from pale yellow to bright orange. Tends to be more streaked white above than Red-fronted Tinkerbird, and lacks that species' white supercilium. Juv. lacks yellow forehead. **Habitat:** Woodland and savanna. **Status:** Common. **Voice:** Continuous 'pop-pop-pop ...' or 'tink tink tink ...', very similar to Red-fronted Tinkerbird's. [C8.32, G4.2.10]

7 RED-FRONTED TINKERBIRD *Pogoniulus pusillus*   9-10 cm
Differs from Yellow-fronted Tinkerbird in having bright red (not yellow) forehead. Is also smaller, with finer bill, and is darker above. Tends to have neater facial pattern, with well-defined black cheek patch and white supercilium extending back from behind eye. Juv. lacks red forehead. **Habitat:** Coastal forests in S, more arid woodland and thickets in N. **Status:** Common, with disjunct populations in S and E Africa. **Voice:** Continuous, monotonous 'pop-pop-pop ...', very similar to Yellow-fronted Tinkerbird's, but slightly faster and higher pitched. [G4.2.9]

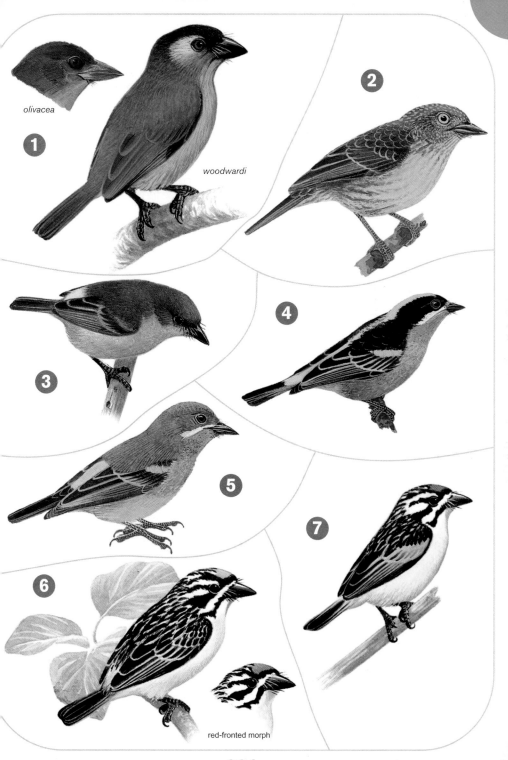

olivacea

1

woodwardi

2

3

4

5

6

7

red-fronted morph

BARBETS & TINKERBIRDS

1 YELLOW-RUMPED TINKERBIRD *Pogoniulus bilineatus*   9-11 cm
A small tinkerbird with a plain black back and crown, and two white stripes on sides of head. Small yellow rump patch is not easy to see in the field. Juv. has black upperparts narrowly barred and spotted yellow-green, and base of bill is paler. **Habitat:** Forest, forest edge and dense woodland; favours more open habitats in areas of overlap with Yellow-throated Tinkerbird. **Status:** Common. **Voice:** 'Pop pop pop pop'; a lower-pitched, more ringing note than that of Red- or Yellow-fronted tinkerbirds, repeated in phrases of 4-6 notes, not continuously. Coastal E Africa *fischeri* has a faster 'pop-trill' call, slightly slower than Green Tinkerbird's. [C8.31, G4.3.1]

2 YELLOW-THROATED TINKERBIRD *Pogoniulus subsulphureus*   10 cm
Similar to Yellow-rumped Tinkerbird, but with yellow (not white) throat and facial stripes (although W African birds have whiter throat). Best separated by song. Tends to occur in more forested habitat, but the two species do occur together at forest edge, in gallery forest or in secondary growth. **Habitat:** Mature forest, gallery forest and secondary growth. **Status:** Common. **Voice:** 'Pyop pyop pyop pyop', faster than Yellow-rumped Tinkerbird's, each note starting with a higher initial element. [C8.30]

3 WHITE-CHESTED TINKERBIRD *Pogonolius makawai*   10 cm
Known only from one bird collected in NW Zambia. Resembles Yellow-rumped Tinkerbird but has clear white throat and breast and lacks white supercilium. Bill is heavy. **Habitat:** Only specimen collected in 'mavunda' dry forest. **Status:** Unknown. **Voice:** Reported to be subtly different from Yellow-rumped Tinkerbird's.

4 RED-RUMPED TINKERBIRD *Pogoniulus atroflavus*   13 cm
A larger tinkerbird with a distinctive red rump and two yellow stripes behind eye. Underparts are much darker yellow-green than Yellow-throated Tinkerbird's. Juv. duller, with pale tips to upperpart feathers. **Habitat:** Mature forest, gallery forest and secondary growth; forages at any height, from canopy to close to ground. **Status:** Fairly common. **Voice:** Slow, regular 'oop oop oop'. [C8.29]

5 BANDED BARBET *Lybius undatus*   16-18 cm
Endemic to Abyssinian highlands. A rather variable barbet with a heavy black bill and red frons. Most races have black head and breast, with narrow white stripe behind eye, and belly barred grey and white or yellow, but N *thiogaster* has grey-streaked breast and spotted belly. White phase has white throat, neck and nape; some have black bellies. All races have back mottled brown with yellow edges to flight feathers; lacks yellow spotting on back of Red-fronted Barbet (p. 304). **Habitat:** Woodland, forest and adjacent scrub; avoids dry acacia scrub. **Status:** Uncommon to locally common. **Voice:** Low-pitched, nasal hooting.

6 WHITE-HEADED BARBET *Lybius leucocephalus*   18-19 cm
The white head, black eye skin and large grey bill are diagnostic. Vaguely resembles White-headed Buffalo-Weaver (p. 654) but lacks red rump and white wing patches. Races vary considerably in amount of white on body: nominate race has mostly black back, belly and tail, whereas *senex* has these parts white. **Habitat:** Riparian woodland and gardens with fruiting trees. **Status:** Locally common, often in groups of 8-10 birds. **Voice:** Duetting consisting of 'cheechee-chaachaa' notes. [C8.39]

7 CHAPLIN'S BARBET *Lybius chaplini*   18 cm
Endemic to Zambia. White head with red facial streaks is diagnostic. Also differs from White-headed Barbet by having yellow edges to flight feathers, forming panel on folded wing. Easily told from Black-backed Barbet (p. 306) by white (not red and black) crown and white (not pinkish) belly. Extent of white on rump and tail is variable. Juv. has paler bill and lacks red face streaking. **Habitat:** Open woodland with scattered fig trees. **Status:** Localised and uncommon; occurs in family groups. **Voice:** Similar duetting to White-headed Barbet.

senex

leucocephalus

1 MIOMBO PIED BARBET *Tricholaema frontata*　　16-18 cm
Endemic to SC Africa. A rather scruffy-looking pied barbet with poorly defined facial pattern. Range does not overlap with that of any similar barbet; scaled (not black) throat separates it from Acacia Pied and Spot-flanked barbets. Juv. lacks red forehead. **Habitat:** Largely confined to tall miombo woodland. **Status:** Locally common; unobtrusive and usually located by call. **Voice:** Nasal, whining call and low-pitched hooting, similar to Acacia Pied Barbet. [C8.36]

2 RED-FRONTED BARBET *Tricholaema diademata*　　14-16 cm
Endemic to NE Africa. Resembles Spot-flanked and Black-throated barbets, but has red (not black) forehead and lacks black on throat. Much larger than Red-fronted Tinkerbird (p. 300), and lacks black moustachial stripe. Juv. lacks red forehead. **Habitat:** Dry woodland, acacia scrub and riverine forest; drier habitats than Spot-flanked Barbet but not as arid as those of Black-throated Barbet. **Status:** Locally common. **Voice:** Series of 4-6 soft, low hoots.

3 ACACIA PIED BARBET *Tricholaema leucomelas*　　16-18 cm
Near-endemic to S Africa. Typical pied barbet with black throat; range does not overlap with other pied barbet species. Much larger than Red-fronted Tinkerbird (p. 300). Juv. lacks red forehead. **Habitat:** Woodland and savanna, especially arid acacia woodland; also gardens. **Status:** Common. **Voice:** Nasal 'nehh, nehh, nehh' (toy trumpet) call, repeated 3-5 times; soft, low-pitched 'poop-oop-oop-oop…'. [G4.2.5]

4 HAIRY-BREASTED BARBET *Tricholaema hirsuta*　　18 cm
Endemic to W Africa. A black-headed forest barbet with a white supercilium and a broad white moustache. Male has a black throat; female's streaked black and white. Intergrades with Streaky-throated Barbet in Nigeria. **Habitat:** Forest canopy to secondary growth; gallery forest. **Status:** Common. **Voice:** Slow, regular series of 10-20 notes: 'oork oork…', roughly 2 notes per second. [C8.34]

5 STREAKY-THROATED BARBET *Tricholaema flavipunctata*　　18 cm
Often considered a race of Hairy-breasted Barbet, but has much plainer and duller plumage, lacking white facial stripes in WC African *flavipunctata* and *angolensis*; widespread *ansorgei* (E Cameroon to W Kenya) has narrow white supercilium and moustache, but is duller than Hairy-breasted Barbet with a streaked throat in both sexes. Intergrades with Hairy-breasted Barbet in Nigeria. **Habitat:** Forest canopy to secondary growth; gallery forest. **Status:** Common. **Voice:** Similar to Hairy-breasted Barbet's, but slower (1 note per second). [C8.35]

6 YELLOW-SPOTTED BARBET *Buccanodon duchaillui*　　16 cm
An unmistakable forest barbet, with a red crown, yellow stripe behind eye, and glossy blue-black body, spotted yellow on back. Yellow underparts are barred with dark blue. Easily distinguished from Yellow-billed Barbet (p. 308) by its short tail and black bill. From below, blue-black breast separates it from Hairy-breasted Barbet. **Habitat:** Forest and secondary growth. **Status:** Common; most often located by strange song. **Voice:** Purring trill, lasting 1-2 seconds, sounding remarkably like someone snoring. [C8.33]

7 BLACK-THROATED BARBET *Tricholaema melanocephala*　　13-14 cm
Endemic to NE Africa. Similar to Red-fronted and Spot-flanked barbets, but black throat, plain, unspotted flanks and dark eye are diagnostic. Black throat extends as long bib down centre of breast onto belly, and in some races ends in reddish spot. **Habitat:** Arid and semi-arid woodland and scrub, often along dry river courses. **Status:** Locally common. **Voice:** Rather distinct: series of 3-6 fast, grating notes, 'kaa kaa kaa kaa'; also nasal call.

8 SPOT-FLANKED BARBET *Tricholaema lacrymosa*　　13-14 cm
Endemic to E Africa. Combination of spotted flanks, black throat and pale eye are diagnostic. Smaller than Red-fronted Barbet, with black (not red) throat. Pale eye and obvious black spots along flanks separate it from Black-throated Barbet. **Habitat:** Various woodland types, generally in moister situations than Red-fronted or Black-throated barbets. **Status:** Locally common. **Voice:** Slightly faster and higher-pitched hooting calls than those of Red-fronted and Black-throated barbets; also nasal call. [C8.37]

1 BLACK-BILLED BARBET *Lybius guifsobalito*   15-17 cm
Endemic to NE Africa. Resembles Red-faced Barbet but red extends onto throat and breast; white-edged wing coverts are diagnostic; ranges do not overlap. Juv. has much less red on the head. **Habitat:** Woodland, including degraded areas and cultivation with fruiting trees. **Status:** Uncommon and thinly distributed, but often conspicuous, with groups calling from tree tops. **Voice:** Duetted 'tooo puudly', similar to Black-collared Barbet's. [C8.40]

2 RED-FACED BARBET *Lybius rubrifacies*   16-18 cm
Endemic to E Africa. An all-black barbet with red streaking on face and yellow edges to secondaries. Lacks red throat and white edges to wing coverts of Black-billed Barbet; ranges not known to overlap. Juv. has less red on its face; bill paler. **Habitat:** Open woodland, forest edge and wooded hill slopes. Avoids dense forest, but occurs in riverine forests. **Status:** Uncommon; most frequently seen in groups on tree tops. **Voice:** Duetting: low-pitched 'kwak aak' answered with higher-pitched 'go baak'.

3 VIEILLOT'S BARBET *Lybius vieilloti*   14-16 cm
A pale brown barbet with diagnostic reddish face, red-streaked pale underparts and pale yellow rump. Range does not overlap with that of any similar barbet except Black-billed Barbet, which has black body. Juv. has extensive red on head and breast. **Habitat:** Dry woodland, scrub and gardens; groups gather at fruiting trees. **Status:** Thinly distributed. **Voice:** Duetting call is series of 'oop-oop-oop' notes; harsher, churring sounds. [C8.38]

4 BLACK-COLLARED BARBET *Lybius torquatus*   18-20 cm
In most areas the bright red face and throat, broadly bordered with black, is diagnostic. Belly is yellow to off-white. Some races have more orange breast, and a rare colour morph has yellow face and throat. Variable *zombae* race (S Malawi to S Tanzania) sometimes lacks red on head, and can have white throat and ear coverts. Juv's head and throat are dark brown, streaked with orange and red. **Habitat:** Forests, woodland, savanna and gardens. **Status:** Common; often in groups. **Voice:** Duet: starts with harsh 'krrr krrrr', followed by ringing 'tooo puudly tooo puudly', the 'tooo' being higher pitched. [C8.41, G4.2.4]

5 BROWN-BREASTED BARBET *Lybius melanopterus*   18-19 cm
Endemic to E Africa. Brown (not black) breast band, white belly and pale (not black) bill separate it from Black-collared Barbet. Red flecking extends onto nape. Juv. is darker, with less red. **Habitat:** Lowland, coastal and riverine forest; around cultivation and villages, especially where there are fruiting trees, where small groups gather. **Status:** Uncommon and local. **Voice:** Far-carrying, rasping 'raak'; other grating calls.

6 BLACK-BACKED BARBET *Lybius minor*   18 cm
Endemic to C Africa. Red frons, white underparts with pinkish wash on belly and black thighs are diagnostic. Two very distinct races were formerly treated as separate species: *minor* (Gabon to NW Angola) has brown upperparts and face; *macclounii* (NE Angola to Malawi) has black back and white face. Juv. is duller; lacks red frons and has darker bill. **Habitat:** Riverine woodland and forest edge and adjacent cultivation. **Status:** Uncommon and unobtrusive. **Voice:** Buzzing trill similar to Double-toothed Barbet's. [C8.42]

7 BLACK-BREASTED BARBET *Lybius rolleti*   21-23 cm
A large, conspicuous barbet with a massive white bill. Black (not red) throat and breast, and white (not yellow) bill separate it from Double-toothed and Bearded barbets (p. 308). Juv. is browner, with more orange belly; lacks faint red wing bar of adult. **Habitat:** Riverine woodland and adjacent cultivation, including eucalypt plantations. **Status:** Uncommon; occurs singly or in pairs on tree tops and around fruiting trees. **Voice:** Harsh and rasping, with whistled notes. [C8.45]

yellow morph

307

1 DOUBLE-TOOTHED BARBET *Lybius bidenatus*   20-22 cm
A large, red-breasted barbet with a large yellow bill. Slightly smaller than both Black-breasted (p. 306) and Bearded barbets, with no black on red underparts and more prominent red wing bar. Juv. is duller. When excited, flicks its tail. Clings to tree trunks when foraging and regularly hawks insects. **Habitat:** Open woodland, forest edge and cultivated areas with fruiting trees. **Status:** Locally common. **Voice:** Harsh 'krrrrrk'. [C8.43]

2 BEARDED BARBET *Lybius dubius*   21-23 cm
Larger than Double-toothed Barbet, with diagnostic black breast band. Also has yellowish (not brown) legs, and lacks red wing bar. Juv. is duller, with darker bill. **Habitat:** Riverine woodland, forest in dry savanna and adjacent farmlands near fruiting trees, where small parties gather. **Status:** Uncommon and localised. **Voice:** Scratchy, rasping 'squaak'; whirring notes when calling together. [C8.44]

3 YELLOW-BILLED BARBET *Trachyphonus purpuratus*   23-26 cm
A long-tailed forest barbet with bright yellow bill and eye-patch, and purple and maroon head, breast and upperparts. Breast is finely spotted silver; belly is yellow (in W African *goffinii*) or mottled black (other races). Long tail and yellow bill easily separate it from Hairy-breasted and Yellow-spotted barbets (p. 304). **Habitat:** Lowland rainforest and dense secondary growth. **Status:** Common, but difficult to see because it keeps to thick tangles in lower and mid-levels. **Voice:** Often-heard popping 'hoop'; also duetting call. [C8.46]

4 CRESTED BARBET *Trachyphonus vaillantii*   23-24 cm
The shaggy crest, yellow face speckled with red, and yellow underparts with broad black breast band are diagnostic. In N, range overlaps with smaller D'Arnaud's and perhaps Red-and-yellow barbets; differs by having crest, unspotted upper back and short, deep, pale yellow bill. Juv. is browner and duller. **Habitat:** Woodland, savanna, riverine forests and gardens. **Status:** Common. **Voice:** Male utters sustained trilling 'trrrrrrrrrrr...'; female responds with repeated 'puka-puka'. [C8.47, G4.3.3]

5 D'ARNAUD'S BARBET *Trachyphonus darnaudii*   16-19 cm
Endemic to NE Africa. Smaller than both Red-and-yellow and Yellow-breasted barbets, with diagnostic speckled face, no red on head and pale pinkish (not red) bill. Is overall drabber bird, with duller yellow and less contrasting black on plumage. S *usambiro* is larger, with darker bill and simpler duet; sometimes treated as distinct species (Usambiro Barbet). **Habitat:** Varied dry to moist woodland and scrub and along dry riverbeds and adjacent farmlands; call is familiar sound of arid habitats in E Africa. **Status:** Common. **Voice:** Duet variable, but mostly 'wit tee toe toe'.

6 RED-AND-YELLOW BARBET *Trachyphonus erythrocephalus*   20-23 cm
Endemic to NE Africa. Larger than D'Arnaud's Barbet, with red on head and red bill. Red ear coverts with diagnostic white patch separate it from Yellow-breasted Barbet. S nominate race has black throat (in male) and more extensive red on head than N races. Female has reduced black breast band and generally lacks black crown. **Habitat:** Dry acacia scrub, open woodland and savanna. Most often in pairs, feeding on ground or duetting from bush tops. **Status:** Locally common. **Voice:** Loud duet 'teee deeedly', repeated monotonously.

7 YELLOW-BREASTED BARBET *Trachyphonus margaritatus*   19-23 cm
A rather neat barbet with a plain yellow face and black crown. Forms a superspecies with Red-and-yellow Barbet, but is paler with no red on face or white ear-covert patch; also lacks a black breast band. Larger than D'Arnaud's Barbet, with reddish bill and no black speckling on face. **Habitat:** Dry riverbeds in arid savanna and surrounding farmlands. Often found near termite hills and earth banks, where they breed. **Status:** Common but thinly distributed. **Voice:** Noisy, duetted 'deee doo', repeated continually. [C8.48]

usambiro

darnaudii

♀

erythrocephalus

♂

Drab, olive-brown birds with stubby bills and prominent white outer-tail feathers. Sexes alike, except Greater Honeyguide. Could be confused with various passerines, but erect stance, undulating flight and prominent white outer-tail diagnostic. Feed on beeswax, and at least some species guide predators to beehives. Brood parasites of hole-nesting birds such as barbets and woodpeckers.

1 SCALY-THROATED HONEYGUIDE *Indicator variegatus*   18-19 cm
A large honeyguide with a streaked throat and mottled breast. Base of lower bill is pinkish. Larger than Lesser Honeyguide (p. 312), and lacks moustachial stripes. Mottled breast separates it from female Greater Honeyguide (which does, however, have scaled throat). At close range, dark forecrown has whitish flecks, unlike uniform forehead of Spotted Honeyguide. Juv. is greener than adult. **Habitat:** Forests and dense woodland. **Status:** Scarce to locally common. **Voice:** Insect-like, ventriloquistic trill, 'trrrrrrr', rising at end and lasting 3-4 seconds, repeated at 1- to 2-minute intervals; calls from within canopy, often returning to same perch. [C8.54, G4.3.5]

2 SPOTTED HONEYGUIDE *Indicator maculatus*   18 cm
Forms a superspecies with Scaly-throated Honeyguide, with very limited overlap in Uganda and Sudan. This species is more richly coloured, with plain (not pale spotted) forecrown. Large and stocky, it has distinctive, dull-yellow spotting on dark olive underparts; upperparts are bright olive-green. **Habitat:** Forest and forest edge. **Status:** Locally common. **Voice:** Male gives long, trilling call similar to Scaly-throated Honeyguide's; also falcon-like 'woe woe woe' call. [C8.53]

3 LYRE-TAILED HONEYGUIDE *Melichneutes robustus*   24 cm
A large honeyguide, best identified at rest by its forked tail. Tail feathers typically are splayed outwards only during aerial display. Difficult to see when perched, as it stays on highest posts in forest canopy, but easy to locate by noisy territorial flight; unmistakable if seen displaying above forest canopy. **Habitat:** Forest, forest edge, gallery forest. **Status:** Scarce to locally common. **Voice:** Flight call 'trr trr'; aerial display uses bizarre tail to generate far-carrying, nasal honking, with 10-30 notes in succession, becoming faster and louder. [C8.52]

4 GREATER HONEYGUIDE *Indicator indicator*   18-20 cm
A large honeyguide. Adult has pale edges to wing coverts and olive shoulders. Adult male has pink bill, black throat and white ear patches. Adult female lacks male's well-marked head and has dark bill; plain breast separates it from Scaly-throated Honeyguide. Juv. is plain brown above, with yellowish throat and breast. **Habitat:** Woodland, savanna and plantations; avoids forests. **Status:** Scarce to locally common. **Voice:** Ringing, repeated 'whit-purr' or 'victor' from regularly used site high in tree; guiding call is harsh, rattling chatter. [C8.55, G4.3.4]

MELIGNOMON **HONEYGUIDES**
Poorly known rainforest honeyguides with yellowish legs and slender bills. Similar to Honeybirds (p. 314). Sexes alike.

5 YELLOW-FOOTED HONEYGUIDE *Melignomon eisentrauti*   12-14 cm
Differs from smaller honeyguides by fine bill, lack of moustachial stripes, plain upperparts and bright yellow feet and lower legs. Paler and greyer than Zenker's Honeyguide, with pale vent and lower belly. Yellow-whiskered Greenbul (p. 418) also has yellow feet, but is darker and lacks white outer-tail feathers. **Habitat:** Lower and mid-level primary rainforest. **Status:** Poorly known; localised and rare. **Voice:** A series of 10-15 notes, descending in pitch and slowing in frequency.

6 ZENKER'S HONEYGUIDE *Melignomon zenkeri*   12-14 cm
Forms a superspecies with Yellow-footed Honeyguide; this species is darker, especially on vent and belly; feet and legs are duller olive-yellow. White outer-tail and lack of yellow gape stripe separate it from juv. Yellow-whiskered Greenbul (p. 418). **Habitat:** Lowland and mid-elevation rainforest. **Status:** Little known; apparently scarce, but easily overlooked. **Voice:** High-pitched, repetitive 'zeet zeet zeet'. [C8.51]

juv.

♀

♂

311

A confusing group of similar honeyguides, best identified by careful examination of head patterns (presence or absence of loral spots and moustachial stripes). Songs usually diagnostic. Sexes alike.

1 LESSER HONEYGUIDE *Indicator minor* 13-15 cm
A medium-sized honeyguide with a short, stubby bill, quite unlike the thin bills of honeybirds. Resembles a grey-headed sparrow (p. 650), but has white outer-tail and streaked, olive wings. Adult has pale loral stripes and indistinct dark moustachial stripes (lacking in juv.). Overlaps with Thick-billed Honeyguide in Uganda and Kenya, but is paler below and less well marked above, and avoids forest interior. Usually located by its far-carrying call. **Habitat:** Well-wooded habitats from forest to dense savanna; has adapted to suburban gardens. **Status:** Common. **Voice:** Characteristic 'frip', repeated 15-40 times at short intervals; same call-site is used regularly. [C8.56, G4.3.6]

2 THICK-BILLED HONEYGUIDE *Indicator conirostris* 14-15 cm
Forms a superspecies with Lesser Honeyguide. Differs by being slightly larger, with a slightly heavier bill, and having darker underparts and more brightly streaked upperparts; in areas of overlap in Kenya and Uganda, is restricted to forest interior. The two species are reported to interbreed in C Nigeria. **Habitat:** Interior of lowland and mid-altitude forest. **Status:** Fairly common but thinly distributed. **Voice:** Similar to Lesser Honeyguide's 'frip' or 'tuip', but deeper and more husky. [C8.57]

3 LEAST HONEYGUIDE *Indicator exilis* 13 cm
A small honeyguide, often with well-streaked flanks. Smaller than Thick-billed Honeyguide, with noticeably smaller bill and more boldly patterned back. Facial pattern is typically strongly developed, with bold black moustachial stripes and prominent white loral spots, contrasting with dark frons. **Habitat:** Forest canopy and tall trees at forest edge and in plantations, often near *Gymnobucco* barbet colonies. **Status:** Locally common. **Voice:** Repeated 'frip', higher-pitched and faster than Lesser or Thick-billed honeyguides. [C8.58]

4 WILLCOCK'S HONEYGUIDE *Indicator willcocksi* 13 cm
A small, plain honeyguide with a short, thick bill. Lack of moustachial stripes and loral spots separate it from Least Honeyguide. In Albertine Rift, typically occurs at lower elevations than Dwarf Honeyguide, and also lacks that species' dark loral spots. **Habitat:** Forest canopy and tall trees at forest edge and in old plantations. **Status:** Uncommon; status in Upper Guinea forests uncertain. **Voice:** Distinctive tri-syllabic call, 'pe-weeel tik', lasting half a second and repeated monotonously; final element is mechanical-sounding snap. [C8.59]

5 DWARF HONEYGUIDE *Indicator pumilio* 10 cm
Endemic to Albertine Rift Mts. The smallest honeyguide. Lacks moustachial stripes of Least and Thick-billed honeyguides. Easily confused with Willcock's Honeyguide, but has distinct, dark loral spots, and generally occurs at higher elevations. Unobtrusive; sometimes joins bird parties. **Habitat:** Mid- and high-altitude forest above 1 500 m, occurring in canopy and mid-stratum. **Status:** Little known; apparently uncommon. **Voice:** Described as 'too-twi'; usually silent.

6 PALLID (EASTERN LEAST) HONEYGUIDE *Indicator meliphilus* 11-13 cm
A small, rather nondescript honeyguide. Resembles small Lesser Honeyguide, but is more greenish on head and nape, faintly streaked on throat, and bill is decidedly smaller. Lacks well-marked moustache of Least Honeyguide, and is paler below than Thick-billed Honeyguide. Short, thick bill eliminates confusion with honeybirds. **Habitat:** Forests and dense woodland. **Status:** Uncommon. **Voice:** Repeated, high-pitched whistle. [C8.60, G4.3.78]

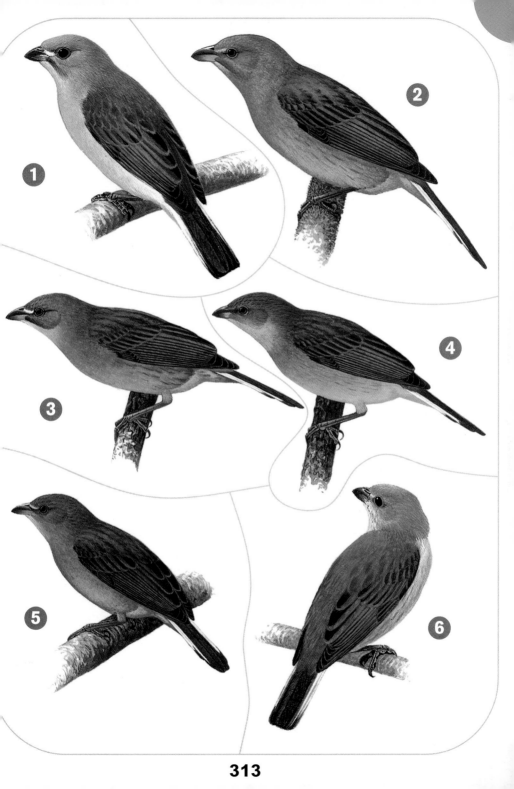

HONEYBIRDS
Small honeyguides with more slender bills; could be confused with *Muscicapa* flycatchers (p. 552). Have erectile white feathers on the sides of the rump, but these are seldom displayed. Don't feed on wax, and parasitise nests of cisticolas, sunbirds and other dome-nesting birds.

1 BROWN-BACKED HONEYBIRD (SHARP-BILLED HONEYGUIDE)
Prodotiscus regulus 13 cm
A drab brown honeyguide with a fine bill that superficially resembles a small flycatcher or warbler, but has diagnostic extensive white outer-tail (with dark tips in adult). Brown back distinguishes it from other honeybirds, and sharp, slender bill distinguishes it from honeyguides. In display, fluffs out white feathers on sides of rump. Juv. has fully white outer-tail. **Habitat:** Woodland, savanna, forest edge and plantations. **Status:** Uncommon to locally common. **Voice:** Rapid churring when perched; metallic 'zwick' during dipping display flight. [C8.50, G4.3.8]

2 GREEN-BACKED HONEYBIRD (SLENDER-BILLED HONEYGUIDE)
Prodotiscus zambesiae 12 cm
Slightly smaller and more stocky than Brown-backed Honeybird, with shorter tail and greenish wash on back and rump. Head appears rounded, with large, dark eye. Differs from Cassin's Honeybird by being paler below and more drab olive above; ranges not known to overlap. Fluffs out white sides of rump in display. Juv. is paler and greyer, with buffy wash on breast. Active forager, taking insects in air or gleaning from leaves. Regularly joins bird parties. **Habitat:** Miombo and other broadleafed woodland; also gardens. **Status:** Uncommon to locally common. **Voice:** Repeated 'skeea' in display flight. [C8.49, G4.3.9]

3 CASSIN'S HONEYBIRD *Prodotiscus insignis* 11 cm
Forms superspecies with Green-backed Honeybird; ranges not known to overlap. Differs by being darker olive below (especially on belly and vent) and brighter yellow-olive above. Separated from sympatric honeyguides by its fine bill. Has distinctive undulating flight that shows off white outer-tail. **Habitat:** Forest, forest edge, gallery forest and tall trees in secondary growth. Generally forages at high levels, hawking insects around trees in blossom. **Status:** Uncommon to locally common. **Voice:** Chatters; utters weak 'ski-aa'.

WRYNECKS
Peculiar birds with wedge-shaped bills and mottled, nightjar-like plumage. Although related to woodpeckers, the tail is soft. Often feeds on the ground or on large branches of trees, with jerky, woodpecker-like movements. Sexes alike.

4 RUFOUS-BREASTED WRYNECK *Jynx ruficollis* 19 cm
Larger than Northern Wryneck, with diagnostic bright rufous throat and breast. Juv. is paler, but still shows rufous wash on breast. Extent of rufous varies; most extensive in Ethiopian *aequatorialis*, which has rufous flanks and vent; NW *pulchricollis* has barred throat and is richer brown above. **Habitat:** Grassland and open savanna, woodland and forest edge; has adapted well to suburban gardens and plantations (especially eucalyptus). **Status:** Locally common within its disjunct range. **Voice:** Series of 2-10 squeaky 'kweek' notes; also repeated, scolding 'peegh'. [C8.61, G4.4.9]

5 NORTHERN (EURASIAN) WRYNECK *Jynx torquilla* 17-18 cm
Similar to Rufous-breasted Wryneck, but lacks rufous breast and is barred (not streaked) below from chin to undertail coverts. Typically has thin black line through eye (absent in Rufous-breasted Wryneck). **Habitat:** Sahelian savannas and cultivated lands. **Status:** Uncommon Palearctic migrant Oct-Mar. **Voice:** Generally silent in Africa. [C3.33]

ruficollis

aequatorialis

315

Distinctive feeders on tree branches, hammering off bark and probing for prey. Sexes differ in amount of red on crown in most species. Flight undulating. Many species use drumming as a non-vocal territorial signal. Key features for identification are face pattern, as well as whether the back is plain or barred and the underparts plain, spotted or streaked.

1 AFRICAN PICULET *Sasia africana* 8-9 cm
A tiny, short-tailed bird, with a strong bill; recalls a short-tailed nuthatch. Dark grey, with olive-green upperparts and red eye-ring and legs. Small white patches on ear coverts visible at close range. Adult male has rufous forehead; juv. is washed rufous below. **Habitat:** Forest understorey, often in dense undergrowth, secondary growth and farmbush, but can be seen in open, on dead branches, at mid-height. **Status:** Locally common, but often overlooked. **Voice:** Weak, high trill; can be located by soft tapping when feeding. [C8.62]

2 GREY WOODPECKER *Dendropicos goertae* 18-20 cm
A medium-sized, plain woodpecker with grey head (red hindcrown in male), golden-olive upperparts and red rump. Belly patch is red, orange or yellow, and sometimes indistinct. Juv. is greener above, more barred below, and has reduced belly patch. Juv. male has reduced red crown, variably mottled with black. Sahel birds (*koenigi*, Mali-Sudan) are paler, with more strongly barred flight feathers and pale tips to wing coverts. **Habitat:** Savannas, open woodland, gardens and mangroves. **Status:** Common. **Voice:** Rattling 'wik-wik-wik-wik-wik'; strident 'skwii-skwii-skwii-skwi'. [C8.81]

3 GREY-HEADED WOODPECKER *Dendropicos spodocephalus* 18-20 cm
Endemic to NE Africa. Often considered a race of Grey Woodpecker, but has larger red (never yellow or orange) belly patch, less barring on wings and tail, brighter yellow-green back, and darker and more uniform grey face. Juv. is darker above, barred below, and has reduced belly patch. **Habitat:** Highland forest, including riparian forest. **Status:** Locally common. **Voice:** Similar to Grey Woodpecker's.

4 OLIVE WOODPECKER *Dendropicos griseocephalus* 17-19 cm
S form of Grey Woodpecker superspecies. Darker and less barred than Grey and Grey-headed woodpeckers; tail is completely unbarred. Underparts are olive-grey, with golden wash on breast. Red belly patch is variable, and absent in *kilimensis* of N Tanzania, which overlaps marginally with Grey-headed Woodpecker. **Habitat:** Forests and dense woodland, often in small forest patches and near forest edge. **Status:** Common. **Voice:** Loud, cheerful 'wir-rit', repeated at intervals; lacks rattling call of Grey and Grey-headed woodpeckers. [C8.81, G4.4.8]

5 GROUND WOODPECKER *Geocolaptes olivaceus* 24-28 cm
Endemic to South Africa. A large, olive-grey and pink woodpecker of open country. Pinkish-red belly and rump, pale eyes and cream-barred wings and tail are diagnostic. Female and juv. have reduced and duller pink on belly and rump. Adult male has red moustachial stripes. **Habitat:** Rocky hill slopes in fynbos, Karoo and grassland; not associated with trees. **Status:** Common; usually in small family parties. **Voice:** Far-carrying 'aargh' or 'pee-aargh'; ringing 'ree-chick'. [G4.3.10]

1 NUBIAN WOODPECKER *Campethera nubica* 21-23 cm
Endemic to NE Africa. Male has full red crown and moustachial stripe, and black-spotted face, neck, breast and flanks. Female has black crown with white spots, red nape and blackish moustachial stripes. Plain throat and heavily marked ear coverts separate both sexes from Speckle-throated Woodpecker, and spotted (not streaked) breast separates adults from Golden-tailed and Mombasa woodpeckers. Juv. is browner and darker above, with black malar stripes; more heavily marked below, sometimes appearing streaked from chin to breast. Replaced in W by Fine-spotted Woodpecker (p. 324); told by its spotted (not barred) upperparts and more boldly spotted breast. **Habitat:** Savanna and acacia woodland. **Status:** Common. **Voice:** Loud duet, accelerating in middle, then slowing down again: 'tyee tyee tyee-tyee-tyee-tyee tee tee'. [C8.64]

2 BENNETT'S WOODPECKER *Campethera bennettii* 20-23 cm
Male has full red crown and moustachial stripes contrasting with plain face and throat. Best told from male Golden-tailed Woodpecker by white throat and spotted (not streaked) breast. Female has diagnostic brown throat and cheek stripe. Sides of neck, breast and flanks are spotted in nominate race, but SW *capricorni* has little spotting, and is paler, with yellow wash on breast. **Habitat:** Broadleafed woodland and savanna; often feeds on ground. **Status:** Scarce to common. **Voice:** High-pitched, chattering 'whirrr-itt, whrrr-itt', often uttered in duet. [C8.65, G4.4.1]

3 SPECKLE-THROATED (REICHENOW'S) WOODPECKER
Campethera scriptoricauda 22 cm
Often considered a race of Bennett's Woodpecker, but has speckled (not plain white) throat and ear coverts. Males are hard to distinguish, but females have very different facial pattern from Bennett's Woodpecker, with lightly speckled (not brown) throat, densely speckled (not white) moustachial stripes and white (not brown) cheek stripe. **Habitat:** Woodland and thickets in savanna. **Status:** Fairly common. **Voice:** Similar to that of Bennett's Woodpecker.

4 GOLDEN-TAILED WOODPECKER *Campethera abingoni* 19-22 cm
Male has full red crown and moustachial stripes, but streaked (not spotted) underparts and ear coverts separate from Bennett's Woodpecker complex. Back is greenish, barred pale yellow, but W African *chrysura* has pale streaked back. Female has white-spotted black crown, red nape, and black speckled moustachial stripes. Most similar to Mombasa Woodpecker but their ranges do not overlap. Paler than Knysna Woodpecker, with streaked (not spotted) underparts. **Habitat:** Woodland, thickets and coastal forests. **Status:** Common. **Voice:** Loud, nasal shriek, 'wheeeeeaa'. [C8.66, G4.4.2]

5 MOMBASA WOODPECKER *Campethera mombassica* 21 cm
Endemic to coastal E Africa. Often considered a race of Golden-tailed Woodpecker, but has brighter green back with only a few small spots (not barred), and pale throat. However, their ranges are not known to overlap. Streaked underparts separate it from Speckle-throated, Nubian and Green-backed (p. 320) woodpeckers. **Habitat:** Forest and coastal woodland. **Status:** Locally common. **Voice:** Very different from Golden-tailed Woodpecker's: accelerating, nasal 'keeoank-yaaaank-yaaank-yaank-yank-yank'.

6 KNYSNA WOODPECKER *Campethera notata* 19-21 cm
Endemic to South Africa. Both sexes are darker than Golden-tailed Woodpecker, with dense, dark brown spotting (not streaks) on underparts. Male's dark red forehead and moustachial stripes are heavily marked with black and are less obvious than those of male Golden-tailed Woodpecker. Female has indistinct black moustachial stripes. **Habitat:** Forests, riparian woodland, euphorbia scrub and mature thickets; often in stands of alien trees (acacias and eucalypts). **Status:** Locally common, but easily overlooked if not calling. **Voice:** Nasal shriek similar to that of Golden-tailed Woodpecker. [G4.4.2]

1

♂

♀

2

♂

capricorni

♀

♂

3

juv.

♀

♂

4

♂

5

♀

♀

♂

juv.

6

♂

1 GREEN-BACKED (LITTLE SPOTTED) WOODPECKER
Campethera cailliautii   15-16 cm
A small woodpecker with a short bill. Plain face, lacking moustachial stripes, separates it from most other species. Male has full red crown; female has red nape. Most races have pale yellow spotting on back and spotted underparts, but W African *permista* has plain back and barred underparts; this race is very similar to Little Green Woodpecker; ranges overlap only slightly in E Ghana. Juv. resembles female but red on crown is reduced or absent. **Habitat:** Forest edge, riparian forest, broadleafed woodland, and thickets near water. **Status:** Uncommon to locally common. **Voice:** High-pitched, whining 'whleeee'. [C8.68, G4.4.4]

2 LITTLE GREEN (GOLDEN-BACKED) WOODPECKER
Campethera maculosa   15-16 cm
Endemic to W Africa (Upper Guinea forests). W counterpart of Green-backed Woodpecker, with bronzy wash on dark back and darker tail lacking yellow shafts. Female lacks red on head; resembles juv. Green-backed Woodpecker but has buffier underparts and black (not brown) tail. Outside narrow area of overlap with Green-backed Woodpecker (E Ghana), is only woodpecker with green back and barred (not streaked) underparts. **Habitat:** Lowland forest, forest edge and adjacent secondary growth; forages low down on trees and underscrub. **Status:** Fairly common. **Voice:** 3- to 4-note ascending phrase, 'teeaay'. [C8.67]

3 GABON WOODPECKER *Dendropicos gabonensis*   15-16 cm
A small, plain-backed woodpecker. Differs from *permista* race of Green-backed Woodpecker by darker face and dark moustachial stripes, and spotted (not barred) underparts. Also has less red on head: only hindcrown and nape in male; absent in female. Birds in SW Cameroon and SE Nigeria intergrade with Melancholy Woodpecker, but differ in rest of range by having spotted (not streaked) underparts, diffusely streaked (not uniformly dark) ear coverts, and more extensive red on the hindcrown (male only). **Habitat:** Canopy of mature forest and gallery forest, and secondary growth; not in forest understorey. **Status:** Common. **Voice:** Buzzy 'dzeeep'. [C8.74]

4 MELANCHOLY WOODPECKER *Dendropicos lugubris*   16-17 cm
Endemic to W Africa. Often considered a race of Gabon Woodpecker, because the two intergrade in SE Nigeria-SW Cameroon; differs by densely streaked (not spotted) underparts, cleaner face markings, with a broad white stripe separating dark moustache and ear coverts, and by having red restricted to nape (male only). **Habitat:** Forest canopy and secondary growth. **Status:** Locally common. **Voice:** Similar to Gabon Woodpecker's; also fast rattle.

5 BUFF-SPOTTED WOODPECKER *Campethera nivosa*   14-16 cm
A small, dark, short-billed woodpecker. Olive-brown above and below, heavily spotted and barred yellowish on underparts. Dark crown contrasts with paler face; male has small red nape. Plain face separates it from larger Brown-eared Woodpecker. **Habitat:** Forest understorey and old secondary growth, generally at lower levels than Brown-eared Woodpecker. **Status:** Locally common. **Voice:** 'Preeuu'; also descending rattling trill, 'dee-dee-dee-dee'. [C8.70]

6 BROWN-EARED WOODPECKER *Campethera caroli*   18-19 cm
A dark brown woodpecker with diagnostic brown facial patches. Male has small red patch on crown (hard to see in the field); absent in female. Upperparts are plain golden-olive; underparts are heavily spotted. W African *arizelus* is duller above and less spotted below. **Habitat:** Forest understorey and mid-strata, forest edge, gallery forest, secondary growth and mangroves. **Status:** Common. **Voice:** 'Kwaa-kwaa-kwaa'; low, trilled 'trrrrrr'. [C8.71]

S races

juv.

♀

♂

① ② ③ ④ ⑤ ⑥

♀ ♂ ♂ ♀ ♂ ♀ ♂ ♀ ♂

1 BROWN-BACKED WOODPECKER *Picoides obsoletus*   13 cm
A small, brown woodpecker with a diagnostic uniformly brown back and well-marked head with clearly defined brown ear coverts, which all help separate it from similar Cardinal Woodpecker. Has white spots on wing coverts and white bars on flight feathers and tail. Whitish underparts are very lightly streaked. Crown is red in male, brown in female. Brown (not red) rump and darker brown plumage separate it from Little Grey Woodpecker. **Habitat:** Arid and semi-arid woodland, savanna and gardens. **Status:** Locally common. **Voice:** Weak, high-pitched trill. [C8.82]

2 CARDINAL WOODPECKER *Dendropicos fuscescens*   14-16 cm
A widespread, small woodpecker with a relatively long bill. Varies geographically, but all races have black moustachial stripes and are streaked underneath. Has very little red in rump and uppertail coverts. S races have barred black-and-white back; NE races are smaller and browner, but still barred; W and C races are greener above, with indistinct barring. Male has red hindcrown and nape; black in female. **Habitat:** Wide range, from thick forests to dry thornveld. **Status:** Common. **Voice:** High-pitched 'krrrek krrrek krrrek'; also makes soft drumming sound. [C8.75, G4.4.5]

3 LITTLE GREY WOODPECKER *Dendropicos elachus*   13-14 cm
A small, pale woodpecker, virtually confined to the Sahel. Resembles a washed-out Cardinal Woodpecker, but has bright red rump and darker ear coverts, and only weakly defined moustachial stripes. Marked back, pale plumage and red rump separate it from Brown-backed Woodpecker. Female lacks red on nape. **Habitat:** Dry woodland along watercourses and adjacent scrub. **Status:** Fairly common; singly or in pairs. **Voice:** Like Cardinal Woodpecker's, but shorter and more abrupt. [C8.72]

4 ABYSSINIAN WOODPECKER *Dendropicos abyssinicus*   16 cm
Endemic to Abyssinian highlands. Similar to Cardinal Woodpecker, but with much darker ear coverts and diagnostic golden-yellow back. Female is duller, with no red on head. **Habitat:** Hagenia and juniper forests and drier euphorbia bush at lower altitudes; forages low down on tree trunks and also on thin vines and shrubs. **Status:** Fairly common; occurs in pairs. **Voice:** Thin, high-pitched shriek during courtship display; responds to tape-recording of Cardinal Woodpecker's call.

5 SPECKLE-BREASTED (UGANDA SPOTTED) WOODPECKER
Dendropicos poecilolaemus   15 cm
Similar to Cardinal Woodpecker, but with only faint spotting (not streaks) confined to breast. Differs further by having red (not yellow-green) rump and rather plain, unbarred back. Spotted (not barred) wing coverts and barred (not plain) flight feathers separate it from Green-backed and Gabon woodpeckers (p. 320). Male has red hindcrown and nape; absent in female. **Habitat:** Moister woodland than Cardinal Woodpecker: forest edge, riverine forest and adjacent woodland. **Status:** Locally common. **Voice:** Dry rattle, 'che che chi chi chichi'. [C8.73]

6 STIERLING'S WOODPECKER *Dendropicos stierlingi*   17-18 cm
Endemic to SC Africa. Striking head pattern recalls a tiny Bearded Woodpecker (p. 324), but has uniform (not barred) olive back, wings and tail. Plain (not barred) upperparts and head pattern separate it from Cardinal Woodpecker. Flight is fast and twisting. **Habitat:** Mature miombo woodland, frequenting larger branches and trunks than Cardinal Woodpecker. **Status:** Uncommon; occurs in pairs and joins bird parties. **Voice:** Loud, wavering rattle; drums louder and faster than Cardinal Woodpecker.

1 BEARDED WOODPECKER *Dendropicos namaquus*　　　　23-25 cm
A large woodpecker with a diagnostic bold black-and-white face pattern. Barred (not plain) back, wings and tail, as well as habitat, separate it from Yellow-crested Woodpecker. Both sexes have dark underparts which are finely barred white (spotted in Yellow-crested Woodpecker). Male has red hindcrown; black in female. Juvs of both sexes have some red in crown. **Habitat:** Woodland, riverine forests and thickets, favouring areas with dead trees; avoids dense forest. **Status:** Common. **Voice:** Loud, rapid 'wik-wik-wik-wik'; drums very loudly. [C8.76, G4.4.6]

2 YELLOW-CRESTED (GOLDEN-CROWNED) WOODPECKER
Dendropicos xantholophus　　　　23 cm
A large forest woodpecker with a boldly patterned head, long bill and uniform dark olive-brown upperparts. Yellow feathers in middle of crown are hard to see in the field. Plain (not barred) back and spotted (not barred) underparts separate it from Bearded Woodpecker. Lack of red on belly distinguishes it from Fire-bellied Woodpecker; ranges are not known to overlap. Female's crown is entirely black. **Habitat:** Tall trees in mature forest and secondary growth, gallery forest. **Status:** Locally common. **Voice:** Loud, piercing 'weeeh weeeh'. [C8.78]

3 FIRE-BELLIED WOODPECKER *Dendropicos pyrrhogaster*　　　　24 cm
Endemic to W Africa. A large forest woodpecker, easily identified by its boldly patterned face and crimson centre of breast and belly. Hindcrown (in male and juv.) and rump are red. Red plumage separates it from similar Yellow-crested Woodpecker; ranges are not known to overlap. **Habitat:** Tall dead trees in forest, gallery forest and old secondary growth. **Status:** Locally common. **Voice:** Noisy and demonstrative: 'wip wi di di di di dit' and drums frequently. [C8.77]

4 ELLIOT'S WOODPECKER *Dendropicos elliotii*　　　　20-22 cm
A fairly large forest woodpecker with uniform bright olive-green upperparts and long, rather pale bill. Black crown (with red nape in male) contrasts with pale, plain face. Buff (in nominate race) or lime-yellow (in *johnstoni*, SE Cameroon highlands) underparts are streaked with long, fine, dark lines (reduced and barely visible in *johnstoni*). **Habitat:** Lowland and montane forest. Feeds on large and medium-sized branches, from understorey to canopy. **Status:** Uncommon, but fairly common in mountains of SW Cameroon. **Voice:** Generally silent; calls reported to be similar to Grey Woodpecker's. [C8.79]

5 TULLBERG'S (FINE-BANDED) WOODPECKER *Campethera tullbergi*　　18-20 cm
A montane forest woodpecker with plain green upperparts and yellowish underparts. Nominate birds in SW Cameroon and Nigeria are finely spotted below, while E races (Fine-banded Woodpecker, *taeniolaema* and *hausburgi*) are finely barred below, resembling large *permista* Green-backed Woodpecker (p. 320). Plain, grey-green face is finely spotted (in nominate race) or barred (in E races). Male's crown and forehead are mottled black and red; nape is red. Female's crown is black, spotted with white. **Habitat:** Montane forest, mostly in canopy. **Status:** Locally common. **Voice:** Loud 'kweek kweek kweek'. [C8.69]

6 FINE-SPOTTED WOODPECKER *Campethera punctuligera*　　　　22 cm
A savanna woodpecker of WC Africa. Similar to Nubian Woodpecker (p. 318), but has finely barred (not heavily spotted) olive upperparts and is only very lightly spotted on breast and flanks; belly is plain. Male has red crown and moustachial stripe; female has black crown, red nape and poorly defined black moustaches. **Habitat:** Savanna and open woodland. **Status:** Common. **Voice:** Querulous 'kweeyer'. [C8.63]

elliotii

johnstoni

325

PITTAS
Brilliantly coloured, unobtrusive forest understorey birds. Sexes alike.

1 AFRICAN PITTA *Pitta angolensis*   18-22 cm
Buff (not green) breast distinguishes it from Green-breasted Pitta; ranges barely overlap. W African *pulih* is smaller, with greener wash to breast and whiter throat. In flight, has white panel in primaries. Juv. duller, with bicoloured bill. **Habitat:** Riverine thickets and forests. When disturbed, flies into mid-storey and freezes. **Status:** Uncommon; resident in W Africa; migratory in E and S Africa; vagrants occasionally stray well outside usual range. **Voice:** Displaying birds utter frog-like 'preert', with initial mechanical purr apparently caused by wings as they jump up from a low perch; after calling, they parachute back to perch, then slowly raise their tail, displaying crimson vent. Call is short, ascending croak. [C8.87, G4.5.1]

2 GREEN-BREASTED PITTA *Pitta reichenowi*   18-20 cm
Similar to African Pitta, but has green (not buff) breast, with small black collar between breast and white throat; green breast can be hard to observe on gloomy forest floor. Smaller than E race of African Pitta (*longipennis*), but similar in size to W African forms, with possible hybridisation in E Cameroon. **Habitat:** Forages over leaf litter in thick tangles of undergrowth in rainforest, sometimes near damp areas. **Status:** Poorly known; shy and furtive, easily overlooked. **Voice:** Bell-like whistle; mechanical 'brrrtt' flight call. [C8.86]

BROADBILLS
Dumpy, phlegmatic flycatcher-like forest birds. Sexes similar; juvs duller.

3 AFRICAN BROADBILL *Smithornis capensis*   12-14 cm
Heavily streaked, buff-white underparts, lacking rufous on breast, distinguish it from other *Smithornis* broadbills. Male has prominent black cap; less well-defined in female and juv. White 'puffball' on lower back is fluffed out during display. **Habitat:** Forests and thickets; avoids primary forest in areas of overlap with other broadbills. **Status:** Uncommon to locally common; easily overlooked when not displaying. **Voice:** Dry, frog-like 'prrrrrrruup' during display, chiefly at dawn and dusk; displaying birds execute short, circular display flights from favoured branches, typically 1-3 m (rarely up to 6 m) above ground. [C8.85, G4.4.9]

4 AFRICAN GREEN (GRAUER'S) BROADBILL *Pseudocalyptomena graueri* 12 cm
Endemic to Albertine Rift. Unmistakable small, green, flycatcher-like bird. Plump, short-tailed shape combined with green and blue plumage is diagnostic. Juv. is duller, with green vent. **Habitat:** Primary rainforest edge and clearings, especially near swamp forest and streams. Occurs higher in canopy than other African broadbills. **Status:** Vulnerable. Uncommon and localised; occurs singly, in pairs or even small groups, sometimes with bird parties. Easily overlooked unless calling. **Voice:** Diagnostic soft, high-pitched 'ptsii ptsii' in display or agitation, with fluffed-out plumage and trembling wings.

5 RUFOUS-SIDED BROADBILL *Smithornis rufolateralis*   12-13 cm
Smaller than Grey-headed Broadbill, with pale tips to wing coverts forming two pale bars at rest, and rufous confined to sides of breast (not across breast). Male's head is uniform dark black-brown, extending well below eye; female's is dark brown (in W) or grey-brown (in E). **Habitat:** Primary rainforest, often near damp areas and streams. **Status:** Locally common; occurs in pairs, and forages with bird parties; more often heard than seen. **Voice:** Similar to African Broadbill's, but higher pitched; display flight from higher perch (4-7 m). [C8.84]

6 GREY-HEADED BROADBILL *Smithornis sharpei*   15-18 cm
Larger and paler than other *Smithornis* broadbills, with a grey-brown crown and grey cheeks in both sexes. Much larger than Rufous-sided Broadbill, with no white spots on wing and more extensive rufous breast band (not confined to sides of breast and neck). Albertine Rift *eurylaemus* has greyer head and more olive breast. **Habitat:** Primary rainforest and montane forest, often near damp areas and streams. **Status:** Locally common. **Voice:** Similar to African Broadbill's, but sharper, more metallic and slightly higher pitched; display and call typically given from lower perches than Rufous-sided Broadbill. [C8.83]

Cryptic, ground-dwelling birds, superficially similar to pipits (p. 368). Sexes alike, but many species show marked geographic variation. Short-lived juvenile plumage has pale-fringed upperparts and larger, more diffuse breast spots in most species. Recent studies suggest several cryptic species have been overlooked.

1 MONOTONOUS LARK *Mirafra passerina* 14 cm
Endemic to SW Africa. A medium to small, compact, stout-billed lark. Shorter tailed and with less distinct facial markings than Melodious Lark. White throat contrasts with relatively plain buff breast, and is prominent when singing. In flight, distinguished from paler Stark's Lark (p. 332) by its chestnut wing patches. **Habitat:** Thornveld and mopane woodland with sparse grass cover. **Status:** Common resident and nomad; summer visitor to S of range; unobtrusive when not calling. **Voice:** Monotonous 'trrp-chup-chip-choop', day and night, usually from bush or tree; short display flight from a perch, rising 15-20 m, calling all the time. [G4.5.3]

2 MELODIOUS LARK *Mirafra cheniana* 12 cm
Endemic to S African grasslands. Small, compact lark with a well-marked face. White throat contrasts with buffy (not white, as in Monotonous Lark) flanks and belly. Smaller than Fawn-coloured Lark (p. 334), with shorter wings and tail. **Habitat:** Grassland and pastures, often on gentle slopes. **Status:** Locally common; unobtrusive when not displaying. **Voice:** 'Chuk chuk chuer'; song jumbled and melodious, often mimicking other birds, given during high, protracted aerial display. [G4.5.2]

3 SINGING BUSH LARK *Mirafra cantillans* 13 cm
A small lark with a short, stubby bill and obvious white outer-tail feathers in flight. Display song is diagnostic. Most easily confused with White-tailed Lark, but is paler above, with a uniform bill that does not appear upturned. Differs from Friedmann's Lark by its paler plumage and less streaked upperparts. Legs are fleshy pink. When flushed, it frequently hovers before landing. **Habitat:** Open grassland with scattered bushes. **Status:** Locally common. **Voice:** Mixture of jumbled chips and warbles, ending in trill; given in hovering flight or from bush top. [C8.88a]

4 WHITE-TAILED LARK *Mirafra albicauda* 13 cm
Darker above than Singing Bush Lark, due to broader dark feather centres; breast spotting darker; bill more bicoloured and appears slightly upturned; in flight, the wings are less rufous. Also darker than Friedmann's Lark, with a weaker bill. **Habitat:** Grassy plains and open savanna. **Status:** Locally common; usually in pairs. **Voice:** High aerial display with varied song of whistles, chuks and tissiks, but lacks the trills of Singing Bush Lark. [C8.89]

5 WILLIAMS'S LARK *Mirafra williamsi* 14 cm
Endemic to N Kenya. Differs from White-tailed, Singing Bush and Friedmann's larks by having an overall more rufous tone, especially across the breast, with much stronger markings above, and by being less streaked below. Occurs in a dark and a rufous morph. **Habitat:** Red lava soils in desert areas. **Status:** Uncommon; shy and secretive; in pairs. **Voice:** Simple, weak mixture of chips and tissiks; laboured, low display flight in early morning with 'sirret' call note.

6 FRIEDMANN'S LARK *Mirafra pulpa* 13 cm
Localised endemic to E Africa. Similar to Singing Bush and White-tailed larks, but is more rufous above, with a heavier bill. Below, streaking is confined to the breast (not throat), and is more heavily streaked on mantle and nape. Lacks the marked face pattern of Athi Short-toed Lark (p. 346). White throat puffed out when singing. **Habitat:** Grasslands in short bush or scrub. **Status:** Rare and little-known species, appearing in years of good rain in S Kenya. **Voice:** Whistled 'see-ree-eoo' given from bush tops or in low-level display flight.

7 KORDOFAN LARK *Mirafra cordofanica* 12-13 cm
A small, compact, stout-billed N African lark. Within its range, differs from Dunn's Lark (p. 340) by being darker overall, especially on the underparts, and has a dark (not pale) bill. In flight, shows a dark-centred tail, rufous middle tail and white outer-tail (Dunn's Lark has a dark-tipped tail). **Habitat:** Grassy plains in semi-desert areas; specific to red soils. **Status:** Common but nomadic in small groups. **Voice:** Short, slightly bubbly series of whistles and trills. [C8.88b]

1 RED-WINGED LARK *Mirafra hypermetra* 21-23 cm
Endemic to NE Africa. A large savanna lark, similar to Rufous-naped Lark but is larger with a thicker and more robust bill, longer tail and obvious dark pectoral patches on sides of neck; flight is laboured, on more rounded wings. **Habitat:** Savanna. **Status:** Common; often seen singing or resting on bush tops. **Voice:** Mimics other birds' songs and calls in complex song; usual call note 'tuu wee tuu' or variations on this.

2 RUFOUS-NAPED LARK *Mirafra africana* 15-18 cm
Large savanna lark with considerable geographic variation, but rufous wings and small crest are consistent features. Most races have rufous nape, but this is lacking in Kenyan *athi*. In E Africa, resembles Red-winged Lark, but lacks dark pectoral patches and is smaller, with a shorter tail. Isolated W African races are generally smaller and darker. **Habitat:** Grassland and savanna; also in cultivated fields. **Status:** Common and widespread. **Voice:** Perched, gives frequently repeated, 3-syllabled 'tree tree-leeooo', sometimes vibrating wings; sometimes mimics other birds' songs, especially during display flights. [C8.90, G4.5.4]

3 SHARPE'S LARK *Mirafra sharpii* 17 cm
Endemic to Somalia. Often treated as a race of Rufuous-naped Lark, but is almost plain rufous above; ranges do not overlap. Within its small range could be confused with Somali Lark (p. 340), but is slightly smaller, with a noticeably shorter bill and buff (not white) outer-tail feathers. **Habitat:** Grassy red sand dunes and grassy plains with scattered bushes on reddish soils. **Status:** Locally common, occurring in pairs. **Voice:** Short, clear whistled 'chuu-lo-leeooo', similar to Rufous-naped Lark's; frequently sings from bushes and anthills.

4 MALBRANT'S LARK *Mirafra malbranti* 17 cm
Endemic to WC Africa. Often treated as a race of Rufous-naped Lark, but song and display differ. Rather pale and unstreaked above, but may intergrade with *kaballii* Rufous-naped Larks of NW Zambia. Larger than Flappet Lark (the only other lark with which it co-occurs) with longer bill and legs, and less heavily patterned back. **Habitat:** Short-grass savanna on sandy plateaux and hills. **Status:** Locally common. **Voice:** Various long, protracted, whistled phrases, often in display flight, which is sometimes direct and straight with wing claps over back. [C8.9.1]

5 ANGOLA LARK *Mirafra angolensis* 16 cm
Intermediate in size between Rufous-naped and Flappet larks; song is diagnostic. Larger than Flappet Lark, with a longer, heavier bill; upperparts darker, with plain (not barred) dark brown feather centres. Dark cap contrasts with paler grey neck. Distinctly smaller and darker above than overlapping races of Rufous-naped Lark, with less rufous in the wings and conspicuous white (not buff) outer-tail feathers. **Habitat:** Grasslands, especially seasonally damp areas dotted with termite mounds. **Status:** Locally common, occurring in pairs. **Voice:** Trilling 'ziii-zuu zi zi-zu', given during a short display flight; call 'trrrp trrrp tee-tu' from termite mounds. [C8.92]

6 FLAPPET LARK *Mirafra rufocinnamomea* 14-15 cm
A medium-sized lark resembling a small, dark Rufous-naped Lark. Smaller than largely non-overlapping Eastern Clapper Lark (p. 332), with slightly longer tail, darker plumage, less rufous in wing and different aerial display. **Habitat:** Grassland, savanna and woodland with at least some openings. **Status:** Common, occurring in pairs. **Voice:** Short 'tuee', given when perched; characteristic display flight includes brief bursts of rapid wing-clapping (2-3 phrases, separated by several seconds), but no song. [C8.93, G4.5.6]

7 MASKED LARK *Spizocorys personata* 14-15 cm
Endemic to NE Africa. A desert lark with an obvious black face mask and large yellow or pink bill. Appears very dark in the field, with buffy outer-tail feathers in flight. Racially variable from greyish to brown, but cinnamon belly always contrasts with greyer breast. **Habitat:** Stony and shrubby black lava deserts. **Status:** Locally common but nomadic; sometimes in small flocks. **Voice:** Short 'chip chip' flight note.

1

2

paler
races

darker races

3

4

5

6

paler
races

7

darker
races

1 EASTERN CLAPPER LARK *Mirafra fasciolata* 15 cm
Endemic to SW Africa. Larger and more rufous than Cape and Agulhas clapper larks, with heavier bill and prominent rufous panels in flight feathers; display differs and ranges not known to overlap. Plumage variable: S grassland birds rich rufous, resembling small Rufous-naped Lark (p. 330); N savanna birds are greyer above, with some races quite pale, but Zambian *jappi* is darker brown. Overlaps slightly with Flappet Lark (p. 330), but occurs in more open habitats and has a slightly shorter tail with paler outer-tail feathers. When displaying, climbs steeply while clapping its wings, then parachutes down, calling. Displays from ground, perches or in flight. **Habitat:** Grassland and open savanna. **Status:** Common. **Voice:** Long, ascending whistle, 'pooooeeee', similar to Cape Clapper Lark, but with less increase in frequency, and preceded by slow wing-clapping (12-14 claps per second). Also mimics other birds' songs. [G4.5.5]

2 CAPE CLAPPER LARK *Mirafra apiata* 15 cm
Endemic to S Africa. Smaller and darker than Eastern Clapper Lark, with faster clapping display. Very similar to Agulhas Clapper Lark, but averages more rufous above, due to broader rufous bars on richly barred black and rufous upperparts. Underparts are rich rufous, with darker breast streaks. Unobtrusive when not displaying; reluctant to flush. **Habitat:** Karoo scrub and coastal fynbos, especially areas rich in restios. **Status:** Common. **Voice:** Long, ascending whistle, 'pooooeeee', preceded by fast wing-clapping (22-28 claps per second).

3 AGULHAS CLAPPER LARK *Mirafra marjoriae* 15 cm
Endemic to South Africa. Smaller and darker than Eastern Clapper Lark, with faster clapping display and distinct song. Best told from Cape Clapper Lark by display and range. Upperparts are darker than Cape Clapper Lark, with narrower rufous bars; appears colder grey-brown from a distance. **Habitat:** Coastal fynbos and fallow fields. **Status:** Common. **Voice:** Two descending whistles, 'peeooo peeeoooo', with rapid wing-clapping (25–28 claps per second).

4 BOTHA'S LARK *Spizocorys fringillaris* 12-13 cm
Endemic to South Africa. A small, pink-billed lark with heavily streaked upperparts. Differs from Pink-billed Lark by its white (not buff) outer-tail feathers, white (not rufous) belly, streaked flanks, and finer bill. **Habitat:** Heavily grazed grassland. **Status:** Vulnerable. Uncommon and localised. Often occurs in small flocks. **Voice:** Cheerful, repeated 'chiree'; 'chuk, chuk', uttered in flight; also reputed to mimic other birds' songs. [G4.6.9]

5 PINK-BILLED LARK *Spizocorys conirostris* 12-13 cm
Near-endemic to S Africa. A small, compact lark with a short, conical, pink bill. Differs from Botha's Lark by its rich rufous-buff underparts, which contrast boldly with the white throat and unstreaked flanks. Breast is lightly streaked. W races are paler below, and can be confused with Stark's Lark, but are less grey, have a shorter bill and lack a crest. **Habitat:** Grassland, pastures and desert scrub. **Status:** Common but nomadic. **Voice:** When flushed, utters a soft 'si-si-si'. [G4.6.8]

6 STARK'S LARK *Spizocorys starki* 13-14 cm
Endemic to SW Africa. A small, compact lark with an erectile crest and a stubby, pale bill. Much paler above and below than Sclater's and Pink-billed larks. Differs from Gray's Lark (p. 340) in having streaked upperparts. **Habitat:** Stony desert scrub, gravel plains and arid grasslands. **Status:** Common but nomadic, with large flocks following rain events. **Voice:** Short 'chree-chree', given in flight; song recalls Skylark, melodious jumble of notes, given in high display flight. [G4.7.1]

7 SCLATER'S LARK *Spizocorys sclateri* 13-14 cm
Endemic to S Africa. A small, compact lark with a remarkably large bill. Darker than Stark's Lark, with buffy (not white) belly. At close range the dark brown 'teardrop' mark below the eye is diagnostic. In flight, has a characteristic dark triangle on the tail (broader at the tip), with the white outer-tail broadening towards the tail base. **Habitat:** Stony plains in arid Nama-Karoo shrublands. **Status:** Uncommon; resident and partial nomad. **Voice:** Repeated 'tchweet-tchweet', given in flight. [G4.6.10]

rufous E races

paler form

darker form

333

1 KAROO LARK *Calendulauda albescens* 16-17 cm
Endemic to South Africa. A medium-sized lark, more heavily streaked above and below, including on the flanks, and with a finer bill than other species. White eye-stripe, dark ear coverts and white throat contrast with boldly streaked breast. Upperparts range from sandy-brown (coastal), through reddish (W Karoo), to dark brown (E Karoo). Has a rather long, dark tail in flight. Hybridises with Barlow's Lark in a narrow contact zone. **Habitat:** Karoo and coastal shrublands. **Status:** Common. **Voice:** Sings from top of bushes or in low aerial display, 'chleeep-chleeep-trrr-trrrrrrr', song shorter and higher pitched than Barlow's Lark's, with only 1-2 lead-in notes; often located by guttural alarm rattle. [G4.6.2]

2 BARLOW'S LARK *Calendulauda barlowi* 17-18 cm
Endemic to S Africa. A medium-sized lark in the Karoo Lark complex; slightly larger and longer-billed than other species. Differs from Karoo Lark in having plain (not streaked) flanks, and often appears 'bull-necked'. Coastal *patae* are pale sand-brown above, inland *cavei* and *barlowi* reddish. Race *barlowi* closely resembles Dune Lark in the north, but is slightly more streaked. Hybridises with Karoo Lark in narrow contact zone between Port Nolloth and Orange River. **Habitat:** Arid scrublands and vegetated dunes. **Status:** Locally common. **Voice:** Similar to Dune Lark's, but with fewer (5-8) lead-in notes and shorter trill.

3 RED LARK *Calendulauda burra* 18-19 cm
Endemic to South Africa. A fairly large lark, with a shorter, deeper bill than species in the Karoo Lark complex (not known to occur with Karoo Larks). Upperpart colour varies from unstreaked red on dunes to brown with darker streaks on the plains. Overlaps with smaller Fawn-coloured Lark in N. **Habitat:** Scrub-covered red sand dunes and Nama Karoo plains. **Status:** Vulnerable. Fairly common but localised. **Voice:** Song similar to Karoo Lark's, but slower and much lower pitched; sings in air or from bush. [G4.6.4]

4 FAWN-COLOURED LARK *Calendulauda africanoides* 14-16 cm
Near-endemic to S Africa. A small to medium lark with relatively long wings and tail. Upperpart colour varies regionally, but the white underparts, slightly streaked breast and well-marked, pale supercilium above a plain face are diagnostic. Overlaps with larger, plainer Red Lark in SW. **Habitat:** Sandy soils in Kalahari scrub, broadleafed savanna and thornveld. **Status:** Fairly common. **Voice:** Jumble of harsh 'chips' and twitterings, ending in buzzy slur, given from tree top or during short display flight; occasionally mimics other birds' songs. [G4.5.7]

5 SABOTA LARK *Calendulauda sabota* 15 cm
Near-endemic to S Africa. A medium-sized lark, more compact than Fawn-coloured Lark. Has a large white eye-stripe which extends from the frons to the nape, giving it a capped appearance. Breast is boldly streaked, contrasting with pale throat and belly. Upperpart colour varies regionally, but always lacks rufous in the wing. Bill size increases from E to W; large-billed W *naevia* may be a distinct species, 'Bradfield's Lark'. **Habitat:** Arid savanna and Nama Karoo. **Status:** Common. **Voice:** Jumbled song of rich, melodious 'chips' and twitterings; mimics other birds; often calls from elevated perch. [G4.5.8]

6 DUNE LARK *Calendulauda erythrochlamys* 16-17 cm
Endemic to Namibia. A medium-sized lark in the Karoo Lark complex; slightly longer-legged than other species. Generally paler, sandy-rufous than Barlow's Lark, with very plain, unstreaked upperparts and fine, rufous (not brown) breast streaks. Some *barlowi* Barlow's Larks around Lüderitz are virtually indistinguishable from Dune Larks, but ranges not known to overlap. **Habitat:** Vegetated areas among dunes in Namib Desert between Lüderitz and Walvis Bay. **Status:** Fairly common. **Voice:** Series of 10+ 'tip-ip-ip-ip' lead-in notes followed by whistle and long, uniform trill. [G4.6.3]

1

inland races

coastal races

2

cavei

barlowi

patae

3

dune form

plains form

4

5

small-billed form

large-billed form

6

335

1 COLLARED LARK *Mirafra collaris*   13-15 cm

Endemic to NE Africa. Narrow black collar on upper breast is diagnostic. Appears reddish, with a white throat and supercilium, blackish nape and buffy underparts. In flight the reddish body contrasts with the black wings and tail. **Habitat:** Dry grasslands on red soils with scattered trees and bushes. **Status:** Uncommon to rare; wary and secretive. **Voice:** Poorly known; in display gives descending whistle and wing-claps like Flappet Lark.

2 FOXY (ABYSSINIAN) LARK *Calendulauda alopex*   14-16 cm

Endemic to NE Africa. Often treated as a race of Fawn-coloured Lark (p. 334), but is longer and darker-billed; ranges do not overlap. Two distinct races with dijunct ranges may be good species: NE *alopex* is plain rufous above; lack black wings and collar of Collared Lark. S & W *intercedens* is heavily streaked with a prominent white supercilium; darker than Gillett's Lark with a rufous (not brown) wing panel and darker brown breast streaks. **Habitat:** Dry grasslands and savanna on reddish, sandy soils. **Status:** Locally fairly common. **Voice:** Jumbled chirpy song given from bushes and trees; flight call sharp 'tchwerp'.

3 GILLETT'S LARK *Mirafra gilletti*   15-17 cm

Endemic to NE Africa. Slightly larger and greyer than *intercedens* Foxy Lark with smaller rufous-brown (not dark brown) breast streaks; lacks rufous wing panel and tail shorter; appears more plump and rotund. Not known to overlap with localised Degodi Lark. **Habitat:** Semi-arid savanna and open grassy areas in thicker bush. **Status:** Locally fairly common. **Voice:** Jumbled, chirpy song similar to Foxy Lark's but with more 'chissik' notes, given from bush top, or when in flight, chasing other birds from territory.

4 DEGODI LARK *Mirafra degodiensis*   14 cm

Little known, small- to medium-sized lark, only known from S Ethiopia. Most obvious features are straight, buffy-white eyebrow, pale rusty ear coverts and distinctive song; has no rufous in wings. Pipit-like, with a thin bill, longish tail and white underparts. Breast is more streaked than Pink-breasted Lark, but not as heavily streaked as Gillett's Lark; also slightly smaller and paler than Gillett's Lark. Superficially similar to Bushveld Pipit (p. 374), but has less heavily streaked underparts. **Habitat:** Dry gravel and stony areas with small acacia trees and bushes. **Status:** Vulnerable. Uncommon and highly local; occurs in pairs. **Voice:** High-pitched 'tsee tsee' and high-pitched trill, 'twill-ill-ill-ill', given from bush top.

5 ASH'S LARK *Mirafra ashi*   15 cm

Endemic to Somalia. Little known, medium-sized lark, similar to Foxy Lark, but is grey (not red-brown) above, with buff-fringed feathers giving a scalloped appearance. Smaller than Somali Lark (p. 340), with a much shorter bill. Outer-tail white, but extent of white variable. **Habitat:** Coastal grassy plains and grassed sand dunes. **Status:** Endangered. **Voice:** Undescribed. Sings from top of stunted bushes.

6 PINK-BREASTED LARK *Calendulauda poecilosterna*   15-16 cm

Endemic to NE Africa. A plain, pipit-like lark with a long tail, slender bill and horizontal stance. Pinkish wash across face, throat and breast, and plain upperparts are diagnostic. Crown greyish. **Habitat:** Savanna and open woodland. **Status:** Common; usually in pairs; frequently perches on top of bushes. **Voice:** Song thin, squeaky jumble of notes; could be confused with a cisticola. Usually sings from an elevated perch; rarely in display flight.

7 RUSTY LARK *Mirafra rufa*   14-15 cm

Endemic to N Africa. Darker than Kordofan Lark (p. 328), especially below, with buff (not white) outer-tail and a blackish (not pale brown) upper mandible. Much darker above and below than Dunn's Lark (p. 340), and lacks a dark tail tip. Tail is longer than both Kordofan and Dunn's larks'. In flight, appears dark reddish with a paler rufous tail with buffy outer-tail feathers. **Habitat:** Arid, stony plains to lightly grassed plains with scattered bushes. **Status:** Uncommon and nomadic; in pairs or small groups. **Voice:** Undescribed.

alopex

1 OBBIA LARK *Spizocorys obbiensis* 13 cm
Endemic to coastal Somalia. Within its restricted range, is unlikely to be confused with any other lark: underparts are heavily streaked, with a dark malar stripe, broad pale eye-ring and broad buff eyebrow stripe. Appears short-legged; shuffles along with a hunched posture. **Habitat:** Dunes and sandy plains. **Status:** Locally common; sometimes in flocks of 30 or more. **Voice:** Short 'tip tip', given in flight.

2 ARCHER'S LARK *Heteromirafra archeri* 14 cm
Endemic to NW Somalia. A small, large-headed lark with a short, thin tail. Upperparts are heavily scaled; underparts are buffy, with dark brown streaking. Erectile crest has a pale median stripe. Outer-tail feathers are white (not pink-buff as in Sidamo Lark). Within its range most similar to Singing Bush Lark (p. 328), but has a shorter tail and no rufous wing patches. **Habitat:** Grassy plains. **Status:** Vulnerable. Uncommon and little known; reported to be secretive. **Voice:** Undescribed, but apparently has aerial display like other *Heteromirafra*.

3 SIDAMO LARK *Heteromirafra sidamoensis* 14 cm
Endemic to S Ethiopia. A small, large-headed lark with a short, thin tail. Diagnostic pale stripe down centre of crown difficult to see. Upperparts are scaled. Outer-tail is pink-buff, not white as in Archer's Lark. Runs rapidly through long grass like a rodent, changing directions erratically. **Habitat:** Short and long grasslands interspersed with stunted whistling acacias. **Status:** Vulnerable. Uncommon and thinly distributed in its small range. **Voice:** Short series of 3- to 5-note melodious whistles given repeatedly in high display flight.

4 RUDD'S LARK *Heteromirafra ruddi* 14 cm
Localised endemic to South Africa. A small, large-headed lark with a short, thin tail. Has an erectile crest with a buff median stripe, but this can be hard to see in the field. Unobtrusive when not displaying. **Habitat:** Short upland grassland, usually near damp depressions. **Status:** Critically endangered due to habitat loss. Uncommon. **Voice:** Bubbling, whistled song, with 3- to 4-note phrases repeated several times, then switching to new variation; display flight very high and protracted (single flight can last up to 30 minutes). [G4.5.9]

5 SPIKE-HEELED LARK *Chersomanes albofasciata* 13-15 cm
A short-tailed, medium-sized lark with a characteristic upright stance and white-tipped tail. Breast and belly coloration varies from rufous (SE) to pale buff (NW), but always contrasts with the white throat Bill is long and slightly decurved. **Habitat:** Wide range, from moist grasslands through Karoo shrublands and semi-desert to gravel plains. **Status:** Common; almost invariably in small groups; one bird often stands sentry on low bush. **Voice:** Trilling 'trrrep, trrrep, trrrep'. [G4.6.6]

6 BEESLEY'S LARK *Chersomanes beesleyi* 11-13 cm
Highly localised endemic to small area west of Kilimanjaro in N Tanzania. Recently split from Spike-heeled Lark; smaller with a more streaked breast. Has a peculiar habit of cocking its tail on alighting. Smaller than Short-tailed Lark, with a short, white-tipped tail, plain face and pale throat contrasting with buff belly. **Habitat:** Short grasslands in rain shadow of Mt Kilimanjaro. **Status:** Fairly common within its very restricted range; population less than 1 000 birds. **Voice:** 'Trrep trrrep' flight call similar to Spike-heeled Lark's.

7 SHORT-TAILED LARK *Pseudalaemon fremantlii* 14 cm
Endemic to NE Africa. The black 'teardrop' face pattern and long, slightly decurved bill are diagnostic. Has dark patches on the sides of the neck. Occurs in a grey and rufous morph, differing in upperpart colour. In flight, tail appears short, square and dark, with white outer-tail feathers. **Habitat:** Dry grasslands, including pastures. **Status:** Locally common, usually in pairs or small groups. **Voice:** Song slow whistle, given from ground; 'chittick' flight call.

range of underpart colouration

1 LESSER HOOPOE LARK *Alaemon hamertoni* 18-20 cm
Endemic to N Somalia. Smaller than Greater Hoopoe Lark, with plain brown wings and a shorter, less decurved bill; ranges are not known to overlap. Fairly nondescript, with uniform sandy upperparts and buffy underparts, with slight streaking on the breast. The long legs, slender body and long tail impart a pipit-like jizz. **Habitat:** Semi-desert and wide expanses of dry grassy plains and desert. **Status:** Uncommon; usually in pairs. **Voice:** Undescribed.

2 GREATER HOOPOE LARK *Alaemon alaudipes* 19-23 cm
A large, long-legged lark with an unmistakable black-and-white face and wing pattern. On the ground it appears sandy-coloured, with unusually long legs, body and tail. Bill is long and decurved. Resembles a long-tailed courser; runs rapidly and is hard to flush. **Habitat:** Open sandy deserts with stunted vegetation. **Status:** Uncommon; sparsely distributed; usually in pairs. **Voice:** Spectacular display flight: bird climbs steeply then suddenly descends, giving series of piping notes and trills. [C3.37]

3 GRAY'S LARK *Ammomanopsis grayi* 13-14 cm
Endemic to Angola and Namibia. A small, pale, compact lark with a fairly stout, pale bill. Plain, unstreaked back and dark tip to outer-tail separate it from Stark's Lark (p. 332); also lacks a crest. Upperparts darker in *hoeschi* (N Namibia) than in S or Angola. Desert form of Tractrac Chat (p. 462) is similar in colour, but has longer legs, a dark, slender bill and an obvious white base to its tail. **Habitat:** Gravel plains. **Status:** Fairly common; nomadic. **Voice:** Short 'tseet' or 'tew-tew', given in flight; song very high-pitched, un-lark-like mixture of descending, metallic-sounding 'tinks' and whistles, normally given before dawn. [G4.7.4]

4 DESERT LARK *Ammomanes deserti* 15-16 cm
Lacks the dark tail bar of Bar-tailed Lark, and has more distinct streaking on breast and throat, and a pale bill with a dark tip (not uniform). Tail is rufous, with dark centre. Could be confused with female Black-crowned Sparrowlark (p. 348), but lacks black tail and underwings. NE race *assabensis* is darker. **Habitat:** More stony and rocky deserts in mountainous areas than Bar-tailed Lark. **Status:** Locally common; usually in pairs or small flocks. **Voice:** Flight call 'tscherr' or 'gshurr'; also slowly repeated 'chee-leep'. [C3.41]

5 BAR-TAILED LARK *Ammomanes cinctura* 13-14 cm
A small, pale, nondescript lark. Most easily confused with Desert Lark, but has a distinct black tail tip and in flight has black tips to primaries; bill colour is uniform (not dark-tipped). Differs from female Black-crowned Sparrowlark (p. 348) by its black tail tip (not all-black tail) and pale (not dark) underwings. **Habitat:** Very arid, flat, sandy or stony deserts; unlike Desert Lark it avoids rocky deserts in mountainous areas. **Status:** Uncommon; occurs in small groups or pairs. **Voice:** 'Cherr' flight notes similar to Desert Lark's; more diagnostic 'bshee' nasal call. [C3.40]

6 DUNN'S LARK *Eremalauda dunni* 14-15 cm
A small lark with a stout, yellowish bill that gives it a large-headed appearance. Streaked upperparts separate it from Desert and Bar-tailed larks. Tail is dark, with rufous centre. Paler and less rufous than Kordofan Lark (p. 328), lacking streaking on underparts; bill is much larger. **Habitat:** Dry grassy plains and desert edge. **Status:** Locally fairly common, but nomadic; usually in pairs or small groups. **Voice:** Throaty, ascending 'dshrooee'; shorter 'chlep' flight note. [C3.44]

7 SOMALI LARK *Mirafra somalica* 19-20 cm
Endemic to Somalia. A large, reddish desert lark. Within its range, differs from Sharpe's Lark (p. 330) by its longer, straight bill and white outer-tail feathers. Red-winged Lark (p. 330) is larger and has a shorter, more robust bill. Sometimes placed in *Certhilauda*. **Habitat:** Grasslands and red dunes on coastal plains. **Status:** Little known, but common in some areas; typically occurs in pairs. **Voice:** Undescribed.

hoeschi

grayi

1 CAPE LONG-BILLED LARK *Certhilauda curvirostris* 20-24 cm
Endemic to S Africa. A large, elongate lark with a long, decurved bill. Grey-brown above, with well-marked dark streaking. White underparts are densely streaked, extending onto flanks and belly. Female is smaller, with a noticeably shorter bill. N form is larger and greyer, with a truly impressive bill. **Habitat:** Coastal dunes and croplands. **Status:** Fairly common. **Voice:** Querulous 'whir-irry' contact call; song far-carrying, descending whistle, 'seeeooooo', given in display or from ground. In S, call 2-noted 'whit seeeooooo'. Display flight common to all long-billed larks: bird flies close to ground then rises vertically 10-15 m, closes its wings just before the top of its climb, calls, and drops, opening its wings just above ground.

2 AGULHAS LONG-BILLED LARK *Certhilauda brevirostris* 18-20 cm
Endemic to South Africa. Similar to S form of Cape Long-billed Lark, but plumage is more buffy, bill and tail are shorter and calls differ; ranges not known to overlap. More buffy brown (not rufous) than Karoo Long-billed Lark, with heavy streaking extending onto its flanks and belly. **Habitat:** Fallow fields, croplands, coastal fynbos and semi-arid Karoo scrub. **Status:** Fairly common. **Voice:** Display song 2-noted 'seeit seeooo'.

3 KAROO LONG-BILLED LARK *Certhilauda subcoronata* 18-22 cm
Endemic to S Africa. Upperpart colour varies from dark chocolate brown in S to reddish in N; hindneck is greyer. Streaking reduces S to N, with a marked reduction in Bushmanland, but belly and flanks are always largely unstreaked. Overlaps marginally with Cape Long-billed Lark near Orange River, but easily told by reddish upperparts and plain belly and flanks. Not known to overlap with Eastern Long-billed Lark, which is less streaked. **Habitat:** Karoo scrub and grasslands W of 25°E; typically in rocky areas. **Status:** Common. **Voice:** At close range, soft 'inhalation' can be heard before long, descending whistle, 'uh-seeeooooo'. [G4.5.10]

4 BENGUELA LONG-BILLED LARK *Certhilauda benguelensis* 18-20 cm
Endemic to Angola and N Namibia. Recognised due to large genetic difference from other long-billed larks, but identification criteria require clarification. Resembles N form of Karoo Long-billed Lark, but tends to be slightly more heavily streaked on the crown, back and breast. **Habitat:** Arid hill slopes and plains, apparently N of Brandberg (exact limit uncertain). **Status:** Common. **Voice:** Slightly quavering, long, descending whistle, 'seeoeeooooo'.

5 EASTERN LONG-BILLED LARK *Certhilauda semitorquata* 16-20 cm
Endemic to S Africa. The smallest and least-streaked form of long-billed lark. Upperparts are reddish, lightly streaked darker brown in W, virtually unstreaked in E. Buffy below, with light streaking confined to the breast. Elongate shape and relatively short, straight bill (especially females) can result in confusion with pipits, but different gait, reddish plumage and lack of pale outer-tail feathers are diagnostic. **Habitat:** Grasslands, generally on rocky hill slopes. **Status:** Fairly common. **Voice:** Long, descending whistle, 'seeeooooo'.

6 SHORT-CLAWED LARK *Certhilauda chuana* 17-19 cm
Endemic to S Africa. Structure similar to long-billed larks, but easily identified by broad, buff-fringed upperparts, and different habitat and range. Lacks the rufous wings and nape of the co-occurring Rufous-naped Lark (p. 330), but has rufous rump visible in flight. The long buff-white eyebrow stripe imparts a capped appearance. **Habitat:** Dry acacia savanna and open, grassy areas with scattered trees. **Status:** Uncommon. **Voice:** Short 'chreep-chuu-chree', given when perched in tree; display flight with descending whistle similar to long-billed larks'. [G4.6.1]

1 BIMACULATED LARK *Melanocorypha bimaculata* 15-17 cm
A medium to large, chunky, short-tailed lark with white tail tips, black patches on the side of the neck (not always visible), a well-marked face and a heavy, thick-based bill. **Habitat:** Stony, arid and short-grassed areas. **Status:** Fairly common Palearctic migrant, mostly Oct-Mar. **Voice:** Complex trilling and rattling song; irregular, cheeping contact call. **Similar species: Calandra Lark** *M. calandra* is larger, with a thicker bill, white trailing edge to wing and white outer-tail (not white tips); Palearctic vagrant to N. **Thick-billed Lark** *Rhamphocoris clotbey* has a massive bill, patterned face and black-spotted breast; flight feathers are black, with broad white trailing edge; rare in extreme N. **Temminck's Horned Lark** *Eremophila bilopha* has a diagnostic black mask, horns and breast band; rare in extreme N.

2 SUN LARK *Galerida modesta* 14-15 cm
A medium-sized, dark-backed lark, with some rufous in the wing in flight. Within its range could be confused with Flappet Lark (p. 330), but breast is heavily streaked, underparts are less rufous, and upperparts are streaked (not scalloped). Crown is dark brown and well streaked, giving a capped look; has a slight crest. **Habitat:** Open grasslands, grassy areas in lightly wooded hillsides and agricultural lands. **Status:** Common; in pairs or small groups. **Voice:** Jumbled mixture of soft and sharp notes, given from perch or in flight; often mimics other birds. [C8.97]

3 CRESTED LARK *Galerida cristata* 16-18 cm
A medium to large lark, easily told from all species except Thekla Lark by its prominent crest. Generally paler than Thekla Lark, with only light streaking above and spotting below; rump and uppertail coverts uniform; crest longer and more pointed; bill is slightly longer. Coloration varies regionally; taxonomy is complex. **Habitat:** Open areas with sparse vegetation cover; prefers dryer, sandier areas than Thekla Lark in areas of overlap. **Status:** Locally common; usually in pairs. **Voice:** 3-note 'tree lee puu' contact call; song similar to Thekla Lark's. [C3.46] **Similar species: Eurasian Skylark** *Alauda arvensis* has much shorter crest, plainer face, white (not buff) outer-tail and white trailing edge to wing; Palearctic vagrant to NW.

4 THEKLA LARK *Galerida theklae* 15-17 cm
Disjunct E African population rather variable, with 6 races described. In areas of overlap, differs from Crested Lark by being darker, with bolder dark streaks on white underparts; rufous-tinged rump contrasts with paler grey uppertail coverts; crest is shorter and more fan-like (less pointed); appears less hunched and stocky. **Habitat:** Lowland populations that overlap with Crested Lark prefer rocky or stony habitats (not sandy soils); also occurs in high-elevation grasslands and fields in Ethiopia, where Crested Lark is absent. **Status:** Locally common. **Voice:** 'Too telli tew telli tee', more melodic than Crested Lark's. [C3.47]

5 LARGE-BILLED LARK *Galerida magnirostris* 18 cm
Endemic to S Africa. A robust, heavily built lark with a relatively short, dark tail and boldly streaked underparts. The thick-based, heavy bill, with a yellow base to the lower mandible, is diagnostic. Small crest is raised when bird is alarmed or singing. **Habitat:** Grassland, arid scrublands, and open and fallow fields. **Status:** Common. **Voice:** Highly vocal; far-carrying, ascending 'troo-lee-liiii', like rusty gate being opened; mimics other species. [G4.7.2]

6 RUFOUS-RUMPED LARK *Pinarocorys erythropygia* 19-20 cm
A large, thrush-like lark; striking facial pattern, heavily spotted breast and obvious rufous rump in flight are diagnostic. Walks slowly, lifting its wings every few metres. Told from Dusky Lark by its rufous rump and flanks. **Habitat:** Lightly wooded grasslands and savannas; often in recently burned areas. **Status:** Fairly common intra-African migrant; in small groups or pairs. **Voice:** Mixture of buzz trills and clear, far-carrying whistled 'epee you'. [C8.94]

7 DUSKY LARK *Pinarocorys nigricans* 19-20 cm
A large, thrush-like lark, with a striking facial pattern, heavily streaked breast and strange wing-flicking behaviour. Lacks the rufous rump and flanks of Rufous-rumped Lark. Smaller than Groundscraper Thrush (p. 438) with whitish legs and no wing bars. **Habitat:** Open woodland and savanna; often in recently burned areas. **Status:** Fairly common intra-African migrant. **Voice:** Sings 'treeoo' from tree top or display flight; soft 'chrrp' in flight. [C8.95, G4.6.5]

1

fresh plumage

worn plumage

2

3

huei
Ethiopia

4

5

ellioti
Somalia

6

7

1 GREATER SHORT-TOED LARK *Calandrella brachydactyla*   13-15 cm
A medium-sized, long-tailed lark with mostly plain, off-white underparts. Crown is streaked; lacks plain reddish cap of Red-capped, Blanford's and Erlanger's larks. Small black patches on the sides of the neck, relatively plain, unstreaked breast and shorter wings separate it from Lesser Short-toed Lark. **Habitat:** Dry grassy and stony plains and old agricultural lands. **Status:** Palearctic migrant, mostly Oct-Mar; locally common, especially in W; occurs in flocks. **Voice:** Short, dry, clipped 'chritt' and 'tcheeleep'. [C3.42]

2 RED-CAPPED LARK *Calandrella cinerea*   14-15 cm
Coloration is very variable but rufous patches on sides of neck, rufous cap (which can be raised in a crest) and plain white underparts are diagnostic. In NE Africa, told from Erlanger's and Blanford's larks by plain (not black) rufous neck patches. Male has a longer crest and larger neck patches than female. Juv. lacks the red cap and neck patches; is dark brown above, with the feathers fringed with white, and the breast is heavily spotted. **Habitat:** Short grassy areas and croplands. **Status:** Common; often found in flocks. **Voice:** Sparrow-like 'tchweerp', given in flight; song sustained jumble of melodious phrases, given during display flight. Also mimics other birds songs. [C8.96, G4.6.7]

3 ERLANGER'S LARK *Calandrella erlangeri*   14-15 cm
Endemic to Ethiopia. Often treated as a race of Red-capped Lark, but has black (not red) patches on sides of neck, a larger rufous cap (which can be raised in a crest) and more heavily streaked back. Darker and more heavily streaked above than Blanford's Lark with larger black neck patches. **Habitat:** Upland grasslands and agricultural lands. **Status:** Common; sometimes in large flocks. **Voice:** Similar to Red-capped Lark's.

4 BLANFORD'S LARK *Calandrella blanfordi*   14-15 cm
Differs from Erlanger's and Red-capped larks by having a much paler rufous cap (which can be raised in a crest), paler sandy-coloured back with reduced streaking, clearer, unmarked underparts, and only a small dark patch at sides of neck. **Habitat:** Dry gravel and stony arid plains with stunted acacia bushes and wooded wadis. **Status:** Common; occurs in small flocks outside breeding season. **Voice:** Sparrow-like 'tchweerps', given in flight.

5 LESSER SHORT-TOED LARK *Calandrella rufescens*   13-14 cm
Differs from Greater Short-toed Lark by the well-streaked breast and the lack of dark neck patches; wings are longer, with primaries extending beyond uppertail coverts; buffy supercilium is shorter and narrower behind the eye, but meets on the forehead, giving a small, pale frons; bill is slightly shorter and stouter. **Habitat:** Grassy and stony plains, very often near coastal areas. **Status:** Rare Palearctic migrant; usually in small flocks. **Voice:** Easily told from Greater Short-toed Lark by buzzing or trilling 'drrrrd' contact note. [C3.43]

6 SOMALI SHORT-TOED LARK *Calandrella somalica*   14-15 cm
Endemic to NE Africa. Birds in N easily recognised by reddish-tinged feather edges on upperparts and pink- (*somalica*) or buff-washed (*perconfusa*) underparts. Birds in S (*megaensis*) are also reddish above, but are more streaked, with a red-brown wash beneath. Sides of breast are lightly streaked. Smaller than Sharpe's (p. 330) and Somali (p. 340) larks. **Habitat:** Dry grassy plains, semi-arid gravel plains and fallow lands. **Status:** Poorly known; apparently resident in Somalia; often in small flocks. **Voice:** Short flight call 'chwer-it'.

7 ATHI SHORT-TOED LARK *Calandrella athensis*   13-14 cm
Endemic to S Kenya and N Tanzania. Often treated as a race of Somali Short-toed Lark, but is colder grey-brown above and whiter (less buffy) below. Buff-brown above, heavily streaked with dark brown. Breast and flanks are washed buff; belly is white. Neat band of streaking across breast contrasts with paler throat. More elongate and finer-billed than Singing Bush Lark (p. 328) with a relatively long tail. **Habitat:** Short and well-grazed grassy plains, avoiding fields of long grass. **Status:** Common; often in flocks. **Voice:** Low 'trrrit' flight call; chittering noise given by flocks on the wing; prolonged, trilling flight song.

Small, compact larks; unusual among African species by being sexually dimorphic. Boldly patterned males are readily identified, but duller females and juvs could be confused with other small larks.

1 BLACK-EARED SPARROWLARK *Eremopterix australis*   12-13 cm
Endemic to S Africa. Male identified by all-black head, underparts and underwings. Female is dark chestnut above and heavily streaked with black below; told from other female sparrowlarks by black secondaries in flight and by lack of a dark belly patch. **Habitat:** Karoo shrublands and grassland, Kalahari sandveld, gravel plains and, occasionally, cultivated lands. **Status:** Locally common; nomadic; usually in flocks. **Voice:** Short 'preep' or 'chip-chip', given in flight; male has butterfly-like aerial display. [G4.7.7]

2 GREY-BACKED SPARROWLARK *Eremopterix verticalis*   12-13 cm
Endemic to SW Africa. Greyish back and wings separate both sexes from Chestnut-backed Sparrowlark. Male also differs in having larger white patch on hindcrown. Female is much greyer than female Chestnut-backed Sparrowlark; black belly patch and unstreaked flanks separate it from female Black-eared Sparrowlark. Male's back colour varies geographically from dark grey (E) to silvery (NW). **Habitat:** Karoo shrublands, semi-desert, grassland, arid savannas and cultivated lands. **Status:** Common but nomadic; usually in groups, often forming huge flocks. **Voice:** Sharp 'chruk, chruk', given in flight. [G4.7.6]

3 CHESTNUT-BACKED SPARROWLARK *Eremopterix leucotis*   12-13 cm
Male's rich chestnut back and wings and contrasting black-and-white head are diagnostic. Female is mottled buff and brown above, darker than other sparrowlarks except Black-eared Sparrowlark; differs from this species by black lower breast and belly, and pale rump. Juv. resembles female but is paler. **Habitat:** Sparsely grassed savanna and cultivated lands, especially recently burned areas. **Status:** Common but nomadic; usually in flocks. **Voice:** Short 'chip-chwep', uttered in flight. [C8.98, G4.7.5]

4 FISCHER'S SPARROWLARK *Eremopterix leucopareia*   11-12 cm
Endemic to SE Africa. Paler than other sparrowlarks within its range; male has mostly white underparts, with only a dark stripe down the centre of the breast and belly. Female is paler than female Chestnut-headed and Chestnut-backed sparrowlarks, with unstreaked underparts with a thin black line down the centre of breast and belly. Lacks pale cheek patch of imm. male Chestnut-headed Sparrowlark. **Habitat:** Semi-desert plains, stony or gravel areas and agricultural lands. **Status:** Common; usually in small flocks. **Voice:** Soft 'tseps' and 'chrup'; display flight is high, with repeated, chipping song.

5 CHESTNUT-HEADED SPARROWLARK *Eremopterix signatus*   11-12 cm
Endemic to NE Africa. Male's chestnut head with white cheeks and crown spot are diagnostic. At a distance the chestnut appears black; could be confused with Black-crowned Sparrowlark, but is richer coloured on the back and has a white crown (not frons). Female is drab, with a buffy eyebrow stripe, diffusely mottled breast and white belly. Imm. male has diffuse band down centre of belly, but can be told from Fischer's Sparrowlark by its pale cheek patch. **Habitat:** Arid stony and grassy plains. **Status:** Uncommon nomad; sometimes locally abundant. **Voice:** Nondescript 'chip' and 'tsssp' flight calls.

6 BLACK-CROWNED SPARROWLARK *Eremopterix nigriceps*   11-12 cm
Overlaps with Chestnut-headed and Chestnut-backed sparrowlarks. Pale grey back and distinctive head pattern separate male from Chestnut-backed Sparrowlark; female lacks a dark belly patch. Male told from Chestnut-headed Sparrowlark by its white frons (not crown). Female has a short, very dark tail and dark underwings in flight. **Habitat:** Semi-desert with sparse vegetation cover and dry wadis. **Status:** Locally common but nomadic; usually in small flocks. **Voice:** Repeated, high-pitched, whistled phrase, given in display flight; descending 'cheeo' also given.

E races

1

2

3

4

5

6

Aerial feeders; told from swifts (p. 258) by angled wings, more flapping flight and ability to perch. Typically forage lower down than swifts. Common names reflect three broad groupings based on upperpart colour: martins (brown), saw-wings (black) and swallows (blue). Sexes alike; juvs duller with shorter tails (usually lacking streamers).

1 SAND MARTIN (BANK SWALLOW) *Riparia riparia*   11-12 cm
Differs from Brown-throated Martin by its white (not brown) throat and brown breast band. Much smaller than Banded Martin, with all-dark underwings, a shallow-forked (not square) tail, and no white eyebrow. Unlikely to overlap with similar Congo Martin; differs by having a better-defined breast band. **Habitat:** Usually over or near fresh water. **Status:** Locally common Palearctic migrant Oct-Mar; scarce in extreme SW. **Voice:** Grating 'chrrr'. [C3.54, G4.9.2]

2 BROWN-THROATED (PLAIN) MARTIN *Riparia paludicola*   11-12 cm
A small, rather compact martin. Lacks breast band of most other martins; colour of belly varies from white to brown; mostly brown morphs occur in E Africa, white in S Africa, and virtually all white in W Africa. Dark morph is smaller than Rock Martin (p. 352) and lacks white tail spots. Juv. paler with pale fringes to secondaries. **Habitat:** Open areas, usually near water; breeds in sandbanks. **Status:** Common. **Voice:** Soft twittering. [C3.53, G4.9.3]

3 CONGO MARTIN *Riparia congica*   11 cm
Endemic to Congo River area. Distinguished from Sand Martin by having a diffuse, greyish-brown breast band, not sharply delimited from the white throat. Much smaller than Banded Martin. Shows distinctly paler throat than Brown-throated Martin; ranges not known to overlap. Juv. has less distinct breast band and pale tips to back feathers. **Habitat:** Congo River and its tributary, the Oubangui. **Status:** Locally common. **Voice:** Not known.

4 BANDED MARTIN *Riparia cincta*   15-17 cm
A large, broad-winged martin. Larger than other martins, with white (not dark) underwing coverts, a small white eyebrow and a square-ended (not forked) tail. Often has a thin brown line across vent. Juv. has upperparts scaled with pale buff, and lacks most of the white eyebrow. **Habitat:** Areas of low vegetation or grassland. **Status:** Locally common resident and intra-African migrant. **Voice:** Flight call is 'che-che-che'; song is jumble of harsh 'chip-choops'. [C9.6, G4.9.4]

5 BRAZZA'S (CONGO) MARTIN *Phedina brazzae*   12 cm
Endemic to Congo Basin. Dull brown upperparts and streaked white underparts are diagnostic within its limited range. Wings are broad; tail lacks white panels of Rock Martin (p. 352). Very similar to migrant Mascarene Martin, but is slightly smaller and tail square (not shallowly forked); ranges are not known to overlap. **Habitat:** Banks of Congo River and adjacent savannas and rocky areas in savanna. **Status:** Local and uncommon. **Voice:** Not known.

6 MASCARENE MARTIN *Phedina borbonica*   14-15 cm
Very similar to Brazza's Martin, but is larger, with a shallow-forked (not square) tail; confusion is unlikely as ranges are mutually exclusive. Could be confused with juv. Lesser Striped Swallow (p. 360) but lacks chestnut crown and pale rump. Juv. has pale fringes to secondaries. **Habitat:** Chiefly over miombo woodland and forests. **Status:** Uncommon to locally common non-breeding visitor from Madagascar May-Sept. Often in mixed swallow flocks. **Voice:** High-pitched shrieks; usually silent in Africa. [G4.9.5]

dark morph

351

1 EURASIAN CRAG MARTIN *Hirundo rupestris* 15 cm

A fairly large, dull brown martin with white windows in the tail coverts. Darker than Rock Martin, with blackish (not grey-brown) underwing. Also has darker belly and vent and uniform rump (not paler than back); at close range the throat is speckled (not uniform). **Habitat:** Dry, mountainous country. **Status:** Uncommon Palearctic breeding migrant Oct-Mar; mostly along Nile Valley. **Voice:** 'Prrrt' contact call is most commonly heard, distinct from Rock Martin's high-pitched 'twee'. [C3.57]

2 ROCK MARTIN *Hirundo fuligula* 12-15 cm

Larger than sand martins (p. 350) with distinctive pale panels in the tail. Northern races overlap with Eurasian Crag Martin, but are slightly smaller, paler and greyer with a plain throat and paler rump. Juv. has pale edges to upperwing coverts and secondaries. **Habitat:** Usually in rocky areas; also breeds in buildings. **Status:** Common. **Voice:** Soft, high-pitched twitterings. [C3.56, G4.8.9]

3 FOREST SWALLOW *Hirundo fuliginosa* 11 cm

A small, dark forest swallow with a short tail. Differs from Square-tailed Saw-wing by its slightly forked (not square) tail, chunkier body and less agile, more rapid and deliberate flight. Rufous throat is only visible in ideal viewing conditions, and is not a reliable field mark. Usually occurs in pairs or family groups, whereas saw-wings are often in larger groups. **Habitat:** Forest canopy, clearings and adjacent savanna; nests under large rocks in forest. **Status:** Local and uncommon. **Voice:** Various 'chwit chwit' calls. [C9.12]

4 SQUARE-TAILED SAW-WING *Psalidoprocne nitens* 11 cm

A typical saw-wing, with alternating flapping and slow gliding flight, the wings stretched or tightened along the body. Type of flight and short, square (not forked) tail distinguish it from very similar Forest Swallow. Usually forages in loose groups. **Habitat:** Clearings and edges of forest, roadsides, plantations and villages in forested areas. **Status:** Common. **Voice:** Soft twitterings; 'tissit' contact notes. [C9.2]

5 AFRICAN RIVER MARTIN *Pseudochelidon eurystomina* 14 cm

Localised endemic to WC Africa. A strange-looking swallow, robust and thick-bodied, with a big head and peculiar shape and behaviour. Easily identified by its entirely dark plumage, red eyes and orange bill, legs and feet. When seen flying high, it has distinctively broad, triangular wings and quite slow flight. **Habitat:** On migration, along large forest rivers and above forest; breeds in coastal savannas (Gabon, Congo) and on large sandbanks of Congo River. **Status:** Locally common; roosts in large numbers. **Voice:** Double-noted nasal call at rest and in flight, 'zzcher zzher'. [C9.1]

1 MOUNTAIN SAW-WING *Psalidoprocne fuliginosa*   12 cm
Endemic to Mt Cameroon and Bioko. A small, drab brown swallow; smaller than Black Saw-wing, with a shallower forked tail and matt-brown (not glossy black) plumage. Matt plumage and forked tail separates it from Square-tailed Saw-wing (p. 352). **Habitat:** Montane forests, mostly at high altitude near tree line. **Status:** Common; in small groups or singly foraging low over canopy, in lee of forest glades and above tree line in open heath and grasslands. **Voice:** Short, wheezy phrases; 'chick' notes. [C9.5]

2 WHITE-HEADED SAW-WING *Psalidoprocne albiceps*   12-15 cm
Endemic to EC Africa. A dark brown saw-wing with a distinctive snowy white head, bisected by a black line running through the eye to the nape. Adult plumages have a slight greenish sheen. Female and juv. have black or grizzled black-and-white crowns. **Habitat:** Open forest glades and wooded slopes. **Status:** Locally common. **Voice:** Soft, weak twittering, with harsher chatters.

3 BLACK SAW-WING *Psalidoprocne pristoptera*   13-15 cm
A variable species, with several of the 12 races often considered to be full species, including Blue *pristoptera* and Brown *antinorii* saw-wings of Ethiopia. WC African races show grey or whitish wing linings, but not as crisp and clear as white wing linings of Eastern Saw-wing. Told from Blue Swallow (p. 358) by its glossy, greenish-black (not dark blue) plumage and less deeply forked tail with shorter tail streamers. Juv. is very dark brown and lacks gloss. **Habitat:** Fringes and clearings in forests and plantations. **Status:** Locally common. **Voice:** Soft 'chrrp' alarm call. [G4.9.6]

4 EASTERN SAW-WING *Psalidoprocne orientalis*   15 cm
Sometimes considered a race of Black Saw-wing, but has conspicuous white (not black or greyish) underwing coverts. Also is more slender and longer tailed. Juv. is very dark brown and lacks gloss of adult. **Habitat:** Over evergreen forests and miombo woodland, and around rivers in these habitats. **Status:** Locally common. **Voice:** Soft twittering; short 'chip'. [C9.4, G4.9.7]

5 FANTI SAW-WING *Psalidoprocne obscura*   15-17 cm
Endemic to W Africa. An all-black saw-wing with a diagnostic long, deeply forked tail (the longest and most deeply forked of any saw-wing) with long outer-tail feathers. Under perfect viewing conditions, greenish glossed plumage is also diagnostic. **Habitat:** Various lowland forest types, mostly near water and often into adjacent lightly wooded and grassland areas. **Status:** Common; sometimes in groups. **Voice:** Mostly silent; high-pitched 'treet' note. [C9.3]

354

1 BARN (EUROPEAN) SWALLOW *Hirundo rustica* 15-18 cm
An abundant, well-known species with a reddish frons and throat. Differs from Angola and Red-chested swallows by having a complete blue-black breast band of relatively uniform thickness. Breeding adults have long tail streamers, but most birds in Africa are rather drab, with shorter tail streamers. Breast and belly colour are variable; usually off-white, but some birds are quite reddish. Juv. is duller, with browner frons and throat, and has shorter outer-tail feathers. **Habitat:** Cosmopolitan, except in closed forest. **Status:** Abundant Palearctic migrant, mostly Oct-April. **Voice:** Soft, high-pitched twittering. [C3.58, G4.7.8]

2 RED-CHESTED SWALLOW *Hirundo lucida* 15 cm
Most easily confused with Barn and Angola swallows. Appears smaller and much bluer than Barn Swallow, with narrower, sometimes incomplete blue breast band and reduced amount of red on forehead; lacks very long outer-tail feathers and has much more white in tail. Differs from Angola Swallow by having white (not grey) breast and belly. **Habitat:** Open grassland and slightly wooded areas; often around bridges and human habitation. **Status:** Locally common; in pairs or small groups, and not usually in large gatherings as in Barn Swallow. **Voice:** Song and calls similar to those of Barn Swallow. [C9.24]

3 ANGOLA SWALLOW *Hirundo angolensis* 14-15 cm
Slightly smaller and more compact than Barn Swallow with red throat extending onto breast and narrowly bordered by an incomplete black band. Upperparts are bluer and appear more iridescent, and underparts are grey (not buff, reddish or white). W population is darker grey below, recalling cliff-swallows (p. 362), but lacks paler rump. Outer-tail streamers are much shorter than Barn Swallow's, and tail is less deeply forked. Juv. has red of adult replaced by pale rufous, and is less glossy above. **Habitat:** Upland grasslands. **Status:** Often breeds under eaves and bridges. **Status:** Uncommon to locally common; range has contracted and numbers have fallen in some areas. **Voice:** Weak twittering song; loud 'tsip' call. [C9.23, G4.7.9]

4 WHITE-THROATED SWALLOW *Hirundo albigularis* 14-17 cm
The white throat and broad, blue-black breast band are diagnostic. Larger than Wire-tailed and Ethiopian swallows, with very obvious breast band. Glossy blue upperparts separate it from much browner martins (p. 352). Juv. is less glossy above, and has brownish forehead. **Habitat:** Closely associated with water; usually breeds under bridges and culverts. **Status:** Common intra-African migrant. **Voice:** Soft warbles and twitters. [C9.22, G4.7.10]

5 ETHIOPIAN SWALLOW *Hirundo aethiopica* 14 cm
Confusion is most likely with Wire-tailed Swallow, but differs by having red confined to forehead (not total cap) and buffy (not white) throat. Differs from Barn Swallow by buffy (not reddish) throat and incomplete black breast band. Unlikely to be confused with either White-throated or Pearl-breasted (p. 358) swallows, both of which are extreme vagrants within its range. **Habitat:** Wide range of open habitats, including forest clearings. **Status:** Common resident and intra-African migrant. **Voice:** Contact call is soft 'cheet'; song is extended, weak twittering. [C9.21]

6 WIRE-TAILED SWALLOW *Hirundo smithii* 13-17 cm
The combination of chestnut crown and plain white underparts is diagnostic. Most similar to Ethiopian Swallow, but entire crown (not just forehead) is chestnut, and has longer outer-tail feathers. Juv's crown is brown, and is less glossy blue above. Flight is extremely rapid. **Habitat:** Usually near water, often breeding under bridges. **Status:** Common resident and intra-African migrant. **Voice:** Call is sharp, metallic 'tchik'; song is twittering 'chirrik-weet, chirrik-weet'. [C9.18, G4.8.2]

1 WHITE-THROATED BLUE SWALLOW *Hirundo nigrita* 12-14 cm
A brilliant dark blue river swallow, with a distinctive white throat patch and white tail panels that are conspicuous in flight. Tail only shallowly forked, lacking tail streamers. Never seen far from water, where it hunts with a rapid and agile flight, generally at low height. **Habitat:** Mainly forest rivers; sometimes on lakes and mangroves. **Status:** Common. **Voice:** Sharp 'chit chit' contact call.

2 BLACK-AND-RUFOUS SWALLOW *Hirundo nigrorufa* 13-15 cm
Localised swallow of SC Africa. Easily identified by the combination of deep blue upperparts and dark rufous underparts. Much smaller than Mosque and Red-breasted swallows (p. 360), with no red rump and shorter tail streamers. Looks dark at a distance in poor light. **Habitat:** Open grasslands, usually near wetlands. **Status:** Uncommon and thinly distributed; most often singly or in pairs, flying very low over grasslands. Rests for long periods on grass stems and low perches. **Voice:** Sharp 'chrik chrik' in flight; soft, tinkling display song. [C9.17]

3 BLUE SWALLOW *Hirundo atrocaerulea* 18-25 cm
The glossy, dark blue plumage and long outer-tail feathers are diagnostic. Differs from saw-wing swallows (p. 354) in having blue (not black) plumage and much longer tail streamers (in male). Flight action is less erratic than saw-wings. Female lacks long tail streamers; juv. has brown throat and generally much less glossy plumage. **Habitat:** Upland grassland, often bordering forests. **Status:** Vulnerable. Uncommon and localised intra-African migrant. **Voice:** Musical 'bee-bee-bee-bee' in flight. [C9.16, G4.8.1]

4 PIED-WINGED SWALLOW *Hirundo leucosoma* 12-13 cm
Endemic to W Africa. Easily identified by the white inner secondaries, forming a white patch along the upperwing on either side of the body. Rest of upperparts dark blue, with white underparts. Juv. is duller and browner above. **Habitat:** Moist wooded savanna. **Status:** Generally uncommon; usually solitary or in pairs. **Voice:** Not very vocal except for soft 'wup wup' and soft twitterings. [C9.19]

5 WHITE-TAILED SWALLOW *Hirundo megaensis* 13-14 cm
Endemic to S Ethiopia. Similar to Pearl-breasted Swallow but with a diagnostic white tail. Lacks red crown of Wire-tailed Swallow (p. 356). Female has less distinctive white tail. Juv. is duller and browner above. **Habitat:** Dry thornbush with large, tall, red-clay termite mounds. **Status:** Vulnerable. Fairly common within its small range; usually seen in pairs. **Voice:** Typical swallow-like twitterings and chirrups.

6 PEARL-BREASTED SWALLOW *Hirundo dimidiata* 14 cm
A small blue-and-white swallow. Told from Wire-tailed Swallow (p. 356) by its lack of tail streamers, white tail panels and its blue (not red) cap. From below it differs from Grey-rumped Swallow (p. 362) and Common House Martin (p. 362) by its white (not dark) wing linings; from above by its dark (not pale) rump. **Habitat:** Grassland, savanna and open woodland; often breeds in buildings. **Status:** Locally common resident and migrant in the S. **Voice:** Subdued chipping note in flight. [C9.20, G4.8.3]

1 GREATER STRIPED SWALLOW *Hirundo cucullata*   20 cm
Larger and paler than Lesser Striped Swallow, with less well-defined striping on the buffy (not whitish) underparts; ear coverts buffy (not orange), and orange rump and crown are paler. Paler overall than Red-rumped Swallow, with an orange (not blue) crown and more pronounced streaking on underparts. Juv. is duller with a reddish-brown crown, and partial brown breast band. **Habitat:** Grassland and vleis. **Status:** Common intra-African migrant. **Voice:** Twittering 'chissick' and querulous, nasal notes. [C9.11, G4.8.6]

2 LESSER STRIPED SWALLOW *Hirundo abyssinica*   15-17 cm
Smaller and darker than Greater Striped Swallow, with heavy, black (not narrow, weak) striping on whiter underparts and darker, more rufous rump. Female has shorter tail streamers than male. Juv. has less blue-black gloss above than adult, and brown (not rufous) crown. **Habitat:** Usually near water. **Status:** Common resident and intra-African migrant. **Voice:** Descending series of squeaky, nasal 'zeh-zeh-zeh-zeh' notes. [C9.10, G4.8.7]

3 RED-RUMPED SWALLOW *Hirundo daurica*   17-18 cm
Similar to Greater Striped Swallow, but has a dark blue (not orange) cap and only faint streaking on underparts. Slightly smaller than Mosque and Red-breasted swallows, and is much paler with a rufous (not dark blue) nape. E and C African *emini* is rufous below, darker towards the vent; W African and Palearctic races are paler beneath, ranging from creamy-buff to whitish, with very fine dark streaks on the breast (only visible at close range). **Habitat:** Chiefly in highland and mountainous areas. **Status:** Locally common resident, with Palearctic migrants in the N. **Voice:** Single-note 'djuit'; twittering song, softer and shorter than that of Barn Swallow. [C3.55, G6.15.3]

4 RED-BREASTED SWALLOW *Hirundo semirufa*   20-24 cm
A large, red-rumped swallow. Slightly larger than Mosque Swallow with a red (not white) throat and breast, dark ear coverts and dark buffy (not white) wing linings. Larger than Red-rumped Swallow, with darker rufous underparts and dark (not rufous) nape. Juv. has creamy white throat and breast; differs from adult Mosque Swallow by buffy (not white) wing linings. **Habitat:** Grassland and savanna. **Status:** Common resident and intra-African migrant. **Voice:** Soft, warbling song; twittering notes in flight. [C9.8, G4.8.4]

5 MOSQUE SWALLOW *Hirundo senegalensis*   20-22 cm
Slightly smaller and paler than Red-breasted Swallow, with white (not buffy-red) underwing coverts and white (not red) throat, face and upper breast. Juv. paler with buffy (not white) underwing coverts, but coverts always paler than Red-breasted Swallow. **Habitat:** Open woodland, often near rivers, and especially near baobabs. **Status:** Locally common. **Voice:** Nasal 'harrrrp'; guttural chuckling. [C9.9, G4.8.5]

emini

1 GREY-RUMPED SWALLOW *Pseudhirundo griseopyga* 13-14 cm
The combination of grey crown and rump contrasting slightly with blue-black upperparts is diagnostic. In flight, could be confused from below with Common House Martin, but is more slender with a longer, more deeply forked tail. Tail is also longer and more deeply forked than Pearl-breasted Swallow (p. 358). Juv. has reddish-brown rump. **Habitat:** Open woodland and grassland, often near water. **Status:** Locally common resident and intra-African migrant. **Voice:** Flight call-note recorded as 'chraa'. [C9.7, G4.9.1]

2 COMMON HOUSE MARTIN *Delichon urbicum* 14 cm
A swallow-like martin with pure white underparts and a diagnostic white rump (in adult). In flight, told from Grey-rumped Swallow by its shorter, less deeply forked tail and broader-based, shorter wings. Juv. has pale greyish rump and is less glossy above. In Africa, many individuals are in moult, appearing somewhat tatty. **Habitat:** Over most open habitats; often feeds higher in the sky than most other swallows. **Status:** Common Palearctic migrant Oct-Apr; has bred in South Africa. **Voice:** Single 'chirrp'. [C3.59, G4.8.10]

3 PREUSS'S CLIFF-SWALLOW *Hirundo preussi* 12-13 cm
The W and C African cliff-swallow. Told from red-rumped swallows (p. 360) by its square tail, lacking tail streamers. Paler on the breast and rump than other cliff-swallows, with plain buff underparts; lacks white tail spots of Red-throated Cliff-Swallow. At close range, adults have a distinctive rufous patch behind the eye. Juv. is duller. **Habitat:** Large rivers and streams in moist wooded savannas, and at N border of forest in C Africa. **Status:** Locally common; often in very large colonies under bridges and buildings. **Voice:** Soft 'peorr' flight call and chittering call at colonies. [C9.13]

4 RED-THROATED (ANGOLAN) CLIFF-SWALLOW *Hirundo rufigula* 12-13 cm
The SW C African cliff-swallow. Smaller, more slender and longer-tailed than South African Cliff-Swallow, with diagnostic white spots in its tail (not always visible in flight) and a uniformly rufous throat and breast (not darkly mottled on the breast); ranges overlap during migration. Juv. is duller. **Habitat:** Large rivers and adjacent savanna; best seen around colony site, generally a bridge; also abandoned buildings. **Status:** Locally common. **Voice:** High-pitched twittering at colonies. [C9.14]

5 SOUTH AFRICAN CLIFF-SWALLOW *Hirundo spilodera* 14-15 cm
Large cliff-swallow, appearing distinctly chunkier, shorter-tailed and broader-winged than Red-throated Cliff-Swallow; lacks white spots on tail. Differs from red-rumped swallows (p. 360) in having only a slight notch in a square-ended tail, and a darkly mottled breast. Told from Barn Swallow (p. 356) by pale rump. Crown is dark brown, slightly glossed in front. Juv. is duller above. **Habitat:** Upland grassland, usually breeding in road bridges. **Status:** Locally common intra-African migrant. **Voice:** Twittering 'chooerp-chooerp'. [C9.15, G4.8.8]

6 RED SEA CLIFF-SWALLOW *Hirundo perdita* 15 cm
Only known from one specimen from near Port Sudan. Most closely resembles South African Cliff-Swallow, but has a grey (not rufous) rump and blacker throat. Unidentified cliff-swallows seen in Ethiopia might be this species, but their field descriptions do not tally with the specimen. **Habitat:** Unknown. **Status:** Unknown. **Voice:** Unknown.

Boldly patterned, long-tailed birds that typically bob their tails as they walk. Sexes alike in black-and-white species, but differ in yellow-breasted species.

1 AFRICAN PIED WAGTAIL *Motacilla aguimp*   20 cm
A distinctive black-and-white wagtail. Differs from White Wagtail in having black (not grey) back and black (not white) frons. Juv. is greyer, but still darker than White Wagtail, with more white in folded wing; told from Cape Wagtail by white-edged wing coverts. Most birds have white underparts, but nominate birds from South Africa have sooty grey flanks. **Habitat:** Large rivers, wetlands and coastal lagoons; also in large gardens near water. **Status:** Locally common. **Voice:** Loud, shrill 'chee-chee-cheree-cheeroo'. [C9.27, G5.12.1]

2 WHITE WAGTAIL *Motacilla alba*   19 cm
A variable black, grey and white wagtail, told in all plumages from African Pied Wagtail by its grey (not black) mantle. Adult differs from Mountain Wagtail by black-and-white (not grey-and-white) facial pattern. Juv. is paler grey, with only narrow black collar; told from other wagtails by two conspicuous white wing bars formed by broad pale tips to median and greater wing coverts. **Habitat:** Open habitats, typically close to water. **Status:** Common Palearctic migrant Oct-Mar. **Voice:** High-pitched, 2-note 'chizzik' in flight. [C3.62]

3 CAPE WAGTAIL *Motacilla capensis*   19-20 cm
A greyish-brown wagtail, darker above than Mountain Wagtail, with a shorter tail, olive-buff (not white) flanks and belly, and less white in wings and outer-tail. Juv. is duller, with more pronounced buff-yellow wash over belly. **Habitat:** Open grassland, usually near water, but also in gardens. **Status:** Common. **Voice:** Clear, ringing 'tseee-chee-chee' call; whistled, trilling song. [C9.25, G5.12.3]

4 MOUNTAIN (LONG-TAILED) WAGTAIL *Motacilla clara*   19-20 cm
Forms a superspecies with Grey Wagtail, but lacks any yellow underparts and has more white in wing and outer-tail. Told from Cape Wagtail by much longer tail, pale grey upper-parts, white (not olive-buff) underparts, and more white in wings and outer-tail. Juv. is browner. **Habitat:** Fast-flowing forest streams. **Status:** Locally common. **Voice:** Sharp, high-pitched 'cheeerip' or 'chissik'. [C9.26, G5.12.2]

5 GREY WAGTAIL *Motacilla cinerea*   19-20 cm
A longtailed species; told from Mountain wagtail by at least some yellow on underparts and less white in wing and outer-tail. Noticeably longer-tailed than Yellow Wagtail, with blue-grey (not green) back, which contrasts with greenish-yellow rump. Tail wagging is more exagger-ated. Breeding male has black throat; throat is speckled in non-breeding plumage. Female has white throat; juv. is similar but duller. **Habitat:** Verges of fast-flowing streams and ponds. **Status:** Locally common Palearctic migrant Oct-Apr. **Voice:** Single, sharp 'tit'. [C3.61, G5.12.5]

6 CITRINE WAGTAIL *Motacilla citreola*   17-18 cm
Slightly larger than Yellow Wagtail, with a greyish back (lacking olive tones); appears slimmer due to longer tail and legs. Breeding male has diagnostic all-yellow head and black nape. Non-breeding adult is easily confused with Yellow Wagtail, but has paler yellow vent, more prom-inent supercilium (extending around ear coverts) and typically bolder white wing bars. Juv. is drab grey, with only buff-yellow wash on breast. **Habitat:** Open grassland near water. **Status:** Scarce Palearctic migrant. **Voice:** Similar to Yellow Wagtail's, but shorter and shriller 'trsiiip'.

7 YELLOW WAGTAIL *Motacilla flava*   16-17 cm
Highly variable; sometimes split into several species. Smaller than Grey Wagtail, with shorter tail and green (not blue-grey) back. Slightly smaller than Citrine Wagtail, with typically olive (not greyish) back and shorter supercilium. Juv. is yellowish-brown above and pale buff below, with narrow blackish breast band. At least 10 races occur in the region: *flava*, *flavissima*, *feldegg*, *lutea*, *beema*, *leucocephala*, *thunbergi*, *iberiae*, *cinereocapilla* and *melanogrisea*; breeding males vary in head colour and amount of yellow on underparts. **Habitat:** Short, cropped, grassy verges of coastal lagoons, sewage ponds and wetlands. **Status:** Locally common Palearctic migrant Oct-Apr; sometimes in flocks. **Voice:** Weak, thin 'tseeep'. [C3.60, G5.12.4]

1

juv.

juv.

2

non-br.

3

juv.

4

br.
♂

br.
♂

5

non-br.

6

non-br.

non-br.

feldegg

lutea

thunbergi

breeding males

7

Fairly large, heavily built ground-dwelling birds related to pipits and wagtails. Their flight is jerky, gliding with the wings angled down. Sexes alike, but females duller in some species. Juvs much duller with reduced black gorgets.

1 YELLOW-THROATED LONGCLAW *Macronyx croceus*   20-22 cm
A large, yellow-breasted longclaw. More heavily streaked than Fülleborn's Longclaw, with black streaking below breast band, lightly streaked flanks, yellower underparts and more extensive white in outer-tail. Slightly larger than Pangani and Cape longclaws, with yellow (not orange) throat; has yellow vent (not white as in Pangani Longclaw). Larger than male Golden Pipit, with brown (not golden) wings and white outer-tail tips. Female is duller, washed buffy below. Juv. lacks black breast band; told from juv. Cape Longclaw by yellow (not buffy-orange) belly and less streaked upperparts. In E Africa, is larger than juv. Pangani and Sharpe's (p. 368) longclaws. **Habitat:** Grassland, often near wetlands and well-grassed savanna woodland. **Status:** Common. **Voice:** Loud, whistled 'phooooeeet' or series of loud whistles, frequently uttered from top of small trees; also calls in flight. [C9.36, G5.13.8]

2 FÜLLEBORN'S LONGCLAW *Macronyx fuellebornii*   20 cm
Endemic to SC Africa. Slightly smaller and more compact than Yellow-throated Longclaw, with no black streaking on breast below black breast band. Adult told from Grimwood's and Rosy-breasted longclaws (p. 368) by yellow (not pink) throat. Juv. is duller and lacks black breast band; has some indistinct streaking on breast, but less than juv. Yellow-throated Longclaw; much less streaked below than juv. Rosy-breasted and Grimwood's longclaws. **Habitat:** Moist grassy areas, often close to water; usually above 1 000 m. **Status:** Locally common. **Voice:** 2-note, trilled 'chree-er'; repetitive, whistled 'gee-o-weee'. [C9.35, G5.13.9]

3 CAPE (ORANGE-THROATED) LONGCLAW *Macronyx capensis*   20 cm
Endemic to S Africa. A compact longclaw. In its range, is the only species with an orange throat (Abyssinian and Pangani longclaws have orange throats but their ranges do not overlap). Female is duller. Juv. has yellow throat with brown-streaked collar; differs from juv.. Yellow-throated Longclaw in having buffy-orange (not yellow) underparts and wing feathers edged with buff (not yellow). **Habitat:** Wide range of coastal and upland grasslands. **Status:** Common. **Voice:** Fairly melodious song, 'cheewit-cheewit', often in flight; nasal 'wheea' alarm call, similar to that of Cape Grassbird; loud, high-pitched 'tsweet' contact call. [G5.13.7]

4 PANGANI LONGCLAW *Macronyx aurantiigula*   19-20 cm
Endemic to NE Africa. A fairly small longclaw; adult typically has orange throat, but yellower in some birds. Yellow-throated birds told from larger Yellow-throated Longclaw by white (not yellow) lower belly and vent. Flanks and sides of breast are conspicuously streaked. Juv. is paler below than juv. Yellow-throated Longclaw, with heavier breast streaking and brighter yellow throat, often with some orange spotting. **Habitat:** Dry grassland with scattered bushes below 1 000 m. **Status:** Common. **Voice:** Song is mixed series of whistled and churred notes, changing every 3-4 notes; high-pitched, whistled 'cheeeeeee' contact call.

5 ABYSSINIAN LONGCLAW *Macronyx flavicollis*   20 cm
Endemic to Abyssinian highlands, where it is the only longclaw. Juv. has creamy-buff throat and belly, with indistinctly streaked breast band; told from pipits by larger size, heavier build and proportionally shorter tail. **Habitat:** Montane grassland and swamp fringes. **Status:** Common above 1 200 m; numbers may be decreasing due to cultivation and heavy grazing. **Voice:** Piping contact call; clear, trilling song.

6 GOLDEN PIPIT *Tmetothylacus tenellus*   13-15 cm
Endemic to NE Africa, but vagrants wander to S Africa. Although this species resembles a diminutive, bright golden Yellow-throated Longclaw, predominantly bright yellow upper- and underwings render it unmistakable. Female and juv. are duller, with whitish underparts and no black breast band; could be confused with Yellow Wagtail, but is smaller, with shorter tail, marked (not plain) mantle and different gait. **Habitat:** Open, dry woodland and savanna. **Status:** Locally common and nomadic. **Voice:** Short burst of scratchy, whistled notes with weaver-like quality. [G5.13.6]

juv.

♂

♀

1 ROSY-BREASTED (PINK-THROATED) LONGCLAW *Macronyx ameliae* 19-20 cm
A slender, dark, heavily streaked longclaw. Smaller than Grimwood's Longclaw; adult has well-defined breast band and pink throat extending onto breast. Has less extensive white tips to inner tail feathers than other longclaws, but almost fully white outer-tail feathers show clearly in flight. At close range has pinkish wash to wrist. Female is duller, with narrower breast band (sometimes incomplete). Juv. has brown-streaked breast band, with creamy throat and only faint rosy hue on belly. **Habitat:** Moist grassland surrounding open areas of fresh water. **Status:** Locally common but patchily distributed. **Voice:** Melodious, rather deep 'cheet errr' or 'cheet eeet eet eet eer'. [C9.37, G5.13.10]

2 SHARPE'S LONGCLAW *Macronyx sharpei*   16-17 cm
Endemic to Kenyan highlands. The smallest longclaw; recalls Yellow-breasted Pipit, but has typical stiff-winged flight of longclaws. Occurs at higher elevations than other longclaws, with only slight overlap with Yellow-throated Longclaw (p. 366); differs by being smaller, with streaked (not solid black) breast band and white in tail confined to outer-tail. Female is duller. Juv. has only faint yellow wash on belly, recalling a large pipit (but does not overlap with Golden Pipit, p. 366). **Habitat:** High-altitude, short grassland above 1 800 m. **Status:** Vulnerable. Uncommon and localised; threatened by cultivation and intensive grazing. **Voice:** Sharp 'tswit'; drawn-out, metallic 'weeeeeeee'; song is rising series of thin whistles.

3 GRIMWOOD'S LONGCLAW *Macronyx grimwoodi*   22 cm
Localised endemic to SC Africa. Larger than Rosy-breasted Longclaw, with brown-streaked (not black) breast band and buffy-brown (not pink) belly. Female has paler pink-buff throat. Juv. undescribed, but presumably told from juv. Fülleborn's Longclaw (p. 366) by lack of yellow on underparts. **Habitat:** Marshy grassland, often with Rosy-breasted and Fülleborn's longclaws. **Status:** Locally common. **Voice:** High-pitched, trilling 'swee-ee-ee-ee-ee'. [C9.38]

PIPITS
Cryptic birds of open country or woodland. Usually on the ground, but may perch in and call from trees. They superficially recall larks, but typically are more slender, with a longer tail and a more horizontal stance. Taxonomy is poorly resolved in some complexes, with geographic variation often exceeding inter-specific differences; this is possibly the most challenging group in the region. Sexes alike in most species.

4 YELLOW-BREASTED PIPIT *Anthus chloris*   17 cm
Endemic to S Africa. Similar to Sharpe's Longclaw, but their ranges do not overlap. Breeding birds have diagnostic yellow throat and breast; upperparts are dark and heavily streaked. In flight, yellow underparts and underwing coverts are conspicuous. In non-breeding plumage, lacks yellow underparts; best identified by boldly scaled upperparts and plain buffy underparts. Juv. is buff below and paler above. **Habitat:** Short grassland; breeds above 1 500 m but moves lower in winter. **Status:** Vulnerable. Local and uncommon. **Voice:** Rapid, repeated 'chip, chip, chip', like call of displaying male Long-tailed Widow; also subdued 'suwiep'. [G5.13.5]

5 AFRICAN ROCK PIPIT *Anthus crenatus*   17 cm
Endemic to S Africa. A drab, uniformly coloured pipit of rocky hill slopes. From a distance, pale eye-stripe is only obvious plumage feature; at close range, faint, narrow breast streaking and greenish edges to wing coverts are visible. Usually located by distinctive song; is fairly secretive when not calling. Juv. is mottled above. **Habitat:** Boulder-strewn, steep, grassy hillsides and Karoo koppies. **Status:** Locally common. **Voice:** Far-carrying 'tseeet-tserrroooo', second note descending; calls with typical erect stance, bill pointed upwards, from low perch. [G5.13.1]

6 STRIPED PIPIT *Anthus lineiventris*   17-18 cm
A fairly plump, heavily built pipit with boldly striped underparts extending over almost the entire belly. At close range, has diagnostic yellow-edged wing feathers; tail is very dark, with conspicuous white outer-tail feathers. Larger and more heavily striped than Tree Pipit (p. 374). Juv. is paler and speckled above. **Habitat:** Boulder-strewn hill slopes in woodland. **Status:** Locally common; flies up into trees when disturbed. **Voice:** Loud, penetrating, thrush-like song, uttered from rock or tree perch. [C9.34, G5.12.12]

br.

juv.

non-br.

1 AFRICAN (GRASSVELD) PIPIT *Anthus cinnamomeus*   16-17 cm
The 'standard' pipit throughout much of the region, against which others should be compared. Typically has streaked back, well-marked face, fairly well-streaked breast and plain belly. Underpart coloration varies from whitish to pale buff; base to lower mandible is yellowish. At close range, white (not buff) outer-tail distinguishes it from Long-billed Pipit complex, but smaller size, weaker bill and stronger breast and face markings are often more useful characters. Streaked back separates it from Plain-backed/Buffy pipit complex (p. 372). Display flight and song distinguish it from all species except Cameroon, Jackson's and Mountain pipits. Juv. is darker above, with more heavily streaked underparts. Sometimes lumped with **Richard's Pipit** *A. richardi*, which may occur as a non-breeding migrant to extreme N. **Habitat:** Open grassland and fields. **Status:** Common. **Voice:** Song is repeated 3-5-note 'trrit-trrit-trrit', uttered in undulating display flight. [C3.63, G5.12.6]

2 MOUNTAIN PIPIT *Anthus hoeschi*   18 cm
Slightly larger than African Pipit, with more bold breast streaking and pink (not yellow) base to lower mandible; in flight, shows buff (not white) outer-tail. Distinguished from Long-billed Pipit by behaviour, display song and heavily marked breast. **Habitat:** Montane grassland above 2 000 m. **Status:** Common breeding visitor Oct-Apr; non-breeding range in C Africa. **Voice:** Display flight song is deeper and slower than African Pipit's. [G5.12.7]

3 JACKSON'S PIPIT *Anthus latistriatus*   16-17 cm
Often treated as a race of African Pipit (or Long-billed Pipit), but is darker, blackish brown above, with rich buff edgings to wing feathers, buff outer-tail, rich buff underparts and heavy streaking extending from breast to flanks. Lower mandible pinkish. White throat contrasts strongly with buff breast and belly. **Habitat:** Short grassland, including lake fringes. **Status:** Poorly known; breeding range unknown. **Voice:** Presumably similar to African Pipit's.

4 CAMEROON PIPIT *Anthus camaroonensis*   17-18 cm
Endemic to W Africa. Often treated as a race of African Pipit, but is slightly larger and darker above, with extensively buff underparts and buff (nominate) or chestnut (*lynesi*) margins to wing feathers. Breast streaking is very strongly pronounced, but told from Jackson's and Bannerman's pipits by having streaking confined to breast (not extending to flanks). **Habitat:** Montane grassland. **Status:** Locally common. **Voice:** Similar to African Pipit's.

5 BANNERMAN'S PIPIT *Anthus bannermani*   16-17 cm
Endemic to W Africa. Often treated as a race of Long-billed Pipit, but is darker overall, with blacker (not brown) streaking on upperparts and bolder streaking on breast and flanks, with some streaking extending to undertail coverts. Streaked flanks also separate it from Cameroon Pipit. Underparts are suffused with buffy-cinnamon, and has pale cinnamon edges to wing feathers. **Habitat:** Montane grassland and rocky slopes. **Status:** Locally common. **Voice:** Probably similar to Long-billed Pipit's.

6 LONG-BILLED PIPIT *Anthus similis*   18 cm
Larger than African Pipit, with a heavier build, longer bill, less distinct facial pattern and breast streaking, and different display and song. At close range, has buff (not white) outer-tail feathers. Fairly well-marked back differentiates it from Plain-backed/Buffy pipit complex (p. 372). Absent from woodland habitat of Woodland Pipit (p. 372), and is paler and less streaked than Bannerman's Pipit. Less well marked than Kimberley Pipit, with malar stripe absent or diffuse. Juv. is paler and more heavily spotted. **Habitat:** Rocky grassland. **Status:** Locally common. **Voice:** High-pitched, 2-3-note song, 'tchreep-tritit-churup', usually from prominent perch; sharp 'wheet' call. [C9.28b, G5.12.8]

7 KIMBERLEY PIPIT *Anthus pseudosimilis*   16-18 cm
Endemic to S Africa. Closely resembles Long-billed Pipit, but is shorter billed, with more prominent supercilium, blackish malar stripe and rufous ear coverts; outer-tail edged buff or white. Appears smaller and longer-legged; often crouches while feeding. Female duller. **Habitat:** Grassland and sparse savanna. **Status:** Little known; locally fairly common. **Voice:** Similar to Long-billed Pipit's, but descending in pitch and usually given in flight.

paler races

371

1 WOODLAND PIPIT *Anthus nyassae*   16-18 cm
Endemic to SC Africa. Often treated as a race of Long-billed Pipit (p. 370), but occurs in woodland rather than open grassland. Tail and bill are shorter than in Long-billed Pipit, with more extensive pale areas in base of outer-tail feathers. Juv. is spotted above, and more heavily streaked below. **Habitat:** Miombo and teak woodland. Forages on ground, but flushes into trees when disturbed. **Status:** Locally common. **Voice:** Song is similar to that of Long-billed Pipit, but more variable and slightly higher pitched. [C9.28a/29, G5.12.9]

2 PLAIN-BACKED PIPIT *Anthus leucophrys*   16-17 cm
A rather heavily built pipit, told from African and Long-billed pipits (p. 370) by its uniform (not streaked) back (although streaking is not obvious in some Long-billed Pipits) and indistinct breast markings; outer-tail is narrowly edged buff. Typically is darker above and below than Buffy Pipit, with yellowish (not pink) lower mandible, and tail wagging is less pronounced. Juv. is heavily mottled above. NE African *goodsoni* and *saphiroi* are paler, closely resembling Buffy Pipit. **Habitat:** Short grass and recently burned areas; also fields. **Status:** Locally common; subject to local movements. **Voice:** Loud, clear 'chrrrup-chereeoo' song, similar to Long-billed Pipit's, but usually 1-2 notes (not 3); often calls in flight, but does not have display flight. [C9.30, G5.12.10]

3 BUFFY PIPIT *Anthus vaalensis*   17-18 cm
Slightly larger than Plain-backed Pipit, but with a pinkish (not yellow) base to the lower mandible. Breast markings are often faint, with rich, buffy belly and flanks. On ground, it stops often, usually remaining horizontal, but occasionally standing boldly erect. Often bobs its tail up and down in a more exaggerated manner than most other pipits, recalling a wagtail. Juv. is mottled above. **Habitat:** Short grassland and fields. **Status:** Uncommon to locally common. **Voice:** Repeated, 2-note song, 'tchreep-churup'; when flushed, gives short 'sshik'. [C9.31, G5.12.11]

4 LONG-LEGGED PIPIT *Anthus pallidiventris*   17-19 cm
A large, plain, pale greyish pipit with very long, pale legs. Averages paler and greyer than Plain-backed and Buffy pipits, with obviously longer legs. Has fairly upright stance, and wags and pumps tail regularly like Buffy Pipit. Due to pale plumage and behaviour, confusion is more likely with Buffy than Plain-backed pipit, but base of lower mandible is yellowish (not pink, as in Buffy Pipit). **Habitat:** Grassland, clearings in rainforest and gardens. **Status:** Common; usually in pairs. **Voice:** 'Duit duit' flight call; other 'tseep' or 'chi chi' notes. [C9.32]

5 LONG-TAILED PIPIT *Anthus longicaudatus*   19 cm
Recently described; apparently endemic to South Africa. A plain-backed pipit, larger and darker than Buffy Pipit, with a long, heavy, square-ended tail. Bill is shorter, and is yellowish (not pinkish) at base (but beware Plain-backed Pipit which also has yellowish lower mandible). Stance is even more horizontal than Buffy Pipit's; wags tail continually, and seldom stands upright, as Buffy Pipit occasionally does. When feeding, head is often held below the horizontal. **Habitat:** Open grassland and arid savanna. **Status:** Locally fairly common in South Africa during winter; recently found with fledged chicks in NW Zambia. **Voice:** Single thin, short call note.

6 TAWNY PIPIT *Anthus campestris*   16-17 cm
A slender, pale pipit with a fairly long tail and a wagtail-like jizz. Paler above than Long-billed Pipit (p. 370), with white (not buffy) outer-tail feathers and smaller, finer bill. Adult is almost unmarked above, with very faint breast streaking. Has prominent pale supercilium that contrasts with dark lores and moustachial stripe, pale-fringed wing coverts and blackish median coverts. Juv. is darker above, and more heavily streaked above and on breast, recalling African Pipit (p. 370); best distinguished by more horizontal (less upright) stance, shorter legs and different call. **Habitat:** Short, dry grassland and mountain slopes. **Status:** Locally common Palearctic migrant Oct-Apr. **Voice:** Loud 'tseuk' on take-off and landing; 'tzeep' in flight. [C3.64]

1 MALINDI PIPIT *Anthus melindae*   15-16 cm
Endemic to coastal Kenya and Somalia. Similar to African Pipit (p. 370), but is greyer and less streaked above, and more heavily streaked below, with streaking extending onto flanks and upper belly. Smaller and less buffy than Long-billed Pipit (p. 370). At close range, shows distinctive yellow-orange legs and base of lower mandible. **Habitat:** Seasonally flooded areas of short grass. **Status:** Locally common. **Voice:** 'Tsweeep' in flight; also 'tirrip-tirrip-tir-rip'; song repetitive 'kwee' from perch.

2 TREE PIPIT *Anthus trivialis*   15 cm
Longer tailed and larger than either Bushveld or Short-tailed pipits, and shows much more contrast between pale throat and dark upperparts. Bill is rather short and weak. Easily confused with non-breeding Red-throated Pipit, but has less clearly streaked underparts and lacks dark brown streaking on rump; at close range, has pale eye-ring. Juv. is buffier. **Habitat:** Grassy areas in open woodland. **Status:** Common Palearctic migrant Oct-May. **Voice:** Soft, nasal 'teeez' in flight or when flushed; song is melodic and canary-like. [C3.66, G5.13.2] **Similar species: Meadow Pipit** *A. pratensis* is slightly smaller, shorter tailed and more olive-brown above than Tree or Red-throated pipits; Palearctic vagrant to N.

3 RED-THROATED PIPIT *Anthus cervinus*   15 cm
In breeding plumage, dull red face, throat and breast are diagnostic. Non-breeding birds lack red throat and could be confused with Tree Pipit, but are more richly coloured and boldly streaked, with heavily streaked underparts and streaked (not uniform) rump. Flank streaks are much broader than those of Tree Pipit. Larger than Short-tailed Pipit, with longer tail and more strongly marked supercilium. **Habitat:** Damp grassland, usually near water and agricultural lands. **Status:** Common Palearctic migrant Oct-Apr; usually occurs at higher altitudes; sometimes in flocks. **Voice:** Clear, penetrating 'chup'; buzzy 'skeeeaz'. [C3.67, G6.15.2]

4 BUSHVELD PIPIT *Anthus caffer*   13-14 cm
Smaller than Tree Pipit, with shorter tail, indistinct supercilium, paler plumage and suffused, less distinct streaking on breast. From a distance, head appears uniform, and lacks Tree Pipit's malar stripe. Slightly larger than Short-tailed Pipit, with longer, broader tail, paler upperparts and less heavy streaking below. Juv. is paler and speckled above. **Habitat:** Acacia savanna and open broadleafed woodland. **Status:** Locally fairly common. **Voice:** Characteristic 'zeet' as it flies from ground to tree; song is 3-note 'zrrrt-zrree-chreee' from perch in tree. [G5.13.3]

5 SHORT-TAILED PIPIT *Anthus brachyurus*   12 cm
A small, squat pipit, very much darker and more heavily streaked above and below than either Tree or Bushveld pipits. In flight, shows noticeably shorter, thinner tail than other small pipits. When flushed, resembles a large cisticola, with white outer-tail feathers showing clearly. **Habitat:** Grassy hillsides and glades in miombo woodland, preferring areas of short grass, including recently burned areas. **Status:** Uncommon resident and local migrant. **Voice:** Similar to Bushveld Pipit's, a buzzy, bubbling 'chrrrt-zhrrrreet-zzeeep'; calls from perch or during circling display flight. [C9.33, G5.13.4]

6 SOKOKE PIPIT *Anthus sokokensis*   12 cm
Endemic to coastal forests of Kenya and N Tanzania. A small, richly patterned and secretive pipit that is heavily streaked above and below. Pale face lacking malar stripes and prominent white wing bars separate it from Short-tailed Pipit; ranges are not known to overlap. **Habitat:** Coastal forests, where spends much time foraging in leaf litter and among root tangles; often flies to high perch when flushed. **Status:** Endangered. Local, uncommon and easily overlooked. **Voice:** Contact call is very high-pitched, almost inaudible 'tsweeer', descending in pitch; display flight song is 2- to 3-note, ascending and descending whistle.

br.

non-br.

Thrush-sized, rather unobtrusive birds that typically move slowly through woodland and forest canopy. Sexes differ. Black males of *Campephaga* could be confused with black flycatchers (p. 548), drongos (p. 380), black boubous (p. 588) or even widowbirds (p. 680), but have a horizontal posture, glossy plumage and yellow gapes.

1 BLACK CUCKOOSHRIKE *Campephaga flava*   18-21 cm
Male is all-black or has a yellow shoulder patch; yellow gape is intermediate in size between Petit's and Purple-throated cuckooshrikes'. Yellow-shouldered male could be confused with a widowbird given a poor view. Female is barred below, with bold yellow edges to wing feathers; is greener above than female Red-shouldered Cuckooshrike, with mostly yellow (not black) undertail. Juv. resembles female but is more heavily barred, including on crown. **Habitat:** Mature woodland and forest margins. **Status:** Locally common resident and local migrant. **Voice:** High-pitched, prolonged 'trrrrrrrr'. [C9.40, G4.9.8]

2 PETIT'S CUCKOOSHRIKE *Campephaga petiti*   19-20 cm
Male is all-black, with a larger yellow gape than either Purple-throated or Black cuckooshrikes. Female is much yellower than female Black or Red-shouldered cuckooshrikes; differs from female Purple-throated Cuckooshrike by yellow (not grey) throat, blackish wings with contrasting yellow feather edges, and some dark bars on upper breast. Juv. resembles female but is spotted on breast, thighs and undertail coverts. **Habitat:** In C Africa, mainly patches of woodland in savannas, mangroves and coastal forests, and secondary growth; in E Africa, forest edge. **Status:** Localised and uncommon. **Voice:** Soft whistle, not often given.

3 RED-SHOULDERED CUCKOOSHRIKE *Campephaga phoenicea*   20 cm
Male is black, with conspicuous red shoulder (not yellow, as in Black Cuckooshrike, but can appear orange-yellow in worn plumage). Female differs from female Black Cuckooshrike by largely black undertail and greyer upperparts. Juv. resembles female but has broader bars (almost spotted) below, and narrower yellow tail tips. **Habitat:** Wooded savannas and gallery forest. **Status:** Common. **Voice:** High-pitched hissing, squeaks and whistles. [C9.39]

4 PURPLE-THROATED CUCKOOSHRIKE *Campephaga quiscalina*   19-20 cm
Male is all dark, with a smaller yellow-orange gape than Black or Petit's cuckooshrikes. In good light, has glossy purple-violet throat and breast; could be confused with small glossy starling, but jizz and behaviour differ. Female is only cuckooshrike with plain olive-green upperparts; head is grey and underparts are yellow (plain in W, lightly barred on breast in E); could be confused with a greenbul (p. 412). Juv. is similar to female but barred above and below, with white tips to wing coverts. **Habitat:** Forest canopy, forest edge, gallery forest and secondary growth with tall trees. **Status:** Uncommon. **Voice:** Whistled 'tseeuu', often repeated, with slight variations. [C9.41]

5 BLUE CUCKOOSHRIKE *Coracina azurea*   20 cm
An unmistakable, electric-blue, forest cuckooshrike. Appears brilliant blue in good light, but is more greyish blue in shade. Male has blackish throat; female is duller, with blue throat. Juv. has white-tipped wing and tail feathers, and some white spotting on underparts. **Habitat:** Forest canopy, forest edge and gallery forest. **Status:** Common; often located by call. **Voice:** Various slurred whistles, 'chip peeooo' or 'pooeet peeooo'. [C9.44]

♂

♂

♀

♀

♀

worn plumage

♂

3

♂

undertail

juv.

♀

4

♂

♂

5

1 WHITE-BREASTED CUCKOOSHRIKE *Coracina pectoralis*   25-27 cm
A large grey cuckooshrike with predominantly white underparts, which separates it from Grey Cuckooshrike. Localised Grauer's Cuckooshrike is smaller and darker; ranges do not overlap. Male has grey throat and upper breast, contrasting with white belly; female and juv. are paler, with whitish throat. Juv. has spotted underparts and barred upperparts. **Habitat:** Tall woodland, especially miombo and riverine forests. **Status:** Uncommon to locally common. **Voice:** 'Duid-duid' by male; 'tchee-ee-ee-ee' by female. [C9.43, G4.9.9]

2 GREY CUCKOOSHRIKE *Coracina caesia*   21-23 cm
The only all-grey cuckooshrike in the region, with a narrow white eye-ring. Larger than White-eyed Slaty Flycatcher (p. 546) and other all-grey flycatchers, with very different jizz. Plumage appears very smooth, with subtle differences in grey shades from darker upperparts to paler underparts. Female is paler and lacks black loral patches. Juv. is barred and mottled. **Habitat:** Forests; mostly at higher elevations in the tropics. **Status:** Uncommon. **Voice:** Soft, thin 'tseeeeep'. [C9.42, G4.9.10]

3 GRAUER'S CUCKOOSHRIKE *Coracina graueri*   22 cm
Endemic to E DRC. A dark grey cuckooshrike with a dark breast contrasting with white belly. Darker above than Grey Cuckooshrike, which lacks white belly. Smaller and much darker than White-breasted Cuckooshrike; ranges are not known to overlap. In good light, upperparts and breast have greenish-blue gloss. Female is paler grey above, with buff vent. **Habitat:** Montane forests and forests edge, 1 200-1 900 m. Forages in canopy and mid-stratum in mixed bird parties. **Status:** Rare and little known. **Voice:** High pitched trill. [C11.1]

4 EASTERN WATTLED CUCKOOSHRIKE *Campephaga oriolina*   18-19 cm
Endemic to C Africa. Resembles a small, black-headed oriole (p. 384), but has a black (not red) bill, large orange gape wattle and is generally silent. Forms a superspecies with Western Wattled Cuckooshrike; male differs in being less richly coloured below and having greenish (not yellow) edges to secondaries; females and juvs are probably inseparable in the field, but ranges are not known to overlap. **Habitat:** Forest canopy. **Status:** Uncommon; easily overlooked as it silently gleans insects from the forest canopy. **Voice:** Unknown.

5 WESTERN WATTLED CUCKOOSHRIKE *Campephaga lobata*   17-18 cm
Endemic to W Africa. A colourful, oriole-like cuckooshrike. Dark bill and black head with prominent orange wattle are diagnostic. Female is duller, with browner head, smaller wattle and yellow underparts. Juv. has white tips to wing feathers and is faintly barred above and below. Male is more richly coloured below than Eastern Wattled Cuckooshrike, and has yellow (not greenish) edges to secondaries; females and juvs are almost identical; ranges are not known to overlap. **Habitat:** Forest canopy. **Status:** Vulnerable. Llocal and uncommon to rare. Difficult to see as it is furtive and silent, keeping in forest canopy. **Voice:** Usually silent; flight call is thrush-lik 'zit'.

379

Noisy, conspicuous black birds with erect posture and variably forked tails. Easily separated from male *Campephaga* cuckooshrikes (p. 376) and black boubous (p. 588) by posture and foraging action. They hawk from perches, taking insect prey in air or from the ground. Most likely to be confused with black flycatchers (p. 548), but have red eyes, heavier bills and typically have forked tails. Frequently join bird parties and harass raptors. Sexes alike.

1 SQUARE-TAILED DRONGO *Dicrurus ludwigii*   18-19 cm
A fairly small drongo with a shallow-forked tail. Smaller and shorter-tailed than Shining Drongo, with less glossy plumage, brighter red eyes and less deeply forked tail. In flight, lacks pale primaries of Fork-tailed Drongo. Heavy bill and red eye separate it from black flycatchers; vertical posture and habits distinguish it from black cuckooshrikes and boubous. Female is duller and greyer in some races; juv. has pale tips to mantle and underpart feathers. **Habitat:** Forests and dense riparian woodland and thickets. **Status:** Locally common; usually in pairs. **Voice:** Strident 'cheweet-weet-weet' and other phrases; often very vocal in bird parties. [C14.4b, G4.10.1]

2 SHINING DRONGO *Dicrurus atripennis*   21-24 cm
A medium-sized forest drongo with glossy blue-black plumage. Much glossier than other African drongos, although this is not always evident in its gloomy forest habitat. Appears intermediate in size and tail-fork depth between smaller Square-tailed and larger Velvet-mantled drongos. Eyes are typically duller red than those of W races of Square-tailed Drongo. Juv. is only slightly glossy, primarily on wings and tail. **Habitat:** Middle canopy and understorey of closed-canopy forest and large gallery forests. **Status:** Common; often joins bird parties, where it is very visible and audible. **Voice:** Noisy: wide variety of loud whistles and buzzy calls; also mimics other species. [C14.5a]

3 FORK-TAILED DRONGO *Dicrurus adsimilis*   23-26 cm
A large drongo with a deeply forked tail (but moult can affect tail shape). Adult is glossy blue-black; less glossy than Shining Drongo, and lacks matt-black back of Velvet-mantled Drongo. In flight, has diagnostic pale primaries that contrast with rest of wing. Typically occurs in more open habitats than other African drongos. May hybridise with Velvet-mantled Drongo. Juv. has buff-tipped wing coverts and underparts, and yellow gape. **Habitat:** Woodland, savanna and plantations. **Status:** Common; often in pairs. **Voice:** Variety of grating or shrill notes; mimics birds of prey, especially Pearl-spotted Owlet. [G4.10.1]

4 VELVET-MANTLED DRONGO *Dicrurus coracinus*   24-26 cm
A forest drongo with a diagnostic matt-black mantle contrasting with glossy wings and nape. Larger than Shining Drongo, with more deeply forked tail and different habitat (unlike Shining Drongo, never enters closed-canopy forest understorey). Apparently occasionally hybridises with Fork-tailed Drongo; differs from this species by habitat and dark primaries in flight. Juv. is duller. **Habitat:** Forest canopy, perching out on tall dead branches or at edge of forest, in gallery forest, secondary growth and village plantations. **Status:** Common. **Voice:** Loud and varied drongo-type calls, sometimes very similar to Shining Drongo's. [C14.6a]

5 PRÌNCIPÉ DRONGO *Dicrurus modestus*   26-28 cm
Endemic to Prìncipé; the only drongo on the island. Often treated as a race of Velvet-mantled Drongo, but is larger and less glossy, with greyish inner webs to flight feathers. Has strong bill and well-forked tail with slightly rounded extremities. **Habitat:** Forest canopy, forest edge, plantations and secondary growth. Hawks insects from mid-canopy down to forest floor, but is mostly seen in secondary forest and perched on exposed dead branches or poles. **Status:** Fairly common. **Voice:** Usual jumble of drongo-like chirps and harsh screeches.

juv.

juv.

Fairly large, boldly plumaged birds of woodland and forest canopy. Often detected by loud, ringing song. Sexes alike or differ; dimorphism is most marked in migrant species. In W and C Africa, beware confusion with convergent wattled cuckooshrikes (p. 378).

1 EURASIAN GOLDEN ORIOLE *Oriolus oriolus*   22-25 cm
Adult male is stunning yellow and black; differs from male African Golden Oriole by black wings and black eye-stripe which extends only marginally behind eye. Female is similar to female African Golden Oriole but is less yellow below, with plain wing coverts (lacking yellow edges), and less extensive dark line behind eye. Juv is whitish below, with dark green streaks; bill is blackish. **Habitat:** Woodland, savanna and exotic plantations. **Status:** Fairly common Palearctic migrant Oct-Apr; scarce in W Africa. **Voice:** Song is liquid 'chleeooop', but chattering subsong and grating 'naaah' calls are more typically heard in Africa. [C4.51, G4.10.3]

2 AFRICAN GOLDEN ORIOLE *Oriolus auratus*   20-21 cm
Brighter golden-yellow than Eurasian Golden Oriole; differs mainly by its yellow edges to the wing coverts and secondaries at all ages, as well as longer black stripe extending behind eye (in adult only). Female is duller than male, but brighter than female Eurasian Golden Oriole. Juv. is streaked below and has dark bill. **Habitat:** Tall woodland (especially miombo) and riverine forest. **Status:** Locally common resident and intra-African migrant. **Voice:** Liquid whistle, 'fee-yoo-fee-yoo'; mewling, up-slurred call. [C13.28, G4.10.4]

3 GREEN-HEADED ORIOLE *Oriolus chlorocephalus*   21-23 cm
Endemic to SE Africa. The moss-green head, yellow collar and green back are diagnostic. From a distance, head appears dark, and might be confused with black-headed orioles, but back is darker. Juv. has dull yellow underparts, breast slightly streaked with olive, and pale olive wash on head and throat. **Habitat:** Forest; usually montane forest, but also down to near sea level in E Africa. **Status:** Locally common. **Voice:** Explosive, liquid song, typical of orioles; distinctive nasal mewing, 'waaaarrr'. [G4.10.6]

4 SÃO TOMÉ ORIOLE *Oriolus crassirostris*   22-24 cm
Endemic to São Tomé, where it is the only oriole. A black-headed oriole with little yellow in plumage; belly is greyish and upperparts are dull grey-green. Has diffuse, pale yellow-grey collar on hindneck. In flight, has conspicuous black tail with yellow tips. Female and juv. are duller, with diffuse paler streaking on black breast. **Habitat:** Forest and old secondary growth from sea level to highest peaks. **Status:** Vulnerable. Remains fairly common in primary forest. **Voice:** Song is deeper and slower than other black-headed orioles'. [C13.33]

juv.

383

1 (EASTERN) BLACK-HEADED ORIOLE *Oriolus larvatus* 20-22 cm

The common black-headed oriole of E and S Africa. Whitish edges to outer secondaries form pale panel in closed wing (not greyish, as in Western Oriole or localised Ethiopian and Mountain orioles). Inner secondaries are edged yellow (not green, as in Western and Ethiopian orioles). Central tail feathers are olive-green above (not black, as in Mountain Oriole). Juv. is duller, with dark brown, slightly mottled head and dark bill. **Habitat:** Mature woodland, especially broadleafed; also forest edge and exotic plantations, up to 2 300 m in E Africa. **Status:** Common. **Voice:** Song is explosive, whistled 'pooodleeoo'; harsher 'kweeer' note. [C13.32, G4.10.5]

2 WESTERN (BLACK-HEADED) ORIOLE *Oriolus brachyrhynchus* 20-21 cm

A black-headed oriole of W and C Africa, differing from sympatric Black-winged Oriole by obvious white spot on primary coverts, grey (not yellow-green) edges to secondaries and green (not black) central tail feathers. In area of overlap with Black-headed Oriole, best told by pattern of folded wing, as well as more forested habitat. Juv. is duller, with paler throat, streaked breast and dark bill. **Habitat:** Forest and forest edge, and gallery forest. **Status:** Common. **Voice:** Rather slow oriole song, with 3-4 notes well separated. [C13.29]

3 BLACK-WINGED ORIOLE *Oriolus nigripennis* 21 cm

Differs from Western Oriole by black (not yellow-green) outerwing, lacking white spots (but some show very narrow white tips to primary coverts), and black (not green) central rectrices. More frequently seen at forest edge and in gallery forest; seldom ventures far into closed-canopy forest. Overlaps with similar Mountain Oriole in Albertine Rift, but lacks white in wing and typically occurs at lower elevations (below 1 500 m). Juv. duller with streaked breast **Habitat:** Forest edge, gallery forest, old secondary growth and mangrove; seldom in primary forest. **Status:** Common. **Voice:** Similar to Western Oriole's, but typically higher pitched, with fewer discrete notes; often duets. [C13.30]

4 ETHIOPIAN ORIOLE *Oriolus monacha* 23-24 cm

Endemic to Abyssinian highlands. Range overlaps marginally in SW with slightly smaller Black-headed Oriole; best distinguished by grey (not whitish) edges to outer secondaries and green (not yellowish) edges to inner secondaries. Juv. is duller and slightly streaked **Habitat:** Damp highland forests (mostly 1 000-2 000 m), overlapping with Black-headed Oriole in juniper forests at lower elevations in SW. **Status:** Locally common to abundant **Voice:** Typical oriole song, somewhat higher pitched than other species'.

5 MOUNTAIN ORIOLE *Oriolus percivali* 19-21 cm

Endemic to E Africa. Differs from similar Black-headed Oriole by being brighter and more contrasting black and yellow, with black (not green) central tail feathers and more extensive black on wings (lacks prominent pale edges to outer secondaries). Juv. duller. **Habitat** Montane forests above 1 500 m, usually at higher elevations than Black-headed Oriole **Status:** Common; usually in pairs or larger groups at fruiting trees. **Voice:** Similar to Black-headed Oriole's. [C13.31]

juv.

1

2

juv.

juv.

3

juv.

4

juv.

5

juv.

Medium to very large passerines with predominantly black plumage (except for aberrant *Zavattariornis*). Often in pairs or small groups. Sexes alike.

1 CAPE (BLACK) CROW *Corvus capensis* 43-45 cm

A fairly large, slender, glossy black crow with a long, thin, slightly decurved bill. Appears more slender than Dwarf Raven (p. 388), with longer, thinner bill and longer tail. Larger than House Crow, and uniformly black (not grey) body. Juv. is duller, lacking glossy blue-black plumage. **Habitat:** Grassland, open country, cultivated fields and dry, desert regions. **Status:** Common; usually in pairs, but sometimes in larger flocks. **Voice:** Deep, cawing, 'kaah-kaah'; astonishing variety of bubbling calls. [C14.7b, G4.10.7]

2 HOUSE CROW *Corvus splendens* 33-38 cm

A rather small, slender, long-tailed crow with a diagnostic grey body and robust, slightly decurved bill. Head, wings and tail are glossy blue-black. Juv. has greyish brown body. **Habitat:** Usually near human habitation, where it scavenges food scraps. **Status:** Common; introduced from Asia, with populations scattered along E coast. **Voice:** Hurried, high-pitched 'kah, kah'. [G4.10.9] **Similar species:** Western Jackdaw *C. monedula* is more compact, with a pale eye and grey confined to head and nape; Palearctic vagrant to NW Mauritania.

3 PIAPIAC *Ptilostomus afer* 35-36 cm

A peculiar, long-legged crow with a stiff, graduated, long tail. Told from long-tailed starlings (p. 602) by heavy, decurved bill and dull red eye. In flight, brownish primaries appear translucent. Juv. has bright pink bill, variably dark-tipped. **Habitat:** Open savanna, grazed grasslands and other short-grass habitats. **Status:** Common; usually in groups of about 8 birds, rarely up to 40. **Voice:** Noisy, especially at dawn and dusk; calls vary from shrill 'pee-ip' to various harsh squeals. [C14.6b]

4 RED-BILLED CHOUGH *Pyrrhocorax pyrrhocorax* 36-40 cm

Localised population restricted to Abyssinian highlands. Adult is unmistakable: a medium-sized, glossy black crow with red legs and a long, decurved, coral-red bill. In flight, has deeply slotted primaries, giving somewhat vulture-like wing profile. Juv. is less glossy and slightly browner, with yellow-pink bill and legs. **Habitat:** Mountain plateaux up to 4 500 m; also forages in cultivated areas. **Status:** Uncommon; probably fewer than 1 300 birds. **Voice:** High-pitched 'chee-aw', but reported to differ from Palearctic populations. [C4.60]

5 STRESEMANN'S BUSH CROW *Zavattariornis stresemanni* 30 cm

Endemic to S Ethiopia. A rather small, starling-like, pale grey and black crow; pale grey plumage may be stained reddish-pink by soil. Larger than Wattled Starling (p. 612), with blue facial skin and no pale rump; plumage pattern is much 'cleaner'. Juv. is washed buffy. **Habitat:** Park-like acacia savannas. **Status:** Vulnerable. Llocally common in highly restricted area of S Ethiopia centred on Yabello and Mega; non-breeding birds (mostly June-Feb) gather in flocks of 6-30. **Voice:** Somewhat nasal, high-pitched 'chek'.

juv.

1 PIED CROW *Corvus albus* 46-50 cm
The only white-breasted crow in the region. From above, has longer tail, more slender wings and smaller head and bill than White-necked Raven. Juv. is slightly duller, with dusky tips to white feathers. In NE, hybridises with Dwarf Raven, producing birds with mottled black-and-white neck and breast. **Habitat:** Virtually all except driest desert areas. **Status:** Common and widespread; often in flocks. **Voice:** Loud 'kwaaa' or 'kwooork' cawing. [C14.7a, G4.10.8]

2 BROWN-NECKED RAVEN *Corvus ruficollis* 52-56 cm
A large, all-dark crow with an indistinct brownish wash on the head, neck and breast. Easily separated from Fan-tailed Raven by much longer tail (extends beyond wing tips at rest). Larger than Cape Crow (p. 386) with heavier bill. Range not known to overlap with that of much smaller Dwarf Raven. **Habitat:** Desert and arid savannas below 2 500 m. **Status:** Common. **Voice:** Deep, guttural 'crrraaarrr'. [C4.65]

3 DWARF RAVEN (SOMALI CROW) *Corvus edithae* 46 cm
Endemic to NE Africa. A medium-sized, all-dark crow with a brownish wash on the head and neck. Sometimes considered a race of Brown-necked Raven, but is much smaller; ranges are not known to overlap. Bill is markedly heavier than Cape Crow's (p. 386), and bird has wedge-shaped (not rounded) tail, and white (not black) bases to neck feathers (visible during display or when ruffled). Tail is much longer and wings more slender than Fan-tailed Raven's; at rest, tail reaches at least to wing tips. Sometimes hybridises with Pied Crow; hybrids have variably mottled white markings on neck and breast. **Habitat:** Arid, from deserts to dry savannas; usually below 2 000 m, but up to 4 000 m in Ethiopia. **Status:** Common. **Voice:** 'Wraaaa', similar to Pied Crow's.

4 WHITE-NECKED RAVEN *Corvus albicollis* 54-56 cm
A large crow with a white crescent on the back of the neck and a heavy, white-tipped bill. Smaller than localised Thick-billed Raven, with shorter tail, smaller bill and white on neck (not nape). In flight, has relatively broad wings and short, broad tail. Juv. is less glossy black. **Habitat:** Restricted to mountainous and hilly areas. **Status:** Locally common. **Voice:** Deep, throaty 'kwaak'. [C14.8b, G4.10.10]

5 FAN-TAILED RAVEN *Corvus rhipidurus* 46-47 cm
Easily separated from other all-dark corvids by its very short tail. At rest, wing tips project well beyond tail tip. In flight, wings are broad, especially inner secondaries, and tail is often fanned, with tertials overlapping outer-tail feathers. Sometimes shows dull brown wash on head and neck. Juv. is duller and browner. **Habitat:** Hilly and mountainous arid areas; also forages in bushy country and cultivated areas. **Status:** Locally common. **Voice:** Croaked 'krroo' or 'krroo-uk'; higher-pitched 'kwaa-kwaa'. [C14.8a]

6 THICK-BILLED RAVEN *Corvus crassirostris* 60-64 cm
Endemic to Abyssinian highlands. A very large black corvid with a massive, white-tipped bill and a fairly small white nape patch. Overlaps with White-necked Raven only as vagrant; is easily distinguished by its enormous bill, longer tail and different white head markings. **Habitat:** Mountainous areas, especially 1 500-3 000 m; also around settlements and in cultivated areas. **Status:** Common; usually in pairs, but flocks gather at rubbish dumps. **Voice:** Grunting 'gwrrrrurrr' or 'harrr-harrr'.

Small, warbler-like tits with short, sharp bills. Confusion is most likely with eremomelas (p. 528). They typically occur in small flocks, and roost together in distinctive, woven nests. Sexes alike.

1 FOREST (YELLOW-FRONTED) PENDULINE-TIT *Anthoscopus flavifrons* 9 cm
The only forest penduline-tit, identified by its dark green upperparts and dull yellowish-green underparts. Differs from Tit-hylia (p. 392) by lacking striping on underparts. Smaller and duller than Forest White-eye (p. 640). Distinguished from other small forest birds mainly by behaviour and bill shape. **Habitat:** Forest canopy, forest edge and secondary growth at lower heights, and plantations with tall trees and shrubs. **Status:** Widespread but generally uncommon. **Voice:** Not usually heard when in canopy; soft 'siis' and 'seee' calls. [C12.58]

2 YELLOW PENDULINE-TIT *Anthoscopus parvulus* 9 cm
A lime-green savanna penduline-tit of W and C Africa with pale fringes to its wing and tail feathers. Confusable with Sennar Penduline-Tit but has much brighter greenish-yellow (not buffy) underparts. Juv. lacks black-streaked frons. **Habitat:** Dry wooded savanna and semi-arid savannas. **Status:** Uncommon to locally common. **Voice:** Buzzy 'tzee tzee' and 'fwip fwip' contact notes. [C12.55]

3 SENNAR PENDULINE-TIT *Anthoscopus punctifrons* 8-9 cm
Differs from Yellow Penduline-Tit by having buffy (not greenish-yellow) underparts. Forehead is paler than rest of crown, with fine black speckles that are visible only at close range. Juv. is duller version of adult, with more grey (not green) on upperparts. **Habitat:** Arid to semi-arid areas, especially along dry riverbeds. **Status:** Common in most of its range. **Voice:** Soft 'tsip'; repeated 'tipuur tipuur' song. [C12.57]

4 MOUSE-COLOURED PENDULINE-TIT *Anthoscopus musculus* 8 cm
Endemic to NE Africa. A tiny and very pale bird, most likely to be confused with Grey Penduline-Tit in S of range, but has whitish (not buff) underparts and brownish (not buffy or whitish) frons. In NW may overlap with Sennar Penduline-Tit, but is browner above, and lacks pale forehead. **Habitat:** Dry acacia woodland and scrub in arid or semi-arid areas. **Status:** Locally common but easily overlooked; usually in small groups or pairs. **Voice:** Short 'tsit tsit' call; wheezy 'tzeee'; song is rattling trill.

5 GREY (AFRICAN) PENDULINE-TIT *Anthoscopus caroli* 8 cm
Lacks distinctive black forehead, eye-stripe and speckled throat of Cape Penduline-Tit and is generally much greyer, with buffier flanks and belly, whitish on breast, and buff on face and forehead. Differs from Mouse-coloured Penduline-Tit by being much darker on underparts. **Habitat:** Broadleafed and miombo woodlands. **Status:** Common; in small groups. **Voice:** Soft 'chissick' or 'tseeep'. [C12.56, G4.11.8]

6 CAPE PENDULINE-TIT *Anthoscopus minutus* 8 cm
Endemic to S Africa. Distinguished from eremomelas (p. 528) by its tiny size, short, more conical bill, rotund body and very short tail. Confusable with Grey Penduline-Tit, but differs in having black forehead extending as eye-stripe, yellowish (not buff) belly and flanks, and speckled throat. Black forehead differentiates it from Yellow-bellied Eremomela (p. 530). Juv. is paler beneath. **Habitat:** Fynbos, Karoo scrub, semi-desert and arid savanna. **Status:** Common. **Voice:** Soft, high-pitched, tinking 'tseep' or 'tsip-eep-eep'. [G4.11.7]

1 TIT-HYLIA *Pholidornis rushiae* 8 cm
A tiny bird of the forest canopy, easily identified by its streaked head and breast, and yellow rump and belly. Was thought to be related to penduline-tits, but recent evidence suggests that it is a warbler related to Green Hylia (p. 534). **Habitat:** Forest canopy and tall trees in secondary growth; often at lower heights in secondary growth and in plantations. **Status:** Widespread; uncommon to locally common. **Voice:** High-pitched, short 'tisk' and 'teeu' contact notes. [C11.62]

TITS
A widespread group of woodland and forest birds. Social and noisy, they occur in small groups and are often key members of bird parties. Sexes alike. Several species complexes are very similar, but ranges typically do not overlap.

2 ACACIA (SOMALI/NORTHERN GREY) TIT *Parus thruppi* 11-12 cm
Endemic to NE Africa, where it is the only greyish tit. White cheeks are enclosed by black line connecting throat patch to hindcrown (unlike in other grey tits). Bill is robust and longer than other grey tits'. **Habitat:** Acacia woodland and scrub, and thickets in dry watercourses in arid and semi-arid areas. **Status:** Common in some areas but uncommon in most of its range. **Voice:** Buzzy, tit-like call and whistled song, but is relatively quiet for a tit.

3 MIOMBO TIT *Parus griseiventris* 13 cm
Endemic to C Africa. Range overlaps with Ashy Tit, but occurs in different habitat, and is paler, with buffy (not white) cheek patch and outer-tail, and a thinner bill. Black lores and lack of complete black border to white cheek patch separate it from Acacia Tit. Distinguished from Grey Tit by blue-grey (not brownish-grey) back and pale blue-grey (not buffy) flanks. **Habitat:** Miombo and adjacent broadleafed woodland. **Status:** Common. **Voice:** Sweet 'tjou-tjou-tjou-tjou' as well as scolding, harsher calls. [C12.62, G4.11.3]

4 ASHY TIT *Parus cinerascens* 13 cm
Endemic to SW Africa. Differs from Grey Tit by its blue-grey (not brownish-grey) back, and blue-grey (not buffy) flanks and belly; ranges do not overlap. Darker than Miombo Tit, with less white in wings. Juv. is duller version of adult. **Habitat:** Thornveld and arid savanna. In area adjacent to Grey Tit's range, it is confined to acacia-lined rivers, whereas Grey Tit occurs in open Karoo scrub. Avoids broadleafed woodland of Miombo Tit. **Status:** Common. **Voice:** Harsher and more scolding Grey Tit.'s. [G4.11.2]

5 GREY TIT *Parus afer* 13 cm
Endemic to S Africa. Distinguished from Ashy and Acacia tits by its distinctive brownish grey (not blue-grey) back, buffy (not grey) belly and flanks, and a proportionally shorter tail. Juv. is browner. **Habitat:** Fynbos and Karoo scrub, often near rocky outcrops and old buildings. **Status:** Common, usually in small groups. **Voice:** Song is ringing, whistled 'klee-klee-klee-cheree-cheree'; harsh 'chrrr' alarm call. [G4.11.1]

393

1 RUFOUS-BELLIED TIT *Parus rufiventris*   14-15 cm
Endemic to C Africa. The dark head and breast and lack of white cheek patches, together with the rufous belly, flanks and vent, are diagnostic. Bright yellow eye is conspicuous at close range, distinguishing it from Cinnamon-breasted Tit. Also differs by richer belly colour. Juv. is duller, with brown eye and buffy edges to wing feathers. **Habitat:** Broadleafed woodland. **Status:** Locally common; often in bird parties. **Voice:** Harsh, tit-like 'chrrr chrrr'; clear 'chick-wee, chick-wee' song. [C12.64, G4.11.6]

2 CINNAMON-BREASTED TIT *Parus pallidiventris*   14-15 cm
Often considered a race of Rufous-bellied Tit, but is duller and paler, with dark (not yellow) eyes and paler, almost greyish underparts; ranges are mostly mutually exclusive. **Habitat:** Chiefly miombo woodland; sometimes climax mopane woodland. **Status:** Local and generally uncommon; in small groups and associated with foraging bird parties when not breeding. **Voice:** Whistles and churrs similar to those of Rufous-bellied Tit.

3 RED-THROATED TIT *Parus fringillinus*   12 cm
Endemic to S Kenya and N Tanzania. Range overlaps slightly with Cinnamon-breasted Tit in Tanzania; differs by having dark cap contrasting with rufous cheek and nape (not all-dark head and breast). Juv. Cinnamon-breasted Tit has pale throat which can impart dark-capped appearance but always lacks cinnamon collar of this species. **Habitat:** Riverine woodland in savannas; frequently forages in fever trees. **Status:** Locally common; often in small family parties and associated with larger bird parties. **Voice:** Often-repeated 'see-er see-er'; harsher, typical tit-like churring notes.

4 STRIPE-BREASTED TIT *Parus fasciiventer*   14 cm
Endemic to Albertine Rift. A black-headed tit with no white cheek patches and with a black stripe down the centre of the pale buff belly. **Habitat:** Mid- to high-altitude forest, both in canopy and undergrowth and extending to heath edge (over 4 000 m) in some areas. **Status:** Common; in small family groups in mixed feeding parties. **Voice:** Whistles and churrs very similar to those of other African black-and-grey tits. [C12.63]

5 WHITE-BACKED TIT *Parus leuconotus*   13-14 cm
Endemic to Ethiopia. A small, all-dark tit with an obvious white triangle on its mantle; the only black tit to have a white back. Male's mantle is bright white; female's and juv's is duller creamy white. **Habitat:** Various highland forest and woodland types, from juniper to *Hygenae* and farmlands. **Status:** Locally common. **Voice:** Usual mixes of tit-like buzzing and churrs with various whistles and chirps.

6 DUSKY TIT *Parus funereus*   14 cm
A widespread forest tit, with all-black plumage. Female is slightly greyer, especially below. Juv. has white-tipped wing coverts, forming two white wing bars. **Habitat:** Forest canopy and tall trees in secondary growth; sometimes occurs in shorter vegetation in degraded habitats. **Status:** Locally common; almost always in groups, and a frequent member of forest bird parties. **Voice:** Very variable tit-like churrs and whistles. [C12.61]

1 WHITE-SHOULDERED BLACK TIT *Parus guineensis* 14 cm
A white-winged black tit of N savannas of W and C Africa. Often treated as a race of White-winged Black Tit, but is slightly smaller, with yellow (not dark) eyes. Range does not overlap with similar Carp's and Southern Black tits. **Habitat:** Various woodland types, from acacia bush to broadleafed woodland, farmlands and forest edge. **Status:** Common but thinly distributed; in pairs or small family groups; often associated with mixed bird parties. **Voice:** Typical tit-like churrs and buzzes; clear, whistled 'chree chree'. [C12.59]

2 WHITE-WINGED BLACK TIT *Parus leucomelas* 15-16 cm
Often treated as a race of White-shouldered Black Tit, but has dark (not yellow) eyes; ranges mostly do not overlap. Differs from similar Carp's and Southern Black tits chiefly by having solid white (not black-and-white striped) shoulder patch; ranges do not overlap. **Habitat:** Range of woodland types, from broadleafed to drier acacia bush; avoids true forest types. **Status:** Common; usually in small groups or pairs; associated with mixed bird parties. **Voice:** Whistled 'chee-er chee-er' and variations on this; harsh, scolding churrs.

3 SOUTHERN BLACK TIT *Parus niger* 15-16 cm
Endemic to S Africa. Within its range, confusable only with Carp's Tit, from which it differs by having barred grey (not black) vent and less white in wings. Female and juv. are paler grey below than other black tits, with less white in wings. **Habitat:** Forest and broadleafed woodland. **Status:** Common; usually in small groups. **Voice:** Harsh, chattering 'chrr-chrr-chrr'; musical 'phee-cher-phee-cher'. [G4.11.4]

4 CARP'S TIT *Parus carpi* 14-15 cm
Endemic to Namibia and S Angola. Confusable only with Southern Black Tit, from which it differs chiefly by lacking grey-barred vent and having more white in wings. Female is duller, but belly is darker than female Southern Black Tit's. Range does not overlap with similar White-winged Black Tit. **Habitat:** Semi-arid savanna woodland. **Status:** Common. **Voice:** Similar to that of Southern Black Tit. [G4.11.5]

5 WHITE-BELLIED TIT *Parus albiventris* 15 cm
Resembles other black tits from above, but is easily identified from below by its contrasting white belly and vent. Juv. is duller, but still shows clear white belly and vent. **Habitat:** Broadleafed and riverine woodland, as well as open woodland and farmlands. **Status:** Common; usually in pairs or small groups; often in company with large mixed parties. **Voice:** Churring preceded by whistled and clicked 'chick-a-dee' call. [C12.60]

SPOTTED CREEPERS
Small, distinctively patterned birds that creep up tree trunks and branches, then drops to the base of an adjacent tree; often placed in its own family or sub-family. Sexes alike.

6 SPOTTED CREEPER *Salpornis spilonotus* 14-15 cm
The only tree-creeper in the region; always seen creeping along large tree branches and trunks. Much smaller than woodpeckers or wrynecks. Thin, curved bill and brown upperparts heavily spotted with white are diagnostic. Juv. is duller. **Habitat:** Miombo woodland in C Africa; range of broadleafed woodlands elsewhere. **Status:** Locally common to uncommon, often joining bird parties. **Voice:** Fast, thin 'sweepy-swip-swip-swip'; harsher 'keck-keck'. W African birds have deeper calls and some authorities treat them as a separate species linked to Indian populations. [C12.65/6, G4.11.9]

396

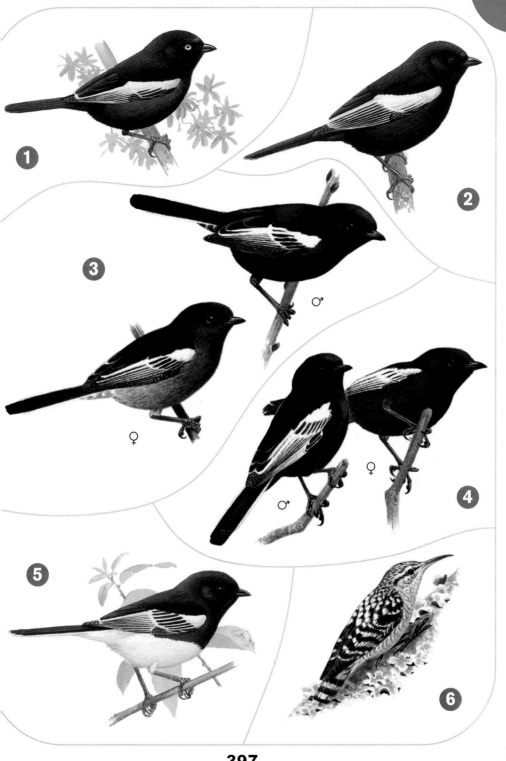

1

2

3

♂

♀

4

♂

♀

5

6

397

1 BOULDER CHAT *Pinarornis plumosus* 25 cm
Near-endemic to Zimbabwe. The brownish-black plumage and white-tipped outer-tail feathers are diagnostic. Occurs in same habitat as Mocking Cliff Chat (p. 472), but lacks chestnut rump and belly. In flight, shows row of small white spots on edge of primary and secondary coverts. Runs and bounds over large boulders, occasionally raising tail well over back when landing. Female is duller. **Habitat:** Well-wooded terrain with large granite boulders. **Status:** Locally common. **Voice:** Clear, sharp whistle; softer 'wink, wink' call, like a squeaky wheel. [G5.1.10]

ROCK-JUMPERS
Large, babbler- or chat-like birds with no close relatives. Restricted to rocky mountain slopes in South Africa and Lesotho. Easily seen when perched up on boulders, they can be overlooked when foraging on the ground among vegetation. They occur in family groups and breed cooperatively, nesting on the ground next to a rock. Sexes differ; juvs resemble dull females.

2 CAPE ROCK-JUMPER *Chaetops frenatus* 24-25 cm
Endemic to South Africa. Darker than Drakensberg Rock-jumper and slightly larger; ranges do not overlap. Male has dark rufous (not orange as in Drakensberg Rock-jumper) belly and rump. Female and juv. are darker buff below than female Drakensberg Rock-jumper, and have more boldly marked head pattern. **Habitat:** Rocky mountain slopes and scree. **Status:** Common but localised; usually in small groups. **Voice:** Series of loud, high-pitched whistles. [G5.2.1]

3 DRAKENSBERG (ORANGE-BREASTED) ROCK-JUMPER
Chaetops aurantius 23-24 cm
Endemic to S Africa. Paler than Cape Rock-jumper and slightly smaller; ranges do not overlap. Male's belly and rump are orange (not dark rufous as in Cape Rock-jumper). Female and juv. are pale buff below and have less distinctly marked heads. **Habitat:** Usually above 2 000 m on rocky slopes. **Status:** Locally common; usually in small groups. **Voice:** Rapidly repeated, piping whistles, like Cape Rock-jumper's. [G5.2.2]

PICATHARTES (ROCKFOWL)
Peculiar, large, slender, strong-legged passerines with no close relatives, restricted to W African forests. Secretive, they are typically found on or near the forest floor, but also venture into adjacent scrub. They build mud-cup nests attached to cave walls and overhanging boulders and cliffs, and breed colonially in areas where there are few suitable nesting cliffs. Sexes alike.

4 WHITE-NECKED PICATHARTES *Picathartes gymnocephalus* 40 cm
Endemic to Upper Guinea forests. Easily identified by the white underparts and bald yellow head with two black cheek patches. Shy and difficult to see in forest undergrowth when foraging; less difficult near caves and rocks where they roost or nest. **Habitat:** Forest understory, with large rocks and caves, although occasionally ventures out of primary forest to forage in adjacent plantations and secondary scrub. **Status:** Vulnerable. Local and uncommon. **Voice:** Usually silent. [G12.53]

5 GREY-NECKED PICATHARTES *Picathartes oreas* 38 cm
Endemic to WC Africa. Dark breast and diagnostic bright blue-and-red naked head separate it from White-necked Picathartes; ranges do not overlap. **Habitat:** Forest understorey; needs large rocks and caves in forest for breeding. **Status:** Vulnerable. Local and uncommon. **Voice:** Usually silent; soft, protracted, sibilant alarm call. [G12.54]

Large, thrush-like birds that are extremely noisy. They occur in small groups of 4-12 birds that maintain contact with continuous raucous babbling. Sexes alike.

1 FULVOUS BABBLER (CHATTERER) *Turdoides fulva*   20-25 cm
The only babbler throughout most of its N African range. Overlaps with White-headed Babbler (p. 402) in E, but is easily separated by lack of white head and pale buff (not brown) body. Paler than Rufous Chatterer (p. 404), with whitish (not dark) throat. **Habitat:** Semi-desert scrub and wadis with acacia thickets. **Status:** Common in small groups; more secretive than other chatterers. **Voice:** Noisy chattering and scolding. [C4.41]

2 BLACK-FACED BABBLER *Turdoides melanops*   21-25 cm
A localised, brown-rumped babbler. Differs from Arrow-marked Babbler by pale yellow-green (not red-rimmed yellow or orange) eye, scalloping (not streaking) on breast, and larger, more sharply defined black lores. Juv. has brown eye. **Habitat:** Broadleafed woodland. **Status:** Uncommon; forages in scattered groups; more furtive than other babblers. **Voice:** Nasal 'wha-wha-wha'; harsh, fast 'papapapa'. [C12.45, G4.12.1]

3 DUSKY BABBLER *Turdoides tenebrosa*   22-24 cm
Localised endemic to NE and NC Africa. A dark brown, white-eyed babbler with very dark upperparts, paler scaled forehead, and rufous-tinged rump and vent. Heavily mottled throat and breast; feathers are edged buff. White eye contrasts with black lores which surround the eye (not confined to lores only, as in Black-lored Babbler). Overall much darker than Black-lored Babbler. **Habitat:** Thickets, scrub and understorey of riverine woodland. **Status:** Uncommon and easily overlooked; occurs in small groups; generally shy and secretive and unusually quiet. **Voice:** Harsh, scolding 'chow'; more nasal 'whachow'.

4 BLACK-LORED BABBLER *Turdoides sharpei*   22-23 cm
Endemic to E Africa. A brown, dark-rumped babbler with a whitish eye. Dark underparts separate it from Northern Pied Babbler (p. 402); *vepres* in C Kenya shows various amounts of white on underparts, especially throat, and may have hybridised with Northern Pied Babbler. White eye separates it from Brown and Arrow-marked babblers. Range meets Dusky Babbler in NW, but is much paler. **Habitat:** Varied: forest edge, thickets and acacia bush. **Status:** Locally common in small groups. **Voice:** Harsh chattering and scolding.

5 SCALY BABBLER *Turdoides squamulata*   22-23 cm
Localised endemic to NE Africa. A mostly brown babbler, differing from White-rumped Babbler (p. 402) by dark (not white) rump. Differs from Brown and Arrow-marked babblers by obvious white crescent-shaped tips to breast and neck feathers (not scalloping or flecks); no overlap in ranges. S birds have dark brown face and ear coverts; N birds are variably white faced. Isolated population in Webi Gestro, Ethiopia, is much paler below, with pale underwing coverts. **Habitat:** Lowland riverine thickets and forest edge. **Status:** Uncommon; furtive, in small groups. **Voice:** 'Che wuk che wuk'; not as noisy as other babblers.

6 BROWN BABBLER *Turdoides plebejus*   21-22 cm
A uniform brown babbler. Although ranges not known to overlap, differs from similar Arrow-marked Babbler by having paler eyes and lores, and broad white chevrons (not pointed arrow marks) on underparts. **Habitat:** Thick bush and undergrowth in riverine woodland and acacia thickets. **Status:** Uncommon; thinly distributed, in small groups. **Voice:** Chattering and cackling, similar to Arrow-marked Babbler's. [C12.43]

7 ARROW-MARKED BABBLER *Turdoides jardineii*   21-24 cm
A uniform brown babbler with white breast streaks that are narrow and pointed. Black (not pale) lores (extending around eye in S) separate it from Brown Babbler. Eye is red-rimmed yellow in S, orange in N. Juv. has less white streaking and darker eye. **Habitat:** Woodland and savanna. **Status:** Common; occurs in groups of up to 12 birds. **Voice:** Noisy; raucous 'chow-chow-chow-chow...', with several birds calling together. [C12.44, G4.11.10]

vepres

1 SOUTHERN PIED BABBLER *Turdoides bicolor* 23-26 cm
Endemic to S Africa, where it is the only babbler with an all-white head, back and underparts. In flight, white wing coverts contrast with blackish-brown flight feathers. Juv. is pale brown, whitening with age; could be confused with other species, but invariably with adults. **Habitat:** Arid savanna, especially acacia thornveld. **Status:** Common; occurs in groups. **Voice:** High-pitched 'kwee kwee kwee kweer' babbling. [G4.12.3]

2 HARTLAUB'S BABBLER *Turdoides hartlaubii* 24-26 cm
The only white-rumped babbler in its African range. At rest, differs from Black-faced Babbler (p. 400) by white lower belly and vent; eye is orange-red to crimson (not yellow). Imm. is paler, especially on throat and breast. **Habitat:** Reedbeds and surrounding woodland. **Status:** Common; occurs in groups. **Voice:** Noisy; loud 'kwek-kwek-kwek' or 'papapapa-papa'. [C12.47, G4.12.2]

3 BARE-CHEEKED BABBLER *Turdoides gymnogenys* 24 cm
Endemic to Angola and Namibia. Differs from Southern Pied Babbler by its brown (not white) back, rufous nape, brown (not blackish) wings, and small patches of bare black skin below and behind eye. Juv. is darker than juv. Southern Pied Babbler. **Habitat:** Arid savanna, favouring taller and denser vegetation along rivers and wooded hills. **Status:** Uncommon; occurs in groups. **Voice:** Typical babbler 'kerrrakerrra-kek-kek-kek'. [G4.12.4]

4 HINDE'S (PIED) BABBLER *Turdoides hindei* 20-23 cm
Endemic to Kenya. The darkest babbler, with a dark brown-black head and breast, scaled with white. Rump is rufous; flanks are buffy. Extent of white plumage is highly variable between individuals; some have white belly and vent. Eye is red. **Habitat:** Forest edge and thickets on farmlands and alongside rivers, generally above 1 000 m. **Status:** Vulnerable. Uncommon to rare; occurs in small groups. **Voice:** Noisy chattering and chuckles from whole group when disturbed.

5 WHITE-HEADED (CRETSCHMAR'S) BABBLER
Turdoides leucocephala 22-25 cm
Localised endemic to NE Africa. Could be confused with white-headed morph of White-rumped Babbler, but lacks white rump, vent and belly. Eye is yellow. **Habitat:** Thick scrub in dry areas alongside wadis and riverine woodland; feeds on or near ground, hiding in thickets when threatened. **Status:** Common; occurs in groups of 5-12 birds; noisy and bold, often following intruder when disturbed. **Voice:** Typical babbler harsh chattering and cackling.

6 WHITE-RUMPED BABBLER *Turdoides leucopygia* 24-27 cm
Endemic to NE Africa. The only white-rumped babbler within its range; does not overlap with Hartlaub's Babbler. Head varies from all-white in N to striking black face and throat edged with white in S. Eye is orange-brown. **Habitat:** Highland forest edge through scrub and swamps to dry riverine woodland; forages in undergrowth and on ground. **Status:** Common; occurs in groups. **Voice:** Noisy chorus of chattering and cackling.

7 NORTHERN PIED BABBLER *Turdoides hypoleuca* 20-23 cm
Endemic to E Africa. The plain brown upperparts and white underparts with an incomplete breast band are diagnostic. The race *vepres* of Black-lored Babbler (p. 400) shows variable amount of white on underparts, but white is not as well defined as in this species. **Habitat:** Thickets and forest edge; also farmlands and gardens with adequate cover. **Status:** Locally common; occurs in groups, foraging in undergrowth and on ground. **Voice:** Loud chattering, cackling and churring noises.

juv.

omoensis

leucopygia

403

1 BLACKCAP BABBLER *Turdoides reinwardtii* 20-22 cm
Unmistakable W African babbler with a black cap and face with a startling pale yellow eye; appears black-headed from some angles. In W has well-defined black cap and little breast streaking, whereas in E black cap extends onto mantle, and has heavier breast streaking. **Habitat:** Forest edge, clearings and adjacent secondary growth. **Status:** Uncommon and thinly distributed; occurs in small groups, foraging on or near the ground. **Voice:** Usual babbler-like chattering given by whole group, especially when going to roost. [C12.46]

2 CAPUCHIN BABBLER *Phyllanthus atripennis* 20 cm
The black-and-silver head contrasting with the bright yellow bill and dark maroon (almost black) body is diagnostic. Extent of black and silver on head varies regionally. **Habitat:** Usually thick undergrowth in deep forest, but also riverine thickets, gardens and plantations. **Status:** Scarce to locally common; noisy groups of 4-12 birds forage close to ground. **Voice:** Group contact call high-pitched babbler-like cackling; song low, slurred whistle. [C12.50]

CHATTERERS
Small babblers with warm brown plumage. Contact calls are softer and higher-pitched than larger babblers. Sexes alike.

3 SCALY CHATTERER *Turdoides aylmeri* 21-22 cm
Endemic to NE Africa. Differs from slightly smaller, commoner Rufous Chatterer by having paler, less rufous underparts, and scaling on the throat and breast. At close range, pale lilac bare skin around eye is visible. Bill is longer than Rufous Chatterer's. **Habitat:** Dry scrub and thickets. **Status:** Uncommon and thinly distributed; fossicks low down and on ground in small groups. **Voice:** High-pitched chatter given by groups; squeaky 'wheeu chu cheeu'.

4 RUFOUS CHATTERER *Turdoides rubiginosa* 19-20 cm
Endemic to NE Africa. Differs from scarcer Scaly Chatterer by its darker plumage with rich cinnamon (not buffy-grey) underparts and lacking bare skin around eye; bill is shorter and less decurved. Uniform cinnamon underparts are diagnostic. **Habitat:** Woodland and thickets, generally in moister areas than Scaly Chatterer. **Status:** Common; occurs in small groups; feeds mostly on ground; is more confiding than Scaly Chatterer. **Voice:** Various cackling and chattering calls given by whole group; softer 'chwer'; high-pitched, descending 'cheeers'.

MOUNTAIN-BABBLERS
Chunky, short-tailed babblers with localised ranges in montane forests. Sexes alike.

5 WHITE-THROATED MOUNTAIN-BABBLER *Kupeornis gilberti* 20-22 cm
Endemic to SW Cameroon and SE Nigeria. White face, throat and upper breast combined with dark chocolate-brown plumage, and pale eyes, bill and legs are diagnostic. Juv. is all-brown. **Habitat:** Primary forest above 900 m; clambers tit-like through vegetation, sometimes hanging upside down. **Status:** Endangered. Locally common within its small range; groups often join bird parties. **Voice:** Noisy; harsh chattering, cackling calls. [C12.48]

6 RED-COLLARED BABBLER *Kupeornis rufocinctus* 20-22 cm
Endemic to Albertine Rift. Easily identified by the rufous collar, throat and breast, and a distinct small black cap. Bill and eye are pale; juv. has dark eye. Range does not overlap with Chapin's Babbler, which is less rufous and lacks black cap. Has a peculiar wing- and tail-flicking action. **Habitat:** High-altitude primary forest; often in wet areas; forages mostly in mid-stratum and canopy, where it gleans bark. **Status:** Locally fairly common; occurs in small groups. **Voice:** Grating 'kakak', 'chjerr' and 'jajajut'; also usual babbler chorus. [C12.49]

7 CHAPIN'S BABBLER *Kupeornis chapini* 20-22 cm
Endemic to E DRC. Differs from similar Red-collared Babbler by lack of a distinct black cap and less rufous plumage; ranges not known to overlap. **Habitat:** Mid- and lowland rainforest at lower elevations than Red-collared Babbler; groups of up to 12 birds frequent mid-stratum and canopy. **Status:** Little known; at least locally common. **Voice:** Unknown.

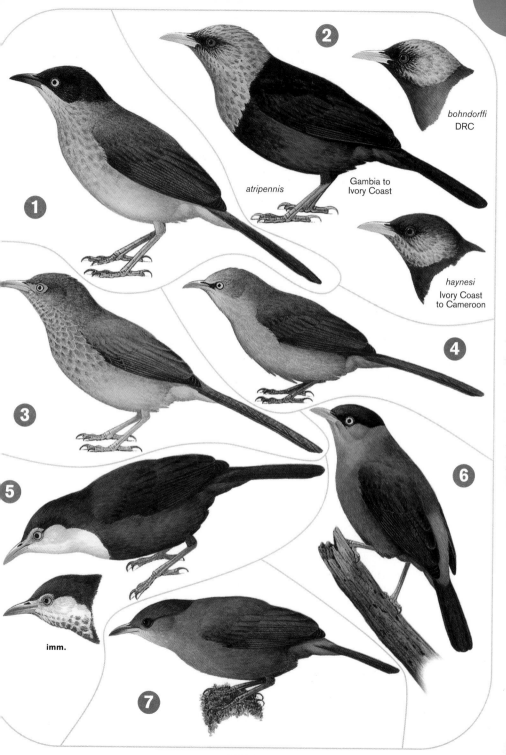

2

bohndorffi
DRC

atripennis

Gambia to
Ivory Coast

haynesi
Ivory Coast
to Cameroon

1

4

3

5

6

imm.

7

Nondescript forest understorey babblers that resemble small thrushes. Secretive; usually seen when foraging among leaf litter. Sexes alike.

1 PALE-BREASTED ILLADOPSIS *Illadopsis rufipennis* 13 cm

Rather small and compact, with a white to greyish-white throat and central belly. Has darker upperparts and colder buff underparts than Brown Illadopsis, which has brown belly in most areas; in C Africa, where Brown Illadopsis has pale belly, can be told by its darker and greyer head, contrasting strongly with white throat. W African *extrema* has brown crown and face, more similar to Brown Illadopsis. Rather short-tailed and round-headed, and its stance is more erect, not as horizontal as Brown Illadopsis's. Tanzanian *distans* has larger bill and different call; may be a distinct species. Juv. has bright orange-yellow base to bill. **Habitat:** Forest understorey, on ground and in lower strata, in dense vegetation. **Status:** Locally common. **Voice:** Harsh 'chack' contact call; grating alarm call; song variable, usually 3-noted whistle (birds in E seldom sing). [C12.36]

2 BROWN ILLADOPSIS *Illadopsis fulvescens* 15 cm

Slightly larger and longer-billed than Pale-breasted Illadopsis, with warmer brown underparts and brown belly through most of range. C and E African *ugandae* has pale central belly, but lacks dark grey head and sharp throat contrast of Pale-breasted Illadopsis, and stance is more horizontal. W African race have browner head, with throat either white (*gularis*: Senegal-Ghana) or ochre (*moloneyana*: E Ghana-Nigeria). **Habitat:** Dense forest understorey, forest edge and old secondary growth. **Status:** Fairly common. **Voice:** Nasal 'chaa' alarm call; song rather mournful 'tik tik ti-fooown', first notes probably given by mate. [C12.35]

3 SCALY-BREASTED ILLADOPSIS *Illadopsis albipectus* 13-16 cm

When present, the scaled breast is diagnostic, but scaling is often absent, especially in W. Unscaled birds differ from Pale-breasted Illadopsis by having less well-defined, greyish (not buffy) breast, less distinct pale throat and slightly longer, paler legs. Juv. has dull pink-yellow base to bill and prominent rufous eye-stripe. **Habitat:** Dense forest undergrowth. **Status:** Locally common; occurs singly, in pairs or in small family groups. **Voice:** Soft, far-carrying, 3-noted, ascending whistle, similar to Pale-breasted Illadopsis's. [C12.38]

4 MOUNTAIN ILLADOPSIS *Illadopsis pyrrhoptera* 12-14 cm

Endemic to E Africa. A plain illadopsis with dark brown upperparts, rufous rump and dark grey face and breast; throat is only very slightly paler. Has obscure pale eye-ring visible at close range. Lacks chestnut back of African Hill Babbler (p. 408), which occurs in mid-storey and canopy. **Habitat:** Montane forests; on ground in dense undergrowth; occurs at high elevation; range overlaps only marginally with those of other illadopsises. **Status:** Locally common, but difficult to see; occurs singly or in small groups, foraging in leaf litter or creeping among tangled branches. **Voice:** Song 3-5 descending whistled notes; sometimes duets.

5 RUFOUS-WINGED ILLADOPSIS *Illadopsis rufescens* 18 cm

Endemic to Upper Guinea forests. A large, thrush-like illadopsis with rufous-brown upperparts and indistinctly marked underparts, with a diffuse, brownish-grey breast band. Grey (not buffy) flanks separates it from Puvel's Illadopsis. Lacks rich orange-buff underparts of Puvel's Illadopsis, and has whitish (not bluish) legs and yellow base to lower mandible (not all yellow). **Habitat:** Closed-canopy forest understorey, on or near ground; seldom in secondary scrub and gallery forest. **Status:** Uncommon to locally common. **Voice:** Repetitive 'tip tip whe-wheee-wheee', last 2 long whistles are ringing and far-carrying. [C12.39]

6 PUVEL'S ILLADOPSIS *Illadopsis puveli* 17 cm

Most easily confused with Rufous-winged Illadopsis, but is warm orange-brown (not greyish-brown) on flanks, and has different habitat preference. Usually the entire lower mandible is pale yellow-horn. Legs are bluish. Contrasting white throat is sometimes puffed out *Criniger*-like. **Habitat:** Dense forest undergrowth, usually in gallery forest and secondary growth. **Status:** Locally common. **Voice:** Muted 'tip tip whe-wheer-wheerr', with 3 last whistled notes descending in pitch; long, loud, descending whistle, 'peeeyaarr'. [C12.40]

moloneyana

1 BLACKCAP ILLADOPSIS *Illadopsis cleaveri* 16 cm
The most distinctive illadopsis, with its black cap contrasting with a broad, pale grey eyebrow and a dark eye-stripe. Flanks are rufous-brown. Could be confused with Brown-chested Alethe (p. 442), but eyebrow is broader and longer, extending onto nape, and ear coverts are dark grey (not brown), contrasting with pale grey (not brown) moustachial stripe and pale throat; upperparts are rather drab olive-brown (not warm brown). **Habitat:** Forest understorey, on or near ground. **Status:** Locally common; usually in pairs and located by song. **Voice:** Song 1-3 mournful, ascending whistles, increasing in volume and lasting roughly 1 second; often preceded by a few 'chip' notes. [C12.37]

2 GREY-CHESTED ILLADOPSIS (BABBLER) *Kakamega poliothorax* 17 cm
Endemic to montane forests of E and C Africa. A large, thrush-like forest babbler, with rich rufous upperparts and a dark grey breast and flanks contrasting with a white throat and belly. Juv. is slightly paler above, with olive-brown wash to breast. **Habitat:** Montane forest understorey, foraging on ground; sometimes attends ant swarms. **Status:** Uncommon to locally common; rather furtive. **Voice:** A rich, fluty whistling song and a nasal alarm call. [C12.33]

3 AFRICAN HILL BABBLER *Pseudoalcippe abyssinica* 15 cm
A small, chestnut-backed babbler with a grey head and breast, buffy flanks and a paler belly. Appears like a small bulbul or robin. Differs from Mountain Illadopsis (p. 406) by having rich chestnut-brown (not plain brown) back, generally uniform grey head and throat, and seldom occurring on ground. Eye is usually dull red, but ranges from brown to bright red. Head colour is variable: 'Ruwenzori Hill Babbler' *atriceps* (Albertine Rift and SW Cameroon) is darker, with almost black head; *monacha* (Mount Cameroon) has slightly darker head and lightly streaked throat; and *stierlingi/stictigula* (Tanzania S) has black face and heavily streaked throat. **Habitat:** Montane forest, and adjacent secondary forest. **Status:** Common but secretive; keeps well hidden in vines and tangles in mid- and lower strata; most often detected by explosive calls and song. **Voice:** Very vocal; loud and far-carrying 'wheeo tu tuweeo', with many variations. [C12.41]

4 SPOTTED THRUSH BABBLER *Ptyrticus turdinus* 18-20 cm
A large, thrush-like babbler with a long bill and strong feet. Identified by its white underparts heavily blotched with brown spots across breast and upper belly. Legs and feet whitish. **Habitat:** Lowland forest, usually near streams or swampy areas; forages on ground. **Status:** Local and uncommon, in pairs or small groups. Generally located by its loud, ringing calls. **Voice:** Oriole-like, fluty, descending whistles, 'chiu-lau-li'; chattering alarm notes. [C12.42]

MODULATRIXES
Two forest understorey species variously linked to babblers, bulbuls or thrushes. Quite secretive; most easily seen at dawn when singing. Sexes alike.

5 DAPPLED MOUNTAIN ROBIN (DAPPLE-THROAT)
Modulatrix orostruthus 16-17 cm
Endemic to Eastern Arc Mts; highly localised. Differs from understorey greenbuls (p. 412) by having brown-mottled (not uniform) yellowish breast (but breast dappling is reduced in *orostruthus* from N Mozambique). Streaked breast is superficially similar to juv. robins or thrushes, but it has plain (not spotted) upperparts. **Habitat:** Dense understorey in montane forests, often near streams. **Status:** Vulnerable. Locally common in some Udzungwa and Namuli forests; rare in East Usambaras. Secretive; best located when singing at dawn. **Voice:** Bulbul-like chattering; fluty, rich, oriole-like song, chiefly at dawn.

6 SPOT-THROAT (SPOT-THROATED MODULATRIX) *Modulatrix stictigula* 14 cm
Endemic to Eastern Arc Mts. Rich chestnut plumage, bare face and mottled throat are diagnostic. Behaviour is more robin-like than understorey greenbuls (p. 412). Differs from slightly larger Dappled Mountain Robin by its dark brown (not mottled) breast and belly. **Habitat:** Undergrowth in montane forests and adjacent secondary growth, and even gardens. **Status:** Locally common but secretive, staying in dense cover, where it forages over leaf litter. **Voice:** 2-note whistle, 'hooo eeee', with last note higher pitched; song loud, rich, thrush-like warbling.

atriceps

abyssinica

monacha

Abundant, distinctive bulbuls with erect stance and short hindcrown crests. Taxonomy is unresolved, with considerable geographic variation. Sexes alike.

1 DARK-CAPPED (BLACK-EYED) BULBUL *Pycnonotus tricolor*   19-22 cm
Often lumped with Common Bulbul, but has a yellow (not white) vent, and typically has sharper contrast between the brown breast and whitish belly. Lacks white neck patch and scaly breast of Dodson's and Somali bulbuls. Black (not red or white) eye-ring separates it from African Red-eyed and Cape bulbuls. **Habitat:** Catholic, ranging from savanna to forest edge and gardens. **Status:** Abundant. **Voice:** Harsh 'kwit, kwit, kwit' alarm call; song is liquid 'sweet sweet sweet-potato'. [G4.12.8]

2 COMMON BULBUL *Pycnonotus barbatus*   19-22 cm
Often lumped with Dark-capped Bulbul, but has a creamy-white (not yellow) vent and typically has less contrast between brown breast and white belly (although Sudanese-Ethiopian populations show greater contrast). Apparently intergrades with Dark-capped Bulbul in WC Africa ('*gabonesis*', Congo-C Cameroon), but elsewhere they meet without interbreeding. Some *arsinoe* (Sudan) have small white neck patch, but much smaller than Dodson's and Somali bulbuls', and lack scaling on breast. Typically has brown breast grading onto belly, but NE populations show greater contrast. **Habitat:** Virtually all habitats with bushes or trees; avoids dense forest and very arid areas. **Status:** Abundant. **Voice:** Similar to Dark-capped Bulbul's. [C3.71]

3 DODSON'S BULBUL *Pycnonotus dodsoni*   18-21 cm
Endemic to NE Africa. Similar to Somali Bulbul, but has a yellow (not white) vent, white tail tips, more heavily scaled breast extending to upper belly, and scaly (not plain) back. Told from Dark-capped Bulbul by white neck patches, white tail tip and scaling, although the two species apparently hybridise in C Kenya. **Habitat:** Dry acacia scrub, other dry wooded areas and along dry river courses'. **Status:** Locally common. **Voice:** Similar to Dark-capped Bulbul's.

4 AFRICAN RED-EYED BULBUL *Pycnonotus nigricans*   19-21 cm
Endemic to SW Africa. Told from Dark-capped and Cape bulbuls by its diagnostic red eye-ring. Head is blacker than Dark-capped Bulbul's, contrasting with greyish collar and breast. Juv. has pale pink eye-ring. Hybridises with Dark-capped and Cape bulbuls in a narrow zone near Grahamstown. **Habitat:** Arid savanna, riverine bush and gardens. **Status:** Common. **Voice:** Liquid whistles, slightly more fluty than Dark-capped Bulbul's. [G4.12.7]

5 SOMALI BULBUL *Pycnonotus somaliensis*   18-21 cm
Endemic to NE Africa. Similar to Common Bulbul, but has a white patch on the side of the neck, scaly breast (formed by paler fringes to dark breast feathers) and paler upperparts. Told from Dodson's Bulbul by white (not yellow) vent. **Habitat:** Dry acacia scrub and other semi-arid bushed country. **Status:** Locally common. **Voice:** Harsher and more grating than Common Bulbul's, with louder 'chwit chwit' alarm.

6 CAPE BULBUL *Pycnonotus capensis*   19-21 cm
Endemic to South Africa. Told from African Red-eyed and Dark-capped bulbuls by its diagnostic white eye-ring and darker underparts extending onto lower belly. Juv. initially lacks white eye-ring, but is darker below than Dark-capped and African Red-eyed bulbuls. **Habitat:** Fynbos, coastal scrub and gardens. **Status:** Common. **Voice:** Song is liquid whistle, 'peet-purt-pater-ta', higher-pitched and sharper than Dark-capped Bulbul's. [G4.12.6]

7 BUSH BLACKCAP *Lioptilus nigricapilla*   15-17 cm
Endemic to S Africa. A distinctive, brown-backed bulbul or babbler of uncertain affinities. Adult's red bill, pink legs and black crown are diagnostic; larger than male Blackcap (p. 492), with red (not greyish) bill and black cap extending below eye. Juv. is duller, with pink bill. **Habitat:** Montane forest and dense scrub; gardens and coastal forest in winter. **Status:** Uncommon resident and altitudinal migrant. **Voice:** Rich, melodious warbling song, 'plik plik toodley-oodley-oodley-ooo'. [G4.12.5]

juv.

Greenbuls are one of Africa's most challenging groups. Many species lack distinctive plumage features, especially in the gloomy forest understorey or backlit in the forest canopy. Vocalisations and behaviour are often the best clues to identification. *Phyllastrephus* is mostly insectivorous; more slender than other genera, with a longer, slender bill and more horizontal stance. Understorey species could be confused with illadopsises (p. 406), but have a longer tail and typically a longer, finer bill. They usually occur in small groups. Several species habitually flick their wings. The sexes are alike, but with greater size differences between males and females than other greenbuls.

1 YELLOW-STREAKED GREENBUL *Phyllastrephus flavostriatus*   18-20 cm
Endemic to SE Africa. A slender, pale greenbul, best identified by its foraging action: creeps up branches, gleaning insects and continually flicking open one wing at a time. Greyish (not brown) head separates it from Sharpe's Greenbul. Faint yellow streaks are visible only at close range and in good light, but merge to form yellow belly in some races (DRC and S Tanzania). **Habitat:** Forest mid-stratum and canopy. **Status:** Locally common. **Voice:** Song is 'klip weet-weet-weet-weaat'; sharp 'kleet kleet kleeat' and dry 'trl-rl-rl-rl' calls. [C9.76, G4.12.10]

2 SHARPE'S GREENBUL *Phyllastrephus alfredi*   18-20 cm
Endemic to SW Tanzania (Ufipa Plateau), NE Zambia and N Malawi. Often treated as a race of Yellow-streaked Greenbul, but has brown (not grey) head and paler, whitish underparts, with brown (not grey) patches on the sides of the breast; ranges do not overlap. **Habitat:** Mid-altitude and highland forests, in mid-canopy; behaviour is similar to Yellow-streaked Greenbul's. **Status:** Common. **Voice:** Similar to Yellow-streaked Greenbul's.

3 GREY-HEADED GREENBUL *Phyllastrephus poliocephalus*   20-23 cm
Endemic to SW Cameroon and SE Nigeria. A large, long-tailed greenbul; the combination of grey head, whitish throat and yellow underparts is diagnostic. Larger and longer-billed than Western Mountain Greenbul (p. 422), with paler head and much brighter underparts. Shows affinities to Yellow-streaked Greenbul, with similar wing-flicking behaviour, but is larger and brighter; ranges do not overlap. **Habitat:** Montane forest. **Status:** Common; usually in noisy and conspicuous groups. **Voice:** Loud 'wurp wurp' and 'kit kit' calls. [C9.77]

4 WHITE-THROATED GREENBUL *Phyllastrephus albigularis*   17-18 cm
Slightly smaller than Yellow-streaked Greenbul, with darker olive-brown upperparts and breast contrasting with white throat; behaviour is similar. Much less yellow beneath than Icterine and Xavier's greenbuls, with obvious white (not yellow) throat. **Habitat:** Forest understorey, forest edge and gallery forest. Creeps among dense tangles, but also gleans from branches and flicks wings when agitated. **Status:** Fairly common in E, uncommon in W. Often in bird parties with Icterine and Xavier's greenbuls. **Voice:** Rapid series of whistled notes; loud, rolling 'trrrp'. [C9.75]

5 ICTERINE GREENBUL *Phyllastrephus icterinus*   15-17 cm
A rather brightly coloured greenbul with olive-green upperparts and dull yellow underparts. Slightly smaller than Xavier's Greenbul, but differences are masked by large size differences between sexes. Icterine averages brighter yellow beneath, with rufous (not greenish) upper-tail coverts and brighter rufous tail, but these features are often hard to observe. Appears to have more rounded head (not flat-crowned) and shorter bill, but best told apart by calls. **Habitat:** Forest and gallery forest, in understorey and mid-stratum. **Status:** Common; in pairs or family groups, often in mixed bird parties. **Voice:** Fast, rattling 'trrrup uupp uupp' and 'trr-rr owp owp owp owp'. [C9.73]

6 XAVIER'S GREENBUL *Phyllastrephus xavieri*   16-17 cm
Slightly larger and duller than Icterine Greenbul; crown appears flatter (less rounded), and male has appreciably longer bill, but female's shorter and overlaps with male Icterine Greenbul's. Best identified by calls. **Habitat:** Forest understorey to mid-stratum, usually at lower levels than Icterine Greenbul. **Status:** Locally common. **Voice:** Loud 'wurp wurp' and nasal 'urrrpp' calls, sometimes descending in pitch; lower and deeper than Icterine Greenbul's. [C9.74]

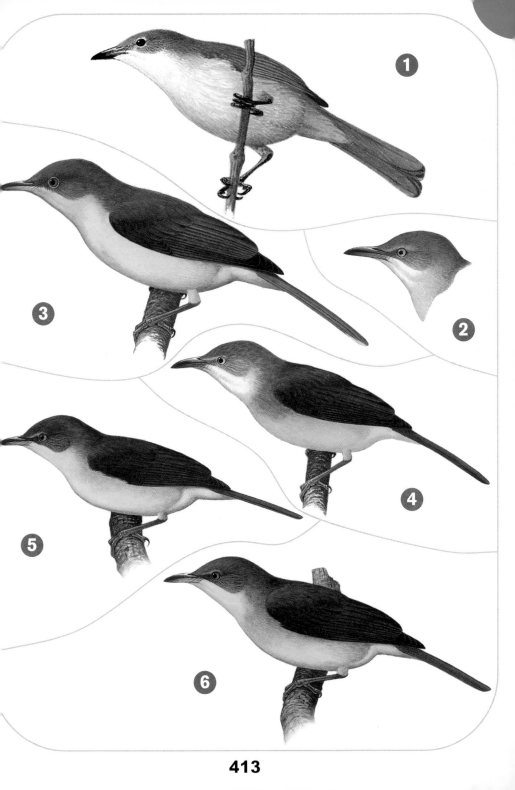

1 CABANIS'S GREENBUL *Phyllastrephus cabanisi*   17-19 cm
Endemic to C Africa, W of Rift Valley. A fairly large, slender, long-tailed greenbul of highland forest understorey; in good light shows a rufous tail. Often treated as a race of Placid Greenbul, but is yellower below, with creamy-yellow (not whitish) throat and dull yellow (not greyish-white) belly; ranges do not overlap. Conspicuous yellowish throat separates it from White-throated Greenbul (p. 412). Flicks wings and raises crest when agitated. **Habitat:** Thickets and tangles in highland forests, often along streams. **Status:** Common; usually in small groups. **Voice:** Noisy: series of harsh, dry 'prrt' calls, with more melodic whistles interspersed. [C9.71]

2 PLACID GREENBUL *Phyllastrephus placidus*   17-19 cm
Endemic to SE Africa, E of Rift Valley. Often treated as a race of Cabanis's Greenbul, but lacks yellowish underparts, and has a creamy-white throat and greyish-white belly; ranges do not overlap. Slightly larger than Grey-olive Greenbul (p. 416), with blue-grey (not pale, fleshy-coloured) legs and different calls. Compared with Terrestrial Brownbul, rufous tail contrasts with brownish back and has olive-brown (not warm brown) flanks. Eye colour varies from pale grey to darker brown. Wing-flicks. **Habitat:** Mid-altitude and highland forest undergrowth, favouring thick tangles. **Status:** Common; usually in small, noisy groups, often joining bird parties. **Voice:** Dry churrs and chuckles, similar to those of Cabanis's Greenbul.

3 FISCHER'S GREENBUL *Phyllastrephus fischeri*   17-18 cm
Endemic to coastal SE Africa. Formerly lumped with Cabanis's and Placid greenbuls, but has pale (not dark) eyes and a longer, straighter bill; ranges do not overlap. Differs from Terrestrial and Northern brownbuls by pale (not red-brown) eyes and olive-brown (not brown or rufous-brown) upperparts, and flanks that contrast with dull rufous tail. **Habitat:** Forest undergrowth and thickets in woodland; forages noisily on or near ground, with wing-flicking and tail-flirting. **Status:** Common; usually in small groups. **Voice:** Variable contact notes of 'prrrt', dry chattering churrs and repeated and rapid 'chweeooo'.

4 TERRESTRIAL BROWNBUL *Phyllastrephus terrestris*   17-19 cm
A fairly large, brown-backed understorey greenbul. Darker and less rufous above than Northern Brownbul, with more strongly contrasting white throat and less rufous tail. Has less olive on back and flanks than Fischer's Greenbul, with red-brown (not pale) eyes. Juv. is paler, with more rufous rump and tail and yellow wash on underparts; best told from Northern Brownbul by accompanying adults. **Habitat:** Forest understorey and thickets. **Status:** Common; in small, noisy flocks, scuffling around on forest floor. **Voice:** Soft, chattering 'trrup cherrup trrup', deeper than Northern Brownbul's. [C9.67, G4.12.9]

5 NORTHERN BROWNBUL *Phyllastrephus strepitans*   16-18 cm
Endemic to NE Africa. Similar to Terrestrial Brownbul, but has a less pronounced white throat and warmer brown upperparts, with a rufous-brown rump and tail. Warmer rufous than Fischer's Greenbul, lacking olive tones to back and flanks. Eye colour varies from pale grey through red to brown. Juv. is more rufous on crown. **Habitat:** Prefers drier, less moist thickets and tangles in forest undergrowth. **Status:** Common; in small, noisy family parties, creeping low down or on ground in thick tangles. **Voice:** Chattering and scolding, higher-pitched and more babbler-like than Terrestrial Brownbul's.

6 RED-TAILED LEAF-LOVE (GREENBUL) *Pyrrhurus scandens*   19-21 cm
A large, grey and rufous greenbul, with affinities to Yellow-throated Leaf-love (p. 424) and Swamp Palm Bulbul (p. 430) as well as *Phyllastrephus*. Best identified by pale grey head, buffy (not yellowish) underparts and bright rufous tail which is fanned regularly. Larger than Pale-olive Greenbul (p. 416). **Habitat:** Understorey of swamp forest, gallery forest and thickets, seldom far from water. **Status:** Locally common; usually in pairs or small groups. **Voice:** Usually located by loud, ventriloquial 'cowp cocowp' calls produced in chorus; variable harsh babbler-like cackling, similar to Swamp Palm Bulbul's. [C9.66]

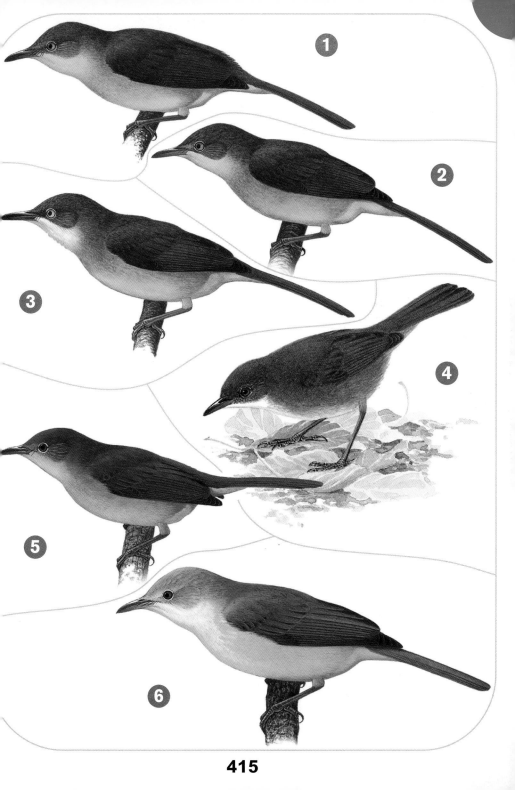

1 GREY-OLIVE GREENBUL *Phyllastrephus cerviniventris*   15-17 cm
A small, rather drab greenbul. Slightly smaller than Placid Greenbul (p. 414), with a less obvious white throat and distinctive pale fleshy (not blue-grey) legs. Lacks yellow throat and belly of Cabanis's Greenbul (p. 414). Smaller and paler than Terrestrial and Northern brownbuls (p. 414), with pale legs and mostly pale bill. **Habitat:** Thick tangles along streams and rivers in forests; keeps to dense cover on or near ground. **Status:** Uncommon; usually in small groups. **Voice:** Distinctive, nasal 'weh weh weh', similar to Yellow-bellied Greenbul's; repeated, harsh 'chekerik cherick'. [C9.68]

2 PALE-OLIVE GREENBUL *Phyllastrephus fulviventris*   17 cm
Endemic to Angola and coastal DRC. Paler below than Grey-olive Greenbul; ranges do not overlap. Nondescript, with rather uniform pale yellow-buff underparts and olive-brown upperparts contrasting with rufous tail. Lacks contrasting white throat of Terrestrial Brownbul (p. 416) or White-throated Greenbul (p. 412). **Habitat:** Coastal forest, gallery forest and patches of woodland. **Status:** Locally common. **Voice:** Short, rapid, querulous 'wher-er-er'; also sharp 'tsik-tschirr-tschirr'. [C9.69]

3 TORO OLIVE GREENBUL *Phyllastrephus hypochloris*   18 cm
Endemic to E Africa. A drab olive greenbul. Most similar to Cabanis's Greenbul (p. 414), but has dark (not pale) eyes, greyish (not yellow) throat, and only a hint of a pale eye-ring. Told from plain olive *Andropadus* greenbuls (p. 418) by long, thin (not short, stubby) bill. **Habitat:** Primary forest among thick tangles in undergrowth near ground and dense thick vines to mid-stratum, usually near streams. **Status:** Uncommon; elusive; usually singly or in pairs. **Voice:** Song is slurred series of descending notes; harsher 'shree shree'. [C9.70, but may be Little Greenbul]

4 BAUMANN'S GREENBUL *Phyllastrephus baumanni*   18 cm
Endemic to W Africa. Sometimes lumped with Toro Olive Greenbul, but ranges do not overlap. Larger than Little Greenbul (p. 418), with paler, more brownish (less olive) underparts, longer, thinner bill, and darker legs. Long, slender bill differentiates it from other plain olive *Andropadus* greenbuls (p. 418). **Habitat:** Tangled undergrowth in mid-altitude forest, especially along streams. **Status:** Poorly known; apparently rare and localised; usually in pairs or small groups. **Voice:** Short, nasal, jumbled song; 'chik' or 'crik' contact calls.

5 CAMEROON OLIVE GREENBUL *Phyllastrephus poensis*   18 cm
Endemic to SW Cameroon and SE Nigeria. Nondescript; olive-brown above, with a greyer face, greyish-brown underparts, paler throat and a fairly long, rufous tail. Relatively long, slender bill distinguishes it from plain olive *Andropadus* greenbuls (p. 418); browner than Cameroon Mountain Greenbul (p. 422), with rufous tail, paler, less olive underparts, and wing-flicking behaviour. **Habitat:** Montane forest, from understorey to canopy. **Status:** Locally common. **Voice:** Harsh, ratchet-like trilling, 'trrrrt'; loud, querulous 'kwerp kwerp kwer kwer'. [C9.72]

6 SASSI'S OLIVE GREENBUL *Phyllastrephus lorenzi*   15-17 cm
Endemic to E DRC. Similar to other olive greenbuls, but with a diagnostic black cap. Much duller beneath and longer-tailed than Blackcap Illadopsis (p. 408); ranges not known to overlap. Most likely to be confused with Toro Olive Greenbul if dark cap is not seen, but reportedly moves slowly, allowing good views. Juv. has less well-defined black cap. **Habitat:** Mid-altitude forest, 1 000-1 800 m, in understorey and mid-strata. **Status:** Little known; usually in small groups, often joining bird parties. **Voice:** Unknown.

7 TINY (SLENDER) GREENBUL *Phyllastrephus debilis*   12-14 cm
Endemic to coastal SE Africa. A small, warbler-like greenbul. Recalls a diminutive Yellow-streaked Greenbul (p. 412), with pale grey head and variably yellow-washed underparts. Eye is usually pale grey or red, but sometimes darker brown. Bill is mostly pale; *albigula* (Usambara and Nguru Mts, N Tanzania) has dark upper mandible, greener crown and less yellow underparts. Juv's crown is greener. **Habitat:** Low- and mid-elevation forest, forest edge and adjacent thickets, gleaning from foliage in dense tangles. **Status:** Common; often in small groups. **Voice:** Nasal, bubbling song, 'kwerr kerr ker ker kr-r-rrrr', increasing in pace and pitch; shrill 'shriiip' call. [G4.13.1]

Mostly frugivorous, these greenbuls are stockier than *Phyllastrephus*, with a shorter, broader bill and more upright stance, but are not as bulky or heavy-billed as *Chlorocichla*. Typically they occur singly or in pairs. Sexes alike.

1 YELLOW-WHISKERED GREENBUL *Andropadus latirostris*   17-18 cm
A dark brown and dull olive-green bulbul with a diagnostic yellow stripe on the side of the throat; stripes are raised in display. Legs and toes are dull orange or yellowish. Dark bill often shows some orange-yellow at cutting edges and gape. Juv. lacks yellow throat stripes; told from other small greenbuls by brighter yellow legs and yellow gape and base to lower mandible. Could be confused with Yellow-footed Honeyguide (p. 310), but lacks white outer-tail feathers. **Habitat:** Forest, gallery forest and secondary growth; occurs in all strata, but usually in lower levels. **Status:** Common; usually single. **Voice:** Various greenbul chatterings and chortles; continual 'chuk chuk' series of notes – a most familiar forest call within bird's range. [C9.55]

2 LITTLE GREENBUL *Andropadus virens*   15-16 cm
A nondescript, small greenbul with a short, stubby bill, plain, rounded head and distinctive, frequently uttered song. Slightly larger than Little Grey and Ansorge's greenbuls, with no suggestion of an eye-ring, and has pale or yellowish gape and yellowish-brown (not dark) legs. Slightly smaller than Plain Greenbul, with olive (not greyish) throat, yellow-brown (not grey-brown) legs and no eye-ring. Legs are duller than juv. Yellow-whiskered Greenbul. **Habitat:** Forest understorey, gallery forest, secondary growth, thickets and plantations; generally in low- and mid-strata. **Status:** Common. **Voice:** Song starts with short chirps, followed by rapid, whistled chortles and ending in a liquid flourish. [C9.49]

3 PLAIN (CAMEROON SOMBRE) GREENBUL *Andropadus curvirostris*   17 cm
Distinguished from Little Greenbul, which shares the same habitat, by having an obvious eye-ring, greyish (not olive) throat, darker legs and slightly longer, decurved bill. Larger than Little Grey and Ansorge's greenbuls, with less obvious eye-ring, grey throat contrasting with darker cheeks, more upright stance and different song. Superficially recalls olive greenbuls (p. 416), but has shorter, heavier bill. Upper Guinea *leoninus* has quite distinct song and may be a different species. **Habitat:** Closed-canopy forest, from low to mid-strata, but usually in higher strata than Little Greenbul. **Status:** Common. **Voice:** Variable harsh trills; short trisyllabic 'wheet tee wher' song. [C9.52/53]

4 LITTLE GREY GREENBUL *Andropadus gracilis*   15 cm
A tiny, grey-olive greenbul with a well-marked white eye-ring, which separates it from slightly larger Little Greenbul. Very similar to Ansorge's Greenbul, but has yellowish (not ginger) belly and patches on sides of breast; song differs. Smaller than Plain Greenbul, with more prominent eye-ring and less contrast between face and throat. **Habitat:** Forest canopy, gallery forest and tall trees in secondary growth. Occurs at lower levels at forest edge or in degraded habitats. **Status:** Common; not furtive; more easily seen than most small greenbuls. **Voice:** Short song, generally rising in pitch, 'a-hut a-whit-whit'; 'chuk' contact call. [C9.50]

5 ANSORGE'S GREENBUL *Andropadus ansorgei*   15 cm
Differs from Little Grey Greenbul by less prominent eye-ring, and being greyer overall on underparts, with gingery-brown wash on flanks and vent; lacks yellowish breast patches and has buffy (not yellowish) wing linings. **Habitat:** Forest canopy and gallery forest, at lower heights at forest edge, along forest trails or in secondary growth. **Status:** Locally common. **Voice:** Short, 3-note 'cheet cher cheet' whistled song; long, rattled trill. [C9.51]

6 SOMBRE GREENBUL *Andropadus importunus*   16-18 cm
A medium-sized, rather plain olive-green greenbul with a diagnostic pale eye and distinctive song. Race *hypoxanthus* (C Mozambique-S Tanzania) is greener above and more yellow below; could be confused with Yellow-bellied Greenbul (p. 424), but has white (not red) eye. Juv. is duller, with dark eye and narrow, pale eye-ring. **Habitat:** Forest and thicket, in canopy and mid-strata. **Status:** Common. **Voice:** Song is piercing 'weeewee', usually followed by a liquid chortle, rendered 'WILLIE, quickly run around the bush and squeeeeze-me'. [G4.13.2]

juv.

juv.

1 SLENDER-BILLED GREENBUL *Andropadus gracilirostris* 18 cm

A slender, long-billed canopy greenbul with diagnostic pale grey underparts which contrast with the olive-brown upperparts. This is especially well marked on face, where there is clear contrast between dark ear coverts and pale creamy-white throat. Structure recalls olive greenbuls (p. 416), but occurs in canopy, not understorey. Typically has upright stance, often stretching neck. Eye is dark red. C Kenya *percivali* has buffy undertail coverts. **Habitat:** Forest canopy, gallery forest and tall trees in secondary growth; keeps mainly to crown of tall trees, in open; is not furtive. **Status:** Common. **Voice:** Long whistled 'teeeooo'; short, jumbled song. [C9.54]

2 SHELLEY'S GREENBUL *Andropadus masukuensis* 16-17 cm

Endemic to Eastern Arc Mts of Tanzania and N Malawi. Slightly smaller and more slender than Stripe-faced, Olive-headed and mountain greenbuls (p. 422), with finer, longer bill and duller olive underparts. Further differs from Stripe-faced and Olive-headed greenbuls by dark (not pale) eye and pale eye-ring. Behaves like Yellow-streaked Greenbul (p. 412), creeping up branches and creepers, frequently flicking wings. **Habitat:** Montane and mid-altitude forest, foraging in mid- and lower strata. **Status:** Fairly common; in pairs or small groups, usually with bird parties. **Voice:** Usually silent; variable 'tchwik tchwik' or nasal 'kew kewa'. [C9.46]

3 KAKAMEGA GREENBUL *Andropadus kakamegae* 16-17 cm

Endemic to Albertine Rift and W Kenya. Often treated as a race of Shelley's Greenbul, but has greyer (not olive) head; ranges do not overlap. Slightly larger than Ansorge's and Little Grey greenbuls (p. 418), with greyer head and longer tail. Smaller and more slender than Olive-breasted Mountain Greenbul (p. 422), with duller olive underparts and less prominent eye-ring. **Habitat:** Forest mid-stratum and undergrowth; regularly clings to tree trunks and branches, where it forages woodpecker-like. **Status:** Uncommon; easily overlooked; very quiet and unobtrusive. **Voice:** Generally silent; call unknown.

4 STRIPE-CHEEKED GREENBUL *Andropadus milanjensis* 19-20 cm

Endemic to E Zimbabwe, N Mozambique and S Malawi (Mt Mulanje). Often lumped with Olive-headed and Stripe-faced greenbuls, but is darker above and below, typically with darker eye and less clearly defined dark cheeks; ranges do not overlap. Slightly larger and stockier than Sombre Greenbul (p. 418), with grey (not olive) head, darker eye, pale eye-ring, and faint white cheek streaks. Juv. has greener crown. **Habitat:** Montane forest and forest edge. **Status:** Locally common. **Voice:** Throaty 'chrrup-chip-chrup-chrup'. [G4.13.3]

5 STRIPE-FACED GREENBUL *Andropadus striifacies* 19 cm

Endemic to S Kenya and Tanzania. Often lumped with Stripe-cheeked and Olive-headed greenbuls, but has brighter yellow underparts and a paler throat, resulting in a more contrasting dark cheek patch. Eyes typically are pale. Larger and more colourful than Shelley's Greenbul; compared to mountain greenbuls (p. 422), has olive (not grey) crown and lacks prominent white eye-ring. Smaller than Yellow-bellied Greenbul (p. 424), with more olive (not brown) upperparts, contrasting dark cheeks and paler eyes. **Habitat:** Forest and forest edge and secondary growth, in mid-stratum and canopy. **Status:** Locally common. **Voice:** Usual greenbul chattering, with loud, low-pitched 'chee kwaaa' and 'tchikuu tchikuu'.

6 OLIVE-HEADED GREENBUL *Andropadus olivaceiceps* 19-20 cm

Endemic to extreme S Tanzania (Mt Rungwe and Poroto Mts), N Mozambique (Serra Jeci) and Malawi. Often lumped with Stripe-cheeked and Stripe-faced greenbuls; ranges do not overlap. Differs from Stripe-cheeked Greenbul chiefly by having paler eyes (much paler when breeding) and slightly paler plumage. Darker above than Stripe-faced Greenbul, with greener (less yellow) underparts, resulting in less contrast with dark cheeks. Larger than Shelley's Greenbul, with more robust bill and dark, contrasting cheek patches. Told from mountain greenbuls (p. 422) by olive (not grey) crown, contrasting with darker cheeks, and less prominent eye-ring. **Habitat:** Forests and forested gullies, in mid-stratum and canopy. **Status:** Locally common. **Voice:** Very vocal: variable low-pitched chortles of mixed 'choops', 'chaas' and 'cherks'.

1 CAMEROON MOUNTAIN GREENBUL *Andropadus montanus* 18 cm
Endemic to SW Cameroon and SE Nigeria. A montane bulbul with uniform olive-green plumage, tinged with yellowish on the underparts. Differs from Western Mountain Greenbul by having olive (not grey) head and olive (not yellowish) underparts. Lacks reddish tail of Cameroon Olive Greenbul (p. 416), with shorter bill and darker olive underparts; does not wing-flick. **Habitat:** Forest understorey, forest edge and secondary growth. **Status:** Locally common; best located by song from low in forest understorey. **Voice:** Nasal chuckling and babbling, with low 'churp churp' rambling chatter. [C9.45]

2 WESTERN MOUNTAIN GREENBUL *Andropadus tephrolaemus* 17 cm
Endemic to SW Cameroon and SE Nigeria. Told from Cameroon Mountain Greenbul by its grey (not olive) head, throat and upper breast, and more prominent white eye-ring (although eye-ring is narrower in nominate race from Mt Cameroon and Bioko). Similar to Olive-breasted Mountain Greenbul, but ranges do not overlap. **Habitat:** Montane forest, from undergrowth to canopy. **Status:** Common; often in small groups. **Voice:** Nasal chirs and chirrups; repeated 'trup trup' song. [C9.47a]

3 OLIVE-BREASTED MOUNTAIN GREENBUL *Andropadus kikuyuensis* 18 cm
Endemic to Albertine Rift and C Kenya. Virtually identical to Western Mountain Greenbul but genetically closer to Black-headed Mountain Greenbul; ranges do not overlap. Larger than Kakamega Greenbul (p. 420), with brighter greenish-yellow underparts and more obvious pale eye-ring. **Habitat:** Forest, forest edge and secondary growth; usually forages higher in canopy than Shelley's and Kakamega greenbuls. **Status:** Locally common. **Voice:** Soft, grating chur; plaintive, bleating call. [C9.47b/48c]

4 BLACK-HEADED MOUNTAIN GREENBUL *Andropadus nigriceps* 18 cm
Endemic to highland forests of S Kenya and N Tanzania. Nominate race has a full black crown; told from Uluguru Mountain Greenbul by white eye-ring. Usambara Mountain Greenbul *usambarae* has black supercilium and grey crown, and perhaps is also best treated as a separate species. Both differ from Olive-breasted Mountain Greenbul by grey (not olive-yellow) belly. Larger and stockier than Shelley's Greenbul (p. 420), with blacker head and more conspicuous pale eye-ring. Told from Stripe-cheeked Greenbul (p. 420) by black-and- grey (not olive) head, pale eye-ring and dark (not pale) eye. **Habitat:** Mid-altitude and montane forests. **Status:** Common. **Voice:** Noisy: various nasal and chirpy phrases.

5 ULUGURU MOUNTAIN GREENBUL *Andropadus neumanni* 18 cm
Endemic to Uluguru Mts, Tanzania. Closely resembles Black-headed Mountain Greenbul, but lacks a pale eye-ring. Larger and stockier than Shelley's Greenbul (p. 420), with blacker head and more conspicuous pale eye-ring. Told from Stripe-faced Greenbul (p. 420) by black-and-grey (not olive) head, pale eye-ring and dark (not pale) eye. **Habitat:** Montane forest. **Status:** Common. **Voice:** Similar to that of other mountain greenbuls.

6 YELLOW-THROATED MOUNTAIN GREENBUL *Andropadus chlorigula* 18 cm
Endemic to S Tanzania (Udzungwa, Ukaguru and Nguru mts). Differs from other mountain greenbuls by having a dull olive-yellow (not grey) throat. Grey (not olive) crown and yellow throat separate it from Stripe-faced Greenbul (p. 420). **Habitat:** Mid-altitude and montane forests. **Status:** Common. **Voice:** Noisy: loud bursts of both nasal 'chzzr' notes and more melodic whistles and chirps. [C9.48b]

7 SOUTHERN MOUNTAIN GREENBUL *Andropadus fusciceps* 18 cm
Endemic to Malawi, N Mozambique and extreme S Tanzania (Mt Rungwe and Poroto Mts). Lacks yellow throat of Yellow-throated Mountain Greenbul. Differs from Stripe-cheeked and Olive-headed greenbuls (p. 420) by having plain grey head with faint black eye-stripe (lacking dark cheeks); eye is dark. Larger than Shelley's Greenbul (p. 420), with grey (not olive) head and more obvious white eye-ring. **Habitat:** Montane forest and forest edge. **Status:** Locally common. **Voice:** Variable greenbul-like chatterings; lower-pitched 'kwo kwor' notes. [C9.48a]

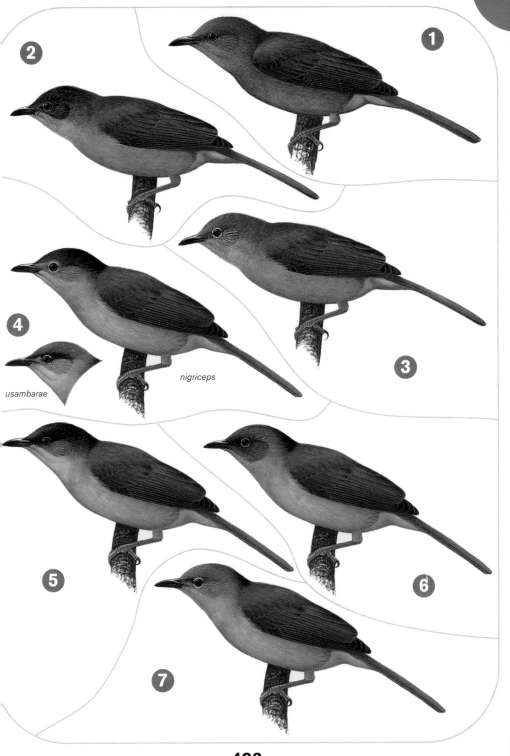

usambarae

nigriceps

Fairly large, stocky greenbuls with strong bills. Most avoid forest, occurring in dense tangles in more open habitats. Often found in small, noisy groups. Sexes alike.

1 SIMPLE GREENBUL (LEAF-LOVE) *Chlorocichla simplex*　　19 cm
A skulking, dark brown bulbul with a conspicuous broken white eye-ring and white throat. Superficially resembles brownbuls (p. 414), but is stockier, with shorter bill and broken white eye-ring; ranges do not overlap. Told from white-throated *soror* Yellow-throated Leaf-love by white eye crescents, behaviour and call. **Habitat:** Forest edge, secondary growth, well-wooded savanna bordering gallery forest and plantations. **Status:** Common. **Voice:** Querulous, soft nasal chattering; short 'kwik' contact notes. [C9.63]

2 YELLOW-THROATED LEAF-LOVE (GREENBUL) *Chlorocichla flavicollis*　21 cm
A large, noisy bulbul with a bright yellow or white throat, which is frequently puffed out. Differs from bearded greenbuls (p. 426) by dark blackish-brown (not paler grey) face, more open habitat and distinctive calls. White-throated *soror* (Cameroon-N DRC and Ethiopia) is told from Simple Greenbul by paler eye, lack of conspicuous white eye-ring and more active, noisy behaviour. **Habitat:** Woodland and gallery forest, secondary growth and thicket clumps in marshy areas. **Status:** Common; usually in small groups. **Voice:** 'Chow' and 'chip chip' nasal contact calls; rambling, chattering song, softer than Swamp Palm Bulbul's. [C9.64]

3 FALKENSTEIN'S (YELLOW-NECKED) GREENBUL *Chlorocichla falkensteini* 20 cm
Large, with a distinctive yellow throat that contrasts with the rest of the pale ashy-grey underparts, bright green upperparts and dark red eye. Greener above than Yellow-throated Leaf-love, with paler, olive-green (not blackish-brown) face; underparts are pale grey (not brownish). Juv. has brown eyes. **Habitat:** Dense scrub, degraded forest and old plantations; very furtive, located mainly by song. **Status:** Locally common. **Voice:** Scratchy, nasal song, 'whit it it-errr it it err', rising in the middle with slight crescendo; nasal alarm calls. [C9.62]

4 YELLOW-BELLIED GREENBUL *Chlorocichla flaviventris*　　20-23 cm
A large, chunky greenbul with olive-brown upperparts and mostly yellow underparts, with a diagnostic narrow white crescent over the eye. Shows more contrast between upperparts and underparts than Joyful Greenbul; ranges do not overlap. Larger than Sombre Greenbul (p. 418), with yellower underparts and red (not pale) eye. Bright yellow underwing coverts are conspicuous in flight. **Habitat:** Thickets, dense woodland and forest edge. **Status:** Common. **Voice:** Monotonous, nasal 'nehr-nehr-nehr-nehr'; 'kwoar-tooarr' call. [C9.61, G4.13.4]

5 JOYFUL GREENBUL *Chlorocichla laetissima*　　20-21 cm
Endemic to E Africa. Similar to Yellow-bellied Greenbul, but is greener above, showing less contrast with the olive-yellow underparts. Has faint yellowish supercilium; lacks white eye crescents. Larger than Golden Greenbul, with dark (not pinkish) bill; also more noisy, frequenting mid-stratum in groups (not singly in canopy). **Habitat:** Forest mid-stratum and secondary growth. **Status:** Common. **Voice:** Noisy: explosive bubbling song, increasing in both volume and pitch; chattering 'whit whit' calls. [C9.60]

6 PRIGOGINE'S GREENBUL *Chlorocichla prigoginei*　　19-20 cm
Endemic to E DRC. Slightly smaller and darker than Joyful Greenbul, with grey lores and a pale eye-ring. Yellow throat contrasts with darker breast and belly. **Habitat:** Forest and riparian thickets, including slightly degraded areas, 1 300-1 800 m; usually in mid-stratum. **Status:** Endangered. Known from only Lendu Plateau and NW of Lake Edward, where it occurs with Joyful Greenbuls. **Voice:** Unknown.

7 GOLDEN GREENBUL *Calyptocichla serina*　　19 cm
A brightly coloured greenbul, superficially resembling Joyful Greenbul, but occurs in forest canopy where it feeds openly; does not skulk. Identified by bright golden-yellow belly and diagnostic long, slender pinkish-brown bill. Frequently perches in the open, remaining inactive for long periods. **Habitat:** Forest canopy, gallery forest and secondary growth, where it occurs closer to ground. **Status:** Common. **Voice:** Song is rather varied, whistled 'white tit tit' ot 'tit teooo'; thin 'tsip' or 'tseet' contact calls. [C9.56]

flavicollis

soror

425

Forest greenbuls with distinctive white or yellow throats frequently puffed out. They have long, hair-like plumes on the nape, visible only at short range. Usually occur in small, noisy groups in low- and mid-strata of forest. Sexes alike.

1 YELLOW-BEARDED GREENBUL *Criniger olivaceus* 18 cm
Endemic to Upper Guinea forests. A warm olive-green greenbul with a bright yellow throat, rufous-washed tail and narrow grey eye-ring. Smaller than Western Bearded Greenbul, with greener plumage, less prominent throat and different call and behaviour: forages higher, often clinging to vertical trunks in search of insects. **Habitat:** Forest. **Status:** Vulnerable. Uncommon. **Voice:** Song is 'chwup wut chweerr', deeper and slower than Red-tailed Greenbul's. [C9.85]

2 WESTERN BEARDED GREENBUL *Criniger barbatus* 22 cm
Endemic to W Africa. Larger and heavier-billed than Yellow-bearded Bulbul, with darker, greyish olive (not olive-green) breast and olive-brown (not uniform olive) head; throat is more puffy and erectile. Nigerian *ansorgeanus* is paler above, with white chin, pale yellow throat and more rufous tail and vent; intermediate with Eastern Bearded Greenbul, but songs differ and ranges do not overlap. Similar to Yellow-throated Leaf-love (p. 424), but has paler, greyish (not blackish-brown) face and occurs in different habitat. **Habitat:** Forest understorey and gallery forest; does not cling to vertical trunks like Yellow-bearded Greenbul. **Status:** Locally common. **Voice:** Song is deep, melodic 3-note 'turrup ree-ruuu'; crisp, clear 'ch-chlu chleree'; jumbled greenbul chattering and high-pitched, sunbird-like 'tsip tsip' contact call. [C9.82]

3 EASTERN BEARDED GREENBUL *Criniger chloronotus* 22 cm
The C African counterpart of Western Bearded Bulbul, with a white (not yellow) throat and brighter rufous tail. Larger than Red-tailed and White-bearded greenbuls, with heavier bill, brighter rufous tail and duller, greyer (not bright yellow) underparts; best told by call. Similar to white-throated *soror* race of Yellow-throated Leaf-love (p. 424), but has paler, greyish (not blackish-brown) face and occurs in different habitat. **Habitat:** Forest understorey and gallery forest. **Status:** Common. **Voice:** Wavering 2-note song, 'churrrr weeerrrr', slower and deeper than Western Bearded Greenbul's; bee-eater-like 'trrp trrp' call. [C9.83]

4 RED-TAILED GREENBUL *Criniger calurus* 18-20 cm
A bright olive-and-yellow greenbul with a startling white throat, which is often puffed out. Smaller then Eastern Bearded Greenbul, with much brighter yellow underparts and less obvious rufous tail (although tail colour varies geographically, and is richest in C and E Africa). Easily told from Western Bearded Greenbul by white (not yellow) throat. Forages higher up and more in the open, often searching for insects on bark of large trees. Extremely similar to White-bearded Greenbul; best differentiated by song, but also has yellowish (not buff-rufous) vent and dark (not whitish) lores. W African *verreauxi* has darker crown. **Habitat:** Forest, from understorey to undercanopy, and gallery forest. **Status:** Common. **Voice:** Short, whistled song, 'weet wheet-oo', similar to Common Bulbul's; 'chisk' alarm call. [C9.84]

5 WHITE-BEARDED GREENBUL *Criniger ndussumensis* 18-19 cm
Extremely similar to Red-tailed Greenbul; both species may occur in the same flock. White-bearded Greenbul has smaller, more slender bill, whitish loral spot, more olive on flanks, and undertail coverts more rufous than yellow. **Habitat:** Forest understorey and gallery forest. **Status:** Locally common. **Voice:** Slow, deep 'chwut hut weerr' song, similar to Yellow-bearded Greenbul's but much deeper and typically slower than Red-tailed Greenbul's; harsh 'chweerrr' call. [C9.86]

6 BLACK-COLLARED BULBUL *Neolestes torquatus* 16 cm
An aberrant bulbul with a diagnostic white throat, black gorget, grey head and plain olive-green upperparts. Recalls a small bush-shrike, but has liquid, bulbul-like song. Is rather sluggish, with upright stance. **Habitat:** Scrub and thickets in woodland, savanna and edge of gallery forest. **Status:** Locally common, but easily overlooked; in pairs or family groups. **Voice:** Rapid, liquid song, similar to Dark-capped Bulbul's; sings from canopy of bushes and trees, sometimes perching in the open. [C9.87]

verreauxi

BRISTLE-BILLS

Large, brightly coloured greenbuls that forage on or close to the ground, often attending ant swarms. Sexes alike; juvs rufous-brown above and paler below.

1 RED-TAILED BRISTLE-BILL *Bleda syndactylus* 23 cm

The only bristle-bill with a rufous tail (conspicuous in flight) and a distinctive, large patch of blue skin above the eye. Larger than other greenbuls with rufous tail (e.g. bearded greenbuls, p. 426) and occurs on or near the ground. Active and fast-moving, often flicking tail. **Habitat:** Forest and gallery forest. **Status:** Common but shy. **Voice:** Short series of wavering whistles, usually descending in pitch; loud, nasal 'chowp' contact call. [C9.78]

2 GREEN-TAILED BRISTLE-BILL *Bleda eximius* 23 cm

Endemic to Upper Guinea forests. Often lumped with Yellow-lored Bristle-bill, but is larger, with smaller yellow tail spots and dark greyish (not yellow) lores; ranges do not overlap. Olive (not grey) head separates it from Grey-headed Bristle-bill. **Habitat:** Forest understorey. **Status:** Vulnerable. Local and uncommon. **Voice:** Series of whistles, usually slightly higher-pitched and less wavering than Red-tailed Bristle-bill's; sharp 'tcheet' alarm call. [C9.79]

3 YELLOW-LORED (LESSER) BRISTLE-BILL *Bleda notatus* 18-21 cm

Often lumped with Yellow-eyed and Green-tailed bristle-bills, but is smaller, with bright yellow lores; size of yellow tail tips is intermediate; ranges do not overlap. Range may overlap with Grey-headed Bristle-bill in W, but has distinctive yellow lores and olive (not grey) crown and nape. **Habitat:** Forest understorey, especially near water. **Status:** Uncommon. **Voice:** Loud series of descending whistles, usually starting with sharp 'tchip chip-oop-oop', and ending in dry trill. [C9.81]

4 YELLOW-EYED BRISTLE-BILL *Bleda ugandae* 20-22 cm

Often lumped with Yellow-lored Bristle-bill, but has larger yellow tail tips and lacks contrasting yellow lores; ranges not known to overlap. Told from Red-tailed Bristle-bill by its yellow-tipped green (not reddish) tail and yellow (not red-brown) eye. **Habitat:** Forest understorey. **Status:** Common. **Voice:** Contact call is 'tak tak'; song is a series of descending whistles similar to those of Yellow-lored Bristle-bill's.

5 GREY-HEADED BRISTLE-BILL *Bleda canicapillus* 22 cm

Grey (not olive) crown, nape and ear coverts, contrasting with olive back, are diagnostic. Outer-tail is broadly tipped yellow, with equally large tips to all four outer feathers (not increasing in size towards edge of tail). **Habitat:** Forest understorey and gallery forest; more often at forest edge and in secondary growth than other bristle-bills. **Status:** Common. **Voice:** Loud 'cheeow cheeow' contact call; song is variable, rich series of whistles, more slurry than Red-tailed Bristle-bill's. [C9.80]

HONEYGUIDE GREENBULS

Similar to *Andropadus* greenbuls (p. 418), but with white outer-tails like honeyguides (p. 310). Sexes similar; juvs duller.

6 HONEYGUIDE GREENBUL *Baeopogon indicator* 19 cm

Distinctive white outer-tail feathers have narrow dark tips (not entirely white, as Sjöstedt's Greenbul). Plain head and throat, and greyish-white (not creamy-buff) belly separate it from Sjöstedt's Greenbul. Male has diagnostic white eye; female and juv. have dark eyes. Juv's outer-tail entirely white. **Habitat:** Canopy of forest, gallery forest and secondary growth. **Status:** Common, but easily overlooked if not calling. **Voice:** Clear series of robin-chat-like whistles, 'treee teee leeeu', descending at end, or red-winged starling-like 'tleeoou'; softer mewing calls. [C9.57]

7 SJÖSTEDT'S GREENBUL *Baeopogon clamans* 19 cm

Paler than Honeyguide Greenbul, with creamy-buff underparts and a paler throat; outer-tail is entirely white (lacking dark tip, but beware juv. Honeyguide Greenbul). Eye dull red (not white, as male Honeyguide Greenbul). **Habitat:** Forest understorey and mid- to lower canopy, gallery forest and forest edge. **Status:** Locally common. **Voice:** Sharp, nasal 'nehr', repeated monotonously; sometimes ends with brief, rollicking flourish. [C9.58]

429

1 SWAMP PALM BULBUL *Thescelocichla leucopleura* 22 cm
A large, dark-backed bulbul related to leaf-loves but with diagnostic broad white tips to the outer feathers of the long, graduated tail. Whitish throat contrasts with grey-streaked face and breast; belly is creamy. White tail tip is conspicuous because it frequently fans its tail as it clambers along branches. Juv. has yellow wash to throat and breast. **Habitat:** Forest and secondary growth, usually near water. **Status:** Common; conspicuous, usually in noisy groups. **Voice:** Querulous, nasal calls; loud, babbler-like chattering. [C9.65]

2 LIBERIAN (WHITE-WINGED) GREENBUL *Phyllastrephus leucolepis* 16-17 cm
Endemic to Liberia. Closely resembles Icterine and Xavier's greenbuls (p. 412), but has creamy white wing spots on the tips of the greater coverts and flight feathers, forming an obvious wing-bar and whitish trailing edge to the wing. Darker below than Spotted Greenbul, with rufous tail (lacking white outer-tail) and plain (not spotted) shoulders, scapulars and rump. Much smaller than Western Nicator, with weaker bill and yellow-olive (not white) underparts. **Habitat:** Forest understorey. **Status:** Critically threatened. Rare, known only from two forests near Zwedru, SE Liberia. **Voice:** Unknown.

3 SPOTTED GREENBUL *Ixonotus guttatus* 17 cm
The pale underparts, white-spotted wings and rump and white outer-tail are diagnostic. Much paler beneath than Liberian Greenbul, honeyguide greenbuls (p. 428) and Yellow-throated Nicator. Smaller than Eastern and Western nicators, and differs from all nicators by white outer-tail (not yellow tips to outer-tail), white (not yellow) spots and noisy, gregarious behaviour. Very active, continuously wing-flicking. **Habitat:** Forest canopy and edge, gallery forest and secondary growth. **Status:** Common; usually in large, vocal flocks. **Voice:** Noisy; dry, high-pitched 'tik tik' calls. [C9.59]

NICATORS
Peculiar greenbuls with convergent similarities to bush-shrikes, including heavy, hook-tipped bills. They could possibly be confused with *Malaconotus* bush-shrikes that also have yellow-spotted wings (p. 594). Skulking, they occur singly or in pairs. Sexes alike; juvs duller, with yellow-tipped primaries in the two larger species.

4 EASTERN (YELLOW-SPOTTED) NICATOR *Nicator gularis* 20-23 cm
Endemic to SE Africa. Fairly large, with prominent yellow spots on the wing coverts and tertials. Yellow tips to outer-tail are obvious in flight. Differs from Western Nicator by buffy-brown (not olive-green) face and lores; ranges do not overlap. **Habitat:** Dense riverine and coastal forests and scrub, particularly on sandy soil. **Status:** Common, but easily overlooked if not calling. **Voice:** Distinctive song is short, rich, explosive, liquid jumble of notes. [G4.12.5]

5 WESTERN NICATOR *Nicator chloris* 20-23 cm
Forms a superspecies with Eastern Nicator, differing by having olive-green (not buffy-brown) face and lores; ranges do not overlap. Larger than Yellow-throated Nicator, with paler face and underparts; at close range, shows small white spot in front of eye but not yellow supra-loral stripe. Skulking behaviour and call distinguish it from Spotted Greenbul. **Habitat:** Forest understorey, gallery forest, edge of forest, and secondary growth, in dense vegetation. **Status:** Common. **Voice:** Explosive liquid song, similar to Eastern Nicator's. [C14.1a]

6 YELLOW-THROATED NICATOR *Nicator vireo* 14-16 cm
Smaller than other nicators, with a diagnostic yellow supra-loral stripe and yellowish throat; from a distance, appears darker-faced than Western Nicator, with darker, greyer underparts. General behaviour and call easily separate it from any spotted greenbuls. **Habitat:** Dense forest understorey, mainly at edges, and thick secondary growth. **Status:** Locally common; even more skulking than Western Nicator. **Voice:** Song is regular series of notes, rising and falling in pitch, quite different from those of other nicators. [C14.1b]

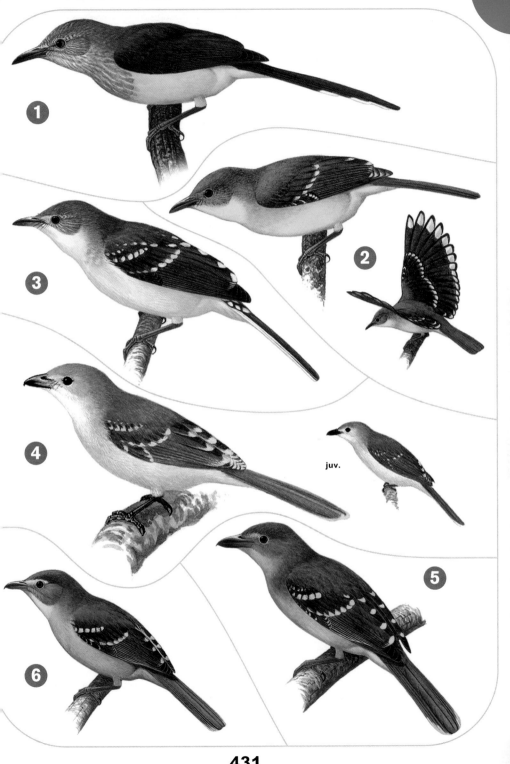

RUFOUS THRUSHES
A peculiar African genus of forest birds, with two thrush-like species (often called ant-thrushes) and two flycatcher-like species (flycatcher-thrushes, often placed in *Stizorhina*). The thrush-like species have longer legs and bill, and are often associated with ant swarms. The two flycatcher-like species have a more vertical posture and a shorter, broader bill. Sexes alike.

1 RED-TAILED RUFOUS THRUSH (ANT-THRUSH) *Neocossyphus rufus* 22 cm
A large thrush of the forest understorey. Rufous outer-tail, warm brown upperparts with little contrast to underparts, and lack of wing bar in flight separate it from White-tailed Rufous Thrush. Thrush-like posture and behaviour and lack of wing bar separate it from Fraser's Rufous Thrush. Juv. is duller. E coast nominate race has paler throat and less grey on breast; call differs. **Habitat:** Forests, usually near ground. **Status:** Common; typically associated with ant swarms. **Voice:** 1-2 whistles, first usually prolonged and descending; may be preceded by sharp crack (C Africa) or 'trrrt' (E coast). [C10.5]

2 WHITE-TAILED RUFOUS THRUSH (ANT-THRUSH)
Neocossyphus poensis 20 cm
A thrush-like rufous thrush, told from Red-tailed Rufous Thrush by its darker upperparts, which show more contrast with rufous underparts, and blackish (not rufous) tail, with white outer tips, obvious in flight. Rufous bases to flight feathers form a conspicuous wing bar in flight. **Habitat:** Forest understorey. **Status:** Common, but shy and very mobile in forest understorey; often associated with ant swarms. **Voice:** Song is long, ascending whistle; flight call is dry 'trrrt'. [C10.6]

3 FINSCH'S RUFOUS THRUSH (FINSCH'S FLYCATCHER-THRUSH)
Neocossyphus finschii 19 cm
Endemic to W Africa, where it replaces Fraser's Rufous Thrush. A flycatcher-like rufous thrush with white inner webs to outer-tail feathers, dark brown upperparts and rufous under-parts. Best told from White-tailed Rufous Thrush by its flycatcher-like (not thrush-like) behaviour, but also is browner (not slaty) above, and lacks rufous wing bars in flight. **Habitat:** Forest, from understorey to lower canopy. **Status:** Common; often in bird parties; sometimes associated with ant swarms. **Voice:** Song of 4 notes, lower pitched and slower than that of Fraser's Rufous Thrush. [C10.8]

4 FRASER'S RUFOUS THRUSH (RUFOUS FLYCATCHER-THRUSH)
Neocossyphus fraseri 19 cm
A flycatcher-like rufous thrush, with shorter bill and legs, and a more vertical posture. Plumage recalls Red-tailed Rufous Thrush, but is darker, with rufous tips to tail (not outer-tail), and paler rufous wing bar in flight; behaviour also differs. Juv. is duller and darker. **Habitat:** Forest, from understorey to lower canopy. **Status:** Common; confident and demonstrative, foraging like a flycatcher from larger branches; sometimes associates with ant swarms. **Voice:** Characteristic song has 4-5 ascending whistles, with last note longest; alarm call is harsh chatter. [C10.7]

ROCK-THRUSHES
Distinctive, open-country thrushes, with marked sexual dimorphism. With the exception of the two Palearctic migrant species, their ranges are restricted, limiting the potential for identification problems.

5 BLUE ROCK-THRUSH *Monticola solitarius* 20 cm
Adult male is overall dark blue-grey, with blackish-brown wings and tail. Female is barred below; darker overall than female Rufous-tailed Rock-Thrush (p. 434), lacking any rufous on tail or rump. Juv. is spotted buff above. **Habitat:** Mountains, including forest inselbergs, quarries and sea cliffs. **Status:** Fairly common Palearctic migrant Sep-May. **Voice:** Penetrating, whistled 'uit-uit'; deep 'tak-tak' contact call. [C3.97]

1 CAPE ROCK-THRUSH *Monticola rupestris* 19-21 cm
Endemic to S Africa. A fairly large rock-thrush with a brownish (not blue-grey) back, longer tail and more horizontal stance than other S African species. Compared to Sentinel Rock-Thrush, male has blue-grey restricted to head (not onto breast and mantle). Female has darker rufous underparts than other female rock-thrushes. Juv. is spotted buff above, scaled blackish below. **Habitat:** Rocky areas in grassland and heaths. **Status:** Common. **Voice:** Song is far-carrying, 'tsee-tseu-tseet chweeeoo' whistle; alarm is harsh grating. [G4.14.1]

2 SENTINEL ROCK-THRUSH *Monticola explorator* 16-18 cm
Endemic to S Africa. A rather small, upright rock-thrush with a shortish tail. Male's blue-grey throat extending onto upper breast separates it from male Cape and Short-toed rock-thrushes; further told from Cape Rock-Thrush by its blue (not brown) back, and from Short-toed Rock-Thrush by its uniform blue-grey head (lacking pale crown). Female is smaller and paler than female Cape Rock-Thrush, with mottled (not uniformly rufous) breast; typically has paler, less rufous breast than female Short-toed Rock-Thrush. Juv. has pale-spotted upperparts and brown-scaled underparts. **Habitat:** Rocky terrain, usually in grassland or short heaths. **Status:** Locally common resident and partial altitudinal migrant. **Voice:** Whistled song similar to that of Cape Rock-Thrush but more varied and not as loud. [G4.14.2]

3 SHORT-TOED ROCK-THRUSH *Monticola brevipes* 16-18 cm
Endemic to SW Africa. Male's pale whitish-blue crown contrasting with darker blue-grey face is diagnostic; some birds have darker blue crown but they usually retain a pale supercilium. E *pretoriae* is duller, with browner crown (sometimes considered a separate species). Blue-grey throat does not extend onto breast as in Sentinel Rock-Thrush. Blue-grey (not brown) back separates it from Cape Rock-Thrush. Female is paler, with whitish throat patch streaked brown, and rufous breast and belly. Juv. is spotted with buff on upperparts and with black below. **Habitat:** Rocky outcrops, often with some bushes; usually in more arid areas than other rock-thrushes. **Status:** Common. **Voice:** Thin 'tseeep'; song of whistled phrases is like those of other rock-thrushes; includes some mimicry of other birds' calls. [G4.14.3]

4 RUFOUS-TAILED (MOUNTAIN/EUROPEAN) ROCK-THRUSH
Monticola saxatilis 18-20 cm
Breeding male (not illustrated) easily identified by its blue-grey head, darker slate-grey wings and white back patch; underparts entirely rufous, distinguishing it from Little Rock-Thrush (breast blue-grey) and Miombo Rock-Thrush (belly whitish). Female and non-breeding male are more extensively barred below (to lower belly) than other species except Blue Rock-Thrush (p. 432); differ from this species by rufous vent and outer-tail. **Habitat:** Grasslands and open savanna, often near boulders, erosion gullies or human settlements. **Status:** Fairly common Palearctic migrant Oct-Apr; scarce in W Africa. **Voice:** Mostly silent in Africa; occasional soft 'chack-chack' or throaty 'kschirrr'. [C3.96]

5 MIOMBO ROCK-THRUSH *Monticola angolensis* 16-18 cm
A woodland rock-thrush. Male has diagnostic black markings on its grey back; lacks white back patch of Rufous-tailed Rock-Thrush, and belly is whitish (not rufous). Female also has distinctly mottled upperparts and blackish malar stripes; rufous wash is limited to breast; belly and vent are whitish, lacking scalloping of female Rufous-tailed Rock-Thrush. Juv. is more heavily mottled below. **Habitat:** Miombo woodland, usually in hilly or rocky areas. **Status:** Locally common, although often fairly unobtrusive. **Voice:** 2-note whistle; song is high-pitched variety of melodic phrases. [C10.30, G4.14.4]

6 LITTLE ROCK-THRUSH *Monticola rufocinereus* 15-16 cm
Endemic to NE Africa. A small, rather chat-like rock-thrush. Smaller than other species, with a plain back and blue-grey throat extending onto the upper breast. Smaller and paler than female Mocking Cliff-chat (p. 472), with different tail pattern: tail and rump are rufous, with dark central tail feathers and tail tips (like Familiar Chat, p. 462). Female resembles male but is duller. Juv. is buff-flecked above and mottled below. Has peculiar habit of 'trembling' its tail, like a Common Redstart (p. 460). **Habitat:** Rocky areas with some trees; also around human settlements. **Status:** Fairly common, but patchy. **Voice:** Song 'tsurr-sureet, skeee, tsee-ee-tsurrrr'.

1 ♂ ♀

2 ♂ ♀

♀ *pretoriae* ♂

3 ♀ ♂ *brevipes*

4 non-br.

5 ♀ ♂

6 juv. ♀ ♂

Rufous-breasted forest thrushes separated from *Turdus* thrushes (p. 438) by their double white wing bars, dark (not yellow) bill and stockier build. Rather skulking, they forage near the ground, but often sing from elevated perches. Sexes alike; juvs duller with dark-spotted breasts and pale-streaked upperparts.

1 ABYSSINIAN GROUND-THRUSH *Zoothera piaggiae*   19-20 cm
Endemic to NE Africa. Lacks dark crown of Orange Ground-Thrush, and has weaker bill, no dark mark across eye, and more extensive orange on belly. Geographic variation, especially in Albertine Rift, is confused; *tanganjicae* differs by having entire crown and nape uniform orange-brown (nape and usually crown are darker in other races); sometimes treated as a separate species, Kivu Ground-Thrush. **Habitat:** Montane forest; usually at higher elevations than Orange Ground-Thrush. **Status:** Common, but easily overlooked unless singing. **Voice:** Contact call is high-pitched 'tseeep'; melodious song of clear, whistled phrases, 'chee-cheeleeroo-chruup'. [C10.35-36]

2 ORANGE GROUND-THRUSH *Zoothera gurneyi*   19-20 cm
Best told from Abyssinian Ground-Thrush (ranges overlap marginally in Kenya) by its more marked head pattern, with a darker crown, grey ear coverts and faint vertical dark bar through eye. White eye-ring is narrower and often broken. **Habitat:** Montane forests; in S, some winter at lower elevations. **Status:** Fairly common. **Voice:** Sibilant 'tseeep'; song is richer, lower pitched and slower than Abyssinian Ground-Thrush's. [C10.32, G4.13.9]

3 OBERLAENDER'S GROUND-THRUSH *Zoothera oberlaenderi*   18-19 cm
Endemic to Albertine Rift. Very similar to Abyssinian Ground-Thrush, but with vertical dark line through eye, which also breaks white eye-ring; best separated by very varied song; also generally occurs at lower altitude. Lacks pale face (contrasting with darker crown) and prominent dark mark on ear coverts of Black-eared and Grey ground-thrushes. **Habitat:** Mid-altitude and lowland rainforest, 700-1 600 m. **Status:** Near-threatened. Uncommon and local. **Voice:** Very varied song; notes are sweet and rich, with little repetition.

4 CROSSLEY'S GROUND-THRUSH *Zoothera crossleyi*   21-22 cm
Localised, montane ground-thrush; forms a superspecies with Orange Ground-Thrush. In E DRC, is larger than Oberlaender's Ground-Thrush, with more extensive black face and lores, and white eye-ring restricted to behind eye. Occurs at higher altitudes than Black-eared and Grey ground-thrushes in W Africa; easily distinguished by lack of two dark bars on face and ear-coverts. **Habitat:** Montane and mid-altitude rainforest, mostly 1 000-2 300 m, but down to 200 m on Mt Cameroon; DRC population at 500 m. **Status:** Near-threatened. Locally common in SE Cameroon. **Voice:** Similar to Orange Ground-Thrush's. [C10.31]

5 BLACK-EARED GROUND-THRUSH *Zoothera camaronensis*   18 cm
Endemic to C Africa. Separated from all other ground-thrushes except Grey Ground-Thrush by its pale face that contrasts with twin vertical black face bars and dark cap. Varies geographically: nominate W African race is orange-chestnut below (much more richly coloured than Grey Ground-Thrush); E African *graueri* is rufous-brown below (approaching Grey Ground-Thrush in colour), best told by buffy (not white) face, lightly streaked breast, and smaller size and more compact shape. Two specimens from Kibale Forest, Uganda, were rufous below; sometimes considered a separate species, Kibale Ground-Thrush *Z. kibalensis*. **Habitat:** Near the ground in primary forest, usually in humid areas. **Status:** Local and uncommon to rare. **Voice:** High-pitched 'tseep' call; song is unknown. [C10.33]

6 GREY GROUND-THRUSH *Zoothera princei*   19-20 cm
A rather large, drab ground-thrush with a conspicuous white face contrasting with olive-brown crown and two vertical black face bars. Larger and more elongate than Black-eared Ground-Thrush, but best told by its greyish-brown (not rufous) underparts. Only ground-thrush in Upper Guinea forests. Could be confused with Forest Scrub-Robin (p. 456), but is larger with distinctive head pattern. **Habitat:** Primary forest understorey, near ground. **Status:** Local and uncommon; furtive and seldom seen. **Voice:** High-pitched 'tseep' call; song is unknown. [C10.34]

1 SPOTTED GROUND-THRUSH *Zoothera guttata*   19-21 cm
The only ground-thrush with a spotted breast. Superficially recalls Groundscraper Thrush, but is easily told by its bold white wing bars, longer tail, more horizontal stance and forest habitat. Pale pink legs are conspicuous. **Habitat:** Forest understorey; from coastal forests in S to montane forests in Malawi. **Status:** Endangered. Rare resident (Malawi) or partial migrant (South Africa and E Africa), wintering to N of breeding areas in coastal forests; populations in DRC and Sudan known from only single specimens. **Voice:** Quiet 'tseeeep' call; song is whistled and fluty, with short phrases of 4-5 notes. [G4.13.8]

2 GROUNDSCRAPER THRUSH *Psophocichla litsipsirupa*   22-24 cm
A distinctive, open-country thrush with a characteristic upright stance and short tail. Has prominent chestnut wing panel in flight, but lacks white wing bars of Spotted Ground-Thrush and has bolder, more contrasting face markings; habitat also differs. Overlaps with Song Thrush in NE; told by bold black-and-white ear coverts. Larger than Dusky Lark (p. 344), with bolder face markings and plain upperparts (lacks pale edges to wing feathers). Abyssinian *simensis* buffy below. **Habitat:** Open woodland, savanna and montane grassland. **Status:** Common. **Voice:** Song is less melodic than those of other thrushes; series of slow notes, 'lit-sit-si-rupa'; also clicking call. [C10.37, G4.13.10]

TURDUS THRUSHES
Large thrushes, usually with some rufous on the belly or flanks. All lack the white wing bars of *Zoothera* ground-thrushes. Sexes alike in most species; the short-lived juv. plumage has the breast and belly mottled with black.

3 SONG THRUSH *Turdus philomelos*   20 cm
The only spot-breasted thrush in most of N Africa. Overlaps with Groundscraper Thrush in NE, but has brown (not black-and-white) ear-coverts, longer tail and more horizontal stance; lacks chestnut wing panel in flight. **Habitat:** Acacia scrub and arid savanna. **Status:** Palearctic migrant Oct-Apr; uncommon inland, fairly common along Red Sea coast. **Voice:** Usually silent; sharp 'tchuk-tchuk' alarm call. [C3.99]

4 SÃO TOMÉ THRUSH *Turdus olivaceofuscus*   24 cm
Endemic to São Tomé, where it is the only thrush. Large, with earth-brown upperparts and distinct brown bars and crescents on white underparts. Underwing coverts are rufous. **Habitat:** Forest understorey, secondary growth and plantations. **Status:** Locally common. **Voice:** Repetitive phrase of 2-3 liquid whistles followed by a few short, sharp notes. [C10.39]

5 PRÌNCIPÉ THRUSH *Turdus xanthorhynchus*   24 cm
Endemic to Prìncipé Island, where it is the only thrush. Often considered a race of São Tomé Thrush, but has very bright orange-yellow (not brown) bill, paler legs and feet, and is whiter beneath, with broader bars. **Habitat:** Remote, primary rainforest. Confined to higher elevations. **Status:** Virtually unknown; only a few recent observations near Table Mountain. **Voice:** Not described.

6 BARE-EYED THRUSH *Turdus tephronotus*   20 cm
Endemic to NE Africa. An arid-country thrush with a diagnostic large orange-yellow patch of bare skin around the eye. Paler grey above than African and Olive thrushes (p. 440), with streaked throat. Range overlaps slightly with Kurrichane Thrush in N Tanzania; told by more rufous belly, more evenly streaked throat and large bare eye patch. **Habitat:** Dry acacia thickets and woodland. **Status:** Locally common but retiring. **Voice:** Song is rather monotonous, bubbling, nasal trill, often followed by 2-3 higher-pitched notes; rattling 'chrrrr' call.

7 KURRICHANE THRUSH *Turdus libonyanus*   21 cm
A pale grey thrush with a white belly and rufous flanks. Black speckling on throat is concentrated into diagnostic broad black malar stripes. Bill is brighter orange than those of most other African thrushes (except Bare-eyed Thrush); has narrow yellow eye-ring, but lacks large bare patch of Bare-eyed Thrush. **Habitat:** Woodland, especially miombo, and parks and gardens. **Status:** Common. **Voice:** Loud, whistling 'peet-peeoo'. [C10.41, G4.13.6]

1 AFRICAN THRUSH *Turdus pelios* 21 cm
A widespread, variable thrush; taxonomy is not well resolved. The only resident thrush throughout most of its range, but overlaps with Mountain Thrush in E; typically is paler, appearing faded, and has yellow (not orange) bill; looks longer legged and more elongate; best told by unbroken song (not in discrete phrases). Zambian *stormsi* is more richly coloured, closer to Mountain Thrush. **Habitat:** Woodland, forest edge and gardens. **Status:** Locally common. **Voice:** Loud, continuous, liquid song. [C10.40]

2 OLIVE THRUSH *Turdus olivaceus* 22 cm
Endemic to S Africa. Recently split from E African forms on genetic differences, but field characters not well resolved, and status of Zimbabwean *swynnertoni* is uncertain; ranges do not overlap. Has much more extensive rufous underparts than Karoo Thrush, with white (not grey) vent. Darker than Kurrichane Thrush (p. 438), with more yellow-orange (not bright orange) bill and no black malar stripes. **Habitat:** Forests, parks, gardens and plantations. **Status:** Common. **Voice:** Sharp 'chink' or thin 'tseeep' call; song is composed of repeated short phrases, 'wheeet-tooo-wheeet'. [G4.13.7]

3 MOUNTAIN THRUSH *Turdus abyssinicus* 22 cm
A variable forest thrush of E Africa. Recently split from Olive, Usumbara and Taita thrushes; ranges do not overlap. Generally darker, with more orange bill than African Thrush, but best told by punctuated (not unbroken) song. Also darker than Kurrichane Thrush (p. 438) with more yellow-orange (not bright orange) bill and no black malar stripes. Generally darker at higher elevations; S and N populations may be distinct species. **Habitat:** Forests; also suburban parks and gardens, and plantations. **Status:** Common. **Voice:** Sharp 'chink' or thin 'tseeep' call; song is similar to Olive Thrush's. [C10.38]

4 USAMBARA THRUSH *Turdus roehli* 22 cm
Endemic to Usambara and Pare Mts, NE Tanzania. Recently split from Olive and Mountain thrushes, with a darker, blackish head and very rich rufous flanks contrasting with white belly. Told from Taita Thrush by streaked (not blackish) throat, paler breast and mottled vent; ranges do not overlap. **Habitat:** Montane forest; forages in leaf litter beneath dense undergrowth; also in mid-canopy. **Status:** Locally common. **Voice:** Soft 'tseeeep' contact call; song is similar to Olive Thrush's.

5 TAITA THRUSH *Turdus helleri* 22 cm
Endemic to Taita Hills, Kenya. Part of the Olive Thrush complex; closest to Usambara Thrush, but has blackish (not streaked) throat, darker breast and plain white (not mottled) vent; ranges do not overlap. Bill, legs and eye-ring are bright orange. **Habitat:** Montane forest. **Status:** Critically endangered by habitat loss. Only 1 350 birds remain in three populations. **Voice:** Soft 'tseeeep' contact call; song is similar to Olive Thrush's.

6 SOMALI THRUSH (SOMALI BLACKBIRD) *Turdus ludoviciae* 23 cm
Endemic to N Somalia. Black head and breast and grey underparts are unique among African thrushes. Female is streaked and mottled, with white throat and streaked breast. **Habitat:** Highland forests, especially Juniper and Hygenea. **Status:** Uncertain; no recent surveys. Assumed to be critically endangered by habitat loss, but was locally common in 1970s. **Voice:** Harsh, Blackbird-like, chattering alarm call; song undescribed. **Similar species: Ring Ouzel** *T. torquatus* is black, with paler wings, and usually has white or pale breast band; imm. is scaled grey; Palearctic vagrant to N.

7 KAROO THRUSH *Turdus smithi* 22 cm
Endemic to S Africa. Recently split from Olive Thrush; differs by being darker beneath, with little rufous (typically restricted to belly), and greyish (not white) vent. Usually has an orange eye-ring, which is absent in Olive Thrush, and bill appears brighter due to contrast with dark breast. May hybridise with Olive Thrush in contact zones, but ranges usually discrete, with Karoo Thrush in more arid areas. **Habitat:** Denser vegetation in semi-arid Karoo scrub, savanna and grassland; also gardens. **Status:** Locally common. **Voice:** Soft 'tseeeep' contact call; song is similar to Olive Thrush's. [G4.13.7]

stormsi

typical races

juv.

441

Medium-sized, drab forest thrushes. Typically skulking and single, several birds may gather to feed at ant swarms. Sexes alike; juvs are buff-spotted above, with scalloped underparts (typically rufous-chestnut feathers with dark brown edges). Recent evidence suggests that the Fire-crested Alethe complex is not closely related to other alethes.

1 WHITE-TAILED ALETHE *Pseudalethe diademata* 18 cm
Endemic to Upper Guinea forests. Larger than Brown-chested Alethe, with a grey head, no pale supercilium, and a bright rufous crown. Underparts are whitish (not buffy-brown), with grey sides to breast. Formerly lumped with Fire-crested Alethe; differs by having white subterminal tips to outer-tail (not rufous outer-tail) and darker brown back; ranges do not overlap. **Habitat:** Primary forest. **Status:** Locally common; often at ant columns. **Voice:** Similar to Fire-crested Alethe's, but usually only 1-2 notes. [C10.3b]

2 FIRE-CRESTED ALETHE *Pseudalethe castanea* 18 cm
Larger than Brown-chested alethe, with a grey head, no pale supercilium, and a bright rufous crown. Underparts are whitish (not buffy-brown), with grey sides to breast. Forms a super-species with White-tailed Alethe; ranges do not overlap. Differs in being warmer brown above and has rufous (not white) outer-tail. **Habitat:** Primary forest. **Status:** Common; often at ant swarms. **Voice:** Most frequent call is monotonous whistle of usually 2-3 ascending notes (one of the characteristic calls of lowland forest); also more varied song with mimicked elements. [C10.3b]

3 RED-THROATED ALETHE *Alethe poliophrys* 15 cm
Endemic to Albertine Rift. Dull red throat, grey supercilium and black crown and face are diagnostic. Occurs at higher elevation than Fire-crested Alethe, but overlaps narrowly with Brown-chested Alethe; best told by rufous (not white) throat. **Habitat:** Montane rainforest and forest edge above 1 300 m, especially near water. **Status:** Common; usually at ant swarms. **Song.** Soft, slightly slurred, single-note 'peeeyooo'; alarm call is soft 'chaa-chaa-chaa'; faint chirping notes. [C10.4a]

4 BROWN-CHESTED ALETHE *Alethe poliocephala* 15 cm
A rather small, robin-like alethe. Buffy-brown breast and flanks contrasting with white throat are diagnostic. Crown is dark, with paler supercilium (most obvious in frontal view). Could be confused with illadopsises (p. 406), but is slightly larger, with paler belly and pale supercilium. **Habitat:** Forest understorey, often near ant columns. **Status:** Locally common, but easily overlooked. **Voice:** Generally silent; song is series of 5-8 descending whistles; harsh calls when feeding at ant swarms. [C10.4b]

5 WHITE-CHESTED ALETHE *Alethe fuelleborni* 18-20 cm
Endemic to SE Africa. A large, rather chunky alethe with diagnostic crisp white underparts contrasting sharply with brown flanks and rich chestnut upperparts. Lacks white tail tips of Thyolo Alethe. **Habitat:** Forest, occurring to coast in S, but only above 900 m in Eastern Arc Mts. **Status:** Uncommon to locally common. **Voice:** Lively, slightly mournful and vibrato 'fweer-her-hee-her-hee-her' series of whistles. [G5.1.5]

6 THYOLO (CHOLO) ALETHE *Alethe choloensis* 18 cm
Endemic to S Malawi and N Mozambique. Forms a superspecies with White-chested Alethe; ranges do not overlap. Differs in having white tail tips and grey-washed (not white) under-parts. **Habitat:** Mid-altitude forest and adjacent secondary growth. **Status:** Endangered. Uncommon at most sites, but fairly common at Namuli. **Voice:** Typical alethe contact 'wheeoo' whistle; short, warbled song, higher pitched and more variable than that of White-chested Alethe.

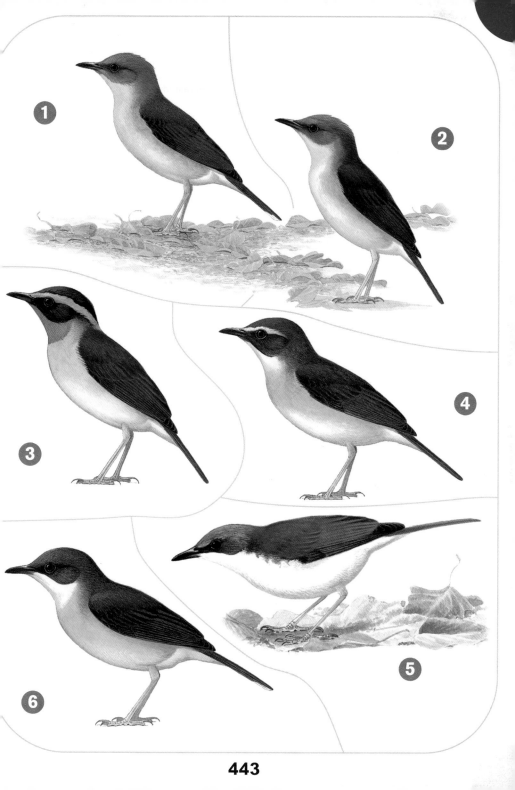

Small, rather short-tailed robins found in the lower strata of forests and dense woodland. Most are rufous-breasted, and could be confused with smaller robin-chats and forest robins; others are brown and nondescript, and can best be told from other forest-understorey groups such as illadopsises (p. 406) by their long legs, upright stance and robin-like gait. Sexes alike; juvs are darker, with spotted plumage. Recent evidence suggests akalats are not a natural group.

1 LOWLAND AKALAT *Sheppardia cyornithopsis*   13 cm
A small, dull robin of W and C African forest understorey. Very similar to Equatorial Akalat, but in E Africa where ranges abut, *lopesi* has brown (not rufous) flanks and typically occurs at lower elevations. W African birds have rufous flanks and could be confused with Bocage's Akalat, but have brown (not rufous) cheeks, no grey on face, and occur at lower elevations. **Habitat:** Forest understorey, often near water or in dense undergrowth; usually below 1 000 m; rarely to 1 500 m. **Status:** Local and uncommon; not shy, but seldom seen. **Voice:** Series of soft whistles, 'whee whiu, whee whiu'. [C9.92]

2 EQUATORIAL AKALAT *Sheppardia aequatorialis*   13 cm
Endemic to E Africa. Very similar to Lowland Akalat, but typically occurs at higher elevations where ranges abut; distinguished by rufous (not brown) flanks and slightly less extensive white on the belly. Range does not overlap with those of other akalats. **Habitat:** Forest understorey, above 1 100 m; usually above 1 600 m. **Status:** Locally common, but retiring and easily overlooked. **Voice:** Soft, purred 'prrrr prrrr'. [C9.93]

3 SHARPE'S AKALAT *Sheppardia sharpei*   12 cm
Endemic to Eastern Arc Mts of Tanzania and N Malawi. A small, rather dull brown akalat with a rufous throat and breast, and pale grey supercilium. Range overlaps with Usambara and Iringa ground robins (p. 446), but is smaller with rufous (not brown) underparts (but can appear drab in poor light). Plain brown above, with wings the same colour as back (unlike East Coast Akalat); lacks yellow in tail of juv. or imm. White-starred Robin (p. 452). **Habitat:** Montane forest and secondary growth. **Status:** Locally common; usually singly or in pairs; most easily detected by song. **Voice:** Soft, thin, high-pitched series of 'sweee tssee' notes, rapidly concluding; contact call is 'chink chink'.

4 EAST COAST (GUNNING'S) AKALAT *Sheppardia gunningi*   11-12 cm
Endemic to SE Africa, with three disjunct populations. Similar to Sharpe's Akalat, but with greyish face, supercilium and shoulders contrasting with brown crown and back; ranges do not overlap; occurs at lower elevations. **Habitat:** Understorey of lowland forest and thickets in dense woodland. **Status:** Vulnerable. Locally common. **Voice:** Alarm is series of piping 'seeep' notes; fast, high-pitched but not loud song of several short phrases, frequently repeated. [G5.1.8]

5 BOCAGE'S AKALAT *Sheppardia bocagei*   13-15 cm
A small, drab brown and dull orange forest robin. Slightly smaller than Grey-winged Robin-Chat, and lacks white supercilium. Orange extends up onto cheek, unlike in Lowland Akalat and White-bellied Robin-Chat (p. 452). N races are darker on crown and have brighter orange underparts; sometimes considered a separate species, *S. insulana*. **Habitat:** Lowland forest in S, montane forest in N. **Status:** Locally common but easily overlooked. **Voice:** Typical akalat high-pitched song of 5-10 notes, last few notes on higher pitch; harsh, rattling squeak, not unlike contact call of African Dusky Flycatcher. [C9.90]

6 GREY-WINGED ROBIN-CHAT *Cossypha polioptera*   14-15 cm
Resembles a large akalat, and has a uniform rufous-brown tail (unlike most robin-chats), but strong, varied song is typical of a robin-chat. Slightly larger than Bocage's Akalat, with brighter orange underparts and a short, white supercilium. W African *nigriceps* has black crown. **Habitat:** Lowland to mid-altitude forest, riverine forest and degraded and secondary forests. **Status:** Locally common, but easily overlooked. **Voice:** Most easily detected by rich, melodic mimicry of whole range of sounds; similar to Red-capped Robin-Chat's, but higher pitched. [C10.1a]

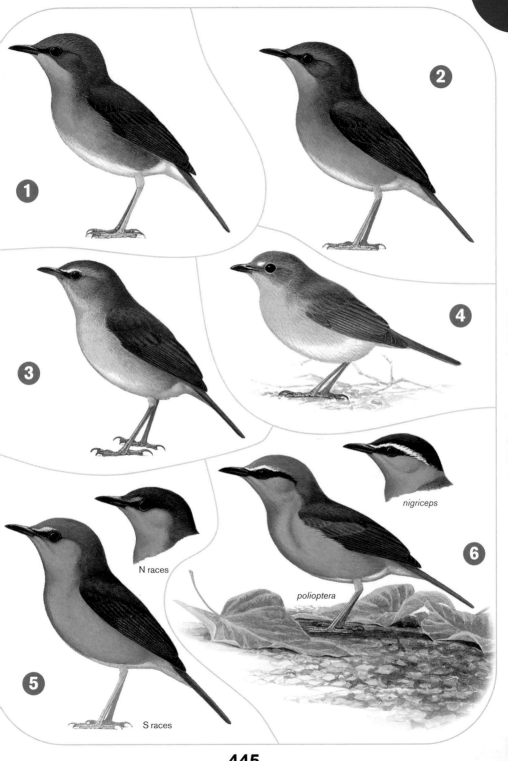

1

2

3

4

nigriceps

N races

polioptera

5

6

S races

1 GABELA AKALAT *Sheppardia gabela* 12-13 cm
Endemic to Angola. A small, drab brown akalat with a brown breast band and paler throat and belly. Smaller than Bocage's Akalat (p. 444), with no orange on underparts. Short, plain brown tail prevents confusion with scrub-robins; smaller than Pale-olive Greenbul (p. 416), with very different stance and gait. **Habitat:** Mid-altitude forest, thickets in secondary growth and understorey in coffee plantations. **Status:** Endangered. Little known. **Voice:** Series of soft, simple descending whistles.

2 USAMBARA GROUND ROBIN (AKALAT) *Sheppardia montana* 13 cm
Endemic to W Usambara Mts, N Tanzania. A nondescript, drab brown akalat with a paler belly. Tail is slightly more rufous than brown upperparts. Appears very lanky as it bounds over forest floor on long legs. **Habitat:** Dense thickets in understorey of montane forest above 1 600 m. **Status:** Endangered. Generally uncommon. Best observed at dawn and dusk. **Voice:** Soft 'tssh' contact note; thin, weak, high-pitched song.

3 IRINGA GROUND ROBIN (AKALAT) *Sheppardia lowei* 13 cm
Endemic to Eastern Arc Mts, S Tanzania. Very similar to Usambara Ground Robin, but ranges do not overlap. Slightly larger and heavier than Sharpe's Akalat (p. 444), with buffy-brown (not rufous) breast, and shorter, buff (not whitish-grey) supercilium. **Habitat:** Dense thickets and drainage lines in understorey of mid-altitude forest. **Status:** Vulnerable. Uncommon and easily overlooked. **Voice:** Alarm note is harsh 'tchak'; whistled 'wree wree'.

FOREST ROBINS
Small, short-tailed robins, similar to akalats but with a narrower bill and a small white spot in front of the eye. Formerly considered a single species, recent work suggests there are four species: two western species with a rich orange breast and white belly, and two eastern species with a paler yellow-orange breast and creamy or yellow belly. Sexes alike; juvs are dull, with spotted plumage; the white eye spots develop before all the juv. plumage is lost.

4 WESTERN FOREST ROBIN *Stiphrornis erythrothorax* 11 cm
Endemic to W Africa. A small, forest-understorey robin, with a blackish face and a conspicuous white spot in front of the eye. Similar to Gabon Forest Robin, with bright orange throat and breast, and white belly, but is distinct in being dark olive-brown (not sooty-grey) above. **Habitat:** Forest understorey. **Status:** Common. **Voice:** High-pitched, fast, repetitive song, 'chi-er err, chi-er err, chi chee-ee'; grating alarm call. [C9.89a]

5 GABON FOREST ROBIN *Stiphrornis gabonensis* 11 cm
Localised endemic to W Africa. Very similar to Western Forest Robin, but is sooty-grey (not tinged olive) above. Female is overall more olive-grey. **Habitat:** Forest understorey. **Status:** Common. **Voice:** Song is like Western Forest Robin's, but usually shorter, 'che-aii, chai-eer', with a more abrupt ending. [C9.89b]

6 EASTERN FOREST ROBIN *Stiphrornis xanthogaster* 11 cm
Differs from other forest robins by having a pale yellow throat which contrasts with the darker yellow-orange breast; belly is cream (not white). **Habitat:** Forest understorey. **Status:** Common. **Voice:** Song is longer than Western and Gabon forest robins', sometimes almost continuous.

7 SANGHA FOREST ROBIN *Stiphrornis sanghensis* 11 cm
A recently described species, only known from Dzanga-Sangha Forest in SW Central African Republic. Belly is yellow (not creamy or white). Breast is yellow-orange, similar to Eastern Forest Robin's, but throat is same colour as breast. **Habitat:** Forest understorey. **Status:** Locally common. **Voice:** Song is similar to Eastern Forest Robin's, with 2 high chirps followed by 3 whistles; rolling trill call.

Medium-sized thrushes, usually with some rufous plumage, especially on the underparts and in the outer-tail. Typically found on or close to the ground in dense vegetation (forest or thickets); crepuscular. Most are accomplished songsters and mimics. Sexes alike; juvs are heavily spotted buff above, and mottled buffy-brown below, but have adult tail patterns.

1 WHITE-HEADED ROBIN-CHAT *Cossypha heinrichi* 22-23 cm
Endemic to WC Africa. A large forest robin with a white head and neck; no other robin-chat has an all-white head. Underparts are rufous-orange. Back and wings are more greyish brown than those of other large robin-chats, and long, graduated tail is reported to be frequently fanned. **Habitat:** Dense undergrowth in gallery forest and adjacent savanna in N Angola; in isolated forest patches in DRC. **Status:** Vulnerable. Known from only two sites, with an unconfirmed sighting further north in DRC. Singly or in pairs, but groups gather to feed on driver-ant columns. **Voice:** Undescribed.

2 SNOWY-CROWNED ROBIN-CHAT *Cossypha niveicapilla* 22 cm
A large robin-chat with a plain, blackish face and white crown. Smaller than White-crowned Robin-Chat, with black frons, orange chin, brown (not red) eye, and orange collar extending around side of neck. Unlike White-crowned Robin-Chat, wing feathers are edged blue-grey (only slightly in SE). White crown is narrow and could be confused with white supercilium of other robin-chats. **Habitat:** Forest edge, gallery forest, dense woodland and thickets in moist savanna. **Status:** Common; skulking in some areas, but familiar and easy to observe in others. **Voice:** Fast, fluty, thrush-like whistle, usually at dusk; also some mimicry. [C10.2b]

3 WHITE-CROWNED ROBIN-CHAT *Cossypha albicapilla* 23-24 cm
The largest robin-chat, with a plain, blackish face and variable white crown. Larger than Snowy-crowned Robin-Chat, with a narrow black chin, white on crown extending onto frons, and red (not brown) eye; lacks orange collar around side of neck. W African nominate race (Senegal-Guinea) has whitish crown, only lightly streaked black; E races have black crown scaled white. **Habitat:** Gallery forest and dense thickets, including gardens. Forages mostly among leaf litter on ground. **Status:** Widespread, uncommon to locally common. Shy, more often heard than seen. **Voice:** Varied, warbling song, often with some raspy notes; generally less melodic than other robin-chats, and not known to mimic. [C10.3a]

4 RED-CAPPED (NATAL) ROBIN-CHAT *Cossypha natalensis* 16-18 cm
The plain rufous face with conspicuous black eyes, and slaty-blue back and wings, are dia-gnostic. Crown and nape are reddish brown. When alarmed, frequently flicks up its tail, then slowly lowers it. **Habitat:** Thickets and tangles in forest and dense woodland. Usually occurs at low elevations, but up to 2 200 m in E Africa. Forages on or near ground, often near water. **Status:** Common. **Voice:** Call is soft, slightly trilled 'seee-saw', often repeated; song is rambling series of melodious whistles, including much mimicry. [C10.2a, G4.15.10]

5 ANGOLA CAVE CHAT *Xenocopsychus ansorgei* 18-19 cm
Endemic to Angola. Unmistakable; the only entirely black-and-white robin-chat, lacking any rufous. Plumage pattern is chat-like, but habits are robin-like: secretive and crepuscular, foraging on or near ground in dense undergrowth, often among rocky outcrops. **Habitat:** Forested hillsides with jumbled rocks and crevices. **Status:** Locally common, singly or in pairs; easily overlooked and best detected by call and song. **Voice:** Melodic, warbled 'pluue pluu pluu'; softer, whistled 'shuee tee tee' contact call; harsh 2-note call.

6 WHITE-THROATED ROBIN-CHAT *Cossypha humeralis* 17 cm
Endemic to S Africa, where it is the only robin-chat with a white wing bar, throat and breast. Upperparts are greyish. Dark-centred, rufous tail differs from those of other robin-chats in having a black tip. Juv. is much darker and lacks white wing bar, but has rufous-and-black tail. **Habitat:** Thickets and riverine scrub in woodland and savanna; usually feeds on ground, but sings from elevated perches. **Status:** Common. **Voice:** Alarm call is repeated 'seet-cher, seet-cher'; song is rather short series of rich whistles; often mimics other birds. [G5.1.2]

E races

albicapilla

1 RÜPPELL'S ROBIN-CHAT *Cossypha semirufa*   18-19 cm
Endemic to NE Africa. Slightly smaller than White-browed Robin-Chat, which it replaces in montane forest; central tail is black (not olive-brown); usually occurs at higher altitudes. Easily told from smaller akalats and robins by its black head with bold white supercilium. **Habitat:** Montane forest, forest edge, secondary growth and gardens. **Status:** Common; bold, venturing from thickets and tangles, especially at dawn and dusk. **Voice:** Loud, rich series of mimicked songs and calls and other noises; repeated contact call of 'zzhree-zzhree-zzhree'.

2 WHITE-BROWED (HEUGLIN'S) ROBIN-CHAT *Cossypha heuglini*   20 cm
A fairly large robin-chat with a prominent white supercilium. Larger and longer-tailed than other white-browed robin-chats. In E Africa, most similar to Rüppell's Robin-Chat, but has olive-brown (not black) central tail feathers, and occurs in thickets usually at lower elevation. Lacks blue shoulder of Blue-shouldered Robin-Chat. In South Africa, occurs at lower elevation than and in different habitat from Chorister Robin-Chat (p. 452), which also lacks white brow. **Habitat:** Dense thickets and tangles, gardens and parks. **Status:** Common. **Voice:** Characteristic, loud, crescendo song of repeated phrases; also is accomplished mimic. [C9.99, G4.15.8]

3 BLUE-SHOULDERED ROBIN-CHAT *Cossypha cyanocampter*   15-16 cm
Similar to White-browed Robin-Chat, but smaller, and with blue (not olive-brown) forewings; also, occurs in dense forest (not thickets and forest margins). **Habitat:** Chiefly lowland rain-forest, but in E ascends to over 2 000 m. **Status:** Common but easily overlooked; one of the most skulking of all forest robins. **Voice:** Explosive, rich song; somewhat less melodic and more rambling than White-browed Robin-Chat; frequently mimics a wide range of calls and other sounds. [C10.1b]

4 CAPE ROBIN-CHAT *Cossypha caffra*   16-17 cm
The grey flanks and greyish white belly are diagnostic. White supercilium is relatively short. Orange throat and breast separate it from all races of Olive-flanked Robin-Chat (p. 452). **Habitat:** Wide range: forest edge, thickets, heaths, scrub, gardens and parks; occurs at higher elevations in N, but common at sea level in S. **Status:** Common. **Voice:** Alarm call is guttural 'wur-da-durrr'; song is series of melodious phrases, often starting 'cherooo-weet-weet-weeeet'. [C9.98, G5.1.1]

5 CAMEROON MOUNTAIN ROBIN (MOUNTAIN ROBIN-CHAT)
Cossypha isabellae   14-15 cm
Endemic to SW Cameroon highlands. A small, short-tailed version of White-browed and Rüppell's robin-chats, which lacks a rufous neck collar; ranges do not overlap. Nominate race from Mt Cameroon has orange belly, separating it from Bocage's Akalat (p. 444) and White-bellied Robin-Chat (p. 452). Elsewhere, *batesi* is browner above, with whitish central belly; best told from White-bellied Robin-Chat by larger size, richer red underparts and less contrasting tail (centre is brown, not black). **Habitat:** Montane forest and secondary growth. **Status:** Common; easily seen, often venturing into open. **Voice:** Short alarm or contact call of 'chrrr'; soft, squeaky, 2-note 'wrreee wrreee' song. [C9.96]

450

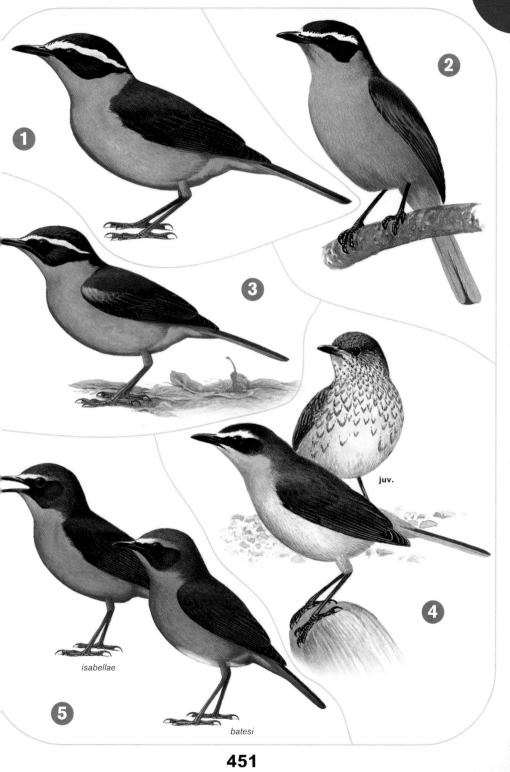

juv.

isabellae

batesi

1 CHORISTER ROBIN-CHAT *Cossypha dichroa* 20 cm
Endemic to South Africa. A large, dark-backed robin-chat with entirely orange underparts and blackish head with no white eye-stripe. Juv. is sooty, mottled tawny-buff above and below. **Habitat:** Forest and coastal thickets. **Status:** Common resident with local movements from interior to coastal forests in winter. **Voice:** Contact call is plaintive 'toy-toy, toy-toy'; song is loud and bubbly, including much mimicry of other forest birds. [G4.15.8]

2 OLIVE-FLANKED ROBIN-CHAT *Cossypha anomala* 14-15 cm
Localised endemic to SE Africa. A dark robin-chat which is unique in lacking any red on throat and breast; only vent, belly and lower flanks are tinged rufous. White throat and white or grey eyebrow contrast with blackish face and dark olive-grey crown and back. Varies geographically, from paler in S to darker in N; isolated *mbuluensis* of N Tanzania is almost black above and on breast. N races have typical robin-chat tail pattern, but contrast between dark centre and rufous outer-tail is less marked in S races. **Habitat:** Montane forest and forest edge. **Status:** Locally common; usually remains well hidden in tangles and thickets within forest. **Voice:** Alarm is short, harsh 'wump' or 'chrupp'; song is varied series of descending whistles.

3 WHITE-BELLIED ROBIN-CHAT *Cossyphicula roberti* 12-13 cm
A small, localised robin-chat of montane forest. Recalls an akalat but has a black-centred (not all-orange) tail. Smaller than Archer's Ground Robin and Grey-winged Robin-Chat (p. 444) with less extensive orange underparts, and lacks contrasting black face; white eye-stripe is much narrower, barely extending behind eye. Spotted juv. is told from juv. akalats by distinctive tail pattern. W race has greyish flanks; these are rufous in E. **Habitat:** Mid-altitude and montane forest. **Status:** Common; usually more confiding than other robin-chats and akalats; sings from exposed perches. **Voice:** Series of rapidly whistled notes, like forest robins. [C9.95] **Similar species:** European Robin *Erithacus rubecula* has red breast extending onto face and forehead, with grey border along neck and flanks; Palearctic vagrant to coastal Mauritania.

4 ARCHER'S GROUND ROBIN (ROBIN-CHAT) *Cossypha archeri* 14-15 cm
Endemic to Albertine Rift. A small to medium-sized robin-chat with a uniform reddish-brown tail (unlike White-bellied and other robin-chats). Similar to Bocage's Akalat (p. 444), but has dark face extending lower onto throat and no grey on head. Slightly larger than Equatorial Akalat (p. 444), with no grey on head, and occurs at higher elevations. **Habitat:** Dense montane forest understorey, especially along streams, 1 600-4 000 m. **Status:** Common. Usually the only small robin found at such high altitudes. **Voice:** Contact call is frog-like 'donk donk'; song is series of trilled whistles. [C9.97]

5 WHITE-STARRED ROBIN *Pogonocichla stellata* 15-16 cm
A striking forest robin. Adult has slate-grey head and throat, yellow-orange breast and belly, and bright yellow tail windows that are conspicuous in flight. Larger than Swynnerton's Robin, with orange (not white) belly and strongly patterned (not uniform) tail. White 'stars' on lower throat and forehead are usually concealed. Juv. is sooty, streaked yellowish buff above and below; some races have dull olive imm. plumage; tail pattern of both is like adult's, but is duller yellow. **Habitat:** Forest understorey. **Status:** Common resident, subject to some altitudinal movements in S. Often rather confiding. **Voice:** Soft 'chuk' or 'zit' note; whistled 'too-twee' contact call, frequently repeated; quiet, warbling song. [C9.88, G5.1.6]

6 SWYNNERTON'S ROBIN *Swynnertonia swynnertoni* 13-14 cm
Localised endemic to SE Africa. Smaller than White-starred Robin, with uniform dark grey tail (lacking yellow windows) and much larger white patch on upper breast, bordered beneath by diagnostic black band. Female duller, with greenish crown and face. Juv. brown above, spotted with buffy yellow; underparts are duller, with throat crescent pale greyish brown. **Habitat:** Montane forest understorey. **Status:** Vulnerable. Uncommon. **Voice:** Song, given by male, is subdued, -syllabled 'zitt, zitt, slurr', last syllable lower pitched; alarm is monotonous, quiet purring. [G5.1.7]

grotei

anomala

juv.

juv.

PALM-THRUSHES
An African genus, also called 'morning thrushes' or 'morning warblers'. Characterised by long, rufous tails and loud, melodious songs; unusual for building mud nests. Sexes alike.

1 RUFOUS-TAILED PALM-THRUSH *Cichladusa ruficauda*   18 cm
Lacks the black breast band of Collared Palm-Thrush, and has dull red (not pale) eyes; crown and back are richer rufous, and cream throat does not extend as far onto breast; ranges do not overlap. Juv. has dark-mottled underparts. **Habitat:** Riverine thickets and *Borassus* palm savanna. **Status:** Locally common. **Voice:** Loud, melodious whistling, including imitations of other birds' songs. [C10.10, G5.1.4]

2 COLLARED PALM-THRUSH *Cichladusa arquata*   18 cm
Forms a superspecies with Rufous-tailed Palm-Thrush. Buff throat and breast with narrow black collar and pale eye are diagnostic. Black collar is often incomplete, and sides of neck and flanks are washed with grey. Juv. is mottled brown below and streaked on crown and nape. **Habitat:** *Hyphaene* or *Borassus* palm savanna. **Status:** Locally common. **Voice:** Explosive, varied song, often including 'weet-chuk' or 'cur-lee chuk-chuk' phrases. [C10.9, G5.1.3]

3 SPOTTED PALM-THRUSH *Cichladusa guttata*   17 cm
Endemic to NE Africa. A small thrush, dark brown above, with a white supercilium and heavily spotted underparts. Could be confused with scrub-robins (p. 456), but has diagnostic rufous tail and lacks any white in wing. E races are darker and more rufous above. Juv. is spotted brown below and more streaked on throat. **Habitat:** Thickets and dense shrubland, often along gullies below 1 600 m; adapts to human habitation such as camp sites and game lodges. **Status:** Common. **Voice:** Song is powerful, varied medley of whistled phrases, incorporating much mimicry; low 'PEE-u-priri-peeu' is given throughout day. [C10.11]

NIGHTINGALES
Small, predominantly brown thrushes, with long, rounded tails that could be confused with large warblers or illadopsises (p. 406). They mostly skulk in thickets. Renowned for their rich and varied song, all species regularly sing in Africa. Sexes alike in nightingales, but the Bluethroat is sexually dimorphic.

4 COMMON NIGHTINGALE *Luscinia megarhynchos*   16-17 cm
Plain brown above, with rump and tail more rufous than the rest of the upperparts. Best told from Thrush Nightingale by plain (not mottled) breast, lack of malar stripes and more rufous rump and tail. Nominate birds (W Africa-Uganda) have warm rufous-brown upperparts, but E races (E Africa) are darker grey-brown, more similar to Thrush Nightingale. **Habitat:** Dense thickets, usually below 1 800 m. **Status:** Common Palearctic migrant Sep-Apr. **Voice:** Song is a complex series of powerful, liquid or bubbling phrases, often repeated; less guttural than Thrush Nightingale's, with fewer rattling phrases. [C3.78]

5 BLUETHROAT *Luscinia svecica*   14 cm
A small, skulking thrush, mostly dark above with a straight creamy-white supercilium and conspicuous russet bases of the outer-tail. Adult has narrow black breast band, usually with some blue above and red below (conspicuous in breeding males). Juv. has pale throat with dark malar stripes. **Habitat:** Waterside vegetation, including thickets and dense grass. **Status:** Locally common Palearctic migrant Oct-Mar. **Voice:** Contact call is harsh 'tacc-tacc', 'turrc' or plaintive 'hweet'; song is loud, melodious and very varied. [C3.79]

6 THRUSH NIGHTINGALE (SPROSSER) *Luscinia luscinia*   16 cm
Similar to Common Nightingale, but has lightly mottled (not plain) breast and faint malar stripes. Generally less rufous above, with less contrast between rump/tail and rest of upperparts. **Habitat:** Thickets in savanna and woodland, often along rivers. **Status:** Locally common Palearctic migrant Sep-Apr; winters further S than Common Nightingale, but both species occur together on passage in E Africa. **Voice:** Rich, warbling song interspersed with harsh, grating notes (unlike Common Nightingale's). [C9.94, G5.1.9]

juv.

1 IRANIA (WHITE-THROATED ROBIN) *Irania gutturalis* 16 cm
Structure and behaviour are similar to those of nightingales. Breeding male is striking, but could be confused with male Common Redstart (p. 460); differs in having narrow white centre to throat (not entirely black), smaller black face, clean white vent and black (not rufous-edged) tail; behaviour is also quite distinct. Non-breeding male, female and imm. have rufous flanks and ear coverts, uniform grey upperparts and long black tail that is often cocked. **Habitat:** Dry thickets and scrub, often along watercourses. **Status:** Locally common Palearctic migrant Oct–Mar. **Voice:** Contact call is grating 'krrrk'; song (often uttered in Africa) is mixture of musical whistles and scratchy notes, reminiscent of *Sylvia* warblers.

SCRUB-ROBINS
Chat-like robins with long tails that are often cocked. All have white tail tips and a well-marked head with a white supercilium; most species also have white in the wing. Sexes alike; the short-lived juv. plumage is spotted buff above and barred or mottled below, but has the adult tail pattern.

2 FOREST (NORTHERN BEARDED) SCRUB-ROBIN *Cercotrichas leucosticta* 15 cm
A shy robin of forest understorey, with diagnostic white tail tips, wing patches and supercilium, dark brown upperparts, and chestnut rump and uppertail coverts. Three disjunct populations: W African nominate race has rufous flanks; these are olive-grey in E races. **Habitat:** Dense undergrowth of forest and forest edge. **Status:** Uncommon to locally common; very furtive, more often heard than seen. **Voice:** Loud, sweet melodious song, but does not mimic other species like robin-chats; alarm call is high-pitched 'chit-it-it' and soft rattle. [C10.12]

3 BROWN-BACKED SCRUB-ROBIN *Cercotrichas hartlaubi* 15 cm
Greyish breast, with diffuse darker streaks, and rufous basal half of the tail separate it from Forest and Miombo scrub-robins. Breast streaks are less prominent than in White-browed Scrub-Robin (p. 458), and back is darker brown, contrasting strongly with rufous rump and diagnostic black tail tip. Wing coverts are very dark, almost black. **Habitat:** Woodland, tall grassland savanna and forest edge; usually in moister habitats than White-browed Scrub-Robin. **Status:** Locally common. **Voice:** Very similar to varied song of White-browed-Scrub-Robin, but sometimes much louder, more musical and in longer snatches; occasionally duets. [C10.14]

4 MIOMBO (CENTRAL BEARDED) SCRUB-ROBIN *Cercotrichas barbata* 16 cm
The plain rufous breast and flanks separate it from all scrub-robins except Bearded Scrub-Robin; in narrow areas of overlap, Miombo Scrub-Robin is greyer on back, has more extensive rufous on underparts and more white on tail tip, and is less boldy marked on head. Habitat also differs. **Habitat:** Miombo woodland; in area of overlap with Bearded Scrub-Robin, occurs in more open habitat (Bearded Scrub-Robin prefers thicker tangles in riverine forest). **Status:** Locally common. **Voice:** Clear, penetrating song of often-repeated, mixed phrases, more continuous than Bearded Scrub-Robin's. [C10.13]

5 BEARDED SCRUB-ROBIN *Cercotrichas quadrivirgata* 16 cm
Very similar to Miombo Scrub-Robin, but is browner above, with a larger white belly patch and less white on tail tip. Told from Brown Scrub-Robin by rufous (not grey-brown) breast and flanks, and rufous (not brown) rump and uppertail coverts. **Habitat:** Thickets and broadleafed woodland; feeds among leaf litter under thickets and dense tangles; favours moister areas than Miombo Scrub-Robin, but drier areas than Brown Scrub-Robin. **Status:** Common, but easily overlooked. **Voice:** Song similar to Miombo Scrub-Robin's, but with short pauses between phrases; alarm call is 1-2 sharp notes followed by 'churr, chek-chek kwezzzzz'. [G5.2.7]

6 BROWN SCRUB-ROBIN *Cercotrichas signata* 16 cm
Endemic to S Africa. A largely brown forest scrub-robin; lacks orange-buff flanks and rufous rump and uppertail coverts of Bearded Scrub-Robin, and has less distinct white supercilium and malar stripes. **Habitat:** Thick tangles of coastal and evergreen forests; shy and skulking, but is readily observed at dawn and dusk when it often forages in open. **Status:** Locally common. **Voice:** Melodious 'twee-choo-sree-sree' introduces varied song; alarm note is sibilant 'zeeeeet'. [G5.2.6]

1 RUFOUS-TAILED SCRUB-ROBIN (RUFOUS BUSH CHAT)
Cercotrichas galactotes   15 cm
A drab scrub-robin with plain, pale greyish or buff underparts. Lacks white wing bars and breast and malar streaks of White-browed Scrub-Robin. Tail is rufous, with black-and-white tip; is frequently cocked and fanned, with wings slightly drooped. Upperpart colour varies racially, from rufous-brown to grey-brown. **Habitat:** Dry bush and riverbeds. **Status:** Breeding resident in Sahel (*minor*) and N Somalia (*hamertoni*); Palearctic migrant in W Africa (nominate) and E Africa (*syriacus*), mostly Oct-Apr. Usually singly or in pairs; sometimes in small groups. **Voice:** Song is long medley of rather soft, querulous notes; thin 'tseeet' contact note. [C3.80]

2 KALAHARI SCRUB-ROBIN *Cercotrichas paena*   15 cm
Endemic to SW Africa. A pale, sandy brown scrub-robin with no white wing bars. Rump, uppertail coverts and most of tail are rufous; tail has broad black subterminal bar and white tips. Lacks breast streaks and white wing bars of White-browed Scrub-Robin. **Habitat:** Dry acacia savanna, favouring thickets and bushy areas. **Status:** Common. **Voice:** Alarm note is harsh 'zzeee'; contact call is whistled 'seeeup'; musical song of whistles and chirps, more varied than those of Karoo or White-browed scrub-robins. [G5.2.5]

3 WHITE-BROWED SCRUB-ROBIN *Cercotrichas leucophrys*   15 cm
A widespread, variable savanna and woodland scrub-robin, but all races have a diagnostic streaked breast and upper belly. Breast is much more heavily streaked than in Brown-backed Scrub-Robin (p. 456). Extent of white in wing varies; NE *leucoptera* (White-winged Scrub-Robin) has wing coverts broadly edged with white, forming large white panel on folded wing. Back colour varies from rufous to brown. **Habitat:** Woodland and savanna; favours drier habitats than most other scrub-robins. **Status:** Common. **Voice:** Harsh 'trrrrrr' alarm note; fluty but repetitive song; characteristic call at dawn and dusk is whistled 'seeep po go'. [C10.15, G5.2.3]

4 KAROO SCRUB-ROBIN *Cercotrichas coryphaeus*   15 cm
Endemic to S Africa. A dark grey-brown scrub-robin with a blackish tail and contrasting white tail tips. Much darker than Kalahari Scrub-Robin, with no rufous in tail. Pale throat contrasts with greyish or grey-brown underparts. Juv. lightly scaled above and mottled on breast. **Habitat:** Karoo and fynbos scrub. **Status:** Common; usually in pairs. **Voice:** Harsh, chittering 'tchik, tchik, tcheet'; song is mixture of whistles and harsh, grating notes. [G5.2.4]

5 BLACK SCRUB-ROBIN *Cercotrichas podobe*   20 cm
A long-legged, all-black scrub-robin with an extremely long, white-tipped tail; vent feathers are tipped white. Often raises tail over back and slowly lowers it, showing white tail tips and white-barred undertail coverts. Base of flight feathers are rufous, forming rufous panel in wings in flight. Body plumage becomes brownish when worn. **Habitat:** Arid scrub and palm-lined wadis. **Status:** Locally common; conspicuous. **Voice:** Far-carrying song of trilling whistles and harsher notes. [C10.16]

leucoptera

leucophrys

REDSTARTS
Dimorphic, chat-like birds. Males usually have some orange-rufous plumage. Juvs resemble females, but have slightly mottled and streaked plumage.

1 COMMON REDSTART *Phoenicurus phoenicurus*   13-14 cm
Breeding male is striking, with its black face and throat, white forecrown, uniform grey upper-parts and red breast. Smaller than male Irania (p. 456), with black throat and red outer-tail. Grey (not blackish) back, smaller black bib and whitish (not grey) forecrown separate it from male Black Redstart. Female and non-breeding male are much duller; could be confused with Familiar Chat (p. 462), but have more extensive red rump and brighter red outer-tail; also, tail is continuously 'trembled' (but bird does not wing-flick). Paler and browner than female Black Redstart. **Habitat:** Semi-arid savanna and woodland. **Status:** Fairly common Palearctic migrant Sep-Apr. **Voice:** Loud 'hooeeet', similar to that of Willow Warbler. [C3.82, G6.15.13]

2 BLACK REDSTART *Phoenicurus ochruros*   15 cm
Race *phoenicuroides* occurs. Slightly larger and heavier than Common Redstart, breeding male is darker above, with black bib extending much further onto breast and greyish (not whitish) forecrown. Female is slightly darker than Common Redstart, with greyer-brown body plumage, especially on underparts. In the hand, P9 is much shorter, giving a more rounded wing. **Habitat:** Rocky, mountainous areas; also juniper forests, mostly 1 200-2 000 m. **Status:** Fairly common Palearctic migrant Oct-Apr. **Voice:** Contact calls 'hweet' and 'twick'. [C3.81]

STONECHATS
Small, compact chats with a short tail and upright stance. Sexually dimorphic; males have a chestnut breast and white wing patches; females and juvs are duller.

3 WHINCHAT *Saxicola rubetra*   13-14 cm
Breeding male differs from female Common Stonechat by its well-defined white supercilium, more extensive white wing bar, white patch at base of primaries, and white sides to base of tail. Female, non-breeding male and juv. also have broad, creamy supercilium, white wing bar and diagnostic white base to outer-tail feathers. Stance is less upright than Common Stonechat's. **Habitat:** Open grassland with patches of stunted scrub. **Status:** Uncommon to common Palearctic migrant Oct-Apr. **Voice:** Scolding 'tick-tick'. [C3.86, G4.15.7]

4 COMMON STONECHAT *Saxicola torquata*   13-14 cm
A highly variable, small chat. Both sexes lack pale supercilium of Whinchat. Male has diagnostic black head, chestnut breast (extent varies geographically) and white neck patch, rump and wing bar. Female is duller; juv. is mottled with buff above, and is paler below than female. Migrant Palearctic birds are browner above, with brown fringes to back and mantle feathers, and may be a distinct species *S. rubicula*. Black-breasted *albofasciatus* (Ethiopia) may also be a good species. **Habitat:** Grassland and open areas with short scrub; also wetland areas. **Status:** Common resident with some local movements; Palearctic migrant in N, mostly Sep-Apr. **Voice:** Song is high-pitched, varied warble; calls 'weet-weet' and harsh 'chak'. [C3.84, G4.15.6]

5 BUFF-STREAKED CHAT *Oenanthe bifasciata*   16-17 cm
Endemic to S Africa. An unusual wheatear, sometimes placed in *Saxicola*. Male's black face, throat and wings and buffy underparts are diagnostic. Female differs from juv. Capped Wheatear (p. 472) in having buff (not white) rump. Juv. is mottled with black and buff on upperparts and underparts, and has rufous rump. **Habitat:** Rock-strewn, grassy slopes. **Status:** Common but localised. **Voice:** Loud, rich warbling, including mimicry of other birds' songs. [G4.14.8]

6 HERERO CHAT *Namibornis herero*   17 cm
Endemic to Namibia and Angola. A peculiar chat-like bird of uncertain affinities. Rufous outer-tail with dark brown central feathers recalls Familiar Chat (p. 462) or robin-chats (p. 448), but has a distinct head pattern, with black face contrasting with white supercilium. Breast streaking is visible only at close range. Juv. is mottled on breast and more streaked above. **Habitat:** Dry scrub and acacia woodland, often near rocks. **Status:** Uncommon. **Voice:** Mostly silent; melodious, warbling 'twi-tedeelee-doo' song when breeding. [G5.2.8]

Small to medium-sized, rather plain chats, best identified by their tail patterns. Sexes alike; juvs spotted buff above and scaled or mottled below, but have adult tail patterns.

1 FAMILIAR CHAT *Cercomela familiaris*   14-15 cm

A widespread, uniform brown chat with a diagnostic rufous outer-tail and rump. Tail has characteristic dark 'T', with rest of tail rufous. Also shows narrow, pale eye-ring and rufous wash on ear coverts. Darker than Tractrac and Sickle-winged chats, with plumper body and more horizontal stance. Closely resembles Brown-tailed and Sombre rock-chats, but is always easily identified by its tail pattern. Invariably flicks wings after landing. **Habitat:** Rocky and mountainous terrain. **Status:** Common. **Voice:** Harsh, scolding 'shek-shek' alarm call; warbling trill. [C10.20, G4.14.9]

2 SICKLE-WINGED CHAT *Cercomela sinuata*   14-15 cm

Endemic to S Africa. Taller and more 'leggy' than Familiar Chat, with a larger eye-ring and more contrast between the grey-brown upperparts and paler underparts; best told by its creamy-orange (not rufous) rump and tail base; black in tail forms broad triangle, not reaching base of tail, rather than 'T' as in Familiar Chat. Tail pattern is similar to that of Tractrac Chat, but generally darker, with warmer, orange-buff (not white or creamy) rump. Common name derives from extremely attenuated outer primary, but this is visible only in the hand. **Habitat:** Grassland, taller Karoo scrub and fields. **Status:** Locally common. **Voice:** Very soft, typically chat-like 'chak-chak'; warbled song. [G4.15.1]

3 KAROO CHAT *Cercomela schlegelii*   16-18 cm

Endemic to SW Africa. Larger and longer-tailed than most *Cercomela*, with a more horizontal posture. Diagnostic white outer-tail feathers framing a dark, triangular central tail separate it from Tractrac and Sickle-winged chats. Much paler than female Mountain Wheatear (p. 466), with pale grey (not white) rump and completely white outer-tail feathers. Upperparts vary from pale grey-brown in arid N to medium grey in S. **Habitat:** Karoo and semi-desert scrub in S; escarpment zone in N. **Status:** Common. **Voice:** Harsh 'chak-chak' or 'trrat-trrat'. [G4.15.1]

4 TRACTRAC CHAT *Cercomela tractrac*   14-15 cm

Endemic to SW Africa. A small, pale chat, very similar to Sickle-winged Chat, but generally paler, with white or creamy (not orange-buff) rump and tail base. Smaller than Karoo Chat, with different tail pattern (broad black tail tip, not white outer-tail). Coloration varies geographically: Namib form is almost white above, with darker wings and tail; S populations are darker. **Habitat:** Karoo and desert scrub, hummock dunes and gravel plains. **Status:** Common; usually in pairs or family groups. **Voice:** Soft, fast 'tactac'; song is quiet, musical bubbling; territorial defence call is loud chattering. [G4.14.10]

5 BROWN-TAILED ROCK-CHAT *Cercomela scotocerca*   14 cm

Similar in posture and size to Familiar Chat, but lacks rufous on tail and rump (S race *turkana* can show some rufous wash on rump and outer-tail, but never as bright as in Familiar Chat). In area of overlap, is paler and greyer than Sombre Rock-Chat, with shorter legs, longer tail, noticeably smaller eyes and less upright posture. Brown (not black) tail and typically darker plumage separate it from Blackstart (p. 464). **Habitat:** Open or treed, rocky, semi-arid areas. **Status:** Locally common. **Voice:** Short 'chruk chrukk' notes; soft, whistled trill. [C10.21]

6 SOMBRE ROCK-CHAT *Cercomela dubia*   14-15 cm

Endemic to NE Africa. Differs from Blackstart (p. 464), Familiar Chat and Brown-tailed Rock-Chat by upright posture, long-legged appearance, short tail and unusually large and rounded eye. Has short brown tail; lacks rufous outer-tail of Familiar Chat or black tail of Blackstart. Most similar to Brown-tailed Rock-Chat, but is darker and browner, with shorter tail and more erect posture. Does not habitually flick wings. **Habitat:** Semi-arid rocky screes with light woodland. **Status:** Uncommon and localised. **Voice:** Soft 'trikk trikk'.

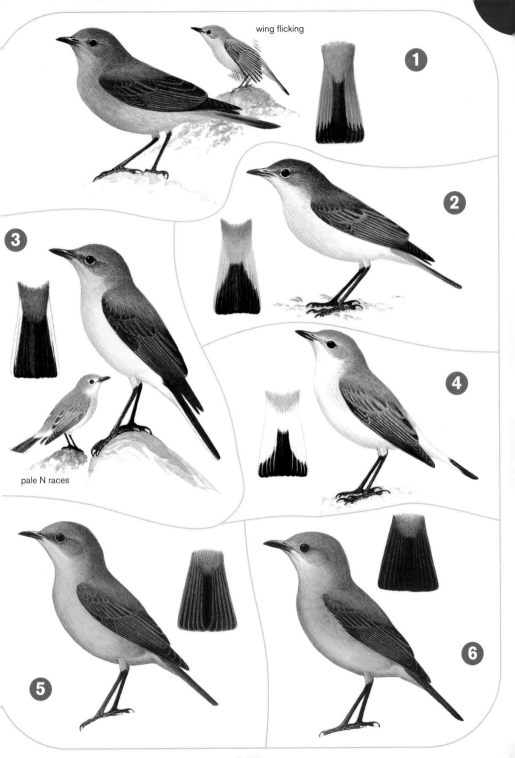

wing flicking

1

2

3

pale N races

4

5

6

1 MOORLAND (ALPINE/HILL) CHAT *Cercomela sordida* 14-15 cm

Endemic to NE Africa. A short-tailed, long-legged, dark brown or grey chat with a black-and-white, wheatear-like tail pattern. At rest, resembles dark-plumaged Familiar Chat (p. 462), but is readily identified in flight by white (not rufous) outer-tail with dark central 'T'. Frequently flicks both wings and tail. Juv. is faintly barred above and mottled dark brown on breast. **Habitat:** High-altitude grasslands and moors, 2 100-5 500 m, mostly above 3 400 m. **Status:** Common. **Voice:** Song is loud, metallic piping; call is chirping 'werp werp'.

2 BLACKSTART *Cercomela melanura* 14 cm

A rather pale, grey-brown chat with a diagnostic all-black tail. Usually paler and greyer than Familiar Chat and Brown-tailed and Sombre rock-chats (p. 462), with whitish belly and throat. Wings are often held drooped to show off slightly fanned black tail; also regularly flicks wings, showing contrast between darker flight feathers and paler grey wing coverts. Some races are browner. **Habitat:** Arid to semi-arid stony areas, screes and cliff bases. **Status:** Locally common to common. **Voice:** Unobtrusive, soft 'tuk tuk'; louder, whistled 'chiree oot'; song is jumbled collection of warbles. [C10.22]

MYRMECOCICHLA CHATS

Medium-sized, chunky chats with short, rounded wings; their flight is fast and buzzy. Males usually have more white plumage than females.

3 CONGO MOOR CHAT *Myrmecocichla tholloni* 18-19 cm

A localised chat, restricted to the grassy plateaux of C Africa. Resembles a washed-out Anteater Chat, with white primary panels in flight and frosty white patches on face and rump. Range overlaps with Sooty Chat, but is brown (not black) and has white (not black) rump. Shows much white in flight; flaps rapidly, with rounded wings, like anteater chats. Juv. is duller and plainer. **Habitat:** Upland grasslands, sometimes slightly wooded; often perches on small bushes and anthills. **Status:** Locally common. **Voice:** Short 'trrep trreep'; short, warbled song, sometimes given in flight or when hovering. [C10.23]

4 (NORTHERN) ANTEATER CHAT *Myrmecocichla aethiops* 17-18 cm

A medium-sized, dark brown or blackish chat with silvery-white primary bases that form a pale panel in flight. Told from Sooty Chat by white wing panels (female Sooty Chat is all dark; male has white shoulders but primaries are dark). Larger and generally browner than White-fronted Black Chat (p. 466); lacks white forecrown of male White-fronted Black Chat, and occurs in more open areas. At rest, appears plump and short tailed, and has upright stance. **Habitat:** Short grasslands and open savanna, 1 500-3 000 m. Usually associated with termite mounds. **Status:** Locally common. **Voice:** Song is mixture of whistles and more guttural notes, reminiscent of reed and marsh warblers'; call is sharp, slightly rasping 'tsuui'. [C10.24]

5 (SOUTHERN) ANT-EATING CHAT *Myrmecocichla formicivora* 17-18 cm

Endemic to S Africa. Slightly browner and more scaly on breast than Anteater Chat; ranges do not overlap. Browner than Sooty Chat, and has conspicuous white patches in primaries. Male has white shoulder patch; female is paler brown and lacks white shoulders. Juv. is more mottled. **Habitat:** Grassland dotted with termite mounds, and open, sandy or stony areas. **Status:** Common; usually in small groups. **Voice:** Short, sharp 'peek' or 'piek' call; song is varied mix of whistles and grating notes. [G4.15.5]

6 SOOTY CHAT *Myrmecocichla nigra* 17-19 cm

Similar to anteater chats, but is blacker and lacks white in the primaries. Male has white upperwing coverts; female and juv. are browner, with all-dark wings. Larger than White-fronted Black Chat (p. 466), with shorter tail and more upright stance. Differs from Arnott's Chat (p. 466) by lacking white on crown or throat, and in having less white in wing coverts and no white in primary bases. **Habitat:** Upland grasslands with scattered bushes and farmland. **Status:** Common; in pairs or small family groups. **Voice:** Dynamic, sharp, whistled song in flight or from atop bush, tree or anthill. [C10.25]

1 RÜPPELL'S BLACK CHAT *Myrmecocichla melaena*   20 cm

Endemic to Abyssinian highlands. An all-black chat that shows white patches in primaries in flight. Larger than White-fronted Black Chat, with more extensive white in wing; also typically occurs at higher elevations. Told from Anteater Chat (p. 464) by its black (not brown) plumage; ranges do not overlap. Has unusual habit of slowly cocking tail up and over back. **Habitat:** Highland cliffs and gorges, partially treed gullies and often close to waterfalls. **Status:** Locally common. **Voice:** Soft, warbled song; short, piercing whistle.

2 WHITE-FRONTED BLACK CHAT *Myrmecocichla albifrons*   15 cm

A small black chat. Male has small white forecrown patch and, in some races, white shoulder patches. Smaller than Arnott's Chat, with much smaller white crown spot; ranges do not overlap. Female is all black, very similar to Rüppell's Black Chat, but is smaller, and lives at lower altitudes and in more treed areas. Both sexes have paler bases to primaries; extent varies but is never as large as in Anteater (p. 464) or Rüppell's Black chats. **Habitat:** Stony areas in well-wooded and treed areas, farmlands and recently burnt areas. **Status:** Locally common; in pairs or family parties. **Voice:** Short chattering notes; sharp whistle. [C10.26]

3 ARNOTT'S (WHITE-HEADED BLACK) CHAT *Myrmecocichla arnotti* 16-18 cm

A compact black-and-white woodland chat. Male is distinguished from black-morph male Mountain Wheatear by entirely black rump and tail. Larger than White-fronted Black Chat, with much larger white crown; ranges do not overlap. Female lacks white cap but has conspicuous white throat and upper breast, often scaled with black. Juv. has black head and white shoulder patch; could be confused with male Sooty Chat (p. 464), but habitat differs and has longer tail. **Habitat:** Miombo and mopane woodland. **Status:** Common. **Voice:** Quiet, whistled 'fick' or 'feee'. [C10.27, G4.15.4]

WHEATEARS

Chat-like birds with distinctive tail patterns. Sexes alike in resident African species, but dimorphic in most Palearctic migrant species, with males having distinct breeding and non-breeding plumages; juvs resemble females or are mottled on the back and breast.

4 WHITE-CROWNED (BLACK) WHEATEAR *Oenanthe leucopyga*   14-15 cm

A mostly black wheatear with a white rump, vent and outer-tail feathers (only central tail is black). Male has white crown; female is greyish black, with dark crown. Superficially similar to Mountain Wheatear, but ranges do not overlap. In NE could be confused with Abyssinian Black Wheatear (p. 470), but has white (not rufous) rump and outer-tail. **Habitat:** Arid and semi-arid areas, dry farmland and stony deserts. **Status:** Uncommon resident and local migrant. **Voice:** Harsh 'chack'; variable wheatear-like melodic song. [C3.87] **Similar species: Black Wheatear** *O. leucura* male lacks white crown; female is browner; both have black 'T' on tail; rare Palearctic migrant to coastal Mauritania.

5 MOUNTAIN WHEATEAR (CHAT) *Oenanthe monticola*   18-20 cm

Endemic to SW Africa. A large, robust, black, grey and white wheatear. Males vary from black to very pale grey, but all have white rump, white sides to tail and white shoulder patch. Some have white cap, resembling male Arnott's Chat, but this species is larger and longer tailed, with white (not black) rump and white outer-tail feathers. Female is uniform sooty-brown except for white rump and outer-tail feathers. **Habitat:** Rocky hillsides and boulders. **Status:** Common. **Voice:** Clear, thrush-like, whistling song, interspersed with harsh chatters. [G4.14.6]

6 HOODED WHEATEAR *Oenanthe monacha*   17 cm

Slightly larger than Mourning Wheatear (p. 470), with mostly white tail, lacking black tail tip. Differs from White-crowned Wheatear by having white (not black) belly. Female differs from female Mourning Wheatear by having buff (not white) tail. **Habitat:** Dry, scrub and arid, stony plains. **Status:** Uncommon to rare resident and migrant. **Voice:** Whistled 'veet' and harsher 'chak' notes.

1

2 ♀ ♂

3 ♂ ♀

4 ♂

5 ♂ ♀ grey morph

black morph

6 ♀ ♂

467

1 NORTHERN (EUROPEAN) WHEATEAR *Oenanthe oenanthe* 15 cm

Breeding male has a diagnostic blue-grey crown and back, and black face. Other plumages are nondescript buffy-brown, best identified by tail pattern: black 'T' pattern has uniformly broad black tip, broader than Black-eared or Pied wheatears', but narrower than Desert Wheatear's. Paler than Botta's and Heuglin's wheatears (p. 470), with narrower black tail tip. Females and non-breeding males are easily confused with Isabelline Wheatear. Smaller than juv. Capped Wheatear (p. 472), with more white on rump and outer-tail, and is usually paler, with plain (not mottled) breast. **Habitat:** Open grassland and dry plains. **Status:** Common Palearctic migrant Sep-Apr. **Voice:** Harsh 'chak-chak' or 'wee-chak'; song is jumbled mix of high whistles and squeaks; seldom sings in region. [C3.89-90, G4.14.5]

2 ISABELLINE WHEATEAR *Oenanthe isabellina* 16 cm

A uniform buffy-brown wheatear with no distinct male breeding plumage. Closely resembles non-breeding Northern Wheatear, but is slightly larger and paler, and looks more upright due to longer legs and shorter tail. Black tail tip is generally broader than in Northern Wheatear, and has white or whitish buff (not grey) underwing coverts. At close range, darker alula is diagnostic. Appears larger-headed, and tends to have more direct flight when flushed. Much paler than Botta's Wheatear (p. 470). **Habitat:** Bush and scrub. **Status:** Common Palearctic migrant Oct-Mar. **Voice:** High-pitched 'wheet-whit' call; song is similar to Northern Wheatear's; seldom heard in Africa. [C3.95, G6.15.12]

3 DESERT WHEATEAR *Oenanthe deserti* 14-15 cm

A small, predominantly sandy-coloured wheatear with a diagnostic black tail (only bases of outer-tail are narrowly white). Uppertail coverts vary from white to buff. Breeding male has black face and throat, resembling Pied Wheatear, but has paler, sandy-coloured back. Differs from black-throated form of Black-eared Wheatear by having black sides of neck linking throat to dark wing. Female and juv. lack black face and throat. **Habitat:** Semi-desert in Sahel; higher elevations in Ethiopia and Somalia. **Status:** Common Palearctic migrant Sep-Mar. **Voice:** Song is mournful, 3- to 4-note, descending whistle. [C3.94]

4 BLACK-EARED WHEATEAR *Oenanthe hispanica* 14-15 cm

A slim, long-tailed wheatear with a narrow tip to the black 'T' on its tail and black outer webs to outer-tail feathers extending almost halfway up tail. Black tip is narrower than Pied Wheatear's. Breeding male has black face, and sometimes throat, but black does not extend to sides of lower neck, or link to black wings (as Desert and Pied wheatears). Other plumages have black underwing coverts, like Pied Wheatear, but upperparts are generally warmer brown. Two races occur: *hispanica* (W Africa) and *melanoleuca* (C and E Africa). **Habitat:** Acacia savanna, rocky plains and fields; regularly hunts from perches. **Status:** Locally common Palearctic migrant Sep-Mar. **Voice:** Harsh, nasal 'tchep'. [C3.91]

5 PIED WHEATEAR *Oenanthe pleschanka* 14-15 cm

Similar to Black-eared Wheatear, but is usually darker above, with a broader black tail tip (but some have narrow tips). Breeding male has black face and throat (rarely white throat). Black throat extends onto upper breast and neck, linking to black wing and back. Non-breeding male has dusky face, buffy breast and belly, and dark brown back. Female and juv. are dusky grey-brown above, darker than other wheatears; lack dark lores of female Northern and Isabelline wheatears. Separation from Cyprus Wheatear is problematic. **Habitat:** Dry, stony areas with scattered scrub. **Status:** Common Palearctic migrant Sep-Mar. **Voice:** Soft 'zack' call; song is a series of soft whistles and harsh 'zack' notes. [C10.17]

6 CYPRUS WHEATEAR *Oenanthe cypriaca* 14 cm

Formerly considered a race of Pied Wheatear, but is smaller and more slender, with a compact body, large head and short wings. Breeding male has duller crown, black throat extending further onto upper breast, smaller white rump and usually darker pink wash on underparts. Breeding female resembles breeding male. Other plumages are little known; presumably similar to Pied Wheatear's. **Habitat:** Dry stony plains, fields and grasslands. **Status:** Uncertain due to identification difficulties. **Voice:** Soft 'tek tek'; song differs from Pied Wheatear's, but silent in Africa.

1 ♀

2 non-br.

br.

3 ♂

4 ♂

5 non-br. ♂

♂

6 ♂

1 BOTTA'S WHEATEAR *Oenanthe bottae* 16 cm
Resembles a large, dark Northern Wheatear (p. 468) with a dull reddish breast and broader black tail tip; sexes are alike. Often lumped with Heuglin's Wheatear but is larger, paler and greyer above, with whiter throat contrasting strongly with more richly coloured breast; ranges abut in W Ethiopia. Underwing coverts are cream (not buffy-pink). **Habitat:** Moorland and grassland, usually above 1 800 m. **Status:** Common in Abyssinian highlands; rare in adjacent lowlands (possible migrants from Arabia). **Voice:** Song is drawn-out, complex and varied, with much mimicry.

2 HEUGLIN'S WHEATEAR *Oenanthe heuglini* 13-14 cm
Smaller and darker than Botta's Wheatear, with darker, browner upperparts and buffy-pink (not creamy) underwing coverts. Breast is less rufous, but throat is washed darker buff, resulting in less contrast between throat and breast. Much darker and slightly smaller than Northern Wheatear. **Habitat:** Open ground, rocky hillsides and outcrops, usually with short, dry grass. **Status:** Uncommon resident and intra-African migrant. **Voice:** Apparently similar to Botta's Wheatear's. [C10.19]

3 MOURNING WHEATEAR *Oenanthe lugens* 15 cm
Breeding male is striking black and white, with pale grey crown contrasting with black head, back, throat and upper breast. Rump and base of tail are white, but differs from Hooded Wheatear (p. 466) by having a broad-tipped black 'T' on the tail (not mostly white tail). Pale crown and mostly white belly separate it from Abyssinian Black Wheatear. Female and juv. resemble washed-out male, with greyish back and crown, and slightly darker grey face and throat. **Habitat:** Bases of rocky hills in acacia scrub and arid savanna. **Status:** Uncommon Palearctic migrant Oct-Mar. **Voice:** Usually silent in Africa; song is scratchy, buzzing 'skeer-reet-siweek-chiurreek'. [C3.92]

4 SCHALOW'S WHEATEAR *Oenanthe schalowi* 15 cm
Endemic to E Africa. Slightly larger than Abyssinian Black Wheatear, with browner upperparts and diagnostic buff-orange (not white) vent. Red-tailed Wheatear also has rufous vent, but has contrasting black face and lacks dark breast. Breeding male has darker, less contrasting cap with less obvious streaking than Abyssinian Black Wheatear; belly always whitish. Dark plumage and orange rump and tail base distinguish it from all other wheatears in its range. Female could be confused with Familiar Chat (p. 462), but is larger, with a different shape; does not habitually flick wings on landing. **Habitat:** Rocky grassland. **Status:** Locally common; usually in pairs. **Voice:** Short, buzzy song.

5 ABYSSINIAN BLACK WHEATEAR *Oenanthe lugubris* 14 cm
Endemic to Abyssinian highlands and N Somalia. Often considered a race of Mourning Wheatear, but has orange-buff (not white) rump and tail base. Male's cap is streaked darker, and black throat extends much further onto breast, usually ending raggedly; some individuals have entire belly black. Female is much darker than Mourning Wheatear, almost black above, with dark grey underparts, streaked black; only central belly and vent are whitish. Slightly smaller than Schalow's Wheatear, with blacker upperparts, white (not orangey) vent and paler, more contrasting crown. N Somalian *vauriei* has paler crown and lacks black-bellied form; affinities are uncertain. **Habitat:** Moorland, grassland and fields. **Status:** Common. **Voice:** Song is series of short phrases, similar to other wheatears'.

6 RED-TAILED WHEATEAR *Oenanthe xanthoprymna* 14 cm
Diagnostic rufous rump and tail separate this from all species except Abyssinian Black and Schalow's wheatears, but is paler brown above, with white breast. Smaller than Red-rumped Wheatear *O. moesta* (not recorded from region); with darker grey-brown back; underwing coverts and axillaries are white (not black or dusky). Most birds in Africa are *chrysopygia*, which have pale throat and grey-brown tail. Male of vagrant nominate race has black face and throat, and white bases to outer-tail. **Habitat:** Rocky hills in acacia savanna. **Status:** Fairly common Palearctic migrant Oct-Mar. **Voice:** Silent in Africa.

1

2

juv.

3 ♂

4 ♀ ♂

5 ♂

6 ♂

471

1 SOMALI WHEATEAR *Oenanthe phillipsi* 14 cm
Endemic to NE Africa. A small, grey-backed wheatear with a diagnostic dark throat and breast (black in male, dark grey in female). Rump and tail base are white, with black 'T', similar to Pied and Northern wheatears' (p. 468). In fresh plumage, white edges to wing feathers form pale wing bar. Sometimes considered a race of Northern Wheatear, but lacks any buff coloration. **Habitat:** Arid to semi-arid plains, farmlands and stony grassland. **Status:** Locally common; singly or in pairs. **Voice:** Low, drawn-out whistle; metallic, clicking call.

2 CAPPED WHEATEAR *Oenanthe pileata* 17-18 cm
A large, striking wheatear, easily identified by its rich brown upperparts, black face and breast band, and contrasting white throat and supercilium; sexes are alike. Juv. could be confused with non-breeding migrant wheatears, but is larger and darker than most, with mostly dark tail and mottled breast band (indistinct in some birds). Juv. could also be confused with female Buff-streaked Chat (p. 460), but has white (not buff) rump. **Habitat:** Barren, sandy or stony areas and short grassland in flat country. **Status:** Common resident with local movements. **Voice:** 'Chik-chik' alarm note; song is loud warbling with slurred chattering. [C10.18, G4.14.7]

CLIFF-CHATS
Large, long-tailed, thrush-like chats (sometimes included in *Myrmecocichla*) associated with rocky areas. Could possibly be confused with rock-thrushes (p. 432), but lack the blue-grey plumage and usually have some white in the wing. Sexes differ. Usually nest in old swallows' nests.

3 MOCKING CLIFF-CHAT *Thamnolaea cinnamomeiventris* 19-21 cm
The male is glossy black, with a bright chestnut belly, vent and rump, and white shoulder patches (size of which varies geographically); black crown separates it from White-crowned Cliff-Chat. Female is dark grey above and chestnut below; differs from White-crowned Cliff-Chat by being greyer above, with distinct grey throat and breast that contrast with chestnut belly. Juv. is duller. **Habitat:** Bases of cliffs and wooded, rocky slopes. **Status:** Common but localised; usually in pairs or family parties. **Voice:** Loud, melodious, whistled song, often with much mimicry. [C10.28, G4.15.2]

4 WHITE-CROWNED CLIFF-CHAT *Thamnolaea coronata* 19-21 cm
Often considered a race of Mocking Cliff-Chat, but male has conspicuous white cap, extending onto nape. Female is browner than female Mocking Cliff-Chat, with paler throat and rufous wash extending onto breast; lacks breast and belly contrast. **Habitat:** Wooded cliffs and gorges. **Status:** Locally common. **Voice:** Alarm is short 'shraat'; song is rich, melodic series of mimicked and original notes. [C10.29]

5 WHITE-WINGED CLIFF-CHAT *Thamnolaea semirufa* 19-21 cm
Endemic to Abyssinian highlands. Range overlaps with Mocking Cliff-Chat, but has diagnostic white patches in primaries at all ages; lacks white shoulder of other two cliff-chats. Female is mostly dark brown, lacking male's chestnut belly. Juv. is heavily spotted buff above and below. **Habitat:** Rocky and wooded gorges, boulders and road cuttings. **Status:** Common to locally common. **Voice:** Melodic song of jumbled mimicry, similar to Mocking Cliff-Chat's.

1 ♂ ♀

2 juv. ♀

3 ♂

4 ♂

5 ♀ ♂

GRASS WARBLERS
Large warblers of uncertain affinities with loud, distinctive songs. Sexes alike.

1 MOUSTACHED GRASS WARBLER *Melocichla mentalis* 18-19 cm
A large, plain grass warbler, easily told from other species by its unstreaked breast and back. Most likely to be confused with Broad-tailed Warbler (p. 478); both species have blackish, broad, rounded tail, but Moustached Grass Warbler is much larger, with black malar stripe, pale (not dark) eyes, more strongly marked face and plain undertail (lacking buff tips to feathers). Rich, varied song is also diagnostic. Juv. is duller, lacking chestnut forehead. **Habitat:** Long, rank grass adjoining forests and in open glades, often near water. **Status:** Locally common. **Voice:** Bubbling 'tip-tiptwiddle-iddle-see'. [C11.38, G5.7.3]

2 CAPE GRASSBIRD *Sphenoeacus afer* 17-19 cm
Endemic to S Africa. Readily identified by its long, pointed tail, chestnut cap and black malar stripes. Heavily streaked plumage eliminates confusion with Moustached Grass Warbler, and is easily told from cisticolas by large size, long, straggly tail and weak flight. Juv. is duller, with more streaked cap. **Habitat:** Fynbos and rank grass on mountain slopes and near water. **Status:** Common; mostly remains in dense vegetation, but easily located by song. **Voice:** Song is stereotyped crescendo, starting as soft series of warbling notes, building in volume, pace and pitch, then ending with loud 'wheeeooo'; nasal 'where' call. [G5.7.1]

3 ROCKRUNNER (DAMARA ROCK-JUMPER) *Achaetops pycnopygius* 16-17 cm
Endemic to SW Africa. A large, ground-dwelling warbler with a heavily streaked dark back, white breast spotted with black, and bright rufous belly and undertail. Long tail, horizontal stance and distinctive behaviour separate it from chats. Juv. is less distinctly marked. Bounds across rocks on long legs; sings from exposed perches. **Habitat:** Boulder-strewn, grassy hillsides and bases of small hills. **Status:** Common, but easily overlooked if not calling. **Voice:** Rich, liquid, melodious song, much more varied than that of Cape Grassbird. [G5.7.2]

LOCUSTELLA WARBLERS
Unobtrusive, skulking warblers with fairly long, graduated tails that appear heavy due to the long undertail coverts, which helps to distinguish them from *Bradypterus* warblers (p. 476). All are non-breeding migrants. Sexes alike.

4 COMMON GRASSHOPPER WARBLER *Locustella naevia* 12-13 cm
The finely streaked upperparts and dark-spotted vent and undertail coverts are diagnostic, although these features are often hard to discern as it creeps through low undergrowth and on the ground. Belly and undertail coverts are whiter than in other *Locustella* warblers in the region. **Habitat:** Dense thickets and tangles, often near water in low-lying areas. **Status:** Little known and easily overlooked Palearctic migrant Nov-Mar, more frequent in W. **Voice:** Insect-like whirring; 'phwit phwit' contact call. [C4.3b]

5 RIVER WARBLER *Locustella fluviatilis* 13-14 cm
A mostly dark brown warbler with a slightly paler belly and somewhat warmer brown rump and tail than the rest of the upperparts. At close range, shows diffuse streaking on throat and breast; undertail coverts are brown with broad white tips. Juv. is warmer rufous above and creamy buff below. **Habitat:** Thickets in woodland and riverine scrub, usually close to water. **Status:** Scarce Palearctic migrant Oct-Apr; readily located only when it sings Mar-Apr. **Voice:** Buzzy, insect-like 'derr-derr-zerr-zerr' song, mainly at dawn; call is sharp, weaver-like 'chick', accompanied by wing- and tail-flicking. [G5.3.7]

6 SAVI'S WARBLER *Locustella luscinioides* 14 cm
The plainest *Locustella* in the region, with a whitish throat and central belly contrasting with the rufous breast and flanks. Lacks streaked throat and breast of River Warbler (although some Savi's Warblers are faintly streaked on upper breast) and has plain buff undertail coverts (not white-tipped). **Habitat:** Swamps and tangled thickets near water. **Status:** Locally common Palearctic migrant Oct-Apr. **Voice:** Harsh 'pitch' and soft 'puitt' contact calls; song is similar to Common Grasshopper Warbler's, but seldom sings in region. [C4.4]

BRADYPTERUS WARBLERS

Skulking warblers with loud, distinctive songs, told from *Locustella* warblers (p. 474) by their longer, broader tail and shorter undertail coverts. They remain close to the ground in dense vegetation. Sexes alike.

1 KNYSNA WARBLER *Bradypterus sylvaticus*   12 cm
Endemic to South Africa. A small, dark olive-brown, nondescript warbler. Smaller and plainer than Barratt's Warbler, with little if any streaking on throat and upper breast. Tail is broad and graduated, but shorter and squarer than that of Barratt's Warbler; best told by distinctive song. **Habitat:** Dense forest understorey; bracken and briar thickets. **Status:** Vulnerable. Uncommon and localised. **Voice:** Song is accelerating series of sharp whistles, ending in dry trill, 'tsip tsip sip sip sip-ip-ip-ip-ip-ip-ip-ir-r-rrrrrrrr'; both sexes make deep 'chuck' contact calls. [G5.4.10]

2 BARRATT'S WARBLER *Bradypterus barratti*   13 cm
Endemic to S Africa. Slightly larger and longer-tailed than Knysna Warbler, with paler underparts and more heavily streaked throat and breast; best identified by song; ranges overlap in S. Also resembles Little Rush Warbler (p. 478), but occurs in forest (not reedbed) and has different song. Juv. has slightly warmer coloration than adult, being more olive above and yellowish below. **Habitat:** Thick, tangled growth on edges of evergreen forests and plantations. **Status:** Locally common resident and altitudinal migrant. **Voice:** Loud, staccato crescendo 'seee-pllip-pllip' song; harsh 'chrrrrr' alarm calls. [G5.4.9]

3 EVERGREEN FOREST WARBLER *Bradypterus lopezi*   13 cm
A dark brown, forest-dwelling warbler varying racially in extent of white on throat, prominence of supercilium and intensity of russet wash to plumage. The only scrub-warbler found in interiors of tropical African forests: Bamboo and Cinnamon Bracken warblers do not penetrate beyond forest fringe and both differ markedly in song. Range does not overlap with that of similar Barratt's Warbler. **Habitat:** Dense undergrowth of montane forests, often near streams; also in rank vegetation at forest edge. **Status:** Locally common; some altitudinal movements 800-3 100 m. **Voice:** Series of 3-10 single or double notes increasing in volume and lasting 2-3 seconds. [C10.49-50]

4 BANGWA SCRUB-WARBLER *Bradyperus bangwaensis*   14 cm
Endemic to highlands of SW Cameroon and SE Nigeria, but absent from Mt Cameroon and Bioko. A brightly coloured scrub-warbler with rich rusty upperparts and breast, contrasting sharply with white belly and lower breast. Formerly considered a race of Evergreen Forest Warbler, but differs in richer plumage, more open habitat and song. Range does not overlap with other scrub-warblers'. **Habitat:** Mostly in rank, low scrub and bracken and briar thickets; less often in forest edge. **Status:** Locally common. **Voice:** Explosive series of 'chitt chit chit' or 'twitick twitick' notes. [C10.51]

5 CINNAMON BRACKEN WARBLER *Bradyperus cinnamomeus*   14 cm
Similar to Evergreen Forest Warbler, but has more rufous cast to plumage, especially on upperparts and tail, and different habitat and song. Less skulking than most other scrub-warblers. **Habitat:** Tangled vegetation in forest clearings and among bamboo; also rank grassland, heather shrubland, marshes, brambles and bracken, 1 300-4 100 m; does not penetrate forest interior. **Status:** Common, but easily overlooked if not calling. **Voice:** Song starts with 1-5 high-pitched whistles, followed by rapid repetition of single note, 'tee'; alarm call is low-pitched 'krrrr'. [C10.46]

6 BAMBOO WARBLER *Bradypterus alfredi*   13 cm
Difficult to separate from other *Bradypterus* warblers except on voice. Most closely resembles *mariae* race of Evergreen Forest Warbler; is slightly paler on central belly and less streaked on breast; best told by song. Greyer-brown (less rufous) than Cinnamon Bracken Warbler. Range does not overlap with that of Barratt's Warbler. **Habitat:** Diverse: bamboo, long grass, marshes and tangles in woodland, 550-2 500 m. **Status:** Rare, localised resident. **Voice:** Male's song is harsh, unmusical 'cheeww-ka'; monotonous, repeated up to 60 times, quite different from that of other *Bradypterus*; also short 'whitt' call. [C10.42]

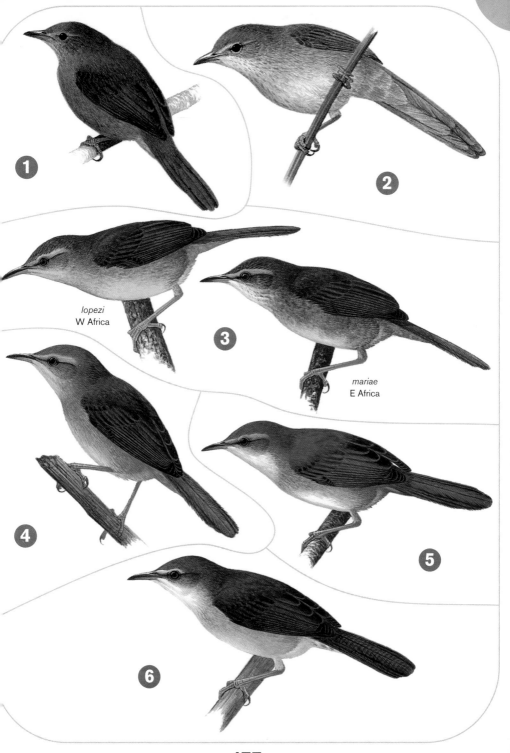

lopezi
W Africa

mariae
E Africa

477

1 LITTLE RUSH WARBLER (AFRICAN SEDGE-WARBLER)
Bradypterus baboecala   14-15 cm

Differs from reed-warblers by its very dark, dusky brown colour, dappled throat and breast, and long, rounded tail. Smaller than White-winged Swamp-Warbler, lacking white wing bars and barred undertail coverts. Slightly smaller than localised Grauer's Swamp-Warbler, with less distinct buffy (not white) supercilium and less boldly streaked breast. Extent of breast streaking and coloration varies geographically. **Habitat:** Reeds and sedges, usually in denser areas further from water than reed-warblers. **Status:** Locally common resident with local movements. **Voice:** Harsh, ratchet-like 'brrrup... brrrup... trrp... trrp... trrp' song, accelerating towards the end and usually accompanied by a wing rattle; also nasal 'wheeaaa'. [C10.43-44, G5.4.8]

2 WHITE-WINGED SWAMP-WARBLER *Bradypterus carpalis*   16-17 cm

Localised endemic to EC Africa. The only *Bradypterus* warbler with a white wing bar and a pale shoulder patch. Underparts are whitish, heavily streaked with brown on chin, throat, sides of breast and flanks; undertail coverts are pale-tipped, appearing barred (not plain, as in other swamp-warblers). Juv. has less distinct underpart streaking, and lacks white wing bar, but has off-white patch at carpal joint. **Habitat:** Dense papyrus beds. **Status:** Locally common, but secretive. **Voice:** Song is series of 'chik', followed by trill, similar to that of Little Rush Warbler, but louder (audible over several hundred metres) and lower pitched. [C10.45]

3 GRAUER'S SWAMP-WARBLER *Bradypterus graueri*   15-16 cm

Endemic to Albertine Rift. Slightly larger than Little Rush Warbler, with a clear white supercilium, heavily spotted chin and throat and an obviously graduated tail, which often appears tatty in the field; song also differs. Range does not overlap with larger Dja River Scrub-Warbler. **Habitat:** Highland swamps, mostly 1 950-2 600 m. **Status:** Endangered due to swamp drainage. Remains locally common. **Voice:** Rapid trill, preceded and sometimes followed by 1-2 guttural 'tchew' notes. [C10.47]

4 DJA RIVER SCRUB-WARBLER *Bradypterus grandis*   19 cm

Endemic to S Cameroon and C Gabon. Distinguished by large size, long graduated tail, black streaks on chest, white underparts, and thin white supercilium. Range does not overlap with smaller Grauer's Swamp-Warbler. **Habitat:** Marshy clearings in forest or at forest edge, where it favours dense sedges. **Status:** Vulnerable. Local and uncommon, very secretive. **Voice:** Short series of 'twiip twiip twipp' notes, followed by trill; gives short display flight similar to that of Little Rush Warbler. [C10.48]

5 VICTORIN'S SCRUB-WARBLER *Bradypterus victorini*   16 cm

Endemic to South Africa. A colourful warbler, easily identified within its restricted range by its cinnamon-orange underparts, blue-grey face and contrasting yellow eye. Juv. is paler below and slightly more rufous above. **Habitat:** Damp, montane fynbos, typically in thick tangles alongside streams and in gullies. **Status:** Common. **Voice:** Quite different from that of other *Bradypterus*; both sexes sing clear, repeated 'weet-weet-weeeo' and rollicking 'whit-itty-weeo, wit-itty weeo', accelerating towards the end; also harsh, pishing alarm call. [G5.5.1]

6 BROAD-TAILED WARBLER *Schoenicola brevirostris*   14-16 cm

A fairly small warbler with a long, broad, black tail which is conspicuous in flight or after heavy rains, when it often perches in the open to dry out its tail and wings. Tail is tipped buff on underside. Flattened head shape is distinctive, with forehead and culmen forming an almost straight line. Juv. has yellowish underparts. **Habitat:** Long, rank grass, usually in damp areas. **Status:** Locally common resident and altitudinal migrant; easily overlooked if not calling. **Voice:** Soft, metallic 'zeenk', repeated at intervals of a few seconds; clear, high-pitched 'peee, peee'. [C11.57, G5.5.2]

A uniform group of reed-warblers that are notoriously tricky to identify. Size, structure, song and leg colour aid identification. Sexes alike.

1 SEDGE-WARBLER *Acrocephalus schoenobaenus*   12-13 cm
One of only two streak-backed *Acrocephalus* warblers, with a short, dark brown tail and a contrasting, unstreaked, rufous rump. Has striking broad, creamy supercilium, with streaked crown lacking central crown stripe of Aquatic Warbler; also is darker above, with shorter streaks and plain rufous (not streaked, straw-coloured) rump. Larger than cisticolas, with shorter tail lacking black-and-white tips. Juv. is yellower and more distinctly marked than adult; sometimes may appear to show pale central crown and could be confused with Aquatic Warbler. **Habitat:** Reedbeds and rank weedy areas bordering wetlands, and thickets sometimes far from water. **Status:** Common Palearctic migrant Nov-Apr. **Voice:** Harsh chattering interspersed with sharp, melodious phrases; 'tuk' call. [C4.6, G5.4.4]

2 AQUATIC WARBLER *Acrocephalus paludicola*   12-13 cm
Similar to Sedge-Warbler, but has a pale median crown stripe, a broader black line above the pale supercilium, and prominent pale stripes down the mantle. Upperparts tend to be paler straw-brown above; rump is straw-coloured and streaked (not plain rufous). Legs are paler than those of Sedge-Warbler, and tail is narrower. Adult's flanks are lightly streaked. **Habitat:** Reedbeds and tall, flooded grasslands; normally forages close to ground. **Status:** Vulnerable. Rare, localised Palearctic migrant Nov-Apr. Secretive and easily overlooked; behaviour recalls *Locustella*. **Voice:** Silent in Africa. [C4.5]

3 EURASIAN REED-WARBLER *Acrocephalus scirpaceus*   12-13 cm
More slender than Marsh-Warbler with a longer bill, paler legs and shorter wing and undertail coverts; typically warmer brown above, with distinctly more rufous rump (although this varies with age and race). Told from African Reed-Warbler with certainty only in the hand (wing formula differs), but typically is colder grey-brown above, and whitish (not buffy) below. **Habitat:** Although there is some overlap, generally favours more aquatic habitats than Marsh-Warbler, frequenting reedbeds and rank vegetation close to water; may occur side by side with African Reed-Warbler. **Status:** Fairly common Palearctic migrant Nov-Apr. **Voice:** Song is typical *Acrocephalus* mixture of musical and harsh notes, 'tchak, tchak, tchak… churr, churr, churr', probably distinguishable from that of African Reed-Warbler only on basis of species mimicked; call notes include low 'churrr'. [C4.7, G5.3.10]

4 AFRICAN REED-WARBLER (AFRICAN MARSH-WARBLER)
Acrocephalus baeticatus   12-13 cm
Told from Marsh-Warbler by its longer bill, warmer brown upperparts, buffy (not greyish) underparts, darker legs and shorter wings (folded wings do not extend beyond rump). Forehead profile is less steep, and is usually found in different habitat. Very difficult to differentiate from Eurasian Reed-Warbler, but generally is warmer brown above and buffy (not whitish) below. Juv. has rufous rump. **Habitat:** Reeds and sedges, rank vegetation and dense gardens. **Status:** Common intra-African migrant. **Voice:** Harsher, more churring and repetitive song than that of Marsh-Warbler, including mimicked phrases of other birds; repeats notes of song 2 to 4 times; song is probably indistinguishable from that of Eurasian Reed-Warbler, except on basis of species mimicked. [C10.52, G5.4.1]

5 (EUROPEAN) MARSH-WARBLER *Acrocephalus palustris*   12-13 cm
Similar to Eurasian and African reed-warblers, but is shorter billed, and longer winged (folded wings extend beyond rump) with long undertail coverts; appears plumper with a more rounded head; plumage typically colder olive-grey above; rump shows little contrast with rest of upperparts; in Africa usually frequents different habitats. Legs average paler pinkish brown (not dark brown). **Habitat:** Rank vegetation, bracken and briar, forest edge, riverine thickets and dense gardens. **Status:** Common Palearctic migrant Nov-Apr. **Voice:** Song differs from songs of African and Eurasian reed-warblers by its clear, melodious phrases, less scratchy than other reed-warblers'; often mimics other birds; call notes include sharp 'chuck'. [C10.53, G5.4.3]

1 GREAT REED-WARBLER *Acrocephalus arundinaceus*   18-20 cm
A large, robust reed-warbler with a fairly prominent buffy supercilium, often located by its harsh, guttural song. Large size readily distinguishes it from most other reed-warblers. Bill is shorter and heavier than equally large Clamorous Reed-Warbler, and wings are much longer, making tail look shorter. Larger and darker than Basra Reed-Warbler; paler and warmer brown above than Greater Swamp-Warbler. Juv. has warmer coloration, underparts with buffy orange wash. **Habitat:** Reedbeds and bush thickets; often near water. **Status:** Common Palearctic migrant Oct-Apr. **Voice:** Prolonged, rambling 'chee-chee-chaak-chaak-chuk-chuk' song, slower than those of smaller reed-warblers. [C4.9, G5.3.8]

2 CLAMOROUS REED-WARBLER *Acrocephalus stentoreus*   18-20 cm
A large reed-warbler, best distinguished from Great Reed-Warbler on shape: appears longer and slimmer due to long, thin bill, which appears very long in the field, and shorter wings which exaggerate length of tail. Primary projection is appreciably shorter than exposed tertials, with wing tip falling well short of ends of undertail coverts. Larger than Basra Reed-Warbler, with warmer brown (not olive-brown) upperparts, and proportionally shorter wing and longer tail. **Habitat:** Reedbeds, papyrus and mangroves. **Status:** Locally common; no evidence of Palearctic migrants entering the region. **Voice:** Song is similar to that of Great Reed-Warbler, but more melodious, higher-pitched and less rhythmic; has variety of short, harsh contact calls.

3 BASRA REED-WARBLER *Acrocephalus griseldis*   14-16 cm
A large, slim reed-warbler with a dark tail and a long bill accentuated by the flat forehead. Slightly smaller than Great Reed-Warbler, with colder, olive-brown (not rufous-brown) upperparts and whitish (not buffy) underparts; build is less robust, closer to that of smaller reed-warblers. Smaller and colder-plumaged than Clamorous Reed-Warbler, with appreciably longer wings (exposed primaries are as long as exposed tertials, with wing tip almost reaching ends of undertail coverts). Narrow, white supercilium with contrasting dark line through eye, as well as unstreaked, white throat and greyish legs, aid in identification. **Habitat:** Reedbeds, thickets and rank vegetation, usually near water. **Status:** Poorly known Palearctic migrant Oct-Apr. **Voice:** Nasal, subdued 'chuc-chuc-churruc-churruc-chuc', similar to contact call of Terrestrial Bulbul. [G5.3.9]

4 LESSER SWAMP-WARBLER (CAPE REED-WARBLER)
Acrocephalus gracilirostris   14-16 cm
A fairly large, slender reed-warbler with a usually fairly prominent supercilium, long bill and dark legs. Pale throat contrasts with darker breast in NE races, but breast is whitish in most areas. Smaller than Greater Swamp-Warbler, with warmer rufous plumage and much more prominent whitish supercilium. Larger than African Reed-Warbler (p. 480), with distinct white supercilium. Wing short and rounded, showing less primary projection than Basra or Great reed-warblers. Dark brown legs appear blackish in the field. Distinct rufous wash on flanks. **Habitat:** Reedbeds, usually over water. **Status:** Common; easily observed; often foraging in the open. **Voice:** Rich, fluty 'cheerup-chee-chiree-chiree' song. [C10.54, G5.4.5]

5 GREATER SWAMP-WARBLER *Acrocephalus rufescens*   16-18 cm
A large, long-billed reed-warbler. Slightly smaller than Great Reed-Warbler, with dark grey-brown (not pale rufous-brown) upperparts, greyish-brown flanks, less prominent supercilium and shorter wings. Larger and darker than Lesser Swamp-Warbler, with greyish (not rufous) flanks and much less prominent pale supercilium. **Habitat:** Papyrus swamps. **Status:** Locally common. **Voice:** Loud 'churrup, churr-churr', interspersed with harsher notes. [C10.55, G5.4.6]

YELLOW WARBLERS

Peculiar flycatcher-like warblers that could be confused with yellow *Hippolais* warblers, but have longer tails, shorter wings and distinctly different head shape and behaviour. Mouth lined orange, which is visible when the bird is singing. Sexes alike.

1 DARK-CAPPED YELLOW WARBLER *Chloropeta natalensis*   14 cm
Readily told from other yellow warblers by its darker brownish or blackish cap that contrasts with the olive-green nape and back; also habitat differs. Intensity of dark cap varies; strongest in E Africa and almost lacking in *major* (Gabon, Angola, DRC and N Zambia), but range does not overlap with those of other species. Female is duller, with less contrast between back and underparts. Juv. has buff wash. **Habitat:** Bracken, sedges and tangled vegetation at forest edge and along streams. **Status:** Locally common, with some seasonal movement. Often inconspicuous, but sings and may hawk insects from exposed perch. **Voice:** Soft 'chip-chip-cheezee-cheezee'. [C10.57, G5.4.7]

2 MOUNTAIN YELLOW WARBLER *Chloropeta similis*   12-14 cm
Lacks the dark cap of Dark-capped Yellow Warbler; olive crown is uniform in colour with nape and back (WC African *major* Dark-capped Yellow Warbler has pale crown, but ranges do not overlap). Also behaves more like a warbler than the flycatcher habits of Dark-capped Yellow Warbler (although bill is broader and more flycatcher-like than that of other species). **Habitat:** Bracken and brier thickets, forest edge, scrub and lightly wooded gullies, usually at higher elevations than Dark-capped Yellow Warbler. Status: Locally common. **Voice:** Loud, particularly melodic song of high and low warbled 'weee weeeo'; harsh 'cha cha' alarm. [C10.58]

3 PAPYRUS YELLOW WARBLER *Chloropeta gracilirostris*   13-14 cm
Differs from other yellow warblers by having a buffy wash on the breast and flanks. Best told by habitat; it is the only yellow warbler found in papyrus swamps; other co-occurring warblers are chiefly brown, grey or buff. **Habitat:** Restricted largely to stands of papyrus beds and sometimes adjacent scrub. Inveterate skulker, it keeps low in swamp vegetation. **Status:** Vulnerable. Uncommon throughout range. **Voice:** Loud, melodic warbling of varied phrases based on 'chwee chwee chweeoo'. [C10.56]

HIPPOLAIS WARBLERS

Medium-large warblers related to reed-warblers, but typically have a more angular crown and square tail. Sexes alike.

4 ICTERINE WARBLER *Hippolais icterina*   13-14 cm
Generally the yellowest *Hippolais* warbler, but some are whitish below and greyish brown above. Told from Melodious and Olivaceous (p. 486) warblers by pale wing panel and blue-grey (not brownish) legs. These features, plus large bill and more angular, sloping forehead, also separate it from smaller Willow Warbler (p. 486). Often shows short yellow supercilium and pale eye-ring. Juv. can appear greyer than adult, with much paler yellow underparts. **Habitat:** Thickets in savanna and arid woodland, plantations and gardens. **Status:** Common Palearctic migrant Oct-Apr. **Voice:** Varied, jumbled notes, including harsh 'tac, tac'. [C10.60, G5.3.5]

5 MELODIOUS WARBLER *Hippolais polyglotta*   12-13 cm
Yellowish morph is most likely to be confused with Icterine Warbler, but is smaller, with a more rounded crown, no pale wing panel, shorter wings and brownish (not blue-grey) legs. On folded wing, primary tips are evenly spaced (not increasing towards wing tip, as in Icterine Warbler). Larger than Willow Warbler (p. 486), with heavier bill. Brown and grey morphs are shorter billed than Olivaceous Warbler (p. 486), and do not flag tail. **Habitat:** Savannas, secondary forest, mangrove woodlands and gardens. **Status:** Common Palearctic migrant Oct-Apr. **Voice:** Contact calls are sparrow-like 'tchuk' and 'trr-trr'; song usually starts with repeated 'twi twi twi twi', developing into rapid, chattering warbles. [C4.12]

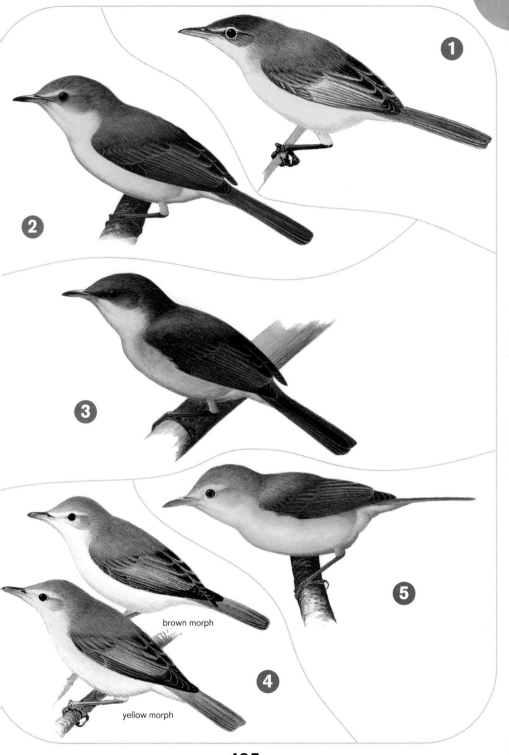

brown morph

yellow morph

1 OLIVACEOUS WARBLER *Hippolais pallida*   12-13 cm
A drab warbler with short wings, no pale wing panel and short undertail coverts that make the square, pale-edged tail appear long. Tail is regularly waved or flagged downwards, but not side to side as Upcher's Warbler; also, tail is shorter and not as dark. Lacks pale wing panel of greymorph Icterine Warbler (p. 484), and has shorter wings. Head is more angular than that of Melodious Warbler (p. 484), and lacks any yellow in plumage. Shorter-winged, paler and longer-billed than Garden Warbler. **Habitat:** Arid and semi-arid open woodland and thicket. **Status:** Common resident and Palearctic migrant Sep-May. **Voice:** Song is busy, scratchy warble, reminiscent of *Acrocephalus* warbler's; contact call is short, sharp, persistent 'tec'. [C4.11]

2 UPCHER'S WARBLER *Hippolais languida*   14 cm
A drab, long-tailed warbler, best identified by its exaggerated, constant side-to-side tail flagging, with tail slightly depressed and fanned. Undertail is noticeably dark, and appears long because of short undertail coverts. Behaviour and indistinct pale wing panel separate it from Olivaceous Warbler. Smaller and darker than Olive-tree Warbler, with smaller bill. **Habitat:** Semi-arid savanna and thickets. **Status:** Uncommon Palearctic migrant Nov-Apr. **Voice:** Song is prolonged musical warble, similar to *Sylvia* warblers'; 'tec tec' call is softer than that of Olivaceous Warbler.

3 OLIVE-TREE WARBLER *Hippolais olivetorum*   15 cm
A large, pale grey warbler with a distinctly angled crown. Larger than Upcher's Warbler, with heavier bill and paler grey upperparts, usually with more prominent pale panel in wing; does not flag tail. Larger and greyer than Olivaceous Warbler, with much longer and heavier bill. Legs are thick, with distinctly robust feet. Could be confused with juv. Barred Warbler (p. 492), but long bill and flat forehead are distinctive. **Habitat:** Dense clumps of thicket in acacia savanna. **Status:** Uncommon Palearctic migrant Nov-Apr. **Voice:** Most easily located by chattering song, which sounds like that of Great Reed-Warbler. [C10.59, G5.3.6]

PHYLLOSCOPUS WARBLERS
Small, active leaf-gleaning warblers. Palearctic migrant species typically found in drier savanna and woodland. Sexes alike.

4 WILLOW WARBLER *Phylloscopus trochilus*   11 cm
The most common *Phylloscopus* in much of Africa. Most are yellow-olive birds from Europe, but paler E *yakutensis* are brown above and whitish below. In N, most similar to Common Chiffchaff, but have paler legs and do not dip tail, plus call differs. Bill is thin and weak compared to Icterine Warbler (p. 484), and yellow is restricted to throat and breast. Juv. has yellow underparts; supercilium and face are much brighter yellow than those of adult. **Habitat:** Wide range of woodland and savanna. **Status:** Abundant Palearctic migrant Oct-Apr. **Voice:** Soft, 2-note contact call, 'hoeet hoeet'; short, melodious song, descending in scale. [C4.31, G5.5.3]

5 COMMON CHIFFCHAFF *Phylloscopus collybita*   10-11 cm
Best told from Willow Warbler by its blackish (not pale brown) legs, more active foraging behaviour and different call. Often dips tail downwards. Smaller and duller than Wood Warbler (p. 488), lacking conspicuous yellowish fringes to wing and tail feathers. Stronger head pattern than Bonelli's warblers, with uniform back, rump and tail. **Habitat:** Savanna in Sahel; highland forest and forest edge in E Africa. **Status:** Common Palearctic migrant Oct-Apr. **Voice:** Song is onomatopoeic 'chiff-chaff-chiff-chaff'; contact call is thin 'hweet' (unlike 2-note call of Willow Warbler). [C4.28/30]

6 WESTERN BONELLI'S WARBLER *Phylloscopus bonelli*   11-12 cm
A rather drab *Phylloscopus* with only a weakly developed supercilium; rump is yellow. Told from Willow Warbler by greenish or golden-brown wing panel, from Wood Warbler (p. 488) by lack of yellow throat, and from smaller Common Chiffchaff by longer primary projection and less bold facial patterning. **Habitat:** Well-treed savannas and dry riverbeds. **Status:** Uncommon to locally common Palearctic migrant Sep-Apr. **Voice:** Song is monotonous, evenly pitched trill, usually lasting less than 2 seconds; contact call is 2-note 'hoo-eet', rising in pitch. [C4.26] **Similar species: Eastern Bonelli's Warbler** *P. orientalis* has paler grey (not brown) upperparts; best told by single-note call; Palearctic migrant to Sudan.

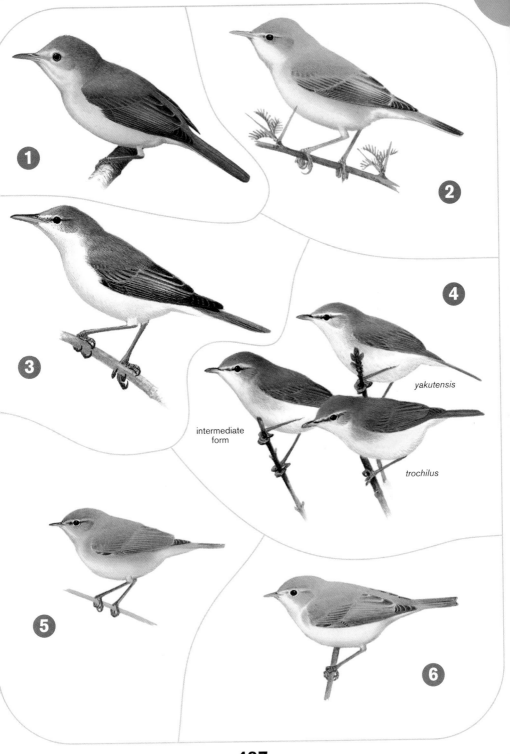

intermediate
form

yakutensis

trochilus

1 WOOD WARBLER *Phylloscopus sibilatrix*   12-13 cm
Distinguished from other *Phylloscopus* warblers by the well-demarcated yellow throat and upper breast, as well as bright green upperparts with an obvious green wing panel. Undertail coverts are white (not yellow as resident woodland-warblers). **Habitat:** Lowland forest and forest fringes, riverine woodland and, occasionally, mangroves. **Status:** Locally common Palearctic migrant Sep-Apr. **Voice:** Song is distinctive, based on single 'tsip' note, starting slowly and then accelerating into descending trill; contact call is soft 'peu' or 'wit-wit-wit'. [C4.27]

2 LAURA'S WOODLAND-WARBLER *Phylloscopus laurae*   10-11 cm
Endemic to SC Africa. Lacks chestnut cap of Yellow-throated Woodland-Warbler. Differs from Willow Warbler (p. 486) by having distinct yellow throat, upper breast and vent contrasting with greyish-white lower breast and belly. **Habitat:** Gallery forest, swamp forest and adjacent secondary growth; montane forest in Angola. Usually in mid-stratum and canopy but sometimes forages in undergrowth. **Status:** Common; usually in pairs and small groups, sometimes in mixed bird parties. **Voice:** Very vocal; loud, warbling, whistled 'tsee tsiree tseee' song, higher pitched and faster than Yellow-throated Woodland-Warbler's. [C10.66]

3 YELLOW-THROATED WOODLAND-WARBLER *Phylloscopus ruficapillus*   11 cm
Endemic to SE Africa. The chestnut crown separates it from Laura's Woodland-Warbler. Told from Willow Warbler (p. 486) by brown crown, forest habitat and greater contrast between greyish belly and bright yellow throat, upper breast and vent. E Tanzanian *minullus* has olive-brown crown; W Tanzanian *ochrogularis* has brownish tinge to yellow face and throat, and could be confused with Red-faced Woodland-Warbler, but has distinctive yellow (not whitish) vent. Juv. is greener on breast. **Habitat:** Evergreen forest, in canopy and mid-strata. **Status:** Locally common. **Voice:** Song is loud 'seee suuu seee suuu'. [G5.5.4]

4 UGANDA WOODLAND-WARBLER *Phylloscopus budongoensis*   10 cm
A small, drab, short-billed woodland-warbler. Differs from Willow Warbler (p. 486) by strongly contrasting white supercilium and black eye-stripe, as well as forest habitat. Smaller and more slender than Green Hylia (p. 534), with thinner bill and different song. Differs from White-browed Crombec (p. 534) by longer tail. **Habitat:** Primary and secondary mid-altitude forest. **Status:** Uncommon to locally common; usually in pairs; frequents bird parties. **Voice:** Distinctive, high-pitched, short phrase, 'chi cher chi chwee'. [C10.65]

5 RED-FACED WOODLAND-WARBLER *Phylloscopus laetus*   10-11 cm
Endemic to Albertine Rift. Told from Uganda and Yellow-throated woodland-warblers by its reddish-brown face and throat, which also distinguish it from Willow Warbler (p. 486) (unlikely in montane forest). Most similar to Brown Woodland-Warbler, but has whitish or grey-white (not buffy-brown) belly and vent. E DRC *schoutedeni* has darker rufous wash over face and darker underparts. **Habitat:** Mid-altitude and montane forests and adjacent secondary growth, especially in bamboo zone. Frequent member of bird parties in mid- and top canopy. **Status:** Common. **Voice:** Short, 2- to 3-phrase 'peetree puutree petree' song. [C10.67]

6 BROWN WOODLAND-WARBLER *Phylloscopus umbrovirens*   11 cm
Endemic to NE Africa. Darker than other *Phylloscopus* warblers, with predominantly brownish plumage. Darker than Red-faced Woodland-Warbler, with buffy-brown (not whitish) belly and vent. Dull olive-brown above, with greenish edges to wing feathers. **Habitat:** Montane forests; gleaning in mid-canopy. **Status:** Common; usually in pairs. **Voice:** Descending series of clear notes, 'tuu tee teeweeo', unlike other woodland-warblers'. [C10.64]

7 BLACK-CAPPED WOODLAND-WARBLER *Phylloscopus herberti*   10 cm
Endemic to SW Cameroon and SE Nigeria. Differs from all other *Phylloscopus* warblers by having a diagnostic black crown and eye-stripe. If crown is not visible, could be confused with Green Hylia (p. 534) (but is smaller) or Uganda Woodland-Warbler (ranges are not known to overlap). **Habitat:** Varied, but usually mid-altitude primary forest and sometimes secondary growth; creeps about in canopy and mid-stratum and sometimes in low undergrowth. **Status:** Locally common; usually in pairs; sometimes joins mixed bird parties. **Voice:** Similar to Uganda Woodland-Warbler's, but shorter, faster and lower pitched. [C10.68]

Small to large warblers with plain backs, rounded heads and short, fairly stout bills; tails usually square with pale outer-tail feathers. Sexes differ in some species.

1 RÜPPELL'S WARBLER *Sylvia rueppelli*   14 cm
Male's black chin and throat, bordered by prominent white moustachial stripe, is diagnostic. Female and juv. much duller; best separated from Subalpine, Sardinian and Ménétries' warblers and Lesser Whitethroat (p. 492) by white-fringed (not buff-fringed or uniform) tertials. **Habitat:** Low vegetation, often in oases. **Status:** Fairly common Palearctic migrant Sep-Mar. **Voice:** Contact call harsh 'chrrr'; song jerky mixture of musical notes and chattering rattles. [C10.62]

2 SARDINIAN WARBLER *Sylvia melanocephala*   13-14 cm
Male lacks the black throat patch of Rüppell's Warbler. Greyer on breast than Ménétrie's Warbler, with sharper contrast between black crown and grey nape; cocks its tail, but does not wave it. Female and juv. are darker and browner above than Rüppell's Warbler, with buff (not white) fringes to greater coverts and tertials. Lower mandible is slate grey (flesh-coloured in Ménétries' Warbler). **Habitat:** Desert scrub, thickets and oases. **Status:** Locally fairly common Palearctic migrant Nov-Mar. **Voice:** Contact call machine-gun-like rattle that starts and ends abruptly. [C4.19] **Similar species: Cyprus Warbler** *S. melanothorax* has shorter tail, black mottling on throat and breast, and white tertial fringes; Palearctic vagrant to NE Sudan.

3 SUBALPINE WARBLER *Sylvia cantillans*   12 cm
A fairly small, plump warbler with a small bill. Chin, throat and breast of male are much more richly coloured than in Ménétries' Warbler, highlighting white moustachial stripe; does not constantly wag its tail. Smaller than Rüppell's Warbler, with less contrasting buff (not white) tertial fringes and pale (not dark grey) lower mandible. Juv. lacks contrast between crown and mantle, unlike juv. Sardinian Warbler. **Habitat:** Dense vegetation in arid savannas; occasionally in reedbeds and mangroves. **Status:** Locally common Palearctic migrant Oct-Apr. **Voice:** High-pitched 'tsee' contact call; song rather musical, largely lacking harsh notes. [C4.20] **Similar species: Tristram's Warbler** *S. deserticola* has shorter wings and rufous wing edgings; rare in extreme N Mali.

4 MÉNÉTRIES' WARBLER *Sylvia mystacea*   13-14 cm
Male differs from Subalpine Warbler by black face and tail contrasting with grey upperparts. Female and juv. are best separated from other *Sylvia* warblers by their habit of constantly wagging their tails up and down and from side to side. Subalpine and Sardinian warblers lack contrast between dark tail and paler rump. **Habitat:** Scrubby vegetation on the coastal plain. **Status:** Uncommon Palearctic migrant Sep-May. **Voice:** Contact call soft 'meek'; song musical and warbling, interspersed with harsh rattles.

5 SPECTACLED WARBLER *Sylvia conspicillata*   12-13 cm
A small, elegant warbler extensively suffused with pinkish below. Within its range, confusion with other *Sylvia* warblers is unlikely. White eye-ring and extensive brown in wings separate it from Subalpine Warbler and Lesser Whitethroat (p. 492). Female duller with buffy throat and browner head and mantle. **Habitat:** Coastal scrub and desert wadis. **Status:** Locally common Palearctic migrant Oct-Apr. **Voice:** Contact call high-pitched 'tsee'; song a warbled mixture of twitters, whistles and rattles. [C4.21]

6 AFRICAN DESERT WARBLER *Sylvia deserti*   11-12 cm
A small, compact, pale sandy warbler. Paler and more uniform above than Asian Desert Warbler; ranges not known to overlap. Frequently flicks and cocks tail. Sexes alike. **Habitat:** Sandy and stony deserts with some vegetation; spends much time on or close to ground. **Status:** Locally common; usually solitary. **Voice:** Bouncy warbling song, starting with rattle and ending with rising whistle; contact call rattling 'krrrrr'. [C4.18]

7 ASIAN DESERT WARBLER *Sylvia nana*   11-12 cm
Head and mantle greyer than African Desert Warbler's, contrasting with brighter rufous-brown-edged wing and tail feathers. Sexes alike. **Habitat:** Arid coastal scrub. **Status:** Fairly common Palearctic migrant, Nov-Feb. **Voice:** Like African Desert Warbler, but mid-part of song is monotonous 'dididididididididi'.

1 BLACKCAP *Sylvia atricapilla*   13-15 cm
A compact, grey-brown warbler, distinguished from other species by its distinctive crown patch, black in male and reddish-brown in female. Juv. like female but duller. If head not seen, could be confused with Garden Warbler (p. 494). **Habitat:** Woodland, forest edge and gardens. **Status:** Common Palearctic migrant Sep-Apr. **Voice:** Call hard 'tac'; song is a series of varied warbles, initially subdued, but becoming more persistent. [C4.15, G6.15.8]

2 GREATER WHITETHROAT *Sylvia communis*   13-15 cm
A slender, long-tailed warbler with obvious rufous wing panels. Grey head of male contrasts with silvery-white throat. Female has brown head; juv. lacks white outer-tail feathers. Larger than Subalpine Warbler (p. 490), with grey-brown (not reddish) eye. Eye-ring is less prominent than in Spectacled Warbler (p. 490), and is almost white (not pinkish-buff) below. **Habitat:** Shrubs in arid savanna, often near water. **Status:** Locally common Palearctic migrant Sep-Apr. **Voice:** Soft 'whit' and grating 'tchack' and 'tchurr' alarm calls; song harsh, snappy mixture of grating and melodious notes. [C4.16, G5.2.10]

3 LESSER WHITETHROAT *Sylvia curruca*   12-13 cm
A small, slim warbler with a dark face mask and white outer-tail. Smaller than Greater Whitethroat, lacking chestnut fringes to wing feathers. Legs are dark, not pale as in Subalpine and Sardinian warblers (p. 490); tail is grey (blackish in orphean warblers); other warblers lack dark face mask. **Habitat:** Arid savannas and waterside thickets. **Status:** Locally common Palearctic migrant, mostly Oct-Mar. **Voice:** Song starts as very subdued musical warble, developing into rattled 'chikka-chikka-chikka'; contact call harsh 'tack tack'. [C4.17] **Similar species: Hume's Whitethroat** *S. althaea* is larger and darker, with different song; melodious 'wheet wheet' contact call. Status unclear; may occur in NE.

4 WESTERN ORPHEAN WARBLER *Sylvia hortensis*   15cm
Larger and duller than Lesser Whitethroat, with a heavier bill and a blackish tail that contrasts with the grey uppertail coverts. Adult's pale eye (brown in juv.) separates it from Arabian Warbler. Juv. has uniform wing coverts, lacking pale tips to the greater and median coverts of juv. Barred Warbler. **Habitat:** Arid savannas. **Status:** Locally common Palearctic migrant Oct-Apr; usually solitary or in small groups. **Voice:** Contact call single 'tek', sometimes repeated rapidly; song rich medley of repeated phrases with thrush-like quality. [C4.13a]

5 EASTERN ORPHEAN WARBLER *Sylvia crassirostris*   15 cm
Recently split from Western Orphean Warbler; ranges probably do not overlap. Male greyer above and whiter below, with a cleaner cap, diffuse dark centres to undertail coverts, and more robust bill. Female and juv. paler and greyer than female Western Orphean Warbler. **Habitat:** Arid savannas. **Status:** Locally common Palearctic migrant Oct-Apr. **Voice:** Contact call single 'tek'; song richer and more varied than Western Orphean Warbler's. [C4.13b]

6 ARABIAN (RED SEA) WARBLER *Sylvia leucomelaena*   14-15 cm
Similar to orphean warblers, but has a dark eye, broken white eye-ring (in male), and shorter primary projection beyond the tertials, appearing longer-tailed; *blanfordi* (Sudan) has white-edged tertials, and stronger contrast between black hood and grey-brown back; these features less pronounced in *somaliensis* (Eritrea-Somalia). Regularly dips its tail, and often hangs upside-down when feeding. **Habitat:** Arid acacia thickets, semi-desert scrub and rocky hillsides. **Status:** Fairly common on coastal plain, scarcer inland. **Voice:** Contact call soft 'tchack'; song slow, loud, far-carrying warble, ending with series of clear, fluty notes.

7 BARRED WARBLER *Sylvia nisoria*   15-16 cm
Adult has grey-brown upperparts with white wing bars, yellow eyes and grey, crescent-shaped barring on pale underparts. Juv. is browner, with grey eye and barring confined to flanks and vent. Larger than Garden Warbler (p. 494), with double wing bar (formed by pale tips to greater and median coverts), pale tertial fringes and whitish (not buff) outer-tail. Pale covert tips and tertial fringes separate it from juv. Orphean Warblers. **Habitat:** Dry woodland, watercourses and thickets. **Status:** Locally common Palearctic migrant, mostly Oct-Apr. **Voice:** Subdued warbling song; contact call rattling 'trrrt' or 'tschurrrr'. [C10.61]

1 GARDEN WARBLER *Sylvia borin*   13-15 cm
A plump, drab greyish or olive-brown warbler, paler below but without marked contrasts or distinctive features. Lacks white outer-tail of Brown Parisoma. Smaller than juv. Barred Warbler (p. 492) with finer bill, plain (not barred) flanks and less prominent pale edges to wing feathers. Differs from Olivaceous Warbler (p. 486) by rounded (not peaked) crown, with indistinct dark eye-stripe and pale supercilium. **Habitat:** Thick tangles in range of forest, bush and riverine habitats. **Status:** Common Palearctic migrant, mostly Sep-Apr. **Voice:** Subdued, monotonous song, interspersed with soft, grating phrases; call harsh 'tec'. [C4.14, G5.2.9]

2 BROWN PARISOMA *Parisoma lugens*   13-14 cm
A dull brown warbler with paler underparts, especially belly and vent. Told from Garden Warbler by its white outer-tail. Occurs at lower elevation (below 2 500 m) than Bale Parisoma in Ethiopia. Much larger and shorter-tailed than Buff-bellied Warbler (p. 524). Eye is dark red-brown. **Habitat:** Usually in tops of acacia trees, especially flat-topped *Acacia abyssinica* and fever trees, at mid- to high altitudes. **Status:** Uncommon and thinly distributed; usually in pairs. **Voice:** Short, loud 'tchwee tchwee' alarm call; song a wheezy trill. [C10.63]

3 BALE PARISOMA *Parisoma griseaventris*   13 cm
Endemic to Bale Mts, Ethiopia. Similar to Brown Parisoma (often lumped with this species), but is greyer, especially on upperparts, with greyish throat and breast, contrasting slightly but merging with off-white belly and vent. **Habitat:** Juniper and *Hygenea* scrub and adjacent bracken and bramble thickets at and above tree-line. Occurs above 3 500 m, much higher than Brown Parisoma in Ethiopia. **Status:** Common; occurs singly or in pairs; territorial. **Voice:** Harsh churs and sharper 'chreek' call than Brown Parisoma's.

4 BANDED PARISOMA *Parisoma boehmi*   12-13 cm
Endemic to NE Africa. Adult has a diagnostic black breast band, pale eyes, dark mottling on throat, white outer-tail and white wing bars. Juv. lacks breast band and has darker eye and buffy wing bars; easily confused with juv. Barred Warbler (p. 492), but is smaller with shorter wings and plain (not barred or mottled) flanks. Larger than Red-fronted Warbler (p. 524) (which can have faint breast band) with a shorter tail that is not cocked. **Habitat:** Canopy of bushes and trees in arid savanna, acacia scrub, and riverine thickets. **Status:** Common; often joins bird parties. **Voice:** Squeaky 'chik-wurra chick wurr'; song jumbled mix of musical whistles, rattles and churrs.

5 LAYARD'S TIT-BABBLER *Parisoma layardi*   14-15 cm
Endemic to S Africa. Paler than Chestnut-vented Tit-Babbler, with a whitish (not chestnut) vent. Pale eye contrasts with dark head, and throat streaking is less pronounced than in Chestnut-vented Tit-babbler. Juv. lacks throat streaking. **Habitat:** Karoo scrub, arid savanna, scrubby areas among grassland, and coastal thicket; often found in rocky, hilly areas. **Status:** Common. **Voice:** Clear 'pee-pee-cheeri-cheeri', similar in quality to that of Chestnut-vented Tit-babbler. [G5.3.2]

6 CHESTNUT-VENTED TIT-BABBLER *Parisoma subcaeruleum*   14-15 cm
Endemic to SW Africa. Differs chiefly from Layard's Tit-babbler by having a chestnut (not whitish) vent. Streaking on throat is bolder and more extensive than in Layard's Tit-babbler. Juv. lacks throat streaking. N races are paler above, with more extensive white underparts. **Habitat:** Savanna, especially acacia thickets, dry watercourses and coastal thicket. **Status:** Common. **Voice:** Loud, fluty 'cheruuup-chee-chee' or 'tjerik-tik-tik'; also imitates calls of other birds. [G5.3.1]

7 ABYSSINIAN CATBIRD *Parophasma galinieri*   14-15 cm
Endemic to Abyssinian highlands. Grey body, chestnut vent and pale grey-white frons are diagnostic. Best located by its explosive song. **Habitat:** Montane forest and edge, adjacent scrub and bracken and bramble cover; occurs in pairs; keeps to cover in undergrowth and mid-stratum. **Status:** Common. **Voice:** Soft, churring alarm note; song varied and loud thrush-like warbling, with more warbler-like higher notes; pairs duet; often sits in open when singing.

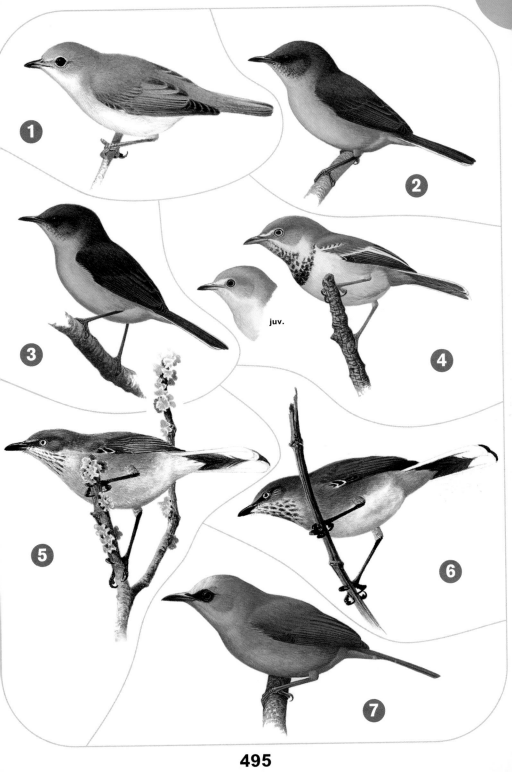

juv.

Cisticolas are a large genus of primarily African warblers that are notoriously difficult to identify. Species are typically grouped on whether they have plain or streaked backs and on tail length, but some plain-backed species have streaked non-breeding plumage, and tails of non-breeders are often longer. Song is often the best character, but with practice and experience most non-calling birds can be identified. Sexes generally alike, although males are much larger in some species. Non-breeders and juvs are often yellower beneath, more rufous above, and may have longer tails.

1 RED-FACED CISTICOLA *Cisticola erythrops* 13-14 cm
A plain-faced, warm buff and rufous cisticola found near water. Brown (not rufous) crown and warm rufous face distinguish it from all other plain-backed species. Wings are brown, uniform with the back; lacks Singing Cisticola's rufous edges to primaries. **Habitat:** Rank vegetation next to pans and streams. **Status:** Common. **Voice:** Male utters a series of piercing whistles, typically descending in pitch in S Africa, ascending in E Africa; also dry 'prrt prrt' calls. Female usually calls with male, deep 'zidit'. Alarm call is thin, high-pitched 'tseeeep'. [C10.90, G5.8.4]

2 SINGING CISTICOLA *Cisticola cantans* 13-14 cm
Rufous edges to primaries form a diagnostic rufous wing panel. Most similar to Red-faced Cisticola, but has rufous (not brown) crown and browner (less rufous) face; underparts often whiter. In C Africa could be confused with plain-backed races of Rattling Cisticola (p. 502) but is duller, and habitat and song differ. Nominate race (Ethiopia) has streaked back in non-breeding plumage. **Habitat:** Rank vegetation, bracken and tall grass with scattered bushes. **Status:** Common. **Voice:** Loud, disyllabic 'jhu-weee' or 'whee-cho'; also dry rattles and croaks. [C10.91, G5.8.3]

3 CHATTERING CISTICOLA *Cisticola anonymus* 12-13 cm
A rather small, plain cisticola told from Whistling Cisticola by habitat and contrast between dull rufous cap and brown-grey to olive-brown back. Looks and sounds like NW races of Rattling Cisticola (p. 502), but is smaller and habitat differs. Darker than Bubbling Cisticola with a more rufous (not buffy) face. **Habitat:** Tall grass at forest edge, humid savanna, marshy clearings, plantations and secondary growth; often in villages and fields. **Status:** Common; demonstrative and confident. **Voice:** Song 'cha cha cha trrrr' similar to Rattling Cisticola's; sings from a prominent perch. Also chattering 'chi titititi' or 'chi chrrrrr' calls. [C10.89]

4 TRILLING CISTICOLA *Cisticola woosnami* 13-14 cm
A large, rather plain cisticola, easily recognised by its song. Rufous cap is only weakly developed, but unlike Whistling Cisticola still shows some contrast with brown back. Larger than Neddicky (p. 500), with a heavier bill and less contrasting crown. **Habitat:** Broadleafed woodland, especially miombo, and grassland; favours drier areas than Whistling Cisticola. **Status:** Common; easily detected during breeding season when males are singing. **Voice:** Song is a long, drawn-out, trilled whistle, sometimes ascending in pitch, usually given from a prominent perch; also dry 'chik-ik' call. [C10.88]

5 WHISTLING CISTICOLA *Cisticola lateralis* 13-14 cm
Plainer than Chattering and Singing cisticolas, with no chestnut cap and a stouter bill. Duller than Trilling Cisticola, with crown uniform with mantle, and with a paler, almost white breast. Behaviour is distinctive: male gives loud, whistling song on top of bushes and small trees for long periods. **Habitat:** Rank vegetation and bracken at forest edge and tall grassland with small trees and bushes. **Status:** Common. **Voice:** Short, melodic, whistled song; 'cha cha' alarm notes are harsher, but are more melodic than other similar species. [C10.87]

6 BUBBLING CISTICOLA *Cisticola bulliens* 13-14 cm
Endemic to coastal Angola, N to S Gabon. Range overlaps with Red-faced Cisticola and, in N, with Chattering and Whistling cisticolas; paler overall with no rufous crown, but best told by its distinctive song. Breeding plumage is slightly warmer rufous-brown. **Habitat:** Grasslands, marshes and drier, wooded grassy areas. **Status:** Little known; apparently locally common in some areas in Angola. **Voice:** Loud 'chee chee chrrrr', similar to Rattling Cisticola.

1 br. non-br.

2 br. non-br.

4

3

5 6

PLAIN-BACKED CISTICOLAS

1 LAZY CISTICOLA *Cisticola aberrans* 13-14 cm
Differs from other plain-backed species within its range by having a pale supercilium, extending well behind eye. Frequently cocks its tail like a prinia; tail lacks dark subterminal bar. Larger than Neddicky or Long-tailed Cisticola (p. 500) with longer, frequently cocked tail and typically a less well-defined rufous cap. Often lumped with Rock-loving Cisticola, but has buffy (not greyish) underparts; ranges do not overlap. **Habitat:** Rocky hillslopes in grassland and woodland. **Status:** Locally common. **Voice:** Bleating 'tzeeee-tzeeee-tzeeee' and scolding, harsh 'cheee-cheee'. [G5.8.9]

2 ROCK-LOVING CISTICOLA *Cisticola emini* 13-14 cm
Often treated as a race of Lazy Cisticola, but has grey (not buffy) flanks and more clearly-defined rufous cap; ranges do not overlap. Differs from other plain-backed species by its pale supercilium and long, plain tail that is often held cocked, like a prinia's. **Habitat:** Grassy and lightly wooded rocky hillsides. **Status:** Localised and uncommon; unobtrusive except when breeding. **Voice:** Ascending 'pee-yah', dry trilling 'tr-r-r-r-r-rt' and harsh, scolding 'skueeee skueeee'; lacks bleating calls of Lazy Cisticola. [C10.86]

DUETTING CISTICOLAS
Rather large cisticolas with plain backs, dark lores and characteristic duetting songs. Occur in pairs or small groups; most in montane grassland. They form a super-species with largely non-overlapping ranges.

3 CHUBB'S (BROWN-BACKED) CISTICOLA *Cisticola chubbi* 14-15 cm
A large highland cisticola; paler than Hunter's Cisticola, with plain (not patterned) back and brighter rufous crown; occurs at lower elevation in area of overlap at Mt Elgon. Recalls Singing Cisticola (p. 496), but slightly larger with uniform brown wings (lacking rufous primary panel). In W Africa is larger than Chattering Cisticola (p. 496), with black lores and brighter rufous crown. W African *discolor* is sometimes treated as a separate species, Brown-backed Cisticola; differs mainly in having darker, grey-buff underparts; song similar. **Habitat:** Tall grasses and shrubs at forest edge in submontane to montane areas; also old fields and rank vegetation. **Status:** Common; conspicuous when duetting. **Voice:** Loud, clear, whistled duet, 'twee dee dee dee' and 'ti-deewit ti-deewit'. [C10.92-4]

4 HUNTER'S CISTICOLA *Cisticola hunteri* 13-14 cm
Endemic to E Africa. A fairly large cisticola of montane grassland and heath, with a dark reddish-brown cap, dark brown upperparts, dark lores, longish tail and distinctive duetting behaviour. Some individuals have streaked backs. Meets Chubb's Cisticola at Mt Elgon, but typically occurs at higher elevation, and is slightly smaller and darker, with less contrasting, duller crown. **Habitat:** Tall grasses and shrubs at forest edge, above 1 600 m. **Status:** Locally common. **Voice:** Rolling, trilling, musical duet from bush tops; male gives 'tweet-errrrr tweet-errrr' and female 'tsee-twit tsee-twit'.

5 BLACK-LORED CISTICOLA *Cisticola nigriloris* 15 cm
Endemic to highlands in S Tanzania and N Malawi. A large, chunky, richly coloured cisticola. The distinct black lores separate it from Trilling and Singing cisticolas (p. 496); also larger and has distinctive 'squeaky-wheel' duetting song. **Habitat:** Highland grasslands, heath tangles of bracken and briar, often near water. **Status:** Common and conspicuous, often in groups of 3-8 birds. **Voice:** Musical 'see-saw' duet, typically comprising 3-note song from one bird and creaking call from the other. Sometimes 3 or more birds join the chorus.

6 KILOMBERO (MELODIOUS) CISTICOLA *Cisticola sp.* 14 cm
Endemic to Kilombero swamp, S Tanzania. A recently discovered species, not formally described. Similiar to Black-lored Cisticola, but with a short white supercilium above the darker lores; habitat quite different, and ranges do not overlap. **Habitat:** Reedbeds, usually tall stands of *Phragmites*. **Status:** Locally common. **Voice:** Loud, musical duet, somewhat more varied than Black-lored Cisticola's.

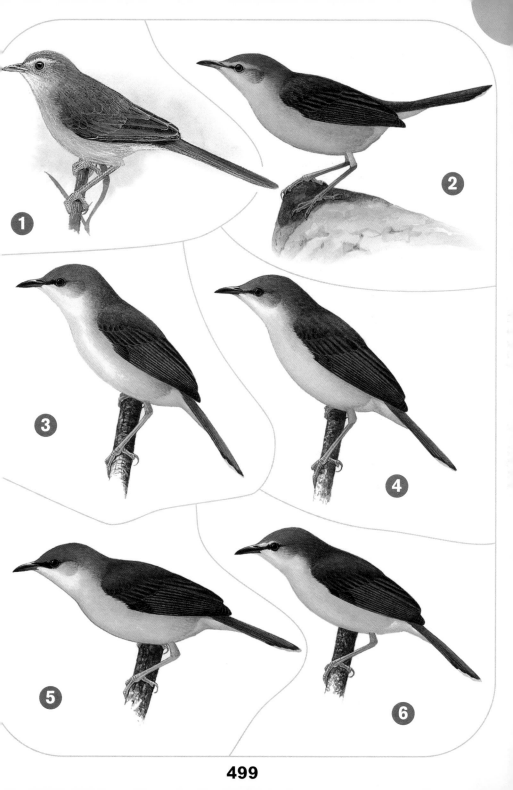

1 NEDDICKY (PIPING CISTICOLA) *Cisticola fulvicapilla*   11 cm
A small, plain-backed cisticola with dark grey (Cape to Natal) or pale buffy-grey underparts, uniform brownish upperparts and chestnut cap. Most similar to Long-tailed Cisticola, but ranges barely overlap (N Zambia), where best told by slightly shorter, less graduated tail and higher-pitched song. Longer-tailed than Short-winged Cisticola, with a distinct chestnut cap and different song. NW *dispar* has a less distinct cap and is darker above, with a darker cap lacking obvious black subterminal tips, but is shorter tailed than Black-tailed Cisticola, with a more contrasting cap and different habitat. **Habitat:** Grassy understorey of woodland and savanna; also mountain fynbos and plantations, especially where there are dead trees. **Status:** Common. **Voice:** Monotonous, high-pitched, frog-like 'tseeep tseeep tseeep' song with ventriloqual qualities and hollow, piping resonance; alarm call is fast, dry 'tictictictic'. [C10.84, G5.9.1]

2 LONG-TAILED (TABORA) CISTICOLA *Cisticola angusticauda*   10-11 cm
Often considered a race of Neddicky, but has a slightly longer, more graduated tail and deeper call (where ranges meet). Longer-tailed than Short-winged Cisticola, with a well-defined cap; occurs in denser woodland. **Habitat:** Broadleafed woodland, especially miombo; forages in rank grass, but flies into trees when disturbed. **Status:** Locally common. **Voice:** Locally variable; piping call is similar to Neddicky's, but is typically deeper in areas of overlap. [C10.85]

3 BLACK-TAILED (SLENDER-TAILED) CISTICOLA *Cisticola melanurus* 10-11 cm
Endemic to NE Angola and SW DRC. Rufous-brown crown merges smoothly into the back, lacking the capped appearance of Neddicky and Long-tailed Cisticola. Long, slender tail is black with grey tip and white outer web (male only). Gleans from tree foliage like an apalis. **Habitat:** Canopy of stunted miombo woodland. **Status:** Poorly known; but not uncommon in Angola. **Voice:** Apparently trembles wings while making unusual purring sound; also soft, wheezy squeak. Jerky display flight accompanied by loud clicking sounds is reportedly similar to that of São Tomé Prinia.

4 SHORT-WINGED (SIFFLING) CISTICOLA *Cisticola brachypterus*   10-11 cm
A small, fairly short-tailed, nondescript cisticola with a plain, open face. Lacks a rufous crown and is shorter-tailed than Neddicky and Long-tailed Cisticola. Breeding birds show slight mottling on backs; more pronounced in non-breeding plumage; E African races tend to be streaked year-round. **Habitat:** Rank grass in open woodland and savanna. **Status:** Locally common. **Voice:** Soft, repeated 'see-see-sippi-ippi' or 'tsip tsip seu'; also slurred warble; sings persistently from high, exposed perches, even during heat of day. [C10.81, G5.8.10]

5 RUFOUS CISTICOLA *Cisticola rufus*   10 cm
Endemic to W Africa. Forms a superspecies with Foxy Cisticola, but is much duller and browner (not bright rufous); ranges barely overlap in SW Chad. Paler and more rufous than Short-winged Cisticola, with plain (not mottled) back and rufous wing panel. **Habitat:** Dry riverbeds, scrub and semi-arid woodlands; often in seasonally damp areas. **Status:** Locally common. **Voice:** Weak, far-carrying 'tsip' or 'tseep' in fast, descending roll, similar to both Short-winged and Foxy cisticolas'. [C10.82]

6 FOXY CISTICOLA *Cisticola troglodytes*   10 cm
A tiny cisticola that cocks its tail like a wren when alarmed. Told from Rufous Cisticola in area of overlap in SW Chad by its much brighter rufous upperparts, and rich buffy-rufous belly and flanks. Much brighter than Short-winged Cisticola, with plain rufous (not streaked brownish) upperparts. **Habitat:** Lightly wooded grasslands and riverine woodland in semi-arid areas. **Status:** Locally common. **Voice:** Similar weak, wispy call notes of Rufous and Short-winged cisticolas, given from tree or bush tops or in short display flight. [C10.83]

7 TINY CISTICOLA *Cisticola nanus*   8-9 cm
Endemic to NE Africa. The smallest cisticola, with a rather plain back (may appear lightly streaked at close range), rufous cap, white supra-loral stripe and pale underparts. Smaller and shorter-tailed than Red-pate (p. 504) and Short-winged cisticolas or Neddicky; ranges barely overlap. **Habitat:** Arid and semi-arid scrub and woodland. **Status:** Common. **Voice:** 2-3 note song of 'chwee' or 'chwit' notes.

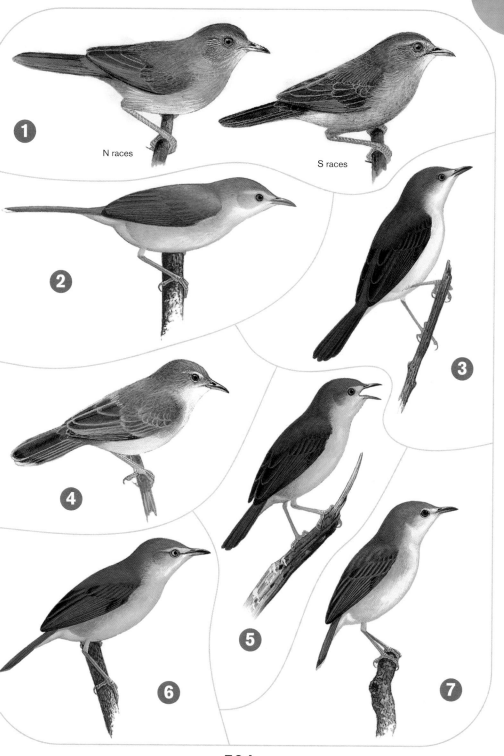

1

N races

S races

2

3

4

5

6

7

501

Most cisticolas have streaked backs and crowns, and can be divided into long-tailed and short-tailed species. Among the long-tailed species, habitat and warmth of plumage are useful cues for identification, but beware seasonal plumage changes. Ultimately song remains the most reliable character.

1 RATTLING CISTICOLA *Cisticola chiniana* 12-14 cm
A rather large, stout cisticola, although female smaller. Has a subdued rufous wash on head, tail and edges of primaries, but duller than Tinkling Cisticola. In E Africa, coastal races are plainer with more prominent rufous wing panels, resembling Singing Cisticola (p. 496), but song and habitat differ. More rufous on crown and wing than Boran Cisticola, and much darker and more rufous than Ashy Cisticola. NW races also plainer above; could be confused with Chattering Cisticola (p. 496), but occur in savanna, not forest edge. **Habitat:** Woodland, savanna and scrub. **Status:** Common to abundant; the most obvious cisticola in SE savannas. **Voice:** Loud, scolding 'chee chee chrrrrr' or 'chee chee chee tup-up-up', uttered from top of bush; 'chree chree chree' alarm call. [C10.78, G5.8.1]

2 BORAN CISTICOLA *Cisticola bodessa* 13-14 cm
Endemic to NE Africa. Similar to Rattling Cisticola but has brownish (not rufous) cap, browner (less rufous) edges to primaries and less bold streaking on mantle; song distinctive. **Habitat:** Broadleafed woodland and thickets; typically in moister areas than Rattling Cisticola. **Status:** Locally common; usually sings hidden in canopy, and often from higher perches than Rattling Cisticola. **Voice:** Loud 'chip' and 'tsip' notes, increasing in pitch and intensity, followed by a short, whistled, liquid song with faint rattling qualities.

3 ASHY CISTICOLA *Cisticola cinereolus* 13 cm
Endemic to NE Africa. A rather pale, grey-brown cisticola, entirely lacking rufous plumage. Paler than Rattling and Boran cisticolas, with pale grey-brown (not rufous or dark brown) crown. Shorter-tailed than Tana River Cisticola, with pale grey-brown (not rufous-washed) crown and entirely whitish underparts (lacking grey sides to the breast). **Habitat:** Usually in drier acacia bush and scrub than Boran or Rattling cisticolas. **Status:** Common; sings from bush tops. **Voice:** Rapid, melodious song, variable but usually ascending and subsequently descending the scale; alarm is repeated 'peee peee'.

4 TANA RIVER CISTICOLA *Cisticola restrictus* 13 cm
Endemic to coastal Kenya. Taxonomic status uncertain; may be a hybrid or variant of Ashy Cisticola, but is slightly browner above, with a rufous wash on the crown and nape, greyish (not white) sides of the breast and longer tail with more prominent subterminal spots. Smaller and much paler than Rattling Cisticola with a longer tail, more streaked back and crown, and no rufous wing panels. **Habitat:** Acacia scrub, often along dry river courses. **Status:** Not seen since 1972; might be extinct. **Voice:** Unknown.

5 TINKLING (GREY) CISTICOLA *Cisticola rufilatus* 12-13 cm
Endemic to SC Africa. A streak-backed cisticola with a diagnostic pale supercilium and bright rufous crown, ear coverts and long, rufous tail. Smaller and appreciably brighter than Rattling Cisticola, with prominent pale supercilium and longer, thinner, rufous tail. Brighter rufous than Grey-backed Cisticola (p. 504), with a more prominent pale supercilium. Female's tail shorter. **Habitat:** Dry, broadleafed woodland, savanna and scrub. **Status:** Uncommon to locally common; shy and easily overlooked. **Voice:** Song is tinkling, bell-like notes 'tseep seep seep seep' and harsher 'chik chik' notes and trills, often accompanied by wing snapping. [C10.77, G5.8.1]

6 CHURRING CISTICOLA *Cisticola njombe* 12-13 cm
Endemic to S Tanzania and N Malawi. A long-tailed cisticola, slightly smaller than Wailing Cisticola (p. 504), with a brighter, unstreaked rufous cap. Most obvious differences are in habitat choice and calls. **Habitat:** Mountain grasslands and tangled, rank growth of bracken and briar, often at forest edge (not rocky hillslopes as Wailing Cisticola, p. 504). **Status:** Common at mid- and high elevations, mostly in pairs or small family parties. **Voice:** Trilling or rattling song on even pitch, quite unlike shrill 'shree' calls of Wailing Cisticola.

non-br.

br.

1 WAILING CISTICOLA *Cisticola lais*   13-14 cm
A long-tailed cisticola with a streaked rufous head, and rufous-brown tail and wing panels contrasting with greyer back. Slightly larger than Grey-backed Cisticola with a heavier bill, warmer buff (not cold grey-buff) belly and brighter rufous head. E Cape *maculatus* has a variably streaked breast. Angolan *namba* has plainer crown and greyer underparts; may be a distinct species. **Habitat:** Rank grass and bracken on rocky hillslopes in moister areas than Grey-backed Cisticola. **Status:** Common. **Voice:** Rattled 'trrrrrrt' and slightly plaintive, drawn-out 'phweeeep', higher-pitched than Grey-backed Cisticola's song. [G5.7.10]

2 LYNES'S CISTICOLA *Cisticola distinctus*   14-15 cm
Endemic to E Africa. Often treated as a race of Wailing Cisticola, but is larger with a stouter bill, more rufous face and darker, browner upperparts; ranges do not overlap. Greyer on back than Rattling Cisticola (p. 502) with a longer, thinner tail and more rufous face; behaviour and habitat also differs. Cocks its tail like Rock-loving Cisticola (p. 498), but has a well-streaked back. **Habitat:** Rocky hillslopes in grassland and savanna. **Status:** Locally common. **Voice:** Shrill 'wheee wheeee', harsher 'sherker sherker', more varied than Wailing Cisticola; alarm note is 'steek steek'.

3 GREY-BACKED CISTICOLA *Cisticola subruficapilla*   12-13 cm
Endemic to SW Africa. S races have a grey back, finely streaked black, and grey-washed underparts, but N races are browner above, and more buffy below. Range overlaps with very similar Wailing Cisticola, but is smaller and finer-billed, with colder, greyish-buff underparts. Breast lightly streaked, especially in SW. **Habitat:** Lowland fynbos, karoo scrub and arid, grassy hillsides, typically in drier habitats than Wailing Cisticola. **Status:** Common. **Voice:** Muffled 'tr-r-rrrrt' and loud, plaintive 'hu-weeeee', deeper than Wailing Cisticola's, given from perch or in air; also harsher 'chee chee' call. [G5.7.9]

4 RED-PATE CISTICOLA *Cisticola ruficeps*   11-12 cm
Fairly small; non-breeding birds are heavily streaked above with bright rufous crowns; breeding birds are duller with plainer backs. Breeding birds are larger and longer tailed than Rufous, Foxy and Tiny cisticolas (p. 500). Differs from both Short-winged (p. 500) and Desert (p. 508) cisticolas by rufous (not brown) cap. Very similar to Dorst's Cisticola; best told by whitish (not buffy) vent and song. **Habitat:** Arid savanna. **Status:** Locally common, but range uncertain due to confusion with Dorst's Cisticola. **Voice:** Fast, high-pitched 'tsweee wir-i-eeee' and lower trill, reminiscent of Grey-backed Cisticola's; also chips and high-pitched 'sweee' alarm call. [C10.79]

5 DORST'S CISTICOLA *Cisticola dorsti*   11-12 cm
Breeding adult differs from Red-pate Cisticola by having buffy (not white or greyish) belly, flanks and vent, less contrasting subterminal tail band and more uniform upperparts; best told by different song. Non-breeding plumage unknown. **Habitat:** Grassy savanna, often in moister areas than Red-pate Cisticola. **Status:** Locally common. **Voice:** High-pitched, insect-like trill, occasionally followed by series of descending whistles 'trrrrrrrrr tsee tseo tseu tseu'; high-pitched alarm call 'sweeoo' descends more than Red-pate Cisticola's. [C10.80]

6 CHIRPING CISTICOLA *Cisticola pipiens*   14-15 cm
Endemic to SC Africa. Slightly larger than Carruther's, Winding, Luapula (p. 506) and Levaillant's cisticolas, with duller brown crown, less boldly streaked back, and buffish (not whitish) underparts. Best told by its song. **Habitat:** Reedbeds and papyrus swamps. **Status:** Locally common. **Voice:** Song loud: 2-3 sharp notes followed by a dry, buzzy trill 'chit chit-it rrrrrrrrrr'; also plaintive 'chwer-chwer-chwer' and sharp 'chit chit' calls. [C10.97, G5.8.6]

7 LEVAILLANT'S (TINKLING) CISTICOLA *Cisticola tinniens*   13-14 cm
The brightest wetland cisticola. Told from the winding cisticola complex (p. 506) by its streaked (not plain) rump and rufous (not grey) tail (but non-breeding winding cisticolas have browner tails); song is diagnostic. Slightly smaller than Chirping Cisticola, with paler underparts and much brighter rufous crown, wing panel and tail. Non-breeding birds have buffy-brown (not greyish) margins to the mantle feathers and streaked crowns. **Habitat:** Reedbeds, sedges and long grass adjacent to wetlands. **Status:** Common. **Voice:** Warbling, musical 'chrip-trrrup-trreee'; wailing 'cheee-weee-weee'. [C10.98, G5.8.7]

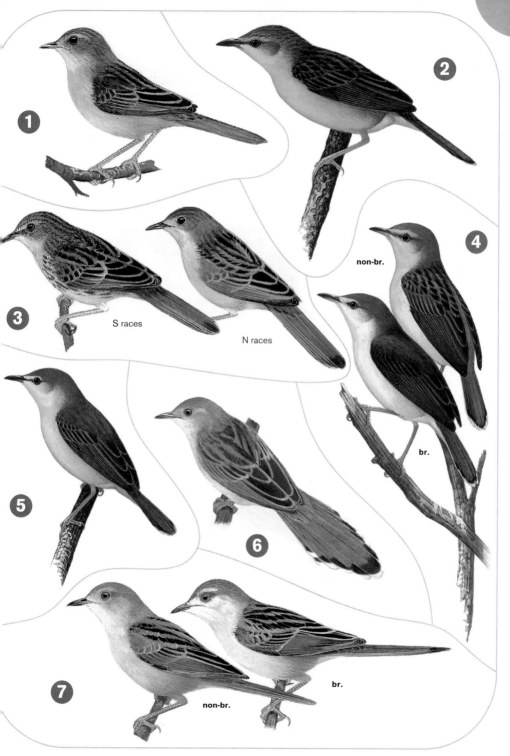

1

2

3 S races

N races

4 non-br.

br.

5

6

7 non-br.

br.

STREAK-BACKED CISTICOLAS

1 CARRUTHERS'S CISTICOLA *Cisticola carruthersi* 12-13 cm
Endemic to E Africa. Similar to Winding Cisticola, but has thinner, weaker bill, blacker tail and duller rufous crown and wing panel; songs differ. Smaller and brighter than Chirping Cisticola (p. 504) with paler underparts. **Habitat:** Papyrus swamps; occurs in other wetlands at higher altitudes where Winding Cisticola is absent. **Status:** Common. **Voice:** Noisy: song is series of loud, rapid, chattered notes, lacking Chirping Cisticola's introductory notes.

2 WHITE-TAILED CISTICOLA *Cisticola sp.* 12-13 cm
Endemic to Kilombero swamp, Tanzania; recently discovered and not formally described. Duller than Coastal Cisticola with darker crown and wing panels and browner tail with diagnostic narrow white edges to outer-tail and no subterminal spots; ranges apparently do not overlap. Best told by its song. **Habitat:** *Phragmites* reedbeds and adjacent rank grass. **Status:** Common; conspicuous when singing from reeds, but also runs on ground. **Voice:** Distinctive song a series of descending notes 'tseoo tseoo tseou tseou' but also has a jumbled song, including notes similar to Coastal Cisticola's; 'szhree szhree' contact note.

3 WINDING CISTICOLA *Cisticola marginatus* 12-14 cm
The only 'black-backed' cisticola of swamps and marshes throughout most of its range. Larger and brighter than Coastal Cisticola, and told from Luapula Cisticola by its distinctive winding call. Seldom occurs together with Carruther's Cisticola, and is brighter with a greyer (not blackish) tail. Told from Levaillant's Cisticola (p. 504) by its greyish (not rufous) tail (although non-breeders have browner tail) and plain grey (not streaked) rump; typically occurs at lower elevations in areas of overlap. Smaller and much brighter than Chirping Cisticola (p. 504), with heavier, blackish (not dark brown) streaking above. **Habitat:** Swamps, marshes and adjacent thickets and scrub. **Status:** Locally common, but patchily distributed, especially in W Africa. **Voice:** Dry, ascending trill, 'zrrrrtttt', likened to winding a watch; also bleating 'cheoo cheoo' calls. [C10.95]

4 COASTAL CISTICOLA *Cisticola haematocephala* 11-13 cm
Endemic to coastal E Africa. Smaller than Winding Cisticola, with a duller rufous crown and wing panel; in worn plumage, crown is brown. Browner above than White-tailed Cisticola, with grey (not brownish) tail and prominent subterminal black spots; lacks white outer-tail. Apparently lacks a non-breeding plumage. **Habitat:** Coastal swamps, marshes and reedbeds, but also coastal scrub away from water. **Status:** Common. **Voice:** Musical 'cherup' and prinia-like, raspy trill, shorter than Winding Cisticola's; 'tic tic' in flight.

5 LUAPULA CISTICOLA *Cisticola luapula* 12-14 cm
Endemic to SC Africa. Has a darker chestnut crown and wing panel than Winding Cisticola and lacks winding song. Slightly smaller than Chirping Cisticola (p. 504) with richer crown and wing panel, greyer tail and more boldly marked back; underparts paler. Told from Levaillant's Cisticola (p. 504) by its plain (not streaked) rump and grey (not rufous) tail. **Habitat:** Swamps and marshes, preferring *Phragmites* reeds to dense papyrus. **Status:** Locally common. **Voice:** Loud 2-note display song 'tid-ick'; also 'tic tic' and 'zrrtttt' calls, sometimes in display flight.

6 RUFOUS-WINGED CISTICOLA *Cisticola galactotes* 12-14 cm
Endemic to SE Africa. Similar to Luapula Cisticola, but duller with greyer crown and nape and different song; ranges do not overlap. Breeding adults told from Levaillant's Cisticola (p. 504) by grey (not rufous) tail, but non-breeders have browner tail; differ in song and plain (not streaked) rump; ranges barely overlap. **Habitat:** Reedbeds, long grass and sedges near water. **Status:** Common. **Voice:** Single-note, musical, ascending 'phweeep' song; also buzzy 'tzeet' or 'trrrt trrrt'. [G5.8.5]

7 ETHIOPIAN CISTICOLA *Cisticola lugubris* 12-14 cm
Endemic to Ethiopia and Eritrea, where it is the only 'black-backed' wetland cisticola. Darker than other members of the complex, with more buffy underparts. Easily identified by its chestnut cap, buffy underparts, heavily streaked black back and chestnut wing panels. **Habitat:** Upland scrub, heath and bracken, often in damp areas. **Status:** Common; usually in pairs and small family parties. **Voice:** Various 'trrt' and 'chit' calls; dry 'zrrrttttttt' note.

LARGE CISTICOLAS

Highly dimorphic cisticolas with relatively short tails. Males are much larger.

1 CROAKING CISTICOLA *Cisticola natalensis* 13-17 cm

The largest cisticola with a robust, decurved bill. Slightly larger than Stout Cisticola with a brown (not rufous) crown; nape the same colour as the back; lacks pale rufous nape and typically occurs at lower elevations. Has a paler tail than Aberdare Cisticola and lacks a rufous crown and nape; altitudinally segregated. **Habitat:** Wide range of grassland types, below 2 200 m (to 2 400 m in Ethiopia). **Status:** Common. **Voice:** Deep, frog-like 'prrrrp', and loud 'prrr-CHINK' bounding display flight or exposed perch. [C10.75, G5.8.8]

2 ABERDARE CISTICOLA *Cisticola aberdare* 12-15 cm

Endemic to C Kenya. Occurs chiefly at higher altitudes than Stout and Croaking cisticolas. Slightly larger than Stout Cisticola, with black-streaked (not plain) rufous nape and longer, blacker tail with a broader buff tip. Told from Croaking Cisticola by smaller, thinner bill, much darker tail and rufous (not brown) crown, nape and wing panel. Chunkier and shorter-tailed than Winding (p. 506) and Levaillant's (p. 504) cisticolas. **Habitat:** Montane grassland and heath. **Status:** Endangered. Locally common above 2 300 m on both sides of the Rift Valley (mostly above 3 000 m in Aberdare Mts). **Voice:** Variable series of trills and sharper 'tchew' notes from atop grass stems or small bushes.

3 STOUT CISTICOLA *Cisticola robustus* 11-14 cm

Slightly smaller than Croaking Cisticola with a bright rufous (not brown) crown and nape, brighter wing panels and less robust bill; typically occurs at higher elevations. Told from Aberdare Cisticola by its plain rufous, unstreaked nape and paler brown tail with a narrower buff tip; mostly occurs at lower elevations. **Habitat:** Grassland with scattered bushes, 1 200-2 700 m, often in damp areas. **Status:** Common. **Voice:** Short, buzzy 'bzee' trill, usually preceded by a few short, sharp introductory notes; higher pitched and more subdued than Croaking Cisticola's. [C10.76]

SHORT-TAILED CISTICOLAS

Small, streak-backed cisticolas with short or medium tails (longer in non-breeding birds in some species). Sexes differ in most species, with females resembling non-breeding males. Identification of silent birds is problematic.

4 ZITTING (FAN-TAILED) CISTICOLA *Cisticola juncidis* 10 cm

A fairly pale, buffy cisticola. Darker and more heavily streaked above than Desert Cisticola, with a paler brown tail that has a prominent dark subterminal band and broad white tip. Paler than Black-backed and Dambo cisticolas (p. 510), especially on the tail. Longer-tailed than other short-tailed species. **Habitat:** Thick grass and fields, often in damp areas. **Status:** Common. **Voice:** Monotonous 'zit zit zit', repeated 1-2 times per second; during display flight, 10-30 m over territory. Does not snap wings. [C4.36, G5.7.4]

5 SOCOTRA CISTICOLA *Cisticola haesitatus* 9-10 cm

Endemic to Socotra, where it is the only cisticola. Resembles a washed-out Zitting Cisticola; ranges do not overlap. Smaller than Socotra Warbler (p. 524), with brown, heavily streaked (not plain, greyish-brown) upperparts. **Habitat:** Widespread in dense, dwarf coastal shrubland below 100 m; also known from one upland site at 850 m. **Status:** Vulnerable. Locally common. **Voice:** Display flight is similar to Zitting Cisticola's, with 'tsip tsip tsip' call, accelerating in pace as the song progresses.

6 DESERT CISTICOLA *Cisticola aridulus* 10 cm

Similar to Zitting Cisticola, but paler overall, with a darker tail lacking an obvious black subterminal bar. Much paler backed than Black-backed and Dambo cisticolas (p. 510), and longer-tailed than other short-tailed species. **Habitat:** Arid grassland and old fields, typically occurs in more arid areas than Zitting Cisticola. **Status:** Common. **Voice:** Song is fast 'zink zink zink', 'sii sii sii' or 'su-ink su-ink su-ink', typically faster than Zitting Cisticola's and interspersed with sharp wing-snapping. Display flight is fairly low and jerky. [C10.74, G5.7.5]

1

♂ br.

non-br.
♂

♀

2

♂

3

non-br.

br.

4

br.

non-br.

5

6

br.

non-br.

1 BLACK-BACKED CISTICOLA *Cisticola eximius*   10 cm
A richly coloured cisticola with a medium-short tail. Much darker than Zitting and Desert cisticolas (p. 508) with a more rufous nape. Breeding male has distinctive plain rufous crown and nape. Has a longer tail and richer plumage than male Wing-snapping Cisticola, and typically occurs at lower altitudes. **Habitat:** Damp savanna, marshes and seasonally flooded grasslands; prefers wetter areas than other short-tailed cisticolas. **Status:** Locally common. **Voice:** Repeated, slightly slurred 'trleeee', faster 'tlee tlee, tlee tlee, tlee tlee' and monotonous, trilling 'trrrt trrrt trrrt', uttered from a perch or low aerial display. Does not wing snap. [C10.72]

2 DAMBO (CLOUD-SCRAPING) CISTICOLA *Cisticola dambo*   11 cm
Endemic to SC Africa. Similar to Black-backed Cisticola, but is browner above, and more rufous below; breeding male has lightly streaked (not plain rufous) crown; ranges do not overlap. Slightly longer-tailed than Pale-crowned and Wing-snapping cisticolas with the distinctive rich buff underparts of breeding males contrasting with the dark streaked back and blackish top of head. Much darker than Zitting and Desert cisticolas (p. 508). **Habitat:** Edges of seasonally flooded grassland, favouring moister areas than Wing-snapping Cisticola, but not as wet as Pale-crowned Cisticola. **Status:** Locally common. **Voice:** Rasping, scolding notes and whistled 'zeee-it' song, similar to Cloud Cisticola's; frequently wing snaps. [C10.73]

3 PALE-CROWNED CISTICOLA *Cisticola cinnamomeus*   10 cm
Forms a superspecies with Pectoral-patch Cisticola; ranges overlap narrowly in S Gabon and Congo. Male in breeding plumage has distinctive black lores contrasting with a pale buffy (not rufous) crown, and occurs in wetter habitats than Pectoral-patch Cisticola in area of overlap. Non-breeding males and females are very similar to Cloud and Wing-snapping cisticolas; probably not separable in the field. **Habitat:** Damp or marshy areas in upland grassland. **Status:** Uncommon and localised. **Voice:** Song is soft, very high-pitched 'tsee-tsee-tsee-itititi-titi'; display flights are at both high and low levels; does not snap wings. [C10.70, G5.7.8]

4 PECTORAL-PATCH CISTICOLA *Cisticola brunnescens*   9-10 cm
Differs from Pale-crowned Cisticola mainly by having pale rufous (not buff) crown and forehead in breeding season; darker pectoral patches are often hard to see in the field. **Habitat:** Upland grasslands, especially over damp or wet areas. **Status:** Common to abundant in many areas. **Voice:** Song is harsher and less wheezy than Pale-crowned Cisticola's, with 'tssk tssk' or 'szisk szisk' notes, Stonechat-like in quality; given in display flight, accompanied with muffled wing-snapping. [C10.69]

5 WING-SNAPPING (AYRES') CISTICOLA *Cisticola ayresii*   9 cm
A very small, short-tailed cisticola. Breeding birds have shorter tails than any species except Cloud Cisticola; distinguished by plain breast (lacking any streaking) and shorter legs; appears more slender. In areas of overlap, breeding male has plain, unstreaked rufous crown (streaked in Cloud Cisticola). Breeding male is shorter-tailed than male Pectoral-patch or Pale-crowned cisticolas, with paler lores, darker crown and less contrasting rump; non-breeding birds probably inseparable in the field. **Habitat:** Short grassland, usually above 1 000 m, but descending to near sea level in the S; also occurs in marshes, especially in winter. **Status:** Common; breeds at much higher altitudes than other small cisticolas. **Voice:** In S Africa, song consists of 3-4 evenly pitched notes, slower and deeper than Cloud Cisticola's. Elsewhere is higher pitched and more jumbled, typically with 3-8 notes. Sings in high aerial display, interspersed with loud, rapid wing snapping. On descending and just before landing, it jinks and loudly snaps its wings. [C10.71, G5.7.7]

6 CLOUD CISTICOLA *Cisticola textrix*   9-10 cm
Near-endemic to S Africa. A very short-tailed cisticola with distinctive, high aerial display. Similar to Wing-snapping Cisticola, but more slender with longer legs and typically some streaking on the sides of the breast; best told by distinctive song. Nominate *textrix* (W Cape) has extensive streaking across the breast; these birds may constitute an undescribed species. **Habitat:** Grassland, fields and lowland fynbos. **Status:** Common. **Voice:** Song is 3-4 whistled notes, typically followed by 3 fast wing snaps 'soo-see-see', uttered by displaying male while cruising at great height; does not snap wings before landing, like Wing-snapping Cisticola. [G5.7.6]

1 non-br.

br.

2

4

non-br.

br.

3 br.

non-br.

5 non-br.

br.

6 non-br.

br.

textrix

A large African genus of long-tailed warblers that glean insects in forest, woodland or thicket vegetation. Many are brightly coloured, often with distinctive throat and breast patterns. Sexes similar in most species, but males are brighter or more strongly marked in some; juvs are duller in some species.

1 RWENZORI (COLLARED) APALIS *Apalis ruwenzorii* — 10 cm
Endemic to Albertine Rift. Told from Black-collared Apalis by its buffy (not white) throat, grey (not balck) breast band, paler flanks and no white outer-tail; ranges do not overlap. Female and juv. have narrower breast bands. **Habitat:** Mid-altitude and montane forests, in canopy and mid-stratum. **Status:** Common; in pairs or small groups, often in bird parties. **Voice:** Very similar to Black-collared Apalis's. [C11.21]

2 BLACK-COLLARED APALIS *Apalis pulchra* — 12 cm
Told from Rwenzori Apalis by its blacker breast band on white (not buffy) underparts and bright orange flanks; ranges do not overlap. Sexes alike; juv. duller with a grey breast band. **Habitat:** Forest undergrowth, dense vegetation and vine tangles; forages low down in undergrowth. **Status:** Locally common; usually in pairs. **Voice:** Diagnostic, far-carrying duet of 'dzee dzee' or 'prrip prrip' at varying speeds, vaguely similar to Bar-throated Apalis's. [C11.20]

3 YELLOW-THROATED APALIS *Apalis flavigularis* — 11-12 cm
Endemic to S Malawi. Often lumped with Bar-throated Apalis, but with brilliant primrose-yellow underparts. Differs from Yellow-breasted Apalis (p. 514) by having dark brown (not grey) crown and different habitat. **Habitat:** Mid- to high altitude forest; forages in mid-stratum. **Status:** Endangered. Locally common within its restricted range. Usually in pairs, frequently in bird parties. **Voice:** Very similar to Bar-throated Apalis's.

4 BAR-THROATED APALIS *Apalis thoracica* — 11-12 cm
A rather variable apalis with a narrow black collar across top of breast, pale eyes and white outer-tail feathers. Upperparts vary from grey to green, underparts from white to greyish or yellow. Pale (not dark) eyes and white (not dark) outer-tail separate it from Rudd's Apalis. Male's breast band is broader than female's. Juv is buffier below, sometimes with incomplete breast band. **Habitat:** Forest, dense woodland and coastal thickets. Restricted to montane forest in N of range. **Status:** Common. **Voice:** Male utters harsh 'krrup-krrup-krrup'; female responds with much higher-pitched 'tilllip-tilllip-tilllip'. [G5.5.5]

5 NAMULI APALIS *Apalis lynesi* — 11-12 cm
Endemic to Mt Namuli, N Mozambique; often lumped with Bar-throated Apalis. Very similar to both Taita and *sanderi* race of Buff-throated Apalis (p. 516) but has yellow (not white) belly and vent; ranges do not overlap. **Habitat:** Montane forests on Mt Namuli, in canopy, mid-stratum and forest edge. **Status:** Vulnerable. Locally common; in pairs or mixed bird parties. **Voice:** Similar to Bar-throated Apalis's.

6 TAITA APALIS *Apalis fascigularis* — 11-12 cm
Endemic to Taita Hills, SE Kenya; often lumped with Bar-throated Apalis. A black-and-white apalis with dark grey upperparts and dark grey to black throat and breast. Eye is silvery white or pale yellow. Similar to *sanderi* Buff-throated Apalis (p. 516), but has pale (not red) eyes. Also resembles Namuli Apalis, but has white (not yellow) underparts; ranges do not overlap. **Habitat:** Montane forest, in tangles in thick undergrowth at forest edge and clearings; forages low down in undergrowth. **Status:** Critically endangered by habitat loss. Uncommon; in pairs and sometimes associated with bird parties. **Voice:** Similar to Bar-throated Apalis's but slower, more slurred and deeper in pitch.

7 RUDD'S APALIS *Apalis ruddi* — 11-12 cm
Localised endemic to S Africa. Lacks white outer-tail feathers and pale eye of Bar-throated Apalis, and has small white stripe in front of and above eye. Lime-green back contrasts strongly with grey head. Female has narrower throat band. Juv. is buffier below. **Habitat:** Sandforest and coastal thickets. **Status:** Common. **Voice:** Male calls fast 'tuttuttuttut', answered by female with slower 'clink-clink-clink'. [G5.5.9]

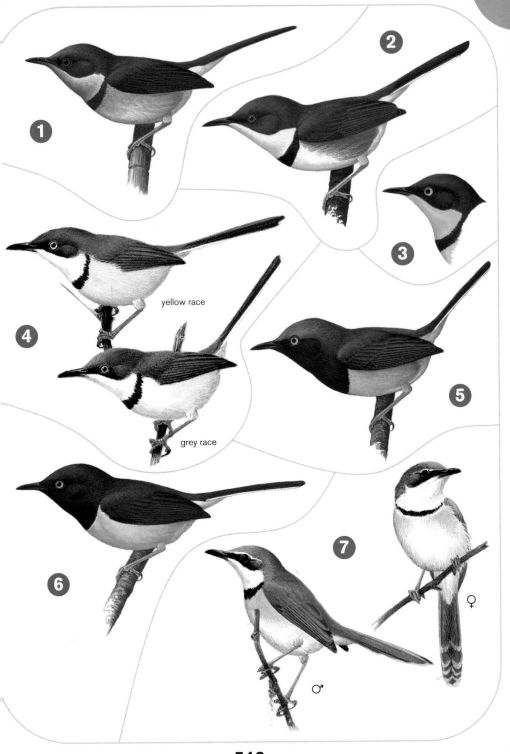

yellow race

grey race

1 BLACK-CAPPED APALIS *Apalis nigriceps*   11 cm
Smaller and shorter tailed than Black-throated Apalis, with white (not black) throat, white (not yellow) underparts and brighter yellow mantle. Female has grey (not black) head and breast band. Juv. is duller and lacks breast band. **Habitat:** Forest canopy and tall trees in cultivated areas, sometimes at lower height in degraded areas. **Status:** Locally common. **Voice:** Even-noted, rapid buzzing, 'zzzrrrr zzzrrrr', repeated continuously. [C11.14]

2 BLACK-THROATED APALIS *Apalis jacksoni*   12 cm
A long-tailed apalis. Differs from Black-capped Apalis by black (not white) throat and bright yellow (not white) underparts. Has distinctive white moustache; told from Lowland and Mountain masked apalises by yellow (not buffy-olive) underparts. Female is duller, with grey head and throat. Juv. is more olive on head than adult. SW Cameroon *bambuluensis* is darker; male has black crown; female sooty throat. **Habitat:** Forest canopy and clearings in forest edge in montane areas; also tall trees in cultivated areas at lower altitude. **Status:** Locally common. **Voice:** Duetting song of 'kruu kree' and variations on this. [C11.11]

3 WHITE-WINGED APALIS *Apalis chariessa*   12-13 cm
Endemic to SE Africa. The combination of black upperparts with obvious white wing panels, white throat with black breast band, and bright golden-yellow underparts make this apalis very easy to identify. Might be mistaken for Black-throated Apalis but lacks that species' black throat and has white wing panels. Female has paler back and lacks breast band but still shows white wing panels. **Habitat:** Montane forest, usually in canopy. **Status:** Vulnerable. Locally common to rare. **Voice:** Rapid, repeated 'tee-luu dee-lu'.

4 LOWLAND MASKED APALIS *Apalis binotata*   11 cm
Distinguished from Black-throated Apalis by duller plumage, buffy-olive and white (not yellow) underparts, and short tail. Head is grey, delineated from black throat and breast by white line; upperparts are olive-green; eye is dark red. Female has less black on breast and broader white moustache. Juv. has olive-green head and pale yellow throat. **Habitat:** Dense vegetation of secondary growth, low trees and shrubs at forest edge; not a forest-canopy apalis. **Status:** Locally common. **Voice:** Harsh, buzzy, clicking song and continuous, hollow-sounding 'tic tic' notes. [C11.9]

5 MOUNTAIN MASKED (BLACK-FACED) APALIS *Apalis personata*   11-12 cm
Endemic to Albertine Rift, where it replaces Lowland Masked Apalis at higher elevations. Differs by being much darker, especially on head, and by having black on throat extending further onto breast and belly. Lacks white malar stripe; instead, has only white spot on side of neck. Female duller with less extensive black on the breast. **Habitat:** Mid-stratum and canopy of montane forests. **Status:** Common. In pairs and associated with bird parties. **Voice:** Very similar to Lowland Masked Apalis's, with 'tuc tuc tuc' or 'tec tec tec', raspy and repeated song. [C11.10]

6 YELLOW-BREASTED APALIS *Apalis flavida*   11-12 cm
The only apalis with a plain yellow breast and no black breast collar, although males of some races have small black bar beneath yellow breast. Crown is grey, contrasting with olive-green back. Juv. has paler yellow breast. Arid NE *viridiceps* has mostly green (not grey) crown, greener breast band and browner tail; sometimes considered a separate species, Brown-tailed Apalis. **Habitat:** Woodland, dense savanna and thickets; avoids montane forest. **Status:** Common. **Voice:** Fast, buzzy 'chizzick-chizzick-chizzick'; pairs often duet. [C11.8, G5.5.8]

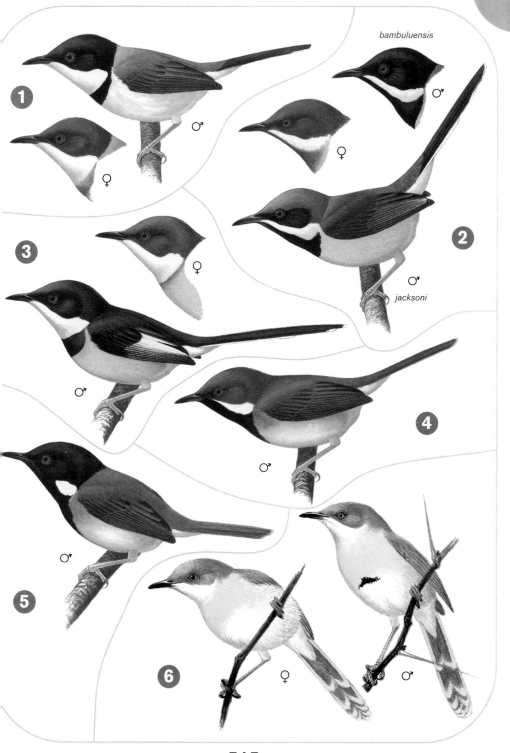

bambuluensis

♂

♀

1

♀

♂

2

3

♀

♂

jacksoni

♂

4

♂

5

♂

6

♀

♂

1 BUFF-THROATED APALIS *Apalis rufogularis* 12 cm
Most closely resembles Sharpe's Apalis, but their ranges do not overlap. NW males have dark head and breast, while other races resemble Grey Apalis (p. 518), but are darker above and paler below with a shorter tail which is fanned regularly. Could be confused with Brown- and Black-headed apalises (p. 518), but has short (not long) tail which is predominantly white underneath (not dark with white tips). Female is similar to female Gosling's Apalis (p. 518), but has white (not dark) undertail. Told from female Chestnut-throated Apalis by reddish wash confined to throat (not extending onto breast). **Habitat:** Mid-stratum or canopy of lowland and highland forests. **Status:** Common; in pairs in bird parties. **Voice:** Diagnostic buzzing trill, very insect-like; best described as often-repeated 'drrritt drrrit' or 'zrree zzrree'. [C11.16]

2 SHARPE'S APALIS *Apalis sharpii* 12 cm
Endemic to Upper Guinea forests with no other similar apalis within its range. Uniformly dark grey, with paler belly and vent and white tail tips; eyes are dark red. Female is dark grey, tinged with olive above, and a reddish throat, but this is not obvious in the field. Juv. is duller, with pale yellow or buff throat. **Habitat:** Forest edge and secondary growth; forages in canopy and mid-stratum, occasionally in tangled undergrowth at forest edge. **Status:** Common; usually in pairs. **Voice:** Rapid but sometimes slurred 'chivi chivi chivi'; more ringing 'pi pi pi pi' in duet. [C11.15]

3 BAMENDA APALIS *Apalis bamendae* 12 cm
Endemic to SW Cameroon. A dull grey apalis with pale yellowish eyes and dark brown tail lacking any white. Within its restricted range could be confused with Grey Apalis (p. 518), but has reddish (not greyish-brown) face and throat. Female is slightly paler. **Habitat:** Riverine forest and thickets. **Status:** Uncommon; usually in pairs or small groups; easily detected by song. **Voice:** Tuneless, often-repeated rattle, sometimes in duet; rendered 'tititi-tititii' or slower 'puuee peee peee'. [C11.18]

4 KUNGWE APALIS *Apalis argentea* 11-13 cm
Endemic to Albertine Rift. Sometimes treated as a race of Buff-throated Apalis, and easily confused with Grey Apalis (p. 518), but tail is shorter with much more white on outer feathers, especially when fanned; crown grey (not greyish-brown). **Habitat:** Canopy and mid-strata of mid-altitude and montane forest; secondary growth. **Status:** Endangered. Little known; usually in mixed parties. **Voice:** Buzzy, tuneless, grating trill, 'drrrrrrrttt', of 3-4 seconds, often repeated.

5 CHESTNUT-THROATED APALIS *Apalis porphyrolaema* 12 cm
Endemic to E Africa. A small grey apalis with a diagnostic small, rust-coloured throat, which separates it from Black-headed and Grey apalises (p. 518). Differs from female Buff-throated Apalis by having paler and less extensive reddish throat patch and short, white undertail (not long dark tail with white tips to undertail). **Habitat:** Montane forest and adjacent secondary growth; riverine forest. **Status:** Common; often in bird parties; most often detected by diagnostic song. **Voice:** Insect-like trilling, 'ti ti trrreeee'. [C11.17]

6 CHAPIN'S (CHESTNUT-HEADED) APALIS *Apalis chapini* 12 cm
Endemic to montane forests of S Tanzania, Malawi and E Zambia. Similar to Chestnut-throated and Buff-throated apalises but ranges do not overlap. Within its restricted range, is the only apalis with reddish face and throat. N nominate race has white chin; chin is rufous in S *strausae*. Vaguely resembles Red-capped Forest Warbler (p. 540), but occurs in canopy (not undergrowth) and has different head shape. **Habitat:** Montane forest, forest edge and adjacent secondary growth, chiefly in canopy but does venture lower. **Status:** Common; usually in pairs; joins bird parties. **Voice:** Often-repeated 'dzzee dzzee', sometimes run together in a trill; higher-pitched, 'tsee tsee', noted in Tanzania.

7 KABOBO APALIS *Apalis kaboboensis* 12 cm
Endemic to Mt Kabobo, E DRC. Often lumped with Chestnut-throated Apalis, but has dark grey (not chestnut) throat and whitish (not buffy) flanks and vent. Within its restricted range, could be confused only with Grey Apalis (p. 518); differs by being darker overall and having grey (not white) throat and breast and pale (not dark) eyes. **Habitat:** Forest canopy and edge. **Status:** Little-known; occurs in bird parties. **Voice:** Dry, buzzy trill with softer ringing quality.

♂ Angola, Zambia, DRC & E Africa

1

♀

2

♂

NW races (Nigeria-Gabon)

3

♂

4

5

6

7

1 BLACK-HEADED APALIS *Apalis melanocephala*   11-13 cm
Endemic to SE Africa. A rather plain apalis with black or dark grey upperparts and white underparts. At close range, yellowish eye contrasts with black cap. Could be confused with Chirinda Apalis, but occurs mostly at lower elevations and has distinct black (not grey) cap. Differs from Grey Apalis by black cap and white tail tips (not outer-tail). Juv. is paler grey above. **Habitat:** Canopy of coastal, riverine and mid-altitude forests. **Status:** Locally common. **Voice:** Piercing, repeated 'wiii-tiiit-wiii-tiiit'. [G5.5.7]

2 CHIRINDA APALIS *Apalis chirindensis*   11-13 cm
Endemic to S Africa. A dull grey apalis with white outer-tail. In poor light could be confused with Black-headed Apalis, but is more uniform grey and lacks black cap. A restless bird, creeps and flits through canopy when foraging and, unlike White-tailed Crested Flycatcher (p. 560), with which it frequently occurs, does not fan tail or swing from side to side on perch. Juv. is tinged yellow-green, with paler bill. **Habitat:** Montane forests. **Status:** Locally fairly common. **Voice:** Repeated 'chipip chipip'. [G5.5.6]

3 GREY APALIS *Apalis cinerea*   12-13 cm
A long-tailed grey apalis. Paler and greyer above than Buff-throated Apalis (p. 516) with longer tail and white throat (males of N & E races of Buff-throated also have pale throat, but are darker above). Also paler above than Black-headed Apalis, with fully white outer-tail (not just tips white). Lacks brown crown of Brown-headed Apalis and has a darker eye. **Habitat:** Mid-altitude and highland forest, secondary growth and riverine forest. **Status:** Common; in pairs; frequents bird parties. **Voice:** Repeated 'chip chip chip chip', sometimes in duet; higher, faster trill sometimes given. [C11.12]

4 BROWN-HEADED APALIS *Apalis alticola*   12-13 cm
Told from Grey Apalis by its chocolate-brown (not greyish-brown) crown, pale (not dark) eye and only white tips to outer-tail feathers (not white outer-tail). Race *dowsetti* in DRC has all-white (not white-tipped) outer-tail feathers, but Grey Apalis does not occur here. **Habitat:** Mid- to high-altitude forest and adjacent secondary growth and riverine forests. **Status:** Common; in bird parties, in small groups or pairs. **Voice:** Very similar to Grey Apalis's 'chip chip' or 'tit tit iti' often-repeated notes. [C11.13]

5 KARAMOJA APALIS *Apalis karamojae*   12 cm
Localised endemic to E Africa. A grey apalis with white underparts and diagnostic white wing panel on folded secondaries. Grey Tit-flycatcher (p. 556) is vaguely similar but has habit of fanning and swaying tail from side to side, and also lacks white wing flashes. **Habitat:** Dry, stunted acacia scrub and thickets and scrub along dry river courses. **Status:** Vulnerable. Rare and little known but observed foraging low down in thickets in small groups. **Voice:** Rapid 'tissik tissik tissik' by foraging groups.

6 GOSLING'S APALIS *Apalis goslingi*   11 cm
A nondescript grey apalis of riverine vegetation in C Africa. Shorter-tailed than Buff-throated Apalis (p. 516), with less white in outer-tail (only tips white). Male has darker face. Juv is paler, with wash of yellow on underparts. **Habitat:** Riverine vegetation of large and medium-sized rivers, from trees to dense bushes. Avoids small forest streams, forest canopy and frequently found foraging low down in gallery forest thickets. **Status:** Locally common. **Voice:** Fast- and slow-delivered series of 'trrit' and 'chwit' notes. [C11.19]

Long-tailed African warblers typically found in woodland or scrub, usually in drier habitats than apalises. They could be confused with plain-backed cisticolas, but typically lack the rufous cap and have longer tails. Sexes alike, or females slightly duller; some species have distinct non-breeding plumages.

1 TAWNY-FLANKED PRINIA *Prinia subflava*   11-12 cm

The most abundant, widespread prinia throughout most of the region. Forms a superspecies with Pale and River prinias, but differs from these species by having warmer brown upperparts and richer buffy flanks (whitish in Pale Prinia, pale buff in River Prinia). Differs from non-breeding Black-chested Prinia by white (not yellow) throat and breast, warm buff flanks and belly, and russet edges to wings. **Habitat:** Woodland and thick, rank vegetation. **Status:** Common. **Voice:** Rapidly repeated 'przzt-przzt-przzt'; harsh 'chrzzzt'. [C11.2, G5.9.3]

2 PALE PRINIA *Prinia somalica*   11-12 cm

Endemic to NE Africa. Similar to Tawny-flanked Prinia, but has paler, buffy-grey upperparts and whiter underparts, with whitish (not buff) flanks (but juv. has slight buff wash on breast and flanks). Nominate race from N Somali is paler above. **Habitat:** Frequents drier scrub and more open vegetation than Tawny-flanked Prinia; forages low down in thickets and very often on ground, where it hops around with tail cocked. **Status:** Common; usually in pairs. **Voice:** Nasal, buzzy 'zhree zhree' or 'zik zik zik' notes.

3 RIVER PRINIA *Prinia fluviatilis*   11-12 cm

Localised endemic to W Africa. Very similar to Tawny-flanked Prinia, but is paler overall, with greyer upperparts and cleaner white underparts; is also longer tailed, and appears more slender. Best identified by specific habitat and song. **Habitat:** Almost always associated with aquatic vegetation alongside rivers and other wetlands; seldom found away from water. **Status:** Uncommon and thinly distributed; usually in pairs. **Voice:** Clear, high-pitched ringing notes, less varied than Tawny-flanked Prinia's, with less grating and slurred notes, 'pleeu pleeu pleeu'. [C11.3]

4 GRACEFUL PRINIA *Prinia gracilis*   14 cm

A small, rotund prinia with an especially long, graduated tail, with black-and-white tips. Streaked crown and back distinguish it from Red-fronted Warbler (p. 524) and Tawny-flanked and Pale prinias; told from cisticolas by very long tail (but beware moulting birds). Undertail is mostly black, with white tips. **Habitat:** Scrub in dry wadis, dune vegetation and, in some areas, mangrove scrub; feeds low in foliage and on ground, with much tail bobbing and wing flicking. **Status:** Common; usually in pairs. **Voice:** Drawn-out contact call of 'zeet' or 'breep'; scolding 'trrrt trrrt'; song is far-carrying 'zwrritt', often repeated; loud wing-snapping when alarmed.

5 BLACK-CHESTED PRINIA *Prinia flavicans*   14-15 cm

Endemic to SW Africa. The only prinia with a broad black breast band. Breast band is usually absent in non-breeding plumage, when it could be mistaken for Tawny-flanked Prinia, but lacks russet edges to wing feathers and is usually yellowish (not creamy-white) below. Breeding female has narrower breast band. Juv resembles non-breeding adult, but is yellower below. Breeding plumage *ansorgei* (Angola & N Namibia) lacks complete breast band; non-breeders have buff flanks. **Habitat:** Arid scrub, savanna, plantations and gardens. **Status:** Common. **Voice:** Loud, repetitive 'zzzrt-zzzzrt-zzzrt-zzzrt'. [G5.9.5]

6 NAMAQUA WARBLER *Phragmacia substriata*   13-14 cm

Endemic to S Africa. Similar to Karoo Prinia (p. 522), but has a more russet-coloured back, a thinner, more graduated tail, and only very narrow streaking confined to the breast. Unlike Karoo Prinia (p. 522), lacks buff tips to undertail feathers. Female has less streaking; juv. is duller. Formerly placed in *Prinia*, but recent work confirms it is distinct. **Habitat:** Acacia woodland, usually with *Phragmites* reedbeds, along wadis, rivers and dams; pairs defend territories year round. **Status:** Common. **Voice:** Distinctive, high-pitched rattling song, 'tit-trrrrrrrrrrrr'. [G5.9.8]

non-br.
ansorgei

br.

non-br.

1 KAROO (SPOTTED) PRINIA *Prinia maculosa* 12-14 cm
Endemic to S Africa. Forms a superspecies with Drakensberg Prinia, but is less yellow below and more heavily streaked, with streaks extending onto the flanks and vent. Much more heavily streaked below than Namaqua Warbler (p. 520), and is greyer brown above, with a broader tail, with buff-tipped (not plain) tail feathers. Female is less heavily spotted; juv. is yellower below. **Habitat:** Fynbos, thickets and taller Karoo scrub. **Status:** Common; usually in pairs and territorial year-round. **Voice:** Wide range of scolding calls, including sharp 'chleet-chleet-chleet' and faster 'tit-tit-tit-tit'. [G5.9.6]

2 DRAKENSBERG PRINIA *Prinia hypoxantha* 12-14 cm
Endemic to S Africa. Formerly lumped with Karoo Prinia, but has a less densely streaked, yellow-washed breast, yellowish supercilium and more reddish-brown upperparts. Streaking on underparts confined to breast. Non-breeding birds are richer orange-buff below. Juv. is paler below. **Habitat:** Forest edge, wooded gullies and bracken tangles, in more mesic areas than Karoo Prinia. **Status:** Common. **Voice:** Similar to Karoo Prinia's. [G5.9.7]

3 SÃO TOMÉ PRINIA *Prinia molleri* 13 cm
Endemic to São Tomé, where it is the only resident warbler. Long-tailed, with grey back and chestnut head, and graduated blackish tail with white tips. Female is paler, with olive back; juv. is duller, with rufous face and yellow-washed underparts. **Habitat:** Any wooded habitat at all elevations; in primary forest, occurs in canopy, clearings and along riverbanks. **Status:** Common. **Voice:** Monotonous, high-pitched 'tswee tswee tswee' song during distinctive territorial flight, accompanied by wing snapping; high-pitched 'sweet-errr sweet-errr' call. [C11.4]

4 BANDED PRINIA *Prinia bairdii* 12 cm
A prinia of forest edge, with distinctive dark barred underparts and conspicuous white wing bars formed by white spots on the wing coverts. Long, graduated tail is often held erect. Nominate birds (C Africa to W Uganda) have finely barred throat; E races have darker head and blackish throat. Juv. is paler and duller, with plain grey underparts. **Habitat:** Forest edge, riverbanks, in low and dense vegetation, and in plantation regrowth. **Status:** Common; inquisitive, but more often heard than seen. **Voice:** Apalis-like 'tillip tillip tillip' song; more typically prinia-like scolding calls. [C11.5]

PRINIA-LIKE WARBLERS
A mixed bag of long-tailed African warblers that superficially resemble prinias, but of mixed affinities. Sexes alike.

5 WHITE-CHINNED PRINIA *Schistolais leucopogon* 13 cm
A common C African warbler, active and noisy. Mainly grey, with conspicuous white throat and blackish-grey area from bill to ear coverts. Belly colour varies geographically from grey (nominate birds in W) to buffy (*reichenowi* in E). Juv. has less streaking on crown and darker eyes. Formerly placed in *Prinia*, but recent work confirms that *Schistolais* is distinct, and not even the closest relative of *Prinia*. **Habitat:** Forest edge, well-bushed savannas along gallery forest and abandoned cultivation; lives at low height, seldom found in high canopy. **Status:** Common; usually in family parties. **Voice:** Groups utter excited 'teeuu teeuu teeuu' song; slightly querulous 'teee teee teee' call. [C11.6]

6 SIERRA LEONE (WHITE-EYED) PRINIA *Schistolais leontica* 13 cm
Endemic to Upper Guinea forests. A small, long-tailed, mainly dark grey warbler, with white eyes and buff flanks. Easily told from White-chinned Prinia by dark chin. Lacks pale spots in folded wing of juv. Banded Prinia. **Habitat:** Forest edge, often along streams and in gullies in mountainous areas; occurs in dense vegetation, near ground. **Status:** Vulnerable. Local and uncommon, in small groups. **Voice:** High-pitched 'tsip tsip tsip' call; sometimes duets, with second bird giving lower call. [C11.7]

juv.

1 ROBERTS' WARBLER *Oreophilais robertsi* 13-14 cm
Endemic to E Zimbabwe highlands and adjacent Mozambique. A dark grey, prinia-like warbler, differing from Tawny-flanked Prinia (p. 520) by its grey throat, lack of a pale eyebrow and grey (not russet) wing. Non-breeding birds are paler below. Pale eye contrasts with dark face, but juv. has dark eye. **Habitat:** Forest edge, and bracken adjoining forests. **Status:** Common; usually in small groups. **Voice:** Raucous chorus of rather babbler-like chattering by all members of group. [G5.9.4]

2 BUFF-BELLIED WARBLER *Phyllolais pulchella* 10 cm
A rather nondescript warbler of the canopy of arid woodlands; best told from vaguely similar eremomelas (p. 530) and Willow Warbler (p. 486) by its longer tail with white outer-tail feathers. Also has smaller head, and thin bill with very pale pinkish-yellow lower mandible. Juv. is yellower below. **Habitat:** Canopy of acacia trees. **Status:** Common; usually in pairs or small groups; unobtrusive as it creeps about gleaning in foliage. **Voice:** Contact call is 'chit chit'; song is buzzy, descending trill. [C11.26]

3 CRICKET (SCALY-FRONTED) WARBLER *Spiloptila clamans* 12-13 cm
A small, long-tailed warbler resembling a prinia. Black-and-white scaling on crown and bold black-and-white wing coverts are diagnostic. Long tail has obvious black-and-white tips. **Habitat:** Dry acacia scrub and other dry thickets; obvious, constantly on the move while foraging and running on ground, with much raising and lowering of tail. **Status:** Locally common; in pairs or small groups. **Voice:** Very vocal: high-pitched, insect-like 'tseeep tseeep' or trilling 'trrrrrt trrrrrt'; lower tinking call; alarm call is short 'zrrt zrrt'. [C11.22] **Similar species:** **Streaked Scrub-warbler** *Scotocerca inquieta* is tiny, ground-dwelling warbler with streaked crown and strong white supercilium and black eye-stripe; lacks well-marked wing coverts of Cricket Warbler; found in arid wadis in N Mauritania.

4 RED-FRONTED WARBLER *Urorhipis rufifrons* 11 cm
A prinia-like warbler with a long, thin tail that is diagnostically flicked from left to right and in a circular motion. Differs from Pale and Tawny-flanked prinias (p. 520) by having distinct rufous forecrown and white edges to wing feathers. Juv's crown is brown. Longer tailed than Long-tailed Cisticola (p. 500), with distinctive white-edged black undertail pattern. **Habitat:** Semi-arid acacia scrub and thicket; forages on or near ground. **Status:** Common; usually in pairs. **Voice:** Fast 'tik tik tik tik' and 'tseeu tseeu tseeu', often several birds calling together; alarm is dry, high-pitched 'trrreu trrreu'. [C11.23]

5 SOCOTRA WARBLER *Incana incana* 13 cm
Endemic to Socotra. Differs from Socotra Cisticola (p. 508) (the only other small warbler on the island) by having uniform (not streaked) greyish-brown upperparts and longer tail. **Habitat:** Various, but usually scrubby bush, thickets and grassland with scattered bushes; runs mouse-like on ground, often with tail slightly cocked. **Status:** Locally common; usually in pairs. **Voice:** Rapid, almost staccato series of 'chip' notes; churring alarm call.

6 RUFOUS-EARED WARBLER *Malcorus pectoralis* 14-15 cm
Endemic to S Africa. A prinia-like warbler with diagnostic reddish ear coverts and a narrow black breast band. Tail is very long and thin. Juv. lacks breast band and has brown face; told from cisticolas by longer tail and lack of rufous cap, and from Karoo Prinia (p. 522) by plain breast and streaked back. **Habitat:** Arid scrub and grassland with scattered bushes; often forages on ground, running swiftly from bush to bush. **Status:** Common. **Voice:** Scolding, high-pitched 'chweeo, chweeo, chweeo...'. [G5.9.9]

1 RED-WINGED WARBLER *Heliolais erythropterus* 13 cm
A long-tailed, prinia-like warbler. Differs from Tawny-flanked Prinia (p. 520) by its bright rufous (not brown) wings, which contrast with the dark brown upperparts, and by the lack of a prominent white eye-stripe. Non-breeding birds are browner above, showing less contrast with rufous wings. Juv. is paler. **Habitat:** Long grass in woodland clearings and alongside streams. **Status:** Locally common. **Voice:** Monotonous, rather prinia-like 'pseep-pseep-pseep'; chattering alarm call. [C11.25, G5.9.2]

2 RED-WINGED GREY WARBLER *Drymocichla incana* 13 cm
A nondescript, small warbler, but easily recognised by its greyish upperparts relieved only by the diagnostic chestnut patch on the folded wing. Range overlaps with Red-winged Warbler, but is much greyer above, with wing panel restricted to primary bases (not extending onto wing coverts). Legs are yellow-pink. **Habitat:** Thickets and shrubby understorey in woodland and riverine scrub, chiefly in damp areas; feeds low down in warbler-like fashion and flicks tail as it creeps about. **Status:** Uncommon to locally common; singly, in pairs or small family groups. **Voice:** Mostly silent; whistled 'tseeoo pilip plip'; pairs duet, with one bird giving double note, 'cherie cherie', while other gives high-pitched 'tip tip tip'. [C11.27]

3 GREY-CAPPED WARBLER *Eminia lepida* 15 cm
Endemic to E Africa. A large, very vocal warbler. The combination of bright green back, black-bordered grey cap and chestnut throat is diagnostic. Most birds also have chestnut vent. Juv. is duller. **Habitat:** Varied, from montane forest and forest edge to lowland forest and thicket, gardens and old cultivation. **Status:** Common but secretive and not easily seen. **Voice:** Loud, melodic, warbling song, usually with repetitive 'whee whee whee' or 'wher cheee wher cheee' elements. [C11.37]

4 GREEN LONGTAIL *Urolais epichlorus* 14 cm
Endemic to SW Cameroon and Bioko. The combination of long straggly tail, olive-green upperparts, paler green underparts and yellowish throat is diagnostic. At close range, face is paler green, with distinct yellow loral stripe and eye-ring. **Habitat:** Dense undergrowth and mid-stratum of montane forest; also forest edge and secondary growth. **Status:** Common but easily overlooked unless diagnostic call is heard. **Voice:** Far-carrying, high-pitched, metronomic 'chip chip chip'; ascending trill, 'tseu tsee-see-se-se-it-t-t-t'. [C11.24]

5 ORIOLE WARBLER (MOHO) *Hypergerus atriceps* 19 cm
A very large, slender, long-tailed warbler. If seen clearly, the black head, green upperparts and yellow underparts are diagnostic. Given poor views, could be confused with a greenbul (p. 412) or even a masked weaver (p. 662). **Habitat:** Gallery forest and forest edge, near ground, in dense vegetation. **Status:** Locally common, but furtive, remaining in dense vegetation. **Voice:** Loud, robin-like, whistled song, 'huee huu he he', or variations, rendered 'here, tea purry'; harsher 'tik-ik-ik' by female. [C11.36]

br.

non-br.

Small, rather short-tailed warblers found in the canopy of woodland, forest and arid scrub. They are considered intermediate between crombecs and apalises. They usually occur in small groups, and regularly join bird parties. The paler species could be confused with penduline tits (p. 390), but are larger and longer billed. The greener species superficially resemble white-eyes (p. 640). Sexes alike.

1 RUFOUS-CROWNED EREMOMELA *Eremomela badiceps*   11 cm
A handsome eremomela of forest canopy. Readily distinguished from all other species except Turner's Eremomela by its bright chestnut cap, white throat and black breast band. Larger than Turner's Eremomela, with entire crown (not just forecrown) chestnut. Juv. is duller, with olive upperparts, yellow wash on underparts and incomplete olive breast band. Diagnostic chestnut cap is less conspicuous, and mostly concentrated on forecrown; probably indistinguishable from juv. Turner's Eremomela. **Habitat:** Forest canopy and at lower height on forest edge and in secondary growth. **Status:** Common. **Voice:** Rapid series of scolding 'ti ti ti ti' notes; short, thin, warbling song. [C11.45]

2 TURNER'S EREMOMELA *Eremomela turneri*   8-9 cm
A highly localised eremomela; recently known only from small forest areas in SW Kenya and E DRC. Smaller than Rufous-crowned Eremomela, with chestnut confined to forehead (not whole crown); ranges overlap in E DRC. Juv. probably indistinguishable from juv. Rufous-crowned Eremomela unless smaller size can be judged accurately. **Habitat:** Mid- and low-altitude forest; occurs in canopy of closed-canopy forest, but ventures to lower strata at forest edge and in disturbed areas. **Status:** Endangered. Uncommon; usually found in small groups; often joins bird parties. **Voice:** Soft, thin 'ssrik ssrik', repeated often and sometimes rolled together.

3 BURNT-NECKED EREMOMELA *Eremomela usticollis*   10 cm
Near-endemic to S Africa. A tiny, rather nondescript eremomela, bluish grey above and pale buff below. Combination of pale yellow eyes and rufous cheeks and ear coverts is diagnostic; small, rusty throat bar is often inconspicuous or absent. Told from Red-capped Crombec (p. 532) by longer tail, pale eye and different foraging action. Female lacks brown on cap and has fainter brown throat bar. Juv. lacks rufous patches on face and rusty throat bar of adult. **Habitat:** Mainly acacia woodland, but also arid broadleafed woodland and dry riverbeds. **Status:** Common; usually in small groups. **Voice:** High-pitched 'chii-cheee-cheee', followed by sibilant 'trrrrrrrrr'. [G5.6.6]

4 BLACK-NECKED EREMOMELA *Eremomela atricollis*   11 cm
Endemic to SC Africa. The striking head pattern, with a black mask, yellow throat, black chest band, and orange-yellow supercilium, is diagnostic. Eye and legs are dark. Juv. is duller, with diffuse breast band and face mask. **Habitat:** Primarily well-developed miombo woodland, but also well-wooded savannas. **Status:** Locally common; usually in small groups in bird parties; often occurs in mixed flocks with Green-capped Eremomelas. **Voice:** Frequently uttered, rasping 'zwee zwee zweee'; similar rasping, buzzy alarm notes to those of Green-capped Eremomela. [C11.42]

5 KAROO EREMOMELA *Eremomela gregalis*   12 cm
Endemic to Karoo scrub in S Africa. A fairly long-tailed eremomela, with olive-green upperparts and grey face contrasting sharply with silvery white underparts. Conspicuous pale eye, yellow flanks and undertail coverts distinguish it from camaropteras (p. 536). Juv. is browner above. **Habitat:** Karoo and semi-desert scrub, usually in bushy areas on open flats; often in areas of taller than average shrubs, but avoids watercourses with acacia trees. **Status:** Uncommon to locally common; almost always in small groups. **Voice:** Monotonous, frog-like 'swee swee swee' song usually uttered before dawn; soft 'pink pink' contact call. [G5.6.4]

juv.

1

2

3

juv.

4

5

1 YELLOW-BELLIED EREMOMELA *Eremomela icteropygialis* 10 cm
A pale, grey-backed eremomela, forming a superspecies with Salvadori's and Yellow-vented eremomelas. Slightly smaller than Salvadori's Eremomela by having grey-brown (not greenish) rump uniform with back. Intensity and extent of yellow on underparts varies geographically, tending to be more extensive and brighter in moister areas. Adults have more extensive yellow belly than Yellow-vented Eremomela, but juv. has duller yellow underparts and is difficult to separate from Yellow-vented Eremomela in narrow area of overlap; best told by larger size and larger, heavier bill. In W Africa, told from Senegal Eremomela by grey (not greenish) upperparts and yellow confined to belly (not extending onto breast). **Habitat:** Semi-arid savanna, broadleafed woodland and scrub. **Status:** Common; usually solitary or in pairs. **Voice:** Song is crombec-like: high-pitched, frequently repeated 'tchee-tchee-tchee', more varied and warbling in N. [C11.39, G5.6.3]

2 SALVADORI'S EREMOMELA *Eremomela salvadorii* 11 cm
Endemic to WC Africa. Often considered a race of Yellow-bellied Eremomela, but is slightly larger and more brightly coloured, with green-washed (not grey-brown) rump and uppertail coverts, and brighter yellow belly. Told from Senegal Eremomela by having yellow confined to belly (not extending onto breast); ranges do not overlap. **Habitat:** Woodland and savanna. **Status:** Locally common. **Voice:** Similar to Yellow-bellied Eremomela's. [C11.40]

3 YELLOW-VENTED EREMOMELA *Eremomela flavicrissalis* 8-9 cm
Endemic to NE Africa. A small, short-tailed eremomela. Slightly smaller than Yellow-bellied Eremomela, with faint yellow confined to vent (not extending onto belly); also, is greyer overall, with much finer, more slender bill. Smaller and paler than Phillipa's Crombec (p. 532), with longer tail, and shorter, dark grey (not pink) legs. Juv. has very little, if any, yellow on vent. **Habitat:** Drier woodland and more arid scrub than Yellow-bellied Eremomela. **Status:** Locally common; usually in pairs or bird parties. **Voice:** Contact call is faint 'tseep'; song is less musical than Yellow-bellied Eremomela's.

4 SENEGAL EREMOMELA *Eremomela pusilla* 10 cm
Endemic to W Africa. Forms a superspecies with Green-backed, Green-capped and Karoo (p. 528) eremomelas. Superficially resembles Yellow-bellied Eremomela but has greener upperparts and more extensive yellow on underparts, extending onto lower breast (not confined to belly). Also differs in habitat (occurs in moister savannas) and behaviour (usually in groups, not solitary). **Habitat:** Moist savanna. **Status:** Common; usually in small groups. **Voice:** Groups utter chattering call; song is regular 'wik wik wik'. [C11.44]

5 GREEN-BACKED EREMOMELA *Eremomela canescens* 11 cm
EC African counterpart of Senegal Eremomela; slightly larger, with brighter plumage and diagnostic black lores and cheek forming broad eye-stripe or mask. The two species' ranges barely overlap, but there is a narrow hybrid zone along E border of Cameroon. In S, range overlaps slightly with Green-capped Eremomela; differs in having grey (not green) crown, broad black eye-stripe and white (not yellow) throat and breast. Juv. is duller. **Habitat:** Wooded savanna. **Status:** Common. **Voice:** Often-repeated 'wik wik' contact note; song is more varied than Senegal Eremomela's, closer to Green-capped Eremomela's. [C11.43]

6 GREEN-CAPPED EREMOMELA *Eremomela scotops* 11 cm
SC African counterpart of Green-backed Eremomela; ranges barely overlap. Readily identified by greenish (not grey) cap and face, merging into grey (not green) back, and bright yellow (not white) throat and breast. Lower breast and belly colour varies geographically from whitish to yellow. Juv. is paler. **Habitat:** Broadleafed woodland, especially miombo, but also in mopane and riverine forests; typically forages in canopy, but sometimes ventures to mid-strata. **Status:** Fairly common; usually in small groups. **Voice:** Repeated 'tweer-tweer-tweer'; rasping alarm note. [C11.41, G5.6.5]

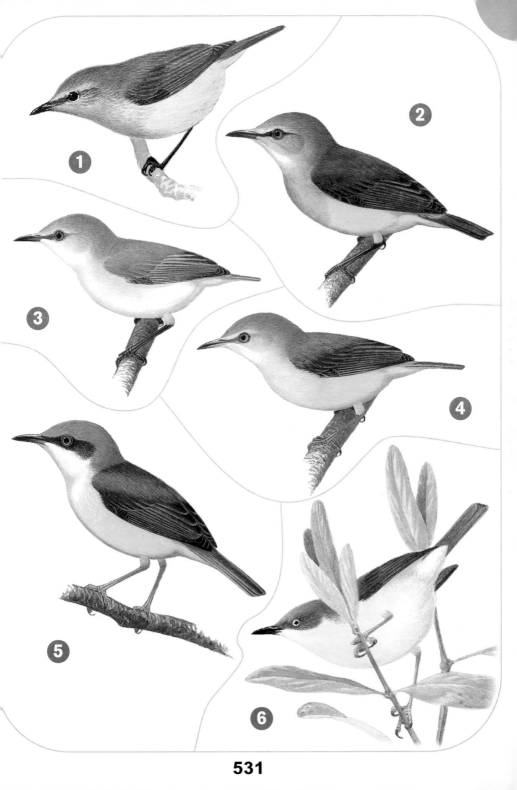

Small, very short-tailed warblers that appear almost tail-less. Similar to eremomelas (pp. 528-530) but have a shorter tail and typically glean from branches rather than foliage. Sexes alike.

1 NORTHERN CROMBEC *Sylvietta brachyura*   8 cm
A small crombec, most likely to be confused with larger Red-faced Crombec, but is paler below, has a pale supercilium and a darker eye-stripe, and a shorter bill. Supercilium and throat vary geographically from creamy to rufous. Smaller than Somali Crombec, with much darker underparts and short bill. Rufous (not yellowish) underparts separate it from Phillipa's Crombec. Juv. has buffy tips to wing coverts. **Habitat:** Varied, from dry woodland to riverine woodland and drier scrub to semi-arid scrub. **Status:** Common; usually in pairs; often joins bird parties. **Voice:** Clear, whistled 'tee uu'; song is short series of jumbled whistles and churrs, 'trrrr tswee tswee tsur-eooo'. [C11.50]

2 PHILLIPA'S (SHORT-BILLED) CROMBEC *Sylvietta philippae*   8-9 cm
Endemic to Somalia and S Ethiopia. Paler than all other crombecs in its range, with the underparts suffused yellow. Could be confused with Yellow-vented Eremomela (p. 530), but has shorter tail, more extensive yellow on underparts and longer, flesh-coloured (not dark) legs. **Habitat:** Short, dry acacia scrub and dry, wooded wadis. **Status:** Fairly common within its limited range. In pairs or small groups, often joining bird parties. **Voice:** Soft churring and chinking calls; 3-noted song, 'ti chureee chrrr'.

3 SOMALI CROMBEC *Sylvietta isabellina*   9-10 cm
Endemic to NE Africa. Forms a superspecies with Long-billed Crombec, but is paler overall and ranges do not overlap. Much greyer than Northern and Red-faced crombecs, with pale greyish buff (not rufous) underparts; also has longer, more decurved bill. Juv. is duller. **Habitat:** Dry acacia scrub and wooded wadis in semi-desert. **Status:** Little known; apparently uncommon through much of its range. Usually in pairs or small groups. **Voice:** Soft 'tissik tissik' contact note; song is unknown.

4 LONG-BILLED CROMBEC *Sylvietta rufescens*   10 cm
Similar to Northern Crombec, but ranges do not overlap. Differs from Red-faced Crombec in having longer bill, brownish (not ashy grey) upperparts, and pale supercilium and dark eye-stripe (not plain rufous face). Lacks chestnut breast band and ear patches of Red-capped Crombec. Bill length varies geographically. Juv. is slightly paler rufous below. **Habitat:** Woodland, savanna and arid scrublands. **Status:** Common. **Voice:** Song is loud, repeated 'tree-rriit, tree-rriit' or 'trree reee rit' whistle; dry 'prrit' contact call is given regularly. [C11.51, G5.6.1]

5 RED-FACED CROMBEC *Sylvietta whytii*   9-10 cm
Pale grey above, with rich rufous underparts. Differs from Long-billed and Northern crombecs in having plain rufous face (lacking dark eye-stripe contrasting with paler supercilium, cheeks and throat). Range barely overlaps with Red-capped Crombec; differs in having uniformly rufous face and underparts (not chestnut ear-coverts and breast band). Juv. is brownish grey above. **Habitat:** Miombo woodland and riparian forests; typically forages in canopy, but ventures into lower strata in areas without Long-billed Crombecs. **Status:** Locally common. **Voice:** Trilling, repeated 'wit-wit-wit-wit...'; thin 'si-si-si-see'. [G5.5.10]

6 RED-CAPPED CROMBEC *Sylvietta ruficapilla*   10 cm
Differs from Long-billed and Red-faced crombecs by its chestnut ear-coverts and breast band; rest of underparts are paler. Forehead and crown vary geographically from chestnut to grey. Back is paler grey than Red-faced Crombec's; ranges barely overlap. Juv. is more buffy above, with buff flecking on wings. **Habitat:** Miombo woodland; typically forages in canopy, but ventures into lower strata in areas without Long-billed Crombecs. **Status:** Locally common. **Voice:** Ringing, repeated 'richi-chichi-chichir'. [C11.46, G5.6.2]

1 LEMON-BELLIED CROMBEC *Sylvietta denti* 8 cm
A forest-canopy crombec. Smaller than Green Crombec, with a shorter bill, darker legs, plainer face and paler plumage (less brown, more olive, and greyer on head). Pale yellow belly is distinctive, but W African race of Green Crombec also has yellow wash on belly. **Habitat:** Forest canopy and edge, secondary growth and gallery forest; remains in canopy of closed-canopy forest, but occurs at lower strata at forest edge. **Status:** Common. **Voice:** Soft series of whistles, 'tsi tsi tsi tswee tswee tswee', descending in scale; often hard to hear when calling from high canopy. [C11.49]

2 GREEN CROMBEC *Sylvietta virens* 9 cm
The most widespread forest crombec. Co-occurs with Lemon-bellied Crombec, but has a more strongly marked head with an indistinct buffy eye-stripe and darker cap, a longer bill and typically a greyish-white (not yellow) belly. W African *flaviventris* has wash of yellow on lower breast and belly. Range overlaps slightly with that of White-browed Crombec, but easily told by much less distinct facial pattern. **Habitat:** Dense vegetation in forest and forest edge, secondary growth, gallery forest and thickets in woodland. **Status:** Common. **Voice:** Dry 'trrt trrt' contact call; song is short, high-pitched 'dee-deu dee-deu dee it it'. [C11.48]

3 WHITE-BROWED CROMBEC *Sylvietta leucophrys* 9 cm
Endemic to E Africa. A montane-forest crombec with a diagnostic broad white eyebrow, dark rufous-brown head and upperparts, greenish wings and light grey underparts. Juv. of nominate race (Kenya and E Uganda) resembles adult, but Albertine Rift *chloronota* juv. lacks white eye-stripe (or it is greatly reduced) and could be confused with Chapin's Crombec; differs by having much darker belly. **Habitat:** Montane forest, in dense vegetation. **Status:** Locally common. **Voice:** Clear series of whistled notes, 'see see su see see'; short 'tii teroo'. [C11.47]

4 CHAPIN'S CROMBEC *Sylvietta chapini* 9 cm
Endemic to Lendu Plateau, E DRC. Often treated as a race of White-browed Crombec, but has a complete chestnut crown (lacking a white supercilium) and yellow-washed (not greyish) underparts. Could be confused with juv. *chloronota* White-browed Crombec, which also lacks white eyebrow, but this species has yellowish (not dark grey) underparts. **Habitat:** Montane forest. **Status:** Poorly known; may be extinct because forest on Lendu Plateau apparently has been destroyed. **Voice:** Similar to that of White-browed Crombec.

5 GREEN HYLIA *Hylia prasina* 12 cm
A small forest warbler with a bold, pale yellow supercilium, black eye-stripe and off-white throat. Olive-green underparts distinguish it from camaropteras and woodland warblers. Longer tail and behaviour separate it from Neumann's Warbler. Bill is slightly decurved; could be confused with female sunbird. **Habitat:** Forest understorey to mid-strata, forest edge, secondary growth and gallery forest; searches for ants on and under leaves and twigs in dense vegetation. **Status:** Common; best located by pure, bi-syllabic whistle. **Voice:** Series of short, rattled 'trrt trrt' notes, followed by loud 'teee heee' whistle. [C11.61]

6 NEUMANN'S (SHORT-TAILED) WARBLER *Hemitesia neumanni* 11 cm
Endemic to Albertine Rift; affinities uncertain. Most obvious field character is black-and-white eye-stripe; does not cock tail like camaropteras. Vaguely resembles Green Hylia, but has much shorter tail, white central belly and unusually large head; stays close to or on ground (not in mid-stratum). **Habitat:** Mid-elevation forest; walks quietly over leaf litter in dark, shady tangles, often near water. **Status:** Uncommon and little known; often in pairs. **Voice:** Loud 2-3 note call, 'wee teee teeeoo' or 'twee chiree'. [C11.52]

Small, active, noisy warblers of forest and thickets. All frequently cock their short tails. They sew living leaves together to form their nests. Sexes alike in most species.

1 GREEN-BACKED CAMAROPTERA *Camaroptera brachyura*   10-11 cm
Differs from Grey-backed Camaroptera in having olive-green (not grey) mantle, back and tail. Lacks distinct breeding and non-breeding plumages. Intergrades with Grey-backed Camaroptera in S Malawi and Mozambique. Juv. is washed yellow below. **Habitat:** Dense undergrowth and tangles in forest and thickets; also gardens. In areas of overlap with Grey-backed Camaroptera, typically occurs in moister habitats. **Status:** Common. **Voice:** Similar to that of Grey-backed Camaroptera. [C11.31, G5.6.7]

2 GREY-BACKED CAMAROPTERA *Camaroptera brevicaudata*   10-11 cm
Often lumped with Green-backed Camaroptera; the two species intergrade in places, but co-occur in others. Differs from Green-backed Camaroptera by having grey (not olive-green) mantle and tail. Angolan escarpment *harterti* has grey back and green tail; sometimes treated as distinct (Hartert's or Green-tailed Camaroptera). Most races have more ashy-brown mantle and back in non-breeding plumage, but W and C African *tincta* lacks distinct breeding plumage. Juv. is washed yellow below. **Habitat:** Dense vegetation in woodland, thicket and forest, including gardens; usually remains in understorey or mid-strata. **Status:** Common. **Voice:** Often repeated, nasal 'neeehhh' (resulting in common name, 'bleating warbler'); loud, snapping 'bidup-bidup-bidup'. [C11.21, G5.6.8]

3 OLIVE-GREEN CAMAROPTERA *Camaroptera chloronota*   10 cm
A nondescript forest camaroptera with a distinctive song. Range overlaps broadly with Grey-backed Camaroptera, but is darker, with olive-green (not greyish) back. Face and breast vary from grey in W to buffy in E. **Habitat:** Dense forest understorey and forest edge; generally in more forested habitat than Grey-backed Camaroptera. **Status:** Common. **Voice:** Long series of loud, piercing notes, descending in scale and fading away, then becoming louder again, before ending abruptly; typical bleating alarm call. [C11.35]

4 YELLOW-BROWED CAMAROPTERA *Camaroptera superciliaris*   10 cm
The most distinctive camaroptera, with a diagnostic bright yellow eyebrow and face with a black line from bill to eye. Bill is longer than in other species. Exposes blue patch on side of throat when it sings. **Habitat:** Dense vegetation of tangles and vines inside forest or at edge, and thick regrowth of abandoned plantations. **Status:** Common, but easily overlooked if not calling. **Voice:** Low-pitched 'naar naar' nasal song. [C11.34]

5 WHITE-TAILED WARBLER *Poliolais lopezi*   11-12 cm
Endemic to SW Cameroon, SE Nigeria and Bioko. A small, short-tailed warbler with diagnostic white outer-tail feathers. Closely resembles camaropteras, but does not sew leaves to form nest. Told from Olive-green Camaropera by shorter tail, with white (not dark) outer feathers. Male is mostly dark grey or olive-grey. Female is greyish brown, with rufous face and crown; could be confused with Red-capped Forest Warbler (p. 540), but has shorter tail with white outer feathers and longer legs; ranges do not overlap. Flight is weak and noisy. **Habitat:** Dense undergrowth of montane forests. **Status:** Fairly common, but easily overlooked; usually in pairs. **Voice:** High-pitched, insect-like chirping song 'tsi-peeuu'; short 'bzzzt' contact call; 'tsee-erp' alarm call. [C11.28]

Dark brown warblers of woodland and semi-arid savanna, closely related to camaropteras; frequently cock their tails and sew living leaves together to form their nests. Sexes alike.

1 STIERLING'S WREN-WARBLER *Calamonastes stierlingi*   13 cm

Often lumped with Pale Wren-warbler; the two species intergrade in a narrow zone in Zambia. Differs from Pale Wren-warbler by cleanly barred underparts, white (not buff) spots on wing coverts, rufous-brown (not grey-brown) upperparts, and song. Range overlaps with Barred Wren-warbler in SW; differs in having cleaner barred underparts, paler, orange-brown eyes, and flesh-coloured (not brown) legs. Juv. is washed yellow below and more rufous above, with dark eyes. **Habitat:** Broadleafed woodland, especially miombo. **Status:** Common. **Voice:** Repeated, fast 'tlip-tlip-lip', recalling cheap cellphone ring-tone. [G5.6.10]

2 BARRED WREN-WARBLER *Calamonastes fasciolatus*   14 cm

Endemic to SW Africa. Breeding male differs from Stierling's Wren-warbler by its brown breast which largely obscures the darker barring. Females and non-breeding males have buff underparts with dusky bars, less well-defined than those of slightly smaller Stierling's Wren-warbler; also has darker brown eyes and brown (not flesh-coloured) legs, and occurs in different habitat. Juv. is more rufous, with yellowish wash on breast. **Habitat:** Dry acacia savanna. **Status:** Common. **Voice:** Soft, tremulous 'trrrreee trrrreee trrrreee'; rather mechanical 'pleelip-pleelip'; chattering alarm call. [G5.6.9]

3 PALE WREN-WARBLER *Calamonastes undosus*   13 cm

Less cleanly barred below than Stierling's Wren-warbler, with grey-brown (not rufous-brown) upperparts, inconspicuous buffy (not white) spots on wing coverts, and different song. Generally paler and more greyish brown than Grey Wren-warbler, with more obvious barring on belly, flanks and throat, and pale fleshy (not dark) legs. Tail is less persistently pumped up and down. **Habitat:** Broadleafed woodland; forages near ground, but sings higher up from open branches. **Status:** Uncommon and thinly distributed. **Voice:** Monotonous 'wheet' or 'weeuu' notes, repeated once per second; less ringing and abrupt than Grey Wren-warbler's. [C11.33]

4 GREY WREN-WARBLER *Calamonastes simplex*   13 cm

Endemic to NE Africa. Darker and more sooty grey than Pale Wren-warbler, with very indistinct barring on belly, flanks and throat. Darker tail contrasts with paler grey back; tail is frequently pumped up and down when bird is alarmed. **Habitat:** Acacia savanna, in drier areas than Pale Wren-warbler; forages on or near ground, but sings from exposed perches. **Status:** Common; more often heard than seen. **Voice:** Sharp, rapid 'chuk chuk chuk', like two stones being struck together.

5 GRAUER'S WARBLER *Graueria vittata*   14-15 cm

Endemic to Albertine Rift. Differs from Banded Prinia (p. 522) by its shorter tail, more diffusely barred underparts, dark eye and uniform brown wing. Occurs in different habitat from Pale Wren-warbler; ranges do not overlap. **Habitat:** Thickets and tangled creepers in forests and forest edge at 1 600-2 500 m; moves slowly and keeps well hidden when foraging. **Status:** Uncommon; little known; most often detected by distinctive song. **Voice:** Soft, slow, frog-like trill, rising in pitch, lasting 1-2 seconds and repeated every 3-4 seconds; recalls song of Scaly-throated Honeyguide. [C11.53]

6 CINNAMON-BREASTED WARBLER *Euryptila subcinnamomea*   14 cm

Endemic to S Africa. A dark brown warbler of arid rocky hillslopes. At close range, rufous breast band, flanks and rump are diagnostic. Juv. is more rufous above. **Habitat:** Scrub-covered, rocky hillsides, in dry river gullies and gorges; creeps among jumbled boulders, often disappearing into crevices. **Status:** Uncommon and localised; unobtrusive unless calling. **Voice:** Song is loud, piercing series of whistles: 1-3 long, ascending 'peeeee' notes, followed by several rapid, short whistles. [G5.6.11]

FOREST WARBLERS (TAILORBIRDS)
Little-known warblers restricted to Eastern Arc Mountains. They possibly have affinities to Asian tailorbirds (and are sometimes placed in *Orthotomus*). Both species have a rounded head with a very fine, spiky-looking bill. Like camaropteras and wren-warblers, they sew leaves together to form their nests. Sexes alike.

1 RED-CAPPED FOREST WARBLER (AFRICAN TAILORBIRD)
Artisornis metopias   10 cm
Endemic to Eastern Arc Mts of Tanzania and N Mozambique. Smaller than Winifred's Warbler, with grey (not rufous) throat and breast. Confusion with Chapin's Apalis (p. 516) is unlikely due to short, dark (not long, white-tipped) tail, grey (not reddish) throat and breast, and different habitat (thick undergrowth, not mid-stratum). **Habitat:** Dense undergrowth and edge of montane forest. **Status:** Common; usually in pairs; easy to overlook if not calling. **Voice:** Duo-syllabic duet, 'tseeu-zizz', often repeated; 'tseeu' part may be given solo.

2 LONG-BILLED FOREST WARBLER (MOREAU'S TAILORBIRD)
Artisornis moreaui   12 cm
Restricted to E Usambaras (N Tanzania) and Serra Jeci (N Mozambique). Much longer-billed than Red-capped Forest Warbler, with rufous restricted to crown (not face), longer tail and greyer upperparts. Most likely to be confused with Brown-headed Apalis (p. 518), but has much longer bill and shorter tail with no white tips. Bill appears exceptionally long and spiky. **Habitat:** Montane forest, usually in lower and mid-canopy, especially where there are vines and thick tangles. **Status:** Critically threatened. Uncommon and local; sometimes in mixed bird parties. **Voice:** Apalis-like, repeated 'peedo peedoo'.

BATHMOCERCUS WARBLERS
Colourful warblers of dense forest undergrowth; rather furtive and easily overlooked if not calling. Sexes differ.

3 BLACK-HEADED (BLACK-CAPPED) RUFOUS WARBLER
Bathmocercus cerviniventris   12 cm
Endemic to Upper Guinea forests. Forms a superspecies with Black-faced Rufous Warbler; distinguished by its fully black head, browner (not rufous) back and tail, and buffy (not grey) belly; ranges do not overlap. Female resembles male, but has pale chin and sides of throat. **Habitat:** Very dense herbaceous vegetation of forest edge and inside forest, often near water; keeps low in dense vegetation, where it is best located by song. **Status:** Uncommon to locally common. **Voice:** High-pitched, penetrating, short, whistled phrases, 'pee pee tee' and variations of this; female gives harsh 'chit chit' calls. [C11.29]

4 BLACK-FACED RUFOUS WARBLER *Bathmocercus rufus*   13 cm
C African counterpart of Black-headed Rufous Warbler, with diagnostic black face and throat. Upperparts and sides of neck and breast are bright rufous (in male) or grey (female). Tail is often cocked when singing. An active bird, best located by song. Juv. is sooty grey-brown, with conspicuous pale gape. **Habitat:** Dense, herbaceous vegetation of marshes and streams in forest, thick vegetation along forest tracks and at forest edge. **Status:** Locally common. **Voice:** Piercing, high-pitched calls similar to those of Black-headed Rufous Warbler, but often more even and monotonous; female gives harsh 'krik krik' notes. [C11.30]

5 WINIFRED'S (MRS MOREAU'S) WARBLER *Bathmocercus winifredae*   13 cm
Endemic to montane forests of Tanzania's Eastern Arc Mts. Lacks black on face and breast of Black-faced Rufous Warbler; ranges do not overlap. Larger than Red-capped Forest Warbler, with rufous (not grey) throat and upper breast. Could possibly be confused with Chapin's Apalis (p. 516) but differs in habitat (thick undergrowth, not mid-stratum) and has short, dark (not long, white-tipped) tail. Female and juv. are duller, with brown back extending onto crown. **Habitat:** Thick tangles in undergrowth in montane forests; occurs close to or on ground, very often in damp areas or alongside streams. **Status:** Vulnerable. Uncommon; difficult to locate except by diagnostic call. **Voice:** High-pitched, far-carrying whistles 'seeee seeee seeee', often repeated, similar to other rufous warblers'. Also variations of 'wheeooo'.

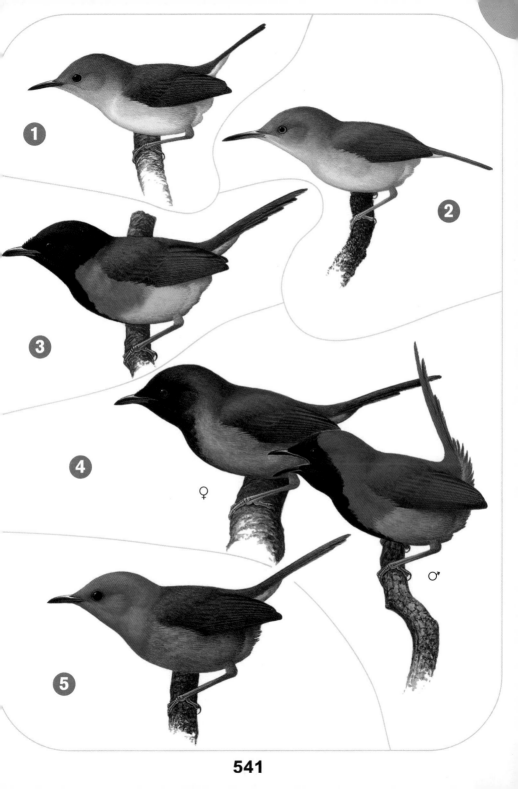

Fairly large, nondescript forest warblers with long, straight, hook-tipped bills. They have short wings, and most have a short tail, giving them a peculiarly unbalanced look. The rump and flank feathers are long and can be erected, but this is seldom observed. Sexes alike.

1 KEMP'S LONGBILL *Macrosphenus kempi*   14 cm
Endemic to W Africa. Forms a superspecies with Yellow Longbill; ranges barely overlap. Adult has greyish underparts with diagnostic chestnut wash on flanks. Juv. is drab olive; best told from Yellow Longbill by its song and yellowish (not whitish) throat. Could be confused with Fraser's Sunbird (p. 624), but has darker face and straight bill. **Habitat:** Canopy and mid-stratum of lowland rainforest; easily overlooked if silent. **Status:** Uncommon to locally common; frequent member of bird parties. **Voice:** Rolling, whistled, slightly descending song, 'chee chur chee chrr chee chur chee cheee'; various warbles and chips given as sub-song. [C11.56]

2 YELLOW LONGBILL *Macrosphenus flavicans*   13 cm
Olive-green above and yellow-olive below, with a diagnostic whitish throat. In good light, greyish crown contrasts with olive back (back and crown are uniform in Grey Longbill). Lacks chestnut flanks of adult Kemp's Longbill. Juv. is browner above, with greyer throat. **Habitat:** Dense vegetation of forest understorey and mid-strata; moves slowly in vegetation. **Status:** Locally common. **Voice:** Song is series of simple whistled notes, descending in pitch and accelerating slightly. [C11.55, but perhaps incorrectly identified]

3 GREY LONGBILL *Macrosphenus concolor*   12 cm
A small, drab olive longbill, with a slightly shorter bill than Yellow and Kemp's longbills. Differs from Yellow Longbill by plainer, olive plumage, darker eye and different song. Lacks chestnut wash on flanks of Kemp's Longbill. **Habitat:** Forest canopy and edge in tangles of lianas; in closed-canopy forest stays in canopy, but ventures lower down in dense vines at forest edge. **Status:** Common; very vocal, but difficult to see if not singing. **Voice:** Rolling, warbled 'wurdley wurdley wurdley', faster and more rolling than that of Kemp's Longbill; also mimicry. [C11.54]

4 PULITZER'S LONGBILL *Macrosphenus pulitzeri*   14 cm
Endemic to W Angola. A fairly short-tailed, thin-billed, drab olive forest warbler with a pale eye and obvious dark lores. Within its limited range, might be confused with Grey-backed Camaroptera (p. 536), but has brownish (not greenish) wings and does not cock tail. Larger and darker than Grey Longbill; ranges do not overlap. **Habitat:** Thick tangles and vines in dry evergreen forests; occurs in secondary growth in coffee plantations. **Status:** Endangered. Very little known, but locally common in some areas. **Voice:** Loud, sharp 'wit chew-it' repeated, or faster 'chew-it chew-it...'.

5 KRETSCHMER'S LONGBILL *Macrosphenus kretschmeri*   14-15 cm
Endemic to coastal SE Africa. Longer tailed than other longbills; could be confused with Grey-olive, Tiny or Little greenbuls (p. 416-418), but has shorter tail, more slender body and longer, thinner bill. Range does not overlap with those of other longbills. Eye colour varies from white to red or brown. **Habitat:** Dense tangles and vines in understorey of low- and mid-altitude forests; ventures into secondary growth. **Status:** Uncommon; best detected by its diagnostic voice. Sometimes joins bird parties. **Voice:** Loud, sharp, piercing, whistled, 4-note phrase, 'weet teuu-peeuu tek'; various warbles and churrs.

6 SÃO TOMÉ SHORT-TAIL (BOCAGE'S LONGBILL) *Amaurocichla bocagei*   9 cm
Endemic to São Tomé. A strange-looking bird, found on or near the ground, usually along streams. Typically walks pipit-like on forest floor or on low branches. Long, thin bill, short tail, long legs, and dark brown plumage are diagnostic. Flight is weak. **Habitat:** Understorey of primary forest; rarely in old secondary forest. **Status:** Vulnerable. Uncommon to locally common. **Voice:** Soft, penetrating 'seeee' or 'teeeee'; sometimes double-noted 'tseee teee'. [C12.52]

Small, active warblers of woodland and forest canopy superficially recalling *Ficedula* flycatchers (p. 556), but have a more horizontal posture, and feed primarily by gleaning rather than hawking prey. They regularly join bird parties. Sexes differ in most species; juvs resemble the females but are duller below, with buff-fringed upperparts.

1 SOUTHERN (MASHONA) HYLIOTA *Hyliota australis*   11-12 cm

Similar to Yellow-bellied Hyliota, but male has matt (not glossy) upperparts, pale yellow underparts and smaller white shoulder patch (restricted to coverts, not extending onto secondaries and tertials). Female is paler and duller; differs from female Yellow-bellied Hyliota by having warm brown (not grey-brown) upperparts. **Habitat:** Miombo and other broadleafed woodland. **Status:** Locally common; usually in pairs or small groups. **Voice:** Similar to Yellow-bellied Hyliota's, but shorter and faster. [C11.59, G5.3.4]

2 YELLOW-BELLIED HYLIOTA *Hyliota flavigaster*   11-12 cm

The most widespread hyliota. Easily told from Violet-backed Hyliota by its prominent white shoulder patch, but is separated with difficulty from Southern Hyliota, and the two species often occur together in SC Africa. Male differs from male Southern Hyliota by having distinctly glossy blue-black upperparts, richer yellow underparts and white in wings extending onto folded secondaries and tertials (in S *barbozae*, which overlaps with Southern Hyliota). Female lacks gloss of male in most races and is duller below; in area of overlap, may be told from female Southern Hyliota by grey-brown (not warm brown) upperparts. **Habitat:** Broadleafed woodland, including miombo. **Status:** Locally common; usually in pairs or small groups. **Voice:** Soft, high-pitched, rather querulous 'tueet tueet'; chittering call. [C11.58, G5.3.3]

3 USAMBARA HYLIOTA *Hyliota usambarae*   12 cm

Endemic to Usambara Mts, NE Tanzania, where it is the only hyliota. Sometimes considered a race of Southern Hyliota, but appears more similar to Yellow-bellied Hyliota, with rich orange-yellow underparts, glossy blue sheen on upperparts and white edges to secondaries forming extended white wing patch. Apparently unique among hyliotas in that the sexes are alike. **Habitat:** Canopy and mid-strata of low to mid-altitude forest and forest edge. **Status:** Endangered. Rare and little known; usually found in pairs and joins bird parties. **Voice:** Uncertain, but a thin squeaky noise has been described.

4 VIOLET-BACKED HYLIOTA *Hyliota violacea*   12 cm

Readily separated from other hyliotas by the virtual lack of white in the folded wing (restricted to only the two inner greater coverts in E nominate race; entirely absent in Upper Guinea *nehrkorni*). Male has whitish underparts, contrasting with glossy violet upperparts, and from a distance could be confused with violet-backed sunbirds (p. 622). Female has rich rufous-tawny underparts. **Habitat:** Forest canopy and tall trees in secondary growth. **Status:** Uncommon to locally common. **Voice:** Short, warbled song; 'tik tik tik' flight call. [C11.60]

violacea

545

Large, long-tailed flycatchers, often lumped with black flycatchers into *Melaenornis* (p. 548). Forage from perches in fairly open habitats, usually onto the ground, less often taking flying insects. Sexes alike; juvs buff-spotted above and mottled below.

1 PALE (MOUSE-COLOURED) FLYCATCHER *Bradornis pallidus* 17 cm
A fairly large, uniform brownish flycatcher. In E Africa, is larger and browner than African Grey Flycatcher, with plain (not streaked) crown. In S Africa, best told from Marico Flycatcher by its buffy brown (not white) underparts. Range overlaps slightly with Chat Flycatcher, but is smaller and paler below. Juv. is paler, mottled with brown and grey. **Habitat:** Moist, broadleafed woodland. **Status:** Locally common. **Voice:** Song is melodious warbling interspersed with harsh chitters; alarm call is soft 'churr'. [C11.63, G5.10.6]

2 AFRICAN GREY FLYCATCHER *Bradornis microrhynchus* 15 cm
Endemic to NE Africa. Smaller than Pale Flycatcher, with more contrast between greyer upperparts and paler underparts. At close range, slight crown streaking is diagnostic. Range does not overlap with that of Marico Flycatcher. Ethiopian *pumilo* is larger, browner and darker; sometimes treated as a distinct species. **Habitat:** Savanna and woodland, usually in drier habitats than Pale Flycatcher. **Status:** Common; conspicuous, hunting from prominent perches. **Voice:** Song is jumbled mix of chitters and warbles; call is soft 'sweeep'.

3 MARICO FLYCATCHER *Bradornis mariquensis* 18 cm
Endemic to SW Africa. Told from Pale and Chat flycatchers by its white (not brownish) underparts contrasting with plain brown upperparts. Usually occurs in more arid habitats. **Habitat:** Semi-arid acacia savanna and sparse woodland. Juv. is more extensively streaked below than juv. Chat Flycatcher. **Status:** Common; conspicuous, often perching in the open. **Voice:** Song is soft 'tsii-cheruk-tukk'. [G5.10.5]

4 CHAT FLYCATCHER *Bradornis infuscatus* 20 cm
Endemic to SW Africa. A large, chat-like flycatcher with long wings and tail. Rather nondescript, with paler edges to wing feathers forming slight panel on folded secondaries. Best told from chats by its long, uniform brown tail. Larger than Marico or Pale flycatchers, with darker brown underparts that contrast less with upperparts. Often lifts its wings and spends more time on the ground than other flycatchers. **Habitat:** Semi-arid and arid shrublands. **Status:** Common. **Voice:** Song is rich, warbled 'cher-cher-cherrip', with squeaky, hissing notes. [G5.10.7]

5 WHITE-EYED SLATY FLYCATCHER *Dioptrornis fischeri* 15-17 cm
Endemic to E and C Africa. The combination of greyish upperparts, paler grey and white underparts and white eye-ring is diagnostic. Dark eye appears large and, together with pale eye-ring, separates it from pale-eyed Abyssinian Slaty Flycatcher; ranges do not overlap. Upperparts vary from bluish grey to slate-grey. Pale eye-ring varies in width and colour; Albertine Rift *toruensis* has much smaller, greyish eye-ring. **Habitat:** Highland forest edge, woodland and farmlands. **Status:** Common but thinly distributed; usually in pairs. **Voice:** Unobtrusive, soft 'tsweep' and chattering; harsher 'zit' alarm call. [C11.64]

6 ABYSSINIAN SLATY FLYCATCHER *Dioptrornis chocolatinus* 15-17 cm
Endemic to Abyssinian highlands. A drab, grey-brown, rather nondescript flycatcher with a creamy yellow eye; lacks white eye-ring of White-eyed Slaty Flycatcher. Pale eye and darker back separate it from Pale and African Grey flycatchers, both of which occur at lower elevations in more arid habitats. Larger, greyer and longer-tailed than African Dusky Flycatcher (p. 554). **Habitat:** High- and mid-altitude forest and woodland edge, farmlands and suburbia. **Status:** Common. **Voice:** Various 'seep' calls; harsher chittering alarm note.

7 ANGOLA SLATY FLYCATCHER *Dioptrornis brunneus* 15-17 cm
Endemic to Angola. The only plain brown flycatcher in its range with a white belly and lower breast. Brown throat is same colour as breast, not pale as in sleeker Pale Flycatcher; lores are paler grey-brown. Browner than other slaty flycatchers, with only very narrow, pale eye-ring. **Habitat:** Edges of montane forest, wooded gullies and adjacent woodland. **Status:** Uncommon. **Voice:** Unknown.

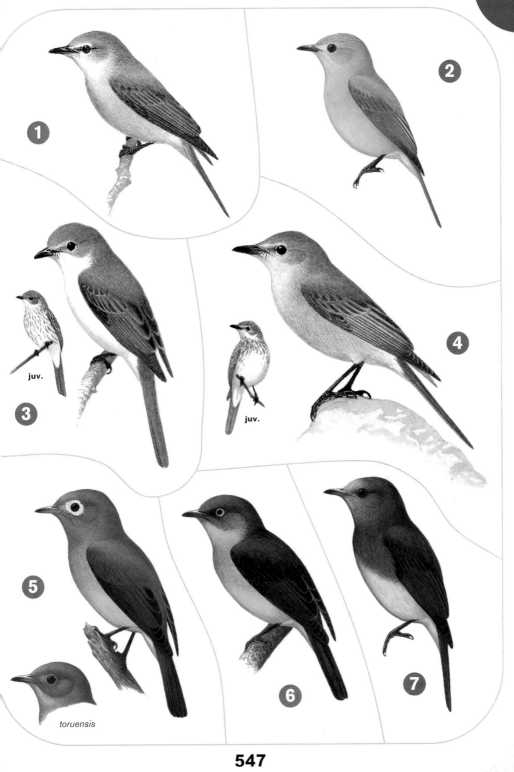

toruensis

547

Large, long-tailed flycatchers that could be confused with drongos (p. 380), but have a square (not forked) tail and dark or pale (not red) eyes. They lack the yellow gape and strongly rounded tail of black cuckoo-shrikes (p. 376), and are longer-tailed and have a more upright stance than black boubous (p. 584). Sexes alike.

1 SOUTHERN BLACK FLYCATCHER *Melaenornis pammelaina* 18-20 cm
An entirely black flycatcher. Differs from Northern Black Flycatcher in being glossy (not matt) black, with a squarer tail; ranges barely overlap. Translucent bases to primaries create paler window in flight. Juv. is dull black, scalloped with brown. **Habitat:** Woodland, savanna and forest edges. **Status:** Common; sallies from perches, taking food from ground. **Voice:** Song is wheezy 'tzzit-terra-loora-loo', faster than Northern Black Flycatcher's. [C11.66, G5.10.4]

2 NORTHERN BLACK FLYCATCHER *Melaenornis edolioides* 18-20 cm
The N counterpart of Southern Black Flycatcher; differs in lacking glossy plumage, and most races are greyer-black. Dark eye and habitat separate it from localised Yellow-eyed Black Flycatcher. Blacker and more slender than Nimba Flycatcher, and occurs in more open habitat. Juv. is very similar to juv. Southern Black Flycatcher. **Habitat:** Woodland and savanna. **Status:** Locally common. **Voice:** Slower and more sibilant than Southern Black Flycatcher's. [C11.68]

3 YELLOW-EYED BLACK FLYCATCHER *Melaenornis ardesiacus* 20 cm
Endemic to Albertine Rift. A deep blue-black flycatcher, with a slight sheen and a diagnostic yellow eye. At a distance, eye appears white or cream, preventing confusion with drongos and Northern Black Flycatcher. Juv. has grey eye and very faint white spotting on underparts. **Habitat:** Montane forests and adjacent secondary growth. **Status:** Fairly common. **Voice:** Various harsh, rasping 'cherr' and 'chip' call notes. [C11.65]

4 NIMBA FLYCATCHER *Melaenornis annamarulae* 19-20 cm
Localised endemic to Upper Guinea forests. Bulkier and greyer below than Northern Black Flycatcher; occurs in forest (not woodland) **Habitat:** Behaviour is very similar to that of Fraser's Forest Flycatcher (p. 550): sallies from perch in mid-canopy and frequently runs along branches, gleaning food. **Habitat:** Mid-stratum of lowland rainforest. **Status:** Vulnerable. Uncommon, in pairs or small groups. **Voice:** Mixed whistles of loud, ringing notes, recalling those of Fraser's Forest Flycatcher or drongos. [C11.67]

5 SILVERBIRD *Empidornis semipartitus* 18 cm
Localised endemic to EC Africa. Diagnostic silvery, blue-grey upperparts contrast with rich, ruddy underparts. Juv. is heavily marked, with dark-tipped chevrons on head, underparts and back; could be confused with non-breeding or juv. rock thrushes, but is smaller, longer tailed and lacks red outer-tail. **Habitat:** Semi-arid acacia savanna with taller trees. **Status:** Locally common; perches conspicuously on wires and tops of bushes and trees. **Voice:** Thrush- or robin-like, short, warbled song.

6 BÖHM'S FLYCATCHER *Muscicapa boehmi* 12 cm
Endemic to SC Africa. A small, compact flycatcher with diagnostic blackish heart-shaped spots on the throat, breast and flanks. Rich brown upperparts are streaked darker, contrasting sharply with white underparts. Juv. has dark chevrons on head, back, breast and flanks. **Habitat:** Miombo woodland, typically in lower strata. **Status:** Uncommon; usually in bird parties. **Voice:** Usually silent; alarm chattering and soft, musical song. [C11.84]

1 FISCAL FLYCATCHER *Sigelus silens*   18-20 cm
Endemic to S Africa. Often mistaken for Common Fiscal (p. 576), but has much more slender bill and shorter tail, and stands taller (not crouched). White in wings is confined to secondaries (not wing coverts). In flight, shows conspicuous white windows in outer-tail. Much larger and longer-tailed than *Ficedula* flycatchers (p. 556). Female is browner above and washed darker grey beneath. Juv. is spotted buff above and scalloped below. **Habitat:** Woodland and thickets, scrub, gardens and plantations. **Status:** Common resident, subject to local movements in winter. **Voice:** High-pitched, chittering song; 'tssisk' alarm call. [G5.10.8]

2 FRASER'S FOREST FLYCATCHER *Fraseria ocreata*   16 cm
A rather large flycatcher with dark slate-grey upperparts and white underparts with dark bars on the breast, throat and flanks. Lacks white supraloral spot of White-browed Forest Flycatcher, and is larger; occurs in canopy and lives in noisy pairs or groups (not solitarily). Frequently flirts its tail. Juv. is browner above, with buff spots; underparts are only very lightly marked on sides of breast. **Habitat:** Canopy of forest, gallery forest and forest edge, and old secondary growth, at highest or intermediate levels (never in closed-canopy forest undergrowth). **Status:** Common. **Voice:** Low, harsh calls, often interspersed with high-pitched whistles; more varied, melodious song. [C11.69]

3 AFRICAN SHRIKE-FLYCATCHER *Megabyas flammulatus*   16 cm
A rather large, dumpy forest flycatcher with a large head and reddish eyes. Sexually dimorphic: male has blue-black upperparts, with white rump and underparts (could be confused with puffbacks; p. 580); female has brown-rufous upperparts, greyish-brown head and diagnostic brown-striped underparts. A sluggish bird, keeping in forest canopy, with characteristic swinging movement of tail. **Habitat:** Forest canopy, and tall trees in degraded or cultivated areas. **Status:** Locally common. **Voice:** Male's song is repetitive, short, melodious 'che-we-wit'; bill-snaps; high-pitched 'tsip-tsip' contact call. [C12.1]

4 WHITE-BROWED FOREST FLYCATCHER *Fraseria cinerascens*   15 cm
Smaller than Fraser's Forest Flycatcher, with a diagnostic white supraloral spot; dark crescents on breast are less neatly demarcated; also is usually solitary (not in pairs or groups) and unobtrusive (not noisy), in dense undergrowth (not canopy); does not flirt its tail. In W Africa, white supraloral spot extends further above eye. Juv. is browner, heavily spotted buff above. **Habitat:** Forest understorey, along rivers and streams. **Status:** Locally common. **Voice:** Long series of insect-like notes, lasting up to almost a minute; high-pitched 'tseep' contact call. [C11.70]

5 DOHRN'S THRUSH-BABBLER *Horizorhinus dohrni*   14 cm
Endemic to Prìncipé. A brown-and-white understorey bird of uncertain affinities; probably related to *Kupeornis* babblers (p. 404). Brown upperparts, white throat, brown breast band and white lower breast and belly washed with yellow are diagnostic. Active and noisy; readily located and identified by song. **Habitat:** Mainly forest understorey, but occasionally forest canopy; also coffee and cocoa plantations. **Status:** Common. **Voice:** Powerful, joyful whistles. [C12.51]

6 BLACK-AND-WHITE (VANGA) FLYCATCHER *Bias musicus*   14-15 cm
Male is unmistakable, with its diagnostic black crest, black throat and bib, and white wing patches. Larger than batises (p. 564) or wattle-eyes (p. 570), with an obvious crest. Female has bright chestnut back and tail, and could be confused with paradise-flycatchers (p. 558), but is stockier, with pale (not chestnut) throat and yellow (not dark) eyes and legs. Juv. resembles female but is duller and streaked on head. Imm. male has blackish breast and rufous back. **Habitat:** Forest and riparian woodland, up to 1 500 m. **Status:** Usually uncommon and local. **Voice:** Song is loud, whistled 'whitu-whitu-whitu'; alarm note is sharp 'we-chip'. [C12.2, G5.10.]

Small, compact flycatchers, usually with a fairly short tail. Most have dull brown or grey plumage. Sexes alike; juvs have a mottled breast and are pale-spotted on the head, nape and back, often with paler edges to the flight feathers.

1 LITTLE GREY FLYCATCHER *Muscicapa epulata*   9 cm
A tiny forest flycatcher, with a white throat and belly. Slightly smaller and paler than Yellow-footed Flycatcher, with dark legs and indistinct broad breast streaks. Much smaller than any other grey flycatcher; lacks white supraloral line of Dusky-blue Flycatcher. Needs open areas in forest for hunting. **Habitat:** Open-canopy forest, forest edge, secondary growth and plantations with dead trees. **Status:** Uncommon to locally common. **Voice:** Series of soft, high-pitched notes. [C11.77]

2 YELLOW-FOOTED FLYCATCHER *Muscicapa sethsmithi*   10 cm
A small forest flycatcher, with diagnostic yellow feet. Slightly larger than Little Grey Flycatcher, with darker blue-grey plumage, plain breast and yellow lower mandible (only base of mandible is yellow in Little Grey Flycatcher). White throat and belly contrast with plain grey breast; lacks white supraloral line of Dusky-blue Flycatcher. Juv. is browner above, with buffy spots. **Habitat:** Closed-canopy forest, with open understorey; also edges of forest tracks and along forest streams. Hunts from exposed branches or lianas, inside forest. **Status:** Locally common. **Voice:** High-pitched, insect-like calls. [C11.78]

3 DUSKY-BLUE FLYCATCHER *Muscicapa comitata*   11 cm
A dark, slate-grey flycatcher with a narrow white supraloral line and a white throat. Much smaller than White-browed Forest Flycatcher (p. 550), with darker underparts lacking any mottling. W African *aximensis* is darker, with buffy throat and belly. **Habitat:** Edges of streams, forest clearings and plantations; often hunts from dead branches. **Status:** Locally common. **Voice:** Series of high-pitched notes, similar to Ashy Flycatcher's. [C11.80]

4 TESSMANN'S FLYCATCHER *Muscicapa tessmanni*   12 cm
A rather sluggish, forest-edge flycatcher. Larger than Dusky-blue Flycatcher, with a larger, heavier bill and no white supraloral line. Underparts are paler grey, with creamy white throat and belly. Habitat and stout bill separate it from Cassin's Flycatcher. Appreciably larger than Yellow-footed and Little Grey flycatchers. **Habitat:** Edges of forest clearings and secondary growth. **Status:** Uncommon. **Voice:** Series of alternating high and low notes. [C11.81]

5 CASSIN'S (GREY) FLYCATCHER *Muscicapa cassini*   13 cm
A forest flycatcher always associated with water. Uniform grey, with darker wings and tail, and paler throat and belly. At close range, has slightly streaked crown and breast. Habitat and longer, more slender bill separate it from Tessmann's Flycatcher. Hunts low down over water, sallying from dead branches and trees or rocks. **Habitat:** Forest rivers and streams, and associated open waters. **Status:** Common; often confiding. **Voice:** Song is varied mix of whistles, trills and chips; buzzy contact call. [C11.76]

6 ASHY (BLUE-GREY) FLYCATCHER *Muscicapa caerulescens*   14-15 cm
Bluer above and greyer below than Grey Tit-flycatcher (p. 556), and lacks white outer-tail feathers. Larger than other *Muscicapa* flycatchers, often in more open habitats (avoids dense forest in much of its range). Behaviour also differs: aerial hawks or sallies to the ground, but does not glean from foliage; does not flirt tail. Juv. is speckled with dark brown and buff. **Habitat:** Riverine forests and moist, open broadleafed woodland. **Status:** Common. **Voice:** Song is soft 'sszzit-sszzit-sreee-sreee', descending in scale. [C11.79, G5.10.1]

7 SWAMP FLYCATCHER *Muscicapa aquatica*   13-14 cm
An aquatic flycatcher, usually found in papyrus swamps. Easily identified by its brown upperparts, white underparts and broad brown breast band. Banded and Sand martins (p. 350) when perched near water or in swamps, might cause momentary confusion. Breast band more diffuse in W and WC African *aquatica* **Habitat:** Near water, especially papyrus swamps and trees overhanging rivers. **Status:** Locally common. **Voice:** Short, sharp 'zwit' notes; soft, high-pitched, 2-note song. [C11.74]

aquatica

553

1 SPOTTED FLYCATCHER *Muscicapa striata*   13-14 cm
A grey-brown flycatcher with a dark-streaked crown, indistinctly streaked breast and long wings extending almost halfway down the tail. Hindcrown is slightly peaked. Larger than Gambaga Flycatcher, with all-dark bill and boldly (not finely) streaked crown. Browner and longer winged than African Grey Flycatcher (p. 546), with streaked (not mottled) breast. Often flicks its wings on landing. **Habitat:** Virtually all wooded habitats, from forest edges to semi-arid savanna. **Status:** Common Palearctic migrant Sep-May. **Voice:** Soft 'tzee' and 'zeck, chick-chick'. [C4.40, G5.9.10]

2 GAMBAGA FLYCATCHER *Muscicapa gambagae*   12-13 cm
Slightly smaller than Spotted Flycatcher, with a pale base to the lower mandible and less defined streaking on breast; crown is only faintly (not boldly) streaked. Also is shorter winged, appearing dumpier; stance is more horizontal and head more rounded. Rarely flicks wings. **Habitat:** Arid acacia woodland and dry riverbeds. **Status:** Uncommon and thinly distributed; usually singly or in pairs. **Voice:** Harsh, short 'zzik' or 'zzzitt' contact notes. [C11.72]

3 AFRICAN DUSKY FLYCATCHER *Muscicapa adusta*   12 cm
A small, compact flycatcher; appears short-winged and dumpy compared with Spotted Flycatcher. Usually the only small, brownish flycatcher in its habitat; typically in more forested habitats than Spotted or Gambaga flycatchers. Slightly smaller and more mottled below than Olivaceous Flycatcher. Colour varies geographically: mostly grey-brown, but some are browner, with buffy supraloral spot in N. Breast and flanks have ill-defined streaking. **Habitat:** Forest edges and glades, riverine forest and well-wooded gardens. **Status:** Common. **Voice:** Soft, high-pitched 'tzzeet' and 'tsirit'. [C11.73, G5.9.11]

4 OLIVACEOUS FLYCATCHER *Muscicapa olivascens*   13 cm
A dull brown forest flycatcher, with no distinctive marks; the only drab brown flycatcher in lowland rainforest throughout its range. At close range, entire lower mandible is yellowish. Lacks any streaks, unlike Spotted Flycatcher. Face and throat are paler, greyish and whitish; centre of belly and undertail coverts are white. **Habitat:** Lowland forest, from understorey to lower canopy. **Status:** Uncommon to locally common. **Voice:** Sings from canopy, mainly in morning; song is rather shrill 'chi chi chree', consisting of 6-10 notes. [C11.75]

5 CHAPIN'S FLYCATCHER *Muscicapa lendu*   13 cm
Localised endemic to E Africa. Very similar to Olivaceous Flycatcher, but occurs at higher elevations; ranges do not overlap. Larger and darker than African Dusky Flycatcher, with plain (not mottled) breast. At close range, has dark loral stripe. Itombwe Mts, DRC, race *itombwensis* has more pointed wings; sometimes regarded as a separate species (Itombwe Flycatcher). **Habitat:** Montane forest, above 1 500 m. **Status:** Vulnerable. Uncommon and thinly distributed; usually in pairs high in canopy or mid-stratum. **Voice:** Hardly discernible, soft 'sweep' or 'tsseeep'.

6 SOOTY FLYCATCHER *Muscicapa infuscata*   12 cm
Endemic to C Africa; forms a superspecies with Ussher's Flycatcher. A very dark brown, small, short-tailed flycatcher. Shows more contrast between dark-streaked rufous underparts and dark brown upperparts than does Ussher's Flycatcher. Long-winged; when hawking insects from dead branches in forest canopy, resembles a small, brown swallow with broad, long wings. Often wags tail when returning to perch. **Habitat:** Forest canopy, on highest dead branches; also secondary growth and clearings with tall trees. **Status:** Common. **Voice:** Usually silent; shrill whistle and trills. [C11.82]

7 USSHER'S FLYCATCHER *Muscicapa ussheri*   12 cm
Endemic to Upper Guinea forests, where it replaces Sooty Flycatcher. Darker beneath than Sooty Flycatcher, with little contrast between upper- and underparts; at close range, pale-barred vent and paler chin are diagnostic. Has same habit of hunting insects from highest posts above forest and same shape of small, dark swallow. **Habitat:** Lowland and gallery forest canopy and edge. Usually perches on highest posts and dead branches. **Status:** Locally common, in pairs or family parties. **Voice:** Usually silent; buzzy 'tsrip'. [C11.83]

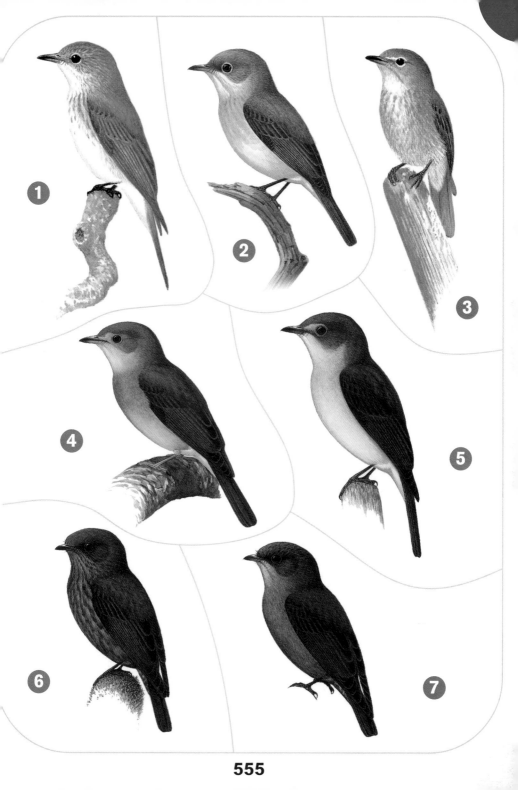

TIT-FLYCATCHERS
Peculiar slender, warbler-like flycatchers that lack the broad bill of flycatchers and typically glean rather than hawk for insects. Stance horizontal, frequently fan and flirt their tails, recalling crested flycatchers. Sexes alike; juvs spotted with brown and buff above and below.

1 GREY TIT-FLYCATCHER (LEAD-COLOURED/FAN-TAILED FLYCATCHER)
Myioparus plumbeus   14 cm
The most widespread tit-flycatcher, with diagnostic white outer-tail and tail tips. Whitish supraloral stripe and narrow eye-ring also separate it from Grey-throated Tit-flycatcher. Warbler-like behaviour, tail fanning and flirting, and white outer-tail distinguish it from Ashy Flycatcher (p. 552). **Habitat:** Dense woodland and savanna thickets, riparian woodland and forest edge. **Status:** Locally common. **Voice:** Soft, tremulous, whistled 'treee-trooo'. [C11.85, G5.10.3]

2 GREY-THROATED TIT-FLYCATCHER *Myioparus griseigularis*   14 cm
The forest tit-flycatcher; told from Grey Tit-flycatcher by its all-dark tail and plain grey face. Superficially resembles Cassin's Flycatcher (p. 552), but has less contrasting throat and different behaviour: moves actively in forest understorey, twisting tail from side to side, showing white undertail coverts. **Habitat:** Dense understorey of forest, often near water. **Status:** Locally common; most often located by song. **Voice:** Mournful series of 2-4 notes, descending in scale but with second note higher in longer calls. [C11.86]

FICEDULA FLYCATCHERS
Migrant Palearctic flycatchers with prominent white wing bars. More compact than hyliotas (p. 544), with longer wings, a rounder head and typical flycatcher hawking behaviour (not warbler-like gleaning). Three common species in Africa require careful observation for identification; range overlap is limited, but vagrants may occur outside the normal range.

3 PIED FLYCATCHER *Ficedula hypoleuca*   13 cm
The darkest *Ficedula*. Breeding male has incomplete white collar, very small white frons spot and limited white primary bases. Amount of white in outer-tail varies racially, but never extends to tail tip (unlike in Semi-collared Flycatcher). Other plumages also show less white in wing than other *Ficedula*, with white primary flash reduced or absent and no pale tips to median coverts. Rump is dark, showing little contrast with back. **Habitat:** Woodland, forest edge and gallery forest. **Status:** Locally common Palearctic migrant Sep-Apr. **Voice:** Contact call is sharp 'vit' or clicking 'tck', shorter and sharper than that of other *Ficedula*. [C4.37] **Similar species: Red-breasted Flycatcher** *F. parva* lacks white in wing and has broad white bases to outer-tail; rare Palearctic vagrant to N.

4 SEMI-COLLARED FLYCATCHER *Ficedula semitorquata*   13 cm
Intermediate in colour between Pied and Collared flycatchers, with diagnostic white outer-tail and white tips to median coverts forming second wing bar. Breeding male has narrow, partial collar, and intermediate-sized forecrown spot and primary base patch. Rump is paler than back, but not whitish as in Collared Flycatcher. Other plumages best identified by paler outer-tail and white tips to median coverts. **Habitat:** Woodland and gallery forest. **Status:** Uncommon to locally common Palearctic migrant Sep-Apr. **Voice:** Calls hard 'tek' or clear 'sjiep', harsher and shorter than Collared Flycatcher's. [C11.71]

5 COLLARED FLYCATCHER *Ficedula albicollis*   12-13 cm
The palest *Ficedula*. Breeding male has prominent, complete white collar, large white forecrown and extensive white primary bases. Rump is pale, but tail is all-dark. Other plumages typically show paler rump; have largish white patch at base of primaries, but lack second white wing bar formed by white tips to median coverts as in the Pied Flycatcher (may be pale tipped, but not white). **Habitat:** Woodland. **Status:** Locally common. **Voice:** Drawn-out 'seep' or soft 'whit-whit-whit'. [C4.38, G5.10.2]

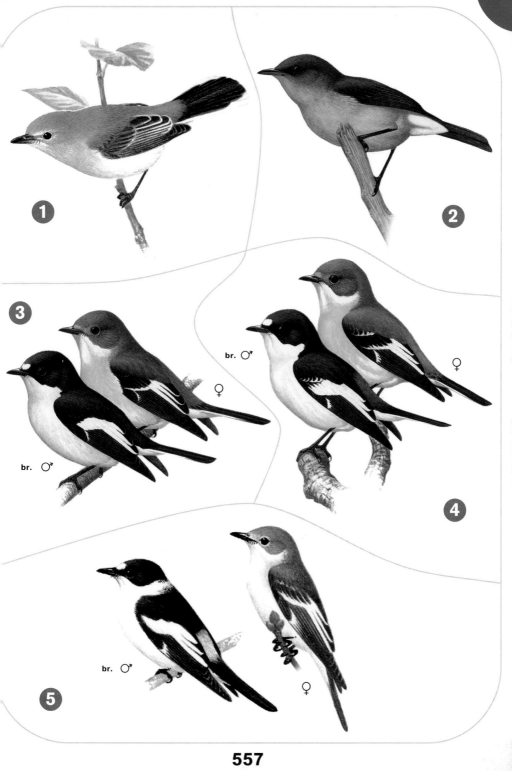

1

2

3
br. ♂
♀

4
br. ♂
♀

5
br. ♂
♀

Spectacular crested flycatchers or monarchs that are only very distantly related to true flycatchers. All have similar 'zweet-errr' contact call; songs more varied. Sexes differ in most species; breeding males typically have elongated central tail streamers.

1 AFRICAN PARADISE-FLYCATCHER
Terpsiphone viridis   17-20 cm (plus 18 cm tail in male)
The most widespread paradise-flycatcher; occurs in more open habitats than other species in areas of overlap. Plumage varies from rufous to white morphs, and may have white wing bar, but always has greyish underparts and strong crest. Some individuals are inseparable from Rufous-vented Paradise-Flycatcher. Breeding male has elongate tail streamers, dark head and breast, and bright blue bill and eye-ring. Female has shorter tail and duller blue soft parts. Juv. duller. **Habitat:** Forest and dense woodland; also gardens. **Status:** Common resident and intra-African migrant. **Voice:** Harsh 'zweet-zweet-zwayt' call; song is loud, whistled 'twee-tiddly-te-te'. [C12.28, G5.11.10]

2 BATES'S PARADISE-FLYCATCHER
Terpsiphone batesi   18 cm (plus 5-10 cm tail in male)
Endemic to C Africa. Both sexes resemble female Rufous-vented Paradise-Flycatcher, but lack crests, and head is blue-grey (not blackish); also, back is more rufous-orange. Male's central tail feathers generally are not elongate, except in some areas of Cameroon and Angola. Tail is rufous; there is no white in wing. **Habitat:** Forest understorey, at intermediate levels to under canopy. **Status:** Common. **Voice:** Song a ringing 'tswee tswee tsweee tswee' or 'tsweee tooo tooo'; contact calls similar to other paradise-flycatchers'. [C12.29]

3 RED-BELLIED (BLACK-HEADED) PARADISE-FLYCATCHER
Terpsiphone rufiventer   18-20 cm (plus 15 cm tail in male of some races)
A variable paradise-flycatcher, but it always has a black head and rufous to orange-rufous underparts. Back colour varies from rufous brown (most races) to slate grey (WC African *neumanni*); W African races have white wing bar and elongate tail streamers; other races lack wing bar and elongate central tail. Tail may be rufous or slate grey. **Habitat:** Primary and secondary forest, at intermediate levels; also gallery forest. **Status:** Common. **Voice:** Song is a ringing 'choo choo, choo choo, t'choo-oo, t'choo-oo', sometimes preceded by a nasal 'whoo whoo'; grating alarm calls like African Paradise-Flycatchers'. [C12.32]

4 RUFOUS-VENTED PARADISE-FLYCATCHER
Terpsiphone rufocinerea   18 cm (plus 11 cm tail in male)
Endemic to C Africa. Differs from African Paradise-Flycatcher by rounder head, short crest, shorter tail (in male) and chestnut undertail coverts and vent. Confusion is possible with female African Paradise-Flycatcher, but habitat and males differ. Male never shows white on wing, and has blue-black head, merging into slate grey from lower breast to belly, and rufous upperparts and tail. Female is paler, with short tail. **Habitat:** Mangroves, coastal forests and riverine forest; also clumps of bushes in open marshes and gardens. **Status:** Locally common. **Voice:** Calls similar to other paradise-flycatchers'. [C12.30]

5 BEDFORD'S PARADISE-FLYCATCHER   *Terpsiphone bedfordi*   20 cm
Endemic to lowland forest of Albertine Rift. An all-grey paradise-flycatcher; larger than Blue-headed or Dusky crested flycatchers (p. 560), with longer tail, no obvious crest and different foraging behaviour (does not fan and flirt tail or droop wings). Some forms of Red-bellied Paradise-Flycatcher are all-dark grey, but usually show some rufous on underparts. **Habitat:** Lowland rainforest and secondary forest and clearings. **Status:** Locally common. **Voice:** Typical paradise-flycatcher whistled song; harsher, more grating alarm notes.

6 ANNOBON PARADISE-FLYCATCHER   *Terpsiphone smithii*   18-20 cm
Endemic to Pagalu Island (Annobon), where it is the only flycatcher. Sometimes lumped with Red-bellied Paradise-Flycatcher. A black-headed flycatcher, with rufous-brown back and rufous body, dark grey wings and grey tail. **Habitat:** Forest, forest edge and secondary growth. **Status:** Vulnerable. Common in its small range. **Voice:** Similar to other paradise-flycatchers'.

neumanni

rufiventer

559

1 SÃO TOMÉ PARADISE-FLYCATCHER
Terpsiphone atrochalybeia   18 cm (plus 11 cm tail in male)
Endemic to São Tomé, where it is the only flycatcher. Male is all glossy blue-black, with long central tail streamers. Female is short tailed, with bluish-grey head, grey underparts, and chestnut upperparts and tail. **Habitat:** Primary forest up to 1 600 m, cocoa and coffee plantations, and secondary growth. **Status:** Common and easy to observe. **Voice:** Usual paradise-flycatcher calls, but this species is not known to sing. [C12.31]

CRESTED **FLYCATCHERS**
Smaller, more conservatively coloured monarchs than paradise-flycatchers. They forage very actively, continuously fanning and flirting their long tails. Sexes differ.

2 BLUE-MANTLED CRESTED FLYCATCHER *Trochocercus cyanomelas* 13-14 cm
The only black-and-white crested flycatcher with a prominent white wing bar; tail is all-dark. Male has glossy black head, crest and throat, contrasting sharply with white lower breast and belly. Female is paler grey, with streaking on throat, and less white in wing. Juv. resembles female, but has shorter crest and buffy wing bar. **Habitat:** Forest, in dense under- and mid-storey. **Status:** Common. **Voice:** Alarm call is harsh 'zweet-zwa', similar to African Paradise- Flycatcher's; song is fluty whistle. [C12.26, G5.11.8]

3 BLUE-HEADED CRESTED FLYCATCHER *Trochocercus nitens*   13-14 cm
A fairly small, dark crested flycatcher. Male has glossy bluish head, crest and throat, sharply demarcated from grey lower breast and belly. Lacks white wing bar of male Blue-mantled Crested Flycatcher, with darker back and grey (not white) belly. Female lacks dark throat and upper breast, and is slate-grey above, with greenish gloss to crest. Continuously fans and flirts tail, which is dark in both sexes. **Habitat:** Lowland primary forest, where it skulks in undergrowth and lower mid-canopy. **Status:** Uncommon and rarely seen. **Voice:** Most often detected by low-pitched, rolling 'dou-dododododo' call. [C12.27]

ELMINIAS
Appear very similar to crested flycatchers, but more closely related to warblers. Sexes similar, although females generally duller.

4 DUSKY ELMINIA (CRESTED FLYCATCHER) *Elminia nigromitrata*   11 cm
A small, all-dark slate-grey crested flycatcher with a black cap and all-dark tail. Dark (not white) belly separates it from White-bellied Crested Flycatcher, which occurs at higher elevations. Female duller; juv. slightly browner on the wings. **Habitat:** Forest understorey, often near streams and in marsh forest. Forages low in understorey; not secretive. **Status:** Locally common; often in pairs. **Voice:** Usually silent apart from raspy contact calls, but can produce varied song, including mimicry of other species. [C12.25]

5 WHITE-TAILED ELMINIA (CRESTED FLYCATCHER)
Elminia albonotata   13-14 cm
The only crested flycatcher with white tail tips. Slightly larger than Dusky or White-bellied crested flycatchers with larger white belly than White-bellied Crested Flycatcher. Dark throat and flanks merge gradually into paler belly; lacks sharp contrast of male Blue-headed or Blue-mantled crested flycatchers; dark throat and upper breast separate this species from female *Trochocercus* flycatchers. Female and juv. duller. **Habitat:** Montane forest. **Status:** Locally common. **Voice:** Song is fast 'tsee-tsee-teuu-choo' and other jumbled notes, including mimicked calls of other birds. [C12.24, G5.11.9]

6 WHITE-BELLIED ELMINIA (CRESTED FLYCATCHER)
Elminia albiventris   11 cm
The montane-forest counterpart of Dusky Crested Flycatcher, with white (not dark) belly. Darker cap extends onto face and throat, giving more of a black-headed appearance than Dusky Crested Flycatcher. Female duller; juv. slightly browner on wings. **Habitat:** Understorey of montane forest, 900-2 500 m. **Status:** Locally common. **Voice:** Raspy contact calls; slow, fluty, warbling song. [C12.23]

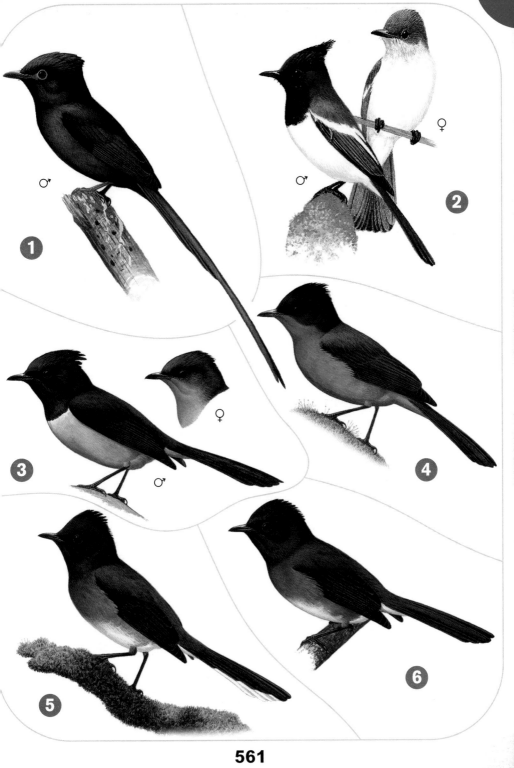

BLUE ELMINIAS (BLUE FLYCATCHERS)
Distinctive powder-blue Elminias. Very active; constantly fan, flirt and cock their long, graduated tails. Sexes similar; females slightly duller.

1 AFRICAN BLUE FLYCATCHER *Elminia longicauda*   14 cm
Pale blue upperparts and breast combined with its longer tail separate it from all other crested flycatchers, except White-tailed Blue Flycatcher, which replaces it in S and E; differs in having all-blue (not white-edged) tail and lack of contrast between blue breast and mantle. Female duller blue, with shorter tail. Juv. greyish, with shorter tail and crest, and pale tips to wing coverts. **Habitat:** Forest edge, clearings and secondary growth; also gardens. Forages in mid- to low canopy with mixed bird parties. **Status:** Common but localised in some areas. **Voice:** High-pitched 'ziink'; nasal 'zseez'; song is high-pitched jumble of wheezy notes. [C12.21]

2 WHITE-TAILED BLUE FLYCATCHER *Elminia albicauda*   14 cm
Forms a superspecies with African Blue Flycatcher, but has white (not uniform blue) outer-tail and paler breast that contrasts with darker mantle; ranges do not overlap. Juv. darker and greyer, with smaller crest. **Habitat:** Riverine forest, well-developed miombo woodland and adjacent secondary growth. **Status:** Locally common; usually in pairs; often joins bird parties. **Voice:** Jumbled, high-pitched warbling song; usual contact notes are high-pitched 'chit chit' and 'treeet'. [C12.22]

ERYTHROCERCUS FLYCATCHERS
An endemic genus of tiny, warbler-like flycatchers. Very active, occurring in small groups that move rapidly through the vegetation gleaning for insects. Sexes alike. Recent evidence suggests they are related to warblers.

3 CHESTNUT-CAPPED FLYCATCHER *Erythrocercus mccallii*   10 cm
A small, warbler-like flycatcher with a diagnostic chestnut tail and cap (streaked white), grey back and buffy throat and breast. Juv. is duller; lacks chestnut forecrown. **Habitat:** Forest canopy and at lower levels along forest edge and in secondary growth. Searches actively for insects in foliage, fanning and flicking tail sideways. **Status:** Common, usually occurs in family groups. **Voice:** Noisy; parties make constant chittering and squeaking calls. [C12.20]

4 LITTLE YELLOW FLYCATCHER *Erythrocercus holochlorus*   10 cm
Endemic to coastal E Africa. A tiny, olive and yellow, warbler-like flycatcher. Constantly fans its tail, with wings drooping. Much smaller than Dark-capped and Mountain yellow warblers (p. 484), and occurs in different habitat. Smaller and daintier than Yellow White-eye (p. 640), with longer tail and no white eye-ring. May overlap slightly with Livingstone's Flycatcher in S Tanzania; differs in having olive (not rufous) tail and yellow (not olive) face. **Habitat:** Thick primary and secondary coastal forests and even in gardens in some areas. **Status:** Fairly common; singly or in small groups. **Voice:** Thin, reedy 'wee seesu' contact call.

5 LIVINGSTONE'S FLYCATCHER *Erythrocercus livingstonei*   11 cm
Endemic to SE Africa. A small, olive and yellow flycatcher with a diagnostic long, rufous tail with an indistinct black subterminal band. Constantly in motion, flicking and fanning tail sideways. S races have blue-grey cap; N *thomsoni* has olive cap. Juv. lacks tail bar. **Habitat:** Riverine and coastal forests. **Status:** Locally common; usually in small groups. **Voice:** Sharp 'chip-chip'; clear, warbled song. [G5.11.7]

6 FAIRY FLYCATCHER *Stenostira scita*   11 cm
Endemic to S Africa. A very small, active, flycatcher-like warbler of uncertain affinities. Predominantly grey, with black mask, and white wing bar and outer-tail. Adults have peachy wash on lower breast and belly. Juv. browner above and lacks peach-coloured flanks. **Habitat:** Karoo scrub and montane heath in summer, dispersing down to acacia savanna in winter. **Status:** Common resident and altitudinal migrant. **Voice:** Wispy, high-pitched 'tisee-tchee-tchee'; descending 'cher cher cher'. [G5.11.6]

Small, active shrike-like flycatchers related to wattle-eyes (p. 570); endemic to Africa. Many species are very similar; taxonomy is poorly resolved. Sexes differ; in many cases females are more distinctive than males. Frequently snap bills and wings.

1 CAPE BATIS *Batis capensis*   13 cm
Endemic to S Africa. A richly coloured batis with rufous wing bars and chestnut flanks in both sexes. Male has black breast band and golden eyes; female has chestnut breast band, discrete chin spot and reddish eyes. No other male batis in range has rufous wing bars. Female is larger and more strongly marked below than female Woodwards' Batis, and generally lacks white supercilium. **Habitat:** Forests, riparian thickets and even well-wooded gardens. **Status:** Common. **Voice:** Soft, pish-like 'shwee ksh ksh ksh ksha'; whistled 'foo-foo-foo'. [G5.10.10]

2 MALAWI BATIS *Batis dimorpha*   13 cm
Endemic to Malawi and N Mozambique. Often lumped with Cape Batis, but male has white (not rufous) wing bar, lacks chestnut flanks, and has broader black breast band. Female resembles female Cape Batis; ranges do not overlap. **Habitat:** Montane forest and secondary growth. **Status:** Fairly common. **Voice:** Similar to Cape Batis's.

3 REICHENOW'S BATIS *Batis reichenowi*   13 cm
Endemic to SE Tanzania. The only forest batis in its range. Sometimes lumped with Malawi and Cape Batises, but may have affinities to Forest Batis. Very short-tailed. Male lacks any rufous plumage, with white wing bar and white underparts, apart from narrow black breast band (narrower than Malawi or Forest batises'). Female appears intermediate between Malawi and Forest batises, with chestnut breast band, faint buff chin spot and rufous-grey flanks. Much larger than Pale Batis (p. 568), and occupies different habitat; male has broader breast band, female has rufous (not white) wing bar. **Habitat:** Forest and secondary growth. **Status:** Little known. **Voice:** Typical batis 'chwerra-werra' call; soft, 2-note whistle.

4 MARGARET'S BATIS *Batis margaritae*   12 cm
Localised endemic to SC Africa. Range overlaps with Chinspot Batis (p. 568); female has black (not chestnut) breast band, white throat lacking chestnut spot, red (not gold) eye and chestnut (not white) wing bar. Male is similar to Chinspot Batis, but is bulkier, with broader black breast band which does not narrow in centre; song also differs. **Habitat:** Lower strata of dry, evergreen forest and adjacent woodland. **Status:** Locally common in NW Zambia; status in Angola unclear. **Voice:** Series of 5-10 short whistles, often with first note slightly higher pitched. [C12.3]

5 FOREST BATIS *Batis mixta*   11 cm
Endemic to E Africa. Smaller and shorter-tailed than Malawi Batis, with a broader white supercilium and red (not gold) eye; ranges do not overlap. Male differs from Chinspot and Pale batises (p. 568) by forest habitat, broader breast band and red (not yellow) eye. Female has rufous (not white) wing bar. Told from Black-headed Batis (p. 568) by grey (not blackish) crown and back. **Habitat:** Forest, up to 2 300 m. **Status:** Locally common; often in pairs in bird parties. **Voice:** Single low whistle.

6 PRIRIT BATIS *Batis pririt*   12 cm
Endemic to SW Africa. Male is black, grey and white; differs from male Chinspot Batis (p. 568) in call and dark mottling on flanks; ranges overlap only marginally. Female and juv. have pale rufous wash over throat and breast, unlike any other batis in its range. **Habitat:** Acacia thickets, arid broadleafed woodland and dry riverine bush. **Status:** Common. **Voice:** Series of numerous, slow 'teuu, teuu, teuu, teuu' notes, descending in scale, often with sharp clicking calls. [G5.11.3]

7 WOODWARDS' BATIS *Batis fratrum*   11 cm
Endemic to SE coastal forests. Both sexes have diffuse, buff-washed breast. Lack of clear breast bands separates it from other batises in its range (Chinspot; p. 568, Pale; p. 568 and Cape batises). Male has white wing bar, resembling female Pririt Batis, but ranges do not overlap. Female has buffy wing bar. **Habitat:** Coastal forests and scrub. **Status:** Locally common. **Voice:** Clear, penetrating whistle, 'tch-tch-pheeeoooo'. [G5.11.4]

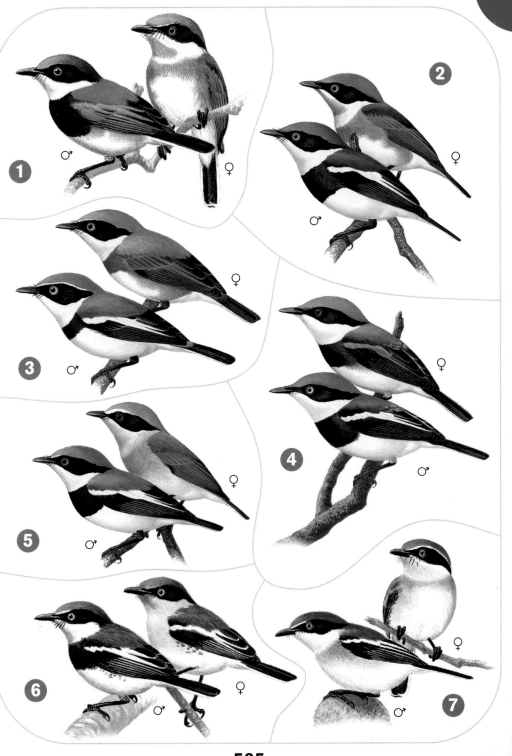

1 SENEGAL BATIS *Batis senegalensis*   10 cm
Endemic to W Africa, where it is the only savanna batis. Female is readily identified by tawny supercilium, nape collar and breast band, which extends down sides of breast. Overlaps narrowly in E with Grey- and Black-headed batises (p. 568); males are very similar and best told by song. May meet West African Batis at forest ecotone; females easily separated; males more similar, but this species is larger, with broader breast band and complete supercilium (not broken over eye). Juv. resembles female but is browner. **Habitat:** Semi-arid and well-wooded savannas. **Status:** Common; usually in pairs. **Voice:** Song a weak buzzy note, sometimes preceded by 1-2 soft whistles; also loud 'tlip tlip tlip' call. [C12.6]

2 WEST AFRICAN BATIS *Batis occulta*   9 cm
The most widespread forest batis of W and WC Africa. Both sexes have a narrow white supercilium, which is often broken over the eye, but extends from behind the eye to the nape (absent or broken in Gabon and Fernando Po batises). Female's neat, clean-cut chestnut breast band distinguishes it from female Gabon Batis (which has grey band) and Fernando Po Batis (band diffuses onto lower breast). Juv. has tawny-washed throat and wing bar. **Habitat:** Forest canopy, forest edge and secondary growth with tall trees. **Status:** Locally common. **Voice:** Song usually a buzzy note followed by 1-2 whistles, often repeated; also a long series of evenly-pitched whistles. [C12.11]

3 FERNANDO PO (BIOKO, LAWSON'S) BATIS *Batis poensis*   10 cm
Endemic to Bioko, Gulf of Guinea, where it is the only batis on the island. Sometimes lumped with West African Batis, but male has darker head with incomplete supercilium; female's breast band is lighter chestnut and diffuses gradually onto lower breast and flanks. **Habitat:** Forest canopy and tall trees in cocoa plantations. **Status:** Uncommon. **Voice:** Unknown; flight is noisy.

4 ANGOLA BATIS *Batis minulla*   9 cm
Endemic to WC Africa. Range overlaps with Black-headed Batis (p. 568), but is smaller, with paler grey crown (contrasting with darker face mask) and incomplete supercilium (usually visible only as loral spot). Female has chestnut breast band, paler than female Black-headed Batis's. Smaller than Chinspot Batis (p. 568); female lacks chin spot; male lacks obvious supercilium, and song differs. **Habitat:** Patches of woodland and gallery forest in savanna. **Status:** Locally common. **Voice:** Male song a series of soft whistles; also a dry buzzing call. [C12.9]

5 GABON (VERREAUX'S) BATIS *Batis minima*   8 cm
Endemic to Gabon and S Cameroon. A tiny batis of forest canopy. Grey breast band of female is diagnostic. Male is smaller than male West African Batis, with broader breast band. Has fairly prominent white loral spot, but narrow, discontinuous supercilium is rarely visible as bird stays in canopy. **Habitat:** Forest canopy, tall trees in secondary growth and cultivated areas. **Status:** Uncommon. **Voice:** Similar to West African Batis's, but lacks buzzy call before whistled notes. [C12.10]

6 ITURI BATIS *Batis ituriensis*   9 cm
Endemic to Albertine Rift, where it is the only batis in lowland forest. A small batis, lacking rufous plumage. Female has narrow white supercilium behind eye, extending onto nape. Smaller than Rwenzori Batis, with narrower black breast band. **Habitat:** Lowland forest canopy below 1 300 m. **Status:** Uncommon and easily overlooked. **Voice:** Undescribed, but likely to be typical whistled notes and churrings.

7 RWENZORI BATIS *Batis diops*   12 cm
Endemic to Albertine Rift, where it replaces Ituri Batis in montane forest. Larger than Ituri Batis, with broader black breast band. **Habitat:** Montane forest above 1 400 m in mid-stratum and, less regularly, canopy. **Status:** Locally common. **Voice:** Soft, mellow, whistled 'heeeoo'; 2-note 'tuuu tuuu'; also bill- and wing-snapping and typical batis-like churring. [C12.4]

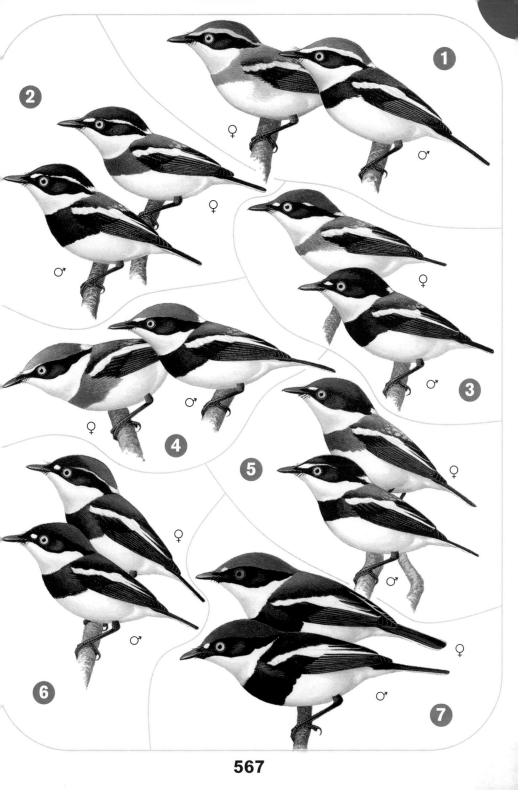

1 CHINSPOT BATIS *Batis molitor* 12-13 cm
A widespread woodland batis. Female has a diagnostic chestnut throat spot and neat breast band; wing bar is white. Larger than female Pale Batis, with darker and better-defined under-part markings. Male is very similar to male Pririt Batis (p. 564), but has white (not dark mottled) flanks; is larger than male Pale Batis, with broader breast band and distinctive song; ranges overlap only marginally. Juv. resembles female, but head and breast are mottled brown. **Habitat:** Broadleafed woodland and acacia savanna. **Status:** Common. **Voice:** Clear, descending 2-4 whistled notes 'teuu-teuu-teuu' ('three blind mice'); harsh 'chrr-chrr' notes. [C12.5, G5.11.1]

2 PALE (MOZAMBIQUE, EAST COAST) BATIS *Batis soror* 10 cm
Endemic to SE Africa. Resembles a small Chinspot Batis but male has narrower black breast band and dappled, grey-and-white (not uniform grey) back; female's breast band is narrower and paler, tawny (not chestnut); chin patch is ill defined. In N, overlaps with darker Black-headed Batis. Smaller than Reichenow's Batis (p. 564), with narrower breast band; female has white (not rufous) wing bar and flanks. **Habitat:** Miombo woodland and lowland forests. **Status:** Common. **Voice:** Soft, frequently repeated 'tcheeo, tcheeo, tcheeo'. [G5.11.2]

3 GREY-HEADED BATIS *Batis orientalis* 10-11 cm
A NE African savanna batis with a well-defined white supercilium. Closely resembles Black-headed Batis, but typically has paler grey crown that contrasts with blackish face mask. However, identification is complicated in coastal E Africa where Black-headed Batis races have greyer crowns; best told here by its drier habitat. Larger than Pygmy Batis, with super-cilium extending behind eye onto nape. **Habitat:** Semi-arid savanna and acacia savanna; generally in drier areas than Black-headed Batis. **Status:** Locally common. **Voice:** Song a series of 4 or more descending whistles. [C12.7]

4 BLACK-HEADED BATIS *Batis minor* 11-12 cm
A very dark batis, with a blackish-grey crown and well-defined white supercilium. Very similar to Grey-headed Batis, but is slightly larger, with darker blackish (not grey) crown that shows little contrast with dark face mask. However, E African coastal races have paler crown and are smaller; best told by distinctive song, moister woodland habitat and female's narrower, darker breast band. **Habitat:** Well-wooded to lightly wooded savanna. **Status:** Common. **Voice:** Song a series of slow whistles at the same pitch; also a buzzing call. [C12.8]

5 PYGMY BATIS *Batis perkeo* 8-9 cm
Endemic to NE Africa. Smaller than Grey-headed Batis, with a short white supercilium that does not extend behind the eye. Female differs from female Black- and Grey-headed batises by having narrower, paler breast band. **Habitat:** Arid and semi-arid thorn scrub and dry riverine woodland. **Status:** Common but thinly distributed. **Voice:** Typical batis churring; also soft, high-pitched, whistled song.

6 WHITE-TAILED SHRIKE *Lanioturdus torquatus* 15 cm
Endemic to N Namibia and SW Angola. A peculiar, large terrestrial batis, with sexes alike; has also been linked to bush-shrikes. The striking black, white and grey plumage, long legs and short, white tail are diagnostic. Upright posture contributes to its almost tail-less appearance. Juv. has mottled crown. **Habitat:** Dry savanna and semi-desert scrub; often seen on ground or hopping over rocks. **Status:** Common. **Voice:** Clear, drawn-out whistles; harsh cackling. [G6.1.2]

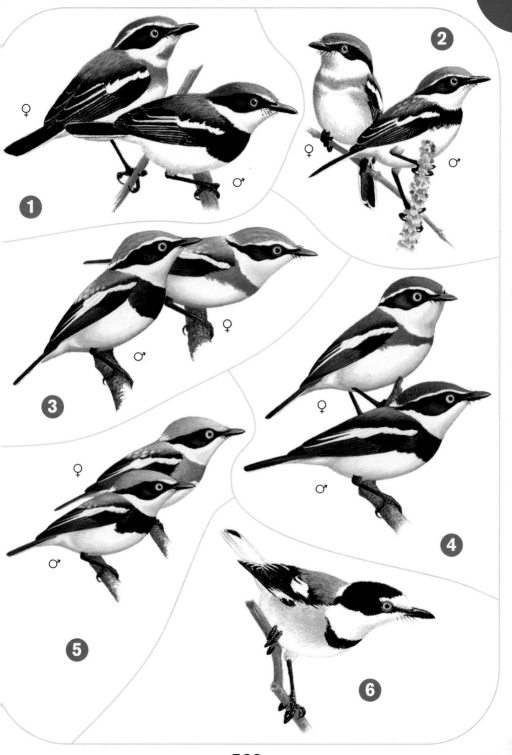

Small, mostly black-and-white flycatchers that typically occur fairly low down in dense vegetation. They could be confused with batises (pp. 564-568), but have dark eyes and conspicuous eye wattles, There are two genera: *Platysteira* is larger, with red eye wattles; *Dyaphorophyia* is smaller and short-tailed, with more colourful plumage and blue, green or violet eye wattles. Sexes differ.

1 BROWN-THROATED (SCARLET-SPECTACLED) WATTLE-EYE
Platysteira cyanea   13 cm

The only red-wattled wattle-eye over most of its range; larger than *Dyaphorophyia* wattle-eyes, with a relatively long tail and different habitat. In E, overlaps with Black-throated Wattle-eye; differs by having white wing bar. Similar to White-fronted Wattle-eye but has black (not grey) back. Female is paler above; told from other female *Platysteira* by its diagnostic chestnut-maroon throat and upper breast. Juv. duller, with buffy wing bar, and is mottled buff on throat and breast. **Habitat:** Wooded savanna, gallery forest, mangroves, gardens and plantations; avoids forest interior. **Status:** Common. **Voice:** Song is a series of clear, descending whistles 'tee teeuu teeu' as well as more warbling variations; also harsher rattling calls. [C12.12]

2 BANDED WATTLE-EYE *Platysteira laticincta*   13 cm
Endemic to Bamenda highlands, SW Cameroon. Often lumped with Black-throated Wattle-eye, but has deep bluish sheen to upperparts and male has broader breast band; ranges do not overlap. Lacks white wing bar of Brown-throated Wattle-eye. **Habitat:** Low and mid-stratum of montane forest. **Status:** Endangered through habitat loss. Still fairly common in remnant forest patches. **Voice:** Various 'chikka chikka' notes; 'zzree zzree' nasal whistle.

3 BLACK-THROATED WATTLE-EYE *Platysteira peltata*   13 cm
The 'wattle-eyed flycatcher' of S Africa. Forms a superspecies with Brown-throated Wattle-eye; best separated by lack of white wing bar. Male also has narrower breast band; female has black (not chestnut-maroon) throat. Lack of wing bar separates it from localised White-fronted Wattle-eye. Lack of gloss on upperparts and narrow breast band (in male) separate it from Banded Wattle-eye; ranges do not overlap. Juv. duller, with throat mottled brown. **Habitat:** Thickets, riparian forest and mangroves. **Status:** Fairly common. **Voice:** Rather dry 'wichee-wichee-wichee-wichee', often repeated. [C12.13, G5.11.5]

4 WHITE-FRONTED WATTLE-EYE *Platysteira albifrons*   11 cm
Endemic to NW Angola. Male resembles a washed-out male Brown-throated Wattle-eye, with grey (not black) upperparts, and a narrow white loral line. White wing bar and paler upperparts separate it from Black-throated Wattle-eye. Female is unique among wattle-eyes in being entirely white below, without any breast band or coloured throat. **Habitat:** Forest edge and patches of woodland in savanna. **Status:** Generally uncommon. **Voice:** Song is a burry 2-noted whistle 'phoo pheeee'; pairs also duet.

5 YELLOW-BELLIED WATTLE-EYE *Dyaphorophyia concreta*   9 cm
A small forest wattle-eye, readily identified by its dark greeny-grey upperparts and at least some yellow on the underparts. Male typically is all-yellow below; female has chestnut wash on throat and breast. Male of W African *concreta* has chestnut breast and belly (throat is yellow); female has discrete dark chestnut bib. Eye wattle is green (blue in Tanzanian *kungwensis*), and larger in male than female. Juv. duller and paler above. **Habitat:** In under-storey of closed-canopy forest. **Status:** Locally common. **Voice:** High pitched 'wheeo' whistle, followed immediately by 2 fast 'chik chik' calls. [C12.14]

kungwensis

1 CHESTNUT WATTLE-EYE *Dyaphorophyia castanea*   10 cm
A small, short-tailed (appearing almost tail-less) wattle-eye; easily identified except in areas of overlap with White-spotted Wattle-eye. Male has large, lilac eye wattle, glossy black upperparts, white rump, and broad black breast band; lacks white face spots and collar of male White-spotted Wattle-eye. Female is mainly chestnut, with white belly and uniform slate-grey head (lacking white malar stripe and darker crown of female White-spotted Wattle-eye). Juv. is mottled grey and chestnut on breast. **Habitat:** Forest understorey to mid-stratum, typically lower than White-spotted Wattle-eye. **Status:** Common; a noisy and active species. **Voice:** Monotonous, hollow-sounding 'chonk chonk chonk…'; also various soft 'chop' or 'chink' notes. [C12.18]

2 WHITE-SPOTTED WATTLE-EYE *Dyaphorophyia tonsa*   9 cm
Similar to Chestnut Wattle-eye, but with a different song and slightly different habitat preference. Male differs from male Chestnut Wattle-eye by having small white spot behind eye and white collar (not easily visible from below). Female has darker crown than cheeks (not uniform, as in female Chestnut Wattle-eye) and more pronounced white malar stripe. **Habitat:** Closed-canopy forest with more open understorey; typically forages at higher levels than Chestnut Wattle-eye, ranging from lower canopy to mid-stratum. **Status:** Locally common. **Voice:** Whistled song in phrases 'chee twee chee', or rather slower continuous notes than Chestnut Wattle-eye. Also 'pee dunk' call note. [C12.19]

3 RED-CHEEKED WATTLE-EYE *Dyaphorophyia blissetti*   9 cm
Endemic to W African forests, E to Mt Cameroon. Often lumped with Black-necked and Jameson's wattle-eyes. Range abuts that of Black-necked Wattle-eye, but has extensive chestnut patches on sides of neck, breast is mostly white, and eye wattle is bluer. Female has paler, less glossy, upperparts. Juv. has tawny throat. **Habitat:** Forest understorey, in closed-canopy forest or secondary forest, gallery forest and plantations. **Status:** Locally common. **Voice:** High, evenly-pitched, 'tee teee tee' whistled song; also harsher, churring calls. [C12.15]

4 JAMESON'S WATTLE-EYE *Dyaphorophyia jamesoni*   9 cm
Endemic to EC Africa. Very similar to Red-cheeked Wattle-eye, but has only very small chestnut patch, restricted to sides of neck (except in juv.); ranges do not overlap. Differs from Chestnut and Black-throated (p. 570) wattle-eyes by black throat and blue-green (not red or lilac) wattles. Juv. has tawny throat. **Habitat:** Forest understorey, at low levels, and secondary growth. **Status:** Locally common. **Voice:** Evenly-pitched whistles 'tsip tsip tseeer'; also a monotonous 'tsip tsip tsip tsip…'. [C12.16]

5 BLACK-NECKED WATTLE-EYE *Dyaphorophyia chalybea*   9 cm
Endemic to C Africa (SW Cameroon, except Mt Cameroon, S to Angola). Has glossy green-black upperparts (rump is white), throat and upper breast; white lower breast and belly tinged with yellow are diagnostic. Often lumped with Red-cheeked and Jameson's wattle-eyes, but black extends further onto breast, lacks chestnut patches on sides of neck, and wattle is green-blue (not blue). Female is less glossy, with smaller eye wattles. Juv. has white-and-tawny throat, and lacks yellow wash on underparts. **Habitat:** Dense undergrowth of gallery forest, riverine forest, secondary growth and old plantations. **Status:** Locally common, but more often heard than seen in its dense habitat. **Voice:** Song a series of descending notes 'tee di-dee-deee dee dee durrr', similar to Brown-throated Wattle-eye's, although not descending in scale as rapidly; also dry rattle call 'tik chee hee'. [C12.17]

Bold, predatory birds with hook-tipped bills. Usually solitary or in pairs, but some social. Sexes differ in many species.

1 RED-BACKED SHRIKE *Lanius collurio* 17-18 cm
A chestnut-backed, grey-crowned shrike with a grey rump and blackish tail. Grey (not rufous) rump and lack of white primary bases separate it from Red-tailed and Emin's shrikes; also differs from Red-tailed in having dark brown (not rufous) tail. Male has black face mask and plain, pinkish underparts; female is duller, with browner mask and faintly barred underparts. Juv. is barred above and below. Female and juv. are darker and more heavily barred than Red-tailed Shrike. Male *kobylini* has grey head extending down back to rump. **Habitat:** Savanna. **Status:** Common Palearctic migrant, mostly Nov-Apr. Scarce in W Africa. **Voice:** Harsh 'chak, chak'; soft, warbler-like song. [C4.52, G5.14.3]

2 RED-TAILED (ISABELLINE) SHRIKE *Lanius isabellinus* 17-18 cm
Formerly considered a race of Red-backed Shrike, but distinguished by rather plain brown upperparts contrasting with rufous (not grey) rump and relatively long, rufous (not mostly dark brown) tail. Female and juv. are paler, greyer and less barred than Red-backed Shrike, with rufous underside to tail. Two races occur, sometimes considered separate species: nominate (which has brown crown and yellowish underparts) and *phoenicuroides* (with rufous crown and white underparts). **Habitat:** Arid savanna and cultivation, mostly below 1 700 m. **Status:** Common Palearctic migrant Oct-Apr. **Voice:** 'Chack' contact and alarm calls. [C13.35]

3 EMIN'S SHRIKE *Lanius gubernator* 15-16 cm
Smaller and darker than Red-backed Shrike, with a rufous (not grey) rump, dark buff (not pinkish) underparts and contrasting white throat. Also has white bases to primaries, forming small white wing patch. Female is duller than male; differs from female Red-backed Shrike by having uniform buffy (not barred) underparts. Juv. is finely barred above and below, with more prominent dark mask than Red-tailed Shrike. **Habitat:** Forest edge and clearings, savanna and farmlands. **Status:** Uncommon; in pairs or small family groups. **Voice:** Generally silent; song undescribed.

4 SOUZA'S SHRIKE *Lanius souzae* 17 cm
A small, slender shrike with a long, thin tail. Recalls female Red-backed Shrike, but with large white shoulder patches and plain (not barred) underparts. Female has pale rufous flanks. Juv. is finely barred; smaller and warmer brown above than juv. fiscals (p. 576). **Habitat:** Miombo and mopane woodlands, feeding mostly in mid-storey. **Status:** Uncommon to locally common; often associated with bird parties. **Voice:** Soft, grating calls. [C13.34]

5 SOUTHERN GREY SHRIKE *Lanius meridionalis* 24-25 cm
A large, pale, grey-backed shrike of N Africa; formerly considered conspecific with Great Grey Shrike *L. excubitor*. Larger than Lesser Grey Shrike, with whitish scapular bar, extensive white edges to secondaries, and little if any black on frons; also has longer and more tapering bill, longer tail and shorter wings (at rest, longest primaries barely reach uppertail coverts). Juv. is washed buff. Several races occur, varying in darkness of back and extent of white supercilium; paler races have prominent white rump. Rare migrant *pallidirostris* has pale bill. **Habitat:** Arid savannas. **Status:** Fairly common resident and local migrant. **Voice:** Slow, staccato mixture of short phrases, both harsh and melodious; a nasal 'gwaaay'. [C13.38] **Similar species. Grey Hypocolius** *Hypocolius ampelinus* is a Palearctic vagrant to NE; female and imm. nondescript, long-tailed greyish birds; male has black mask and white-tipped black primaries.

6 LESSER GREY SHRIKE *Lanius minor* 20-22 cm
A pale grey-backed shrike with a bold black face mask. Lacks the white scapular bars of most other grey-backed shrikes. Smaller than Grey-backed Fiscal (p. 576), with much shorter tail and fully white outer-tail feathers. Female is duller, often with less black on forehead, and may show light barring on flanks. Juv. is barred above, plain buffy below. **Habitat:** Arid savanna and semi-desert scrub. **Status:** Common Palearctic migrant Sep-Apr; southward migration is further W than return migration. **Voice:** Soft 'chuk'; warbled song, heard before return migration. [C13.37, G5.14.1]

1

♀

♂

juv.

♀

♂

2

3

4

5

6

pallidirostris

575

1 GREY-BACKED FISCAL *Lanius excubitoroides* 24-26 cm

A large, social, noisy fiscal with a pale grey hindcrown, nape and back. Longer tailed than Lesser and Southern grey shrikes (p. 574), with black face mask extending onto side of neck and diagnostic white basal half of outer-tail feathers. Juv. is darker, finely barred above and below, with pale-based bill; tail browner. **Habitat:** Arid scrub in W, acacia savanna, fields and gardens in E. **Status:** Common resident and short-distance migrant. **Voice:** Groups give clanging, grating chorus. [C13.39]

2 LONG-TAILED FISCAL *Lanius cabanisi* 27-31 cm

Endemic to NE Africa. A large fiscal with a diagnostic long, graduated black tail. Dark grey and black above, lacking white scapular bars, but with contrasting white rump. Female has small chestnut flank patches. Juv. is paler grey above, and finely barred above and below, but has paler rump and long black tail. **Habitat:** Arid savannas and cultivated areas, usually in drier areas than Grey-backed Fiscal. **Status:** Common up to 1 600 m. **Voice:** Harsh 'chit-er-row'; scolding and chattering.

3 TAITA FISCAL *Lanius dorsalis* 20-21 cm

Endemic to NE Africa. The black crown and facial mask, pale grey back and striking white scapular patches distinguish it from all except Somali Fiscal; differs by having smaller white patch in primaries, black- (not white-) tipped secondaries and narrow (not broad) white edge to tail. Undertail is dark brown, with white spots towards tip. Female has chestnut flanks. Juv. is lightly barred above and below; upperparts greyish (not brown); undertail is predominantly brown (not white); lacks white tips to secondaries. **Habitat:** Arid savanna up to 1 500 m. **Status:** Common. **Voice:** Song is mixture of churrs, pops and ticks.

4 SOMALI FISCAL *Lanius somalicus* 20-21 cm

Endemic to NE Africa. Similar to Taita Fiscal, but with white tips to secondaries and tertials, more extensive white on sides of tail, a wholly white undertail (when closed), and a larger white flash at base of primaries. Female lacks chestnut flank streaking. Juv. is browner above, and has more white in wings and tail. **Habitat:** Very arid open country with little vegetation. **Status:** Uncommon to locally common. **Voice:** Song is less varied than Taita Fiscal's, most often 'bur-er-er, bit-it-it'; alarm call is low churr.

5 MACKINNON'S FISCAL (SHRIKE) *Lanius mackinnoni* 20-21 cm

A grey-backed fiscal with prominent white scapulars and no white patches in the primaries. Adult differs from Lesser Grey Shrike (p. 574) by neat white supercilium. Female has chestnut flanks. Juv. is browner and barred above and below. **Habitat:** Forest edge, woodland and wooded farmlands. **Status:** Uncommon and thinly distributed; chiefly singly or in pairs. **Voice:** Song is melodious mixture of whistles and mimicry; alarm call is simple 'chrrikee'. [C13.36]

6 COMMON FISCAL *Lanius collaris* 21-23 cm

Apart from the localised Uhehe Fiscal, this is the only black-backed fiscal. Several boubous (p. 584) are superficially similar, but differ in behaviour and structure. In S Africa, told from Fiscal Flycatcher (p. 550) by its white scapulars and white outer-tail, as well as heavier bill, longer tail and crouching posture when perched. Female has chestnut flanks in some races. Juv. is greyish brown, with darker crescentic barring above and below. SW *subcoronatus* has conspicuous white supercilium, but intergrades with other races. **Habitat:** Widespread throughout except dense forest. **Status:** Common. **Voice:** Most frequent is harsh, grating call; song is melodious and jumbled, often with harsher notes and mimicry of other birds' calls. [C13.40, G5.14.2]

7 UHEHE FISCAL *Lanius marwitzi* 21-23 cm

Endemic to S Eastern Arc Mts of Tanzania; poorly known. Similar to Common Fiscal, but has white supercilium and more extensive white on lower back and rump; beware white-browed *subcoronatus* Common Fiscal in SW Africa. Female apparently lacks chestnut flanks. Juv. is similar to juv. Common Fiscal, although reputed to be darker and more heavily barred. **Habitat:** Occurs at higher elevations than Common Fiscal, in wooded grassland and farmland. **Status:** Common but localised. **Voice:** Similar to Common Fiscal's.

juv.

subcoronatus

577

1 SÃO TOMÉ (NEWTON'S) FISCAL *Lanius newtoni* 23 cm
Endemic to São Tomé. The only forest shrike and the only bird with black upperparts and white underparts on São Tomé. At close range, white underparts are tinged with yellow, less on throat. **Habitat:** Open forest understorey in primary forest, where it hunts from low branches; generally below 700 m. **Status:** Critically threatened. Scarce in SW São Tomé. **Voice:** Series of 10-12 plaintive 'pew' notes, roughly one per second; metallic 'tink' notes. [C13.41]

2 MASKED SHRIKE *Lanius nubicus* 17 cm
A slim, delicate shrike, reminiscent of a long-tailed Brubru (p. 584). Front of face is white, with dark loral stripe. Upperparts are pied black and white. Underparts are white, with peach-coloured flanks. Lack of chestnut on head and black (not white) rump distinguish it from Woodchat Shrike. Juv. is lightly barred above and below; told from most other juv. shrikes by large, pale frons and supercilium, which give it pale-faced appearance. Greyer than juv. Woodchat Shrike, with dark rump and no chestnut on head. **Habitat:** Arid savannas and wooded oases, including palm groves. **Status:** Locally common Palearctic migrant, mostly Sep-Apr. **Voice:** Quiet 'krrit krrit' while foraging; churring alarm call. [C13.42]

3 MAGPIE (LONG-TAILED) SHRIKE *Corvinella melanoleuca* 40-50 cm (incl. tail)
A large, very long-tailed shrike with black underparts. White scapular bars and whitish rump are conspicuous; in flight has prominent white bases to primaries. Female and juv. have pale flanks and shorter tail. Juv. is dull black-brown, with fine barring. E African *aequatorialis* has shorter tail. **Habitat:** Acacia savanna. **Status:** Common; often in small groups of 4-8 birds. **Voice:** Liquid, whistled 'peeleeo'. [G5.14.5]

4 SOUTHERN WHITE-CROWNED SHRIKE *Eurocephalus anguitimens* 23-25 cm
Endemic to SW Africa. A large, brown-and-white shrike with a prominent white crown. Similar to Northern White-crowned Shrike, but has paler back and dark rump; ranges are not known to overlap. Juv. is paler, with mottled crown, less extensive dark face patch and yellow bill. **Habitat:** Mixed dry woodland and acacia savanna. **Status:** Common; usually in groups of 3-6 birds. **Voice:** Shrill, whistling 'kree, kree, kree'; bleating and harsh chattering. [G6.1.6]

5 WOODCHAT SHRIKE *Lanius senator* 18-19 cm
A rather chunky, medium-sized shrike, easily identified by its bold, black-and-white plumage and bright chestnut hindcrown and nape. Female is duller, with larger pale frons. Told from Masked Shrike in flight by white (not black) rump. Juv. is sparsely barred above and on flanks. **Habitat:** Open plains and arid savannas; also cultivated areas with scattered trees. Often found close to water, including on floodplains and around lake margins; also in forest clearings in W Africa. **Status:** Fairly common Palearctic migrant Aug-Apr. **Voice:** Usually silent in region; contact call is 'kwikwik'. [C4.56]

6 YELLOW-BILLED SHRIKE *Corvinella corvina* 30-40 cm (incl. tail)
A large, long-tailed shrike with greyish-brown, heavily streaked plumage and dark eye mask. At close range, yellow bill and eyelids are diagnostic. In flight, shows rusty patches in wings. Juv. has heavily barred (not streaked) plumage. **Habitat:** Open woodland, farmlands and shrubby grassland. **Status:** Locally common; in family groups, foraging on ground and in trees. **Voice:** Generally very noisy; series of harsh, grating shrieks and buzzes; shorter 'chizz chizz'. [C13.43]

7 NORTHERN WHITE-CROWNED SHRIKE *Eurocephalus rueppelli* 20-21 cm
Endemic to NE Africa. Differs from Southern White-crowned Shrike by dark brown (not pale grey-brown) back, contrasting with white uppertail coverts; ranges are not known to overlap. In flight, broad wings and clumsy flight recall babblers. Juv. has brown breast band, scalloped brown crown, and dark mask and moustachial stripe; bill is pinkish. **Habitat:** Dry woodlands, especially acacia and *Commiphora* woodland, mostly below 1 600 m. **Status:** Common; usually in groups of 3-6 birds. **Voice:** Harsh, repetitive 'chrrk, wirl-wirk, yerk-yerk, wuk-wuk, yerk...'.

aequatorialis

Small, arboreal bush shrikes that resemble small boubous (p. 584), but are more compact, with shorter tails, and most have red (not dark) eyes. There are two main groups: those with plain backs and those with pale edges to the wing feathers. Sexes differ; males are mostly black and white, with a grey or white rump, which is puffed out enormously in display; females typically more rufous.

1 NORTHERN PUFFBACK *Dryoscopus gambensis*   18-19 cm
A large puffback with black wings edged grey-white, a greyish rump and orange eyes. Forms a superspecies with Black-backed Puffback; male is told by greyer scapulars and rump. Separated from Red-eyed Puffback by black-and-white (not black) wings. Female has brown or grey-brown upperparts and pale rufous underparts; lacks pale supercilium of female Black-backed Puffback. **Habitat:** Wooded savanna. **Status:** Common. **Voice:** Sharp 'keeu keeu', faster than Black-backed Puffback's. [C13.46]

2 BLACK-BACKED PUFFBACK *Dryoscopus cubla*   16-18 cm
The only puffback over most of its range. Male is more boldly black and white than Northern or Pringle's puffbacks. Female and juv. are duller, often with buffy wash, but always have diagnostic pale supercilium. Juv. has brown eyes. Coastal E African *affinis* lacks white edges to wing feathers, with only bold white scapular bar; resembles a small boubou (p. 584). **Habitat:** Woodland, thickets and forest canopy. **Status:** Common. **Voice:** Sharp, repeated 'chick, weeo'; in flight, male utters loud 'chok chok chok'. [C13.45, G5.14.10]

3 PRINGLE'S PUFFBACK *Dryoscopus pringlii*   13-14 cm
Endemic to NE Africa. Smaller than Northern or Black-backed puffbacks, with pale lower mandible. Male has greyish scapulars, like Northern Puffback; lacks crisp black-and-white look of Black-backed Puffback. Female is grey, with white fringes to wing coverts; resembles large *Sylvia* warbler (p. 490) but has crimson (not dark) eyes, large bill and white lores. **Habitat:** Dry acacia scrub and thickets. Skulks and keeps very low in undergrowth; joins bird parties. **Status:** Uncommon and thinly distributed. **Voice:** Main contact call is sharp, clipped 'teeu'.

4 RED-EYED (BLACK-SHOULDERED) PUFFBACK
Dryoscopus senegalensis   16-18 cm
A plain-backed puffback with prominent red eyes. Male is black above and white or creamy-white below; separated from Pink-footed and Sabine's puffbacks by red (not dark) eyes and black (not brownish) wings, and from Pink-footed Puffback by white (not grey) rump. Female is paler above, with white lores; lacks rufous underparts of female Sabine's and Pink-footed puffbacks. **Habitat:** Forest and forest edge, clearings, and old, overgrown farmlands. **Status:** Common but localised; forages in mid-canopy with mixed bird parties. **Voice:** Very vocal; most often heard before seen; call is sharp whistle, 'tueet', often repeated. [C13.47]

5 PINK-FOOTED PUFFBACK *Dryoscopus angolensis*   15-16 cm
A plain-backed puffback of montane and submontane forest, identified by the combination of dark (not red) eyes, grey (not black) back and pale grey breast and flanks. Female rich rufous below; could be confused for a robin-chat (p. 448) or akalat (p. 444), but typically occurs higher in the canopy and behaviour differs; it has greyer upperparts (head, mantle and rump) and a smaller bill than female Sabine's Puffback; also, wing feathers have paler margins. Legs and feet pink in both sexes. **Habitat:** Mainly montane and submontane forest, in canopy and at edge of forest. **Status:** Locally common. **Voice:** Loud, repeated 'chow chow chow'; various chukking calls; dry rattle, 'trrrrrrrr'. [C13.48]

6 SABINE'S (LARGE-BILLED) PUFFBACK *Dryoscopus sabini*   18-20 cm
A large, plain-backed puffback with a heavy bill. Male differs from Red-eyed Puffback by its dark eye; the two species meet only at forest edge and in gallery forest. White (not grey) rump and underparts separate it from male Pink-footed Puffback. Female has plain rufous-brown (not grey, as in female Pink-footed Puffback) mantle and rump, and uniform wings; in most of range, the two do not overlap. **Habitat:** Forest canopy, edges of forest and gallery forest. **Status:** Locally common. **Voice:** Series of 10-12 descending notes of increasing length, 'pip pip pee pee peep peep peeer peeer'; also harsh, scolding calls. [C13.49]

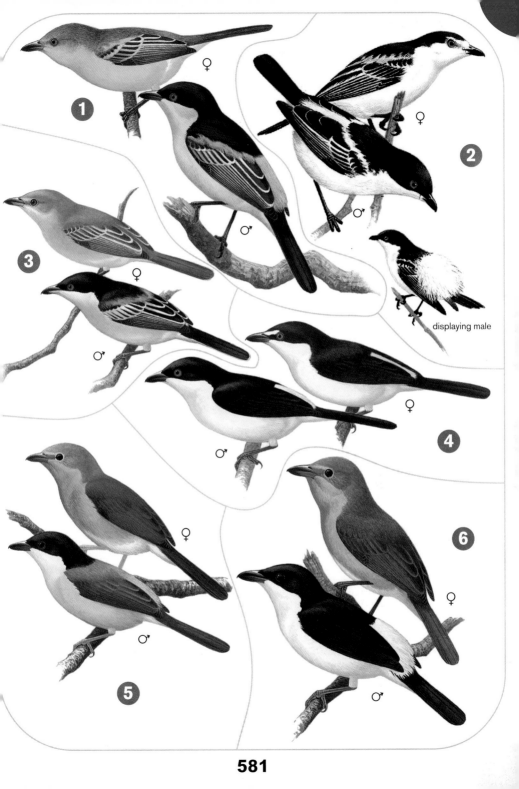

displaying male

Buffy-grey bush shrikes with warm rufous wings and diagnostic head patterns. All have dark brown tails with white tips to the outer feathers. They remain close to the ground, and have loud, distinctive calls uttered during short display flights. Sexes alike in most species. Marsh tchagras sometimes placed in *Antichromus*.

1 MARSH TCHAGRA *Tchagra minuta*   15-18 cm
A small tchagra of rank grassland, identified by its black cap, chestnut upperparts and creamy-buff underparts; blackish tail is tipped buff. Sometimes considered conspecific with Anchieta's Tchagra, but has diagnostic black 'V'-mark on mantle and scapulars, and different call and habitat. Female has broad white supercilium. Juv. resembles female but has off-white median crown stripe. **Habitat:** Rank, long grasslands, often in damp areas and low shrub in swamps near forest edge. **Status:** Uncommon and localised. **Voice:** Contact call is harsh 'qurrr'; fluty song in display flight over long grass. [C13.50]

2 ANCHIETA'S TCHAGRA *Tchagra anchietae*   16-19 cm
S form of Marsh Tchagra; lacks conspicuous black 'V' on mantle and scapulars, and has different calls and habitat; ranges are not known to overlap. **Habitat:** Rank bracken and sedges growing in damp hollows, and marshy areas with long grass. **Status:** Uncommon. **Voice:** Shrill, trilling song in display flight. [G5.15.5]

3 BROWN-CROWNED (THREE-STREAKED) TCHAGRA
Tchagra australis   17-19 cm
A medium-sized tchagra with a brown (not black, as in Black-crowned Tchagra) central crown, bordered by black lateral crown stripes (often obscuring the brown crown if viewed from below). Smaller and shorter-billed than localised Southern Tchagra, and black lateral crown stripes are absent in Southern Tchagra. Underpart colour varies regionally from grey to off-white. Juv. is duller. **Habitat:** Thick tangles and undergrowth in savanna and woodland. **Status:** Common. **Voice:** Aerial display flight and song are very similar to those of Southern Tchagra. [C13.51, G5.15.3]

4 BLACK-CROWNED TCHAGRA *Tchagra senegalus*   20-23 cm
A large, widespread tchagra, told from most other species by its black forehead and central crown. Larger than female marsh tchagras, with broad white (not buff) tips restricted to outer-tail. Underpart colour varies regionally from grey to off-white. Juv. has mottled crown and horn-coloured bill. **Habitat:** Savanna, thickets and riverine scrub. **Status:** Common; less skulking than other tchagras. **Voice:** Song is characteristic, slightly mournful, loud, whistled 'whee-cheree, cherooo, cheree-cherooo' on descending scale, becoming slurred towards end. [C4.57, G5.15.4]

5 THREE-STREAKED (JAMES'S) TCHAGRA *Tchagra jamesi*   16-17 cm
Endemic to NE Africa. A small tchagra, paler and greyer than other species. Head is largely grey, with diagnostic dark central crown stripe (sometimes very narrow and hard to see); lacks paler buffy supercilium of other species. Juv's crown stripe is shorter. **Habitat:** Dry thorn scrub and acacia thickets. **Status:** Uncommon and thinly distributed; unusually skulking and difficult to see. **Voice:** Descending series of slurred whistles in flight, similar to Black-crowned Tchagra's.

6 SOUTHERN TCHAGRA *Tchagra tchagra*   20-22 cm
Endemic to South Africa. A large, long-billed tchagra with a grey-brown crown. Larger and darker than Brown-crowned Tchagra, with no black stripes between its buff supercilium and brown crown. Juv. is duller. **Habitat:** Coastal scrub, forest edges and thickets. **Status:** Common. **Voice:** Song, given in aerial display, is 'wee-chee-chee-cheee', descending in pitch. [G5.15.2]

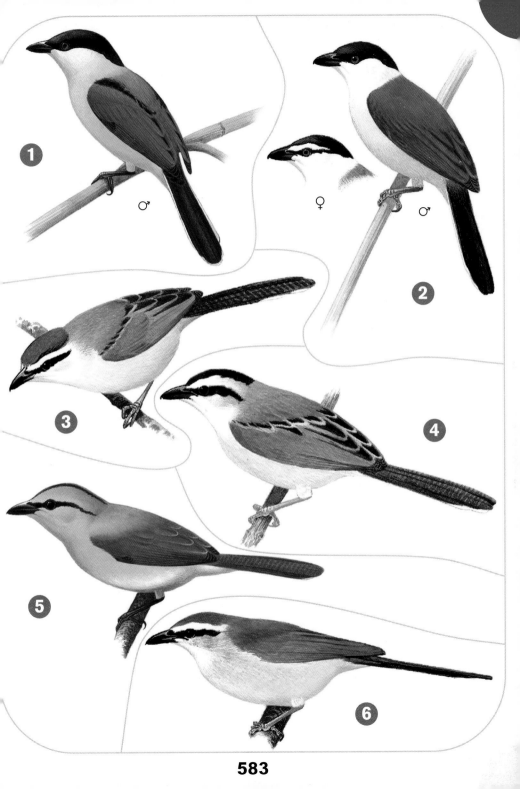

A diverse group of shrike-like birds that are not closely related to the true shrikes. Most are rather retiring, preferring to remain in dense cover, but are highly vocal. Sexes alike in most species.

1 TROPICAL BOUBOU *Laniarius aethiopicus*   19-23 cm
The most widespread boubou, with a variably pink or cream-washed breast. Paler below than Southern Boubou, with more marked contrast between black upperparts and pinkish-white underparts; never pure-white below, as Swamp Boubou. Juv. is duller, spotted with buff above and below. NE races have white in wing restricted to coverts; coastal E African *sublacteus* lacks white wing bar; also occurs in all-black morph which is glossy black (not dark slate-grey, like Slate-coloured Boubou, p. 588). **Habitat:** Thickets, riverine and evergreen forests, and gardens. **Status:** Common. **Voice:** Loud, ringing duet, typically 'wee hooo' or 'wee hooo hooo'; also various whistles and harsh, croaking calls. [C13.53, G5.14.7]

2 SWAMP BOUBOU *Laniarius bicolor*   23-24 cm
Slightly larger than Southern and Tropical boubous with diagnostic pure white underparts; bill more slender. Juv. is spotted with buff above and barred below. N races sometimes placed in Tropical Boubou. **Habitat:** Thickets, dense scrub and poapyrus swamps; often near water. In S Africa always occurs near water. **Status:** Common; usually in pairs. **Voice:** Duets of whistled 'hoouu'; harsh, rattling calls. [C13.55, G5.14.8]

3 SOUTHERN BOUBOU *Laniarius ferrugineus*   20-22 cm
Endemic to S Africa. More richly coloured beneath than Tropical Boubou, with buff-rufous (not pinkish) wash concentrated more on belly than breast. Female is greyer above, with darker, more extensive rufous wash on underparts. Juv. is mottled buff-brown above and barred below. **Habitat:** Forest edge, thickets and dense coastal scrub. **Status:** Common. **Voice:** Variable duet with basic notes of 'boo-boo' followed by whistled 'whee-ooo'; also harsh, scolding calls. [G5.14.6]

4 TURATI'S BOUBOU *Laniarius turatii*   20-21 cm
Localised endemic to W Africa. Black wing lacking white bar across coverts is diagnostic. Range does not overlap with similar E African *sublacteus* Tropical Boubou. Rump and lower back are spotted white; throat and breast are washed creamy buff. **Habitat:** Impenetrable thickets and undergrowth, not necessarily near water. **Status:** Uncommon. **Voice:** Duetted ringing notes, similar to other boubous'. [C13.54]

5 BRUBRU *Nilaus afer*   12-15 cm
A small, black-and-white arboreal shrike with chestnut flanks. Widespread, but with considerable geographic variation. Typically black above, with chequered back and prominent white or buff wing bar and supercilium, although some races lack latter. Relatively large size and thick bill prevent confusion with batises. Female is duller. Juv. is mottled and barred with buff and brown above and below. **Habitat:** Dry acacia savanna and open broadleafed woodland. **Status:** Common. **Voice:** Soft, trilling 'prrrrr' given by male, often answered 'eeeu' by female. [C13.44, G5.15.1]

6 BULO BURTI BOUBOU *Laniarius liberatus*   20 cm
Known from only one individual caught and released in Somalia. Similar to Red-naped Bush Shrike, but with fully black (not chestnut) crown and buff (not white) supercilium and breast. **Habitat:** Acacia thicket in dry riverbeds; forages on ground and deep within thickets. **Status:** Critically threatened. **Voice:** Low 'chack' and ascending soft whistle 'poo-eeeh' given in captivity.

7 RED-NAPED BUSH SHRIKE *Laniarius ruficeps*   18 cm
Endemic to NE Africa. A grey-and-white bush shrike with a prominent white supercilium and an inconspicuous chestnut hind-crown and nape. In similar habitat might be confused with smaller Pringle's Puffback (p. 580), but lacks black cap and supercilium imparts markedly different appearance. Female is browner above. Juv. is much drabber, with obvious white wing bar. **Habitat:** Dry acacia scrub and general dry thickets and bush. **Status:** Locally common but thinly distributed. Skulks low down in thickets and is reluctant to show itself except when singing. **Voice:** Duets a repeated 'creeo creeo'; harsher, scolding 'churr' notes.

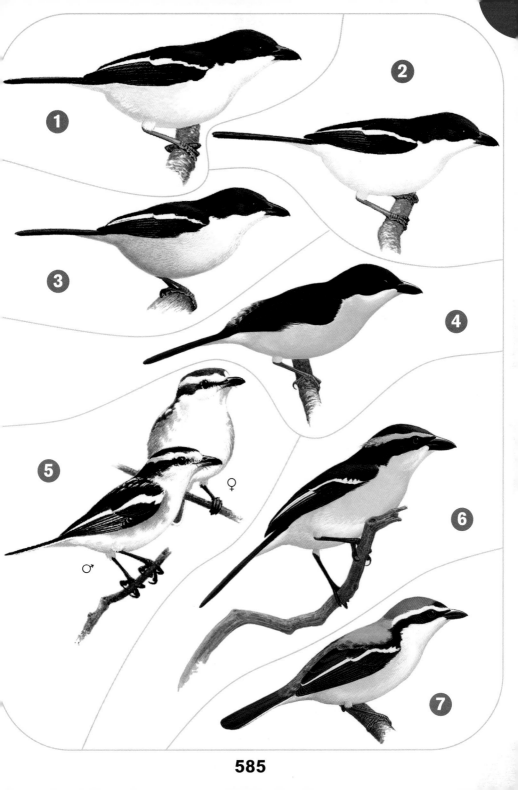

1 YELLOW-BREASTED BOUBOU *Laniarius atroflavus* 20 cm
Endemic to SW Cameroon and SE Nigerian highland forests. A striking black-and-yellow boubou with no white wing bar. Juv. has browner upperparts and duller yellow underparts. **Habitat:** Montane forest, forest edge and thickets. **Status:** Common; demonstrative and bold for a boubou, often sitting out in open on exposed perches. **Voice:** Typical whistled duetting, similar to other boubous'. [C13.53]

2 CRIMSON-BREASTED SHRIKE *Laniarius atrococcineus* 23 cm
Endemic to SW Africa. A striking crimson-and-black boubou with a white wing bar. Rare yellow morph has yellow (not crimson) underparts. Juv. is barred with greyish brown below, with varying amounts of crimson, and is finely barred black and buff above. **Habitat:** Acacia thickets in arid savanna, dry river courses and semi-arid scrub. **Status:** Common. **Voice:** Harsh 'trrrrr'; whistled 'qwip-qwip' duet. [G5.14.9]

3 BLACK-HEADED GONOLEK *Laniarius erythrogaster* 21-22 cm
Similar to Crimson-breasted Shrike, but lacks white in the wings (occasionally has a few white spots), and has yellow (not dark) eyes and buffy vent; ranges do not overlap. Black (not yellow) crown separates it from Yellow-crowned and Papyrus gonoleks. Juv. is mottled red and black on underparts. **Habitat:** Riverine thicket, dense acacia scrub, grassy woodland and farmlands. **Status:** Common; in pairs or family groups. **Voice:** Male whistles loud, far-carrying 'wheeoo'; female replies with harsh 'quurr'. [C13.57]

4 PAPYRUS GONOLEK *Laniarius mufumbiri* 19-20 cm
Endemic to E Africa. Very similar to Yellow-crowned Gonolek but with a white wing bar, and is confined to papyrus swamps; ranges don't overlap. Yellow (not black) crown separates it from Black-headed Gonolek. Juv. is matt-black above, with dull red-and-buff underparts. **Habitat:** Rarely leaves papyrus swamps except to fly over open water. **Status:** Common in large stands of suitable habitat; usually in pairs. **Voice:** Loud gonolek-type whistled duets. [C13.58]

5 YELLOW-CROWNED (COMMON) GONOLEK *Laniarius barbarus* 22-25 cm
A crimson-breasted gonolek of W Africa with a prominent yellow crown. Lacks white wing bar of Papyrus Gonolek; ranges do not overlap. Yellow (not black) crown separates it from Black-headed Gonolek. Juv. is much duller, mostly barred brown, with yellow wash on crown and patches of red on underparts. **Habitat:** Riverine thicket, dry acacia savanna and farmlands. **Status:** Common; often in open, but prefers to skulk in thick undergrowth. **Voice:** Noisy: whistled duet of 'whee-uu' and harsh 'chak chak' notes. [C13.56]

6 ROSY-PATCHED BUSH-SHRIKE *Rhodophoneus cruentus* 22-24 cm
Endemic to NE Africa. A large, dun-coloured shrike with a white-tipped tail and diagnostic pink central breast and rump. Males typically have pink extending up onto throat, but male of S race *cathemagmena* has black gorget and pink throat. Female has black gorget and white throat. Juv. has whitish throat, and only a few pink and black feathers on breast. **Habitat:** Arid and semi-arid scrub, acacia thickets and old farmlands. **Status:** Locally common; frequently in pairs; sometimes perches high in bush when singing but usually seeks cover in thickets and undergrowth. **Voice:** Duets are simple but loud, 'tsuee tsuueee'.

yellow morph

juv.

♂

cathemagmena ♂

♀

1 BRAUN'S BUSH-SHRIKE *Laniarius brauni* 17 cm
Endemic to N Angola. The rusty cap and bright orange-red underparts separate it from closely related Lühder's and Gabela bush-shrikes; ranges are not known to overlap. Juv. is undescribed; probably similar to Lühder's Bush-Shrike. **Habitat:** Forest and forest edge; occurs in dense tangles in mid-stratum and undergrowth. **Status:** Endangered. Current status little known. **Voice:** Throaty 'waark' and 'whoook' as well as soft 'bou-bou' whistle.

2 LÜHDER'S BUSH-SHRIKE *Laniarius leuhderi* 17 cm
Localised, with apparently disjunct distribution. Adult has a diagnostic rich tawny head and breast with a broad black mask. Wings have broad white stripe. Juv. is drab olive above, with pale olive-yellow underparts, rufous rump, and buff edges to wing feathers forming indistinct wing bar. **Habitat:** Forest, secondary growth and old farmlands up to 2 300 m; often near streams and damp areas. **Status:** Common; usually in pairs; more often heard than seen. **Voice:** Frog-like, resonant 'wuurrk' and 'shrik shrik' duet. [C13.52]

3 GABELA BUSH-SHRIKE *Laniarius amboimensis* 17 cm
Endemic to Gabela region of WC Angola. Very similar to closely related Lühder's and Braun's bush-shrikes, but with white underparts (not buff or rufous breast). Differs from Swamp Boubou (p. 584) by having chestnut cap. Juv. is undescribed; probably similar to Lühder's Bush-Shrike. **Habitat:** Forest mid-stratum and undergrowth and forest-edge thickets; also in riverine thickets among coffee plantations. **Status:** Endangered. Locally common within remaining forest patches. **Voice:** Frog-like 'waak-ik' and soft 'pop-op' whistle as well as harsh clicks and rattles when disturbed.

4 LOWLAND SOOTY BOUBOU *Laniarius leucorhynchus* 21-22 cm
Replaces Slate-coloured Boubou in W and C Africa; habitats are mutually exclusive. In good light, is darker than Slate-coloured Boubou, appearing all-black; also is slightly larger, with longer, heavier bill. Juv. is duller, with whitish bill. **Habitat:** Rainforest, secondary growth, forest clearings and old farmlands; keeps to thick undergrowth in forests, close to ground. **Status:** Fairly common but easily overlooked; more often heard than seen. **Voice:** Duetted series of clear whistles and harsher notes, similar to other black boubous'. [C13.63]

5 SLATE-COLOURED BOUBOU *Laniarius funebris* 18-20 cm
Endemic to NE Africa. A dull, dark grey boubou; skulking habits and shape separate it from black flycatchers (p. 548), drongos (p. 380) and male cuckoo-shrikes (376). Best told from other black boubous by head being darker than dark grey body and relatively arid habitat; there is no overlap in range. Matt, sooty grey (not glossy black) body separates it from black-morph *sublacteus* Tropical Boubou (p. 584) in coastal E Africa. Juv. is browner, finely barred below. **Habitat:** Dry to semi-arid bush, thicket and riverine woodland. **Status:** Locally common; usually in pairs; keeps well hidden unless singing from exposed perch. **Voice:** Duets 'kidunk kidunk', answered with harsh 'chruk chruk'.

6 MOUNTAIN SOOTY BOUBOU *Laniarius poensis* 18-20 cm
An all-black boubou restricted to Albertine Rift, SW Cameroon and Bioko highland forests. Sometimes treated as conspecific with Fülleborne's Boubou; ranges do not overlap. Occurs at higher elevations than Lowland Sooty Boubou. **Habitat:** Montane forests and forest edge and clearings above 600 m (rarely 450 m) in Cameroon, generally above 1 200 m in Albertine Rift. **Status:** Locally common but rarely seen, keeping to undergrowth and thickets, close to ground. **Voice:** Very varied duets, similar to those of Fülleborne's Boubou. [C13.60-62]

7 FÜLLEBORNE'S (BLACK) BOUBOU *Laniarius fuelleborni* 20 cm
Endemic to Eastern Arc montane forests of Tanzania, N Malawi and NE Zambia. Resembles other all-black boubous, but range and habitats are mutually exclusive. Birds in N are glossy black; further S are grey-black. Female is greyer, with olive wash on belly in S. Juv. is grey-brown above, grey-olive below, faintly barred in very young birds. **Habitat:** Montane forests, clearings and forest edge. **Status:** Locally common; usually in pairs; keeps to undergrowth and thickets but will ascend through creepers to canopy to duet. **Voice:** Typical boubou-like duetting, but with considerable variation.

1 GREY-GREEN (BOCAGE'S) BUSH-SHRIKE *Telephorus bocagei* 16 cm
A small, grey-and-white bush-shrike that could be confused with male Pink-footed Puffback (p. 580), but has an obvious white supercilium, black face mask and buffy breast. Juv. is more olive, with faint grey barring on underparts and olive-buff feather tips above. **Habitat:** Lowland and mid-altitude forest, forest edge and clearings, and old, overgrown farmlands. **Status:** Locally common; usually in canopy, where it moves slowly when gleaning; often in bird parties. **Voice:** Distinctive, rapid 'chwee ee eee eee'; slower, often repeated 'whee-eeuu'. [C13.64]

2 MOUNT KUPE BUSH-SHRIKE *Telephorus kupeensis* 18 cm
Endemic to Kupe and Bakossi mts, SW Cameroon. A forest bush-shrike with an unmistakable, striking head pattern, with a broad black mask extending onto the frons, white throat and narrow black breast band. Juv. lacks black breast band. **Habitat:** Montane forest slopes in canopy and mid-stratum. **Status:** Endangered. Rare and localised. **Voice:** 3-note whistle, ascending in scale. [C13.68]

3 ORANGE-BREASTED BUSH-SHRIKE *Telophorus sulfureopectus* 16-18 cm
Differs from all other bush-shrikes by its conspicuous yellow forehead and supercilium, yellow throat and orangey breast. Much smaller than *Malaconotus* bush-shrikes (p. 594), with dark (not yellow) eyes. Female is duller, with paler grey face mask. Juv. has drab grey head, pale yellow throat and little orange on breast. **Habitat:** Acacia savanna and riverine forests. **Status:** Common. **Voice:** Song is frequently repeated 'poo-poo-poo-pooooo', fading towards end; deeper 'pu pu pu pu'; harsher 'titit-eeezz'. [C13.65, G5.5.15.8]

4 OLIVE BUSH-SHRIKE *Telophorus olivaceus* 17-19 cm
Near-endemic to S Africa. Ruddy or grey morph has a grey head, black mask and peach-coloured breast, and usually a whitish supercilium. Olive morph is entirely olive-green above, with more orange breast and yellow supercilium. In area of overlap with Black-fronted Bush-Shrike (p. 592), identification is easy because only ruddy-morph Olive Bush-Shrike and red-breasted-morph Black-fronted Bush-Shrike occur together. Female and juv. of both morphs lack black mask; juvs are faintly barred below. **Habitat:** Evergreen and riverine forests. **Status:** Common. **Voice:** Varied series of whistles, such as 'wheee hoo hoo hoo hoo'; call is similar to Orange-breasted Bush-Shrike's 'poo-poo-poo-poooo'; harsh, rattling alarm call, 'krrrr krrrr krrrrr'. [G5.15.10]

5 BOKMAKIERIE *Telophorus zeylonus* 22-23 cm
Endemic to arid SW Africa, with an isolated population in E Zimbabwe. The grey head, yellow underparts and broad black gorget are diagnostic within its range. In flight, yellow tip to dark tail is conspicuous. Juv. lacks black gorget, and is dull olive-green, with reduced yellow tail tips. **Habitat:** Shrublands, Karoo scrub, grassland with scattered bushes and suburban gardens. **Status:** Common. **Voice:** Very varied whistles, but usually duetted 'bok-bok-kik'. [G5.15.6]

1

2

3

juv.

olive
morph

juv.

ruddy morph

juv.

4

♀

5

juv.

591

1 MANY-COLOURED BUSH-SHRIKE *Telephorus multicolor*   18-19 cm
A forest bush-shrike with several colour morphs; breast is orange, buff, scarlet or black; belly typically is yellow, but is scarlet in some black-chested birds and buff in buff-breasted birds (S Albertine Rift only). Forms a superspecies with Black-fronted Bush-Shrike; ranges do not overlap. In E Africa, where two ranges are closest, Many-coloured Bush-Shrike always has diagnostic white frons and supercilium. **Habitat:** Primary and secondary forests, up to 2 500 m, foraging high in canopy and at mid-stratum. **Status:** Common; often found in bird parties; more often heard than seen. **Voice:** Diagnostic call of 'choop' followed quickly by ascending 'sshweet'. [C13.66]

2 GORGEOUS (FOUR-COLOURED) BUSH-SHRIKE *Telophorus quadricolor*   18 cm
A stunning, olive-backed bush-shrike with a red throat, black gorget and yellow central breast and belly. Yellow (not red) frons and supercilium separate it from Doherty's Bush-Shrike. Sometimes lumped with Perrin's Bush-Shrike, but has yellow-orange (not red) central breast, belly and vent. Female is duller, with narrower breast band. Juv. has yellow throat and lacks black breast band; differs from juv. Orange-breasted (p. 590) and Black-fronted bush-shrikes by olive (not grey) upperparts. **Habitat:** Dense tangled thickets. **Status:** Common; more often heard than seen. **Voice:** Often-repeated 'kong-kon-kooit'. [G5.15.7]

3 BLACK-FRONTED BUSH-SHRIKE *Telophorus nigrifrons*   18-19 cm
Forms a superspecies with Many-coloured Bush-Shrike; ranges do not overlap. Occurs in several colour morphs: buff-breasted morph is similar to ruddy-morph Olive Bush-Shrike (p. 590), but has black frons (this morph does not occur in area of overlap); never has pale supercilium (as in Orange-breasted (p. 590) and Many-coloured bush-shrikes). Female is duller, with less black on frons. Juv. has buff-olive, barred underparts and pale edges to wing feathers. **Habitat:** Forest canopy and mid-stratum, especially where there are dense tangles of creepers and lianas. **Status:** Fairly common; less skulking than many other bush-shrikes. **Voice:** Harsh 'tic-chrrrr'; ringing 'oo-pooo' call. [C13.67, G5.15.9]

4 DOHERTY'S BUSH-SHRIKE *Telophorus dohertyi*   18 cm
Endemic to E Africa. Differs from Gorgeous and Perrin's bush-shrikes by having a bright red (not yellow and green) forecrown, and yellow (not orange-red) lower breast; ranges do not overlap. Rare yellow morph has bright yellow forecrown and throat, resembling small Bokmakierie (p. 590). Juv. lacks breast band, and has yellow throat and olive-yellow breast and belly. **Habitat:** Montane forests. **Status:** Locally common; very secretive and skulking, rarely coming into open. **Voice:** Rapid version of Gorgeous Bush-Shrike's call. [C13.70]

5 PERRIN'S BUSH-SHRIKE *Telophorus viridis*   18 cm
The W form of Gorgeous Bush-Shrike, with the red extending down the central breast and belly to the vent. Rest of underparts are olive-green (not yellow); ranges do not overlap. Juv. resembles juv. Gorgeous Bush-Shrike. **Habitat:** Dense woodland and thickets, often along watercourses. **Status:** Locally common; very furtive, keeping low in thickets and dense cover. **Voice:** Often repeated variations of 'con qu-eet qu-eet', similar to Gorgeous Bush-Shrike's. [C13.69]

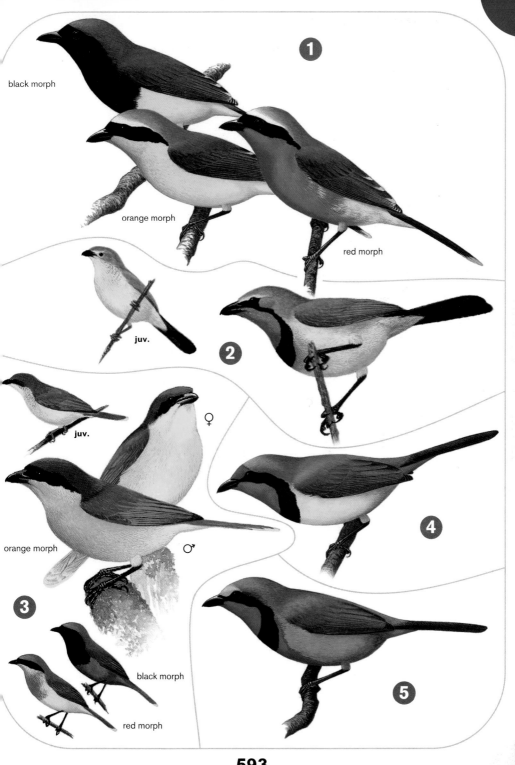

black morph

orange morph

red morph

1

juv.

2

juv.

♀

orange morph

♂

3

black morph

red morph

4

5

593

1 GREY-HEADED BUSH-SHRIKE *Malaconotus blanchoti*   24-26 cm
A large, massive-billed bush-shrike of woodland and riparian thickets. Differs from other large-billed bush-shrikes by habitat, as well as yellow (not whitish) eyes, white lores (not extending behind eye) and variable orange wash across breast. Wing coverts and tertials are narrowly tipped pale yellow-green. Does not occur alongside Lagden's and Monteiro's bush-shrikes so confusion is unlikely with these forest species. Juv. has greyish, barred head and is pale yellow below. **Habitat:** Thickets in acacia savanna and broadleafed woodland. **Status:** Common. **Voice:** Drawn-out 'oooooop' (hence colloquial name 'Ghostbird'); 'tic-tic-oooop'. [C13.74, G6.1.1]

2 MONTEIRO'S BUSH-SHRIKE *Malaconotus monteiri*   25-27 cm
Larger and heavier than Grey-headed Bush-Shrike, with a dark grey (not yellow) eye, yellow (not orange) breast and white lores extending behind and below the eyes. Bill is proportionately larger and thicker. May be more closely related to Fiery-breasted or even Green-breasted bush-shrikes. Juv. is undescribed. **Habitat:** Montane and mid-altitude forests. **Status:** Rare and little known, but locally common in Angolan scarp forests. **Voice:** Ghostly whistle, sometimes accompanied by bill-rattling; very similar to Grey-headed Bush-Shrike.

3 LAGDEN'S BUSH-SHRIKE *Malaconotus lagdeni*   25-26 cm
A montane-forest form of Grey-headed Bush-Shrike, with bright yellow edgings to blackish wing coverts and tertials. W African birds have orange throat; Albertine Rift birds lack orange wash on throat and breast. Differs from rare yellow phase of Fiery-breasted Bush-Shrike by having grey (note pale) lores, yellow-tipped (not plain) wing coverts and no black subterminal tail band. Juv. is grey-brown above and paler below, with whitish throat and faint barring on flanks. **Habitat:** Mid-altitude and montane forests, usually high in canopy. **Status:** Uncommon and little known; easily overlooked unless calling. **Voice:** 1-note whistle, similar to Grey-headed Bush-Shrike's. [C13.72]

4 FIERY-BREASTED BUSH-SHRIKE *Malaconotus cruentus*   25 cm
A large forest bush-shrike with a heavy bill, grey head and mantle, bright orange throat and breast and uniform wing coverts (but has black-and-yellow-tipped tertials). Most widespread large bush-shrike of lowland forest, distinguished from local Lagden's Bush-Shrike by uniform (not yellow-spotted) wing coverts, pale (not grey) lores and black-and-yellow-tipped (not uniform green) tail. Rare yellow morph lacks orange on underparts. Juv. has whitish throat and rufous crown. **Habitat:** Forest canopy, gallery forest, forest edge and secondary growth, sometimes near ground. **Status:** Locally common. **Voice:** 2 bell-like whistles; series of faster whistles, 'ho ho ho ho ho ho'. [C13.71]

5 ULUGURU BUSH-SHRIKE *Malaconotus alius*   22-24 cm
Endemic to Uluguru Mts, Tanzania. A large forest bush-shrike with a diagnostic black head and yellow throat; upperparts are uniform olive. Much larger than yellow morph Black-fronted Bush-Shrike (p. 592), with no orange on the breast. Juv. undescribed. **Habitat:** Montane forest above 1 300 m. **Status:** Endangered. Uncommon and thinly distributed. **Voice:** Haunting 3-5 note whistle with slight rise on last note.

6 GREEN-BREASTED BUSH-SHRIKE *Malaconotus gladiator*   28 cm
Endemic to SW Cameroon and SW Nigeria montane forests. A huge, plain, predominantly green bush-shrike with a grey head and moss-green underparts. Upperparts are uniform olive-green, lacking any yellow feather edgings on wing. Juv. is undescribed. **Habitat:** Montane forest and forest edge, mainly in canopy. **Status:** Vulnerable. Uncommon to locally common. **Voice:** Long, even, mournful whistles, similar to Grey-headed Bush-Shrike's. [C13.73]

juv.

1

2

3

4

5

6

Endemic African family. Social; flight slow on broad wings. Sexes alike; juvs duller.

1 GREY-CRESTED HELMET-SHRIKE *Prionops poliolophus* 24-26 cm
Localised endemic to E Africa. Larger than co-occurring White Helmet-Shrike (*poliocephalus*), with tall, erect, grey hindcrest, black patches on sides of breast and no eye-wattles. **Habitat:** Dry acacia scrub and open woodland. **Status:** Locally common, in small flocks. **Voice:** Bill-snapping; various churring and clicking sounds.

2 WHITE HELMET-SHRIKE *Prionops plumatus* 18-24 cm
A widespread, black-and-white helmet-shrike with an erect whitish forecrown, grey hind-crown, broad white collar, yellow eye-wattles and pink legs. N races have long, forward-curved crest.; smaller than Grey-crested Helmet-Shrike with eye-wattles and entirely white breast. Some E African races lack white wing bars. Juv. is duller, with brown eyes; lacks yellow eye-wattle and black ear coverts. **Habitat:** Mixed woodland and acacia savanna. **Status:** Common resident, with local movements and occasional invasions beyond its normal range. **Voice:** Repeated 'cherow', often taken up by group in chorus. [C14.2a, G6.1.3]

3 YELLOW-CRESTED HELMET-SHRIKE *Prionops alberti* 22-24 cm
Endemic to Albertine Rift. The slightly glossy-black plumage relieved only by a brilliant golden crest makes this species unmistakable (any all-black forest starling or drongo lacks diagnostic yellow crown). **Habitat:** Montane and mid-altitude forest, in mid-storey and forest canopy. **Status:** Vulnerable. Rare and little known; in small groups. **Voice:** Undescribed.

4 GABELA HELMET-SHRIKE *Prionops gabela* 17-18 cm
Endemic to W Angola. Slightly smaller than Retz's Helmet-Shrike, with grey (not brown) back, grey (not black) belly and lower breast, and white wing bar restricted to outer primaries; ranges do not overlap. **Habitat:** Forest, forest edge and woodland. **Status:** Endangered. Little known. **Voice:** Similar to Retz's Helmet-Shrike's.

5 RETZ'S (RED-BILLED) HELMET-SHRIKE *Prionops retzii* 19-21 cm
A black-bodied helmet-shrike with brown back and wing coverts, and red bill and legs. Larger and darker than Chestnut-fronted Helmet-Shrike, with black crown and red (not blue) eye wattles. Very similar to localised Gabela Helmet-Shrike. Juv. is paler, with brown eye-ring, bill and legs; difficult to separate from juv. Chestnut-fronted Helmet-Shrike. **Habitat:** Woodland, and riparian forest. **Status:** Common; in groups of 2-10 birds, often in bird parties. **Voice:** Harsh grating calls. [C14.4a, G6.1.4]

6 GABON (RUFOUS-BELLIED) HELMET-SHRIKE *Prionops rufiventris* 20-22 cm
Often treated as a race of Red-billed Helmet-Shrike, but has grey throat, more richly coloured belly sharply divided from narrow white breast band, and smaller bill; ranges do not overlap. **Habitat:** Lowland and mid-altitude forest. **Status:** Locally common; in small, noisy family groups; frequently in bird parties. **Voice:** Bubbling, popping and churring notes. [C14.3b]

7 CHESTNUT-FRONTED HELMET-SHRIKE *Prionops scopifrons* 16-18 cm
Superficially similar to Retz's Helmet-Shrike, but is smaller and greyer, and has diagnostic bristly chestnut forehead and blue (not red) eye-wattles. Juv. is uniform grey, and lacks chestnut forehead; difficult to separate from juv. Retz's Helmet-Shrike. **Habitat:** Lowland forests. **Status:** Uncommon, in small groups; often joins groups of Retz's Helmet-Shrikes. **Voice:** Repeated 'churee', with bill-snapping and other notes. [G6.1.5]

8 RED-BILLED HELMET-SHRIKE *Prionops caniceps* 20-22 cm
Endemic to W Africa. The glossy-black upperparts, blue-grey head and rich buff-and-white underparts are diagnostic. Black throat, larger red bill and broad white breast merging gradually into buffy belly separate it from Gabon Helmet-Shrike; ranges do not overlap. In flight, has white wing bar. Nominate race in W has black cheeks; *E harterti* has grey cheeks. Juv. is browner, with whitish crown. **Habitat:** Lowland and mid-altitude forest, in mid-storey and forest canopy. **Status:** Locally common; in small, noisy flocks, often with bird parties. **Voice:** Very vocal: chorus, pops and bill-snapping. [C14.3a]

Medium-large passerines, often with some glossy plumage. Most are fairly easy to identify, but care is needed with the red-winged complex, and especially the glossy starlings, where identification often depends on subtle tones of iridescent plumage, which varies with light conditions and angle. Often gregarious. Sexes alike in most species; juvs duller.

1 COPPER-TAILED STARLING *Lamprotornis cupreocauda* 21 cm
Endemic to Upper Guinea forests. A small forest glossy starling identified by its rather short tail, broad wings, dark purple head and breast, and dark blue upperparts. Differs from Purple-headed Starling by having yellow (not dark) eyes and dark blue (not dark green) back; ranges do not overlap. Much smaller and shorter-tailed than Splendid Glossy Starling. Juv. duller, blackish brown. **Habitat:** Forest canopy, gallery forest and forest edge. **Status:** Locally common. **Voice:** Usual flight call is 'chreet'; other chirps and warbles at roosts. [C14.15]

2 PURPLE-HEADED STARLING *Lamprotornis purpureiceps* 20 cm
Closely resembles Copper-tailed Starling but has dark (not yellow) eyes and dark green (not dark blue) back; ranges are not known to overlap. Best told from much larger Splendid Glossy Starling by its dark eyes, short tail, and dark purple head and breast. In flight, has a distinctive shape due to its broad wings and relatively short tail. Juv. duller. **Habitat:** Forest canopy, gallery forest, tall trees in secondary growth and plantations. **Status:** Common. **Voice:** 'Chink chink' flight call; chirps and warbles when roosting. [C14.16]

3 PRÌNCIPÉ GLOSSY STARLING *Lamprotornis ornatus* 30 cm
Endemic to Prìncipé Island. Slightly larger than Splendid Glossy Starling with dark blackish-green (not dark blue) underparts and bronze (not dark blue) wing coverts. Both species have white eyes and make a whooshing flight noise. Juv. duller with blackish-brown underparts, darker below than juv. Splendid Glossy Starling. **Habitat:** Forest, plantations, secondary growth and gardens. **Status:** Common. **Voice:** Similar range of notes as Splendid Glossy Starling. [C14.23]

4 BLACK-BELLIED STARLING *Lamprotornis corruscus* 18-21 cm
Endemic to E coast forests. The smallest and least glossy of the glossy starlings, with a black belly and flanks. Male has bronze gloss on belly which is visible at close range, and has red (not yellow-orange) eyes for short period during breeding season. Female and juv. are duller; appear black in the field. **Habitat:** Coastal and riverine forests. **Status:** Locally common; irregular visitor in extreme S of range. **Voice:** Harsh, chippering notes interspersed with shrill whistles. [G6.2.8]

5 SPLENDID GLOSSY STARLING *Lamprotornis splendidus* 25-28 cm
A large, short-tailed glossy starling with extravagantly glossy plumage. Longer-tailed than Purple Glossy Starling, with white (not orange) eyes. Differs from Prìncipé Glossy Starling by having dark blue (not bronze) wing coverts and dark blue (not dark blackish-green) under-parts. In flight, wings make loud whooshing noise. Female has less prominent bronzy breast band and coppery neck patches are much smaller. Juv. duller, with paler brown underparts than juv. Prìncipé Glossy Starling. **Habitat:** Lowland and mid-altitude rainforest, secondary growth and adjacent farmlands and gardens. **Status:** Locally common to abundant, sometimes in large flocks. **Voice:** Very noisy in flocks: drawn-out, cat-like, nasal 'mi aaar' and 'cho waaaa'; parrot-like 'kreee-aaak'. [C14.24]

6 PURPLE GLOSSY STARLING *Lamprotornis purpureus* 26 cm
A savanna glossy starling of W and C Africa, easily identified by its flat head, long bill, disproportionately large orange eye and short tail. It is entirely glossy purple on head and underparts. Appears short-tailed and broad winged in flight. Juv. duller with grey eyes and sooty underparts. **Habitat:** Wooded savanna and galleries in savanna. **Status:** Common. **Voice:** Jumbled series of warbles and chirps; 'skaar' call. [C14.17]

1 CAPE (RED-SHOULDERED) GLOSSY STARLING *Lamprotornis nitens* 25 cm
A compact glossy starling that differs from blue-eared starlings by its uniformly glossy green ear patches and head and glossy green belly and flanks (lacks blue or magenta flanks). Larger than Black-bellied Starling (p. 598), with much brighter, shinier plumage; belly glossy green (not dull black). Juv. is duller, with straw-yellow (not bright orange-yellow) eyes. **Habitat:** Savanna, mixed woodland and gardens; often in quite arid regions. **Status:** Common. **Voice:** Song is slurred 'trrr-chree-chrrrr'. [C14.18]

2 BRONZE-TAILED STARLING *Lamprotornis chalcurus* 20-23 cm
Similar to Greater Blue-eared Starling, but with darker orange-yellow eyes and a shorter tail which has a bronze (not bluish) iridescence. Other features are bluer upperparts, brighter purple belly, and purple rump which contrasts with tail. Blue-green (not purple) head and breast separate it from Purple-headed Starling (p. 598). Juv. dull sooty brown with grey eye. **Habitat:** Savanna, usually in more mesic areas than Greater Blue-eared Starling. **Status:** Locally common, often in flocks with Lesser Blue-eared Starlings. **Voice:** Similar to Greater Blue-eared Starling's, but harsher and more raspy. [C14.19]

3 GREATER BLUE-EARED STARLING *Lamprotornis chalybaeus* 23-24 cm
Larger than Lesser and Miombo blue-eared starlings, with broader ear patch and blue (not magenta) belly and flanks. Longer-tailed than Bronze-tailed Starling, with a paler yellow eye. Distinguished from Cape Glossy Starling by its broad, dark blue (not green) ear patch and blue (not green) belly and flanks. Juv. is less glossy; is blue (not chestnut) below, which separates it from Lesser and Miombo blue-eared starlings. **Habitat:** Savanna and mopane woodland. **Status:** Common. **Voice:** Distinctive, nasal 'squee-aar' (unlike any call of Cape Glossy Starling); warbled song. [C14.20, G6.2.5]

4 MIOMBO BLUE-EARED STARLING *Lamprotornis elisabeth* 18-20 cm
Smaller than Greater Blue-eared Starling, with a more compact head and a finer bill. Dark blue ear patch is less extensive; appears as black line through the eye. Belly and flanks are magenta (not blue). Juv. has distinctive rusty-brown underparts (darker than juv. Lesser Blue-eared Starling), becoming mottled blue-and-brown in imms. Formerly considered a race of Lesser Blue-eared Starling; ranges do not overlap. **Habitat:** Confined to miombo woodland. **Status:** Common. **Voice:** Higher pitched than that of Greater Blue-eared Starling; 'wirri-girri' flight call. [C14.21, G6.2.6]

5 LESSER BLUE-EARED STARLING *Lamprotornis chloropterus* 18-20 cm
Recently split from very similar Miombo Blue-eared Starling; ranges do not overlap. Smaller than Greater Blue-eared Starling, with a more confined and narrower blue ear patch and shorter, thinner bill. Juv. has diagnostic chestnut underparts, paler than juv. Miombo Blue-eared Starling's. **Habitat:** Favours wooded savanna but is found in wide range of wooded and bushed areas. **Status:** Locally common, in flocks outside breeding season. **Call.** Higher pitched than Greater Blue-eared Starling's and less slurred; flight call 'wirrri-girrri'.

6 SHARP-TAILED STARLING *Lamprotornis acuticaudus* 26 cm
Endemic to SC Africa. Difficult to distinguish from the other short-tailed, glossy starlings unless the diagnostic wedge-shaped tail is seen. In flight, underside of primaries appears pale (not black as in other glossy starlings). Male's eye is red, female's is orange. Juv. is duller, greyish below with buff-edged feathers. **Habitat:** Dry, broadleafed woodland and dry riverbeds. **Status:** Generally uncommon; often in small flocks. **Voice:** Reedy 'chwee-chwee-chwee' in a flock. [C14.22, G6.2.7]

1 BURCHELL'S STARLING *Lamprotornis australis*   32-34 cm
Endemic to S Africa. The largest glossy starling. More heavily built than Meves's Starling, with broader, more rounded wings and shorter, broader tail. Eye dark. At close range has finely barred tail. Juv. duller with sooty black underparts. **Habitat:** Savanna and dry broadleafed woodland. **Status:** Common. **Voice:** Song is jumble of throaty chortles and chuckles. [G6.2.2]

2 MEVES'S STARLING *Lamprotornis mevesii*   34-36 cm
Endemic to SC Africa. Smaller-bodied than Burchell's Starling, with much longer tail. Dark (not pale) eye separates it from Rüppell's Starling; tail longer and more pointed. Female is smaller. Juv. duller with brownish head and underparts, but long, pointed tail is evident. Very rare pale grey morph could be confused with Ashy Starling. **Habitat:** Tall mopane woodland and riverine forest. **Status:** Locally common. **Voice:** Harsh 'keeeaaaa' and churring notes. [G6.2.3]

3 LONG-TAILED STARLING *Lamprotornis caudatus*   34 cm
The only long-tailed glossy starling of W and C Africa, with glossy green upperparts and violet tail. Range overlaps slightly with Rüppell's Starling in Sudan; differs by its larger size, longer tail, green (not violet-blue) upperparts and tail. Eye whitish. **Habitat:** Dry wooded savanna, with some seasonal movements to the S. **Status:** Common. **Voice:** Variable glossy-starling-like squeaks and chortles. [C14.25]

4 RÜPPELL'S STARLING *Lamprotornis purpuropterus*   27-31 cm
Endemic to NE Africa. A large, long-tailed glossy starling with pale eyes. Less brightly coloured and iridescent than Splendid and Purple glossy starlings (p. 598), with a much longer, graduated tail. Overlaps with Long-tailed Starling in Sudan; differs in shorter, violet (not green) tail and blue (not green) back. Smaller and shorter-tailed than Meves's Starling, with pale (not dark) eyes. Juv. duller with dark eyes. **Habitat:** Open woodland, farmland, old cultivation and around human habitation. **Status:** Common. **Voice:** Variable harsh shrieks and whistles, with some very parrot-like screeching. [C14.26]

5 GOLDEN-BREASTED STARLING *Cosmopsarus regius*   30 cm
Endemic to NE Africa. Arguably the best-looking starling; adult is unmistakable, with golden lower breast, belly and undertail coverts, and long, graduated tail. Juv. duller, with shorter tail and grey (not white) iris. **Habitat:** Arid and semi-arid bushed grasslands, mostly below 1 200 m. Habituated around some safari lodges. **Status:** Locally common; usually in skittish, small groups. **Voice:** Drawn-out 'cherrreeeeeta-cherrreee'.

6 ASHY STARLING *Cosmopsarus unicolor*   28-30 cm
Endemic to Tanzania. A long-tailed starling with diagnostic grey-brown plumage and long, graduated tail. Could be confused with aberrant grey morph of Meves's Starling. At close range, shows greenish gloss on wing coverts and tail, and pale creamy eye. Juv. is more brownish-grey with a darker head. **Habitat:** Dry bush and open woodland, farmlands and wooded grasslands. **Status:** Locally common, in small groups or pairs. **Voice:** Usually silent; soft 2-note whistle and harsher, more grating call in flocks in flight.

1 CHESTNUT-BELLIED STARLING *Lamprotornis pulcher*   18 cm
The only rufous-bellied starling in most of its range. Pale (not red) eyes and brownish (not glossy) head separate it from Hildebrandt's and Shelley's starlings; lacks white breast band of Superb Starling. Shows pale panel in primaries in flight. Vaguely resembles juv. Lesser Blue-eared Starling (p. 600), but has distinct dark head and breast. **Habitat:** Arid Sahelian acacia savanna. **Status:** Common resident and intra-African migrant; numbers decreasing in E of range. **Voice:** Warbled song; 'whirri whirri' contact call. [C14.27]

2 SUPERB STARLING *Lamprotornis superbus*   18 cm
Endemic to NE Africa. Differs from Shelley's and Hildebrandt's starlings by its white band across breast, white (not dark) vent, and white (not dark) eye. Juv. has dark eye and lacks white breast band, but has white (not dark) vent. Range does not overlap with Chestnut-bellied Starling. **Habitat:** Open scrub and woodland, including gardens and cultivated areas, mostly below 2 200 m. **Status:** Common. **Voice:** Protracted warbling song that includes trilling and chattering; mimics other birds.

3 SHELLEY'S STARLING *Lamprotornis shelleyi*   16 cm
Endemic to NE Africa. Darker and slightly smaller than Hildebrandt's Starling with much darker rich-chestnut (not pale rufous) lower breast and belly. Lacks white breast band of Superb Starling. Juv. has dark vent (not white, as in juv. Superb Starling). Juv. is distinguished from juv. Hildebrandt's Starling by its grey-brown (not brown) head and back. **Habitat:** Semi-arid scrub and woodland, usually below 1 000 m. **Status:** Uncommon intra-African migrant breeding in N of range. **Voice:** Similar to Superb Starling's but louder and harsher.

4 HILDEBRANDT'S STARLING *Lamprotornis hildebrandti*   18 cm
Endemic to E Africa. Adult could be confused with adult Shelley's Starling, but has pale rufous (not rich chestnut-brown) lower breast and belly. Differs from juv. Superb Starling by having dark (not white) vent. Juv. is distinguished from juv. Shelley's Starling by brown (not grey-brown) head and back. **Habitat:** Open bush and savanna; also around human habitation; mostly 700-1 700 m. **Status:** Locally common resident. **Voice:** Song is slow and varied, alternating creaking sounds and whistles: 'cherrah-cherrah, squirk, kwerra-kwerra, eeeeek, querk'.

5 FISCHER'S STARLING *Spreo fischeri*   17-19 cm
Endemic to NE Africa. An unmistakable grey-and-white starling. Vaguely resembles non-breeding Wattled Starling (p. 612) but has dark (not pale) rump and a clearly demarcated dark breast. Lacks white wing patches of imm. Magpie Starling (p. 606), and is grey (not brownish). Smaller than White-crowned Starling, with white (not brown) belly. **Habitat:** Open, semi-arid woodland, farmlands and old cultivations. **Status:** Locally common, sometimes in flocks. **Voice:** Flocks chatter incessantly; song is series of high-pitched trills.

6 AFRICAN PIED STARLING *Spreo bicolor*   27-28 cm
Endemic to S Africa. A large, dark brown starling with a conspicuous white vent and under-tail coverts. At close range, has exaggerated yellow gape, creamy white eyes and glossy sheen on wings. In flight, has paler panels in primaries. Juv. is matt black, with dark eye. **Habitat:** Grassland and Karoo scrub, often around farmyards and stock. Frequently perches on sheep and other animals. **Status:** Common; usually in flocks. Breeds colonially in holes in banks. **Voice:** Loud 'skeer-kerrra-kerrra'; warbling song. [G6.1.9]

7 WHITE-CROWNED STARLING *Spreo albicapillus*   23 cm
Endemic to NE Africa. A large starling with a distinctive white crown and wing bar, dull bronze upperparts and white-streaked brown throat, breast and belly. Eyes white. Much larger than Fischer's Starling, with cleanly defined white crown. Juv. has dark iris and pale tawny crown, brown-tipped yellow bill and reduced streaking below. **Habitat:** Arid and semi-arid bush up to 1 500 m; also around cattle pastures and human settlements. **Status:** Locally common resident. **Voice:** Shrill 'tschurreeet' or 'chew-chew, tshurreeet'.

juv.

605

1 SHARPE'S STARLING *Pholia sharpii* 15-17 cm

Endemic to NE Africa. An unmistakable black-and-white forest starling, told from Abbott's Starling by its white (not black) throat and breast. Lacks black throat and white in wings of Magpie Starling. Belly washed buff. Female less glossy above. Juv. resembles female Violet-backed Starling but differs by being less well streaked on underparts and having much darker upperparts. **Habitat:** Mid-altitude and montane forests. **Status:** Uncommon and thinly distributed, usually in small flocks. **Voice:** Diagnostic sharp 'chiink'; song is series of musical notes, similar to Forest Weaver's song.

2 ABBOTT'S STARLING *Pholia femoralis* 16-18 cm

Endemic to E Africa. Appears similar to Magpie Starling, but occurs in highland forests (not arid savanna); differs also by lacking white in wings and has pale yellow (not red) eyes. Black throat and breast separate it from Sharpe's Starling. Female and juv. browner with streaked belly. **Habitat:** Mid-altitude and montane forests. **Status:** Vulnerable. Uncommon and localised in Kenya and Tanzania; sometimes in large flocks at fruiting trees, but usually in small groups. **Voice:** Song is jumbled series of whistled and scratchy phrases, similar to Dark-backed Weaver's.

3 VIOLET-BACKED (PLUM-COLOURED, AMETHYST) STARLING
Cinnyricinclus leucogaster 15-17 cm

Male readily identified by its stunning, glossy amethyst upperparts, throat and upper breast; this colour may vary with wear from bluish to coppery. Female and juv. are unique among African starlings in having heavily streaked plumage; more likely to be confused with other passerines. **Habitat:** Most woodland, but avoids dense forest. **Status:** Common resident and intra-African migrant. **Voice:** Soft but sharp 'tip, tip'; song is short series of buzzy whistles. [C14.29, G6.2.1]

4 EMERALD STARLING *Coccycolius iris* 19 cm

Endemic to Upper Guinea region. A small, short-tailed starling with bright emerald green plumage, dark purple ear patches, and purple lower breast to belly. Its brown eyes and green plumage distinguish it from all savanna glossy starlings. **Habitat:** Wooded savanna and forest-savanna mosaic. **Status:** Local and generally uncommon. **Voice:** Usually silent; long, raspy whistle before flying.

5 WHITE-COLLARED STARLING *Grafisia torquata* 23 cm

A small, compact, localised starling usually found in tree canopies. Male is the only starling with a conspicuous white band across the breast (recalls Ring Ouzel). Female is grey-brown, with indistinct mottling on upperparts and scaling on underparts. Both sexes have conspicuous yellow eyes. **Habitat:** Grassy savanna with palm trees, well-wooded savanna, edge of forest at higher altitudes, gallery forest in savanna country, forest clearings on migration. **Status:** Locally common. **Voice:** Variable soft chortles and whistles.

6 MAGPIE STARLING *Speculipastor bicolor* 17-19 cm

Endemic to NE Africa. Most likely to be confused with Abbott's Starling, but has obvious white wing patches and red (not pale yellow) eyes, and occurs in very different habitat. Much smaller and darker than Fischer's Starling (p. 604), with distinctive white wing patches. Male glossy balck above and on breast; female grey-brown. Juv. might be confused with non-breeding Wattled Starling (p. 612), but shows white wing patches. **Habitat:** Dry thorn-bush and open wooded savanna. **Status:** Locally common resident, nomad and intra-African migrant; non-breeding visitor to S of range; usually in small groups. **Voice:** Jumbled babbling and twittering.

juv.

1 RED-WINGED STARLING *Onychognathus morio*   27-30 cm
The common rufous-winged starling of S and E Africa. Much smaller and shorter-tailed than Bristle-crowned Starling (p. 610), and lacks the forward-facing crown feathers. Larger-bodied and shorter-tailed than Slender-billed Starling, with a heavier bill. The bright chestnut flight feathers and dark red (not orange) eyes separate it from Pale-winged Starling (p. 610). Female has ash-grey head and upper breast. Juv. resembles male but has dark head. **Habitat:** Rocky ravines, cliffs and gardens. Disperses widely when not breeding. **Status:** Common. **Voice:** Clear, whistled 'cherleeeeoo'; variety of musical whistles and harsh, grating alarm call. [C14.12, G6.2.9]

2 NEUMANN'S STARLING *Onychognathus neumanni*   25 cm
The only rufous-winged starling of the N savannas of W and C Africa, generally limited to rocky areas. Formerly considered a race of Red-winged Starling, but has a heavier bill and forward-facing feathers covering the nostrils like Bristle-crowned and White-billed starlings (p. 610). Female has grey head. **Habitat:** Savannas with rocks and cliffs for breeding; near towns in some parts of range. **Status:** Locally common. **Voice:** Whistles similar to Red-winged Starling's. [C14.12]

3 SÃO TOMÉ CHESTNUT-WINGED STARLING *Onychognathus fulgidus*   35 cm
Endemic to São Tomé; often considered a race of Chestnut-winged Starling, but is larger. A large forest chestnut-winged starling, with a heavy, long bill and long graduated tail. Female's head streaked and grey. Juv. duller. **Habitat:** Forest canopy, plantations and secondary growth, from sea level to 1 500 m. **Status:** Common. **Voice:** Various loud whistled 'tuip' and harsher 'ah raap' notes, quite unlike Chestnut-winged Starling.

4 CHESTNUT-WINGED STARLING *Onychognathus hartlaubi*   30 cm
The common chestnut-winged forest starling of W and C Africa. Habitat and more slender bill separate it from Neumann's Starling. Much larger than Narrow-tailed Starling (p. 610), and has much longer, graduated tail than Waller's Starling (p. 610). Female's head is grey, streaked with black. **Habitat:** Forest canopy, gallery forest, edge of forest, tall trees in secondary growth and plantations. **Status:** Common. **Voice:** Loud, whistled 'tuwee'. [C14.13]

5 SLENDER-BILLED STARLING *Onychognathus tenuirostris*   29-33 cm
Differs from other similar-sized rufous-winged starlings by its very long and thin bill and relatively long tail. Longer tailed than Red-winged Starling, with a longer and thinner bill; usually occurs at higher elevations. Much smaller than Bristle-crowned Starling (p. 610), with a shorter tail and no forward-facing feathers forming a bump on its forehead. **Habitat:** Associated with rivers and waterfalls; sometimes breeds on bridges. **Status:** Locally common, but patchily distributed. **Voice:** Similar 'chleeoo' whistles to Red-winged Starling's; jumbled song of repeated whistled notes. [C14.14]

6 SOMALI STARLING *Onychognathus blythii*   28-30 cm
Endemic to NE Africa. Differs from both Slender-billed and Red-winged starlings by having the two central tail feathers projecting well beyond the end of the long, graduated tail. Appears longer tailed than other red-winged starlings except much larger Bristle-crowned Starling (p. 610). At close range, head of female is uniform greyish brown, lacking streaking of related starlings. **Habitat:** From sea level to high mountains. Feeds on nectar of flowering Lobelias and Knipofias. **Status:** Little known but locally common. **Voice:** Similar to fluty whistles of Red-winged Starling.

7 SOCOTRA STARLING *Onychognathus frater*   25 cm
Endemic to Socotra Island. Similar to Somali Starling, but smaller, with a relatively short (not long and graduated) tail, and lacks grey on head. Sexes alike. **Habitat:** Favours wooded areas, but also found on rocky cliffs and in agricultural areas, towns and villages. **Status:** Uncommon. **Voice:** Far-carrying 'tyooooo'.

609

1 BRISTLE-CROWNED STARLING *Onychognathus salvadorii*   40-42 cm
Endemic to NE Africa. The largest rufous-winged starling, with an extremely long tail and noticeable bump on its forehead formed by its bristle of forward-facing feathers. Female has a shorter tail, greyish head and smaller bump on forehead. **Habitat:** Cliffs and gullies, usually in semi-arid areas. **Status:** Locally common; in small groups. **Voice:** Short, repeated whistles; harsher, raspy call.

2 WALLER'S STARLING *Onychognathus walleri*   23 cm
The smallest of the rufous-winged forest starlings, with a rather short tail and dark glossy plumage. Larger than *Poeoptera* starlings, with dark red (not pale) eyes, more conspicuous rufous wing patches and broader tail. Female is greyer, less glossy on head and underparts. **Habitat:** Montane forest canopy and forest edge, 900-3 000 m. **Status:** Common. **Voice:** Far-carrying, whistled 'wee-ooo' and harsh 'chwaa' notes. [C14.11]

3 PALE-WINGED STARLING *Onychognathus nabouroup*   26-28 cm
Endemic to SW Africa. Told from Red-winged Starling (p. 608) by its whitish (not chestnut) patches in primaries (visible only in flight), square (not graduated) tail and bright orange (not dark red) eyes. Sexes alike; juv. duller. **Habitat:** Rocky ravines and cliffs in semi-arid and arid regions; non-breeding flocks wander to more mesic areas. **Status:** Common resident and local nomad; sometimes forms mixed flocks with Red-winged Starlings. **Voice:** Ringing 'preeoo' in flight. [G6.2.10]

4 WHITE-BILLED STARLING *Onychognathus albirostris*   25 cm
Endemic to Abyssinian highlands, where it is distinguished from all other rufous-winged starlings by its short, square tail and white bill. Male has all-black head; female has head and underparts ashy grey; juv. resembles male. **Habitat:** Cliffs and gorges above 1 800 m, usually near waterfalls; also in moorland with Giant Lobelias. **Status:** Locally common resident; flocks in non-breeding season (up to 40 birds), feeding on juniper fruits and figs, sometimes together with White-collared Pigeons. **Voice:** Typically a whistled 'cheee-up', shorter and less melodious than Red-winged Starling's; alarm call is harsh 'charr'.

5 NARROW-TAILED STARLING *Poeoptera lugubris*   24 cm
A tiny forest starling, much smaller than rufous-winged starlings. In Albertine Rift, told from Stuhlmann's Starling by its long, narrow, pointed tail. Male has dark blue-black plumage with greyish (not rufous) wings; female is greyer, with narrow rufous primary bases, visible only in flight. **Habitat:** Forest canopy and tall dead trees in secondary growth, often in association with *Gymnobucco* barbets. **Status:** Locally common. **Voice:** Whistled 'chuwee'; high-pitched trills. [C14.9]

6 KENRICK'S STARLING *Poeoptera kenricki*   18-19 cm
Endemic to E Africa. Smaller and more slender than similar Waller's Starling, with a narrower tail. Male all dark; female has small rufous wing patch (smaller than rufous-winged starlings). Range does not overlap with very similar Stuhlmann's Starling. **Habitat:** Mainly in canopy of various forest types, chiefly mid-altitude and montane. **Status:** Common, sometimes in large flocks around fruiting trees. **Voice:** In flocks, gives continuous, musical murmur; distinctive 'pleep pleep' flight call.

7 STUHLMANN'S STARLING *Poeoptera stuhlmanni*   17-18 cm
Endemic to NE Africa and Albertine Rift. Could be confused with Waller's Starling, but is smaller and more slender, with a longer and narrower tail. Kenrick's Starling is almost identical, but male has blue-black (not sooty black) plumage; ranges do not overlap. Male all dark; female has small rufous wing patch (only visible in flight). **Habitat:** Various forest types, mainly in high canopy and frequently perching on dead emergent branches. **Status:** Common in some areas, sometimes abundant in fruiting-treed regions. **Voice:** Usual flight call is bee-eater-like 'trrup'; song is jumbled whistles and chirrups. [C14.10]

1 WATTLED STARLING *Creatophora cinerea* 19-21 cm
Breeding male is unmistakable: very pale grey body, with black-and-yellow head, and black wattles, wings and tail. Female and imm. are darker grey, with characteristic whitish rump. Juv. is browner. **Habitat:** Grassland, savanna and open woodland. Often perches on livestock. **Status:** Common resident and nomad; often in large flocks; breeds colonially; regularly joins flocks of other starlings. **Voice:** Various hisses and cackles; 'sreeeeo' note. [C14.30, G6.1.10]

2 WHITE-WINGED BABBLING STARLING *Neocichla gutturalis* 18-20 cm
Localised endemic to C Africa, with several disjunct populations. An unusual starling, most similar to Wattled Starling, but is browner, with conspicuous white wing patches and blackish bib. **Habitat:** Mainly miombo woodland with little or no undergrowth. When alarmed, will fly into mid-canopy to scold intruders. **Status:** Common but thinly distributed; usually in groups, feeding on ground. **Voice:** Loud, wheezy chattering.

3 COMMON (EUROPEAN) STARLING *Sturnus vulgaris* 20-22 cm
Introduced from Europe to S Africa. Male is easily identified by its yellow beak and by glossy black plumage speckled with white. Female has paler abdomen and is more speckled. Juv. resembles female Wattled Starling but is uniformly grey, lacks pale rump, and has dark bill. **Habitat:** Wide range, from cities to open farmland, but always close to human habitation. **Status:** Common in S Africa; Palearctic migrant in N Mauritania. **Voice:** Song includes mimicry, whistles and chattering. [C4.67, G6.1.7]

4 COMMON (INDIAN) MYNA *Acridotheres tristis* 25 cm
Introduced from Asia; restricted to S Africa in region. Easily identified by its chestnut plumage, white wing patches, white tail tips and bare yellow facial skin. Moulting adults sometimes lose most of their head feathers and head then appears all yellow. Juv is paler. **Habitat:** Urban and suburban regions. **Status:** Locally common. **Voice:** Jumbled titters and chattering. [G6.1.8]

OXPECKERS
Slender, long-winged and long-tailed relatives of starlings. Specialists, gleaning ticks and other ectoparasites from large mammals, with laterally compressed bill; also take blood and tissue from wounds. Roost communally, usually in dead trees. Flight is swift and direct. Sexes alike; juvs duller.

5 YELLOW-BILLED OXPECKER *Buphagus africanus* 19-22 cm
Paler than Red-billed Oxpecker and easily identified by its deeper, bright yellow bill with a red tip, as well as by the pale lower back and rump. Juv. has brown (not black) bill and is paler than juv. Red-billed Oxpecker with a paler rump. **Habitat:** Savanna and broadleafed woodland, often near water. Frequently found in association with buffalo, rhino, hippo and livestock. **Status:** Locally common; usually in flocks. **Voice:** Short, hissing 'kriss, kriss'. [C14.31, G6.3.1]

6 RED-BILLED OXPECKER *Buphagus erythrorhynchus* 19-21 cm
Distinguished from Yellow-billed Oxpecker by its all-red bill, the bare yellow skin around the eyes and the dark (not pale) rump. Juv. has paler base to blackish bill and is darker than juv. Yellow-billed Oxpecker, with dark (not pale) rump. **Habitat:** Savanna, in association with game and cattle. **Status:** Locally common; usually in flocks. **Voice:** Scolding 'churrrr'; hissing 'zzzzzzist'. [C14.32, G6.3.2]

1 br. ♂ non-br.

2

juv.

non-br.

br.

3

4

5

6

SUGARBIRDS

Large, long-tailed nectar-feeding birds, superficially similar to Australasian honey-eaters. Distantly related to sunbirds, but usually placed in their own family, endemic to S Africa. Sexes similar, but females and juvs have shorter tails.

1 GURNEY'S SUGARBIRD *Promerops gurneyi*   m 25-29 cm; f 23 cm
Endemic to S Africa. Smaller than Cape Sugarbird, with a shorter tail, and conspicuous russet breast and crown; lacks malar stripes. Ranges only rarely overlap in E Cape. **Habitat:** Stands of flowering proteas and aloes in mountainous regions. **Status:** Common, localised resident; some move to lower altitudes in winter. **Voice:** Rattling song, higher pitched and more melodious than Cape Sugarbird's. [G6.3.4]

2 CAPE SUGARBIRD *Promerops cafer*   m 34-44 cm; f 28 cm
Endemic to South Africa. Resembles a giant sunbird with a long, shaggy tail. Differs from Gurney's Sugarbird by distinct malar stripes and lacks russet breast and crown. Male's tail length varies, 1,5-3 times body length; female and juv. tail usually 1-1,5 times body length. Often has yellow, pollen-stained crown. **Habitat:** Fynbos; visits gardens and coastal scrub after breeding. **Status:** Common. **Voice:** Rattling song, including starling-like chirps and whistles; harsh, grating noises. [G6.3.3]

SUNBIRDS

Small, active, warbler-like birds with decurved bills adapted for taking nectar from flowers. Most species have some iridescent plumage. Sexes differ in most species; juvs usually resemble females, and some males have a drab eclipse plumage.

3 GIANT SUNBIRD *Dreptes thomensis*   18-23 cm
Endemic to São Tomé. Sexes are alike. A huge, dark blue-black sunbird with whitish tail tips. Remarkably long, curved bill used creeper-like to probe bark for insects. **Habitat:** Montane and lowland forest, from understorey to canopy. **Status:** Vulnerable. Locally common. **Voice:** An atypical sunbird song; rather deep and melodious 'swee woo wee woo wee'. [C12.76]

4 NEWTON'S (YELLOW-BREASTED) SUNBIRD *Anabathmis newtonii*   11 cm
Endemic to São Tomé; the only small sunbird on the island. Male has a glossy blue-and-violet throat and upper breast contrasting with a bright yellow lower breast. Female has grey-brown throat, streaked breast and pale yellow belly. Both sexes have small white outer-tail tips. **Habitat:** Forest, plantations, secondary growth and gardens. **Status:** Common. **Voice:** High pitched 'swit-errr swit-errr' and 'chip chip' chitter. [C12.75]

5 PRÌNCIPÉ SUNBIRD *Anabathmis hartlaubii*   14 cm
Endemic to Prìncipé. Male is dull olive, with a glossy dark-blue throat and upper breast. Pectoral tufts and underwing coverts are whitish; tail is graduated, with whitish outer-tail tips. Female is drab olive-brown; darker than Olive Sunbird (p. 622), with a graduated tail and white outer-tail tips. **Habitat:** Forest, plantations and secondary growth. **Status:** Common. **Voice:** Ascending 'sweet sweet'; also high pitched 'wit wit' call. [C12.74]

6 ORANGE-BREASTED SUNBIRD *Anthobaphes violacea*   m 15 cm; f 12 cm
Endemic to South Africa. The dark green head, orange-yellow breast and belly, and elongated central tail feathers of male are diagnostic. Female is olive-green above and yellow-green below (not grey-brown like female Southern Double-collared Sunbird; p. 638). **Habitat:** Fynbos and adjacent gardens. **Status:** Common. **Voice:** Call metallic, nasal twang; rapid 'ticks' given in pursuit flight; song subdued jumble of notes; mimics other species. [G6.3.7]

7 GOLDEN-WINGED SUNBIRD *Nectarinia reichenowi*   m 24 cm; f 13 cm
Endemic to E Africa. Both male and female have golden edges to the wing and tail feathers, forming a large wing patch. Male has a bronze head and body, and elongate central tail streamers. Bill is sickle-shaped, with a deep base. Juv. is duller, but has yellow wing patches. **Habitat:** Forest edge, gardens and fields, 1 200-3 000 m. **Status:** Locally common. **Voice:** Continuous 'cher cher cher' and harsher, clipped 'chik chik' notes. [C13.23]

1 MALACHITE SUNBIRD *Nectarinia famosa* m 25 cm; f 14 cm
A large, long-billed sunbird. Breeding male has metallic-green plumage with yellow pectoral tufts (only visible when displaying) and elongated central tail feathers (shorter and thicker than Scarlet-tufted Sunbird's tail streamers). Female is rather pale, with diffuse streaking on the breast, a small supercilium, a prominent pale yellow moustachial stripe and white outer-tail; lacks pectoral tufts. Eclipse male resembles female, but often has a few green feathers. **Habitat:** Fynbos, grassland and mountain scrub; sea-level in S to 3 500 m in N. **Status:** Common resident and local migrant. **Voice:** Piercing 'tseep-tseep'; song series of twittering notes. [C13.20, G6.3.5]

2 SCARLET-TUFTED SUNBIRD *Nectarinia johnstoni* m 27 cm; f 14 cm
Endemic to E Africa. Male is larger and deeper metallic green than Malachite Sunbird, with longer, whispier tail streamers. If seen, the red tufts are diagnostic. Female is darker than other large female sunbirds; tail is square-tipped, with no white outer web; also has orange-red pectoral tufts. Eclipse male has brown body, but retains greenish wings and tail streamers. **Habitat:** Heath, moorland and montane forest edge, 2 000-4 500 m; occurs at higher elevation than Malachite Sunbird (except on Nyika, N Malawi). **Status:** Uncommon. **Voice:** Higher pitched and more scratchy than Malachite Sunbird's.

3 BRONZY (BRONZE) SUNBIRD *Nectarinia kilimensis* m 22 cm; f 12 cm
Bill is strongly decurved, shorter than that of Tacazze or Malachite sunbirds, longer than Purple-breasted Sunbird. Male is metallic bronze-green, appearing black unless seen in good light; no purple in plumage (especially in N races). Angolan *gadowi* is dark glossy-green, but its range does not overlap with Malachite and Scarlet-tufted sunbirds'. Female is smaller than female Tacazze and Malachite sunbirds, and has a paler throat, lacking clear moustachial stripes. Male has no eclipse plumage. **Habitat:** Evergreen forest edges, bracken and adjoining grassland. **Status:** Locally common, 1 000-2 800 m. **Voice:** Loud, piercing 'chee-wit', repeated every half-second; also high-pitched twittering. [C13.22, G6.3.6]

4 TACAZZE SUNBIRD *Nectarinia tacazze* m 22 cm; f 15 cm
Endemic to NE Africa. Bill is long and relatively straight. Male has reddish or purple iridescence on breast and mantle, especially S *jacksoni*, which overlaps with Bronzy Sunbird. Female is darker and less yellow below than female Malachite and Bronzy sunbirds, with mottled (not streaked) underparts (but juv. Bronzy Sunbird is more mottled). **Habitat:** Highland grassland, heath, forest edge, gardens and cultivation, 1 800-4 000 m. **Status:** Common; aggressive, chasing other birds away from flowers. **Voice:** Slow, slurred 'chew chew chew'; twittering, unmusical song.

5 PURPLE-BREASTED SUNBIRD *Nectarinia purpureiventris* m 22 cm; f 14 cm
Endemic to Albertine Rift, where it overlaps with Bronzy Sunbird; differs by having a shorter, less decurved bill; male has a purple (not blackish) breast and belly and a deep mauve-pink (not green-black) back and rump. Female has a longer, more graduated tail than female Bronzy Sunbird, with plain underparts and little, if any, pale eye-stripe. Eclipse male resembles female. **Habitat:** Montane forest canopy, forest edge and clearings, 1 500-2 500 m. **Status:** Locally common to abundant. **Voice:** Long series of twittering and rattles; contact call 'chay chay' and harsher 'tzitt'. [C13.21]

6 BOCAGE'S SUNBIRD *Nectarinia bocagei* m 19 cm; f 14 cm
Localised, little known sunbird. Short, relatively straight-billed. Overlaps with Bronzy Sunbird in Angola, where it can be told by male's smaller size and blackish coloration, with relatively short tail streamers and bronze (not greenish) metallic iridescence. Female best told from female Bronzy Sunbird by its shorter bill; lacks pale tail tip of female Copper Sunbird (p. 618). **Habitat:** Clearings in miombo woodland, often around dambos; also scrubby, swampy areas. **Status:** Uncommon to locally common. **Voice:** Calls 'wisp wisp' and 'trik trik'.

non-br.

1

♂

♀

2

♂

♂

3

♂

♀

4

♀

♂

5

♀

♂

6

♀

♂

617

1 COPPER (COPPERY) SUNBIRD *Cinnyris cupreus* 13 cm
A relatively small, long-tailed, short-billed sunbird. Male is dark, with coppery iridescence, but lacks elongated central tail feathers of Bronzy, Tacazze or Bocage's sunbirds (p. 616). Female has a pale supercilium contrasting with dark lores and ear coverts; tail is blue-black, with white tip. Eclipse male retains coppery wing coverts and rump. **Habitat:** Woodland, forest edges and clearings. **Status:** Uncommon to locally common. **Voice:** Harsh 'chit-chat' call; soft, warbling song. [C13.19, G6.3.8]

2 BUFF-THROATED SUNBIRD *Chalcomitra adelberti* 12 cm
Endemic to W Africa. Male has a diagonistic cream throat and chestnut breast and belly; iridescent green forecrown and moustachial stripes. Female lacks pale eye-stripe of female Green-throated Sunbird, and has a shorter bill and thinner breast streaks. **Habitat:** Forest canopy, gallery forest, edge of forest, secondary growth and gardens. **Status:** Common. **Voice:** Rather deep, melodic 'ti choo-it' or 'che-chi choo-it' song. [C12.85]

3 CARMELITE SUNBIRD *Chalcomitra fuliginosa* 15 cm
Male is rich dark brown, with an iridescent violet-purple forehead and throat (visible only in good light) and yellow pectoral tufts. No eclipse plumage, but worn birds have a noticeably paler hindcrown and mantle. Overlaps marginally with Amethyst Sunbird in E, but is altogether much browner (not blackish), with smaller glossy throat and violet (not green) forecrown. Female is dull; can be told by pale moustache, dark throat and dark blotches on breast. **Habitat:** Mangroves, coastal thickets, secondary growth, gardens and riverine habitats. **Status:** Locally common. **Voice:** Rather deep, melodic warbling song; also high-pitched trilling 'chit-er-er-er-r-r-r-r' call. [C12.86]

4 GREEN-THROATED SUNBIRD *Chalcomitra rubescens* 12-14 cm
Male is dark blackish-brown, with an iridescent green forehead (tinged violet posteriorly), throat and upper breast, and a narrow pink-violet breast band. Can look all dark in poor light; bill is shorter than Amethyst Sunbird's. No eclipse plumage. Male *crossensis* of Nigeria and SW Cameroon has a brown throat (may be hybrid with Buff-throated Sunbird). Female is dark brown above, with a pale eye-stripe and yellowish underparts with large diffuse dark streaks. Juv. male resembles female but has a dark throat. **Habitat:** Forest canopy, gallery forest, tall trees in secondary growth and adjacent savanna. **Status:** Common; often joins bird parties. **Voice:** Loud 'chip chip', often repeated and accelerating into a slow trill. [C12.87]

5 AMETHYST (BLACK) SUNBIRD *Chalcomitra amethystina* 13-15 cm
At a distance, male appears all black, but in good light shows an iridescent greenish fore-crown and violet-purple throat and shoulder patches. Lacks pectoral tufts. Rump is violet in S races, matt black in N. No eclipse plumage. Female is paler above than female Green-throated Sunbird, with less streaking below. Female Scarlet-chested Sunbird lacks pale eye-stripe and has paler, streaked (not mottled) underparts. Juv. male has a purple throat; can be confused with Marico Sunbird (p. 632). **Habitat:** Woodland, forest edge and gardens. **Status:** Common. **Voice:** Quite deep, fast, twittering song; loud, harsh calls. [C12.88, G6.5.2]

6 SCARLET-CHESTED SUNBIRD *Chalcomitra senegalensis* 13-15 cm
Male has scarlet breast and iridescent green crown and throat. In E Africa, told from Hunter's Sunbird by its green (not black) throat and lack of a violet shoulder. No eclipse plumage. Female is darker than female Hunter's Sunbird; lacks the pale eye-stripe of female Green-throated and Amethyst sunbirds. **Habitat:** Woodland, savanna and suburban gardens. **Status:** Common. **Voice:** Loud, whistled 'cheeup, chup, toop, toop, toop' song. [C12.89, G6.5.1]

7 HUNTER'S SUNBIRD *Chalcomitra hunteri* 13-14 cm
Endemic to NE Africa, replacing Scarlet-chested Sunbird in arid habitats. Male told from Scarlet-chested Sunbird by its iridescent violet (not green) rump and shoulder patches (only visible in good light), black (not green) throat and brighter red breast with metallic bluish bands. Female is paler than female Scarlet-chested Sunbird, with grey (not yellowish) under-parts. **Habitat:** Dry acacia scrub and woodland, below 1 000 m. **Status:** Locally common. **Voice:** Chipping call notes similar to Scarlet-chested Sunbird's.

1 GREEN-HEADED SUNBIRD *Cyanomitra verticalis*　　　　13-15 cm
A medium-sized, dark-bodied sunbird. Male has an iridescent blue-green head and upper breast and yellow pectoral tufts; larger than Bannerman's Sunbird with a longer, more decurved bill and greener head. Female has glossy green confined to the head and crown, and lacks pectoral tufts. **Habitat:** Forest edges, clearings, gallery forest, secondary growth and well-wooded savanna. **Status:** Common. **Voice:** Loud, rapid 'chip-ip-ip-ip-ip' song; also a nasal 'wher' call. [C12.79]

2 BANNERMAN'S SUNBIRD *Cyanomitra bannermani*　　　　13 cm
Localised endemic to C Africa. Slightly smaller than Green-headed Sunbird, with a shorter, straighter bill; male tends to be more blue on the head and has slightly less extensive glossy plumage on the breast; female has iridescence on the head restricted to feather tips, often appearing plain-headed; ranges overlap in Angola **Habitat:** Forest edge, especially riverine forest; also in adjacent miombo woodland. **Status:** Uncommon; usually singly or in pairs; often joins bird parties. **Voice:** Nasal, slurred 'djoowi', also high-pitched 'chit'. [C12.80]

3 BLUE-HEADED SUNBIRD *Cyanomitra alinae*　　　　12-14 cm
Endemic to Albertine Rift Mts. Sexes alike; both have pale yellow pectoral tufts. Differs from Green-headed Sunbird by having the iridescent sheen of the head extend well onto breast; belly sooty with yellow wash on vent and flanks, mantle yellowish-brown (not olive). **Habitat:** Montane forest, 1 300-2 300 m; overlaps only narrowly with Green-headed Sunbird at low elevation. Usually in the canopy, but visits flowering shrubs at forest edge. **Status:** Common. **Voice:** High-pitched 'tsee see'; rapid song of chipping notes. [C12.83]

4 CAMEROON (BLUE-HEADED) SUNBIRD *Cyanomitra oritis*　　　　12-13 cm
Endemic to SW Cameroon, SE Nigeria and Bioko. The only blue-headed sunbird with olive-yellow underparts and a plain hindcrown. Resembles Olive Sunbird (p. 622) but has an iridescent green-blue (not dull olive) forecrown, throat and upper breast. Female lacks the yellow pectoral tufts and has reduced glossy area on head. Juv. is duller, with glossy blue parts being sooty grey; streaked on breast and belly. **Habitat:** Montane forest and clearings. **Status:** Common. **Voice:** High-pitched chittering rattle; also dry 'wheet' call. [C12.82]

5 REICHENBACH'S SUNBIRD *Anabathmis reichenbachii*　　　　12-14 cm
A peculiar sunbird, distinguished by the pale tips to the long, graduated tail. Bill is relatively short. Sexes alike; adults have an iridescent dark-blue head, throat and breast, and a yellow lower belly, vent and uppertail coverts. The olive-brown back is lightly scaled. Juv. is drab olive-yellow below; best identified by diagnostic tail pattern. **Habitat:** Mangroves, coastal forest, thickets and adjacent clearings, and riverine forest. **Status:** Locally common. **Voice:** Fairly deep 'swoozy-sweezy swoozy-sweezitty' song; also a melodic 'tooee' call. [C12.73]

6 BLUE-THROATED BROWN SUNBIRD *Cyanomitra cyanolaema*　　　　14-15 cm
A large, dark sunbird. Male has a dark metallic-blue forehead and throat, but this is visible only in good light; can appear dark brown with a pale grey belly. Pectoral tufts are creamy. Female is paler olive-brown, with two white stripes above and below the eye; larger and more olive than Mangrove Sunbird (p. 624), with a much longer bill. **Habitat:** Forest canopy and edge, gallery forest and secondary growth. **Status:** Common; active. **Voice:** Noisy; song a rapid series of high whistles, usually descending in pitch. [C12.81]

1 OLIVE SUNBIRD *Cyanomitra olivacea* 12-15 cm
A dull olive sunbird. Much greener than Grey Sunbird, with less contrast between the dark upperparts and paler underparts. Juv. has a rust-coloured throat. Sexes alike, although females of some races lack yellow pectoral tufts (usually concealed). Populations W of Rift have been split as Western Olive Sunbird *C. obscura*, but this is not supported by genetic evidence. **Habitat:** Coastal, riverine and montane forests. **Status:** Common; usually the most abundant forest sunbird in its range. **Voice:** Call sharp 'tuk, tuk, tuk'; song series of descending, piping notes, accelerating in pace, and sometimes increasing in pitch at end. [G6.4.10]

2 GREY (MOUSE-COLOURED) SUNBIRD *Nectarinia veroxii* 12-14 cm
A nondescript sunbird, restricted to E coast. Sexes alike. Dark grey back contrasts with paler grey underparts; differs from Olive Sunbird by its grey (not green) colour, red (not yellow) pectoral tufts and call. At close range, crown, back and wing coverts are faintly washed blue-green. Juv. is more yellow-olive below; more similar to Olive Sunbird. **Habitat:** Coastal and riverine forests. **Status:** Locally common. **Voice:** Song loud series of well-spaced 'chreep chreep choop' phrases; call harsh, grating 'tzzik, tzzik'. [G6.4.9]

3 WESTERN VIOLET-BACKED SUNBIRD *Anthreptes longuemarei* 13 cm
A small, short-billed sunbird. Male has violet upperparts, head and throat; appears blackish in poor light. Differs from male Eastern Violet-backed Sunbird by violet (not blue-green) rump and from Uluguru Violet-Backed Sunbird by its white (not greyish) underparts. Female is brown above, with a conspicuous white eye-stripe; belly is yellow (not whitish, as in female Eastern Violet-backed Sunbird) and tail is violet (not blue). Juv. has pale yellow underparts. **Habitat:** Woodland; occurring in moister habitats than Eastern Violet-backed Sunbird. **Status:** Uncommon to locally common. **Voice:** Sharp 'chit-chit' or 'skee'. [C12.67, G6.5.5]

4 EASTERN VIOLET-BACKED SUNBIRD *Anthreptes orientalis* 12 cm
Endemic to E Africa. Male is similar to male Western Violet-backed Sunbird but has a blue-green (not violet) rump. Told from Uluguru Violet-backed Sunbird by its violet (not brown) nape and white (not grey) below. Female has a blue (not violet) tail and whitish underparts; at most, a yellow tinge on the central belly. **Habitat:** Thickets in arid savanna, often near water; occurs in drier areas than Western and Uluguru violet-backed sunbirds. **Status:** Fairly common. **Voice:** Nasal 'chwee'.

5 VIOLET-TAILED SUNBIRD *Anthreptes aurantium* 11-13 cm
Endemic to C Africa. A small, very short-billed sunbird. Male has iridescent violet and blue-green upperparts and throat, buffy-white underparts and orange pectoral tufts. Female is green above, with a white eyebrow, blue tail and yellow belly. **Habitat:** Coastal and riverine forest and scrub; also mangroves; invariably close to water. **Status:** Locally common. **Voice:** Harsh 'chip' call.

6 ULUGURU VIOLET-BACKED SUNBIRD *Anthreptes neglectus* 12 cm
Localised endemic to E Africa. Differs from other violet-backed sunbirds by being greyish, not white below. Male and female both have a violet crown and back, with a brown nape; female lacks a white eye-stripe and has a pale yellow wash on the belly. Juv. is duller above, with a white eye-stripe and more extensive yellow underparts. **Habitat:** Lowland and mid-altitude forests; unlikely to occur alongside other violet-backed sunbirds. **Status:** Uncommon; often joins bird parties. **Voice:** Calls 'tssp' and 'chissik'.

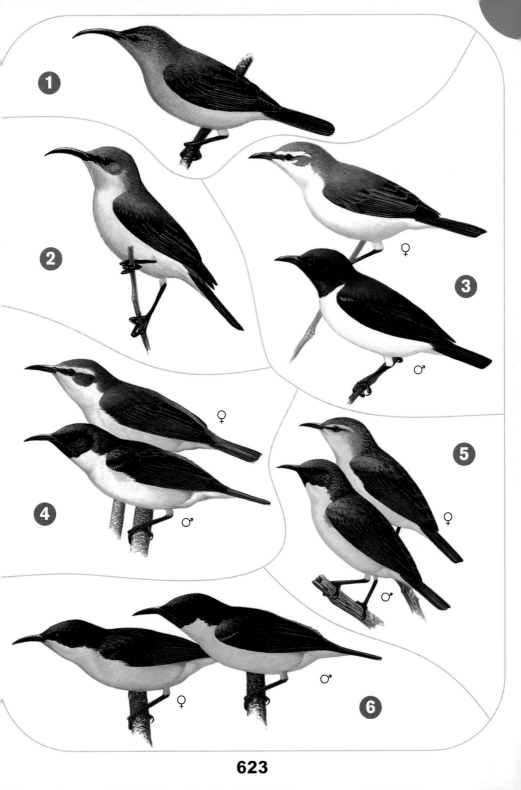

1 MANGROVE (BROWN) SUNBIRD *Anthreptes gabonicus*   10-11 cm
Endemic to W and C Africa. Sexes alike. A small, brown, grey and white sunbird with a short, relatively straight bill. Has diagnostic crisp white lines above and below the eye, white carpal edge and white tail tips. Juv. olive-brown above, washed yellow below. **Habitat:** Mangroves and riparian vegetation; seldom seen far from water. **Status:** Common. **Voice:** High-pitched 'tsip tsip tsip' call. [C12.68]

2 LITTLE GREEN SUNBIRD *Anthreptes seimundi*   9-10 cm
A very small, short-tailed sunbird. Sexes alike. Differs from Bates's Sunbird by its straighter bill, curved only at the tip. Also has a narrow, pale yellow eye-ring. In areas of overlap, tends to have greener underparts with a distinctive yellow centre to the belly. Overall more yellow-green (not grey-olive) than Bates's Sunbird. Juv. is duller. **Habitat:** Canopy of lowland forest, gallery forest and secondary growth; occurs in lower strata at forest edge. **Status:** Locally common. **Voice:** High-pitched 'tseep tseep tseep' call. [C12.71]

3 BATES'S SUNBIRD *Cinnyris batesi*   9-10 cm
A very small, drab sunbird with a short, dark tail and an indistinct pale eyebrow; resembles a very small, short-tailed Olive Sunbird (p. 622). More grey-olive than Little Green Sunbird, and the short bill curves uniformly from base to tip. Typically a forest edge species (Little Green Sunbird prefers canopy). Sexes alike, but only male has red pectoral tufts. Often has an upright stance. **Habitat:** Lowland and gallery forest, tall secondary growth. **Status:** Locally common. **Voice:** 'Tsip tsip tsip' call; also a soft rattling trill. [C13.17]

4 URSULA'S (MOUSE-COLOURED) SUNBIRD *Cinnyris ursulae*   9-10 cm
Endemic to SW Cameroon and Bioko. A small sunbird, similar to Bates's Sunbird, but with red-orange pectoral tufts in both sexes (not only male) and a brownish (not olive) throat that contrasts weakly with the grey (not olive) breast. At close range, shows some iridescent blue on the crown. Juv. is paler and lacks pectoral tufts. **Habitat:** Montane forest, forest edge and secondary growth, 1 000-2 000 m. **Status:** Locally common. **Voice:** Fast, high-pitched trilling song. [C13.18]

5 FRASER'S (SCARLET-TUFTED) SUNBIRD *Deleornis fraseri*   11-13 cm
A small, olive-green sunbird, with a medium-long, straight, pale bill, and a diagnostic pale yellow eye-ring. Male has orange-red pectoral tufts, but these are seldom visible in the field. Resembles a small warbler or a greenish white-eye with a long bill. Gleans leaves for insects. **Habitat:** Lowland and gallery forest, and old secondary growth from understorey to lower canopy, but mostly in mid-strata. **Status:** Common; often in small groups; regularly joins bird parties. **Voice:** Plaintive 'sweeit' and 'tsu-tsweeet'; also an even series of 4-6 notes. [C12.70]

6 GREY-HEADED SUNBIRD *Deleornis axillaris*   11-13 cm
Endemic to Congo basin. Often treated as a race of Fraser's Sunbird, but male has a grey (not olive-green) head. Female and juv. have olive-green head; best separated from Fraser's Sunbird on range. The two species apparently meet without hybridising in W DRC. **Habitat:** Lowland and gallery forest. **Status:** Common. **Voice:** Not known to differ from that of Fraser's Sunbird.

7 ANCHIETA'S (RED-AND-BLUE) SUNBIRD *Anthreptes anchietae*   10-12 cm
Endemic to SC Africa. The bright red-and-yellow lower breast, red vent and iridescent blue fore-head, throat and upper breast are diagnostic. Rest of upperparts and belly brown. Female and juv. are duller, with less extensive iridescent blue on the forehead. **Habitat:** Miombo woodland. **Status:** Locally common; often joins bird parties. **Voice:** Distinctive, vaguely tit-like 'chew ti teeu teeu teeu'; also usual sunbird chips and chissiks. [C12.72]

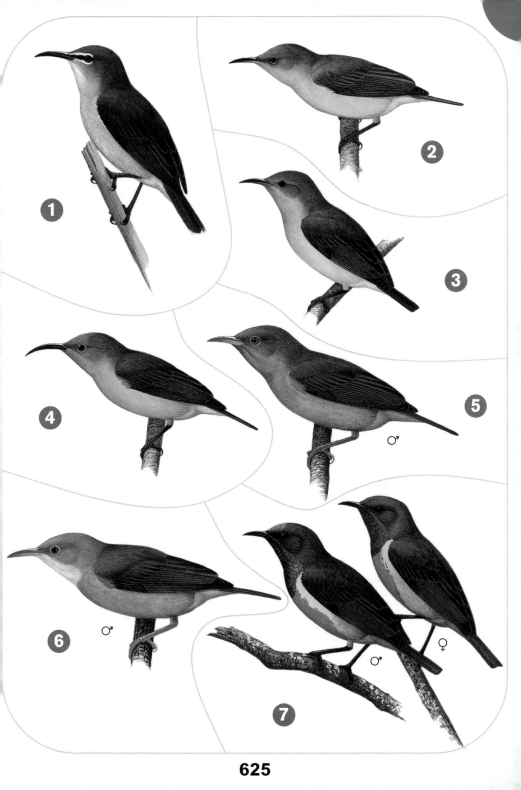

1 GREY-CHINNED (GREEN) SUNBIRD *Anthreptes rectirostris*   9-10 cm
A small sunbird with a short, straight bill. Male is iridescent green above and across breast, with grey (E of Dahomey gap *rectirostris*) or yellow (Upper Guinea *tephrolaema*) chin. Narrow orange band across lower breast is inconspicuous; pectoral tufts are yellow. Best told from Collared Sunbird by chin colour (Collared Sunbird's is iridescent greenish) and pale yellow-grey (not bright yellow) belly. Female is nondescript olive-green; looks like a small warbler. **Habitat:** Canopy of lowland and gallery forest; also in lower strata of secondary growth and forest edge. **Status:** Common. **Voice:** High-pitched trilling song; loud 'tseep' call. [C12.69]

2 COLLARED SUNBIRD *Hedydipna collaris*   9-10 cm
A small, short-billed sunbird with metallic green upperparts. Male has an iridescent green throat and upper breast, separated from the yellow belly by a purple band (very narrow in some races). Pectoral tufts yellow. Smaller and much shorter-billed than yellow-bellied form of Variable Sunbird (p. 628); also throat is green (not violet-blue), and extends less far onto breast. Female is yellow below, with a dusky throat in some races. **Habitat:** Forest, dense woodland and gardens. **Status:** Common. **Voice:** Soft 'tswee'; a harsh, chirpy song. [C12.77, G6.5.3]

3 AMANI SUNBIRD *Hedydipna pallidigaster*   8-9 cm
Localised endemic to E Africa. A small, short-billed sunbird. Male resembles male Collared Sunbird, but has a whitish (not yellow) belly and is dark iridescent blue-green above, tinged with violet on the head (can appear black); pectoral tufts orange. Dark throat extends onto breast; lacks the white throats of violet-backed sunbirds (p. 622). Female is grey above, sometimes with violet highlights; tail is dark blue-black. Told from female Plain-backed Sunbird (p. 628) by pale grey-white (not olive) underparts. **Habitat:** Coastal miombo woodland in Kenya, and low- and mid-altitude forest in Tanzanian Eastern Arc Mts. **Status:** Endangered. Uncommon. **Voice:** High-pitched 'sereeet sereet'; jumbled song.

4 BANDED (GREEN) SUNBIRD *Anthreptes rubritorques*   8-9 cm
Endemic to Eastern Arc Mts, Tanzania. A small sunbird, iridescent green above and greyish below. Much shorter billed than double-collared sunbirds; male has very thin (not broad) red breast band and grey (not iridescent green) throat. Female is duller and lacks red breast band and reddish pectoral tufts; differs from Collared Sunbird by its grey-green (not yellow) underparts. **Habitat:** Montane forest canopy and forest edge, 300-1 600 m. **Status:** Vulnerable. Locally common; sometimes joins bird parties. **Voice:** Far-carrying, chirping call.

5 NILE VALLEY SUNBIRD *Hedydipna metallicus*   m 17 cm; f 9 cm
Similar to Pygmy Sunbird but has blue-green (not golden-green) head and upperparts, with a violet rump and lower back. Males lacking tail streamers are more slender than male Collared Sunbird, with a violet (not green) back and rump; occurs in much more arid habitats. Female is similar to female Pygmy Sunbird, but often has a more pronounced pale eye-stripe. **Habitat:** Arid savanna, riparian thickets, parks and gardens. **Status:** Locally common resident and local migrant; usually in pairs. **Voice:** Usual jumbled chittering sunbird-like song; nasal 'chwee weee' alarm call.

6 PYGMY SUNBIRD *Hedydipna platurus*   m 17 cm; f 9 cm
Tiny, short-billed sunbird. Adult male is easily recognised by long, central tail streamers. Range overlaps with Nile Valley Sunbird in Sudan, where males lacking tail streamers resemble male Collared Sunbird; differs from both by lacking a purple band across the breast, and is more golden-yellow below, and golden-green (not blue-green or green) above (but uppertail coverts are violet). Female is drab brown above and paler than Nile Valley Sunbird; yellow-olive below, with weak, pale eye-stripe. **Habitat:** Arid savanna and riparian thickets. **Status:** Locally common resident and local migrant; usually in pairs. **Voice:** Soft, nasal 'sooay'; jumbled and typical sunbird chittering song. [C12.78]

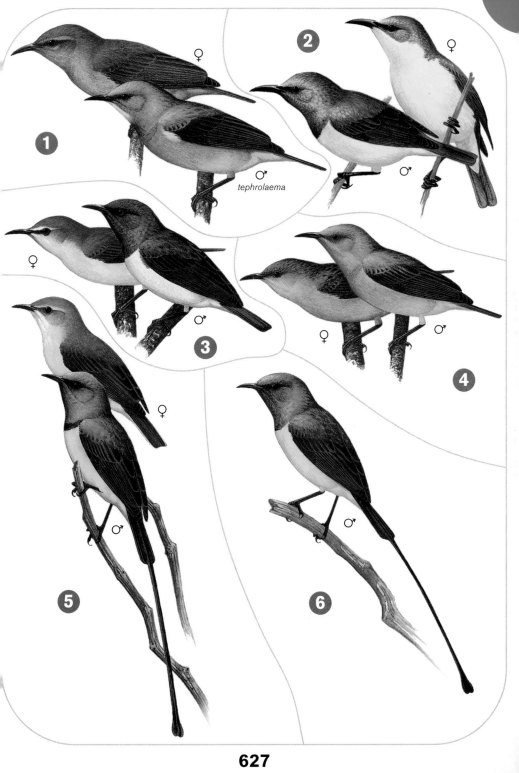

tephrolaema

1 PLAIN-BACKED (BLUE-THROATED) SUNBIRD *Anthreptes reichenowi* 10-11 cm
Endemic to E coast. A slender, warbler-like sunbird, with a relatively short bill. Male is pale yellow below with dull, brownish-green upperparts and an iridescent blue-black throat patch and forehead; can be confused with imm. male Variable and White-bellied sunbirds moulting into adult plumage. Female is duller, lacking the iridescent throat patch; plain olive-brown (not iridescent greenish) upperparts distinguish it from female Collared Sunbird (p. 626). **Habitat:** Mixed moist woodland and coastal forests. **Status:** Uncommon to locally common. **Voice:** Loud 'tsweep tsweep twit tweet tweet' warbling song; soft 'tik-tik' call. [G6.5.4]

2 VARIABLE (YELLOW-BELLIED) SUNBIRD *Cinnyris venustus* 10-11 cm
Male is iridescent blue-green above, with a violet-blue crown and throat, and purple upper breast band. W African birds are greener on the back and throat. Lower breast and belly typically yellow but some orange (Albertine Rift) or white (arid NE); pectoral tufts yellow or orange. Yellow-bellied forms have a longer, more decurved bill and more extensive dark breast than Collared Sunbird (p. 626). White-bellied forms do not overlap with Oustalet's and White-bellied sunbirds. Female is grey-olive above and plain yellow-olive below; has blackish tail with white tail tip (lacking in female White-bellied Sunbird). Juv. male has blackish throat, but told from Plain-backed Sunbird by having some iridescence on wing coverts. **Habitat:** Woodland, forest edge, gardens and plantations; also mesic savannas in W Africa. **Status:** Common. **Voice:** 'Tsui-tse-tse'; trilling song. [C13.13, G6.4.5]

3 WHITE-BELLIED SUNBIRD *Cinnyris talatala* 10-12 cm
Near-endemic to S Africa. Male has an iridescent green back, head and breast, a purple breast band and a white belly. Does not overlap with white-bellied form of Variable Sunbird. Has a longer, more decurved bill than Oustalet's Sunbird, with a duller green head, narrower, less distinct maroon breast band and yellow (not orange) pectoral tufts. Female is grey-brown above and off-white (rarely yellowish) below; told from female Dusky Sunbird by its indistinctly streaked (not plain) breast, and only outer-tail feathers are tipped pale (not whole tail). Juv. male has a blackish throat. **Habitat:** Dry woodland, savanna and gardens. **Status:** Common. **Voice:** Loud 'pichee, pichee', followed by rapid tinkle of notes. [C13.12, G6.4.6]

4 OUSTALET'S SUNBIRD *Cinnyris oustaleti* 10-11 cm
Localised endemic to SC Africa. Bill is shorter and less decurved than White-bellied Sunbird's, with a brighter green head and a broader, more distinct maroon breast band, and orange (not yellow) pectoral tufts. Female is slightly darker than female White-bellied Sunbird, especially on throat and breast, which is more heavily streaked. **Habitat:** Miombo woodland, often in open, degraded areas, where it forages low down in undergrowth. **Status:** Locally common. **Voice:** Distinctive, soft, high-pitched 'tsip'.

5 DUSKY SUNBIRD *Cinnyris fusca* 10 cm
Endemic to SW Africa. Male has a glossy black head, throat and back, contrasting with a white belly; pectoral tufts are orange. Female is light grey-brown above and off-white below; paler below than female Southern Double-collared Sunbird (p. 638); lacks the light breast streaking of female White-bellied Sunbird. Juv. male has a blackish throat. Imm. has a black line extending onto the breast. **Habitat:** Arid savanna, acacia thickets and Karoo scrub. **Status:** Common; wanders into more mesic areas in some years. **Voice:** 'Chrrrr-chrrrr'; short, warbling song. [G6.4.8]

6 SOCOTRA SUNBIRD *Chalcomitra balfouri* 15 cm
Endemic to Socotra, where it is the only sunbird. Male has grey-brown streaked upperparts and white underparts, with a dark chin and heavily barred breast; the yellow pectoral tufts are rarely seen. Female is similar, but is less clearly marked on the underparts and lacks pectoral tufts. **Habitat:** Arid woodland. **Status:** Locally common. **Voice:** Jangled, short song; various 'zee', 'zii' or 'tchee' contact notes.

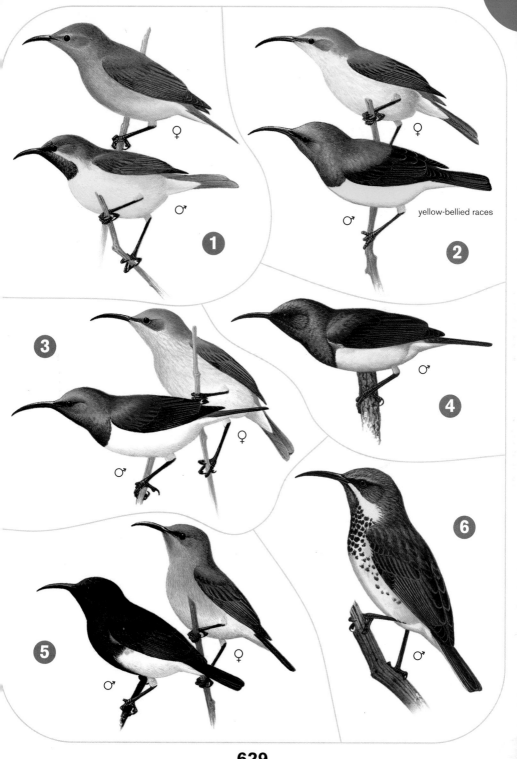

yellow-bellied races

1 ♀ ♂

2 ♀ ♂

3 ♂ ♀

4 ♂

5 ♂ ♀

6 ♂

1 BEAUTIFUL SUNBIRD *Cinnyris pulchellus*　　　m 14-17 cm; f 9-11 cm
A tiny sunbird. Male has obvious yellow sides to the broad red breast band, and has much longer tail streamers than Black-bellied Sunbird. Nominate race has green belly; S Kenya and Tanzania *melanogastra* has black belly; sometimes considered a distinct species. Female is duller (not bright yellow) below than Pygmy and Nile Valley sunbirds (p. 626), with a longer, more decurved bill. **Habitat:** Woodland, arid acacia scrub, gardens and mangroves. **Status:** Common. **Voice:** Weak 'chip chip'; variable, high-pitched, jumbled song. [C13.8]

2 BLACK-BELLIED SUNBIRD *Cinnyris nectarinioides*　　　m 13 cm; f 10 cm
Endemic to NE Africa. Male is smaller than Red-chested Sunbird, with a paler breast band. Nominate race (C Kenya to Tanzania) has orange breast band with yellow pectoral tufts; N *erlangeri* has a reddish breast band and no pectoral tufts. Female is grey-brown above, pale yellow below, lightly streaked darker; within its range, resembles female Tsavo Sunbird (p. 632), but is less heavily streaked. **Habitat:** Arid savanna, acacia thickets and adjacent gardens. **Status:** Locally common; usually in pairs. **Voice:** Rapidly repeated 'tsit stit tsit'; harsher 'tzrit' contact note.

3 RED-CHESTED SUNBIRD *Cinnyris erythrocercus*　　　m 15 cm; f 12 cm
Endemic to NE Africa. Male has a black belly and deep red-crimson breast band, lacking yellow sides (as in Beautiful Sunbird). Occurs further W and in different habitat from Black-bellied Sunbird. Female has a graduated, blue-black tail with pale tips, and is heavily streaked below, with yellow fringes to wing feathers; is larger, darker and more streaked below than female Beautiful Sunbird. **Habitat:** Shrubs and woodland alongside swamps, streams and lake edges; also adjacent gardens and fields. **Status:** Common; occurs in pairs, usually foraging low down. **Voice:** Song high-pitched, soft twittering; contact note harsh 'jik jik'.

4 CONGO (BLACK-BELLIED) SUNBIRD *Cinnyris congensis*　　　m 19 cm; f 11 cm
Endemic to Congo River. Male is only sunbird in its range with elongated central tail feathers. Told from male Olive-bellied Sunbird (p. 636) by its black belly. Female is brownish-olive above, with a pale yellow belly, and a greyish, lightly streaked breast and throat. **Habitat:** Riverine forest and adjacent clearings. **Status:** Locally common. **Voice:** Unknown.

5 SHELLEY'S SUNBIRD *Cinnyris shelleyi*　　　9-13 cm
Endemic to SE Africa. Male told from Miombo Double-collared Sunbird (p. 638) by its sooty (not olive-grey) belly. Eclipse male has paler belly. Female told from female Miombo Double-collared Sunbird by its lightly streaked (not plain) underparts; shorter billed, greyer above and duller beneath than female Marico Sunbird (p. 632). Tanzanian *hofmanni* is smaller with a jet black belly; sometimes treated as a separate species, Hofmann's Sunbird. **Habitat:** Nominate usually in miombo woodland; *hofmanni* in riverine scrub and gardens. **Status:** Locally common, with local movements. **Voice:** 'Didi-didi'; a nasal 'chibbee-cheeu-cheeu' song. [G6.4.1]

6 SHINING SUNBIRD *Cinnyris habessinica*　　　13 cm
Endemic to NE Africa. A large, arid-country double-collared sunbird. Male has diagnostic black belly and a purple sheen on forecrown and chin. Female is pale greyish brown with a pale eye-stripe; underparts slightly paler with diffuse breast streaking. Juv. male has dark throat. **Habitat:** Arid to semi-arid scrub and woodland, agricultural lands and gardens. **Status:** Common. **Voice:** A sharp and short 'stik stik'; low warbled and jumbled mixture of harsh and soft notes.

7 NEERGAARD'S SUNBIRD *Cinnyris neergaardi*　　　10-11 cm
Endemic to S Africa. Rather small, with a short, thin bill, it is the only double-collared sunbird in its range. Male has a blackish belly. Female's upperparts are greyish brown and the underparts a pale, dull yellow, not streaked like female Purple-banded Sunbird (p. 632). **Habitat:** Acacia savanna and sand forest. **Status:** Common but very localised. **Voice:** Thin, wispy 'weesi-weesi-weesi'; short, chippy song. [G6.4.2]

8 TOHA SUNBIRD (not illustrated)
3 yellow-crowned sunbirds (male, female and juv.) photographed in Djibouti remain unresolved; tentatively described as a new species; may be aberrant Shining or Marico (p. 632) sunbirds.

1 MARICO SUNBIRD *Cinnyris mariquensis* 11-14 cm
A fairly large, dark sunbird. Male has a black or sooty-grey belly, and violet-blue and purple-maroon breast bands. Most races have broader purple than violet breast band, but *osiris* (N Kenya and Uganda to Eritrea) has narrower purple band. Larger than Purple-banded Sunbird, with a longer, thicker bill. Female has grey-brown upperparts and pale yellow, dusky-streaked underparts; tail is dark grey, with white tips and edges. **Habitat:** Woodland and savanna, often in fairly arid areas. **Status:** Common. **Voice:** Long series of rapid 'tsip-tsip-tsip'; fast, warbling song. [G6.3.9]

2 ORANGE-TUFTED SUNBIRD *Cinnyris bouvieri* 10-12 cm
A dark, purple-banded sunbird restricted to savannas around the Congo basin forest. Overlaps with Purple-banded and Marico sunbirds; intermediate in size, with a long, relatively straight bill. At close range, has a violet (not green) forecrown and chin, and golden-green (not bluish-green) head and upperparts; pectoral tufts orange-yellow. Female is dull brown above and olive-yellow below, with indistinct dusky streaks and a dark throat. **Habitat:** Shrubby savannas, secondary growth and grassy clearings close to forest edge. **Status:** Locally common but patchily distributed. **Voice:** Typical sunbird 'tsip sweety-sweety-sweety-sweet' song, sometimes accompanied by a harsh trill. [C13.9]

3 PALESTINE SUNBIRD *Cinnyris osea* 8-9 cm
Localised, very small, dark sunbird which, within its restricted range, could be confused with Purple-banded and Marico sunbirds; differs from both by being smaller and shorter billed and lacking the purple breast band. Range does not overlap with Orange-tufted Sunbird. Female is nondescript drab olive and lacks the streaking and mottling of larger female Marico and Purple-banded sunbirds. **Habitat:** Semi-desert woodland, wooded wadis and dry forests; also agricultural lands and gardens. **Status:** Common; in pairs, sometimes with mixed bird parties. **Voice:** Rather harsh, chittering song; harsh 'choo-eet' and 'chit' calls. [C13.10]

4 PURPLE-BANDED SUNBIRD *Cinnyris bifasciatus* 9-11 cm
Smaller than Marico and Violet-breasted sunbirds, with a thinner, shorter and less decurved bill. Male often has narrower purple breast band than Marico Sunbird, but this is variable; always has a broader purple band than Tsavo Sunbird. Female is pale yellow below with less streaking than Marico Sunbird. Eclipse and juv. male resemble female but have a dark throat. **Habitat:** Woodland, moist savanna and coastal scrub. **Status:** Common. **Voice:** High-pitched 'teeet-teeet-tit-tit' song, not sustained as call of Marico Sunbird. [C13.11, G6.3.10]

5 PEMBA SUNBIRD *Cinnyris pembae* 9-10 cm
Endemic to Pemba Island, where it is the only small, dark sunbird. Smaller than other purple-banded sunbirds; male has fairly narrow violet breast band. **Habitat:** Virtually all habitats, even small offshore coral islets, avoids dense primary forest. **Status:** Common. **Voice:** Repeated 'tslink tslink' call; jumbled song.

6 VIOLET-BREASTED SUNBIRD *Cinnyris chalcomelas* 11-12 cm
Endemic to NE Africa. Male has a broad violet-blue breast band and bluer throat; lacks the purple-maroon breast band of other purple-banded sunbirds. Slightly larger than Purple-banded and Tsavo sunbirds, with a longer, more decurved bill, but smaller than Marico Sunbird. Female is larger than other purple-banded sunbirds, with less well-defined streaking on underparts and no pale eye-stripe. **Habitat:** Coastal forest and scrub. **Status:** Locally common. **Voice:** Buzzy calls; twittering song.

7 TSAVO SUNBIRD *Cinnyris tsavoensis* 9-11 cm
Endemic to E Africa. Often treated as a race of Purple-banded Sunbird, but has a very thin purple breast band (sometimes absent or present only at the sides of the breast). Range and arid habitat assist identification. Slightly smaller than Violet-breasted Sunbird. Female has a more obvious white malar stripe, contrasting with its grey throat, than female Violet-breasted and Purple-banded sunbirds; more streaked below than female Black-bellied Sunbird (p. 630). No male eclipse plumage. **Habitat:** Drier savanna than Purple-banded Sunbird. **Status:** Locally common. **Voice:** 'Tissik' contact note and song similar to Purple-banded Sunbird's.

1 SPLENDID SUNBIRD *Cinnyris coccinigastrus* 13-14 cm
A fairly large, long-billed sunbird with a fairly short tail. Male is brilliantly coloured, with a violet-purple head, throat and breast, and a black belly. Most birds have a blue vent, but some Ivory Coast birds have a green vent and bluish breast band. The pale yellow pectoral tufts are seldom visible. Female is olive-brown above and olive-yellow below, with light dusky streaks on the breast and flanks, a whitish, lightly barred throat and a pale eye-stripe. **Habitat:** Moist woodland and savanna, gallery forest, secondary growth, plantations and gardens. **Status:** Common. **Voice:** Series of 3-4 loud, descending whistles; also scolding 'cheer cheer' calls. [C13.15]

2 SUPERB SUNBIRD *Cinnyris superbus* 14-16 cm
A large sunbird with a very long, slightly decurved bill. Male has an iridescent blue-green (not green, as Johanna's Sunbird) crown and rump, a violet throat and upper breast, and a dark maroon belly; lacks pectoral tufts. Female has uniform yellowish underparts and orange undertail coverts; long, pale eye-stripe contrasts with darker face and whitish throat. **Habitat:** Forest canopy, gallery forest, secondary growth, moist wooded savanna, plantations. **Status:** Common. **Voice:** Similar to Splendid Sunbird, but has 2-3 notes of more even pitch. [C13.16]

3 JOHANNA'S SUNBIRD *Cinnyris johannae* 12-14 cm
Slightly smaller than Superb Sunbird, with a more strongly decurved bill. Crown is iridescent green; lacks blue hues of Superb Sunbird. Belly is dark crimson. Male has yellow pectoral tufts (seldom visible). Female has large, regular stripes on the pale yellow breast and belly, contrasting with white throat; is dark olive-brown above, with a pale eye-stripe and white tail tips. **Habitat:** Forest canopy and edge, gallery forest, secondary growth and adjacent savanna. **Status:** Common. **Voice:** Squeaky series of warbling notes, faster, longer and higher-pitched than song of Superb Sunbird; also 'teeuuu' call. [C13.14]

4 ROCKEFELLER'S SUNBIRD *Cinnyris rockefelleri* 12 cm
Endemic to Albertine Rift Mts. Male has a very broad red breast band, extending well onto the belly; lower belly is grey, with a scarlet vent. Bill is longer than Regal Sunbird's; also lacks yellow sides to breast (but has yellow pectoral tufts). Female is longer-billed than female Regal Sunbird, with a slight pale eye-stripe and metallic tips to mantle feathers. **Habitat:** Montane forest, bamboo and heath, often along streams, 2 000-3 300 m. **Status:** Vulnerable. Little known. **Voice:** Harsh 'schick schick' contact call; song unknown.

5 REGAL SUNBIRD *Cinnyris regius* 10-11 cm
Endemic to Albertine Rift Mts. Bill is medium to long. Male is easily identified by the bright yellow sides to the broad, scarlet breast band, which extends well onto the belly. Lower belly is olive, with scarlet vent. Female is very plain; more olive-yellow than double-collared sunbirds and lacks any metallic wash on mantle (unlike female Rockefeller's Sunbird, which has metallic tips to mantle feathers). **Habitat:** Montane forest, clearings and bamboo, 1 500-3 000 m. **Status:** Uncommon; usually in pairs; joins bird parties. **Voice:** Typical sunbird 'chik', 'tchizzik' notes; jumbled song. [C13.6]

6 LOVERIDGE'S SUNBIRD *Cinnyris loveridgei* 12 cm
Endemic to Uluguru Mts, Tanzania, where it is the only double-collared sunbird. Male has broad, orange-red breast band, extending onto the yellowish belly; sides of the breast yellow. Superficially similar to Regal Sunbird, but bill rather long and lacks a red vent; ranges do not overlap. Larger than Moreau's Sunbird (p. 638), with distinctive breast pattern. **Habitat:** Montane forest and forest edge, 800-2 000 m. **Status:** Common. **Voice:** Usual sunbird song of jumbled twittering and a harsh 'szzit' call.

1 OLIVE-BELLIED SUNBIRD *Cinnyris chloropygius*   10-11 cm
The common lowland red-breasted sunbird of W and C Africa. Male typically lacks blue band between red breast and green throat characteristic of double-collared sunbirds (some C African birds may show slight band). Rump is olive. Bill is longer and more curved than Tiny Sunbird's; also has a golden-green (not bluish-green) head and upperparts, and differs by habitat, very vocal behaviour and low foraging height. Female is olive-green above and olive-yellow below, with a pale eye-stripe. **Habitat:** Forest edge, secondary growth, plantations, gardens and woodland; avoids dense forest. Feeds in low strata. **Status:** Common. **Voice:** High-pitched rapid trilling song; 'tseeep' call. [C13.1]

2 TINY SUNBIRD *Cinnyris minullus*   8-10 cm
Smaller than Olive-bellied Sunbird, with a shorter, less decurved bill (lower mandible appears almost straight). Male has a narrow blue band above the red breast, and is more bluish-green above. Tends to be less vocal. Female is olive-green above, dusky olive-green or olive-yellow below. **Habitat:** Forest canopy, gallery forest, forest edge and secondary growth. Generally feeds in canopy and higher strata than Olive-bellied Sunbird. **Status:** Locally common, but patchily distributed in Congo Basin. **Voice:** Loud, chipping song, accelerating, but shorter and slower than Olive-bellied Sunbird. [C13.2]

3 NORTHERN DOUBLE-COLLARED SUNBIRD *Cinnyris preussi*   11-12 cm
A short-billed double-collared sunbird. Male has a broader red breast band than Olive-bellied Sunbird, which lacks a violet breast band and rump. Smaller and shorter-billed than Rwenzori Double-collared Sunbird, with a darker belly. Darker blue-green above than Eastern Double-collared Sunbird (p. 638), with a shorter bill and tail and a narrower breast band. Female lacks pale eye-stripe of female Olive-bellied Sunbird; best told from female Rwenzori and Eastern double-collared sunbirds by its smaller bill. **Habitat:** Mid-altitude and highland forests and adjacent scrub and gardens. **Status:** Locally common. **Voice:** Harsh 'jii jii jii' and clipped 'chip chip'; song jumbled mixture of buzzy and sweet notes. [C13.3]

4 GREATER DOUBLE-COLLARED SUNBIRD *Cinnyris afrea*   14-15 cm
Endemic to S Africa. Much larger than Southern Double-collared Sunbird (p. 638) with a longer, heavier bill. Male has a broader red breast band. Female grey-brown above, paler below; best separated from female Southern Double-collared Sunbird by its larger size and longer, heavier bill. **Habitat:** Tall shrubs, forest fringes, clearings and gardens. **Status:** Common. **Voice:** Harsh, frequently repeated 'tchut-tchut-tchut'; a fast, twittering song. [C5.13a, G6.4.5]

5 LUDWIG'S DOUBLE-COLLARED SUNBIRD *Cinnyris ludovicensis*   12-13 cm
Disjunct populations variously lumped with Greater and Rwenzori double-collared sunbirds. Overlaps with Miombo and Forest double-collared sunbirds (p. 638), but is slightly larger with a shorter, broader-based bill. Male has a broader red breast band than N Miombo Double-collared Sunbird, with blue rump and brown (not olive) belly of Forest Double-collared Sunbird. **Habitat:** Montane heath and forest edge on Nyika Plateau, Malawi; gallery forest and riparian scrub in Angola. **Status:** Locally common; usually in pairs. **Voice:** Song jumbled chittering with harsh 'ziit' and 'cheet' notes.

6 RWENZORI (STUHLMANN'S) DOUBLE-COLLARED SUNBIRD
Cinnyris stuhlmanni   13-14 cm
Endemic to the Albertine Rift. A large, montane double-collared sunbird. Overlaps at lower elevations (up to 2 500 m) with the smaller Northern Double-collared Sunbird; has a thicker, longer bill, longer tail, slightly broader red breast band and paler grey belly. Female similar to female Northern Double-collared Sunbird; best told by structure and elevation. SE DRC *prigogenei* is smaller and may be closer to Malawi population of Ludwig's Double-collared Sunbird; sometimes treated as a distinct species. **Habitat:** Montane heath, scrub and forest edge, 2 000-4 000 m. **Status:** Locally common. **Voice:** A rapid twittering song and harsher 'chit' or 'sjeep' calls. [C5.13b]

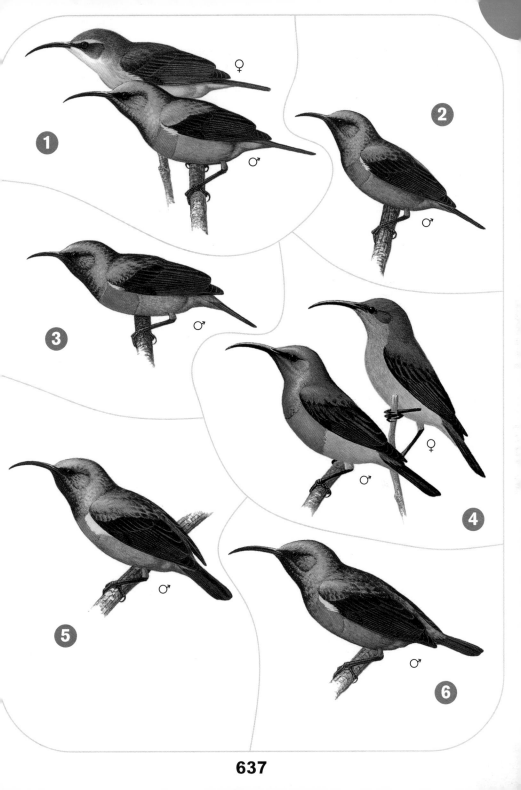

1 SOUTHERN DOUBLE-COLLARED SUNBIRD *Cinnyris chalybeus* 12 cm
Endemic to S Africa. Smaller than Greater Double-collared Sunbird (p. 636), with a shorter, more slender bill; male has a narrower red breast band. Female is grey-brown (not olive-green, as female Orange-breasted Sunbird; p. 614), darker above than below, but not as pale below as female Dusky Sunbird (p. 628). **Habitat:** Coastal and Karoo scrub, fynbos and forests (in NE and extreme W). **Status:** Common. **Voice:** Harsh 'chee-chee' call; song rapid, high-pitched twitter, rising and falling in pitch. [G6.4.3]

2 MIOMBO DOUBLE-COLLARED SUNBIRD *Cinnyris manoensis* 13 cm
Similar to Southern Double-collared Sunbird; in S male has smaller blue uppertail coverts and corresponding broader olive rump; ranges do not overlap. N *pintoi* lacks blue rump and uppertail coverts of Ludwig's Double-collared Sunbird (p. 636), and its red breast band is narrower. Belly is pale olive-grey, not blackish as Shelley's Sunbird (p. 630). Female is grey-brown above and pale grey below, often with a yellowish wash on the central belly. Mt Gorongoza, Mozambique *amicorum* is larger, and has been linked to greater double-collared sunbirds (p. 636). **Habitat:** Miombo woodland, gardens and edges of montane forest. **Status:** Common. **Voice:** Similar to Southern Double-collared Sunbird's. [G6.4.4]

3 EASTERN DOUBLE-COLLARED SUNBIRD *Cinnyris mediocris* 11-12 cm
Endemic to E Africa. A montane-forest sunbird; seldom overlaps with other double-collared sunbirds. Has longer bill and tail and a narrower red breast band than Northern Double-collared Sunbird (p. 636), and occurs at higher altitude than Olive-bellied Sunbird (p. 636) in narrow area of overlap. Red breast band broader than Usambara Double-collared Sunbird, with blue (not violet) uppertail coverts. Female rather dark with paler belly. **Habitat:** Montane forest and forest edge, 1 500-3 700 m (rarely to 700 m). **Status:** Common. **Voice:** High-pitched, jumbled song. [C13.7]

4 USAMBARA DOUBLE-COLLARED SUNBIRD *Cinnyris usambaricus* 11-12 cm
Endemic to S Pare and Usambara Mts. Formerly treated as a race of Eastern Double-collared Sunbird, but genetically highly distinct. Male has narrower red breast band, violet (not blue) uppertail coverts and is more bronzy-green above. **Habitat:** Montane forest and forest edge. **Status:** Common. **Voice:** Not known to differ from Eastern Double-collared Sunbird.

5 FOREST DOUBLE-COLLARED SUNBIRD *Cinnyris fuelleborni* 11-12 cm
Formerly treated as a race of Eastern Double-collared Sunbird, but genetically highly distinct. Habitat, violet uppertail coverts and belly colour separate it from Miombo Double-collared Sunbird. At Nyika Plateau, smaller than Ludwig's Double-collared Sunbird (p. 636), with a narrower red breast band and shorter, thinner bill. Southern *bensoni* has darker belly. **Habitat:** Montane forest. **Status:** Common. **Voice:** Not known to differ from Eastern Double-collared Sunbird.

6 RUFOUS-WINGED SUNBIRD *Cinnyris rufipennis* 12 cm
Endemic to Udzungwa Mts, Tanzania. Male is dark iridescent blue above, with bright rufous wing patches; throat is bronze, with narrow blue and broader red breast bands and a grey belly. In dark forest interior can be mistaken for Forest Double-collared Sunbird, but has a paler belly and rufous wing patches. Female is grey-brown, paler and slightly streaked below, but also has the diagnostic rufous wing patches. **Habitat:** Montane forests, above 1 000 m, rarely down to 600 m. **Status:** Vulnerable. Uncommon; forages mostly in low- and mid-storey, sometimes joining bird parties. **Voice:** Loud 'chow' or 'tchew'; song similar to Eastern Double-collared Sunbird's.

7 MOREAU'S SUNBIRD *Cinnyris moreaui* 11-12 cm
Endemic to Eastern Arc Mts, Tanzania. Range may meet Forest Double-collared Sunbird in N Udzungwas. Differs in having plain olive rump (not iridescent green), yellow sides to the red breast band and a more yellow wash to the belly. Once thought a hybrid between Loveridge's (p. 634) and Forest Double-collared sunbirds, but genetic studies confirm its species status. **Habitat:** Montane forest and forest edge, 1 300-2 000 m. **Status:** Common, from N Udzungwas to Nguu Mts. **Voice:** Chittering, chissik song and harsher contact notes.

Small, greenish-yellow warblers with prominent white eye-rings. They usually occur in small flocks and could be confused with penduline-tits (p. 390) or eremomelas (p. 528). Traditionally linked to sunbirds, they are probably related to warblers. Sexes alike; juvs duller, with smaller eye-rings.

1 CAPE WHITE-EYE *Zosterops capensis*   12 cm
Endemic to S Africa. Overlaps marginally with African Yellow White-eye in N and E; told by its darker, olive-green (not yellow-green) upperparts, more extensive green flanks and greater contrast between green crown and yellow throat. Darker green above than Orange River White-eye, with grey or yellow-green (not peach-coloured) flanks; calls also differ. Occurs in two forms: grey-bellied 'Cape White-eye' *capensis* in SW and yellow-green-bellied 'Green White-eye' *virens* in E, but with broad intergradation. Both have yellow throat and vent, which usually contrast with breast and belly, but some E birds have yellowish breast and central belly. Both forms hybridise with Orange River White-eyes in the Free State. **Habitat:** Woodland, forests, thickets, plantations and gardens. **Status:** Common to abundant. **Voice:** Remarkably loud warbling song uttered mostly at dawn; also constant chittering contact calls. [G6.5.6a]

2 ORANGE RIVER WHITE-EYE *Zosterops pallidus*   11-13 cm
Endemic to arid S Africa. Formerly considered a race of Cape White-eye, but distinguished by its diagnostic peach-coloured flanks and different call. Hybridises with both forms of Cape White-eye in narrow overlap zone in the Free State. **Habitat:** Riparian woodland and thickets in semi-arid and arid Karoo. **Status:** Common; some birds wander, occurring as vagrants outside the normal range. **Voice:** Higher pitched and more trilling than Cape White-eye's. [G6.5.6b]

3 AFRICAN YELLOW WHITE-EYE *Zosterops senegalensis*   11-12 cm
A bright yellow white-eye. Upperpart coloration varies geographically from pale yellow-green to darker green, but generally paler than other white-eyes; underparts mostly yellow, with limited green on the flanks. The only white-eye in most areas, but identification is complicated in C Africa, where it is told from Forest White-eye by paler green upperparts and mostly yellow (not green) flanks; lacks contrasting yellow frons and lores. In S Africa told from green form of Cape White-eye by paler upperparts, limited green on flanks and plainer head. In E Africa it co-occurs with the Abyssinian and Montane white-eye complex (p. 642); best told by its bright yellow underparts and relatively narrow white eye-ring. **Habitat:** Woodland, scrub, forest and gardens. **Status:** Common. **Voice:** Loud 'tweee-tuuu-twee-twee' song; starts hesitantly; notes are slurred in W and N Africa, purer in S. Groups make continuous twittering contact calls. [C13.26, G6.5.7]

4 FOREST (GREEN) WHITE-EYE *Zosterops stenocricotus*   12 cm
Often treated as a race of African Yellow White-eye, which it replaces in C Africa forests; ranges not known to overlap. Differs by being darker green above, with bright yellow forehead and crisply defined yellow lores extending above eye as short eye-stripe; also has more extensive green flanks. Brighter overall and larger than Forest Penduline-Tit (p. 390). **Habitat:** Forest canopy and gallery forest. **Status:** Locally common. **Voice:** Song notes are pure, clear whistles, not slurred. Vocally considered closer to the montane white-eye complex (p. 642). [C13.27]

5 PEMBA WHITE-EYE *Zosterops vaughani*   10 cm
Endemic to Pemba and adjacent islets, where it is the only white-eye. A small, bright yellow white-eye with a black loral stripe and narrow white eye-ring. **Habitat:** Almost all, from woodlands to agricultural and urban habitats. **Status:** Common. **Voice:** Song is high-pitched, melodious 'sreet, seweet-sureeteet-twerila-eeta-eet'.

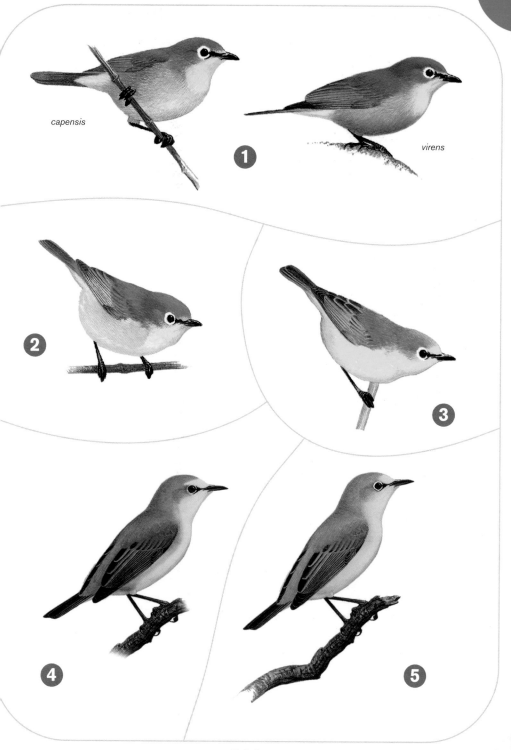

capensis

virens

1

2

3

4

5

1 ABYSSINIAN (WHITE-BREASTED) WHITE-EYE *Zosterops abyssinicus* 10 cm
Endemic to NE Africa. A small white-eye with a relatively narrow white eye-ring, green crown lacking a yellow forehead, and with less black on the lores than other white-eyes. Breast and belly colour vary from pale grey in N, grading to pale lemon-yellow from S Ethiopia to Tanzania. Yellow-breasted races have paler yellow underparts than African Yellow White-eye (p. 640) and lack green flanks. Eye-ring is narrower than Montane White-eye, and yellow-breasted race lacks green flanks; generally occurs at lower altitudes. **Habitat:** Woodland, thickets and gardens below 1 800 m. **Status:** Locally common; undergoes local movement in S. **Voice:** Calls 'teeyu'; typical, undulating white-eye song.

2 MONTANE (BROAD-RINGED) WHITE-EYE *Zosterops poliogastrus* 11-12 cm
Endemic to NE Africa. A montane-forest white-eye with a broader white eye-ring than African Yellow (p. 640) and Abyssinian white-eyes. Most races have yellow underparts and conspicuous yellow foreheads, but *eurycricotus* (Kilimanjaro and Mt Meru) has dark green underparts and yellow-green frons. Race *poliogaster* (C Ethiopia N) has greyish buff flanks and white central belly. **Habitat:** Montane forest and woodland, 1 500-3 400 m. **Status:** Common. **Voice:** Typical, undulating white-eye song.

3 KULAL WHITE-EYE *Zosterops kulalensis* 11-12 cm
Endemic to Mt Kulal, N Kenya, where it is the only montane white-eye. Might overlap with African Yellow (p. 640) and Abyssinian white-eyes on lower slopes, but is darker, with grey underparts and a broader white eye-ring. Grey belly has pale centre. Formerly lumped with Montane and African Yellow white-eyes. **Habitat:** Montane forest, 1 500-2 300 m. **Status:** Vulnerable. Common within its small range. **Voice:** Typical white-eye song and calls.

4 TAITA WHITE-EYE *Zosterops silvanus* 11-12 cm
Endemic to Taita Hills, SE Kenya, where it is the only montane white-eye. Told from Montane and African Yellow (p. 640) white-eyes by its grey underparts, which are darker than South Pare White-eye's, with no pale central belly stripe. Formerly lumped with Montane White-eye. **Habitat:** Montane forest, 800-1 700 m. **Status:** Endangered. Common, but restricted to small and fragmented forest patches. **Voice:** Song is slow, undulating warble, 'see tee tew chew'; typical white-eye calls.

5 SOUTH PARE WHITE-EYE *Zosterops winifredae* 11-12 cm
Endemic to South Pare Mts, NE Tanzania, where it is the only montane white-eye. Darker than African Yellow (p. 640) and Abyssinian white-eyes, with grey underparts and a broader white eye-ring. Grey underparts are slightly paler than Taita White-eye's, with pale central belly stripe. Formerly lumped with Montane White-eye. **Habitat:** Montane forests, 2 000-2 500 m. **Status:** Vulnerable. Common, but highly localised. **Voice:** Typical white-eye songs and calls.

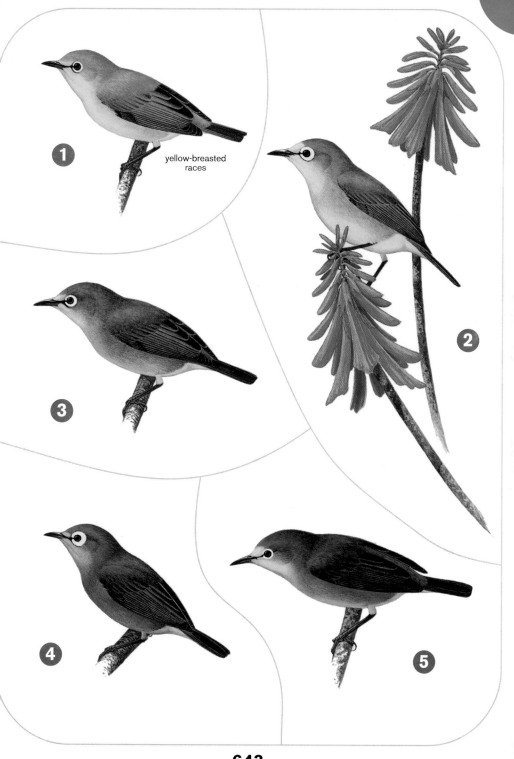

yellow-breasted
races

1 SÃO TOMÉ (PRÌNCIPÉ) WHITE-EYE *Zosterops ficedulinus* 11 cm
Endemic to São Tomé and Prìncipé. A drab white-eye, olive-green above and pale yellow-grey below. Smaller than the islands' speirops, with olive (not brown) upperparts. São Tomé *feae* is darker olive above, greyer below. **Habitat:** Forest and forest edge; also in plantations on São Tomé. **Status:** Vulnerable. Uncommon to locally common on São Tomé; uncommon on Prìncipé. **Voice:** Typical white-eye warbling song.

2 ANNOBON WHITE-EYE *Zosterops griseovirescens* 12 cm
Endemic to Pagalu (Annobon); the only white-eye on the island. A large, drab, olive-green white-eye with black lores and pale yellow supra-loral stripes. **Habitat:** Forest, plantations and shrubby areas. **Status:** Vulnerable. Common in its small range. **Voice:** Typical white-eye warbling song; 'plik-plik' flight call.

SPEIROPS

Large, grey-brown warblers, closely related to white-eyes, that are restricted to Mt Cameroon and islands in the Gulf of Guinea. Their ranges do not overlap, but they could potentially be confused with white-eyes.

3 MOUNT CAMEROON SPEIROPS *Speirops melanocephalus* 13 cm
Endemic to Mt Cameroon; sometimes treated as a race of Black-capped Speirops. A grey-brown warbler with buff belly and white thighs. Pale bill, frons, throat and eye give it a naked-faced appearance. **Habitat:** Chiefly in heath and scrub above forest line, 1 800-3 000 m; seldom reaches forest edge. **Status:** Vulnerable. Locally common in small groups. **Voice:** Whispy series of twittering notes by foraging flocks and in flight. [C13.25a]

4 BLACK-CAPPED (SÃO TOMÉ) SPEIROPS *Speirops lugubris* 13-15 cm
Endemic to São Tomé; sometimes treated as a race of Mount Cameroon Speirops. A large, dark brown warbler with a black cap and pale eye-ring, lores and base of bill. Flanks when fluffed are pale grey to white. Larger than São Tomé White-eye; lacks any green plumage. **Habitat:** Primary forest, secondary growth, gardens and scrub. **Status:** Common. **Voice:** Contact calls 'truer' and 'took'. [C13.25b]

5 FERNANDO PO SPEIROPS *Speirops brunneus* 12-13 cm
Endemic to Bioko (Fernando Po). A very dark, greyish-brown warbler with slightly paler underparts, a dark head, grey throat and prominent whitish flanks. Lacks white eye-ring. **Habitat:** Montane heath, scrub and forest edge, 1 900-3 000 m. **Status:** Vulnerable. Locally common; usually in small groups. **Voice:** Long, trilling 'trrrrrruuuuu'; rapid 'tric tric tric'.

6 PRÌNCIPÉ SPEIROPS *Speirops leucophaeus* 12-13 cm
Endemic to Prìncipé. A pale grey warbler that appears white-headed at a distance. At closer range, head is pale grey, which avoids confusion with olive-headed São Tomé White-eye. Eye is golden brown, with very narrow, white eye-ring. Wings and tail are dark brown; mantle and underparts are grey, with white flanks and central belly. **Habitat:** Primary forest, secondary growth, plantations and gardens. **Status:** Locally common; often in small groups. **Voice:** White-eye-like twittering and churring. [C13.24]

Familiar, finch-like birds with stout, conical bills. Sexes differ, and some species have a distinct male breeding plumage.

1 HOUSE SPARROW *Passer domesticus* 14 cm

Male is easily recognised by its grey crown and rump, reddish-brown back, black throat and white cheeks. Smaller than Great Sparrow (p. 648), and lacks bright chestnut rump. Female and juv. are dull grey-brown and show narrow, off-white eye-stripe; smaller than Yellow-throated Petronia (p. 652), with shorter, stouter bill. **Habitat:** Towns, cities and gardens; usually close to human habitation. **Status:** Introduced; locally common; sometimes forms flocks of up to 50 birds which may occur away from built-up areas. **Voice:** Various chirps, chips and 'chissick' [C4.69/14.33, G6.6.1]

2 SPANISH SPARROW *Passer hispaniolensis* 15-16 cm

Similar to House Sparrow, but slightly larger and with a heavier bill. Breeding male may be told from House Sparrow by chestnut (not grey) crown and extensive black blotching on sides of breast and flanks. Blotching is reduced in non-breeding plumage. Female closely resembles female House Sparrow, but is lightly streaked (not plain) below, and has slightly paler, more conspicuous supercilium, larger bill and more conspicuous pale stripe on mantle. **Habitat:** Open, arid country, often close to water. **Status:** Locally common Palearctic migrant Oct-Mar. **Voice:** Similar to House Sparrow's, but calls are louder and deeper. [C4.70]

3 SOMALI SPARROW *Passer castanopterus* 13-14 cm

Endemic to NE Africa. Breeding male is distinguished from House Sparrow and Kenya Rufous Sparrow (p. 648) by chestnut (not grey) crown and nape; rump is grey, and cheeks and underparts are washed yellow. Female is duller, very similar to female House Sparrow, but belly is washed yellow. Dark (not pale) eyes and drabber upperparts (lacking chestnut) distinguish it from female Kenya Rufous Sparrow. **Habitat:** Dry, open country with scattered bushes up to 1 500 m, also along rocky coasts; frequently in association with humans. **Status:** Common to locally abundant. **Voice:** 'Chirrup', very similar to House Sparrow's.

4 DESERT SPARROW *Passer simplex* 13-14 cm

Male is extremely pale grey or buffy-grey above, with contrasting black bill, bib and loral stripe. Female is sandy above, with largely unmarked head and pale fawn base to black-tipped bill. Paler than Pale Rock Finch (p. 652), and lacks malar and moustachial stripes. Pale wing bar, whitish rump and two-tone bill distinguish it from all plumages of Yellow-spotted Petronia (p. 652). **Habitat:** Sandy plains at desert fringes; also oases and around human settlements. **Status:** Uncommon resident and nomad. **Voice:** Song is finch-like, trilling and melodious; some calls are reminiscent of House Sparrow's; also soft 'chu' and shrill 'chip-chip'. [C4.73]

5 SUDAN GOLDEN SPARROW *Passer luteus* 12-13 cm

Breeding male has a bright yellow head and underparts contrasting with mostly brown upperparts. Brown (not yellow) mantle separates it from Arabian Golden Sparrow. Female and non-breeding male are duller and rather nondescript; could be confused with drab female finches or widowbirds, but are washed yellow on head and breast; told from Arabian Golden Sparrow by dark streaking on mantle and scapulars (not plain). **Habitat:** Arid scrub, open savanna and cultivated areas; does not normally forage around settlements. **Status:** Common resident and nomad; breeds colonially and often roosts communally in towns. **Voice:** Dry 'chirp' or 'chirrup'; also rapid, repeated 'chi chi chi' in flight. [C14.36]

6 ARABIAN GOLDEN SPARROW *Passer euchlorus* 13 cm

Breeding male is bright yellow, with dark wings and tail, easily told from Sudan Golden Sparrow by yellow (not brown) mantle and scapulars. Female and non-breeding male are washed yellow on face and breast; told from Sudan Golden Sparrow by plain (not streaked) mantle and scapulars. The two species are not known to co-occur, but their ranges are separated by less than 100 km. **Habitat:** Dry, open country and savanna, mostly below 600 m. **Status:** Locally common resident and nomad. **Voice:** Dry 'chirp', similar to that of Sudan Golden Sparrow.

1 CHESTNUT SPARROW *Passer eminibey* 11-12 cm

Endemic to NE Africa. A small sparrow. Breeding male is entirely chestnut, with darker face and wings; smaller than male Chestnut Weaver (p. 672), with shorter bill, no sharp contrast between head and body, and very different stance and behaviour. Female and juv. resemble female House Sparrow (p. 646), but are more richly coloured, with chestnut wash to supercilium, throat, scapulars and rump; much smaller than rufous sparrows. Imm. male has chestnut head, streaked brown upperparts and whitish underparts with scattered chestnut feathers. **Habitat:** Open thorn scrub and savanna below 2 200 m; often at human settlements. **Status:** Locally common resident and nomad. **Voice:** Soft chirping; males give twittering call at nest.

RUFOUS SPARROWS

A complex of closely related sparrows with largely non-overlapping ranges. Often treated as a single species; we highlight their differences. Sexes differ; females could be confused with Bush Petronia (p. 652), but have dark throats and paler ear coverts.

2 GREAT SPARROW *Passer motitensis* 15 cm

Endemic to SW Africa. Larger than House Sparrow (p. 646), with a bright chestnut back and sides of head, and chestnut (not grey) rump. Female and juv. are larger and much redder on back and shoulders than female House Sparrow. Told from female Cape Sparrow (p. 650) by dark eye-stripe, buffy wash to supercilium and dark-streaked (not plain) chestnut mantle. **Habitat:** Semi-arid acacia woodland; not usually associated with human habitation. **Status:** Locally common. **Voice:** 'Cheereep, cheereeu', similar to that of House Sparrow. [G6.6.2]

3 KENYA RUFOUS SPARROW *Passer rufocinctus* 13-14 cm

Endemic to Kenya and Tanzania. Larger than House Sparrow (p. 646), with distinctive pale (not dark) eye and rufous (not grey) rump. Pale eye separates it from other rufous sparrows; also has reduced dark eye-stripe, and grey crown and nape extend further onto mantle. **Habitat:** Dry grassland and savanna, often in association with man. **Status:** Common; usually in pairs. **Voice:** Song is high-pitched and metallic, interspersed with lower-pitched chirps; contact calls are sharp 'tsui', squeaky 'tsweeet' or loud 'tchewp'. [C14.34]

4 SHELLEY'S RUFOUS SPARROW *Passer shelleyi* 14-15 cm

The palest rufous sparrow; range is not known to overlap with those of other species. Differs from Kenya Rufous Sparrow by having dark (not pale) eye, more prominent dark eye-stripe and paler buffy-chestnut supercilium. Larger than House Sparrow (p. 646) and more richly coloured, with distinctive chestnut-and-grey head pattern and chestnut (not grey) rump. **Habitat:** Dry bush and scrub, adjacent grasslands and fields; seldom in association with humans. **Status:** Nowhere common and thinly distributed; often in mixed weaver and finch flocks. **Voice:** Similar to House Sparrow's but more metallic and with harsher contact calls.

5 KORDOFAN RUFOUS SPARROW *Passer cordofanicus* 14-15 cm

Endemic to Sudan and E Chad; range is not known to overlap with those of other rufous sparrows. Darker and more richly coloured than Shelley's Rufous Sparrow, with whiter, more contrasting ear coverts and underparts; most closely resembles Great Sparrow. Larger than House Sparrow (p. 646) and more brightly coloured, with distinctive head pattern. **Habitat:** Dry woodlands and scrub; seldom in association with humans. **Status:** Uncommon and thinly distributed; in pairs or small groups mixed with weavers and finches. **Voice:** Typical House Sparrow-like chirruping and chissiks.

6 SOCOTRA SPARROW *Passer insularis* 14-15 cm

Endemic to Socotra and Abd-el-Kuri islands. A large, brightly coloured sparrow that differs from other rufous sparrows by having grey on crown extend over back to rump. **Habitat:** Dry scrubby and bushed areas. **Status:** Uncommon and thinly distributed; usually in pairs or small groups. **Voice:** Typical House Sparrow-like chirrups and chissiks.

GREY-HEADED SPARROWS
A complex group of sparrows; sometimes treated as a single, geographically variable species, but some populations co-occur without interbreeding. Sexes alike; juvs slightly duller and paler. Bills black when breeding, paler when not breeding.

1 NORTHERN GREY-HEADED SPARROW *Passer griseus*   15 cm
Slightly larger than Southern Grey-headed Sparrow, with darker grey head contrasting with darker rufous mantle. Has more extensive grey on upper breast, whiter throat and slightly heavier bill. Also shows reduced or sometimes absent white shoulder stripe. Has white throat and less contrasting rump than Swainson's Sparrow. **Habitat:** Diversity of fairly open habitats, up to 2 500 m; much more commensal with man than Southern Grey-headed or Swahili sparrows. **Status:** Common. **Voice:** Similar to Southern Grey-headed Sparrow's, but often more variable, with higher-pitched notes. [C14.35]

2 SOUTHERN GREY-HEADED SPARROW *Passer diffusus*   14-15 cm
Slightly smaller than Northern Grey-headed Sparrow and paler overall (especially on the belly), with a less contrasting white throat and slightly thinner bill. Much paler than Swahili Sparrow, especially on the underparts. Paler and smaller-billed than Parrot-billed Sparrow. Juv. duller. **Habitat:** Prefers mixed woodland; occurs in gardens in some areas but generally avoids urban areas. **Status:** Common. **Voice:** Various chirping notes, 'tchep tchierp tchep'; brief alarm rattle. [G6.6.4]

3 SWAHILI SPARROW *Passer suahelicus*   14-16 cm
Told from Northern Grey-headed Sparrow by its greyish-brown mantle uniform with nape, crown and face, and darker underparts. Much darker beneath than Southern Grey-headed Sparrow. Smaller and paler than Parrot-billed Sparrow, with smaller bill. Range differs from that of Swainson's Sparrow, so confusion is unlikely. **Habitat:** Dry wooded grasslands, farmlands and villages. **Status:** Locally common; usually in pairs, but also in small flocks when not breeding. **Voice:** Slower and more varied in pitch than other grey-headed sparrows'.

4 SWAINSON'S SPARROW *Passer swainsonii*   14-16 cm
Endemic to NE Africa. Darker than Northern Grey-headed Sparrow, especially on head and throat; pale chestnut tail and rump contrast more strongly with back. Smaller and more compact than Parrot-billed Sparrow, and has much smaller bill. Range does not overlap with that of Swahili Sparrow. **Habitat:** Dry wooded grasslands, farmlands and villages; the common sparrow in Ethiopian towns. **Status:** Common to abundant in some areas. **Voice:** Typical chips, cheroops and chissiks.

5 PARROT-BILLED SPARROW *Passer gongonensis*   15-17 cm
Endemic to NE Africa. The largest, most heavy-set of the grey-headed sparrows, with a noticeably large, robust, chunky bill. Overall, is more smoky grey than other similar sparrows, with typically dark grey underparts, but the huge bill is the best character. **Habitat:** Dry to semi-arid bush or scrub; rarely around villages. **Status:** Locally common; usually in pairs or small flocks. **Voice:** Usual sparrow-like calls; long, low-pitched 'choooop' note.

6 CAPE SPARROW *Passer melanurus*   15 cm
Endemic to SW Africa. Male is unmistakable: it is the only sparrow with a mostly black head, throat and upper breast, with a distinct white 'C' extending from the eye across the ear coverts. Female and juv. differ from female House (p. 646) and Great (p. 648) sparrows by chestnut back, and grey head with paler 'C' like male. **Habitat:** Grassland, fields and large gardens; common in urban areas in some parts of range, but not in others. **Status:** Common. **Voice:** Series of musical cheeps, usually alternating in pitch, 'chirp chroop, chirp chroop'; short, rattled alarm call. [G6.6.3]

PETRONIAS
Superficially sparrow-like birds, petronias may be more closely related to pipits and wagtails. Their bill typically is longer and more slender than that of true sparrows. Often found in trees, walking along larger branches. Sexes alike in most species.

1 YELLOW-SPOTTED PETRONIA *Petronia pyrgita* 15 cm
A plain, grey-brown petronia with a small yellow spot at the base of the white throat (visible only under ideal conditions). Lacks obvious pale supercilium of Yellow-throated Petronia. Supercilium is also less marked than that of Bush Petronia, and is greyer (less brown) above, with less marked wing bars. Most likely to be confused with Pale Rock Finch (especially W *pallida*), but lacks malar and moustachial stripes and has greyish (not orange-brown) legs. E nominate is darker, with grey-washed underparts; W *pallida* is paler, with buffy-washed breast. **Habitat:** Lightly vegetated dry grasslands and steppes; spends more time in trees than on ground. **Status:** Locally common resident and nomad. **Voice:** Sparrow-like chirps, but higher pitched; generally silent. [C14.37]

2 YELLOW-THROATED PETRONIA *Petronia superciliaris* 15 cm
The only petronia within its range, although almost overlaps with Yellow-spotted Petronia in extreme NE; readily identified by its broad, creamy-white supercilium. Yellow throat spot is visible only under ideal conditions; absent in juv. Smaller than White-browed Sparrow-weaver (p. 656), with less contrasting plumage and no white rump. **Habitat:** Dry woodland, savanna and riverine bush. **Status:** Locally common. **Voice:** Loud, sparrow-like chipping. [C14.38, G6.6.5]

3 BUSH PETRONIA (LESSER ROCK SPARROW) *Petronia dentata* 13 cm
A dull brown petronia with a yellow spot at the base of a well-defined white throat. Confusion is most likely with larger Yellow-spotted Petronia, which has plain face; male Bush Petronia has pale chestnut supercilium extending from behind eye to curve around ear coverts; female has broad, conspicuous buffy-white supercilium behind eye. Darker above than Pale Rock Finch, with greyish (not orange-brown) legs. **Habitat:** Arid, lightly vegetated valleys and hillsides. **Status:** Locally common resident and nomad. **Voice:** Soft 'chewee' in flight; song is rapid twittering, sometimes rising and falling in pitch like that of a bunting. [C14.39]

4 PALE ROCK FINCH (SPARROW) *Carpospiza brachydactyla* 14 cm
A rather nondescript, sandy-coloured, pale-billed petronia. The poorly defined moustachial and malar stripes, lack of a clear white throat, and orange-brown (not greyish) legs distinguish it from Bush and Yellow-spotted petronias. **Habitat:** Arid plains and hillsides with rocky outcrops; also in grain crops, especially millet. **Status:** Locally common Palearctic migrant Sep-Apr, but easily overlooked. **Voice:** Nasal 'tsweee' or 'twee-oo'.

AMADINA FINCHES
Fairly large finches, related to waxbills, but recall small sparrows. Sexes differ.

5 CUT-THROAT FINCH *Amadina fasciata* 10-11 cm
The male's pinkish-red band across the throat is diagnostic. Female and juv. are smaller than female Red-headed Finch, with more boldly barred head, and distinctly streaked and mottled back; tail lacks white tips to outer-tail. Pale bill separates it from most waxbills; readily told from silverbills by more heavily barred and mottled plumage, and paler wings and tail. **Habitat:** Various dry woodlands. **Status:** Locally common. **Voice:** 'Eee-eee-eee' flight call. [C15.51, G6.11.5]

6 RED-HEADED FINCH *Amadina erythrocephala* 13 cm
Endemic to SW Africa. Male has distinctive bright red head; its barred or scalloped underparts distinguish it from male queleas. Female is larger than female Cut-throat Finch, with larger, more rounded head, uniform grey-brown (not boldly barred) head and mantle, lightly scalloped (not chevroned) underparts and white tips to outer-tail. Juv. is duller. **Habitat:** Dry grassland, acacia and broadleafed woodland. **Status:** Common resident and nomad, occasionally erupting outside normal range. **Voice:** Soft 'chuk-chuk'; 'zree, zree' flight call. [G6.11.6]

juv.

BUFFALO-WEAVERS

Large, heavy-billed weavers with large, untidy nests of mostly dead sticks. Sexes differ in *Bubalornis*, which is renowned for the male having a penis.

1 WHITE-BILLED BUFFALO-WEAVER *Bubalornis albirostris*   21-24 cm
A very dark, blackish-brown buffalo-weaver with variable whitish streaks below. Told from Red-billed Buffalo-Weaver by black (non-breeding male and female) or whitish (breeding male) bill. Female is browner. Juv. has more extensive streaking below, but is much darker than juv. Red-billed Buffalo-Weaver, with blackish (not dull red) bill. **Habitat:** Dry woodland and savanna. Groups build bulky, multi-chambered nests in large trees. **Status:** Locally common; sometimes in large flocks. **Voice:** Very vocal at nest: dry, rattling calls and rapid, more musical 'chuk chuka' notes. [C14.40]

2 RED-BILLED BUFFALO-WEAVER *Bubalornis niger*   21-24 cm
Male is similar to White-billed Buffalo-Weaver, but has a diagnostic orange-red bill. Female is browner and slightly scaled. Juv. is paler beneath, with quite prominent scaling; paler than juv. White-billed Buffalo-Weaver, with dull red (not blackish) bill. Plain (not scaled) upperparts and brown (not rufous-edged) wings and tail separate it from Rufous-tailed Weaver. **Habitat:** Dry woodland and savanna. Breeds communally in large trees or on electricity pylons. **Status:** Common resident and local migrant. **Voice:** Song is 'chip-chip-doodley-doodley-dooo'; also harsh calls. [G6.5.8]

3 WHITE-HEADED BUFFALO-WEAVER *Dinemellia dinemelli*   18-19 cm
Endemic to NE Africa. Easily recognised by its white head and underparts, orange-red rump and vent, and blackish upperparts with contrasting white wing patches. N nominate race has browner upperparts and tail than Tanzanian *boehmi*. Juv's rump is paler orange. **Habitat:** Dry woodland and savanna. Breeds singly or in small groups; nest is untidy large ball of grass and sticks. **Status:** Common; often in mixed flocks with starlings and other weavers. **Voice:** Parrot-like screech; variable chucks and whistles from noisy breeding and roosting colonies.

4 RUFOUS-TAILED WEAVER *Histurgops ruficauda*   20-22 cm
Endemic to N Tanzania. A very large, scaly brown weaver with a silver eye and rufous edges to the flight feathers. More scaly than female and juv. Red-billed Buffalo-Weavers, with broad white edges to wing coverts and dark (not red) bill. Larger than Donaldson-Smith's Sparrow-weaver (p. 656), with scaly brown (not creamy white) rump and throat. **Habitat:** Dry woodland and acacia savanna and grasslands. Breeds in loose colonies; nest is untidy grass ball with side entrance, similar to sparrow-weavers' but larger. **Status:** Common and confiding; feeds in flocks on ground. **Voice:** Noisy: nasal 'vizzeee'; raucous 'skwer'.

SPOROPIPES FINCHES

Small, sparrow-like finches with dark moustachial or malar stripes and speckled forecrowns. Sexes alike.

5 SPECKLE-FRONTED WEAVER *Sporopipes frontalis*   11-12 cm
The black-and-white speckled forehead, moustachial stripes and rufous nape, extending as a partial collar, are diagnostic. Juv. is duller, with tawny nape. **Habitat:** Dry acacia savanna and grasslands with scattered bushes. Builds large, scruffy grass nest with side entrance in bush. **Status:** Uncommon to locally common; often in small groups. **Voice:** High-pitched 'sip sip' and trilling flight call; song is high-pitched series of ascending trills. [C14.41]

6 SCALY-FEATHERED FINCH *Sporopipes squamifrons*   10 cm
Endemic to SW Africa. Lacks rufous nape of Speckle-fronted Weaver and has more contrasting white-edged blackish wing and tail feathers; ranges do not overlap. Broad black malar stripes make it appear rather displeased. Juv. lacks black malar stripes and freckling on forehead. **Habitat:** Dry savanna, bushy desert watercourses and fields. Builds ball nest of grass with side entrance, sometimes on disused nests of other birds. **Status:** Common resident and nomad; often in small groups; joins flocks of other seed-eaters. **Voice:** Soft 'chizz, chizz, chizz' flight call, deeper and harsher than Speckle-fronted Weaver's. [G6.6.6]

SPARROW-WEAVERS

Fairly large, sparrow-like weavers that breed in loose colonies, building untidy grass nests with side entrances. Sexes alike.

1 WHITE-BROWED SPARROW-WEAVER *Plocepasser mahali*   16-18 cm
A boldly patterned, dark-brown and white sparrow-weaver. Darker above than Chestnut-crowned Sparrow-Weaver, with conspicuous white (not brown) rump and different head pattern. Male's bill black; female's horn-coloured; juv's is pinkish-brown. SE African *pectoralis* has faint dark breast spotting; NE African *melanorhynchus* has white breast with brown partial collar. **Habitat:** Acacia savanna and dry woodland. **Status:** Common; in small groups. **Voice:** Harsh 'chik-chik'; loud, liquid 'cheeoop-preeoo-chop' whistle. [G6.5.9]

2 CHESTNUT-CROWNED SPARROW-WEAVER *Plocepasser superciliosus* 15-17 cm
Told from White-browed Sparrow-Weaver by its chestnut (not dark brown) head, paler brown mantle, brown (not white) rump and different head pattern. Back is colder grey-brown than Chestnut-backed Sparrow-Weaver's, and head pattern is completely different; ranges do not overlap. **Habitat:** Open woodland, often on rocky slopes. **Status:** Uncommon; easily over-looked. **Voice:** Usually silent; rather metallic trilling call; song is softer, higher pitched and more squeaky than White-browed Sparrow-Weaver's. [C14.42]

3 CHESTNUT-BACKED SPARROW-WEAVER *Plocepasser rufoscapulatus* 17 cm
Endemic to SC Africa. The combination of black striped head, rufous back and white wing bars is diagnostic. Head pattern is quite different from Chestnut-crowned Sparrow-Weaver's; ranges do not overlap. Male's bill whitish; female and juv. have dark bill. **Habitat:** Miombo woodland. Feeds on ground but flushes into trees. **Status:** Locally common. **Voice:** Short, high-pitched 'tseep' or 'trrrrt' call; song is higher-pitched than Chestnut-crowned Sparrow-Weaver's. [C14.43]

4 DONALDSON-SMITH'S SPARROW-WEAVER *Plocepasser donaldsoni* 16-17 cm
Endemic to NE Africa. Resembles a dowdy White-browed Sparrow-Weaver but has creamy cheeks with a dark malar stripe; lacks broad white supercilium and large white wing bars. Smaller and paler than Rufous-tailed Weaver or juv. White-billed Buffalo-Weaver (p. 654), with prominent white rump. **Habitat:** Dry acacia bush areas and open grasslands with scattered bushes. **Status:** Uncommon; usually in small flocks. **Voice:** Warbled, chippy, starling-like song.

SOCIAL-WEAVERS

Medium to small, sparrow-like weavers of arid savanna. *Pseudonigrita* usually builds individual nests; *Philetairus* builds spectacular communal nests. Sexes alike.

5 GREY-CAPPED SOCIAL-WEAVER *Pseudonigrita arnaudi*   10-12 cm
Endemic to NE Africa. A small, plain brown weaver with a pale grey cap and white-tipped tail. Differs from Black-capped Social-Weaver by dark (not pale) bill, brown (not white) under-parts and pale (not dark) cap. W *dorsalis* has blue-grey back. Juv. is duller, with paler bill and brown crown. **Habitat:** Dry acacia bush, scrub and adjacent fields. **Status:** Locally common; sometimes in large flocks. **Voice:** Very variable; mostly chattered 'spi chew spi chew'.

6 BLACK-CAPPED SOCIAL-WEAVER *Pseudonigrita cabanisi*   13 cm
Endemic to NE Africa. A brown and white sparrow-like weaver with a diagnostic black cap, face and tail. Differs from Grey-capped Social-Weaver by white (not brown) underparts, with black flank stripe, dark cap and pale bill. Juv. lacks black cap and has darker bill; told from juv. Grey-capped Social-Weaver by dark tail (lacking white tip) and paler underparts. **Habitat:** Dry acacia, savanna. Occasionally builds small communal nests. **Status:** Locally common; sometimes in large flocks. **Voice:** Noisy chattering at colonies; clipped 'chittik' flight call.

7 SOCIABLE WEAVER *Philetairus socius*   14 cm
Endemic to S Africa. The pale bill, black face mask, scaled black flanks and scaly back are diagnostic. Juv. is duller, lacking black chin and flanks. **Habitat:** Semi-arid savanna and Karoo scrub. Gregarious; builds huge, communal thatched nests in trees and on telephone poles. **Status:** Common. **Voice:** Chattering 'chicker-chicker' call. [G6.5.10]

A diverse group of fairly large, sparrow-like finches renowned for weaving complex, ball-like nests. Sexes usually differ. Males of most open-country species have an eclipse plumage and are often hard to identify outside the breeding season; most forest and woodland species lack an eclipse plumage and have more distinctive females.

1 GOLDEN WEAVER (HOLUB'S GOLDEN WEAVER) *Ploceus xanthops* 15-17 cm
The largest 'golden' weaver, with diagnostic pale yellow eyes and a large, heavy bill. Male has yellow head, lacking orange tinge of other 'golden' weavers, with orange-brown wash on throat. Lacks eclipse plumage. Female is duller, with olive wash on head and underparts; lacks whitish belly of most other female weavers. Juv. has brown eyes. **Habitat:** Woodland and savanna. Breeds solitarily or in small groups, usually over water; nest is rather compact, with a short entrance tube. **Status:** Locally common. **Voice:** Typical weaver-like 'chuk' and swizzling calls. [C14.53, G6.7.6]

2 YELLOW WEAVER (AFRICAN GOLDEN WEAVER) *Ploceus subaureus* 12-14 cm
Endemic to coastal SE Africa. Breeding male is smaller and brighter yellow than Golden Weaver, with a smaller, shorter bill and a red (not yellow) eye. Told from other male 'golden' weavers by red (not dark) eyes and orange wash confined to face and throat. Non-breeding male and breeding female are duller, with olive crown and cheeks contrasting with yellow supercilium. Non-breeding female and juv. have white belly and pale bill. **Habitat:** Woodland, savanna and gardens. Breeds colonially in reedbeds and trees near water; nest virtually lacks an entrance tube. **Status:** Locally common; in flocks. **Voice:** Softer 'chucks' and swizzling than other, larger weavers. [G6.7.7]

3 GOLDEN PALM WEAVER *Ploceus bojeri* 14 cm
Endemic to S Somalia and Kenya. Breeding male lacks an eclipse plumage; told from Yellow Weaver by dark (not red) eyes and orange wash over entire head (not confined to face and throat). Smaller than Golden Weaver, with dark (not pale) eyes and much more extensive orange on head and breast. Female is duller; told from female Yellow Weaver by bi-colored bill and dark (not red) eye; belly is yellow. **Habitat:** Swamps and riverine vegetation, especially palms. Breeds colonially, often with Yellow Weavers; nests are similar. **Status:** Locally common. **Voice:** High-pitched swizzling song.

4 ORANGE WEAVER *Ploceus aurantius* 14 cm
Male lacks an eclipse plumage; is bright orange-yellow on head and underparts; back is greener than Yellow Weaver's. Grey (not dark) eye, black lores and slender, pinkish bill separate it from other 'golden' weavers. Smaller and much brighter than Golden Weaver. Female is much duller, with mostly whitish underparts; best told from other female weavers by pale, slender bill and pale eye. **Habitat:** Wetland areas, but generally avoids large swamps and reedbeds. Breeds singly or colonially; nest is compact, with a very short entrance tube. **Status:** Locally common. **Voice:** Usually silent; chattering when breeding. [C14.54]

5 TAVETA WEAVER *Ploceus castaneiceps* 14-15 cm
Endemic to S Kenya and N Tanzania. Male lacks an eclipse plumage, resembling Golden Palm Weaver, but with golden-brown patches on the nape and breast, contrasting with a yellow (not orange) face; ranges do not overlap. Differs from Golden and Yellow weavers by having dark (not pale or red) eyes. Female is duller; told from female Yellow Weaver by bi-coloured bill and dark eye; belly is yellow. **Habitat:** Woodland and savanna. Breeds over swamps and pools in large colonies; nest has virtually no entrance tube. **Status:** Locally common; in loose colonies and in foraging flocks away from breeding areas. **Voice:** Noisy chattering in colonies.

6 PRÌNCIPÉ WEAVER *Ploceus princeps* 16-18 cm
Endemic to Prìncipé, where it is the only weaver. A large weaver; male has orange head, yellow underparts and greenish back; eyes are pale. Female is duller. **Habitat:** Most abundant along coast in disturbed areas; avoids primary rainforest. **Status:** Abundant. **Voice:** Usual weaver-like squizzles and chips. [C14.55]

1 SOUTHERN BROWN-THROATED WEAVER *Ploceus xanthopterus*   15 cm
Breeding male is bright yellow, with a distinctive chestnut (not black) bib confined to the face and throat, not extending onto the forecrown as in Northern Brown-throated, Rüppell's and Cape weavers. Eye is dull red-brown. Breeding female has yellow underparts and brown eyes; non-breeding birds are duller, with horn-coloured bill, buff breast and flanks, and white belly. **Habitat:** Forest and scrub. Breeds over water in reedbeds; nest is rather scraggly, with no entrance tube. **Status:** Locally common. **Voice:** Soft 'zweek, zweek'; swizzling notes. [G6.7.8]

2 NORTHERN BROWN-THROATED WEAVER *Ploceus castanops*   14 cm
Endemic to E Africa. Male differs from male Southern Brown-throated Weaver by chestnut face extending onto forecrown and pale (not dark) eye; ranges do not overlap. Chestnut face is less extensive than in Rüppell's Weaver, not extending behind pale (not reddish) eye. Lacks black eye-stripe of female Spectacled Weaver and has darker, better defined bib. Female told from female Black-headed Weaver (p. 672) by pale (not dark) eyes and longer, more slender bill. **Habitat:** Swamps, reedbeds and adjacent bush. Nest is compact, with no entrance tube. **Status:** Locally common. **Voice:** High-pitched chatters and squizzles.

3 RÜPPELL'S WEAVER *Ploceus galbula*   14 cm
Breeding male has chestnut (not black) face mask. Told from male Northern Brown-throated Weaver by chestnut mask extending behind reddish (not pale) eye. Face mask paler than Northern Masked Weaver's (p. 662), and chestnut is confined to face and throat (not entire head, as Juba Weaver; p. 672). Female and non-breeding male are duller, with dark eyes (darker than female Southern Masked Weaver; p. 672) and horn bill. **Habitat:** Dry acacia savanna. Colonial breeder; nest compact, with no entrance tube. **Status:** Nomadic; often in large flocks. **Voice:** Typical squizzles and chucks.

4 KILOMBERO WEAVER *Ploceus burnieri*   14-15 cm
Endemic to Kilombero marsh, Tanzania. Breeding male is more olive above than male Southern Brown-throated Weaver, and face mask is darker, blackish edged chestnut. Brighter yellow above than male masked weavers, with smaller face mask, not extending behind eye. Female and non-breeding male resemble female Southern Masked Weaver (p. 662). **Habitat:** Reedbeds and adjacent scrub. **Status:** Vulnerable. Locally common. **Voice:** Typical chucks and squizzles.

5 CAPE WEAVER *Ploceus capensis*   17 cm
Endemic to S Africa. A large weaver with a long, pointed bill. Breeding male is less yellow above than 'golden' weavers, with chestnut wash on face and throat, but lacks well-defined bib of Southern Brown-throated Weaver; eyes are pale (not red). Female and non-breeding male are olive above and dull yellow below; lack pale belly of female Southern Masked Weaver (p. 662). Female has brown eyes. **Habitat:** Grassland and scrub. Colonial breeder in reeds and trees. **Status:** Common. **Voice:** Harsh, hysterical swizzling song; 'chack' contact call. [G6.7.3]

6 BOCAGE'S WEAVER *Ploceus temporalis*   16 cm
Endemic to SC Africa. Sometimes considered a race of Cape Weaver, but breeding male has brownish wash confined to ear coverts; throat is yellow; ranges do not overlap. Dark face and more slender bill separate it from Golden Weaver (p. 658). Female is duller, with pale eyes; larger and longer-billed than female Lesser Masked Weaver (p. 662). **Habitat:** Mixed woodland and grassland; breeds in small colonies over water. **Status:** Little known. **Voice:** Similar to Cape Weaver's.

7 SPECTACLED WEAVER *Ploceus ocularis*   14-15 cm
Both sexes are bright yellow, with olive-green back, slender, slightly decurved bill, black eye-stripes and whitish eyes. Lacks eclipse plumage. In W of range, *crocatus* is easily confused with *brachypterus* Black-necked Weaver (p. 670), but has thinner bill and yellower crown; male has less chestnut wash on head and breast. Male has black throat, extending onto central breast in some races. Variable chestnut-brown wash on face and breast. Juv. lacks eye-stripe. **Habitat:** Forest edge, moist woodland, thickets and gardens. Breeds singly; nest is finely woven, with a long entrance tube. **Status:** Common; usually in pairs. **Voice:** Distinctive, descending 'dee-dee-dee-dee-dee'; harsh trills and swizzling song. [C14.50, G6.6.9]

crocatus ♂

1 VILLAGE (SPOTTED-BACKED) WEAVER *Ploceus cucullatus*   14-16 cm
A large, heavy-billed masked weaver. Extent of black on breeding male's head varies geographically, but all races have mottled black-and-yellow back; eye is dark red. Crown ranges from mostly yellow (S), through forecrown black (NC), to entire head and nape black (SC & W). Female and non-breeding male have prominent yellow supercilium, throat and breast; belly is whitish; back is dull, mottled greyish; eye is red-brown. **Habitat:** Savanna, fields and gardens. Breeds colonially in trees, palms and reedbeds; nest is rather untidy, with a short entrance tube. **Status:** Common; often in large flocks. **Voice:** Throaty 'chuck-chuck'; buzzy, swizzling notes. [C14.63, G6.7.1]

2 SOUTHERN (VITELLINE/AFRICAN) MASKED WEAVER *Ploceus velatus* 13-14 cm
Told from most other masked weavers by its red eyes and narrow black line above the bill. Amount of chestnut wash on head and breast varies, but black mask is always more clearly defined than in Northern Masked Weaver. Has narrower black band on forehead than Tanzania Masked Weaver, with yellower (less orange) underparts. Back is more uniform than Village Weaver's. N *vitellinus* has smaller black throat. Female and non-breeding male are much duller, with buffy-yellow breast and white belly. Bill is paler and eye is duller red-brown in non-breeding birds. **Habitat:** Savanna, grassland, fields and gardens. Breeds singly or in small colonies in trees or reeds; nest is neat ball with a short entrance tube. **Status:** Common and widespread. **Voice:** Sharp 'zik, zik'; usual swizzling weaver notes. [C14.58/59, G6.7.4]

3 TANZANIA MASKED (LAKE LUFIRA) WEAVER *Ploceus reichardi*   12-14 cm
Endemic to S Tanzania and NE Zambia. Sometimes considered a race of Southern Masked Weaver, but breeding male has a black frons (not a narrow black line above the bill) and is more orange-yellow below, with a ginger border to the black face mask. 'Katanga Masked Weaver' *katangae* (NE Zambia and SE DRC; orange wash confined to breast) and 'Ruwet's Masked Weaver' *ruweti* (upper Lufira River, SE DRC; even less orange) are intermediate; their specific status is uncertain. Female and non-breeding male are not separable in the field from Southern Masked Weaver. **Habitat:** Swamps and adjacent areas. **Status:** Locally common; often in small flocks. **Voice:** Similar to Southern Masked Weaver's.

4 NORTHERN MASKED WEAVER *Ploceus taeniopterus*   12-13 cm
Endemic to NE Africa. Breeding male has black mask and forecrown, merging through chestnut into yellow hindcrown and breast. Told from other masked weavers by dark (not pale or red) eyes; broad dark forecrown separates it from Heuglin's and Southern masked weavers. Female and non-breeding male are more tan and buff (less olive) than other masked weavers, especially on underparts, with prominent pale supercilium. **Habitat:** Semi-arid savanna. Breeds colonially in reeds and low vegetation over water, foraging in adjacent areas. **Status:** Common; often in large flocks. **Voice:** Usual chucks and squizzles. [C14.56]

5 HEUGLIN'S MASKED WEAVER *Ploceus heuglini*   11-13 cm
Breeding male has entirely yellow crown, but is smaller than Speke's and Fox's weavers (p. 664), with plainer, greener back and shorter, more compact bill. Told from male Southern Masked Weaver by pale (not red) eyes and black mask extending onto central breast. Female and non-breeding male have pale eyes, but more prominent supercilium than female Speke's and Fox's weavers; told from female Lesser Masked Weaver by pinkish (not blue-grey) legs. **Habitat:** Dry savanna. Breeds in small colonies or singly; nest is small, with a short entrance tube. **Status:** Uncommon and nomadic; usually in pairs. **Voice:** Typical swizzling song. [C14.60]

6 LESSER MASKED WEAVER *Ploceus intermedius*   13-14 cm
Breeding male is the only pale-eyed masked weaver with the mask extending onto the forecrown; Heuglin's Masked Weaver and Speke's and Fox's weavers (p. 664) all have yellow crown. Mask has narrow extension onto central breast, and has notch above eye, like Little Weaver (p. 664). Female and non-breeding male are nondescript, with pale eyes; yellower below than most female masked weavers. Legs are blue-grey (not pink-brown). Juv's eye is brown. **Habitat:** Savanna and woodland. Breeds colonially in trees and reeds near water; nest is rather untidy, with a short to medium entrance tube. **Status:** Locally common. **Voice:** Typical swizzling song. [C14.57, G6.7.5]

1 nigriceps

S races ♂ ♀

2 ♀ ♂ S races

3 reichardi ♂ katangae ♂

4 ♀ ♂

5 ♀ ♂

6 ♀ ♂

1 SPEKE'S WEAVER *Ploceus spekei*   14-15 cm
Endemic to NE Africa. Larger and heavier-billed than Heuglin's Masked Weaver (p. 662); male has spangled black-and-yellow (not rather plain olive-green) mantle; ranges do not overlap. Longer winged and longer tailed than Fox's Weaver, with paler upperparts due to broader yellow feather edges. Female is greyer than female Village Weaver (p. 662), with plain head (lacking buffy yellow supercilium) and pale (not red) eye. Lacks eclipse plumage. **Habitat:** Savanna, towns and gardens. Breeds colonially, usually in acacia trees; nest is very untidy, with a short entrance tube often angled to the side. **Status:** Locally common; often in large, mixed foraging flocks. **Voice:** Noisy at colonies; various chucks and chewps.

2 FOX'S WEAVER *Ploceus spekeoides*   14-15 cm
Endemic to Uganda. Has darker upperparts than Speke's Weaver, due to narrower yellow feather edges; also has shorter wings and tail, preferring swamps to savanna. Larger and heavier-billed than Heuglin's Masked Weaver (p. 662), with darker upperparts. Female is yellower below than female Speke's Weaver, with pale yellow (not white) belly. Lacks eclipse plumage. **Habitat:** Usually near water or foraging over savanna close by. Breeds in trees and reeds in swamps. **Status:** Locally common. **Voice:** Usual chucks and squizzles of weavers in breeding colony.

3 LITTLE WEAVER *Ploceus luteolus*   10-11 cm
A tiny weaver. Breeding male has a shorter, stubbier bill than male Slender-billed Weaver, with lemon-yellow (not orangey) underparts. Smaller than Lesser and Northern masked weavers (p. 662), with dark eyes and distinctive notch in crisply defined black mask above eye. Female and non-breeding male are nondescript; best told by small size and stubby bill. **Habitat:** Acacia savanna and woodland. Nest is small, with or without an entrance tube. **Status:** Locally common; usually singly or in small groups; sometimes joins bird parties. **Voice:** Soft 'seep' contact call; song of high-pitched squizzles and chucks; displaying male does not tremble wings. [C14.47]

4 SLENDER-BILLED WEAVER *Ploceus pelzelni*   11 cm
As small as Little Weaver, but has a noticeably longer, thinner bill. Male is more orange below than male Little Weaver. Female is rather bright yellow, with plain yellow face; much brighter than female Little Weaver. Lacks eclipse plumage. **Habitat:** Swamps, mangroves and adjacent areas. Gleans insects in warbler-like fashion. Breeds in small colonies; nest is small, with a short entrance tube. **Status:** Fairly common. **Voice:** Various high-pitched squizzles and buzzing 'zzzzzzzzzzrt'. [C14.46]

5 LOANGO WEAVER *Ploceus subpersonatus*   12-14 cm
Endemic to WC Africa. Slightly larger than Slender-billed Weaver, with a heavier bill. Male has darker orange-chestnut wash on nape and underparts. Female is duller, with less extensive black forecrown; shows less contrast between back and underparts than female Slender-billed Weaver, with olive-buff (not yellowish underparts). Juv. has paler bill. **Habitat:** Coastal palm scrub, mangroves and adjacent areas. **Status:** Vulnerable. Uncommon; usually in pairs or small groups. **Voice:** Harsh chatter; soft, warbling song. [C14.48]

6 COMPACT WEAVER *Pachyphantes superciliosus*   13-14 cm
A short-tailed, dumpy weaver with a large, robust bill. Breeding adults have black mask that only just extends above dark, dull red eyes. Male has chestnut forecrown; female has dark olive crown, separated from face mask by broad golden supercilium. non-breeding birds resemble dull breeding females, but with face mask reduced to broad eye-stripe; face and underparts are buff; bill is paler. **Habitat:** Damp grassland in woodland or forest. Breeds singly in reeds or tall grass; nest is finely woven, with a side entrance near the top, like small Thick-billed Weaver's. **Status:** Uncommon and local; in small flocks. **Voice:** Rather sparrow-like 'chip' and chittering calls. [C14.67]

1 BAGLAFECHT WEAVER *Ploceus baglafecht*   14-15 cm

Geographically variable. Adults have prominent pale eyes, small black mask with yellow throat and broadly yellow-edged wing feathers, but crown colour and upperparts vary greatly. Most males have yellow crown and dark nape, but some have dark crown. Females have black, grey or olive crown, matching nape and mantle, and grading into black mask behind eye. Upperparts vary from olive through grey streaked black, to black in distinctive *reichenowi* (Kenya, N Tanzania). Belly is yellow in most races, but white in NW races. Lacks eclipse plumage. Juv. is duller. **Habitat:** Forest edge, woodland gardens and towns. Breeds singly, building loosely woven nest, usually in foliage of trees and bushes. **Status:** Common and confiding; usually in pairs; often aggressive to other birds. **Voice:** Harsh 'chut'; usual weaver squizzles. [C14.44]

2 BLACK-CHINNED WEAVER *Ploceus nigrimentum*   15-17 cm

Endemic to WC Africa. Similar to *reichenowi* Baglafecht Weaver but has black (not yellow) throat and yellow (not dark) rump; ranges do not overlap. Bold gold-edged wing feathers separate it from other dark-backed weavers; black back separates it from Village Weaver (p. 662). Male has golden crown and collar; female's head is all black. **Habitat:** Forest edge and wooded grassland. **Status:** Uncommon and local; in pairs or small flocks. **Voice:** 'Shrip' or 'chittick' contact notes; jumbled song without squizzles.

3 BERTRAND'S (BERTRAM'S) WEAVER *Ploceus bertrandi*   15 cm

Endemic to highlands of SE Africa. Male resembles a masked weaver (p. 662), but has diagnostic orange-chestnut crown, black nape patch and pale eyes. Lacks eclipse plumage. Female has entirely black head and pale eyes. Both sexes are easily told from Baglafecht Weaver by black (not yellow) throat. **Habitat:** Montane forest edge and adjacent scrub; forages low down and in mid-stratum, where it creeps nuthatch-like on larger limbs. **Status:** Uncommon; usually in pairs. **Voice:** Sparrow-like chirp; male has usual squizzles in display.

4 BATES'S WEAVER *Ploceus batesi*   14 cm

Endemic to S Cameroon. Male has diagnostic chestnut head bordered by a black-and-yellow collar; upperparts are plain olive-green. Female is equally distinctive, with black head and yellow throat. In poor light could be confused with Dark-backed Weaver (p. 668), but back is olive (not brown) and throat is yellow (not speckled brown). Lacks eclipse plumage. Juv. has mottled olive-black head and paler bill. **Habitat:** Lowland forest and secondary forest; forages nuthatch-like. **Status:** Endangered. Apparently rare; often in bird parties. **Voice:** Undescribed.

5 BANNERMAN'S WEAVER *Ploceus bannermani*   13-14 cm

Endemic to highlands of SW Cameroon and SE Nigeria. Both sexes have a black face mask and pale yellow eye. Black throat and yellow-orange (not partly olive) crown separate it from male Baglafecht Weaver. Told from male Heuglin's Masked Weaver (p. 662) by plain (not pale-edged) wings, yellow (not olive) nape and black mask confined to throat (not onto upper breast). **Habitat:** Forest edge and adjacent scrub; often forages low down in vegetation. **Status:** Vulnerable. Uncommon; usually in pairs. **Voice:** Usual call is 'chrik chrik'; displaying male whistles and squizzles. [C14.45]

6 SÃO TOMÉ WEAVER *Ploceus sanctithomae*   14 cm

Endemic to São Tomé. A slender-billed weaver that gleans from branches like a nuthatch. Male has diagnostic orange-buff face and underparts, with contrasting dark crown. Female is paler and duller. **Habitat:** Widespread in all wooded areas. **Status:** Common; usually in small groups. **Voice:** Contact 'chink' or 'wik'; rapid, descending, rattled trill. [C14.72]

7 BAR-WINGED WEAVER *Ploceus angolensis*   13 cm

Endemic to SC Africa. A slender-billed, brown-and-white weaver with diagnostic white wing bars, creamy white mantle, yellow rump and white underparts tinged with yellow on belly. Sexes are alike. **Habitat:** Miombo woodland and dry riverine forest; creeps along branches, nuthatch-like, probing bark and lichens. **Status:** Uncommon; usually in pairs in bird parties. **Voice:** Squeaky contact call; melodic, ascending song ending in a squizzle. [C14.71]

reichenowi

♂

♀

emini

♂

♀

♂

1

♀

♂

2

♀

3

♂

♀

♂

4

5

6

7

1 DARK-BACKED (FOREST) WEAVER *Ploceus bicolor* 13-15 cm
The dark, blackish-brown upperparts contrast sharply with the golden-yellow breast and belly. Back is grey in some races; throat is variably grizzled grey. Told from Strange and Usambara weavers by golden (not chestnut) breast; dark back lacks olive tones of Strange Weaver. Differs from Clarke's Weaver by uniform (not yellow-edged) wings and richer underparts. Sexes alike; lacks eclipse plumage. Juv. is duller, with grizzled forehead and throat. **Habitat:** Forest and dense woodland. Breeds singly; nest is finely woven from vines and creepers, with a long entrance tube. **Status:** Locally common; usually in pairs; often joins bird parties. **Voice:** Song is musical, squeaky duet, with buzzing notes interspersed; soft, high-pitched 'tseep' call. [C14.68, G6.6.8]

2 STRANGE WEAVER *Ploceus alienus* 14 cm
Endemic to Albertine Rift. Told from Dark-backed Weaver by black head contrasting with olive (not blackish-brown or grey) back and wings, and by duller underparts, with chestnut breast and olive-washed flanks. Sexes are similar, but female has chestnut breast extending onto lower throat. Juv. is duller, with olive head. **Habitat:** Montane forests, where it forages in undergrowth and mid-stratum. Breeds singly. **Status:** Uncommon and easily overlooked. **Voice:** Soft 'cheet' and 'trrt' notes when foraging. [C14.52]

3 OLIVE-HEADED WEAVER *Ploceus olivaceiceps* 14 cm
Endemic to SE Africa. Differs from Dark-backed Weaver by its olive (not blackish-brown) upperparts and pale (not dark) eyes. Paler than Usambara Weaver, especially on head. Male has olive-yellow crown and broad chestnut breast band. Female has olive head and smaller chestnut breast patch. Juv. is paler. **Habitat:** Miombo woodland; gleans nuthatch-like among epiphytic lichens in canopy. Breeds singly; nest is made of lichens and is well camouflaged. **Status:** Uncommon to locally common; usually in pairs, often joining bird parties. **Voice:** Soft, whistled contact calls; short song.

4 USAMBARA WEAVER *Ploceus nicolli* 13-14 cm
Endemic to Eastern Arc Mts of Tanzania. Paler than Dark-backed Weaver, with chestnut (not golden) breast. In good light, dark, olive-brown (not blackish) head contrasts with blackish brown back and wings. Male's forehead is dull yellow, recalling dark male Olive-headed Weaver; ranges do not overlap. **Habitat:** Montane forests; clambers along larger limbs and forages, nuthatch-like, in mid-stratum and canopy, sometimes hanging upside-down. Breeds singly. **Status:** Endangered. Uncommon to rare; often in mixed bird parties. **Voice:** Soft, whistled 'swee-ti see see'.

5 WEYNS'S WEAVER *Ploceus weynsi* 15 cm
Endemic to EC Africa. Male is striking; told from Dark-backed Weaver by its black (not golden) breast, chestnut flanks, yellow-edged wing feathers and pale eye. Much richer below than Clarke's Weaver, with pale eyes; ranges do not overlap. Female differs from female Vieillot's Black Weaver (p. 674) by paler belly and broader, more yellow edges to wing feathers. Juv. is duller. **Habitat:** Forest, forest edge and secondary growth, often foraging in canopy. **Status:** Locally common but nomadic and unpredictable. **Voice:** High-pitched squizzling song; dry 'chip' contact call.

6 CLARKE'S WEAVER *Ploceus golandi* 13-14 cm
Endemic to coastal Kenya. Male resembles a washed-out male Weyns's Weaver, but with a dark eye and more slender bill. Paler underparts and yellow edgings to wing and tail feathers separate it from Dark-backed Weaver. Lacks eclipse plumage. Female has olive (not dark brown) head, breast and mantle, but retains bright yellow wing edgings. **Habitat:** Miombo woodland and adjacent forest, foraging in canopy. **Status:** Endangered. Uncommon; in large flocks and often joins mixed bird parties; breeding range unknown. **Voice:** Groups are noisy, making usual squizzling and 'chip' calls.

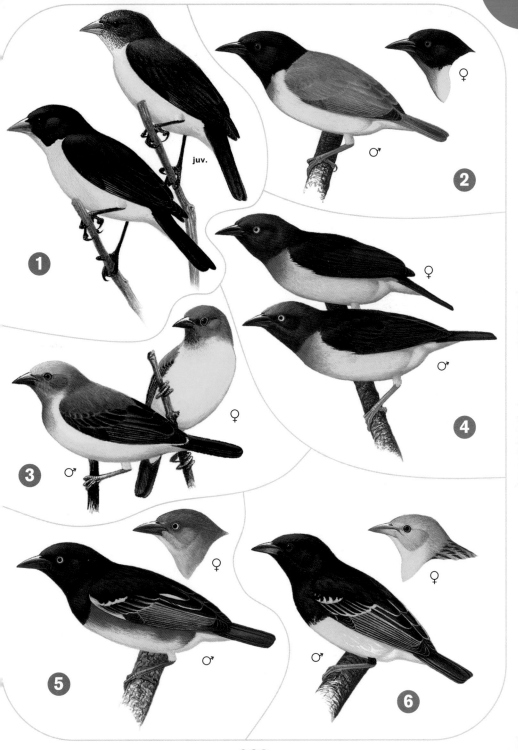

1 BROWN-CAPPED WEAVER *Ploceus insignis* 13-14 cm
A brightly coloured forest weaver. From below, recalls Dark-backed Weaver (p. 668), but has bright yellow mantle, back and rump. Male has diagnostic chestnut crown and nape; female's head is all dark blackish brown. Both sexes lack golden-orange crown of Preuss's Weaver; differ from Yellow-capped Weaver by yellow (not black) rump and distinct head pattern. Lacks eclipse plumage. Juv. has mottled yellow throat. **Habitat:** Montane forest; forages nuthatch-like along large, epiphyte-covered branches. Breeds singly; nest with a long entrance tube is slung under a branch. **Status:** Fairly common; usually in pairs in bird parties. **Voice:** Loud, sharp 'weet' contact call; song is series of soft whistles followed by 2-3 louder whistles and a squizzle. [C14.69]

2 PREUSS'S (GOLDEN-BACKED) WEAVER *Ploceus preussi* 14 cm
Endemic to W Africa. Mostly orange crown separates it from Brown-capped Weaver. Differs from Yellow-capped Weaver by having yellow (not black) rump and entire throat black (not just chin). Male has entire crown golden-orange, with chestnut breast patch; female has black forecrown and less intense orange wash on crown and breast. Juv's head is golden mottled black. **Habitat:** Lowland forest; forages nuthatch-like. **Status:** Uncommon and local; in pairs, often in bird parties. **Voice:** Harsh 'chwep' call; song not recorded. [C14.70]

3 YELLOW-CAPPED WEAVER *Ploceus dorsomaculatus* 14 cm
Endemic to C Africa. Male is similar to Preuss's Weaver but has a black (not yellow) rump, less orange crown and smaller black chin with no chestnut patch on breast; foraging action differs. Female has black crown and face; nape and throat are golden. **Habitat:** Lowland forest canopy; gleans foliage and hawks insects, but not known to forage nuthatch-like on branches. **Status:** Uncommon; usually in pairs in bird parties. **Voice:** Not recorded.

4 BLACK-NECKED WEAVER *Ploceus nigricollis* 15-17 cm
E and C African races have distinctive, blackish back. Male's head is golden, washed chestnut, with black eye-stripe and throat; female has dark cap and broad yellow supercilium. W African *brachypterus* (Senegal to W Cameroon) has olive upperparts, closely resembling Spectacled Weaver (p. 660), but has thicker bill; male has more chestnut wash on head and breast; female has olive crown defining clear yellow supercilium. **Habitat:** Forest, thickets and riverine scrub **Status:** Locally common; usually in pairs. **Voice:** Soft 'chek' contact notes; subdued squizzling song. [C14.49]

5 BLACK-BILLED WEAVER *Ploceus melanogaster* 14 cm
A mostly black weaver with a yellow head and a long, slender black bill. Male has black throat and hindcrown; female has yellow throat. Male *stephanophorus* (E Africa) lacks yellow breast band. Juv. duller, with yellow-olive underparts and dusky crown. **Habitat:** Forest and secondary growth; creeps through vines mostly in low forest strata. **Status:** Fairly common but easily overlooked; in pairs. **Voice:** Short, sharp 'chwit', querulous 'chwert' and squeaky calls. [C14.51]

6 GIANT WEAVER *Ploceus grandis* 22-24 cm
Endemic to São Tomé. Huge, with prominent pale eyes and a slightly decurved bill. Much larger than other weavers on the island (São Tomé Weaver, p. 666 and Southern Masked Weaver, p. 662). Female is much duller than male, with whitish belly. **Habitat:** Forest and secondary growth, plantations, gardens and dry woodland. **Status:** Fairly common. **Voice:** Various loud chatters and weaver-like squizzles.

7 THICK-BILLED (GROSBEAK) WEAVER *Amblyospiza albifrons* 15-17 cm
A large, dark brown weaver with a massive bill and large head. Male has white frons and wing patches; N races have chestnut head and paler back. Female and juv. are whitish below, heavily streaked brown, with paler bill. Appears long-tailed in flight. **Habitat:** Forest edge and rank vegetation, usually near water. Builds neat, finely woven nest attached to several vertical reeds, with a side entrance near the top; larger than Compact Weaver's nest. Breeding nests have smaller entrances than roosting nests. **Status:** Common. **Voice:** Harsh chattering; high-pitched 'tweek tweek' or 'pink pink' flight call. [C14.98, G6.6.7]

brachypterus

stephanophorus

melanogaster

S races

1 CINNAMON WEAVER *Ploceus badius* 15 cm
Endemic to Sudan. Breeding male is similar to Chestnut Weaver, but has yellowish (not chestnut) rump; wings and tail are edged yellow (not whitish). E nominate has yellow vent; vent is blackish in W *axillaris*. Female is nondescript; similar to female Black-headed Weaver, but more buff (not whitish) on underparts. **Habitat:** Dry savanna, open grassland and fields. **Status:** Locally common to abundant nomad. **Voice:** Usual weaver-like chucks and squizzles.

2 CHESTNUT WEAVER *Ploceus rubiginosus* 15 cm
Breeding male has a distinctive chestnut body and black head. Told from localised Cinnamon Weaver by whitish (not yellow) edges to wing and tail feathers; no yellow tinge to rump. Much larger and heavier-billed than Chestnut Sparrow (p. 648), with well-defined black head. Female and non-breeding male are drab, brown and tan, heavily streaked above; best told by reddish eye and heavy bill. Juv. has streaked breast. **Habitat:** Arid savanna and grassy woodland. Breeds in large colonies in trees; nest is untidy, with a short entrance tube. **Status:** Locally common. **Voice:** Melodic 'whut whut'; harsh 'chuk' and swizzling weaver notes. [G6.7.2]

3 GOLDEN-BACKED WEAVER *Ploceus jacksoni* 12-13 cm
Endemic to E Africa. Smaller than Juba Weaver, with a more slender bill. Breeding male has more clearly defined black head and richer chestnut underparts. Told from Black-headed Weaver by bright yellow (not olive) back, black (not yellow) nape and deeper chestnut underparts; eye is brighter red. Female and non-breeding male are nondescript; told from female Black-headed Weaver by its yellow (not buffy) underparts. **Habitat:** Savanna and open woodland, usually near water. Small colonies breed in trees and reedbeds. **Status:** Locally common. **Voice:** Males give wheezy chatter at colonies.

4 JUBA (SALVADORI'S) WEAVER *Ploceus dicrocephalus* 13-14 cm
Endemic to NE Africa. Large-billed; male has dark chestnut-black head contrasting with yellow mantle. Differs from Golden-backed Weaver by having dark head grading gradually into chestnut breast; belly is yellow (not chestnut); ranges do not overlap. Lacks narrow yellow nuchal collar of male Black-headed Weaver. Female and non-breeding male recall female masked weavers, but with dark eye and buffy breast. **Habitat:** Riparian woodland in arid savanna. Colonies breed in trees over water. **Status:** Locally common. **Voice:** Soft chattering.

5 BLACK-HEADED (YELLOW-BACKED) WEAVER *Ploceus melanocephalus* 13-15 cm
Breeding male has a black head and narrow yellow nuchal collar. Plain olive-green back separates it from Village Weaver (p. 662). Most similar to Golden-backed Weaver, but has paler underparts, yellow collar only (not entire back) and black on hindcrown not extending onto nape. Female and non-breeding male told from female Golden-backed Weaver by its buffy (not yellow) underparts. Told from female Southern Masked Weaver (p. 662) by dark brown (not red) eye and darker bill. **Habitat:** Close to water, often in fairly arid savanna. **Status:** Locally common; in loose colonies. **Voice:** Noisy chattering and nasal 'zhree'. [C14.64]

6 YELLOW-MANTLED WEAVER *Ploceus tricolor* 13-15 cm
Told from black weavers (p. 674) by its diagnostic yellow crescent on the mantle and dark (not pale) eyes. Told from Golden-naped Weaver by black (not reddish brown) crown, brownish (not olive-grey) belly and yellow (not golden-orange) mantle. Male's underparts are deep chestnut-brown; female is slightly paler beneath in W African nominate race, dark brownish-black in E African *nigroscapularis*. Juv. has paler chestnut head, mantle and underparts. **Habitat:** Lowland and mid-altitude forest; gleans from branches like a nuthatch. Breeds singly; nest has a fairly long, angled entrance tube. **Status:** Uncommon; in pairs or small groups. **Voice:** Usually silent; soft 'chissik', whistles and musical squizzles. [C14.65]

7 GOLDEN-NAPED WEAVER *Ploceus aureonucha* 13-14 cm
Endemic to Ituri Forest, E DRC. Told from Yellow-mantled Weaver by its reddish-brown (not black) cap and golden-orange nape with yellow stripe extending down the back. Breast is dark chestnut; belly is dark olive-grey. Female is duller, with paler crown, orange-brown nape and greyish breast. **Habitat:** Montane forests; forages along branches like a nuthatch. **Status:** Endangered. Little known and rare. **Voice:** Unknown.

1 VIEILLOT'S BLACK WEAVER *Ploceus nigerrimus*   15-16 cm
Slightly larger than Maxwell's Black Weaver. In E & C Africa, male differs by having pale yellow (not grey) eye; prefers more open areas. In W Africa, easily separated because male *castaneofuscus* (Guinea-SE Nigeria) has chestnut-brown back, rump and belly. Female is dark olive, streaked blackish above, with pale eyes and weak supercilium. **Habitat:** Forest edge, secondary growth and villages. Breeds in colonies, often with Village Weavers; nest compact, with no entrance tube. **Status:** Common. **Voice:** Harsh 'chak'; weaver-like squizzles. [C14.61/62]

2 MAXWELL'S BLACK WEAVER *Ploceus albinucha*   13-14 cm
Smaller than Vieillot's Black Weaver; sexes are alike. In E & C Africa, told from male Vieillot's Black Weaver by pale grey (not pale yellow) eyes and forest-canopy habitat. Nominate race (Upper Guinea) has greyish nape. Smaller than female Cassin's and Red-crowned malimbes (p. 676), with pale (not dark) eyes. Juv. is dark olive, with paler throat and vent; less streaked above than female Vieillot's Black Weaver. **Habitat:** Canopy of lowland forest. Breeds singly. **Status:** Uncommon to locally common; usually in pairs; joins bird parties, often with malimbes. **Voice:** Soft 'chit chat' calls; swizzling song. [C14.66]

3 YELLOW-LEGGED WEAVER *Ploceus flavipes*   16-18 cm
Endemic to Ituri Forest, E DRC. Larger than Vieillot's and Maxwell's black weavers, with white eyes and diagnostic bright yellow legs and feet. In good light, male has scaly greenish gloss on head and mantle; vent is brownish. Female is duller, lacking green gloss. Juv. is paler, with olive underparts and faint yellow collar. **Habitat:** Lowland forest canopy. **Status:** Vulnerable; uncommon; in pairs; sometimes joins bird parties. **Voice:** Unknown.

4 RED-HEADED WEAVER *Anaplectes rubriceps*   13-14 cm
Distinguished from all other weavers by its long, slender red bill. Breeding male has scarlet head and breast, but varies geographically: nominate (SE Africa) has small black eye-stripe and yellow-edged wing feathers; *leuconotus* (W, C & E Africa) has black face and red edges to wing feathers; *jubaensis* (extreme NE) is all red. Nominate non-breeding male, female and juv. have lemon-yellow face and breast; head is darker in other races, with buffy breast. **Habitat:** Woodland, savanna and gardens. Builds a thin-walled nest with a very long entrance tube, suspended from branches or wires. **Status:** Locally common. **Voice:** Squeaky 'cherra-cherra'; harsh calls and high-pitched swizzling. [C14.80, G6.7.9]

MALIMBES
Large, stout forest weavers with striking red- or yellow-and-black plumage. Breed singly, and forage in pairs or small groups. Sexes differ; juvs duller, with paler bills.

5 RED-BELLIED MALIMBE *Malimbus erythrogaster*   17 cm
The only malimbe with a red belly. Male has black face mask including throat; female is more orange-red, with red throat. Juv. is duller, with greyish mask and grey-brown belly. **Habitat:** Canopy of lowland forest and old secondary growth. **Status:** Locally common but patchily distributed. **Voice:** Sharp 'chissik' or 'sisek' contact call. [C14.78]

6 RACHEL'S MALIMBE *Malimbus racheliae*   17 cm
Endemic to WC Africa. A striking red, yellow and black malimbe; range does not overlap with that of Gola Malimbe, the only other yellow-plumaged species. Male differs from male Red-vented Malimbe (p. 676) by yellow-orange (not red) sides of breast and vent. Female lacks male's orange nape and crown. Juv. has orange throat and pale bill. **Habitat:** Lowland forest, usually in canopy. **Status:** Uncommon to locally common. **Voice:** Usual squizzling weaver-like song; harsh contact call similar to Blue-billed Malimbe's.

7 GOLA (BALLMANN'S) MALIMBE *Malimbus ballmanni*   17-18 cm
Endemic to Upper Guinea forests; range does not overlap with that of Rachel's Malimbe. The only yellow-and-black malimbe; can appear orange-yellow, but never red. Female lacks male's yellow nape. **Habitat:** Lowland forest and old secondary growth. **Status:** Endangered. Rare to locally common; in pairs and small family groups; often joins bird parties. **Voice:** Similar to Village Weaver's.

1 ♀ ♂ C & E Africa

2 ♂

3 ♂

4 leuconotus ♂

4 ♀ rubriceps ♂

5 ♂ ♀

6 ♂ ♀

7 ♀ ♂

1 RED-CROWNED MALIMBE *Malimbus coronatus*   17 cm
Endemic to WC Africa. Male is all-black, with a distinctive red cap that does not extend onto nape and mantle (as in Red-headed Malimbe). Female is entirely black; not separable from female Cassin's Malimbe unless male is present. Larger than Maxwell's and Vieillot's black weavers (p. 674), with dark (not pale) eyes. Juv. male has dull orange cap. **Habitat:** Lowland forest canopy. **Status:** Uncommon. **Voice:** Sharp, buzzy squeaks and swizzles. [C14.79]

2 RED-HEADED MALIMBE *Malimbus rubricollis*   17-18 cm
Combination of black underparts and red crown, nape and mantle is diagnostic. Always has more red on nape than male Red-crowned Malimbe. Male has entire crown red; female has black forecrown. Juv's crown is duller orange-brown. **Habitat:** Lowland rainforest and secondary growth; the only malimbe that gleans from large branches like a nuthatch. **Status:** Fairly common. **Voice:** Weaver-like squizzling; harsh 'zheet'. [C14.77]

3 BLUE-BILLED (GRAY'S) MALIMBE *Malimbus nitens*   17 cm
An all-black malimbe, apart from a red breast and throat. Similar to female Red-vented Malimbe, but has black (not red) vent; also red breast has spurs extending onto neck. Rather long, blue-grey bill is diagnostic. Female has slightly smaller red breast patch. Juv. is duller, with red-brown breast extending onto face and lores. **Habitat:** Lowland forest and mangroves, almost always close to water; forages sometimes very low in undergrowth. Nest is rather untidy, with a fairly short, angled entrance tube; habitually suspended over water. **Status:** Fairly common. **Voice:** Noisy, with harsh 'tzeeek' and 'waaak' calls; unremarkable weaver-like squizzling song. [C14.73]

4 CASSIN'S (BLACK-THROATED) MALIMBE *Malimbus cassini*   17 cm
Endemic to WC Africa. Male told from male Red-vented Malimbe by black (not red) vent. Not safely separable from male Ibadan Malimbe; ranges do not overlap: records from Ghana may be Ibadan Malimbe. Female is all-black, like female Red-crowned Malimbe; only identifiable if male is present. **Habitat:** Lowland forest and adjacent secondary growth. Typically breeds in small forest palms; nest has an extremely long entrance tube. **Status:** Fairly common. **Voice:** Harsh 'tuk tuk' contact notes; weaver-like squizzling. [C14.75]

5 IBADAN MALIMBE *Malimbus ibadanensis*   17 cm
Endemic to SW Nigeria, although may wander to Ghana. Male is similar to male Cassin's Malimbe, but typically has more extensive red on breast, with black notch in centre of lower margin of breast band; ranges do not overlap. Female is like male, but with much narrower red breast band. **Habitat:** Lowland forest, secondary growth, oil palm plantations and gardens. **Status:** Endangered. Uncommon to rare. **Voice:** Short series of whistles followed by wheezy swizzle.

6 RED-VENTED MALIMBE *Malimbus scutatus*   17 cm
Endemic to W Africa. Red vent is diagnostic in both sexes; always redder than yellow-orange vents of Rachel's and Gola malimbes (p. 674). Female of nominate race (Upper Guinea) has continuous red breast patch; E *scutopartitus* has two red patches divided by vertical black line. **Habitat:** Rainforest, old secondary growth and gallery forest. Breeds singly; finely woven nest is usually suspended from a palm frond, with a very long tube, flaring at the entrance. **Status:** Fairly common. **Voice:** Loud, buzzy 'tzee tzzee' and 'chuk chuk tzzzz' calls. [C14.76]

7 CRESTED MALIMBE *Malimbus malimbicus*   17 cm
Male has obvious crest and smaller black face mask than Cassin's and Ibadan malimbes, with red breast extending onto throat. Female lacks crest but has diagnostic small black face patch, often with narrow black line extending from eye to nape. Juv. male has dull brownish head with dark throat and no crest. Upper Guinea *nigrifrons* has smaller crest. **Habitat:** Mid-canopy of lowland forest, often in clearings and along roads. **Status:** Fairly common. **Voice:** Similar to Blue-billed Malimbe's harsh 'tzeek' note; variable chirps and whistles. [C14.74]

QUELEAS

Small, weaver-like finches. Non-breeding males and females could be confused with female bishops (p. 680), indigobirds and whydahs (p. 708), even small weavers (p. 568) or sparrows (p. 646). Usually in flocks; often mix with other seed-eating species.

1 CARDINAL QUELEA *Quelea cardinalis* 10-11 cm

Slightly smaller than other queleas. Breeding male told from male Red-headed Quelea by red head extending further onto upper breast, and black (not dark brown) bill. S *rhodesiae* has brown nape (not red, as in Red-headed Quelea), but nominate birds have red nape. Non-breeding male and female have head narrowly streaked with tawny and black, with well-marked buff supercilium; throat and breast are yellowish, and bill is horn-coloured. Juv. is buffier below, with dusky streaking on breast. **Habitat:** Grassland and cultivated areas, often near water. **Status:** Locally common nomad. **Voice:** Sizzling chatter, sometimes ending in nasal 'where' note. [C14.81, G6.8.3]

2 RED-HEADED QUELEA *Quelea erythrops* 11-12 cm

Slightly larger than Cardinal Quelea. Breeding male has red head extending only slightly onto breast and dark brown (not black) bill; in S, red nape is diagnostic. Breeding female has face and throat washed with pale orange. Non-breeding birds and juv. are very similar to Red-headed Quelea, but are slightly larger, with paler throat. **Habitat:** Damp grassland and adjoining woodland. **Status:** Locally common nomad and intra-African migrant. **Voice:** Sharp 'chip' call; flocks make twittering chorus at roosts. [C14.82, G6.8.2]

3 RED-BILLED QUELEA *Quelea quelea* 11-13 cm

The most abundant quelea. Adult has distinctive waxy-red bill (yellow in breeding female). Breeding male typically has black face and throat contrasting with buff crown and breast, often tinged pink; smaller and less colourful than Red-headed Weaver (p. 674). Some birds in W Africa have white head. Non-breeding male and female are nondescript, with strong whitish supercilium and paler underparts than other queleas, and distinctive red bill and pink legs. Juv. has pale brown bill. **Habitat:** Savanna, favouring drier areas than other queleas; also fields, where it is a significant pest. **Status:** Common nomad; at times abundant, in flocks numbering millions. **Voice:** Song is jumble of harsh and melodious notes; flocks make chittering noise. [C14.83, G6.8.1]

4 CUCKOO FINCH (PARASITIC WEAVER) *Anomalospiza imberbis* 11-13 cm

A small, short-tailed weaver-like finch with a distinctive short, stubby bill. Male could be confused with a yellow weaver (p. 658), but is smaller, brighter yellow (especially below) and has distinctly stout black bill. Female and juv. are buffy, with heavy dark brown streaks above; told from female bishops (p. 680) and queleas by relatively plain buffy face and heavy bill. **Habitat:** Open grassland, especially near damp areas. **Status:** Uncommon resident and intra-African migrant. **Voice:** Swizzling song; soft, chipping flight calls. [C14.97, G6.7.10]

5 BOB-TAILED WEAVER *Brachycope anomala* 11 cm

Endemic to WC Africa. A diminutive weaver of uncertain affinities with a distinctively short tail. Male superficially resembles male Cuckoo Finch, but has black-mottled face, buffy (not yellow) belly, shorter tail and slightly longer bill. Female is buffy-brown, with heavily streaked back; lacks darker crown of female Cuckoo Finch and queleas, and has distinctively short tail. Juv. resembles female but is paler. **Habitat:** Open areas along rivers in Congo basin, including villages. **Status:** Locally common; often in pairs. **Voice:** Sharp 'chik chik' call; song with melodious trill. [C14.84]

6 TRUMPETER FINCH *Rhodopechys githagineus* 12-13 cm

A small, plump, superficially lark-like finch. Most plumages are rather plain, pale greyish brown, with darker flight feathers, short pinkish legs and distinctive stubby yellow-horn bill. Breeding male is more distinctive, with grey head and pinkish face, red bill and pinkish flush on underparts and flight feathers. **Habitat:** Stony semi-desert areas and adjacent farmlands; comes to water to drink. **Status:** Uncommon and local. **Voice:** Nasal, buzzy 'neh', sometimes drawn out to metallic ring; short 'veechp' on being flushed. [C4.85]

1

♀

♂
cardinalis

2

♂ ♀

black morph

non-br. ♂

white morph

♀

♂
red morph

3

4

♀

♂

5

♀

♂

6

♀

♂

Sexually dimorphic, sparrow-like seed-eaters related to weavers (p. 658). They frequently form mixed-species flocks with other seed-eaters, especially when not breeding. Breeding males have predominantly black plumage with distinctive red, yellow or white plumage patterns. Bishops are smaller and fluff their plumage when displaying; male widowbirds have longer tails, coloured shoulder patches and are larger than females. Females are hard to identify and could be confused with other small seed-eaters, including non-breeding queleas, whydahs and weavers. Non-breeding male bishops resemble females, but non-breeding male widowbirds retain distinctive shoulder patches. Juvs typically are buffier than females.

1 NORTHERN RED (ORANGE) BISHOP *Euplectes franciscanus*   10-11 cm
Breeding male differs from Southern Red Bishop by more extensive black crown (not confined to forecrown) and very long upper-tail coverts that almost cover the whole tail. Smaller than Black Bishop, with red (not black) throat and rump. Black (not red) crown and brown (not blackish) wings separate it from Black-winged Bishop. Non-breeding male and female are smaller than female Black-winged Bishop, with smaller bill; probably indistinguishable from non-breeding Southern Red Bishop. **Habitat:** Grassland, savanna and fields; breeds colonially in reedbeds and seasonally flooded grasslands. **Status:** Locally common. **Voice:** Advertising males give wheezy, buzzy song; soft 'chip' call. [C14.88]

2 SOUTHERN RED BISHOP *Euplectes orix*   10-11 cm
Breeding male has throat black (S) or red (N); less black on the crown (confined to fore-crown) than Northern Red Bishop and shorter uppertail coverts. Told from male Black-winged Bishop by black (not red) forecrown and brown (not black) primaries. Non-breeding male and female are smaller than female Black-winged Bishop, with smaller bill; slightly larger than Zanzibar Red Bishop; indistinguishable from non-breeding Northern Red Bishop. **Habitat:** Grassland, savanna and fields, usually associated with water; breeds colonially in reedbeds. **Status:** Common; highly gregarious. **Voice:** Advertising males give buzzing, chirping song; 'cheet-cheet' flight call; nasal 'wheet' contact call. [C14.87, G6.8.4]

3 BLACK-WINGED (FIRE-CROWNED) BISHOP *Euplectes hordeaceus* 11-12 cm
Slightly larger than other red bishops, with a heavier bill. Breeding male is told from Southern and Northern red bishops by full red crown (lacking black forecrown), and from Zanzibar Red Bishop by red (not black) breast. In flight, diagnostic black flight feathers are conspicuous. Non-breeding male retains blackish flight feathers. Female closely resembles other non-breeding red bishops, but is larger, with heavier bill. **Habitat:** Damp grassy areas, reedbeds and fields. **Status:** Locally common. **Voice:** Buzzing chatter, similar to that of other red bishops. [C14.86, G6.8.5]

4 ZANZIBAR RED BISHOP *Euplectes nigroventris*   10 cm
Breeding male differs from all other red bishop males by the black (not red) breast. Full red crown separates it from other species except Black-winged Bishop. Non-breeding male and female are similar to other non-breeding red bishops, but are slightly smaller, with darker head markings, especially ear coverts. Told from non-breeding Yellow-crowned Bishop (p. 682) by buffy (not whitish), less streaked underparts. **Habitat:** Breeds in flooded grassland and reedbeds; non-breeding birds join mixed weaver/bishop flocks in grassland and fields. **Status:** Locally common. **Voice:** Usual bishop-like squizzling song and chittering calls.

5 BLACK BISHOP *Euplectes gierowii*   14-15 cm
The largest red bishop. Breeding male is easily identified by the black (not red) rump, narrow breast band and orange-red mantle; vent is streaked (not plain). In Kenya and N Tanzania, could be confused with red-naped form of Red-collared Widowbird (p. 684), but has much shorter tail and red extends further down back. Extent of orange on back varies geographically; greatest in *friederichseni* (Kenya and N Tanzania). Non-breeding male and female are larger than other red bishops and are overall darker, with heavy spotting on breast; more likely to be confused with female widowbirds. **Habitat:** Variable grass and crop types, especially sugar cane and mature corn. **Status:** Locally common; breeds singly; joins bishop and weaver flocks outside breeding season. **Voice:** Squizzling 'zee zee zee' in puffed-up display flight.

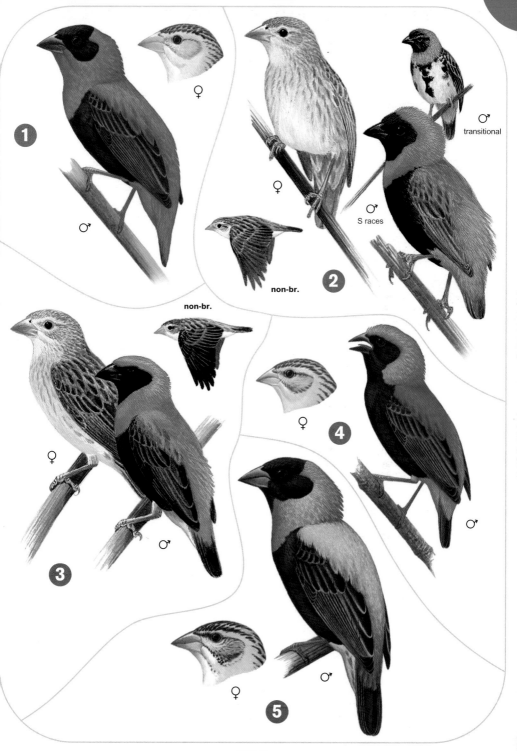

1 ♀

♂

2 ♀

♂ transitional

♂ S races

non-br.

non-br.

3 ♀

♂

4 ♀

♂

5 ♀

♂

1 FIRE-FRONTED BISHOP *Euplectes diadematus*   10 cm
Endemic to NE Africa. Breeding male has a distinctive spangled yellow back, red forehead and golden rump and vent. Non-breeding male and female resemble female red bishops (p. 680), but are smaller, with more prominent yellow-edged wing feathers. Could also be confused with non-breeding queleas, but have weaker bill and no moustachial stripes. **Habitat:** Breeds in small colonies in acacia scrub and woodland after rains; forages in grassland and fields. **Status:** Nomadic and locally common but unpredictable. **Voice:** Sharp 'zee zee'; swizzling song.

2 YELLOW-CROWNED (GOLDEN) BISHOP *Euplectes afer*   10 cm
A small, compact bishop. Breeding male has a diagnostic yellow (not black or red) crown. Displaying birds appear almost spherical, with greatly fluffed-out golden back and rump feathers. Non-breeding male and female are similar to red bishops, but smaller than most, with whiter (less buffy) underparts and prominent buffy-yellow supercilium. **Habitat:** Flooded grassland, vleis and marshes; breeds in small colonies, usually low down in grass or reeds. **Status:** Locally common. **Voice:** Buzzing and chirping notes. [C14.85, G6.8.6]

3 GOLDEN-BACKED BISHOP *Euplectes aureus*   11-12 cm
Endemic to Angola. Breeding male superficially resembles Yellow-crowned Bishop, but has entirely golden-yellow back (not black mantle) and black head (lacking gold crown). Smaller than Yellow Bishop, with no yellow shoulder and much more extensive yellow back. Non-breeding male and female are richer buff above and on breast, with lemon supercilium and throat. **Habitat:** Flooded grassland and marshes in Angola, but drier grassland on São Tomé. **Status:** Locally common in Angola; introduced to São Tomé, where it is abundant in the N. **Voice:** Fast, often-repeated 'bzik bzik bzik' by breeding male. [C14.89]

4 JACKSON'S WIDOWBIRD *Euplectes jacksoni*   14 cm (br. m 30 cm)
Endemic to Kenya and N Tanzania. Breeding male has dull reddish-brown (not red-orange) shoulders and long, noticeably downcurved tail. Non-breeding male retains dull shoulder. Female has paler underparts than other female widowbirds and lacks dusky underwings of female Long-tailed and Marsh widowbirds (p. 684). Males gather in leks, leaping up into the air with tails raised. **Habitat:** Open grasslands when breeding; in flocks over farmlands and open plains when not breeding. **Status:** Locally common. **Voice:** High-pitched, buzzing 'shreep shreep' song.

5 YELLOW BISHOP (CAPE/YELLOW-RUMPED WIDOW) *Euplectes capensis* 15 cm
A large bishop with yellow shoulder patches, forming a link to widowbirds. Smaller than Yellow-mantled Widowbird, breeding male has much shorter tail, and yellow rump and lower back (not yellow mantle). Non-breeding male is heavily streaked buffy-brown, but retains bright yellow rump and shoulder. Female is more heavily streaked than female Yellow-mantled Widowbird, with dull yellow rump; appreciably larger and more streaked than female red bishops. Bill size varies dramatically between races. **Habitat:** Damp grassy areas and heathlands. **Status:** Common. **Voice:** Displaying males give high-pitched 'zeet, zeet, zeet' or harsh 'zzzzzzzzt' calls; song of isolated SW Cameroon *phoenicomerus* is quite different: a dry rattle followed by 'swit-err, swit-err'. [C14.90, G6.8.7]

6 YELLOW-MANTLED (YELLOW-BACKED) WIDOWBIRD
Euplectes macrourus   13 cm (br. m 20 cm)
Breeding male's combination of a fairly long black tail and yellow shoulders and mantle is diagnostic, although breeding male of *macrocercus* (Uganda, W Kenya and Abyssinian highlands) has black (not yellow) mantle; sometimes considered a separate species, Yellow-shouldered Widowbird. Has longer tail than Yellow Bishop, with black (not yellow) lower back and rump; lacks white wing panels of White-winged Widowbird (p. 684). Non-breeding male retains yellow shoulders and is larger, longer tailed and less heavily streaked than male Yellow Bishop. Female is less heavily streaked on breast and lacks dull yellow rump of female Yellow Bishop. **Habitat:** Damp grassland and marshy areas. **Status:** Locally common. **Voice:** Buzzing twitter. [C14.92, G6.8.10]

transitional ♂

1 ♀ ♂

2 ♀ ♂ non-br. ♂

3 ♀ ♂

non-br. ♂

♀ ♂ non-br. ♀

4 ♂ ♀

5 ♂

6 ♂ macrourus

1 LONG-TAILED WIDOWBIRD *Euplectes progne*   16-19 cm (br. m 60 cm)
The largest widowbird. Breeding male has very long tail and large blackish wings with bright red shoulders bordered by whitish-buff. In display, male flies slowly, with trailing tail laterally compressed. Non-breeding male has black flight feathers; larger than Fan-tailed Widowbird, and with redder shoulders than Marsh Widowbird. Female and juv. are larger than other female widowbirds. **Habitat:** Open grassland, especially in valleys and damp areas. **Status:** Common. **Voice:** Male gives 'cheet, cheet' and harsher 'zzit, zzit'. [C14.95, G6.9.2]

2 RED-COLLARED WIDOWBIRD *Euplectes ardens*   12 cm (br. m 25 cm)
A small widowbird characterised by breeding male's long, wispy tail and lack of a coloured shoulder patch. Extent of red on head varies: nominate *ardens* (SE Africa) has red throat collar, "Red-naped Widowbird" *laticauda* (NE Africa) has red collar extending onto nape and crown, and "Black Widowbird" *concolor* (W Africa E to Uganda) lacks any red at all, but is larger, with heavier, darker bill than Steel-blue Whydah (p. 710). Female and non-breeding male have bold, black-and-buff striped head, and unstreaked, buffy underparts; male retains black primaries. **Habitat:** Rank grassland and fields. **Status:** Locally common. **Voice:** Fast, high-pitched 'tee-tee-tee-tee-tee' by displaying male. [C14.94, G6.9.1]

3 FAN-TAILED (RED-SHOULDERED) WIDOWBIRD *Euplectes axillaris* 15-17 cm
Breeding male is the only small, short-tailed widowbird with a red shoulder and buff-orange greater coverts, but could be confused with males of other, longer-tailed species coming into breeding plumage when they have shorter tail (such as *humeralis* Marsh Widowbird). Tail is fanned only in display. Non-breeding male retains black primaries and red epaulettes. Female is heavily streaked above, with chestnut-brown wash on face, throat and breast, and reddish shoulder patches. **Habitat:** Reedbeds, rank grassland and stands of sugar cane. **Status:** Common. **Voice:** Various twittering and chirping sounds by male during display. [C14.91, G6.8.8]

4 MONTANE WIDOWBIRD (MOUNTAIN MARSH WIDOWBIRD)
Euplectes psammocromius   15 cm (br. m 35 cm)
Endemic to N Malawi and S Tanzania. Breeding male is long-tailed, with yellow-orange shoulders. Sometimes considered a race of Marsh Widowbird, but has much more extensive creamy buff panels on wings, due to buff greater coverts (not just edged buff); ranges do not overlap. Non-breeding male retains distinctive shoulders. Female is larger and darker than female Yellow Bishop (p. 682). **Habitat:** Montane heath and marshes. **Status:** Locally common. **Voice:** Similar to Marsh Widowbird's.

5 (HARTLAUB'S) MARSH WIDOWBIRD *Euplectes hartlaubi*   15-20 cm
Breeding male is larger than Fan-tailed Widowbird, with an obviously longer tail. Shoulders are yellow in S nominate race; orange-buff in shorter-tailed N *humeralis*. Nominate birds differ from Montane Widowbirds by smaller buff wing panel formed by mostly black greater coverts with buff fringes (not entire feathers buff). Non-breeding male retains distinctive shoulder patches. Female is larger than female Fan-tailed Widowbird and lacks dull red shoulder. **Habitat:** When breeding frequents flooded grasslands, marshes with short reedbeds and surrounds of lakes and dams; when not breeding, joins mixed flocks of weavers or widows and bishops in open grasslands and farmlands. **Status:** Locally common. **Voice:** Rather deep, harsh 'cheerskkk' song, as well as higher-pitched swizzles. [C14.96]

6 WHITE-WINGED WIDOWBIRD *Euplectes albonotatus*   15-19 cm
Male has diagnostic white wing panels formed by largely white primary coverts and outer greater coverts; other coverts and tertials are edged white or buff. Breeding male has longer tail than Yellow Bishop (p. 682) and black (not yellow) back. Shoulder patch varies from yellow (S and W *albonotatus*) to chestnut brown (NE *eques*). Non-breeding male is buffy brown but still has distinctive shoulders and white wing patches. Female is pale below, and is less streaked than other widows. Male Angolan *asymmetrura* has longer tail. **Habitat:** Tall grass in savanna, marsh edges and rank vegetation. **Status:** Common; usually in flocks. **Voice:** 'Zeh-zeh-zeh'; repetitive 'witz-witz-witz'. [C14.93, G6.8.9]

1

♂

non-br.

♀

2

laticauda

ardens

♂

non-br.

♂

♀

3

non-br. ♂

♂

4

♀

hartlaubi

♂

5

♂

♀

albonotatus

♂

♀

6

OLIVEBACKS
Tiny, olive-backed finches with mostly grey underparts. Sexes differ in most species.

1 SHELLEY'S (FERNANDO PO) OLIVEBACK *Nesocharis shelleyi* 8-9 cm
Endemic to SW Cameroon, SE Nigeria and Bioko. Smaller and shorter-tailed than White-collared Oliveback, and male has white collar confined to sides of neck; ranges do not overlap. Female and juv. have entire underparts grey. **Habitat:** Forest edge and clearings in montane areas, down to sea level on Bioko. **Status:** Locally common; often in small groups. **Voice:** Thin, high-pitched 'chit', repeated rapidly. [C15.7]

2 WHITE-COLLARED OLIVEBACK *Nesocharis ansorgei* 10 cm
Endemic to E Africa. Slightly larger than Shelley's Oliveback, with a longer tail; ranges do not overlap. Male has larger white neck collar which extends across throat. Female lacks white collar and has uniform grey breast and belly. **Habitat:** Forest edge and rank vegetation, often near water, 1 000-2 000 m. **Status:** Locally common; often in small groups. **Voice:** Short, high-pitched, insect-like trill. [C15.6]

3 GREY-HEADED (WHITE-CHEEKED) OLIVEBACK *Nesocharis capistrata* 14 cm
A large oliveback with a diagnostic white face and black throat. Readily told from other olive-backs by its mostly grey head. Sexes alike; juv. duller with a grey face. **Habitat:** Grassy edges of gallery forest and moist savanna. **Status:** Uncommon. **Voice:** High-pitched insect-like series of 6-8 notes, 'tit-it-it it tit tit', slowing and descending in pitch. [C15.8]

NIGRITAS (NEGROFINCHES)
A peculiar group of slender-billed finches that vaguely resemble antpeckers (p. 688), but occur higher in the canopy. Sexes alike in most species.

4 WHITE-BREASTED NIGRITA *Nigrita fusconotus* 10 cm
A very small nigrita, easily identified by its white underparts, contrasting black head and brown upperparts. Superficially resembles Black-crowned Waxbill (p. 706), but lacks red plumage and usually occurs singly or in pairs (not small flocks). **Habitat:** Forest canopy, gallery forest, forest edge and secondary growth, mostly in canopy and mid-strata. **Status:** Common; usually located by call. **Voice:** High-pitched trill, descending and often slowing at end. [C15.5]

5 CHESTNUT-BREASTED NIGRITA *Nigrita bicolor* 12 cm
A brown nigrita with diagnostic rich mahogany underparts and face and grey-brown upper-parts. Looks all-dark in poor light. Could be confused with male Red-fronted Antpecker (p. 688), but has heavier bill and different habits. W birds are slightly smaller and have slate-grey upperparts. Juv. is much paler; told from juv. antpeckers by finch-like bill. **Habitat:** Forest, from understorey to canopy, gallery forest, forest edge and secondary growth; often in lower levels. **Status:** Common. **Voice:** Song is series of 10-15 clear whistles. [C15.4]

6 GREY-HEADED NIGRITA *Nigrita canicapillus* 15 cm
Larger than Pale-fronted Nigrita, with black (not cream) forecrown. At close range, has yellow-red (not dark) eye, distinctive white spotting on wing, and paler grey rump. Juv. is duller, mostly sooty with greatly reduced white spotting and dark eye; could be confused with Dusky Tit (p. 394) or juv. Pale-fronted Nigrita, but still has washed-out head pattern of adult. **Habitat:** Forest and secondary growth. **Status:** Common. **Voice:** Distinctive, far-carrying, mournful, descending whistle, 'tseeu seuuu huuuu', often given from exposed perch. [C15.2]

7 PALE-FRONTED NIGRITA *Nigrita luteifrons* 11 cm
Superficially similar to Grey-headed Nigrita, but is smaller, with a creamy (not black) fore-head, unspotted wings and dark (not red) eyes; grey rump is less contrasting. Male is black below; female is dark grey, with black face and shorter pale supercilium. Juv. is sooty grey; smaller than juv. Grey-headed Nigrita, with uniform head; behaviour and small size distin-guish it from Dusky Tit (p. 394). **Habitat:** Forest edge, gallery forest, secondary growth, dense woodland and mangroves; usually in canopy. **Status:** Locally common. **Voice:** Descending series of 4-6 whistles. [C15.3]

ANTPECKERS
Small, warbler-like finches that glean ants in forest understorey. Sexes differ; juvs duller.

1 WOODHOUSE'S (RED-HEADED) ANTPECKER *Parmoptila woodhousei*   11 cm
Sometimes lumped with Red-fronted Antpecker, but is paler brown above. Both sexes have a creamy breast and belly, heavily barred and spotted dark brown. Told from female Red-fronted Antpecker by rufous face and throat. Male has plain rufous forecrown; female's forecrown is browner and lightly barred. Juv. is dull brown, with paler, more buffy underparts than juv. Red-fronted Antpecker. **Habitat:** Forest understorey, often near streams. **Status:** Generally uncommon; often joins mixed bird parties. **Voice:** Soft 'tsip' or 'tsee'; louder 'tik' call. [C15.1]

2 RED-FRONTED ANTPECKER *Parmoptila rubrifrons*   11 cm
The male has a distinctive bright red forecrown and rich chestnut underparts. Nominate race from Upper Guinea forests has grey-speckled face; E *jamesoni* has chestnut underparts extending onto face and chin. Range overlaps with Woodhouse's Antpecker in DRC, but lacks spotted underparts. Female lacks red forecrown and is cream below, intensely barred and spotted dark brown. Juv. is nondescript, with dark brown upperparts and warmer brown underparts; darker than juv. Woodhouse's Antpecker. **Habitat:** Forest understorey. **Status:** Uncommon; often joins bird parties. **Voice:** Rather loud 'swit'; hoarser 'sweet' calls.

PYTILIAS
Colourful savanna and woodland finches with barred bellies and red rumps and tails. Sexes differ; juvs duller.

3 RED-WINGED PYTILIA (AURORA FINCH) *Pytilia phoenicoptera*   12-13 cm
A grey-backed pytilia with distinctive red edges to the wing feathers. Male typically lacks red face, and is paler grey than male Yellow-winged Pytilia (which may show orange wings). Female and juv. have red-edged wing feathers. **Habitat:** Semi-arid savanna, open woodland and thickets. **Status:** Uncommon to locally common. **Voice:** Usually silent except for chirp flight call; song is squeaky, slurred 'krik, tu-weeooorr'. [C15.12]

4 LINEATED PYTILIA *Pytilia lineata*   12 cm
Endemic to Ethiopia. Often treated as a race of Red-winged Pytilia, but male and female have red bill and darker eye, and are darker grey, with heavier barring on belly; ranges do not overlap. Juv's bill is grey, becoming pink. **Habitat:** Semi-arid savanna and thickets. **Status:** Locally common. **Voice:** Similar to Red-winged Pytilia's.

5 YELLOW-WINGED (RED-FACED) PYTILIA *Pytilia hypogrammica*   12-13 cm
Endemic to W Africa. Similar to Red-winged Pytilia, but with golden-yellow (rarely orange-red) wing edges, darker grey body and some black in tail. Male has red (not grey) face. Female and juv. have yellow-edged wing feathers. **Habitat:** Dry scrub, woodland and thickets in dry riverbeds. **Status:** Rare to uncommon; little known; usually in pairs in mixed foraging groups of waxbills and finches. **Voice:** High-pitched 'tsip tseep tseep'. [C15.11]

6 GREEN-WINGED PYTILIA (MELBA FINCH) *Pytilia melba*   12 cm
A green-backed pytilia with a red bill. Told from Orange-winged Pytilia by uniform olive-green (not golden) wings. Male typically has boldly barred belly, but not in W and C African *citerior*, which also has red (not grey) lores. Male breast colour also varies geographically, from green to yellow or orange. Juv. is browner above and plain below, with pinkish bill. **Habitat:** Acacia savanna and dry woodland. **Status:** Common. **Voice:** Dry chittering song with trilling whistles, often rising and falling in pitch; short 'wick-ick-ick' call. [C15.9, G6.9.4]

7 ORANGE-WINGED (GOLDEN-BACKED) PYTILIA *Pytilia afra*   11 cm
Smaller and shorter-tailed than Green-winged Pytilia, with diagnostic golden-yellow edges to the wing feathers; typically is less distinctly barred on the belly and flanks. Male has less crisply defined red face patch, and green back extends onto nape. Juv. is browner above, with only faint yellowish wing panel. **Habitat:** Thick, tangled scrub and understorey of miombo woodland. **Status:** Locally common. **Voice:** 'Seee, seee' piping whistle; sharp 'tik' call. [C15.10, G6.9.3]

Rather large, colourful finches with white-spotted bellies. Sexes differ in most species; juvs duller and lack spots. Recent work suggests that the Green and Brown twinspots are not particularly closely related to the other species.

1 DYBOWSKI'S TWINSPOT *Euschistospiza dybowskii*   12-13 cm
The grey head and breast, dark red back and rump, and black belly spotted with white are diagnostic. Paler grey on head and breast than Dusky Twinspot, with crimson (not dark grey) mantle and much more obvious white spots on flanks. Female is duller, with mottled chestnut mantle. Juv. is duller and browner above, with grey, unspotted underparts. **Habitat:** Tall-grass savannas with bushes, often in rocky areas, or at edge of gallery forest. **Status:** Widespread but generally uncommon. **Voice:** Usually silent, but utters soft 'wit wit'. [C15.21]

2 DUSKY TWINSPOT *Euschistospiza cinereovinacea*   11-12 cm
Endemic to Angola and Albertine Rift. Appears dark grey, with large, bright red rump; white spots are hardly noticeable in the field. Darker than Dybowski's Twinspot, with dark grey (not crimson) mantle, reduced belly spotting and crimson (not black) flanks; ranges do not overlap. Could be confused with Dusky Crimsonwing (p. 692), but lacks any red on head or mantle. **Habitat:** Rank grass at forest edge, 1 500-2 000 m. **Status:** Poorly known but fairly common in some areas. **Voice:** Contact call described as 'tssip tssip'; unremarkable twittering song.

3 RED-THROATED (PETERS'S) TWINSPOT *Hypargos niveoguttatus*   12-13 cm
Male differs from Pink-throated Twinspot by grey (not brown) crown and deep red (not pink) face, throat and breast. Female has pinkish-orange wash across breast and down centre of belly (not grey-brown, as in female Pink-throated Twinspot). Juv. is dull brown, darker than juv. Pink-throated Twinspot, with blackish belly. **Habitat:** Dense thickets, rank growth and forest edge; prefers moister habitats than Pink-throated Twinspot. **Status:** Locally common. **Voice:** High-pitched, insect-like trill, longer than Pink-throated Twinspot's; song includes mournful, slurred whistles and 'chink' notes. [C15.18, G6.9.9]

4 PINK-THROATED TWINSPOT *Hypargos margaritatus*   12-13 cm
Endemic to S Africa. Male is paler than male Red-throated Twinspot, with a pinkish face, throat and breast; crown is brown (not grey). Female has light grey-brown throat, breast and belly; differs from female Red-throated Twinspot in having no trace of orange or pink on throat and breast. Juv. is brown above and pale grey-buff below; paler than juv. Red-throated Twinspot, and lacks any black on belly. **Habitat:** Dense thickets, thornveld and coastal scrub. **Status:** Locally common. **Voice:** Soft, high-pitched, insect-like trill. [G6.9.8]

5 BROWN TWINSPOT *Clytospiza monteiri*   13 cm
An unmistakeable small finch with diagnostic orangey-brown underparts heavily spotted with white (all other twinspots have white-spotted black underparts). Male has grey head and red throat; female has white throat. Juv. has brown underparts lacking spots. **Habitat:** Damp grassy areas and thickets, forest edge and overgrown farmlands. **Status:** Locally common; in pairs or small family groups. **Voice:** Loud, nasal 'neh neh neh'; harsh alarm call of 'chek chek'; song is variable jumble of twitters, trills and mimicry. [C15.20]

6 GREEN TWINSPOT *Mandingoa nitidula*   10 cm
A tiny twinspot. Easily told from olivebacks (p. 686), the only other green-backed finches in the region, by white-spotted underparts and lack of black on the head. Male has red face and black belly, boldly spotted white. W and C African *schlegeli* has orange throat and breast. Female has buff face and olive-grey belly, spotted white. Juv. is duller, with unspotted, pale grey-green underparts. **Habitat:** Forest, usually near clearings or areas with dense undergrowth; in winter, ventures into woodland and coastal scrub. **Status:** Locally common, but secretive and easily overlooked. **Voice:** Soft, rolling, insect-like 'zrrreet' and whistled notes; call is very high-pitched 'zeet'. [C15.19, G6.9.5]

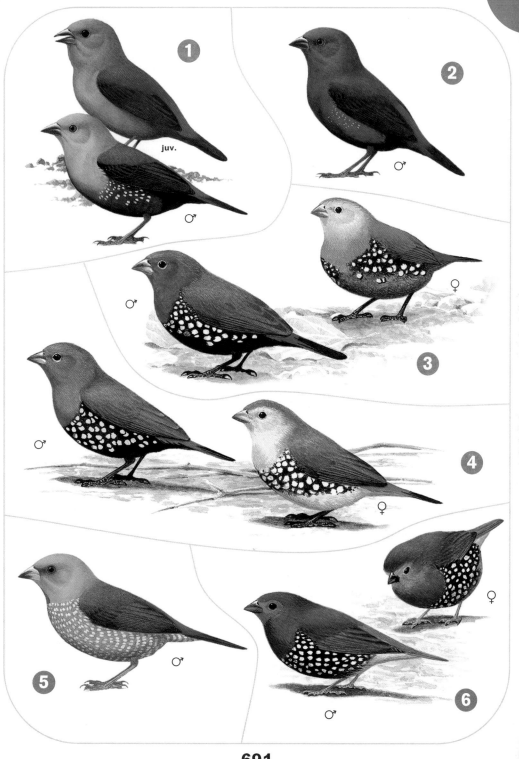

CRIMSONWINGS
Secretive forest finches with reddish backs. Pairs or small groups occur in forest clearings, but retreat to dense cover when disturbed. Sexes differ; juvs duller.

1 RED-FACED CRIMSONWING *Cryptospiza reichenovii* 11-12 cm
Greener than Abyssinian Crimsonwing, with a distinct face patch: red in male, buffy-yellow in female. Smaller than Lesser Seedcracker (p. 696), with black (not reddish) tail and dull red (not brown) back and wings. Juv. has less red on upperparts. **Habitat:** Forest understorey; in E Africa, generally occurs below 2 000 m (rarely to 2 500 m). **Status:** Locally common but easily overlooked. **Voice:** Soft, high-pitched trills or single 'zeet' calls. [C15.13, G6.9.6]

2 ABYSSINIAN CRIMSONWING *Cryptospiza salvadorii* 11-12 cm
Endemic to NE Africa. Greyer than Red-faced Crimsonwing, with no distinct face patch. Male has darker lores than female, and has small red patch on flanks. Juv. is slightly greyer (less olive) than juv. Red-faced Crimsonwing, but not reliably separable in the field. **Habitat:** Forest understorey, in thick tangles along streams and damp areas, generally above 2 000 m. **Status:** Locally common but elusive and shy. **Voice:** Soft, repeated 'zeet'; harsher 'pip pip pip'.

3 SHELLEY'S CRIMSONWING *Cryptospiza shelleyi* 12-13 cm
Endemic to Albertine Rift. The largest, brightest crimsonwing, with a red (not black) bill and olive-green underparts washed orange on the flanks; vent is black. Male has reddish mantle extending onto head; female's head is olive-green. Juv. is duller. **Habitat:** Forest, forest edge and bamboo, 1 500-2 800 m; often near water. **Status:** Vulnerable. Uncommon; shy and elusive, feeding on ground. **Voice:** High-pitched 'chit-it-it'; twittering call, rising and falling in pitch.

4 DUSKY CRIMSONWING *Cryptospiza jacksoni* 11-12 cm
Endemic to Albertine Rift. Darker and greyer than Abyssinian and Red-faced crimsonwings, with blackish (not red) wing coverts and red face in both sexes; male has red extending onto crown. Red face and grey (not white-spotted) flanks separate it from Dusky and Dybowski's twinspots (p. 690). Juv. has grey head, with duller mantle and rump; darker and greyer than juv. Abyssinian and Red-faced crimsonwings; more likely to be confused with juv. Dusky or Dybowski's twinspots. **Habitat:** Mid-elevation forest, 1 500-2 700 m. **Status:** Locally common but easily overlooked. **Voice:** Soft 'trrit trrit' contact call; trilling 'zee zee zee' call.

FIREFINCHES
Small red-and-brown finches, most with distinct male, female and juv. plumages.

5 BAR-BREASTED FIREFINCH *Lagonosticta rufopicta* 10-11 cm
Sexes alike, similar to male Red-billed Firefinch, but pink-red is confined to face, not washing onto crown, nape and mantle. Has white crescents (not spots) on flanks; vent is pale. Redder below than Brown Firefinch, with red (not grey) rump. Juv. has dark bill and distinctive pinkish flush to breast. **Habitat:** Thickets in woodland and villages. **Status:** Locally common. **Voice:** Sharp 'tzek tzek' contact call; song is variable, with short, jumbled notes. [C15.22]

6 RED-BILLED FIREFINCH *Lagonosticta senegala* 10 cm
The adult's mostly red bill, prominent yellow eye-ring and brown (not blackish) vent and tail separate it from most other firefinches. Male has pink wash on sides of neck, nape and mantle, lacking sharp demarcation between face and neck of Bar-breasted Firefinch. Female is sandy brown, with only lores, rump and uppertail pink. Juv's bill is dark; lacks yellow eye-ring and white spots. **Habitat:** Semi-arid woodland, especially near water; also gardens. **Status:** Common. **Voice:** Fairly melodic, slurred 'sweet er-urrrrr', sharp, fast 'vut-vut chit-it-errrr'; various dry, chittering or rattling calls. [C15.24, G6.10.2]

7 BROWN FIREFINCH *Lagonosticta nitidula* 10 cm
A red-billed species, told from all other firefinches by its grey-brown (not red) rump; vent is pale. Male has pinkish-red face, throat and upper breast, with small white spots on sides of breast. Female is duller. Juv. is all-brown, with dark bill. **Habitat:** Thick scrub and reeds close to water. **Status:** Locally common. **Voice:** High-pitched chittering; nasal 'urp' call; 'tsiep, tsiep' flight call. [C15.23, G6.10.3]

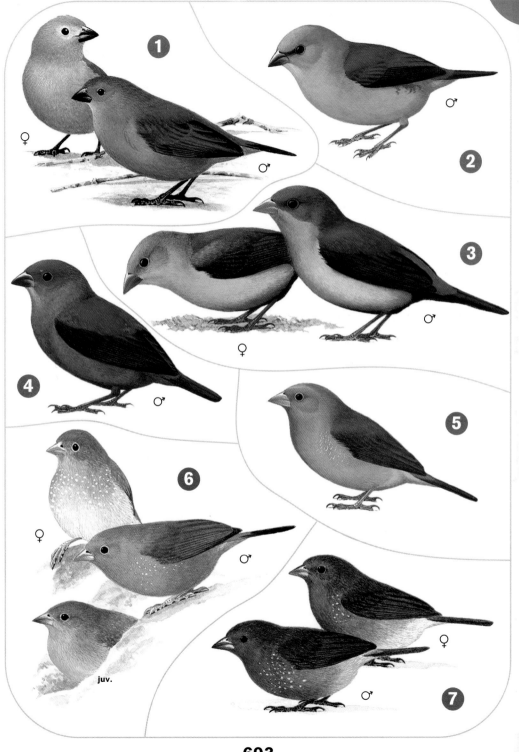

1 AFRICAN (BLUE-BILLED) FIREFINCH *Lagonosticta rubricata*   10-11 cm
A dark, richly coloured firefinch with a mostly dark bill and blackish vent and tail. Male is redder (less pink) than male Jameson's Firefinch, with brown back and wings lacking any pink wash. Most races have distinctive grey (not pink) crown and nape. Female is pinkish brown below, darker than female Jameson's Firefinch. Juv. is brown above and buff yellow below; only rump is red. W Angolan *landanae* has pinkish sides to upper mandible and is brighter, with pink extending onto crown; sometimes considered a separate species, Pale-billed Firefinch. **Habitat:** Thickets in woodland, savanna and riverine scrub. **Status:** Common. **Voice:** Fast, dry 'trrt-trrt-trrt-trrt' and higher-pitched trills; song includes various whistles, including clear 'wink-wink-wink' and faster trills. [C15.26, G6.9.10]

2 JAMESON'S FIREFINCH *Lagonosticta rhodopareia*   10 cm
Paler pink than African Firefinch, with the crown, nape, back and wing coverts suffused pink. Dark bill, vent and tail separate it from Red-billed Firefinch (p. 692). Male is pink below. Female is pinkish buff, with red lores. Juv. duller; lacks red lores. W Angolan *ansorgei* is brighter in both sexes. **Habitat:** Thickets and grassy tangles in savanna and dry woodland. **Status:** Common. **Voice:** Dry trill, interspersed with sharp 'vit-vit-vit' and 'sweet sweet sweet' whistles. [G6.10.1]

3 MALI (KULIKORO) FIREFINCH *Lagonosticta virata*   10 cm
Endemic to Mali. Very similar to male African Firefinch, and ranges partly overlap, but is duller, with red (not greyish) frons and few white breast spots. Female is slightly paler, but much brighter than female African Firefinch. Juvs probably indistinguishable. **Habitat:** Grassy savanna, typically in rocky areas. **Status:** Uncommon. **Voice:** Plaintive, whistled 'tseeoouu'; fast 'chew chew chew'; sharp, dry 'pit pit pit'. [C15.29]

4 ROCK FIREFINCH *Lagonostica sanguinodorsalis*   11-12 cm
Endemic to Jos Plateau and Mandara Mts, Nigeria. Similar to Jameson's and Chad firefinches, but ranges do not overlap. Dark bill has distinctive paler grey base to lower mandible. Male has grey crown. Female is duller, with red lores. Juv. is duller; lacks red lores. **Habitat:** Thickets and scrub on rocky outcrops. **Status:** Locally common. **Voice:** Various 'treee', 'chew' and 'chwee' calls. [C15.28]

5 CHAD (REICHENOW'S) FIREFINCH *Lagonosticta umbrinodorsalis*   10-11 cm
Endemic to Chad and Cameroon. Formerly treated as a race of Jameson's Firefinch, but has crown and nape grey (not pinkish); ranges do not overlap. Differs from Red-billed Firefinch (p. 692) by grey (not reddish) bill, dark vent and pinkish-red (not brown) mantle. Female is only slightly duller than male. Juv is similar to juv African Firefinch. **Habitat:** Rocky areas in arid savanna. **Status:** Little known; locally common in SW Chad, rare in NE Cameroon. **Voice:** Dry trills, soft 'swit swit swit' or sharp 'vit vit vit'. [C15.27]

6 BLACK-BELLIED FIREFINCH *Lagonosticta rara*   11 cm
The only firefinch with no white flank spots. Male is washed pinkish red above, with black vent extending onto central belly. Darker than Jameson's, Chad and Rock firefinches, with distinctive pink base to lower mandible. Female has grey head and red loral spot; has darker central belly than other female firefinches. Juv is drab, with pale vent and belly, but has pinkish bill base. **Habitat:** Savanna and woodland thickets; farmland. **Status:** Locally common. **Voice:** Dry trill; melodic 'wheet wheet wheet'; nasal 'neyh'; sharp 'chrek chrek'. [C15.25]

7 BLACK-FACED FIREFINCH *Lagonosticta larvata*   11-12 cm
Male is easily identified by its black face; has shorter tail than Black-faced Waxbill (p. 704), with plain (not barred) wings. Female lacks black face, but is the only pale-vented firefinch with dark bill (beware juv red-billed species). Breast colour varies geographically: deep red in *larvata* (E Sudan-Ethiopia), mauve-pink in *vinacea* ('Vinaceous Firefinch', Senegal-Mali), lavender-grey in *nigricollis* ('Cameroon Firefinch', Ghana-S Sudan). **Habitat:** Ranges from dry thicket to tall grasslands and bamboo. **Status:** Nowhere common and thinly distributed; in pairs or small groups, often associated with waxbills. **Voice:** Soft, nasal whistles, 'wheet-err sur-eeet'. [C15.30]

Large, heavy-billed, finches. Brightly coloured but retiring, they skulk in dense cover if disturbed and, with only a brief view, could be confused with malimbes (p. 674). Seedcrackers have a reddish tail, bluebills a black tail. Sexes differ.

1 CRIMSON SEEDCRACKER *Pyrenestes sanguineus* 14 cm
Endemic to Upper Guinea forests of W Africa. Range may meet that of Black-bellied Seedcracker in E Ivory Coast; male differs by brown (not black) back, wings and belly. Female is olive-brown, with red head and tail; juv. lacks red on head; in the field, they are inseparable from female and juv. Black-bellied Seedcracker. **Habitat:** Dense grassy areas at forest edge and along streams, and marshy areas. **Status:** Generally uncommon. **Voice:** Sharp 'tuit' call; song is soft warble. [C15.16]

2 BLACK-BELLIED SEEDCRACKER *Pyrenestes ostrinus* 15 cm
The male is the only seedcracker with a black back, wings and belly. Reddish tail and blue-grey bill distinguish it from bluebills. Female is olive-brown, with red head, upper breast and tail; juv. is olive-brown, with reddish tail. Bill size of three morphs differs independently of sex or age. **Habitat:** Grassy areas at forest edge and along forest roads, marshy clearings, reedbeds, plantations, gardens, and humid savannas. **Status:** Fairly common, but easily overlooked. **Voice:** Sharp, metallic 'chink' call; song is short warble or series of descending notes. [C15.14]

3 GRANT'S BLUEBILL *Spermophaga poliogenys* 14 cm
The male is stunning red and black; slightly smaller than Red-headed Bluebill, with black back extending onto nape and hindcrown, and brighter red rump. Distinguished from Western Bluebill by mostly red (not black) crown. Slightly smaller than male Black-bellied Seedcracker, with black tail and smaller, red-and-blue bill. Female told from other female bluebills by dark grey head and cheeks, and lack of red on flanks. Juv. is sooty grey, with redder rump than other juv. bluebills. **Habitat:** Dense vegetation of forest undergrowth, often near water. **Status:** Generally uncommon. **Voice:** Soft 'tseep'; seldom calls.

4 LESSER SEEDCRACKER *Pyrenestes minor* 13 cm
Sometimes considered a race of Black-bellied Seedcracker, but is smaller and male lacks black plumage. Male is very similar to female Black-bellied Seedcracker, but ranges are not known to overlap. Female has less extensive red on head than male, and juv. lacks red on head. Much larger than Red-faced Crimsonwing (p. 392), with brown (not reddish) wings and reddish (not black) tail. **Habitat:** Thickets along streams, and forest clearings. **Status:** Uncommon to locally common. **Voice:** 'Tzeet'; sharp, clipped 'quap'. [G6.9.7]

5 RED-HEADED BLUEBILL *Spermophaga ruficapilla* 15 cm
The reddest of the bluebills; both sexes have all-red head, breast and flanks. Male has black belly; belly is spotted white in female. Male is larger than male Grant's Bluebill, with red nape and duller rump. Male differs from male Black-bellied Seedcracker by black (not reddish) tail and less massive, bi-coloured bill. Red head distinguishes female from other bluebills. Imm. is sooty grey, with dull red lower rump, and red-washed head. Isolated E Usambara *cana* is dark grey (not black) and has slate hindcrown. **Habitat:** Grassy areas and dense vegetation at forest edge, and clearings. **Status:** Locally common. **Voice:** Generally silent; very soft, high-pitched call; song is soft warble.

6 WESTERN BLUEBILL *Spermophaga haematina* 15 cm
The darkest bluebill. Male has a black head and face. Female has white-spotted belly and dusky face; told from female Grant's Bluebill by larger size and red flanks. Juv. is sooty grey, with red wash on breast and flanks. Nominate birds (W Africa-Nigeria) have entire face and rump black; C African *pustulata* has red rump and red wash on cheeks. **Habitat:** Dense vegetation in forest understorey, along forest streams or at forest edge, gallery forest and plantations. **Status:** Common. **Voice:** Soft, metallic 'tsip' contact call; sharp 'tak' alarm call; song is varied series of warbles and trills. [C15.17]

QUAILFINCHES
Small, ground-dwelling grassland finches with boldly barred black-and-white flanks. Usually seen when flushed, giving distinctive flight call. Sexes differ.

1 AFRICAN QUAILFINCH *Ortygospiza atricollis*   9 cm
Adult told from Black-chinned Quailfinch by its small white chin spot and duller red bill; in area of overlap, African Quailfinch has white spectacles; W African & Ethiopian races have plain black faces; NE *ugandae* is paler, often with a narrow eye-ring. Female is duller, with plain grey face and darker upper mandible. Juv. is paler, with only faint barring on thighs; bill is dark. **Habitat:** Grassland and fields, often near water. **Status:** Common. **Voice:** Distinctive, tinny 'chink-chink' in flight. [C15.45, G6.11.2]

2 BLACK-CHINNED (RED-BILLED) QUAILFINCH *Ortygospiza gabonensis* 9 cm
Adults always lack white spectacles; told from African Quailfinch by their black chin and brighter orange-red bill. Male's cheeks brown in most races, blackish in SE *fuscata*. Female has grey cheeks and lacks black around bill. Juv. is similar to juv. African Quailfinch. **Habitat:** Short-grass savannas, from coast to hilly plateaux. **Status:** Locally common. **Voice:** Similar to African Quailfinch's, but shriller. [C15.46]

3 LOCUSTFINCH *Ortygospiza locustella*   9 cm
A primitive finch, superficially similar to quailfinches. Male appears black and red, with distinctive red face, throat, breast, wings and rump. At close range, shows fine white bars on thighs and white spots on back (absent in N *uelensis*). Female is white beneath, but easily told from female quailfinches by rufous wings. Juv. is streaked black and brown above, with grey face and buff wash on underparts; more strongly marked than juv. quailfinches and differs from adult quailfinches by buffish edges to wing feathers and dark bill. **Habitat:** Moist grassland. **Status:** Uncommon. **Voice:** Fast 'tinka-tinka-tinka' in flight. [C15.44, G6.11.3]

MANNIKINS
Dark brown finches with a blackish head and barred flanks. Occur in small flocks, feeding on grass seeds. Sexes alike; juvs dull, with darker bills.

4 BRONZE MANNIKIN *Spermestes cucullata*   9 cm
A small, brownish mannikin, lacking the bold plumage of Black-and-white or Red-backed mannikins. Smaller than Magpie Mannikin, with much shorter bill and barred (not plain) rump. Juv. is uniformly dun brown, paler than juv. Black-and-white Mannikin, and lacks reddish-brown back of juv. Red-backed Mannikin. **Habitat:** Grassy areas in woodland, forest edges and gardens. **Status:** Abundant. **Voice:** Soft, buzzy 'chizza, chizza'; dry 'krrr krrr'. [C15.48, G6.11.7]

5 BLACK-AND-WHITE MANNIKIN *Spermestes bicolor*   10 cm
A strikingly black-and-white mannikin with a pale bluish bill. Black back and wing coverts are diagnostic. W African nominate birds have black wings and rump; C African *poensis* has white barring on flight feathers and rump. Juv. is dull brown, darker and greyer above than other juv. mannikins. **Habitat:** Tall-grass savanna close to forests or thickets, plantations and villages. **Status:** Common. **Voice:** Plaintive 'wheet wheet' or shorter 'whit whit' calls. [C15.49]

6 RED-BACKED MANNIKIN *Spermestes nigriceps*   10 cm
Often treated as a race of Black-and-white Mannikin, but has diagnostic chestnut back and wing coverts; ranges do not overlap. Juv. differs from other juv. mannikins by reddish-brown back. **Habitat:** Moist woodland and forest edge. **Status:** Common; often in small flocks. **Voice:** Sharp 'whit weet weet'; soft 'seeet-seeet' when flushed. [G6.11.8]

7 MAGPIE (PIED) MANNIKIN *Spermestes fringilloides*   12-13 cm
The largest mannikin, with a distinctly long bill; the black head and throat barely extends onto the upper breast. Black triangular spot on sides of breast and rufous marks on flanks are diagnostic. Juv. is grey-brown above, larger than other juv. mannikins. **Habitat:** Tall-grass savanna and bamboo at forest edge, marshy areas, plantations and villages. **Status:** Locally common. **Voice:** Chirruping 'peeoo-peeoo'. [C15.50, G6.11.9]

1

♂ W & NE Africa

S & C Africa

♂

♀

2

♂ fuscata

♂ gabonensis

3

♀

♂

4

juv.

5

6

juv.

7

juv.

Distinctively-plumaged waxbills. Sexes differ in cordonbleus and grenadiers.

1 AFRICAN (WARBLING) SILVERBILL *Euodice cantans*   10 cm
A pale brown waxbill with a fairly long black tail, black rump and blue-grey bill. At close range, shows fine barring on mantle, wing coverts and tertials; this is more prominent in *orientalis* (Sudan E). Juv. is slightly paler, with little barring above. Closely related to Asian munias; probably a recent arrival in Africa. **Habitat:** Dry wooded savanna to semi-arid savanna, cultivations and villages. **Status:** Locally common; often in small flocks. **Voice:** Nasal chattering call; sharper, higher-pitched 'chit-it-it' flight call. [C15.47]

2 GREY-HEADED SILVERBILL *Odontospiza griseicapilla*   10-15 cm
Endemic to NE Africa. Larger than African Silverbill, with a white (not black) rump, grey head speckled with white, and pinkish-buff breast. Juv. is duller, with less contrasting grey head and creamy-buff rump. Closely related to mannikins (not munias). **Habitat:** Dry grassy scrubland and old fields; regularly drinks at waterholes. **Status:** Locally common; in pairs and small groups. **Voice:** Soft, high-pitched trill.

3 BLUE WAXBILL (SOUTHERN CORDONBLEU) *Uraeginthus angolensis* 13 cm
The only blue waxbill through most of its range; lacks the distinctive red cheek patch of male Red-cheeked Cordonbleu; told from Blue-capped Cordonbleu by greyish (not pink-red) bill. Harder to tell from female Red-cheeked Cordonbleu, but in areas of overlap has slightly shorter tail and typically more blue on underparts. Female has less blue on flanks in S. Juv. is paler, with blue restricted to face and throat. **Habitat:** Dry woodland, savanna and gardens. **Status:** Common. **Voice:** Soft 'kway-kway-sree-seee-seee-seee'. [C15.41, G6.10.4]

4 RED-CHEEKED CORDONBLEU *Uraeginthus bengalus*   11-12 cm
Male has a diagnostic red cheek patch. Female differs from Blue-capped Cordonbleu by dull pinkish bill with blackish tip (not pink-red); in areas of overlap has longer tail and typically less blue on underparts than female Blue Waxbill. Extent of blue on female varies geographically: restricted to face and throat in S *katangae*; only on breast and flanks in Kenyan *brunneigularis*. Juv. is like other juv. cordonbleus. **Habitat:** Variable, from dry, open bush to moister areas and thickets, villages, road verges and farmlands. **Status:** Common. **Voice:** Various 'swee swee' notes; harsher 'tseek'. [C15.42]

5 BLUE-CAPPED CORDONBLEU *Uraeginthus cyanocephalus*   13 cm
Endemic to NE Africa. Male is readily identified by its entirely powder-blue head, including crown and nape; brighter blue than other cordonbleus. Female has paler belly than other female cordonbleus, with pink-red bill. Juv. has dark bill and blue restricted to face; possibly told from other juv. cordonbleus by paler belly. **Habitat:** Drier savanna than Red-cheeked Cordonbleu, extending into semi-desert. **Status:** Locally common. **Voice:** 'Swee swee' notes, similar to those of Red-cheeked Cordonbleu.

6 PURPLE GRENADIER *Granatina ianthinogaster*   14 cm
Endemic to NE Africa. Adults have blue (male) or mauve (female) crescents around the eye (not mauve ear coverts of Violet-eared Waxbill); ranges do not overlap. Male's belly and lower breast are blue; female has white-scaled flanks. Juv. has black bill and plain russet head and flanks; darker than juv. Violet-eared Waxbill. **Habitat:** Dry bush, grassy woodland and thickets. **Status:** Common; often in small groups or pairs. **Voice:** Various buzzing and trilling notes; high-pitched, rattling alarm call.

7 VIOLET-EARED WAXBILL (COMMON GRENADIER) *Granatina granatina* 15 cm
Endemic to SW Africa. Male's red bill, chestnut body, mauve cheeks and brilliant blue rump are diagnostic. Female is paler, with tan head and creamy underparts. Both told from Purple Grenadier by violet ear coverts. Juv. has black bill and pale tan face; paler than juv. Purple Grenadier. **Habitat:** Acacia woodland and savanna. **Status:** Common. **Voice:** Dry, buzzy 'tziit'; whistled 'tu-weoowee'. [G6.10.5]

A diverse group of small, colourful, seed-eating finches, often found in flocks. Sexes alike in most species.

1 ORANGE-BREASTED (ZEBRA) WAXBILL *Amandava subflava* 9 cm
A tiny, short-tailed waxbill with a prominent orange-red rump, which separates it from superficially similar quailfinches and Locustfinch (p. 698). At close range, orange-yellow underparts with olive-barred flanks are diagnostic. Male has orange-red supercilium; female is paler yellow below. Juv. is duller, with dark bill and no flank streaks; browner than juv. Yellow-bellied Waxbill. **Habitat:** Grassland and weedy areas, especially near water. **Status:** Common; sometimes in large flocks. **Voice:** Soft, clinking 'zink zink zink' flight call; rapid 'trip-trip' on take-off. [C15.43, G6.11.4]

2 YELLOW-BELLIED WAXBILL (EAST AFRICAN SWEE)
Coccopygia quartinia 9-10 cm
A tiny, olive-backed waxbill with a bright red rump, greyish head and breast and yellow-washed belly. Adult's two-tone bill is diagnostic. Sexes are alike in E African races, but males of isolated Angolan *bocagei* have black face and finely barred backs and wings; perhaps warrants species status. Range does not overlap with that of Swee Waxbill. Juv. is duller, with black bill; told from other juv. waxbills by olive-tinged back. **Habitat:** Forest edge and plantations with rank vegetation. **Status:** Locally common. **Voice:** Soft 'swee-swee' in flight. [G6.11.1]

3 SWEE WAXBILL (BLACK-FACED SWEE) *Coccopygia melanotis* 9-10 cm
Endemic to S Africa. Often treated as a race of Yellow-bellied Waxbill, but male has a distinctive black face; lacks barred back of *bocagei* Yellow-bellied Waxbill. Female is indistinguishable in the field from Yellow-bellied Waxbill; ranges do not overlap. Juv. is duller, with all-black bill. **Habitat:** Forest edge and densely wooded areas with rank vegetation; also gardens. **Status:** Locally common. **Voice:** 'Swee swee' notes, similar to Yellow-bellied Waxbill's. [C15.34, G6.10.10]

4 LAVENDER WAXBILL *Estrilda caerulescens* 10 cm
A pale grey waxbill of N savannas, with a dark red rump, vent and tail. Easily told from other grey waxbills by red (not black) tail; tail is shorter than Grey Waxbill's, and has darker bill than Cinderella Waxbill, with grey (not red) thighs. Juv. is duller, with less pronounced black eye-stripe and less red on undertail coverts. **Habitat:** Wooded to dry savannas. **Status:** Common. **Voice:** Contact call is soft 'tik tik tik'; louder 'tsreeeu'. [C15.31]

5 GREY (BLACK-TAILED) WAXBILL *Estrilda perreini* 11 cm
Longer-tailed than other grey waxbills, with darker grey plumage in most races. Easily told from Lavender Waxbill by black (not red) tail and vent; ranges do not overlap. Black (not reddish) bill and grey (not red) thighs separate it from Cinderella Waxbill. Much longer-tailed than Yellow-bellied and Swee waxbills, with grey (not olive) back. Female has slightly paler vent. Juv. is duller and lacks black eye-stripe. SE *poliogastra* is paler grey; range does not overlap those of other grey waxbills. **Habitat:** Edges of evergreen forests, and thick coastal and riverine forests. **Status:** Locally common. **Voice:** Soft, whistled 'pseeu, pseeu'. [C15.32, G6.10.8]

6 CINDERELLA WAXBILL *Estrilda thomensis* 11 cm
Endemic to Angola and extreme NW Namibia. Shorter-tailed and paler than Grey Waxbill, with red-based bill and red (not grey) thighs. Told from Lavender Waxbill by black (not red) tail. Male has pinkish wash to breast and blackish vent. Female is duller, with grey vent. Juv. lacks red on flanks. **Habitat:** Semi-arid savanna and scrub; in drier areas than Grey Waxbill. **Status:** Locally common. **Voice:** Thin but penetrating, reedy 'sweee-sweee-sweeeooo-swoooo'; short, repeated 'trrt-tsoo'. [C15.33, G6.10.9]

703

1 FAWN-BREASTED WAXBILL *Estrilda paludicola* 11 cm
A plain, orange-billed waxbill; forms a superspecies with Orange-cheeked Waxbill, but has plain grey (not orange) face. Most races have grey crown and face contrasting with plain brown back, but *roseicrissa* (S Uganda-NW Tanzania) has brown crown, extending down to eye in *marwitzi* (C Tanzania). All races are much paler below than Abyssinian Waxbill. Female is slightly duller. Juv. has black bill and duller red rump. **Habitat:** Grassy savannas and rank vegetation, often near water. **Status:** Locally common. **Voice:** Nasal 'wehk'; sharper 'chit' call notes. [C15.35]

2 ABYSSINIAN WAXBILL *Estrilda ochrogaster* 11-12 cm
Endemic to Ethiopia and E Sudan. Sometimes considered a race of Fawn-breasted Waxbill, but has rather uniform tan-brown head and rich buffy wash on underparts. Compared with adjacent nominate Fawn-breasted Waxbill, has brown (not grey) crown; ranges do not overlap. Female is paler. Juv. has black bill. **Habitat:** High-altitude grasslands, scrub and heath; also villages and fields. **Status:** Locally common; in small flocks or pairs; sometimes flocks with Common Waxbills. **Voice:** Nasal 'chrek'; harsher 'chek chek' notes.

3 ANAMBRA WAXBILL *Estrilda poliopareia* 11-12 cm
Endemic to S Nigeria. Sometimes considered a race of Fawn-breasted Waxbill, but has buffy (not whitish) underparts and pale (not dark) eyes; ranges do not overlap. Lacks distinctive orange face of Orange-cheeked Waxbill. Easily told from Common Waxbill (p. 706) by red (not brown) rump and plain face (lacking red eye-stripe). At close range, shows finely barred upperparts. **Habitat:** Grasslands and scrub at forest edge, usually near streams and swamps. **Status:** Vulnerable. Little known; uncommon within small region on Niger Delta. **Voice:** Typical waxbill-like 'trrrt' calls.

4 ORANGE-CHEEKED WAXBILL *Estrilda melpoda* 11 cm
A plain waxbill with a bright, orange-red bill, grey head and diagnostic orange face. Intensity of orange face varies considerably, being brightest in N Cameroon and DRC. Juv. is duller, with black bill, but still has pale orange face. **Habitat:** Tall-grass savanna at forest edge, secondary growth, villages and plantations. **Status:** Common. **Voice:** Rapid, trilling 'tsit tsit tsit', cleaner and sharper than Fawn-breasted Waxbill's. [C15.36]

5 BLACK-FACED WAXBILL *Estrilda erythronotos* 12 cm
A striking grey-and-red waxbill with barred wings and a prominent black face. Superficially recalls Black-faced Firefinch (p. 694), but has longer, black (not reddish) tail and barred (not plain) wings. In E Africa, is easily confused with Black-cheeked Waxbill, but typically is darker grey, with larger black chin; male has black (not grey) central belly and vent. Female is duller, with grey vent. Juv. is duller, with darker bill. **Habitat:** Grassy areas and thick tangles in dry savanna. **Status:** Common. **Voice:** High-pitched 'chuloweee'. [G6.10.7]

6 BLACK-CHEEKED WAXBILL *Estrilda charmosyna* 10-11 cm
Endemic to NE Africa. Sometimes treated as a race of Black-faced Waxbill; but is paler grey, with a pinkish wash on the body plumage. Most birds lack black chin (or it is very small) and both sexes (not just females) have grey (not black) central belly and vent. Juv. is duller, with less pink wash on body plumage. **Habitat:** Dry to semi-arid thorn scrub, usually on ground under thickets. **Status:** Uncommon and local; in pairs or small groups, often with other waxbills. **Voice:** Similar to Black-faced Waxbill's, but harsher.

1 CRIMSON-RUMPED WAXBILL *Estrilda rhodopyga* 10 cm

Endemic to NE Africa. Similar to Common Waxbill, but has dark red (not brown) rump and red-edged greater coverts and tertials; eye-stripe is darker red; bill is darker. Juv. is duller, with reduced barring, black bill and no eye-stripe, but still shows distinctive reddish rump and wing edges. **Habitat:** From tall-grass savannas with shrubs and bushes, at edge of forest, to dry wooded savanna, secondary growth and plantations. **Status:** Common. **Voice:** Similar to Common Waxbill's, but more nasal and with clear 'chee wee' notes.

2 BLACK-RUMPED WAXBILL *Estrilda troglodytes* 10 cm

Slightly paler and plainer (less barred) than Common Waxbill, with a black (not brown) rump and tail, and white (not blackish or brown) undertail-coverts, obvious in flight. Outer-tail feathers are edged white. Male has diffuse pink wash on underparts. Female is duller. Juv. has black bill and diffuse dark eye-stripe. **Habitat:** Semi-arid savanna; typically occurs in drier areas than Common Waxbill, although the two species form mixed flocks on the margins of their ranges. **Status:** Locally common. **Voice:** Plaintive 'chwee' call; soft 'wup' or 'tup' contact call. [C15.37]

3 COMMON WAXBILL *Estrilda astrild* 11-12 cm

A rather drab brownish waxbill with a red eye-stripe and bill. Brown rump and tail exclude most other species, including Black-rumped and Crimson-rumped waxbills. Red (not black) eye-stripe separates it from localised Black-lored Waxbill. Adults typically have reddish belly stripe; most pronounced in C Africa *rubriventris*, which is washed pink over most of body plumage. At close range, shows finely barred upperparts and flanks. Vent is blackish or barred brown. Juv. is duller, with less barred plumage and black bill. **Habitat:** Long grass, rank vegetation, reeds and scrub, usually near water. **Status:** Common; almost always in small groups. **Voice:** Nasal 'chee-chee-cherrr' song, descending slightly on last note; distinctive, high-pitched 'pink, pink' flight note. [C15.38, G6.10.6]

4 BLACK-LORED WAXBILL *Estrilda nigriloris* 10-11 cm

Endemic to SE DRC. Similar to Common Waxbill, but has black (not red) eye-stripe and more diffuse pink wash over breast (lacks reddish central belly stripe). Juv. is undescribed, but probably has black bill. **Habitat:** Grass and reedbeds and adjacent scrub. **Status:** Little known; recorded only from Lualaba River and Lake Upemba. **Voice:** Unknown; presumably similar to Common Waxbill's.

5 BLACK-CROWNED (BLACK-CAPPED) WAXBILL *Estrilda nonnula* 11 cm

A distinctive grey-and-white waxbill with a black crown, red rump and black tail. Told from darker Black-headed Waxbill by white or pale grey (not black or sooty-grey) vent and belly; appears much paler, particularly on face and underparts. Female has smaller red flank patches and brown wash on upperparts, but is still paler above than Black-headed Waxbill. Juv. is browner, with plain upperparts, buffy flanks and dull red rump. **Habitat:** Tall grass at forest edge and in clearings, secondary growth and plantations. **Status:** Locally common. **Voice:** High-pitched, sibilant 'swee' or 'tsee'. [C15.39]

6 BLACK-HEADED WAXBILL *Estrilda atricapilla* 10 cm

Darker than Black-crowned Waxbill, especially on the underparts: vent is blackish and belly is dark grey (not whitish). Male has more extensive crimson flanks. Female is more grey-brown, with paler red flank patch. Juv. is darker than female, with wash of red on flanks. WC African *avakubi* is whiter below, but still has black vent. EC African *graueri* has finely barred underparts and female is more olive above; sometimes considered a separate species, Kandt's Waxbill. **Habitat:** Dense herbaceous vegetation at forest edge, marshy clearings, plantations and villages in forested areas; often at higher elevations than Black-crowned Waxbill. **Status:** Locally common. **Voice:** High-pitched 'tseep' or 'tseep-eep', similar to Black-crowned Waxbill's. [C15.40]

Brood-parasitic finches that each parasitise one (rarely more) estrildid finch, the presence of which may help to identify the indigobird. Bill and leg colour are useful in some areas, but many species have a whitish bill and pale purple legs; identification depends on subtle plumage tones of breeding males and is probably reliable only if mimicked host calls are heard or a juv. is seen with a host. Ranges of many species poorly known. Males have a scratchy territorial song, irrespective of species. Sexes differ; juvs are plain brown, with a paler supercilium and belly.

1 VILLAGE INDIGOBIRD (STEEL-BLUE WIDOWFINCH) *Vidua chalybeata* 11 cm
Parasitises Red-billed and Brown firefinches. In SE Africa, red bill, legs and feet differentiate both male and female from other indigobirds. Elsewhere, has white or pinkish-white bill, but orange-red (not pale purple, although sometimes pinkish) legs are distinctive. Breeding male has blackish wings, darker than those of most other male indigobirds, with narrow white edges; body plumage has bluish sheen, except greenish nominate race (Upper Guinea). Non-breeding male and female are streaked brown above, paler beneath, with striped head; told from non-breeding Pin-tailed Whydah (p. 710) by pink (not dark) legs and less boldly striped head. **Habitat:** Woodland and savanna. **Status:** Common. **Voice:** Mimics dry, rattling calls and clear, whistled 'wheeet-wheeetoo' song of Red-billed and Brown firefinches. [C15.52, G6.12.6]

2 PURPLE (DUSKY) INDIGOBIRD (PURPLE WIDOWFINCH)
Vidua purpurascens   11 cm
Parasitises Jameson's Firefinch. In S Africa, the combination of white or pinkish-white bill, legs and feet distinguish both male and female from other indigobirds. In E and C Africa, is easily confused with Variable Indigobird, which has paler pink legs in this area; breeding male may show more purple gloss on plumage, but certain identification depends on hearing mimetic calls of host. **Habitat:** Savanna, especially acacias. **Status:** Common. **Voice:** Mimics purring calls, whistles and trills of Jameson's Firefinch. [C15.53, G6.12.5]

3 VARIABLE (DUSKY) INDIGOBIRD (BLACK WIDOWFINCH) *Vidua funerea* 11 cm
Parasitises African Firefinch. Throughout most of range, has whitish bill and pink or pale purplish legs, like many other indigobirds, but in South Africa has distinctive red or orange-red legs. Breeding male is black, with slight bluish gloss (typically less than Purple Indigobird, but many individuals are inseparable on plumage alone); wings are dark brown. **Habitat:** Forest edge, woodland and moist savanna. **Status:** Common. **Voice:** Short, canary-like jingle and scolding 'chit-chit-chit' mimicry of African Firefinch's call. [C15.56, G6.12.4]

4 ZAMBEZI (PETERS'S TWINSPOT) INDIGOBIRD *Vidua codringtoni*   11 cm
Parasitises Red-throated Twinspot. Breeding male is glossy greenish (rarely bluish), with black (not dark brown) wings. Bill is whitish; legs and feet are orange-red. Lacks pale primary edges of other male indigobirds, and in good light shows matt, dark grey breast. Non-breeding male and female are similar to other indigobirds but have grey (not buffy) breast. **Habitat:** Moist woodland and forest edge. **Status:** Little known; apparently scarce. **Voice:** Mimics trill call and song of Red-throated Twinspot.

5 JAMBANDU (GOLDBREAST) INDIGOBIRD *Vidua raricola*   11 cm
Parasitises Orange-breasted Waxbill. Breeding male is glossy blue-green, with dark brown wings; bill is whitish; legs and feet are pale purple. Male's plumage is slightly greener than other indigobirds within its range, but certain identification depends on hearing mimetic song. **Habitat:** Grassy plains, flooded meadows, swamps and adjacent woodland. **Status:** Locally common. **Voice:** Mimics calls of Orange-breasted Waxbill.

6 BAKA (BLACK-FACED FIREFINCH) INDIGOBIRD *Vidua larvaticola*   11 cm
Parasitises Black-faced Firefinch. Breeding male is glossy blue-black, but can show greenish gloss in certain light; wings are brown; bill is whitish; legs and feet are pale purple. Unless mimetic song is heard, is very difficult to separate from other indigobirds with white bill and purplish legs. **Habitat:** Grassy woodland and moist thickets, often near water. **Status:** Poorly known, but fairly widespread. **Voice:** Mimics calls of Black-faced Firefinch. [C15.55]

1

W, C & NE Africa

♂

transitional

♂

SE Africa

♂

2

♀

♀

♂ non-br.

4

3

♀

♂

♂

5

♂

6

♂

709

1 WILSON'S (PALE-WINGED) INDIGOBIRD *Vidua wilsoni* 11 cm
Parasitises Bar-breasted Firefinch. Breeding male has purplish gloss to plumage, with dark brown flight feathers narrowly edged whitish. Bill is whitish; legs and feet are purplish. Identification is very difficult unless mimetic song is heard. **Habitat:** Dry scrub and grassland, often near swamps and rivers. **Status:** Poorly known; apparently uncommon; sometimes flocks with waxbills. **Voice:** Mimics warbling song of Bar-breasted Firefinch. [C15.58]

2 JOS PLATEAU INDIGOBIRD *Vidua maryae* (not illustrated) 12 cm
Endemic to Nigeria. Parasitises Rock Firefinch. Breeding male is glossy greenish black, with rather pale brown wings; bill is whitish; legs and feet are pale purple. Slightly larger than Quailfinch Indigobird. **Habitat:** Dry woodland and scrub on rocky outcrops and boulder-strewn areas. **Status:** Little known. **Voice:** Mimics song of Rock Firefinch. [C15.57]

3 QUAILFINCH INDIGOBIRD *Vidua nigeriae* (not illustrated) 11-12 cm
Parasitises quailfinches. Breeding male is greenish black, with rather pale brown wings narrowly edged white; bill is whitish; legs and feet are pale purple. Smaller than Jos Plateau Indigobird, but very difficult to identify unless mimetic song is heard. **Habitat:** Breeding birds occupy open grassy plains associated with river floodplains and adjacent woodland. **Status:** Locally common. **Voice:** 'Chick chick chak' song, similar to that of quailfinches. [C15.59]

4 CAMEROON INDIGOBIRD *Vidua camerunensis* (not illustrated) 11 cm
Apparently parasitises African and Black-bellied firefinches and Brown and Dybowski's twinspots, although each male specialises on a single species. Breeding male is glossy blue-black, with dark brown wings, narrowly edged white; bill is whitish; legs and feet are pale purple. Identification probably depends on hearing mimetic song. **Habitat:** Woodland, savanna and forest edge. **Status:** Poorly known. **Voice:** Mimicry of host species. [C15.60]

WHYDAHS
Brood parasites, mostly of waxbills and pytilias. Breeding males have long tails; females, non-breeding males and juvs resemble indigobirds.

5 PIN-TAILED WHYDAH *Vidua macroura* 12 cm (br. m 34 cm)
Parasitises various waxbills and warblers. Breeding male unmistakable. Non-breeding adult has pink-red bill and boldly striped, black-and-buff head; told from other whydahs and indigo-birds by dark legs. **Habitat:** Savanna, grassland, scrub, parks and gardens. **Status:** Common. **Voice:** Sharp 'chip-chip-chip', often fluttering in air with tail vertical. [C15.61, G6.11.10]

6 SHAFT-TAILED WHYDAH *Vidua regia* 12 cm (br. m 34 cm)
Endemic to SW Africa; parasitises Violet-eared Waxbill. Breeding male is unmistakable. Female and non-breeding male have streaked head markings (not bold black stripes of similarly plumaged Pin-tailed Whydah). Juv. is dull brown, with dark streaking on back and dark bill. **Habitat:** Grassy areas in acacia savanna. **Status:** Common. **Voice:** High-pitched, squeaky and slurred whistles; mimics Violet-eared Waxbill. [G6.12.1]

7 STRAW-TAILED (FISCHER'S) WHYDAH *Vidua fischeri* 10-11 cm (br. m 28 cm)
Endemic to NE Africa; parasitises Purple Grenadier. Breeding male is unmistakable. Non-breeding male and female have streaked back but much plainer head than other whydahs and indigobirds; bill is pinkish. Juv. plain brown, with dark bill. **Habitat:** Dry bush, open grassy plains and farmlands; generally avoids moister areas. **Status:** Locally common. **Voice:** Various thin, squeaky and trilling whistled notes; mimics Purple Grenadier.

8 STEEL-BLUE WHYDAH *Vidua hypocherina* 10-11 cm (br. m 28 cm)
Endemic to NE Africa; parasitises Black-faced and Black-cheeked waxbills. Breeding male is unmistakable. Birds resembling breeding males recorded in S Africa have been ascribed to whydah-indigobird hybrids. Non-breeding males and females are similar to other whydahs and indigobirds, but have greyish-white bill and legs. Juv. is plain brown, with paler belly. **Habitat:** Dry scrub and bush and farmlands. **Status:** Uncommon. **Voice:** Various chirps, chiks and trills by male in display.

1 EASTERN PARADISE-WHYDAH *Vidua paradisaea*   12 cm (br. m 36 cm)
Parasitises Green-winged Pytilia. Breeding male may be told from Broad-tailed Paradise-Whydah by more slender, elongate tail and darker nape patch and breast; range is not known to overlap with those of other paradise-whydahs. Non-breeding male and female are streaked grey-brown above, with black and whitish striped head; typically have darker bill than Broad-tailed Paradise-Whydah and more marked head, with two dark crescents on ear coverts. Juv. is plain brown, with paler belly; slightly smaller than juv. Broad-tailed Paradise-Whydah. **Habitat:** Woodland and acacia savanna. **Status:** Common, with local movements. **Voice:** Sharp 'chip-chip'; mimics chittering calls and high-pitched whistles of Green-winged Pytilia. [C15.64, G6.12.2]

2 SAHEL PARADISE-WHYDAH *Vidua orientalis*   12 cm (br. m 36 cm)
Parasitises Green-winged Pytilia, like Eastern Paradise-Whydah, but breeding male's tail is shorter and more rounded, and non-breeding male and female lack dark cheek mark; ranges are not known to overlap. Tail is shorter than in Exclamatory and Togo paradise-whydahs and is broadest in the middle, tapering to the tip. Non-breeding male and female are reputed to have darker bill and legs than Exclamatory Paradise-Whydah, but are not known to differ from Togo Paradise-Whydah. Juv. is probably indistinguishable from other juv. paradise-whydahs. **Habitat:** Open woodland and old farmlands. **Status:** Uncommon. **Voice:** Sharp 'chip-chip'; mimics chittering calls and mournful whistles of Green-winged Pytilia. [C15.62]

3 TOGO PARADISE-WHYDAH *Vidua togoensis*   12 cm (br. m 40 cm)
Endemic to W Africa; parasitises Yellow-winged Pytilia. The longest, most slender-tailed paradise-whydah. Breeding male's tail is uniformly narrow along most of its length (not broadest in middle, as in Sahel Paradise-Whydah), and more slender than Exclamatory Paradise-Whydah's; also has paler golden-yellow (not chestnut) nape patch. Non-breeding male, female and juv. are undescribed; probably are indistinguishable from other paradise-whydahs. **Habitat:** Slightly wooded savanna and old farmlands. **Status:** Uncommon and thinly distributed. **Voice:** Mimics high-pitched 'tseep' calls of Yellow-winged Pytilia.

4 EXCLAMATORY PARADISE-WHYDAH *Vidua interjecta*   12 cm (br. m 38 cm)
Parasitises Red-winged Pytilia and, from Nigeria E, Yellow-winged Pytilia. Formerly considered a race of Broad-tailed Paradise-Whydah, but breeding male's tail is much longer; ranges do not overlap. Tail is longer and broader than Sahel Paradise-Whydah's, and is broadest towards tip (not in middle); tail is shorter and broader than Togo Paradise-Whydah's, and has darker orange-chestnut nape patch. Non-breeding male and female reportedly have pinkish (not dark) bill and legs. Juv. is probably indistinguishable from other paradise-whydahs. **Habitat:** Wooded savannas and adjacent farmlands. **Status:** Uncommon to locally common. **Voice:** Mimics harsh, rattling calls of Red- and Yellow-winged pytilias. [C15.63]

5 BROAD-TAILED PARADISE-WHYDAH *Vidua obtusa*   12 cm (br. m 27 cm)
Parasitises Orange-winged Pytilia. Breeding male has shorter, much broader tail than male Eastern Paradise-Whydah, with a darker head and breast; nape is orange-chestnut (not golden-yellow). Tail is much shorter than Exclamatory Paradise-Whydah's; ranges do not overlap. Female and non-breeding male typically have paler bill than Eastern Paradise-Whydah, with plainer ear coverts (lacking dark crescents). Juv. probably is indistinguishable from other juv. paradise-whydahs. **Habitat:** Miombo and other broadleafed woodland. **Status:** Locally common. **Voice:** Mimics piping whistles and sharp 'chip' calls of Orange-winged Pytilia. [G6.12.3]

Large group of seed-eating birds, mostly in *Serinus*. There is little consistency in the use of common names, although canaries tend to be yellower and seed-eaters browner. Sexes differ in some species (typically those that flock when not breeding); juvs duller and more streaked.

1 YELLOW-FRONTED CANARY *Serinus mozambicus*　　　　11-12 cm
The typical canary in much of Africa. A fairly small species, with a well-defined blackish malar stripe and bright yellow frons extending as a broad supercilium, contrasting with the darker green crown. Smaller than Brimstone or Yellow canaries, with more strongly marked face, bright yellow rump and white tail tips. In flight, yellow rump and white tail tips are conspicuous, recalling Black-throated Canary complex (p. 716), but is overall much yellower. Female is duller; juv. has buffy yellow, lightly streaked underparts. **Habitat:** Open woodland, savanna and gardens. **Status:** Common to abundant; gregarious. **Voice:** Sweet, rather monotonous 'zeee-zereee, zeee-zereee chereeo', with occasional trills and flourishes. [C15.71, G6.12.8]

2 YELLOW CANARY *Serinus flaviventris*　　　　13-14 cm
Endemic to SW Africa. Slightly larger than Yellow-fronted Canary, with less strongly marked face, rump the same colour as back (not much brighter yellow) and no white tail tips. Smaller than Brimstone Canary, with markedly smaller bill; usually found in drier or more open habitats. Upperparts are darker green in S; paler yellow-green in N. Female is much duller olive-grey above, and paler whitish, greyish or pale lemon below, streaked darker brown in most races. Juv. is more heavily streaked than female. **Habitat:** Karoo, coastal scrub and semi-desert. **Status:** Common; often in large flocks with other seed-eaters and sparrows. **Voice:** Song is similar to that of Yellow-fronted Canary, but faster and typically more varied. [G6.13.8]

3 WHITE-BELLIED CANARY *Serinus dorsostriatus*　　　　12-13 cm
Endemic to NE Africa. Forms a superspecies with Yellow Canary, but has a diagnostic white lower belly and undertail coverts. Larger than Yellow-fronted Canary, lacking its well-marked head and white tail tips. White belly and smaller bill separate it from Brimstone Canary. Head is more marked than Yellow-crowned Canary (p. 718); and wings greenish (not black and yellow). Female is duller, with streaking on breast and flanks. Juv. is browner above, with buffy breast. **Habitat:** Semi-arid savanna, acacia scrub, grasslands and thickets. **Status:** Locally common; usually in pairs or small flocks. **Voice:** Usual canary-like twittering song; 'tsuuweee' flight call.

4 BRIMSTONE (BULLY) CANARY *Serinus sulphuratus*　　　　13-15 cm
Larger than Yellow-fronted Canary, with much heavier bill and no white tail tips. In E Africa, told from grosbeak-canaries by horn-coloured (not pink) bill, and from smaller White-bellied Canary by yellow belly and larger bill. In S Africa, is larger than Yellow Canary, with much heavier bill. Nominate birds (S South Africa) are darker green and have largest bill. Female is duller; juv. is lightly streaked below. **Habitat:** Woodland, mesic thickets and gardens. **Status:** Common; usually in pairs; seldom in flocks. **Voice:** Rich song of deeper, slower notes, 'zwee zwee duid duid duid tweer weerr', more like that of larger seed-eaters than canaries. [C15.72, G6.13.7]

5 NORTHERN GROSBEAK-CANARY *Serinus donaldsoni*　　　　14-15 cm
Endemic to NE Africa. A very large canary with a huge pink bill. Darker and more heavily streaked above than Brimstone Canary, with pink (not horn-coloured) bill. Darker above than Southern Grosbeak-Canary and much more sexually dimorphic; ranges do not overlap. Female is olive-brown above, with whitish underparts, streaked on breast and flanks. **Habitat:** Dry, open acacia scrub and woodland. **Status:** Uncommon; usually in pairs. **Voice:** Song is repeated 'tseuu'; flight call is 'cheeaa'.

6 SOUTHERN GROSBEAK-CANARY *Serinus buchanani*　　　　14-15 cm
Endemic to S Kenya and N Tanzania. Often considered a race of Northern Grosbeak-Canary but is paler and less streaked above, and has much less sexual dimorphism; ranges do not overlap. Larger than Brimstone Canary, with larger pink (not horn-coloured) bill. Female is slightly more streaked below. **Habitat:** Dry acacia scrub, woodland and gardens. **Status:** Uncommon and local; usually solitary or in pairs. **Voice:** Similar to Northern Grosbeak-Canary's; contact call is slurred 'tweeleet'.

N races

S races

N races

sulphuratus

1 BLACK-THROATED CANARY *Serinus atrogularis* 11 cm

A pale grey-brown canary, heavily streaked with dark brown on the upperparts, with a bright lemon-yellow rump and white tail tips. Told from Reichenow's and Yellow-rumped Seed-eaters by blackish throat; ranges do not overlap. Also less streaked below than Reichenow's Seed-eater, with less well-defined supercilium. Black throat is most obvious during breeding. Female has less black on throat; juv. has only a few black spots on throat and is more streaked below. **Habitat:** Acacia savanna, dry woodland and fields in dry regions, often near water. **Status:** Common resident and local nomad; usually in flocks. **Voice:** Prolonged series of wheezy whistles and chirrups. [C15.70, G6.12.9]

2 REICHENOW'S (KENYA YELLOW-RUMPED) SEED-EATER
Serinus reichenowi 11-12 cm

Endemic to NE Africa. Often treated as a race of Black-throated Canary, but has whitish (not blackish) throat. Browner above than both Black-throated Canary and Yellow-rumped Seed-eater, with more prominent buffy-white supercilium and white cheek patch, as well as obvious streaking on breast and flanks; ranges not known to overlap. **Habitat:** Open woodland and fields. **Status:** Locally common; sometimes in small flocks, often with Yellow-fronted Canaries. **Voice:** Song is like Black-throated Canary's; flight call is thin 'sueee'.

3 (ABYSSINIAN) YELLOW-RUMPED SEED-EATER *Serinus xanthopygius* 11-12 cm

Endemic to Ethiopia and Eritrea. Often treated as a race of Black-throated Canary, but has white (not blackish) throat. Greyer and paler above than Reichenow's Seed-eater, with much less distinct streaking on underparts, much weaker supercilium and uniform brownish face (lacking whitish cheek patch); ranges are not known to overlap. Distinct white throat contrasts with greyish-brown breast. **Habitat:** Semi-arid scrub, woodland and fields. **Status:** Uncommon. **Voice:** Very similar to that of Reichenow's Seed-eater.

4 WHITE-RUMPED SEED-EATER *Serinus leucopygius* 10-11 cm

A drab, greyish-brown canary with a diagnostic white rump. White (not yellow) rump and lack of white tail tips separate it from Yellow-fronted Canary (p. 714) and all species in Black-throated Canary complex. In addition, nominate birds that might overlap with Reichenow's and Yellow-rumped seed-eaters have greyish-brown (not white) throat. W races have paler throat. Sexes are alike; juv. is more streaked on breast. **Habitat:** Dry acacia scrub, open woodland, fields and gardens. **Status:** Common to locally common; in small groups or pairs, often with other finches and waxbills. **Voice:** Rich, jumbled canary song; slightly deeper and more melodious than those of other small canaries; 'veeep' contact call. [C15.69]

5 YELLOW-THROATED SEED-EATER *Serinus flavigula* 10-11 cm

Endemic to Awash region, C Ethiopia. A drab grey-brown canary with a yellowish rump and a diagnostic pale yellow throat patch, extending onto the upper breast. Slightly smaller than Yellow-rumped Seed-eater, with buffy-brown (not white) tail tips and less bright rump. Yellow throat patch is smaller than that of Salvadori's Seed-eater, and lacks black collar on upper breast (but may be indistinguishable from juv. Salvadori's Seed-eater); ranges are not known to overlap. **Habitat:** Dry acacia scrub on hillsides. **Status:** Vulnerable. Uncommon and little known; occurs in small flocks. **Voice:** Soft 'chewee' or 'tsree' flight calls; jumbled, chirpy song.

6 SALVADORI'S SEED-EATER *Serinus xantholaemus* 11-12 cm

Endemic to Ethiopia. Similar to Yellow-throated Seed-eater, but has more extensive yellow patch on the lower throat and upper breast, with a diagnostic black collar across the upper breast. Collar is variable in width, and is broken in centre in some birds. Told from Reichenow's Seed-eater by distinctive breast markings and lack of white tail tips. Juv. has smaller yellow breast patch, lacking black collar; could be confused with Yellow-throated Seed-eater, but ranges are not known to overlap. **Habitat:** Semi-arid acacia scrub and juniper forest edge, dry thickets in wadis, and adjacent dry, bushed grassland. **Status:** Little known, but is locally common at a few sites. **Voice:** Flight call is similar to Yellow-throated Canary's; typical jumbled, canary-like song.

1 LEMON-BREASTED CANARY *Serinus citrinipectus* 11 cm

Endemic to SE Africa. Superficially intermediate between Yellow-fronted (p. 714) and Black-throated (p. 716) canaries. Male has pale lemon throat and upper breast, pale peachy-buff flanks and white belly. Has bold head markings of Yellow-fronted Canary, but with white (not yellow) cheek and supraloral patch. Female resembles Black-throated Canary but is peachy-buff below, with more strongly marked head and no black on throat. **Habitat:** Palm savanna and adjacent acacia woodland and grassland. **Status:** Locally common. **Voice:** Song is similar to Black-throated Canary's, but higher pitched and less melodious, with shorter phrases. [G6.13.1]

2 ETHIOPIAN (BLACK-HEADED) SISKIN *Serinus nigriceps* 11-12 cm

Endemic to Abyssinian highlands. Male is easily identified within its limited range by its sooty black head. Female and juv. could be confused with African Citril (p. 720), but have darker forehead, no pale supercilium, paler face, more diffuse streaking on underparts and darker flight feathers. Told from Yellow-crowned Canary by much darker head and upperparts, and less prominent yellow wing bars. **Habitat:** Grassland, scrub and fields, usually above 2 000 m. **Status:** Common; flocks of hundreds gather outside breeding season. **Voice:** Canary-like twitters and chissiks.

3 YELLOW-CROWNED CANARY *Serinus flavicollis* 11-13 cm

Often considered a race of Cape Canary, but is brighter yellow, lacking grey on the head, and with much brighter black-and-yellow wings; ranges do not overlap. Male is easily identified by almost plain yellow head, with only slightly darker hindcrown and eye-stripe. Belly is white, but boldly marked wings and plain face separate it from White-bellied Canary (p. 714); habitat also differs. Female is duller, with heavier streaking on upperparts and some flank streaks, but has distinctive yellow supercilium and bold wings. Juv. is brownish, heavily streaked above and below. **Habitat:** Montane grasslands, scrub and heath; also gardens and fields above 1 600 m. **Status:** Locally common; in pairs or small flocks. **Voice:** Jumbled canary song; twittering 'trrrrreet' in flight.

4 CAPE CANARY *Serinus canicollis* 11-13 cm

The only canary with a smooth blue-grey hindcrown, nape, mantle and sides of the neck. Wings are olive-green, narrowly edged yellow (not blackish with broad yellow edges, as in Yellow-crowned Canary). Male has mustard yellow frons, face and throat; female is duller, lightly streaked above and on flanks, with grey wash on face and breast. Juv. is browner above and greenish yellow below, with heavy brown streaking. **Habitat:** Fynbos, grassland, coastal dunes and gardens. **Status:** Common; often in small flocks. **Voice:** Male gives protracted, warbling canary song from prominent perch or in display flight; flight call is distinctive 'su-wi-wi-wi'. [C15.65, G6.13.2]

5 DRAKENSBERG SISKIN *Pseudochloroptila symonsi* 13 cm

Endemic to S Africa. Sometimes considered a race of Cape Siskin, but has white outer-tail feathers (not white tail tips) and lacks white tips to primaries; ranges do not overlap. Female is duller, lacking yellow in plumage (unlike female Cape Siskin). Juv. is drab brown, heavily streaked on head, mantle and breast. **Habitat:** Montane scrub and grassland. **Status:** Locally common. **Voice:** Similar to Cape Siskin's, but more strident; contact call is sharper 'voyp-vwip'. [G6.13.5]

6 CAPE SISKIN *Pseudochloroptila totta* 12 cm

Endemic to South Africa. A rather dull-coloured canary with a diagnostic warm brown back and wing coverts and a blackish tail with white tips. Very similar to Drakensberg Siskin but has white tips to primaries and tail feathers (not white outer-tail feathers); ranges do not overlap. Female is duller, with streaked throat and less extensive white tips to primaries (often not visible in the field). Juv. is heavily streaked on head and breast. **Habitat:** Montane fynbos, forest margins, and sometimes along coast; also exotic pine plantations. **Status:** Locally common. **Voice:** Diagnostic, querulous 'voyp-veeyr' contact call, often given in flight; canary-like song is rather wispy, often incorporating contact call. [G6.13.4]

1 AFRICAN CITRIL *Serinus citrinelloides*   11-12 cm

Endemic to NE Africa. Formerly treated as a single, polytypic species, but now split into three, with close links to other streaked canaries. Told from Western Citril by very small supercilium, restricted to area above and behind eye. Female and juv. lack black face and are much more heavily streaked on crown, breast and flanks. More heavily streaked than female Ethiopian Siskin (p. 718), with darker face, slight supercilium and paler forehead. Female probably is inseparable from female *kikuyuensis* Western Citril, but told from female *frontalis* by streaked (not plain) underparts. **Habitat:** Mid- and high-altitude forest edge, villages, farmlands and road verges. **Status:** Locally common. In small groups or pairs. **Voice:** Sweet, melodic whistles and more typical, jumbled canary-like song; 'chuwee' contact and flight calls.

2 WESTERN CITRIL *Serinus frontalis*   11-12 cm

Endemic to EC Africa. Often treated as a race of African Citril, but has a very prominent yellow supercilium. Told from Southern Citril by black (not grey) face and prominent supercilium. Range abuts Black-faced Canary's in SW, but is darker green above, with less bright yellow underparts, smaller black face, blackish (not olive-green) flight feathers and more slender, pointed bill. W nominate race is brighter, with supercilium extending forward to form yellow frons; E *kikuyuensis* rarely has any yellow on frons. Female is duller; nominate is plain below, with prominent supercilium; *kikuyuensis* is heavily streaked below, similar to female African or Southern citrils, but is slightly darker and more streaked above. **Habitat:** Moist woodland, forest edge, adjacent grassland and gardens. **Status:** Common. **Voice:** Similar to African Citril's. [C15.66a]

3 SOUTHERN CITRIL *Serinus hypostictus*   11-12 cm

Endemic to SE Africa. Often treated as a race of African Citril, but has greyish or olive (not black) face. Told from Western Citril and Forest Canary by very small (not large) supercilium and lack of black face. Very similar to Papyrus Canary; best told in narrow area of overlap (SW Kenya) by longer, more slender bill and different habitat. Less sexually dimorphic than other citrils; female is only slightly duller and more streaked. **Habitat:** Forest edge, moist woodland, rank growth and gardens. **Status:** Locally common; in small groups or pairs. **Voice:** Similar to African Citril's. [C15.66b]

4 PAPYRUS CANARY *Serinus koliensis*   11-12 cm

Endemic to E Africa. Told from male Western and African citrils by olive-grey (not black) face, lack of a yellow supercilium and streaked underparts in both sexes. Separation from male Southern Citril and female citrils depends primarily on stouter, slightly paler bill and specialised habitat. Lacks yellow supercilium of female Black-faced Canary. Sexes are similar; female is slightly more streaked below. **Habitat:** Papyrus swamps and adjacent vegetation. **Status:** Locally common but unobtrusive and easily overlooked; usually in pairs or small groups. **Voice:** Rather brief warbling song, often including series of dry trilling notes, 'tit-it-it-it-it-it'. [C15.68]

5 BLACK-FACED CANARY *Serinus capistratus*   12 cm

Endemic to WC Africa. Similar to citrils, but has a stouter, less pointed bill; prominent supercilium separates it from all citrils except Western Citril. Male differs from male nominate Western Citril by more extensive black face, brighter yellow underparts, and plainer, paler green upperparts with olive-green (not blackish) flight feathers. Female has greenish face bordered by yellow, and lightly streaked throat, breast and flanks. Juv. is paler and more streaked below. **Habitat:** Tall-grass wooded savanna at edge of forest and along gallery forest, villages and plantations. **Status:** Locally common. **Voice:** Variable canary-like twitterings; 'chissik'. [C15.67]

6 FOREST CANARY *Serinus scotops*   13 cm

Endemic to S Africa. A dark, heavily streaked canary with a black chin and greyish cheeks that contrast with the pale-based bill; presumably closely related to citrils. Differs from Southern Citril by prominent yellow supercilium and throat. Female and juv. have little or no black bib. **Habitat:** Forest, forest edge and clearings. **Status:** Locally common. **Voice:** Often located by soft, high-pitched 'tseeek' contact call; quiet, jumbled song is seldom heard. [G6.13.3]

1 STREAKY SEED-EATER *Serinus striolatus*   14-15 cm
A large, heavily streaked, brown canary. Told from Yellow-browed Seed-eater by white (not yellow) supercilium and throat. Similar to Kipengere Seed-eater, but has more heavily streaked upperparts and more strongly marked face. Larger than Reichard's and Streaky-headed seed-eaters (p. 724), with much heavier bill, white patterned face and prominent malar stripe. Differs from heavily streaked female widowbirds by darker plumage, relatively shorter wings, longer tail and different behaviour. **Habitat:** Forest edge, adjacent secondary growth and gardens. **Status:** Common. **Voice:** Rich, often fairly slow, thrush-like song; also loud, melodic 'si-wioouu' call. [C15.76]

2 YELLOW-BROWED SEED-EATER *Serinus whytii*   14-15 cm
Often considered a race of Streaky Seed-eater, but has yellow (not white) supercilium, face and throat; ranges do not overlap. Also has streaked (not plain) ear coverts and much more prominent yellow edges to secondaries and tail. **Habitat:** Mid- and high-altitude forest edge and adjacent thickets and secondary growth. **Status:** Nowhere common; thinly distributed; usually in pairs. **Voice:** Song is similar to Streaky Seed-eater's, but lower pitched; call is 'si-wuuee'.

3 THICK-BILLED SEED-EATER *Serinus burtoni*   15-16 cm
A large, dark brown canary with a diagnostic huge, pinkish-white bill, blackish-brown face and brownish breast. Extent of white on forehead varies from white forehead through a supraloral spot to absent (CE Africa *tanganjicae*). Larger than Kipengere Seed-eater, with brown (not white) throat, two white wing bars and less heavily streaked underparts. Juv. is paler, with grizzled black-and-white face and darker bill. **Habitat:** Chiefly at higher altitudes in forest edge, clearings and adjacent secondary growth and farmlands. **Status:** Common but not in great numbers; usually singly or in pairs. **Voice:** High-pitched 'seeeet' call; song is jumbled mix of whistles and chissiks, higher pitched than Streaky Seed-eater's. [C15.77]

4 KIPENGERE SEED-EATER *Serinus melanochrous*   14-15 cm
Endemic to S Tanzania. Sometimes considered a race of Thick-billed Seed-eater, but is smaller, with a whitish throat and cleaner white underparts with heavy dark brown streaking; lacks white wing bars and white forehead, but has thin white lines around eye. Less streaked above than Streaky Seed-eater, with less strongly patterned face. **Habitat:** Highland forests and adjacent secondary growth. **Status:** Uncommon, and easily overlooked. **Voice:** Apparently a long series of jumbled rattling notes, quite different from Thick-billed Seed-eater's.

5 WHITE-THROATED CANARY *Serinus albogularis*   15 cm
Endemic to SW Africa. A large, pale, unstreaked canary with a white throat and diagnostic greenish-yellow rump. Lacks blackish face of Protea Seed-eater. Paler than Streaky-headed Seed-eater, with paler face, less prominent supercilium and smaller bill. Larger than female Yellow Canary (p. 714), with much larger bill and plain (not streaked) breast. Juv. is lightly streaked above and on breast. **Habitat:** Coastal thicket, Karoo scrub and semi-desert. **Status:** Common. **Voice:** Song is rich jumbled mix of melodious notes; usual contact call is querulous 'tsuu-eeeee'. [G6.13.9]

6 PROTEA SEED-EATER *Serinus leucopterus*   15 cm
Endemic to South Africa. A drab brown canary with a diagnostic blackish face that contrasts with the pale bill and whitish throat. In flight, lacks greenish-yellow rump of White-throated Canary. Narrow white edgings to secondary coverts result in two diagnostic white wing bars, but these are only visible at close range. **Habitat:** Thick, tangled scrub and dense fynbos, not especially near proteas; more abundant in drier areas. **Status:** Uncommon to locally common. **Voice:** Contact call is 'tree-dili-eeee'; song comprises contact call with rather harsh, repetitive elements. [G6.13.10]

tanganjicae

1 STREAKY-HEADED SEED-EATER *Serinus gularis* 14 cm
A fairly large, drab canary with a relatively long, slender bill and a broad, whitish supercilium. Dark grey (not black) face, plain (or very lightly streaked) breast, creamy (not white) supercilium and warmer brown upperparts separate it from Black-eared Seed-eater. Differs from Reichard's Seed-eater by plain (not streaked) breast. Darker above than White-throated Canary (p. 722), with darker face, more prominent supercilium, and brown (not greenish) rump. Juv. more heavily streaked above and below. **Habitat:** Woodland, thickets and dense scrub, often in hilly areas; frequently associated with aloes in drier areas. **Status:** Common. **Voice:** Short, rather deep, melodious song; 'trrreet'. [C15.75b, G6.14.1]

2 WEST AFRICAN SEED-EATER *Serinus canicapillus* 14 cm
Often considered a race of Streaky-headed Seed-eater, but is darker, with buffy underparts; ranges do not overlap. In E overlaps with Reichard's Seed-eater, but has plain or only very faintly streaked breast. Larger than White-rumped Seed-eater (p. 716) with a prominent supercilium and brown (not white) rump. Female has faint breast streaks. Juv. duller, with paler supercilium and more streaked underparts. Isolated E African *elgonensis* is rich buff below; affinities uncertain. **Habitat:** Edges of gallery forest, wooded savannas, fields and villages. **Status:** Locally common. **Voice:** Typical canary-like jumbled song; 'tseuu' contact call. [C15.74]

3 REICHARD'S (STRIPE-BREASTED) SEED-EATER *Serinus reichardi* 14 cm
Often considered a race of Streaky-headed Seed-eater, but has more heavily streaked breast. Told from Black-eared Seed-eater by grey-brown (not black) ear coverts, warmer brown upperparts and longer, more slender bill. Smaller than Streaky Seed-eater (p. 722), with more suffuse breast streaking and no bold malar stripe. N *striatipectus* is more extensively streaked above and below; may be a distinct species. **Habitat:** Miombo woodland (nominate) and wooded escarpments (*striatipectus*). **Status:** Locally common. **Voice:** Contact call is 'tsweer' and 'tsu-we-err'; jumbled, canary-like song from elevated perch. [C15.75a]

4 BLACK-EARED SEED-EATER *Serinus mennelli* 14 cm
Slightly paler and colder grey above than Streaky-headed and Reichard's seed-eaters, with distinct black cheeks, crisp white (not creamy) supercilium and more crisply streaked black-and-white crown; bill is also heavier. Breast is more heavily streaked than Streaky-headed Seed-eater's. Female and juv. have dark grey cheeks, but retain prominent white supercilium, colder plumage and heavily streaked breast. **Habitat:** Miombo and mopane woodland. **Status:** Uncommon to locally common; often associated with bird parties. **Voice:** Twittering whistle, 'teeu-twee-teeu, twiddy-twee-twee'. [C15.73, G6.14.2]

5 BROWN-RUMPED SEED-EATER *Serinus tristriatus* 13 cm
Endemic to Abyssinian highlands and N Somalia. A drab, uniform brown canary with a small white supercilium. Smaller than Reichard's Seed-eater; ranges do not overlap. Juv. has faint, fine streaking on underparts. **Habitat:** Widespread, ranging from highland heath and forest edge to fields, gardens and even city centres. **Status:** Common. **Voice:** 'Chuwee' or 'sirreee' contact call; usual jumbled canary-like song.

6 PRÌNCIPÉ SEED-EATER *Serinus rufobrunneus* 12 cm
Endemic to São Tomé and Prìncipé. A small, short-tailed seed-eater, rufous-brown (Prìncipé) or grey-brown (São Tomé). Much smaller than São Tomé Grosbeak (p. 730), with a smaller bill and grey-brown (not chestnut) plumage. **Habitat:** Forest, plantations and secondary growth on São Tomé; forest on Prìncipé. **Status:** Common on São Tomé; uncommon on Prìncipé. **Voice:** Harsh, whistled 'tztreee'; jumbled, canary-like song. [C15.78]

7 ANKOBER SERIN *Serinus ankoberensis* 12-13 cm
Endemic to W Rift Valley scarp in Ethiopia. Much smaller than Streaky Seed-eater (p. 722), with plainer head, smaller, finer bill and denser streaking. Told from juv. Yellow-crowned Canary (p. 718) by brown upperparts with no yellow on wing edges, and slender, pointed bill. **Habitat:** Tussock grass and heath on steep slopes and cliffs. **Status:** Endangered. Patchily distributed but locally common; often in small flocks. **Voice:** Double-noted 'tree tree' contact call; flight call is 'weet weet weet'.

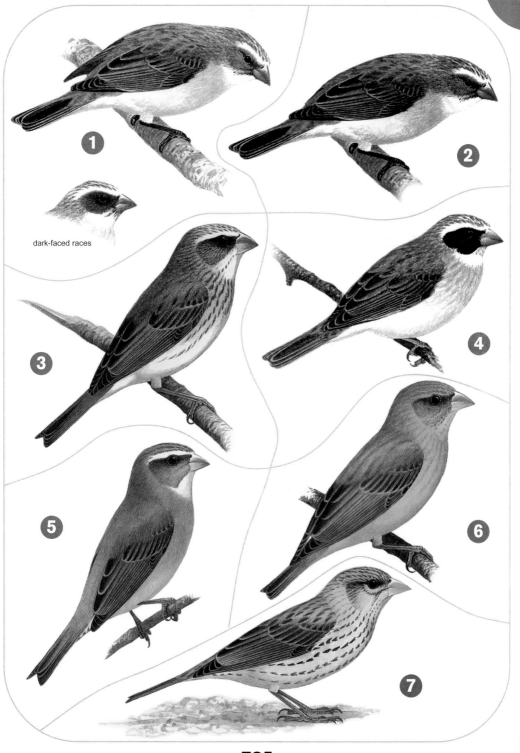

dark-faced races

1 BLACK-HEADED CANARY *Serinus alario* 12 cm
Endemic to S Africa. A small canary with sparrow-like coloration. Male's bold plumage is diagnostic; lacks white face markings of male Damara Canary. Female lacks black-and-white head and breast markings, but has distinctive chestnut back and tail. Told from female Damara Canary by uniform grey head, lacking faint white face pattern. Juv. has streaked breast. **Habitat:** Karoo scrub, usually in better vegetated areas, and fields; visits water to drink. **Status:** Locally common. **Voice:** Soft 'sweea' or 'tweet'. [G6.13.6]

2 DAMARA CANARY *Serinus leucolaema* 12 cm
Endemic to S Africa. Often treated as a race of Black-headed Canary, but they apparently do not hybridise despite broad range overlap. Male has pied (not black) head. Female has faint shadow of male's head pattern. Pairs tend to remain together throughout year, even when flocking. **Habitat:** Arid plains, mountain scrub and fields. **Status:** Fairly common; nomadic, occasionally irrupting S. **Voice:** Song is fast, jumbled canary twitter; 'sooeee' contact call.

BUNTINGS
Short-legged, mostly ground-feeding seed-eaters, superficially similar to canaries. Most have boldly marked head patterns. Sexes similar in most species.

3 LARK-LIKE BUNTING *Emberiza impetuani* 14 cm
Endemic to SW Africa. Rather nondescript, superficially lark-like, but with a long tail, short legs and hopping (not walking) gait. Pale cinnamon wash on underparts and rufous-edged wing feathers are diagnostic. Female and juv. are paler. **Habitat:** Semi-desert plains, Karoo scrub and arid savanna; gathers in large numbers at waterholes to drink. **Status:** Locally abundant nomad; subject to local movements. **Voice:** Song is short series of buzzy notes, accelerating and ending in dry trill; soft 'tuc-tuc' call. [G6.14.7]

4 CINNAMON-BREASTED (ROCK) BUNTING *Emberiza tahapisi* 14-15 cm
A dark, richly coloured bunting. Male darker than male House Bunting, with black (not grey-striped) throat and crown. Female and juv. duller, with less bold brown-and-white head markings; could be confused with male House Bunting but have entire breast cinnamon (not striped grey on upper breast) and wing coverts are less broadly edged rufous. Both sexes differ from Cape Bunting by black or greyish (not white) throat and cinnamon (not grey) underparts. **Habitat:** Rocky slopes in grassland and open woodland. **Status:** Common. **Voice:** Short, dry rattling song in S and E; more melodic in W; querulous 'where-wheer' call. [C15.80, G6.14.6]

5 HOUSE BUNTING *Emberiza striolata* 13-14 cm
Smaller and paler than Cinnamon-breasted Bunting. Male has less striking head pattern, grey and black in W Africa, whitish and black in E. Throat is striped grey and black, extending onto neck and upper breast. Female is much duller, with brown-and-buff (not black and white) head pattern and brown breast streaking. Both sexes have wing feathers broadly edged rufous, forming rufous panel on folded wing. **Habitat:** Arid savanna and desert, usually in rocky areas. **Status:** Locally common nomad; in pairs or small groups. **Voice:** Harsh 'chwik' and nasal 'zswee'; song is jumbled range of nasal burrs and rasps. [C4.92]

6 SOCOTRA BUNTING *Emberiza socotrana* 15 cm
Endemic to Socotra Island. Much paler than Cinnamon-breasted Bunting, with mostly white face and whitish underparts only lightly washed rufous on the breast. Shows white band across rump in flight. **Habitat:** Breeds above 700 m on grassy slopes with rocks and scattered trees, then disperses to coastal plain. **Status:** Vulnerable. Patchy within its small range. **Voice:** 1-3 high-pitched whistles followed by soft gurgle, 'tseep gurguruguru'.

7 CAPE BUNTING *Emberiza capensis* 16 cm
The pale greyish breast and chestnut wing coverts are diagnostic. White (not dark) throat and greyish (not cinnamon) underparts separate it from Cinnamon-breasted Bunting. Juv. is duller. Intensity of grey wash on underparts varies geographically, and is slightly buffy in some races. **Habitat:** Rocky hill slopes and scrub. **Status:** Common in S, local and uncommon in N. **Voice:** Nasal 'wa-meh-ma-meh' call; song is a series of accelerating chirps. [G6.14.5]

1 CABANIS'S BUNTING *Emberiza cabanisi*   16-17 cm
Differs from other golden-breasted buntings by its solid black cheeks, lacking a white stripe below the eye. Female is slightly duller; juv. is paler, with slightly streaked plumage. N nominate race is darker above, with solid black crown; S races (*orientalis* and *cognomitata*, Three-streaked Bunting) have narrow pale median crown stripe and broad chestnut edges to back and wing feathers, appearing paler and more streaked above. **Habitat:** Woodland and moist savanna. **Status:** Locally common. **Voice:** Clear 'tsseeoo' contact note; song is described as 'wee-chidder-chidder-wee'. [C15.82, G6.14.3]

2 GOLDEN-BREASTED BUNTING *Emberiza flaviventris*   15-16 cm
Differs from Cabanis's Bunting in having a white stripe below the eye and a richer yellow breast, washed with orange. Browner (less grey) above than Somali Bunting, with narrower white head stripes. Prominent white wing bars and grey (not brown) rump separate it from Brown-rumped Bunting. Female is slightly duller; juv. is paler, with slightly streaked plumage. **Habitat:** Woodland and moist savanna. **Status:** Common; usually in pairs. **Voice:** Nasal, buzzy 'zzhrrrr'; song is varied 'weechee, weechee, weechee'. [C15.81, G6.14.4]

3 BROWN-RUMPED BUNTING *Emberiza affinis*   13-14 cm
Similar to Somali and Golden-breasted buntings, but lacks prominent white wing bars, has brown (not grey) rump and has the golden-yellow underparts extending onto lower belly, flanks and undertail coverts. Head pattern is closer to Somali Bunting's, with broader white stripes than Golden-breasted Bunting. White stripe across cheek below eye separates it from Cabanis's Bunting. Juv. is paler. **Habitat:** Arid and semi-arid savanna. **Status:** Uncommon and local. **Voice:** Flight note is short 'chip'; song is short series of metallic notes, ending in trill. [C15.83]

4 SOMALI (GOLDEN-BREASTED) BUNTING *Emberiza poliopleura*   15 cm
Endemic to NE Africa. Paler than Golden-breasted Bunting, with grey-fringed back feathers (not chestnut-brown), broader head stripes and white (not buffy yellow) flanks. Also paler than Brown-rumped Bunting, with prominent white wing bars and grey (not brown) rump. White stripe across cheek below eye separates it from Cabanis's Bunting. Female is slightly duller; juv. is paler, with spotted breast. **Habitat:** Semi-arid savanna; usually in drier areas than Golden-breasted Bunting. **Status:** Locally common. **Voice:** Song is simple series of 'suweet tweest' notes or variations on this.

5 ORTOLAN BUNTING *Emberiza hortulana*   16 cm
A plain, grey-headed bunting with a pink bill and narrow white eye-ring. Slightly larger than Cretzschmar's Bunting, with more olive-grey head and yellow (not rusty) moustache and throat. Larger than juv. Cinnamon-breasted and House buntings (p. 726), with plain face and white outer-tail feathers. Juv. is more streaked, with buffy throat and moustache; paler below than juv. Cretzschmar's Bunting, with grey-brown (not rufous) rump. **Habitat:** Semi-arid scrub and grassland, often in rocky areas. **Status:** Locally common Palearctic migrant Nov-Mar. **Voice:** Dry 'prit prit' when flushed. [C4.91]

6 CRETZSCHMAR'S BUNTING *Emberiza caesia*   15 cm
Slightly smaller than Ortolan Bunting; adult has cinnamon-buff (not yellow) moustache and throat. Larger than House Bunting (p. 726), with plain face and white outer-tail. Juv. has buffy head and is more streaked; told from juv. Ortolan Bunting by warmer plumage with rufous (not grey-brown) rump. **Habitat:** Dry grassland and rocky hillsides. **Status:** Uncommon Palearctic migrant Nov-Mar. **Voice:** 'Chik' or 'prit' flight calls, similar to those of Ortolan Bunting.

7 CINEREOUS BUNTING *Emberiza cineracea*   16-17 cm
A large, pale bunting with a grey bill and narrow, pale eye-ring. Male has diagnostic greenish-yellow wash on head and breast. Female is duller, with only faint yellow wash on face and throat and fine breast streaking. Juv. is more streaked below, with buffy face and throat, pale buff underparts and greyish-brown upperparts; paler than juv. Ortolan Bunting, with grey (not pinkish) bill. All ages have obvious white outer-tail. **Habitat:** Stony grasslands, coastal vegetation and dunes. **Status:** Scarce Palearctic migrant Nov-Mar. **Voice:** 'Chirp' and 'chulp' contact calls.

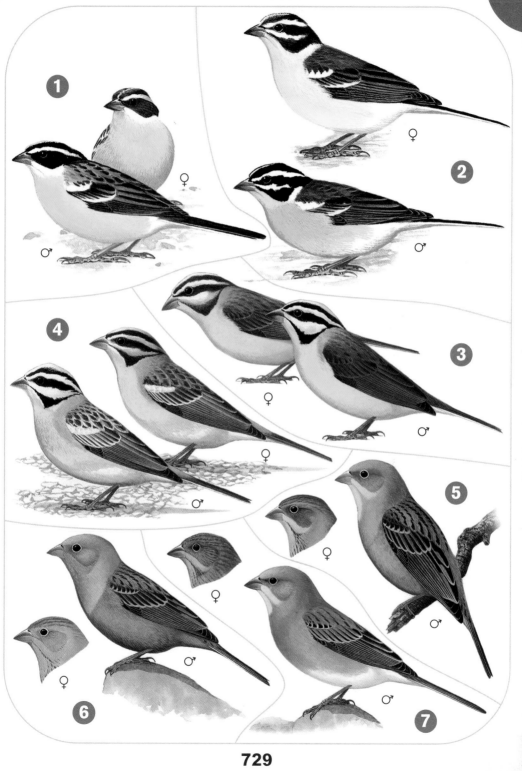

1 SÃO TOMÉ GROSBEAK *Neospiza concolor*   20 cm
Endemic to São Tomé. A large finch with a massive, parrot-like bill. Much larger than Prìncipé Seed-eater (p. 724), with warm chestnut-brown (not grey-brown) plumage. Sexes alike. **Habitat:** Primary forest. **Status:** Critically endangered. Very rare, known only from a few sightings in SW of island, near Rio Xufexufe. **Voice:** Reputed to be a series of 4-5 thin whistles.

2 ORIOLE FINCH *Linurgus olivaceus*   12-13 cm
Male has a distinctive black head and large orange-pink bill; superficially resembles black-headed (p. 384) orioles or masked weavers (p. 662), but is much smaller, with distinctive bill. Males vary geographically: W African *olivaceus* olive above with yellow nuchal collar; NE *elgonensis* much yellower above; C *prigoginei* more orange below; SE *kilimensis* darker above with no nuchal collar, green flanks and no orange on the breast. Female is olive-green, with dull grey-washed head and yellow-pink bill. Juv. resembles female but is paler below, lightly streaked, and has grey bill. **Habitat:** Undergrowth and canopy of montane forest and forest edge. **Status:** Locally common, but unobtrusive; usually in pairs or small family groups. **Voice:** Very high-pitched 'tzzree' or 'tzit' calls; song is canary-like, rapid series of high-pitched 'seee see' and 'shree chree' notes. [C15.79]

3 SOMALI GOLDEN-WINGED GROSBEAK *Rhynchostruthus louisae*   14-15 cm
Endemic to N Somalia. A chunky finch with a blackish head, bright yellow secondaries, greater coverts and base of the tail. Female duller. Juv. is streaked above and below, and has less extensive yellow in the wings. **Habitat:** Varied highland areas, from juniper forest edge to dry wadis and semi-arid acacia and *Euphorbia* scrub. **Status:** Uncommon; usually in pairs or small groups, especially outside breeding season. **Voice:** Soft 'titee', 'chip' and 'tink' calls; song is series of jangled notes given from inside a bush or in fluttering display flight.

4 SOCOTRA GOLDEN-WINGED GROSBEAK *Rhynchostruthus socotranus*   14-15 cm
Endemic to Socotra Island. Often treated as a race of Somali Golden-winged Grosbeak, but has more extensive black on the head, with large white ear patches; bill larger. Female head browner. Juv. is duller, with less extensive yellow in wings, and is streaked above and below. **Habitat:** Similar to that of Somali Golden-winged Grosbeak. **Status:** Uncommon. **Voice:** Not known to differ from Somali Golden-winged Grosbeak's.

5 WARSANGLI LINNET *Carduelis johannis*   12-13 cm
Endemic to N Somalia. A distinctive pale grey finch, with white underparts and rump, and rufous brown lower back and thighs. In flight, black wings show conspicuous white primary bases. Female is slightly streaked above. Juv. is much browner and heavily streaked above and on breast; could be confused with juv. canary but shows white flash at base of blackish-brown primaries. **Habitat:** Highland heath and juniper woodlands. **Status:** Endangered. Locally common at two sites, but threatened by clearing of junipers. **Voice:** Calls described as 'tsee wit', 'tweek' and 'sis sis sis'; song is jumbled, canary-like twittering.

6 COMMON CHAFFINCH *Fringilla coelebs*   14-16 cm
Introduced to Cape Peninsula, South Africa. Male is the only finch with a pinkish face and breast, a blue-grey head, and conspicuous white wing bars. Female and juv. are dowdy, grey-brown and sparrow-like, but still show prominent white wing bars. **Habitat:** Pine and oak plantations, and well-wooded gardens. **Status:** Fairly common on Cape Peninsula; vagrant to Mauritania. **Voice:** Sharp 'pink, pink, pink' call; short, hurried song typically is uttered from high in a tree. [G6.12.7]

7 JAVA SPARROW *Padda oryzivora*   16 cm
Introduced to Pemba and Zanzibar islands, Tanzania. The dark head with large white ear coverts and massive pinkish bill are diagnostic. Juv. is brown above, buff below with a white throat and dusky tip to the bill. **Habitat:** Villages and adjacent scrub and grasslands. **Status:** Localised and fairly common, usually around towns and villages. **Voice:** Tinkling bell-like notes; sharp 'tak'.

olivaceus

♀

♂

♀

♂

Handbooks (provide information on more than identification)
The Birds of Africa, edited by Hilary Fry, Stuart Keith and Emil Urban (Academic Press, London, 1982, 1986, 1988, 1992, 1997, 2000) is the standard handbook for Africa. Six volumes are already published, with the final volume to be published shortly. Until the final volume is released, one has to resort to regional guides for information on sparrows, weavers, finches and canaries. The series has grown in quality with each volume. Volume 1 (ostrich to falcons) was rather weak, especially for seabirds.
Del Hoyo, J., Elliott, A. & Sargatal, J. (eds). 1992, 1994, 1996, 1997, 1999, 2001, 2002. *Handbook of the birds of the world.*
   Lynx Edicions, Barcelona. 7 volumes published, covering all non-passerines; volumes on passerines are in the pipeline.
Mackworth-Praed, C.W. & Grant, C.H.B. 1952. *Birds of eastern and north eastern Africa* (2 vols). Longmans, Green & Co., London.
Mackworth-Praed, C.W. & Grant, C.H.B. 1962. *Birds of the southern third of Africa* (2 vols). Longmans, Green & Co., London.
Mackworth-Praed, C.W. & Grant, C.H.B. 1970. *Birds of west central and western Africa* (2 vols). Longmans, London.
Maclean, G.L. (1993) *Roberts' birds of southern Africa.* John Voelcker Bird Book Fund, Cape Town.
In addition, the many family guides in the Helm and Oxford University Press series provide excellent information. The volume on Finches and sparrows (Clement, P., Harris, A. & Davis, J. 1993. Helm, London) is especially useful, because is covers birds not yet treated by Birds of Africa.

Regional field guides
Aspinwall, D.R. & Beel, C. 1998. *A field guide to Zambian birds not found in southern Africa.* Zambian Ornithological Society,
   Lusaka.
Barlow, C., Wacher, T. & Disley, T. 1997. *A field guide to the birds of the Gambia and Senegal.* Pica Press, Sussex.
Borrow, N. & Demey, R. 2001. *Birds of western Africa.* Christopher Helm, London.
Christy, P. & Clarke, W.V. 1998. *Guide des Oiseaux de São Tomé et Príncipe.* ECOFAC, São Tomé.
Newman, K., Johnstone-Stuart, N. & Medland, B. 1992. *Birds of Malawi – a supplement to Newman's birds of southern Africa.*
   Southern Books, Halfway House.
Sinclair, I., Hockey, P. & Tarboten, W. 2002. *SASOL Birds of southern Africa* (3rd ed.). Struik, Cape Town.
Stevenson, T. & Fanshawe, J. 2002. *Field guide to the birds of east Africa.* T & AD Poyser, London.
Van Perlo, B. 1995. *Collins illustrated checklist birds of eastern Africa.* HarperCollins, London.
Van Perlo, B. 1999. *Collins illustrated checklist birds of southern Africa.* HarperCollins, London.
Van Perlo, B. 2002. *Collins illustrated checklist birds of western and central Africa.* HarperCollins, London.
Zimmerman, D.A., Turner, D.A. & Pearson, D.J. 1996. *Birds of Kenya and northern Tanzania.* Croom Helm, London.

Atlases and annotated checklists
Ash, J.S. & Miskell, J.E. 1998. *Birds of Somalia.* Pica Press, Sussex.
Benson, C.W., Brooke, R.K., Dowsett, R.J. & Irwin. M.P.S. 1971. *The birds of Zambia.* Collins, London.
Benson, C.W. & Benson, F.M. 1977. *The birds of Malawi.* Montfort Press, Limbe.
Carswell, M., Pomeroy, D., Reynolds, J. & Tushabe, H. in press. *Bird Atlas of Uganda.* BOU, Tring.
Cheke, R.A. & Walsh, J.F. 1996. *The birds of Togo.* BOU, Tring.
Dean, W.R.J. 2000. *The birds of Angola.* BOU, Tring.
Elgood, J.H. et al. 1994. *The birds of Nigeria.* BOU, Tring.
Gatter, W. 1997. *Birds of Liberia.* BOU, Tring.
Gore, M.E.J. 1990. *Birds of the Gambia.* BOU, Tring.
Grimes, L.G. 1987. *The birds of Ghana.* BOU, London.
Harrison, J.A., Allan, D.G., Underhill, L.G., Herremans, M., Tree, A.J., Parker, V. & Brown, C.J. (eds). 1997. *The atlas of southern
   African birds* (2 vols). BirdLife South Africa, Johannesburg.
Lewis, A. & Pomeroy, D. 1989. *A bird atlas of Kenya.* AA Balkema, Rotterdam.
Parker, V. 1999. *The atlas of the birds of Sul do Save,* southern Mozambique. Avian Demography Unit & Endangered Wildlife
   Trust, Cape Town & Johannesburg.

Extra-limital books
Southern Ocean seabirds: *Handbook of Australian, New Zealand and Antarctic birds* (vol. 1A, eds Marchant, S. & Higgins,
   P.J. 1990 & vol 3, eds Higgins, P.J. & Davies, S.J.J.F. 1996, Oxford University Press, Melbourne).
Palearctic migrants and N African species that extend their ranges into the Palearctic: Snow, D.W. & Perrins, C.M. (eds). 1998.
   The birds of the western Palearctic, concise edition (2 volumes). Oxford University Press, Oxford. Or, for really detailed
   information, you might also refer to the 9 volume full edition of *Birds of the Western Palearctic.* In addition, several excellent
   western Palearctic field guides are useful for migrant and N African species.

Adult. Reproductively active individuals; the final plumage birds acquire.

Aerial. Forage on the wing.

Aigrettes. Lacy plumes on the back acquired by egrets in breeding plumage.

Alien. Species introduced outside their natural range by human actions.

Allopatric. Species with non-overlapping ranges.

Colonial. Species that form dense aggregations, usually referring to breeding behaviour.

Convergent. Species that appear similar.

Crepuscular. Active at dawn and dusk.

Critical. The highest threat status; these species face an extremely high risk of extinction in the wild in the immediate future.

Cryptic. Camouflaged plumage coloration.

Cursorial. Adapted for running on the ground.

Diurnal. Active during daylight hours.

Eclipse plumage. Drab, female-like plumage that males acquire outside the breeding season (e.g. some ducks, sunbirds, weavers and bishops).

Endangered. A species thought to face a high risk of extinction, but this is less serious than Critical species.

Endemic. A species whose entire range is confined to a particular region.

Epaulettes. Showy feather tufts at the base of the wing that are raised in display (e.g. sunbirds).

Feral. Species that have established populations from domestic birds (e.g. pigeons, ducks).

Flight feathers. The primaries, secondaries and tertials on the wing, and major tail feathers.

Flush. Put to flight.

Fulvous. Reddish yellow or tawny.

Gorget. A distinctively coloured throat or upper breast band.

Immature. Plumage(s) attained between juvenile and adult plumages.

Introduced. Species introduced outside their natural range by human actions.

Irruption. Rapid and usually short-term expansions of a species' range.

Jizz. General impression of size, shape and behaviour, useful to identify species lacking definitive plumage characters.

Juvenile. The first fully feathered plumage of a young bird.

Leucistic. Unusually pale individuals, resulting from the absence of pigments. The extent of leucism can be either partial or complete. Most 'albinos' are usually leucistic birds that retain some pigmentation at least in their soft parts.

Melanistic. Unusually dark individuals, resulting from high levels of the pigment melanin. In some species (e.g. some herons, egrets and raptors) these variants are common enough to be termed dark morphs.

Migrant. A species that undertakes regular, seasonal flights between its breeding and non-breeding areas.

Mirrors. White spots near the tips of gull outer primaries.

Montane. Pertaining to mountains.

Morph. A variant within a species, usually referring to colour morphs which are independent of geographic variation.

Nearctic. The new world Holarctic, comprising North America.

Nocturnal. Active at night.

Nomadic. Species that undergo irregular movements in response to environmental conditions (e.g. rainfall events).

Non-breeding plumage. Basic plumage; the plumage some adult birds acquire when not breeding.

Nuchal. Describes a bird's nape (i.e. the back of the neck).

Palearctic. The old world Holarctic, comprising North Africa, Greenland, Europe and Asia north of the Himalayas.

Pelagic. Organisms of the open ocean surface.

Race. A geographically-distinct population of a species; a subspecies.

Range. The area where a species occurs regularly, at least for part of the year.

Raptor. A bird of prey.

Rectrices. Tail feathers.

Remiges. Flight feathers of the wing (primaries, secondaries and tertials).

Resident. A species that remains in the same area all year.

Rufous. Reddish brown.

Speculum. A patch of colour on a duck's secondaries.

Sub-adult. A bird intermediate in age and plumage between immature and adult.

Sympatric. Species whose ranges overlap.

Vagrant. An individual outside a species' usual range.

Vulnerable. A species with a significant extinction risk, but less threatened than Critical or Endangered species.

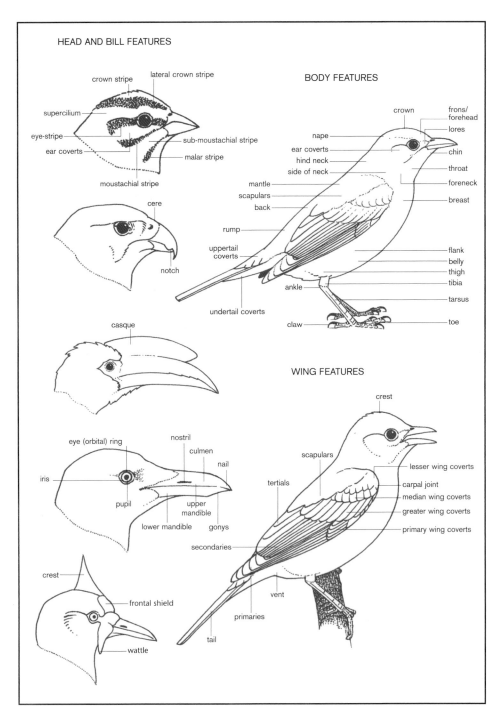

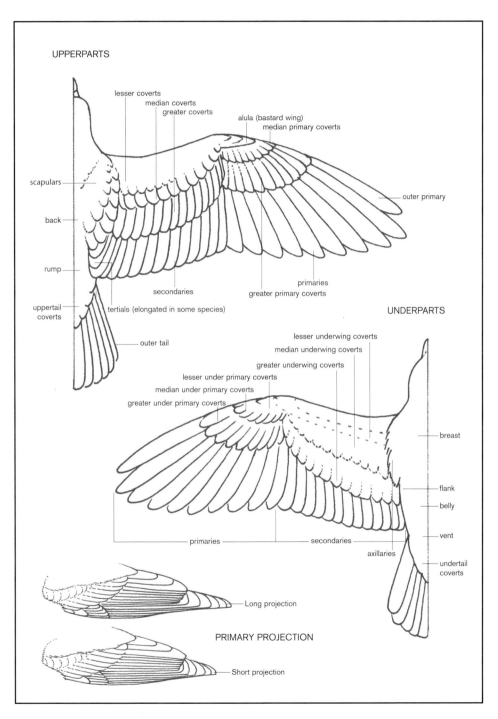

UPPERPARTS

lesser coverts
median coverts
greater coverts
alula (bastard wing)
median primary coverts
outer primary
scapulars
back
rump
primaries
greater primary coverts
uppertail coverts
secondaries
tertials (elongated in some species)
outer tail

UNDERPARTS

lesser underwing coverts
median underwing coverts
greater underwing coverts
lesser under primary coverts
median under primary coverts
greater under primary coverts
breast
flank
belly
vent
primaries
secondaries
axillaries
undertail coverts

Long projection

PRIMARY PROJECTION

Short projection

LIST OF SUBSCRIBERS

Sponsors' Edition

Arlott, Norman
Browne, TL
Chamberlain, David
Chamberlain, Philip
Day, John Edward & Margaret
Dixon, Tony & Maureen
Gallo, Peter

Greaves, Peter
Hathorn, Jenny
Jacobson, Merwyn
Johnstone, Ken & Margie
Jörnvall, Hans
Letaka Safaris Botswana
Marais, Johan
McLuskie, James

Reitz, Elizabeth
Roche, Royden
Ryan, Peter
Sheldrake Family
Sinclair, Ian
Such, Jonathan & Carol
Walker, Joe

Collectors' Edition

Ardington, Tony
Barrell, Alex A
Berard, Dr & Mrs RMF
Blythe-Wood, Colin
Boettger, Linda T
Carter, Ivan
Christy, Patrice
De Goede, Ken & Helen
Dixon, Tony & Maureen
Edge, John SR
Eisler, Mike & Maidie
Fourie, Dr Pieter
Fourie, Wim

Frost, Willem P - Matlabas
  Game Lodge
Goss, Pat & Karin
Hartshorne, Keith & Penny
Hawton, DA
Hickson, GN
Hockey, Phil
Hudson, Andrew & Dee
Jacobs, Mr PT
Keeley, Mr MF
Logan, Micheline
Louw, Peter & Margo
Macaulay, William & Linda

Maclean, Eleanor
Marais, Johan
Marvin, Nigel
McFarlane, Ian
Naylor, Graeme A
O'Hagan, Derrick & Peggy
Oosthuizen, James
Pauwen, Paul
Peddle, Diane Susan
Peile, Simon
Porteus, OM
Price, Simon
Robson, Brenda

Roche, Christopher
Samuel, JM
Scott, David
Skinner, Mark
Stellenbosch University
  Library Service
Taylor, Vincent
Tyldesley, Patricia Audrey
Wilson, Derric H

Standard Edition

ABC Bookshop
Aberdein, Robin
Aiston, Garth
Alberts, M
Alexander, Ian & Gill
Allin, Graham M
Alston, David & Ann
Amadwala Lodge Honeydew
Ambrose, David
Anderson, Mark D
Antonites, Mitchell
Arnold, Greg & Maureen
Artemides, CB
Ashton, Peter J
Aucamp, Hennie & Wanda
Badenhorst, Dr JCW
Baikoff, Jane & Fromenteau,
  Jean-Claude
Bailey, Derek W & Marneweck,
  Gary C
Bakker, Bert
Balderson, CJ
Baldwin, GM
Baldwin, OS
Barker, Peter
Barnes, Neville & Thalia

Barrell, Don
Barrett, Mrs Adriana
Bath, David & Cathy
Baumbach, EJM
Baxter, Darryl L
Beckmann, Roderick & Carol
Beetge, JC
Beeton, Frank & Di
Benjamin, Michael
Bennett, David R
Bennett, DH & JM
Berard, Dr & Mrs RMF
Berger, Lee
Bernitz, Drs Herman & Zephné
Beukes, Prof. Gerhard & Isolde
Bird, Henry A
Birkenmayer, RA
Blackburn, Cheryl
Blair, Steve
Bloch, Laurel
Blomeyer, EF
Bloy, Keith & Wendy
Blum, Werner
Bohme, Elke
Bollaert, Ronnie
Boon, Richard

Booth, EM & PA
Boshoff, Willem & Elfrieda
Botha, André
Botha, Dr Lukas J
Botha, Liesbeth
Botha, Patti
Botha, Rudolph
Böttger, Walter A
Boucher, Jonathan & Laureen
Bouwman, Henk, Charl & Bibi
Bouwer, Mrs K
Bowley, Valerie
Bradbury, DS
Bramwell-Jones, Mr & Mrs TH
Branch, Bill
Branch, Matthew
Branch, Thomas
Branfield, Dr Andy
Bredenkamp, I
Breero, Marinus
Brenchley, Pat
Breytenbach, Carel & Lucill
Bridgeford, Mike & Caroe
Brinkcate, Bob
Britten, Antony
Bromfield, Dave & Pati

Brooker, Arthur
Brooks, Peter
Brophy, Sue & Smith, George
Brown, AD
Brown, Marianne
Brown, Reg
Browne, TL
Bruwer, Pieter Guillaume
Buchholz, Theo & Eva
Buckle, MG
Buckley, Jean & Robin
Budai, Rick
Bulcock, Hugh
Bullen, Karen & Gerald
Burden, Susan Isabel
Burman, Lee
Burnett, Emma, Nick & Neil
Burnett, Rob & Wendy
Burscough, Dean
Bursey, Mary
Calenborne, Alan
Calenborne, Wade
Carnaby, Trevor
Carr, Charles
Carr-Hartley, Kenneth P
Carruthers, Vincent

Carter, Ken
Caulton, Mark & Jean
Cavanagh, Anthony
Cave, Alan
Chiawa Camp - Lower Zambezi
 National Park, Zambia
Chown, Steven
Clark, Johnny
Clark, Joshua
Clarkson, ACV
Claus, Dr CE (Zulu)
Coetzee, Adriaan
Coetzee, Deon
Coetzee, Marius & Almari
Coetzee, Rynetta E
Colley, Roger & Wendy
Collins, Steve
Combrink, C
Connor, Margôt
Cooke, Graham
Cooke, John & Margaret
Cooper, Antony
Cope, Dennis
Cordes Family
Corrans, Roy & M
Cottino, Christian FG
Counihan, TC
Cousins, Mr & Mrs GC
Cousins, SD
Cowan, David
Cowie, Don
Cowie, Keith
Cox, Graham & Jillian
Cox, WL
Cristensen, Dave
Cronje, Pierre & Evelyn
Crosbie, Rob & Chloe
Crosby, Trevor & Family
Crow, JB
Crowther, Jonathan
Crundwell, Mavis
Currie, Don & Rose
Cyrus, Digby & Rose
Dabrowski, Ralph
Dalrymple, HH
Daphne, Chris
Darling, Gregg
Davey, Robin & Wally
Davidson, Naomi
Davies, Laura Leigh
Day, Deryck H
De Beer, Kobus & Elizabeth
De Kock, C
De la Harpe, Derek

De la Rey, Jean-Pierre
De la Rey, Sean-Luc
De Villiers, Dr Jake
De Villiers, Hennie
De Vries, J
Deacon, Braam
Dedekind, Edna
Dedekind, Hartwig
Deetlefs, Darryl
Deighton, Dave
Dennill, Michael, Ingrid,
 Gabriella & Rafaela
Ditchfield, Gary
Divall, Peter & Anita
Dixon, Dr David
Dixon, Karen V
Dixon, Maggie
Dixon, Tony & Maureen
Dominican Sisters,
 St Vincent Convent
Dorse, Cliff
Dott, Graeme
Dowd, Dennis & Gaylyn
Driver, Ralph & Chris
Drowley, John G
Drummond, IM Mck
Du Buy, Dr Wendel
Du Plessis, Esmé D
Du Plessis, Pieter & Natacha
Du Plessis, Tertius
Du Plooy, Neale
Du Randt, Francois & Ronelle
Du Toit, Fanus
Du Toit, Lynette
Du Toit, Pierre
EcoPort - RSA
Egan, Mike & Janine
Ehlers, Eric & Jacqui
Ellis, Elizabeth
Ellmer, Arno
Engelbrecht, Ina
Erken, Dagi & Einhard
Evans, Keith & Gail
Faiola, Luciano
Feather, Dr Clive
Fellingham, Oliver
Ferguson, Mr & Mrs AD
Ferreira, Khakie
Findlay, James BR
Fishley, Marlene
Fitzgerald, D
Fletcher, Alex & Douglas,
 Richard
Fordyce, Bruce & Gill

Forrest, ARD
Forssman, Captain Bill
Foulis, Ian
Fourie, Jan H
Fraser, Kim & Anne
Freestone, Neil & Lynne
Friedman, Russel, Bonnie &
 Gabriella
Froneman, Dr Mark & Louw,
 Ms Delana
Funston, Jane
Funston, Paul
Garner, ESC
Garrard, Francis
Gavin Blair Safaris
Geldenhuys, Elsa & Conrad
Geringer, Huey & Elna
Geyser, Mimi
Gibbons, Bradley
Gibbs, Dalton & Tracy
Gie, Howard & Monica
Gill, Terry & Joan
Gjerstad, Mr Dag
Glasson, Ashwell
Godschalk, Seakle KB
Goulding, KC
Gous, Tertius
Graham, Ian & Lynne
Grannum, Richard & Amelia
Grant, Adrian
Gray, Neil
Greaves, Peter
Green, Howard
Greig, Donald
Greig, Nicolas
Greig, Tamsin
Greyling, Derick & Minette
Greyvensteyn, Mavourneen
Grieve, G, K, A & J
Griffioen, Margaret & Gerrie
Grohovaz, Anthony
Hall, David & Heather
Hammond, Dr Christopher A
Hammond, Margaret
Harman, Mike
Harris, Leigh
Harris, Sandra
Harrop, Shaun, Muriel, Kieran,
 Tristan & Erin
Hart, JOC
Hastie, Rodrick
Hatton, Chris
Hawthorne, Barry & Margie
Hayden, Stefan

Hazell, Ronnie & Renée
Hengherr, Berthold
Hennig, Conrad
Henning, Alta
Hennings, Claus & Penelope
Henry, KO
Hepple, Rob
Herbst, Dries & Ria
Heritage, Kathy, Mike & Bernard
Herrmann, Eric
Hersov, Basil
Hester, AW
Heurlin, Catherine & Jarl
Heywood, JF
Hickson, GN
Hill, Margaret & Dennis
Hislop, Paul
Hitchins, Peter & Stella
Hoal, Mr & Mrs EHO
Hochfeld, Sally
Hodgson, John
Hodgson, Robert
Hofmeyr, Hamish & Dianne
Hofmeyr, Pierre & Bronwyn
Holder, Stephen
Holtshausen, Gordon
Home, Bruce J
Home, Ian, Carolynn & Meghan
Home, John & Maggie
Honiball, Frank
Hook, Clint David & Hook,
 Natalie Ingrid
Hooker, Barbara
Hopcroft, Clive
Horley Family
Horne, SK
Howe, D & Family
Hubert, Gwynneth & Graham
Huizinga, Piet
Hulshof, Rénier
Human, David
Human, Heinrich
Hutson, Doug & Jane
Huxter, JG
Hyslop, Nan
IBBRG Library
Irons, Pete
Irwin, Terry
Jackson, Neels & Louise
James, Richard & Karen
James, Steve
Janse van Rensburg, Theresa
Jarvis, Mark & Bradley, Sean
Joffe, Pitta & Leon

LIST OF SUBSCRIBERS

Johnston, Dr John
Jolliffe, Kevin G
Joubert, Francois
Joubert, Noel
Joubert, Salomon CJ
Kahn, Sidney H
Kaiser, Jan B
Kalis, Pierre Jean
Kaplan, Clive
Kay, Martin Allan
Keighley, Hon WG & Mrs K
Kelly, Lyle
Kelly, Pat & Family
Kenig, Maja
Kennaird, Norman & Elisabeth
Kewley, HC
Kilpin, Alastair & Petro
Kindler, Bernd MR
Kirkman, John
Klasen, Wayne Nigel
Klinck, Johan
Knott, David & Noleen
Knott, Fred & Harriet
Kok, Rynhard
Kontominas, George
Koornhof, Pieter GJ
Kotze, Mr Ian
Kotzee, DJ
Kragh, Vibeke
Krone, Franci & Mariaan
Kruger, Gustav Hugo
Kure, Nils
Kwaan, Beatrice
Laas, Derrick & Jonne
Labuschagne, Rian & Lorna
Laing, Bruce A
Langenhoven, Hanno & Emsè
Langton, Mrs I
Laubscher, BD
Laubscher, Nico & Maud
Lauderdale, John & Moira
Laursen, Mr SKA
Lawes, Mike
Lawrie, RM
Lawson, Peter
Le Feuvre, Philip
Le Roux, Johan
Le Roux, Margaret
Leach, Charles & Bev
Leach, Geoff & Peggy
Ledgard, Sylvia
Lee, Chris & Elaine
Lee, Michael Standish
Lehmann, Wolfgang & Toni

Lello, Mr MG
Lemmer, GJ
Lenferna, CJ
Leroy, Jean-Marie & Astri
Liebenberg, Prof. H
Lilje, Markus
Livingstone, Dawn
Lloyd, Graeme
Lock, Greg
Logan, Ken & Stephanie
Lombard, Jaun
Londolozi Rangers
Longworth, Jennifer
Loppnow, AA
Loubser, Johann D
Louw, George & Caroline
Low, Derek
Lowrie, Ronda
Lubbe, Bradley
Lubke, Roy A
Lund, Angela
Maartens, JA
Maartens, MM
Maartens, PG & JJ
Macdonald, Peter
Machado, Ricardo
Mackay, Alice
MacLarty, Ian & Karin
Maclean, Gordon
MacRobert, Marianne
Mair, Lyn
Mair, Mike & Christine
Malan, Thys & Carina
Malherbe, André P
Maltby, Charles
Marais, Deon & Penny
Marshall, AP
Marshall, Jimmy
Marshall-Smith, AG
Martin, Dave & Jess
Masson Safaris - Sallie & Ewan
Matthis, Tom & Maggie
Mauff, Lorraine & Alfred
Maynier, Simon
Mc Ferren, Doug
McBurnie, Heather K
McCall, Ian
McCallum, Ian
McCleland, Warren
McDonald, Kevin & Loreen
McDonald, Ron
McDonogh, Michael
McFarlane, Ian & Barbara
McIntosh, Candace E

McKenzie, Duncan
McLean, FD
McSweeney, Lu-Anne
Meaker, Johanna & Louis
Meano, Maurice
Meddows-Taylor, Mike & Marion
Meintjes, Drs PG & S
Melville, Marion
Mercer, David
Merryweather, FR
Mervyn-Smith, Joan
Meter, Ingrid
Meyer, Magdalena
Michie, Margaret
Michler, Ian
Miles, Jonathan
Millar, Prof. R Scott
Mills, Gus
Mills, Stephen
Mills, Toby
Minnaar, Beryl & Van den Oever,
    Anneke
Mitchell, David & Carol
Monadjem, Ara
Moncur, Cam & Gill
Morant, Patrick
Morel, Gerard
Morgan, Clifton Dennis
Morrison, Bruce, Sharon,
    Brett & Nicole
Morrison, David
Morton, Doug
Moses, Peter
Mostert, Dalena
Mountain, Peter N
Mulholland, Giles
Muller, Charles
Müller, Harry & Müller,
    Hermann Jnr
Munnik, Ann
Munro, Neil
Murrell, Clive
Musto, Andy & Sue
Myers, Michael
Mynhardt, Ria & Christa
Nabarro, David
Nathoo, Dr J
Naudé, Lize
Naudé, Wilhelm & Alta
Nel, Allan & Jolanda
Nel, Dr Otto
Nel, JP
Nevill, HMD
Neville, John

Niemand, Lukas
Nieuwoudt, Schalk
Norman, Charles
Norman, Justine
Norris, Paul & Muff
Oatley, Terry
Ochse, Andy, Pat & Family
Odendaal, Pieter
Ogilvie, Adrian
Olivier, Harry & Alta
Opperman, Gert J
Orford, Dr Jock
Orrock, Anthony & Lizanne
Oude Stasie Wakkerstroom
Outlook Small Group
    Explorations
Outram, Ian
Owen, Anne
Page, Bruce R
Parsley, Jeff & Bev
Paterson, John
Patterson, Claire
Patterson, Heather
Peacock, Faansie
Peard, Shaun
Pearman, Craig
Peek, Richard
Pelican Safaris
Pellegrini, Franco
Penman, Mike
Penryn College
Pienaar, Jan
Pierce, Rob
Piper, Prof. SE
Pirow, Piers
Poacher, Anne & John
Podmore, Kevin & Glynis
Poliza, Michael
Pope, Mike, Gill, Sean
    & Jaden
Porter, Barry
Power Family
Prentice, George & Sally
Preston, Gill
Pretorius, BD
Price, Pauline
Prins, Frans & Sue
Quick, Ken
Radcliffe, Gordon
Radford, Brian
Rae, John
Rahn, Heather
Randell, D
Rands, Tim

738

Ranger, Gray
Rankin, Alistair
Rasmussen, Irene
Raymond, RF
Rayner, HW
Rayner, Lorna
Rech, A E
Reed, Brent
Rees, DHFH
Reid, Don
Rens, Jeanette
Retief, Dr François P
Richardson, Howard & Tina
Richter, Dr Muriel B
Ridley, MT
Riley, Adam
Ringdahl, Fiona & Peter
Rip, Kirsten & Jason
Robbertze, Clare
Roberts, B
Roberts, Vincent Paul
Robinson, DM
Robinson, Richard & Bridget
Rogan, Rosemary
Rollinson, Dominic
Roos, Prof. CJ
Ross, Dugald & Ginny
Rossiter, Dr & Mrs JB
Roux, Margaret
Rowan, Gary
Rushworth, Dave & Julienne
Rutherfoord Family
Ryder, Marc & Lorna
SafariWise
Salkinder, Alan & Myra
Sandrock, Mary Catherine
Sandy, Glynn & Hannetjie
Sargent, Sandra
Sarkin, Roy, Debbie, Kim & Lee
Sauer, Erik H
Scholtz, GD & MA
Schroeder, C
Schurz, Günther
Schutz, Hans & Ute
Scott, Jonathan & Christine
Scribante, Ryno S
Selfe, Gavin
Shamley, Patrick Roger
Shankman, Errol
Shantikumar, M
Shaw, Kevin & Carma
Shaw, Kevin Fearnley Thomas
Shearer, Stuart
Sievers, JFK

Simms, Chenay
Simms, Gavin
Sinangwana Edition
Slabber, JL
Smith, Edward & Smith, Marlene
Smith, GC & BA
Smith, GH Vivian
Smith, RB
Snow, CE
Snyders, Derek
Snyman, Trevor
Soares, Victor
Sobey, Maureen & John
Sole, Dr Kelwyn
Sonnenberg, D
Sonnenberg, W
Spangenberg, Prof. IJJ
Spencer, Derek William
Stainthorpe, Andrew
Stanford, Deirdre
Stanford, WP
Stanley, Richard & Barbara
Stannard, June
Stern, Anne
Stewart, Anne-Marie E
Stewart, Patsy & Charles
Steyn, Danie Du P
Steyn, David J
Steyn, Gert
Steyn, Jannie G
Stjernstedt, Robert
Stojakovic, Dael
Street, B & C
Stretton, Sandy
Strydom, Don
Strydom, Ebeth
Styles, Tom & Lorna
Sullivan, Peter
Summersgill, Colin
Susman, SN
Sutherland, Andrew & Vanessa
Swanepoel, Wessel
Swart, Paddy & Theo
Taljaard, JJ
Taljaard, Ollie
Tame, Barry
Tattersall, Pat & Fieldwick,
   Roger
Taylor, Grant C
Taylor, Neil C
Taylor, Vincent & Pam
Tennant, Mark
Terraplan Medewerkers
Thalwitzer, Milaan

Theron, Stefan
Thesen, Guy
Thomas, Ian
Thompson, Garth
Thompson, Peter & Ginette
Thomson, Robert L
Thomson, Ron & Debi
Thornton-Smith, Mr & Mrs S
Thorpe, Bradley
Tonking, Thomas & Christine
Topp, Raymond
Trent, Clive G
Triegaardt, Elizabeth
Trollip, SWK
Tucker, Andrew
Tucker, Stewart & Colleen
Turner, Dave
Turner, John
Turner, Nan & Jeremy
Ueckermann, Mariè
Uhlmann, Victor
Valentine, Colin
Van Berkel, Nicola
Van Brakel, Prof. Pieter
Van Coller, Peg & Sam
Van de Wetering, Aro & Marissa
Van den Berg, GJ
Van den Broeck, Jan
Van der Jagt, Dick & Liz
Van der Linde, Gerhard
Van der Merwe, Dr Roelof
Van der Merwe, François
Van der Merwe, Schalk W
Van der Steene, JF
Van der Vyver, BC
Van der Walt, André & Elma
Van der Walt, B
Van Deventer, Lisl
Van Dijk, Ineke
Van Dyk, Karel & Karen
Van Niekerk, Beyers & Clare
Van Niekerk, JP
Van Niekerk, Johann Snr & van
   Niekerk, Johann Jnr
Van Putten, Rick & Pam
Van Rensburg, Dr HJ
Van Rensburg, Koos & Drinie
Van Rooyen, Dr RA
Van Rooyen, Kate & Dave
Van Schaik, Theo
Van Schoor, Dr MCE
Van Vught, Lex
Van Wieringen, John & Ilse
Van Wilgen, Jane & Brian

Van Wyk, André & Theresa
Van Wyk, Ben
Van Wylick, Huguette
Van Zijl, Helm & Gillian
Vandewalle, Louis & Bain, Anne
Veenhuis, Derik & Dorly
Veldman, Mich
Venetia Limpopo Nature
   Reserve
Venter, Hennie
Venter, Nicholas
Venter, PJ & Ellen
Venter, RH
Vickery, Hazel
Viljoen, George
Viljoen, Henri & Maureen
Viljoen, Mark & Judy
Visser, Attie & Rencia
Visser, Bjinse
Vlok, Etienne & Susann
Vlok, Willie & Joan
Von Rahden, Richard
   & Maureen
Wakely-Smith, Rex & Ethne
Walker, Cleve & Julie
Walluschnig, Mario Roland
Waterkloof House
   Preparatory School
Weakley, Dr S
Weaver, Alex, Meryl, Ryan
   & Matthew
Weaver, David, Gill, Emma
   & Olivia
Weber, Masterman Carl
Weideman, Mrs ACF (Cathy)
Wentzel, HE
Wentzel, Kobus
Wheeler, KH
White, SM
Wickham, James & Michael
Wilkes, MC
Wilkinson, Chris
Willan, Ken & Jennifer
Williamson, Pete & Margie
Willis, Nigel
Wilson, Derric H
Wilson, PIT
Withers, Cranston
Wodrich, Anette
Woermann, D & E
Wolfaardt, Francois & Marianne
Wolstenholme, B Nigel
Yaldwyn, Emma
Yates, Stuart

INDEX TO SCIENTIFIC NAMES

741

745

INDEX TO SCIENTIFIC NAMES

INDEX TO SCIENTIFIC NAMES

INDEX TO COMMON NAMES

751

753

INDEX TO COMMON NAMES

Vegetation Map of Africa

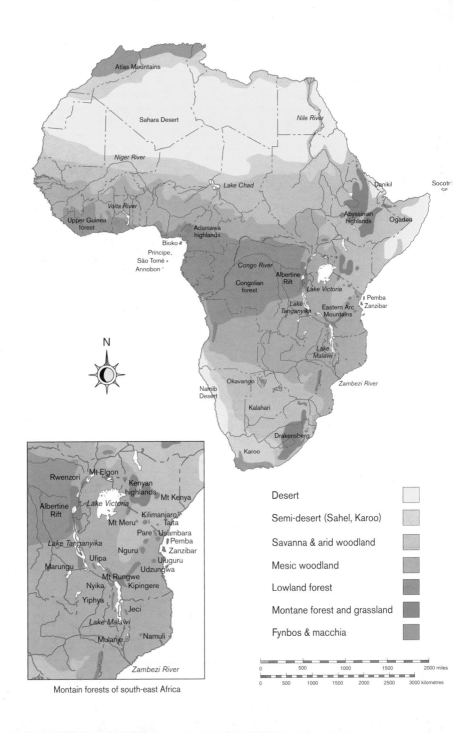

Atlas Mountains

Sahara Desert

Nile River

Niger River

Lake Chad

Volta River

Danikil

Socotr

Upper Guinea forest

Adamawa highlands

Abyssinian highlands

Ogaden

Bioko

Principe,
São Tomé
Annobon

Congo River

Albertine Rift

Congolian forest

Lake Victoria

Pemba
Zanzibar

Lake Tanganyika

Eastern Arc Mountains

Lake Malawi

Namib Desert

Okavango

Zambezi River

Kalahari

Drakensberg

Karoo

Montain forests of south-east Africa

Rwenzori

Mt Elgon

Kenyan highlands

Mt Kenya

Albertine Rift

Lake Victoria

Kilimanjaro

Mt Meru

Taita

Pare Usambara

Pemba

Lake Tanganyika

Nguru

Zanzibar

Ufipa

Uluguru

Marungu

Udzungwa

Mt Rungwe

Nyika

Kipingere

Yiphya

Jeci

Lake Malawi

Mulanje

Namuli

Zambezi River

Desert	
Semi-desert (Sahel, Karoo)	
Savanna & arid woodland	
Mesic woodland	
Lowland forest	
Montane forest and grassland	
Fynbos & macchia	

0   500   1000   1500   2000 miles

0   500   1000   1500   2000   2500   3000 kilometres